APPLIED MICROECONOMICS

AN INTERMEDIATE TEXT

Jonas Prager
New York University

IRWIN

Homewood, IL 60430
Boston, MA 02116

© RICHARD D. IRWIN, INC., 1993

Senior sponsoring editor: *Gary Nelson*
Developmental editor: *Joan Hopkins*
Marketing manager: *Ron Bloecher*
Project editor: *Jess Ann Ramirez*
Production manager: *Ann Cassady*
Designer: *Mercedes Santos*
Cover designer: *Janet Cunniffe*
Cover illustration: *Nancy Serensky*
Art manager: *Kim Meriwether*
Compositor: *BiComp, Inc.*
Typeface: *10/12 Times Roman*
Printer: *R. R. Donnelley & Sons Company*

Library of Congress Cataloging-in-Publication Data

Prager, Jonas.
    Applied microeconomics : an intermediate text / Jonas Prager.
        p.   cm.
    Includes index.
    ISBN 0-256-05780-X
    1. Microeconomics.   I. Title
HB172.P68   1993
338.5—dc20   92–25194

Printed in the United States of America
1 2 3 4 5 6 7 8 9 0 DOC 9 8 7 6 5 4 3 2

To My Parents, of
blessed memory

THE IRWIN SERIES IN ECONOMICS

Appleyard and Field
International Economics

Baily and Friedman
Macroeconomics, Financial Markets, and the International Sector

Barron and Lynch
Economics
Third Edition

Blair
Urban and Regional Economics

Bornstein
Comparative Economic Systems: Models and Cases
Sixth Edition

Brown and Moore
Readings, Issues, and Problems in Public Finance
Third Edition

Colander
Economics

Colander
Microeconomics

Colander
Macroeconomics

Denzau
Microeconomic Analysis: Markets & Dynamics

Hyman
Economics
Second Edition

Hyman
Microeconomics
Second Edition

Hyman
Macroeconomics
Second Edition

Hyman
Modern Microeconomics: Analysis and Applications
Third Edition

Katz and Rosen
Microeconomics

Lehmann
Real World Economic Applications: The Wall Street Journal Workbook
Third Edition

Lindert
International Economics
Ninth Edition

Maurice and Phillips
Economic Analysis: Theory and Application
Sixth Edition

Maurice, Thomas, and Smithson
Managerial Economics: Applied Microeconomics for Decision Making
Fourth Edition

Nadler and Hansen
Microcomputer Macroeconomics with IBM Disk

O'Sullivan
Urban Economics
Second Edition

O'Sullivan
Essentials of Urban Economics

Peterson
Principles of Economics: Micro
Eighth Edition

Peterson
Principles of Economics: Macro
Eighth Edition

Prager
Applied Microeconomics: An Intermediate Text

Rima
Development of Economic Analysis
Fifth Edition

Roger and Daniel
Principles of Economics Software Simulation

Rosen
Public Finance
Third Edition

Schwarz and Van Dyken
Manager: Managerial Economics Software

Seo
Managerial Economics: Text, Short Cases
Seventh Edition

Sharp, Register, and Leftwich
Economics of Social Issues
Tenth Edition

Shepherd
Public Policies Toward Business
Eighth Edition

Shugart
The Organization of Industry

Slavin
Introduction to Economics
Third Edition

Streifford
Economic Perspective

Walton and Wykoff
Understanding Economics Today
Third Edition

PREFACE

A Marketing Problem

As the manager charged with marketing a new textbook, you are aware of stiff competition from existing texts. You're convinced that you have an excellent text that, if given the opportunity, will be a best-seller. Your challenge: sell this obviously superior product!

Analysis

Your challenge is compounded by the odd nature of the college textbook market. First, the market is very fragmented. You must reach individual faculty members, who rightly cherish their independence in textbook selection. Mass sales by appealing to a few key players in the market is not in the cards. Second, students who shell out the bucks and who benefit most from a suitable choice and suffer the most harm from an ill-fated one have no direct impact on the purchasing decision. Thus, third, price is not a strategic variable. It's highly unlikely that undercutting the competition will attract much faculty interest, although a price that's very much above the competition will turn potential adopters off. Fourth, professors are no different than most of us as creatures of habit. Changing texts, while hardly as traumatic as divorce and remarriage, requires overcoming inertia. Fifth, convention precludes using common merchandizing incentives. The marketing department can't employ price inducements or prizes. It cannot violate the integrity of faculty by offering monetary payments for ordering the text, nor can it place the faculty member's name in a contest limited to those who have adopted it. Sure, the marketing staff will advertise, offer free sample texts, visit the professors, and make available a variety of ancillaries such as test banks and teaching aids. But the competitors are doing the same, and so that offers no competitive edge.

How can you, the marketing manager, convince faculty members teaching the course that the swap is in both their best interest and that of their students?

The Response

Persuade the author to write a preface that so clearly points out the virtues of the text that it simultaneously entices professors to give the text serious consideration and encourages students to urge faculty to adopt it.

So that's why I'm writing this preface. I believe this microeconomics text is unique and better serves a broad audience than do its competitors. I'll try to tell you why without exaggerating its qualities but also avoiding the sin—in this particular instance—of immodesty.

To the Student

1. The Audience

You, the reader, like most of your classmates enrolled in the intermediate microeconomics course, will not make economics your career. Even if you're an economics major, you're likely to seek opportunities among the broad range of occupations open to college graduates, although you'll probably be looking for a job related to economics in one way or another. This text recognizes students' pragmatic approach to microeconomic theory and tries to answer in a straightforward manner: What practical knowledge can I take away with me? What will prove useful for me later? This approach implies . . .

2. Stress on Principles, Not Techniques

No microeconomic theory text can avoid technical detail. Nevertheless, I view technique as a means to an end, not an end in itself. I am convinced that most students can be taught the methods of microeconomic analysis even at a sophisticated level without getting so bogged down in the technique that they lose sight of its applicability to real issues that they'll face over their lifetimes. Moreover, students' basic intuition about economic problems is an asset that needs to be nurtured, not repressed. That, in turn, leads to . . .

3. An Applications-Centered Approach

You've just been exposed to a sample in this preface. A practical case is outlined, analyzed, and then applied. Each chapter opens with one or two issues—from stratospheric pricing of an AIDS drug to competition between Pepsi and Coke. Each chapter explores the analytic techniques appropriate to the issue and then reexamines the case in light of the analysis. I have found that students become more enthusiastic and are more likely to retain the fundamental principles when they clearly see them in the context of an issue. Focusing on some real issues implies coping with . . .

4. Uncertainty

Economics courses often leave students puzzled. Textbooks frequently resolve real-life economic problems with precise answers that students intuitively feel are oversimplified. This confusion stems in part from the certain world inhabited by the economic models characteristic of most intermediate texts in contrast with the uncertain environment beyond the classroom. This quandary is not satisfactorily resolved by a chapter on uncertainty near the end of the text, which is rarely taught and even less frequently internalized by students. The present text introduces uncertainty in almost every chapter, because I am convinced that you and your classmates need to come to grips with uncertainty and its implications whenever possible. That should help you appreciate the value of economic analysis long after this text has gathered dust. The real world is also driven home by paying attention to . . .

5. The Quantitative Dimension

Economics prides itself on dressing qualitative relationships in quantitative clothes. Quantitative estimation plays a role in this theory text because of my belief that students of intermediate microeconomic theory need to be shown in as many ways as possible the practical face of microeconomics. So, wherever it has been possible to do so, the text reports econometric estimates. Another way to demonstrate the usefulness of microeconomics is by . . .

6. Straying from the Narrow Path

For instance, most theory texts give short shrift to problems of industrial structure. This text differs, because students interested in reality should be exposed to the competitive posture of modern industry. Thus, Chapter 12 on monopoly and especially Chapter 14 on oligopoly examine public policy issues well beyond the superficial treatment found in most intermediate microeconomics texts. (These chapters may prove especially appealing to business majors but should not be ignored by those interested in applied microeconomics in general.) Similarly, Chapter 10, which deals with environmental and public goods issues where market solutions are not optimal, follows the discussion of perfect competition. That's because the analysis of market failure is needed to counterbalance the tangible achievements of the market economy. The last chapter is entirely a problems chapter, asking you to act as an economist. Aside from being unusual in a micro text, it also furthers another objective of this book . . .

7. *Learning by Doing*

Students rightly view intermediate microeconomics as among the toughest courses in college. The abstract, often subtle ideas combined with technical analysis—mathematical or geometrical—require both comprehension and discipline. You may discover that the better the teacher, the more difficult the course. That's because as you follow your professor's lecture attentively, you'll be convinced that you understand it. And well you may. But you, like many students, will all too frequently discover that the ingenious construction turns into a nightmare when you're asked to replicate its complexity on an exam or apply it in a different context.

Most texts don't address this problem at all. They rely instead on questions at the end of the chapter or workbook problems. While you'll find these features in this text as well, it differs in one important aspect. You are frequently challenged to test your understanding right then and there. This might involve filling in a blank, completing a table, drawing a diagram, or shifting a curve on an existing diagram. If you're conscientious, you'll work it out and then check your response with the correct answer found at the end of the chapter. Perhaps that's one reason that a student of mine called this text . . .

8. *User-Friendly*

He may also have been referring to the conversational style of the writing, the relief offered by an informative box or a cartoon, or the orientation toward relevance. This version is even more user friendly because each diagram appears with a grid in the background, so that you can trace points to the relevant axes. More crucial, each figure uses numbers (not letter references) to facilitate your understanding. No "area *ABCD*"; instead, it's $(40 \times 10) = 400$. That's clearly important in a text relying heavily on a diagrammatic rather than mathematical approach, which suggests that . . .

9. *This Text Is Not For Everyone*

True, both economics and business students should embrace the text's emphasis on application and its target audience of students who do not intend to become professional economists. But there's a flip side. The text is highly inappropriate for those who intend to pursue graduate-level degrees in economics. Such students need a technical, mathematical approach that will teach them first and foremost the tools and techniques of the profession. For them at this stage of their education, applications are of secondary importance. Moreover, they will find the text too intuitive and less rigorous than a more technical approach would take. But, . . .

10. *It May Just Be For You*

If you want to apply basic microeconomic principles, are concerned with using economics as a tool that enables you to draw qualitative and quantitative conclusions about practical issues, learn best by actually testing your understanding along the way, and are helped by such features as learning objectives at the start of each chapter and questions testing both your understanding and your ability to apply the lessons, all wrapped in a tasteful literary and diagrammatic package, then you've found the right book.

By the way, you'll find suggested answers to even-numbered questions at the end of the book. If you want the answers to odd-numbered questions, you'll have to get your hands on the *Instructor's Manual* that is sent to faculty members who adopt this text. While it would be counterproductive to provide you with these answers, you're urged to acquire the accompanying *Study Guide* for a very elementary reason: The more exercises you do, the better you'll understand the material.

That's the sales pitch. A final comment, however, is in order. This text seems to have found an appreciative if captive audience in successive intermediate microeconomics classes at New York University. I owe these men and women a special debt of gratitude for their comments and tolerance.

To the Instructor

Since the fundamental objectives, target audience, and characteristics of this text have been outlined in the previous pages, my comments here relate to a few teaching aspects that you may wish to consider. First, the scope of the course. I have learned that I cannot do justice to all the topics covered in contemporary intermediate micro texts, this one included. I must either omit some topics (my practice) or treat some very superficially. If you elect not to follow the sequence of the text and stop at whatever point you've reached by the semester's end, you might want to adapt by:

1. Leaving Chapter 10 on externalities and public goods for the end. This option will be more to the liking of faculty who adhere to a more traditional micro course sequencing. Nevertheless,

you might like to try the text's sequence in light of current concerns and misconceptions about environmental issues.

2. Omitting the parts of Chapters 12 and 14 that deal with industry structure.

3. Omitting the relationship between the short- and long-run cost curves (pp. 234–237). While this analysis is both interesting and fruitful, the opportunity cost of the time spent on this brief section may be too expensive.

Second, challenge your students. Insist that they write in the text where responses are called for or diagrams need to be drawn or curves shifted. And urge them to go beyond the Review Questions at the chapters' end and digest some of the Food for Thought. As you know, the more involved they are, the better they'll understand the material and the greater will be your teaching pleasure. Chapter 20's problems could either be reserved for the end of the course or used where appropriate. For the same reason, you might want to consider using the *Study Guide,* thoughtfully written by Errol Glustoff of the University of Tennessee.

Third, as has become traditional, Irwin has supplied a test bank both in hard copy and on disk to those who adopt the text. These come in addition to the *Instructors' Manual,* which contains additional questions, answers to the odd-numbered questions, and additional hints capably prepared by Elias C. Grivoyannis of Seton Hall University.

Thanks

Publishing a textbook is a team effort. Once the author has completed the first draft, reviewers scrutinize the content as the publisher's staff deals with form. These professionals share in common anonymity, for it's the author's name that appears on the title page and the royalty check that's sent to his or her address. Their meager recognition comes in the preface, which, unfortunately, is not unlike the trailer of a movie that flashes by on the screen as the audience exits the theater. Nevertheless, since this text would have been a poorer product without their contributions, it is only right that I recognize them by name. My thanks to those who reviewed the prospectus:

Larry Blume	University of Michigan
Faye Duchin	New York University
Edward R. Kittrell	Northern Illinois University
James C. Loughlin	Central Connecticut State University
George Palumbo	Canisius College

And those who reviewed all or portions of the text:

Louis A. Dow	University of Alabama
David Feldman	College of William and Mary
Michael Gurantz	California State University, Northridge
H. Youn Kim	Western Kentucky University
Michael Magura	The University of Toledo
Lawrence Martin	Michigan State University
James Meehan	Colby College
William C. Mitchell	University of Oregon
Jacob Paroush	Bar Ilan University
Joel B. Prager	Debevoise and Plimpton
Joseph Schachter	York College-CUNY
Ken Slaysman	Dickinson College
Bruno Stein	New York University
Bernard Wasow	New York University
Lawrence A. Wohl	Gustavus Adolphus College

There were difficult times when it seemed as if the book would never see the light. Gary Nelson, as a stalwart sponsoring editor and a constant source of encouragement, deserves much of the credit for this text's publication. And I appreciate the commitment of several developmental editors who worked with me through the process. Kris Rabe and Doris Hill were most helpful at the initial stage. Joan Hopkins bore the brunt of the editorial work, so it is to her that my debt is greatest. Joan's cheerful overall supervision has made palatable the distasteful tasks that take up an author's time and try his tolerance. I suspect Joan carried more of the burden than she let on, and she well deserves my warm thanks. My appreciation also to Jess Ann Ramirez, who facilitated and coordinated the production end. Finally, my children surely deserve some credit for tolerance, but let's not go overboard. They've been immunized to me writing textbooks and have learned not to let it disturb their lifestyles. Neither Sharon's marriage to Yudi nor Yossi's decision to work abysmally long hours had anything to do with this text. My wife-helpmate-significant other, Helen, on the other hand, patiently bore the burden of my sour moods when the writing wasn't going well. I know they all share my satisfaction at seeing this book finally out of the way.

In dedicating this book to my late parents, I also wish to express their lifelong gratitude to our great country. They found refuge here from Nazi Germany in 1934, arriving penniless during the Great Depression.

Through determination, hard work, much self-sacrifice, and an abiding faith in God, they set me on the right path. I pray that my children carry on their traditions and commitments, although they could be spared the poverty.

Jonas Prager

CONTENTS IN BRIEF

CONTENTS

APPLIED MICROECONOMICS

AN INTERMEDIATE TEXT

AN INTRODUCTION THAT REFRESHES

Students hone themselves to a fine edge as they prepare for final exams. But it is only natural that the edge dulls as time elapses. And, of course, the more time that has passed and the more complex the original subject matter, the less that's retained in a student's memory.

You and many of your fellow classmates now enrolled in intermediate microeconomics will have taken the principles micro course at least a semester ago. Some of you will have last visited micro principles a year ago or even earlier. If you're like my intermediate micro students at NYU, you'll welcome the review of basic principles in the two chapters that constitute Part I. The initial chapter lays out the ground rules of the course by focusing on the key assumptions of microeconomics. The second chapter reviews and elaborates on the basic demand and supply curves, looking at them in the context of a free market as well as when they're subject to constraints.

1

WHAT MICROECONOMICS IS ALL ABOUT

Economics is stating the obvious in terms of the incomprehensible.
Anonymous

Obviously crime pays, or there'd be no crime.
G. Gordon Liddy, Convicted Watergate Conspirator (1986)

Learning Objectives

You will benefit most from reading this introductory chapter by focusing on the:

- Role of scarcity and choice in economic decisions.
- Four key assumptions of microeconomic analysis: self-interest, rational decision making, absence of frictions, and certainty.
- Adjustments that have to be made when the key assumptions are violated.
- Applicability of economic models: understanding how models can be used and what their limitations are.

Crime as a Way of Life: Two Introductory Cases

Here is Sam, on the life of the professional passer of false checks:

> I like the money. The money drives you. You look over and see a store just sitting there. It's just sitting there and all you have to do to get yourself either $50 or $75 is to walk in there and get it. You don't have to have a gun, you don't have to have anything but a ball point pen.

It's kind of nerve-racking [though]. You have to be on your toes so much of the time. It's kind of like selling, you have to keep smiling all the time. After a while your face gets real tired.

Something else; they don't get *mad* at you. The police, the law enforcement officers, they don't get mad about bad checks. If they catch you, fine; but they're not really going out of their way. Corpus Christi, for instance, has a population of about 200,000 and they have a check detail of *one* man. He handles all the checks. Now that's all the protection they have. He can't be in all those stores at one time. And the descriptions that people give are so varied that it's hard to bust a check man unless you bust him right in the place.

The only reason I stopped writing checks was because I had so much heat on me.[1]

And here's Joey, on being a hit man:

It doesn't bother me, not one bit. This is my job. It is my business. I shoot people and that's it. I never think of it in terms of morality. By most standards of morality what I do would be considered wrong. But this doesn't bother me.

Because I have the ability to pull the trigger I can do what I like to do, go where I want to go, live comfortably, eat well, be what I want to be. I do my job like a guy lays brick, a guy tends bar, a guy cuts hair.

[My first] job paid $5,000. It seemed like a billion. My older brother was working 10 hours a day in a warehouse and bringing home $24 a week.

Every hit begins with a contract. A contract is always a verbal agreement, but these contracts are as strong as any written agreement in the world. The money is paid in advance. The full amount. After the contract is out, the man who put it out can rescind it, but none of his money will be returned.

There is a guarantee in the contract covering the unlikely situation that I'm caught. I will not talk. Not a word. Not a sound. Not a peep. To ensure that, the party with whom I've made my deal must pay all legal fees, support my family the entire time I'm in jail, and have something waiting for me the day I get out.

Why do I do it? There are a number of reasons. Obviously, the money. [And] I like the status it brings. And girls. I also see killing as a test of loyalty and courage. And finally, I guess I do it because I enjoy it.

What makes a good hit man? Pride and confidence. A good hit man goes out, does his job, comes home to his family and can sit down and eat his dinner without any problems. After all, no one likes to bring his work home with him.[2]

No, you didn't pick up a book on criminology mistakenly published with an economics cover! But you certainly have the right to wonder what these two stories are doing in a **microeconomics** text. The truth is, they illustrate marvelously a number of microeconomics issues: goal setting, scarcity, and choice. And they'll serve to distinguish economics from ethics, religion, and politics on the one hand, and the social and physical sciences on the other.

An excellent starting point is the definition of economics suggested by Lord Robbins in 1936, prior to the Keynesian revolution, when all of economics was microeconomics. The definition may be familiar to you, for in one form or another it has found its way into virtually all principles of economics texts. Robbins wrote, "Economics is the science which studies human behavior as a relationship between goals and scarce means which have alternative uses."[3] The focal points of this definition are three:

- A *relationship* between goals and scarce means.
- Scarce means.
- Alternative uses.

1. *Economics and goals.* Economists do not set goals. Whether they work for governments or businesses, economists are rarely the commanding generals; they mostly serve as executive officers. While a commander sets the overall strategy, an executive devises the best tactics to achieve the goal. The economist employed by IBM may be asked to consider how to implement the planned increase in PC manufacturing capacity decided on by the board of directors. Should new plants be built, or should existing ones be expanded? If the former, where should the new plants be sited: at home or abroad? If the latter, which of the factories now in use should be targeted for expansion? The economist is trained to fashion the manner in which these goals can be best accomplished and then to inform the decision makers, who hold the ultimate responsibility.

2. **Scarcity**. Surely you recall the importance of scarcity in defining the economic problem. Adam and Eve lived an idyllic existence, having their wants satisfied by the mere taking. Nothing (except the tree of the knowledge of good and bad) was denied them. However, none of us lives in Eden, and few of us are in the billionaire category; on an individual level, our desires exceed our ability to satisfy our wants. (My grandmother always told me that an alternative to having more was wanting less. A wise woman, she. Perhaps that's the secret of the Garden of Eden.) Limited ability to fulfill wants is a fact of life not only for most individuals but also for business firms, not-for-profit institutions, governments, and societies as a whole.

3. *Alternative uses.* Scarcity is a necessary—but not sufficient—condition for economic decision making. If resources were scarce but each resource had only one use, then the solutions would be absurdly simple. If the only use for acrylic were manufacturing salt shakers and the only use for paper were printing economics books, then we would produce as many shakers and economics books as our supplies of acrylic and paper would allow. Of course, acrylic can be used to make a cornucopia of products from backscratchers to airplane components, and the same is true for paper. The issue then becomes far more complex, for allocation

decisions have to be made regarding which products, using which resources in which combinations, will be produced.

The Robbins definition, consequently, can be summarized as follows: *Economics is concerned with choice under conditions of scarcity.*

Obviously, religion and ethics are positioned on a different plane; they deal with individual and societal goals. And in the highest sense of the calling, so does politics. Whether it is fair to benefit one social group at the expense of another is a question of ethics. Whether business executives are acting properly when they sell unwary customers shoddy goods and whether politicians are behaving suitably when they decide to pander to the insistent but perhaps unjustified claims of a particular interest group are ethical questions. Politics deals with the objectives of government; our political leaders decide the goals of the state. Economists can equally serve—at least insofar as their professional qualifications are concerned—the democrat and the tyrant, the just and the unjust, the good and the bad.

The social sciences in general are similar to economics in the sense that they deal not with the formation of ultimate societal goals, but with the methods of achieving those objectives. Sociologists study social behavior—people in a group setting; psychologists examine, for the most part, individual behavior; political scientists tend to be concerned with how political decisions are fashioned; and historians try to understand the past. In general, clear-cut distinctions can be made between those aspects of study dealing with goal setting and those concerned with attaining those goals. Ethics, religion, and politics fall into the former category; economics and the other social sciences belong to the latter.

Let's go back to Sam and Joey. Ethics concerns itself with the fundamental question, Is criminal activity right or wrong? Whether you believe in God or in an organized religion, or are an atheist or an agnostic, somehow you're going to have to make a decision on this question. The politician takes a stand based on ethical considerations, deciding that since, for example, taking another's life or property by force is wrong and since it is in the interest of the state to minimize such involuntary population reductions or redistributions of wealth, policies will have to be instituted to prevent murder and robbery and to punish murderers and robbers. The politician now turns to the scientists and asks, "How can we minimize crime in our community?" And here, not surprisingly, a plethora of advice with be forthcoming, each suggestion reflecting the profession of the respondent. Practitioners of the various sciences tend to see the causes differently and consequently are likely to propose different and perhaps conflicting solutions.

A sociologist may well explain crime by suggesting that the neighborhood exerts a disruptive effect on individuals; urban poverty is a fertile breeding ground for crime. The psychologist may point to a criminal having a warped psyche, being a social misfit, or perhaps even suffering from a genetic mutation (encroaching on the turf of the geneticist). The political scientist may suggest that the legal system is not working properly and so encourages some people to violate the law. The historian will probably tell you that crime is nothing new; it's always been around and will continue till doomsday. The physical scientists, too, may get into the act, saying that genetic deformities or hormonal imbalances are at fault.

The economist takes a different slant. While not denying any of the other possible causes, the economist suggests that criminals face choices just as the rest of us do. Indeed, the life of crime is merely a specific case of occupational choice. Criminality resolves the problem of scarcity—in this case, inadequate income to satisfy the individual's wants. The solution is to choose a profession that will provide sufficient income to enjoy life. That is what Sam is saying: "The money drives you." And Joey confirms it: "Why do I do it? . . . the money."

So Sam and Joey are both facing an economic problem. They are obviously not concerned about the ethics of murder or of cheating store owners by passing fraudulent checks. Nor do they seem to be crazy or, aside from their occupations, social misfits. They appear throughout their stories as sensible, balanced people, capable of—and indeed, making—rational choices. So, crime is an economic problem in the broad sense of choice in the face of scarcity.

The preceding paragraph highlights two fundamental assumptions implicit throughout the study of microeconomics: self-interest and rational decision making. It's appropriate at this point, then, to consider these and a number of other assumptions used by microeconomics theorists.

Microeconomic Models and Their Key Assumptions

Humans are amazingly complex creatures. Each one of us is an amalgam of emotions and intelligence, passion and reason. We are a product of heredity yet are buffeted and shaped by our environment. People are at times predictable and at other times entirely perverse, random, and capricious. Despite these peculiarities, social scientists have to believe certain fundamental regularities do exist and can be discovered. In that sense, economists do not differ from physicists, who seek to uncover the rules by which the physical universe operates. True, there is the abnormal. But the abnormal is just that: unusual. In addition, economists take solace in the fact that even if individuals do not behave uniformly, when you get enough of them together, predictable behavior will dominate over the unexpected.

In microeconomic theory, economists find it convenient to accept two assumptions that we all know are not the whole truth:

- People are exclusively motivated by self-interest.
- People act rationally.

Two additional assumptions also prove useful:

- Actions tend to be smooth and frictionless.
- All decisions are made in a context of certainty.

Let's take a closer look at all four assumptions.

1. *Self-interest: the egocentric imperative.* Economic beings are devoid of those attributes that make humanity synonymous with compassion. Indeed, the stereotypic "economic man" thinks only of himself (perhaps also of his family as an extension of himself), decides on the basis of what's best for himself, and acts accordingly. Surely this is what Edmund Burke, the 18th-century British statesman, had in mind when he declared, "The age of chivalry is gone; that of sophisters, economists, and calculators has succeeded." Thus, employers seek to hire workers at the lowest possible wage, while employees try to obtain the highest possible wage. Customers search out the lowest prices; sellers attempt to achieve the highest profits.

2. **Rational choice:** *the analytic imperative.* To be consistently selfish requires reasoning out the consequences of any plan. A question that must be asked continuously is, Will this course of action lead to the goal I think best for myself? Only if the answer is yes should that course be pursued. Thus, the economic man is not only egocentric but also calculating, always weighing the pros and cons of all alternatives. Emotion is not an element in the decision-making process of the economic man. Where reason dominates, feelings are not even subordinate, they're nonexistent.

3. *The grease of economic theory: the absence of frictions.* You should be familiar with **comparative statics** from earlier courses in economics. Given normal supply and demand curves and a price determined at the intersection of the two curves, you know that if demand should rise so, too, will price. You've considered the initial equilibrium and the final equilibrium, and you've ignored how you got from the start to the end. That's perfectly legitimate in a comparative statics context.

In **comparative statics**, economists are concerned with the "before" and the "after," but not the "in-between."

But in real life, shifts from one equilibrium to another are neither immediate nor smooth. Consider the following situation: The failure of a major security firm drops a slew of highly paid professionals—security analysts, computer scientists, stock and bond brokers—on the job market. Comparative statics predicts that in the absence of new demand for their skills, these men and women will be reabsorbed into the work force only at reduced salaries. But in the real world, wages are sticky and adjust downward very reluctantly. The newly unemployed may be unwilling to accept offers at lower wages; they may at first believe that their luck will soon turn and they will be reemployed at their previous salaries. Moreover, accepting lower salaries immediately would put them into a poor bargaining position for future increases should the failure of their old firm be an isolated instance rather than an extensive decline in the industry.

What would be the consequences of these reactions if indeed demand in general has fallen? Attempting to maintain higher wages in the face of reduced demand will retard and perhaps even halt the absorption of the unemployed. A disequilibrium persists until workers and employers recognize the permanence of the demand shift. Only then will wages adjust and the new equilibrium be achieved.[4]

4. *The certainty postulate: no doubts ever.* Existence is clouded with uncertainty, and economic life is no exception. Nevertheless, it is traditional in microeconomics to deal with a world in which uncertainty is banished; everything is known by everyone. Thus, buyers know all prices on the market and will avoid the high prices charged by some greedy sellers. Producers can calculate to the penny the cost of production and thus can determine their prices. They can accurately judge the relative prices and productivities of inputs and so make rational choices among them.

Although certainty facilitates economic theorizing, it unfortunately distances economic analysis from the real world. Consumer and producer behavior can't be comprehended unless economists shift their focus to reactions under conditions of uncertainty. Fortunately, economic science has made significant strides in that direction and has clarified much that was ignored previously.

These four assumptions—self-interest, rational choice, absence of frictions, and certainty—are basic to economic thinking. They are ways in which we can bring some order into a complicated world inhabited by complex human beings. Moreover, they deliver conclusions that are plausible if not universally correct.

Adapting the Fundamental Assumptions

But what happens if we drop some of the fundamental assumptions of microeconomic theory? Be forewarned: some of the neat conclusions become messy, and occasionally they are even reversed.

1. Altruism. The converse of self-interest is altruism, doing something without anticipating a reward. Obviously, we are often compassionate, merciful, willing to help a friend in need (denying the aphorism ''A friend in need is a pest''!), and even willing to assist total strangers in times of crisis. Is there any room for such behavior in economic theory?

If theory is to be more than a mere exercise in logical thinking, the answer to the above question must be yes. Yet if we accept that economic theory must find room for altruistic behavior we must then confront a host of subissues: What precisely does altruism consist of? When do individuals and groups behave altruistically, and when do they act out of self-interest? How do you analyze actions that combine self-interest with altruism (e.g., tax-deductible charitable donations)? Economists have not shied away from dealing with altruistic behavior, but the conclusions allowing for altruism necessarily lack the precision of those involving only the simpler principle of egoistic behavior.

The assumption of self-interest is retained throughout this text. It permits clearer and cleaner exposition than dealing with altruism would allow. Moreover, despite the obvious existence of the charitable impulse even on the part of corporate America—consider sponsorship of public television programs and contributions to the arts by major corporations—self-interest is not altogether out of step with reality. If you consider that building a benign image is a goal of massive industrial and commercial firms and that the government foots a good part of the expense as deductions from taxable income, you must wonder how important a factor altruism is.[5]

But to be overly cynical is wrong, too. Not everyone is always motivated by greed, and so insisting on self-interest as the unique motive comes at a cost: some loss of realism and applicability. What you must always keep in mind, then, is that the conclusions of the analysis might have to be modified insofar as the underlying assumption is not fully operative.

2. Emotions and Microeconomic Theory. Economists are human. (Really!) They realize that people are not rational, calculating machines who act only on the basis of the results generated by the fixed program that sits in the computer known as the brain. People often do things by habit (although that can be explained rationally, as you'll see later on), through passion, or by instinct. Sometimes out of stubbornness, we act precisely opposite to the dictates of reason. (Surely you can think of examples from your own life where perversity itself proved satisfying, at least for the moment.)

Yet despite these reservations about the universality of reasoned actions, rational behavior permits us to reach important and basically valid conclusions. These conclusions will not be right all of the time nor in all circumstances. But, fundamentally, the characteristic that differentiates humans from lower animals is the ability to reason, and for the most part, we do use our reasoning facilities. Moreover, when we're dealing with large groups—market behavior rather than individual action—the legitimacy of the rationality assumption should be evident. Even if some of us don't act in conjunction with the dictates of reason, people in general do.

3. Frictions. Why can't we find a decent mechanic? Consider the alternatives in the following figure:

	Honest	Dishonest
Skilled	I	II
All thumbs	III	IV

Some mechanics are honest and capable; they're the ones in Box I. Those in Box II are skilled but dishonest; they're the kind who can repair a hole in a radiator but will tell the gullible customer that the entire radiator is unrepairable. (To add insult to injury, they'll then seal the hole, spray-paint the part, reinstall it, and charge for a new one.) The third category, in Box III, consists of the incompetent but honest; these mechanics think they know how to diagnose and repair the problem, but all too frequently they are wrong. Their intentions are praiseworthy, but the execution is faulty. Box IV, the final category, which in a sense is the worst, comprises the incapable and dishonest; they don't know how to fix the radiator, and they'll charge you double. So, in three of the four options you either get a lousy job, pay an unfair price, or both.

The problem is simple: How do you find a Box I mechanic? How nice it would be to provide you with a method for finding a simple, reasonably priced solution. The objective here is different, however. You've just been introduced to the world of **asymmetric information.** Not everyone has the same amount of knowledge or the same quality of information. Quite obviously, those who have better or more information can take advantage of those who have less or worse.

Asymmetric information occurs when two individuals or groups possess uneven knowledge about an event or a situation.

Microeconomic theory has typically assumed that information is distributed symmetrically; what is known to the seller is also grasped by the buyer. In recent years, however, economists have expanded their horizons to deal with very real problems that occur when information is not evenly disseminated. Uneven knowledge explains the emergence of services such as house inspection, in which investigators determine the structural soundness of a prospective purchase for the potential home buyer. Similarly, **search costs** have become more significant in economic analysis to explain limits on the volume of information individuals and firms seek to acquire.

Search costs are the expenses, including time and money, involved in obtaining information.

Conclusions will have to be modified once frictions of various sorts are introduced. For example, workers at one firm may not immediately quit their jobs just because the firm's competitors are paying higher wages. The employees may not know about the higher potential earnings, and even if they have good information, many are reluctant to give up the known for the unknown. So, unless the differential suffices to overcome such hesitance, higher wages may not lead to worker shifts. Again, this represents an attempt to use the tools of economic analysis to deal with real-life problems.

4. Uncertainty.   Because we can't really make believe that our world is characterized by certainty, economic theorists have begun to grapple with the complexities of uncertainty. For example, in a certain world, in which profitable and unprofitable firms can be easily identified, it would be a simple decision to invest only in the profitable ones and steer away from the losers. In an uncertain world, however, you can't really know whether today's profit makers will continue as such in the future. The opposite is, of course, true for firms presently in the red. Nevertheless, you have to deal with uncertainty to make investment decisions. Diversifying your portfolio by not risking everything on one firm is a strategy that makes sense only in an uncertain environment; it's something you'll be exposed to in Chapter 3.

To summarize: Theory abstracts from reality but in doing so attempts to focus on the critical variables, ignoring the secondary. We obtain a sharper image of the real world by squeezing out its essence. But we also lose some of the fuzziness that constitutes reality. The advantage is manageability; the cost, imprecision.

In order to keep the economic analysis manageable, the two central abstractions—self-interest and rational economic behavior—are pretty much maintained throughout this text. The other two assumptions—the absence of frictions and certainty—are used but often discarded.

The Applicability of Economic Models

In their theories, economists approach reality but never reach it. Typically, economists move from simple models to more complex theories, from the undefined to the defined, from description to prescription. You may improve your overall understanding of this text and of your micro course in general by spending a short while on considering how economists' thought processes work.

Short-Run and Long-Run Models

Let's begin by focusing on the distinction between short-run and long-run economic models. Usually, the short run involves a shorter time period than does the long run, which involves a longer time period. (Obviously! But take care; Chapter 7 introduces a notable exception to this rule.) The important implication that follows is that in the long run, participants in the particular decision have more time to consider their alternatives. The best course of action in the short run may not prove to be the optimal long-run response.

For example, a competitor lowers the price of fashion sunglasses, a product that you, too, are producing. Your customers start ringing you up to find out whether you're going to match the price cut. In the short run, you may have no choice; you either meet the lower price or find yourself stuck with inventories that will soon become dated and out of style. However, upon reflection (unintended pun!), you may implement a strategy to prevent this unexpected shrinkage in your profit margin. You may call up your competitor and suggest that his price-cutting was a foolish move, since, after you matched the reduction, neither of you would be better-off. Why not get together one afternoon and discuss pricing, you say. Although such collusion is of course unlawful, businesspeople occasionally commit illegal acts. However, other alternatives do exist. You might consider starting an advertising campaign to solidify customer allegiance. If you convince customers that your product is better or more fashionable or whatever, then the next time your competitor cuts his price, you may be able to maintain your old price and your old clients. Or you might decide that you no longer wish to worry about competition and just leave the industry. Thus, your long-run supply decision differs from your short-run reaction.

Perhaps the most important implications of the distinction between the short run and the long run crop up in the policy area. The temptation of public policymakers to achieve societal objectives by intervening in the economic process is legendary. All too often, however, policymakers are myopic; they consider only the short-run consequences of their actions without taking into account the long-run responses. Examples are easy to find; the ignorance of policymakers is more difficult to comprehend.[5] Just reflect on the well-known case of rent control. Rents kept low to satisfy tenants are often insufficient to provide landlords with an incentive to maintain their buildings. The short-run impact of rent control is to shift wealth from landlords to tenants; the long-run consequence is a reduction in the supply of housing, harmful both to landlords and tenants.

Comparative Static versus Dynamic Models

The short-run/long-run distinction is characteristic of comparative statics, or the before-after analysis. This type of economic comparison is often useful, and its conclusions are frequently sensible. But remember that comparative statics ignores the interim (or the in-between), which may be important per se. Thus, economists often consider **dynamic models,** which zero in on the route by which we go from here to there. Business-cycle theories are by their very nature dynamic; such models trace out the path on which the economy rolls from one stage of the cycle to the next. In microeconomics, too, dynamic models are oftentimes considered; Chapter 2 looks at the famous cobweb model, which takes into account the time lapse between production decisions and actual output.

The time pattern of reactions is considered explicitly in a **dynamic model.**

For example, students who select majors on the basis of current opportunities and salaries, which form the basis for their best estimate of postgraduation income, may find themselves disappointed when they enter the job market. The dynamics of the cobweb demonstrate that a long-run equilibrium may never be attained.

Estimating Models

You're lost and you need directions. The Good Samaritan who tells you that you're headed the wrong way and advises a U-turn conveys useful information. Yet much more welcome would be a local who tells you, "Turn around, continue for 3.5 miles until you reach a Y in the road, take the left fork for another half a mile until the gas station. Turn right there, go for two miles, and you'll see your destination on your left."

Econometrics involves devising testable economic models and testing them statistically.

Qualitative statements were the bread and butter of generations of economists. By pointing out directions, such statements often served a useful function, since what was clear to economists often proved not very obvious to others. Thus, politicians had to be told that a new excise tax would not lead to treasury revenue collections equal to the tax times previous sales because the tax-induced price rise would cause sales to fall. With the rise of **econometrics** in recent decades, economists have been equipped with powerful tools for fashioning quantitative estimates. It is now possible to estimate more precisely expected government tax revenue from a tax change. This, of course, is not meant to imply that econometrics is easy or totally accurate. (In Chapter 2, you'll be introduced to some elementary econometrics and some of the problems involved in econometric testing.) Yet even at an elementary level, you should be able to appreciate the importance of quantitative information.

Positive versus Normative Economics

While **positive economics** deals with describing and analyzing economic issues, **normative economics** is concerned with economic policy goals.

Until now, the discussion of economic theory was framed in terms of **positive economics.** Theory is neutral; it describes in an analytic framework how people, organizations, companies, and markets adjust and react to scarcity and choice. Yet a next step seems to be inevitable: from description one easily moves to prescription, from *what is* to *what ought to be*. A theoretical model that demonstrates how taxes lower consumption easily turns into the statement "We *should* control alcoholism by placing taxes on whiskey, liquor, and beer." By inserting the word *should*, you have crossed the boundary of positive economics and entered the territory of **normative economics.**

Normative economics involves opinions as to desirability and appropriateness; it considers norms or goals, not merely what is. In a sense, when economics becomes normative it enters the realm of ethics, religion, and politics. Consequently, while most economists agree about positive economics—if the theory is formulated properly and analyzed logically, there's little to disagree about—the room for controversy in normative economics is broad indeed.

For the most part, this text, like most other micro texts, is neutral insofar as norms are concerned. The basic focus is on teaching you how to apply economic analysis. What you do with this knowledge is truly your business. Sometimes, however, the line demarcating positive from normative is fuzzy; you'll have to pay attention throughout this text to make sure that normative statements do not appear in the dress of positive ones.

The Economics of the Criminal Lifestyle

Let's return now to Sam and Joey, and apply to them the lessons implicit in this introductory chapter. We'll build a model of criminality; see if it can be quantified; discover the implications of its conclusions; and point out the how those conclusions, deriving from economic analysis, differ from those drawn from other professions.

Begin with fundamentals mentioned on pages 9–10. Criminals, like other people, are devoted to furthering their own interests and will do so by rational means. Selecting a life of crime suggests that the criminal believes it more profitable in some sense than the alternative, the lifestyle of the square. What might have led Sam and Joey to this conclusion?

"Yup. This is dial-a-hitman. Who do you want vaporized?"

SOURCE: Reprinted from *The Wall Street Journal*; Permission Cartoon Features Syndicate.

Any economic decision begins by listing the benefits and the costs. Crime pays. Sam's income consisted of all the revenue he picked up from passing false checks, while Joey's came from contract murder. But legitimacy also pays. On balance, it's not clear which pays better; much depends on the individual in question and the opportunities he or she faces. Sam could have been a salesman (in fact, in the citation that begins this chapter, Sam likens passing bad checks to selling), but he opted otherwise.

When it comes to costs, generally a whole slew of costs that do not have to be taken into account by the noncriminal have to be considered by the criminal. Perhaps the most important one stems from the fact that a convicted criminal faces free room and board for some finite period under state supervision. On the simplest plane, the time spent in prison means the loss of income that could have been earned outside. In other words, the **opportunity cost** of a jail sentence is, at a minimum, the income lost during incarceration. The wages of crime have to exceed the rewards of legitimate earnings by at least enough to offset this opportunity cost.

Opportunity cost is the return that could have been obtained had some course of action other than the one actually chosen been pursued.

Enter now uncertainty. If all criminals were caught and sentenced, the full loss of income would have to enter into the criminal versus legitimate occupation decision. But not all criminals are apprehended, nor are all of those caught imprisoned—which was crucial in Sam's decision to pass bum checks: "If they catch you, fine; but they're not really going out of their way." He didn't think he was going to get caught and offers a reasonable explanation for why he wouldn't. Moreover, the term spent in jail for nonviolent crime is relatively brief. And the crime itself is nonthreatening; the check passer hasn't done anything to raise the ire of the law enforcement community, so basically he is treated civilly by the police and prison personnel.[7]

In short, Sam, weighing the criminal versus the legitimate lifestyle, has made a rational calculation; all things considered, the benefit/cost ratio favors criminality over a legitimate lifestyle. Indeed, Sam has even calculated that check forging is more profitable and less risky than alternate criminal occupations. He was a safecracker for a while, but as he says, "There's no problem beating a safe, the only problem is finding the one with the money in it. But with a check, the money is already there, you know it's there, you just have to go in." (Lest you are seriously inclined to replicate Sam's exploits, consider that he gave this interview from prison!)

Joey's calculations are not terribly different. Morals aside, being a hit man is a clean way to earn a living. He's paid in advance and, being skillful at his profession, discounts the possibility of being caught. Moreover, as a member of organized crime, his opportunity costs are significantly lower than are Sam's. Recall his insurance: should he be caught, his family will be supported and he will receive a lump sum subsidy when he is finally released from prison.

Economists have developed a model of criminal choice along the lines intimated here. Representative of them is the seminal article by Isaac Ehrlich,[8] who followed his theoretical section with econometric testing. Using state crime data for 1940, 1950, and 1960 for seven types of crime, running from violent felonies such as murder and rape to property offenses such as burglary and auto theft, Ehrlich came to the following conclusions:

- The empirical evidence is consistent with the theoretical explanation: criminals do appear to measure costs versus benefits.
- Of the two variables over which society has direct control—the probability of being jailed and the severity of punishment—the certainty of imprisonment was typically a stronger deterrent than the severity of the penalty.
- An improvement in the relative income positions of lower-income groups would reduce property crime much more than either increases in the probability of apprehension or the severity of punishment. Thus, in addition to any ethical considerations income inequality may pose, Ehrlich suggested that a more equal income distribution would also mean less crime.[9]

The economic approach to criminality is clearly at variance with sociological, psychological, genetic, or pathological explanations of crime, especially with regard to "crimes of passion." What economists are saying, in effect, is that if the penalty is sure enough and significantly severe, passion will be controlled; make the costs substantial enough to the criminal, and he or she will be less likely to commit crime.

Three other interesting conclusions demonstrate the advantage of the economic analysis of criminality over noneconomic theories. First, the idea of dividing society into two classes, criminal and noncriminal, is probably wrong. In essence, everyone is capable of violating the law, and a person will do so providing the benefit/cost ratio is in his or her favor. This fundamentally pessimistic view of human nature may be borne out by considering (1) petty crimes, such as stealing a few cents' or dollars' worth of something (for example, using the office phone for personal calls or calling in sick just to have a day off), and (2) cheating on income taxes. The general impression we all have is that both types of crime—and crimes they are—are common. While few people would actually take money out of a cash register when the clerk was not looking, most people do not think either committing petty crime or ripping off the IRS is morally reprehensible. And, since the chances of getting caught are slight and the penalties often negligible, people who otherwise would not consider themselves criminal become thieves.

Second, recidivism—the repeated criminal acts by one who has already paid the penalty for his or her criminality—is easily explained. If

---

Uncertain Risks, Uneasy Criminals

The basic theory of criminal justice is that crime can be deterred through certain, swift, and severe punishment. But modern America has too much crime and too little law enforcement to make punishment very certain. Since 1978, in fact, the total number of police officers in big cities has been declining, while both serious and minor crimes have surged.

There are several ways for police to adapt to this problem of scarce resources. The common method is to set "triage" priorities, in which lesser offenses are given very little attention, so that resources can be concentrated on more serious problems. In Manhattan, for example, police do not usually investigate burglaries unless the value of property lost exceeds $10,000. In other cities, pot smoking, public drinking, and even domestic violence have been virtually legalized by police inattention. These practical compromises are all seen as necessary ways to have enough police and prison space for armed robbers, narcotics pushers, rapists, and murderers.

The unfortunate consequence of this triage approach is that it makes the risks of getting caught all too predictable for criminals. They can reliably predict that the chances of being punished for killing a police officer, for example, are enormous, and will avoid that offense if they are at all rational. But they also can be certain that the risks of being caught and punished for most stranger-to-stranger crimes—like armed robbery, residential burglary and car thefts—are low.

Thus we need to make Rand Corp. economist Peter Reuter's important distinction between the *risk* of getting caught and the *certainty* about what that risk is for any given offense on any given day. Criminal deterrence is premised on high certainty of a high risk of punishment. What we offer criminals instead is a high certainty of a low risk of arrest for most offenses. But for the same dollar cost, we could create high *uncertainty* about whether the risk of arrest is high or low—and perhaps reduce crime substantially. . . .

---

the basic economic conditions and calculations that led to a commitment to the criminal lifestyle have not changed, why should the criminal's behavior be altered? If it was rational before apprehension—and remember that the criminal explicitly considered the probability of being caught and imprisoned—then the decision remains sensible upon release. (That was true for both Sam and Joey.)

A third implication relates to effective use of resources to prevent crime. Should society, in trying to reduce the crime rate, hire more policemen so that more criminals can be caught, hire more judges so that more criminals can be sentenced, build more prisons to hold more prisoners, or strengthen penalties to deter crime? Econometric analysis of the role of each element in the criminal deterrent and law enforcement system can be an important ingredient not only in improving our understanding of the

MicroBits 1.1 continued

Even if scarce resources have to be rationed according to priorities, the priorities don't have to remain fixed. Police can crack down on street crime in one neighborhood today and in another tomorrow, or on "crack" dealers this week and drunken drivers the next. They can stake out holdup-prone liquor stores one night and gas stations the next.

For limited periods for each type of offense, police can make the risk of getting caught extremely high. Police cannot afford to focus on each type of offense very often. But they can increase the uncertainty criminals face in predicting the risk of arrest on every day in between these intermittent crackdowns. . . .

The mathematics shows a broad range of possible options. Suppose we have only enough resources to catch criminals after 5 percent of all criminal acts. We could spread that 5 percent risk over all offenses, or permanently increase it for some offenses and reduce it for others (triage). But we could also vary the risk over time, from 50 percent or 60 percent on some days to zero on many others, so that the *average* risk of arrest for each type of offense is 5 percent. This would entail no increase in cost, but it would mean that the "worst-case scenario" for a calculating criminal would become considerably more painful. . . .

Some police argue that such crackdowns merely push crime around. But the "supply" of crimes is not fixed, and it arguably can be reduced by police making the risks of the "production" process more uncertain. Others may argue that alternating crackdowns create unconstitutionally selective enforcement. But as long as crackdown targets are selected without regard to race, religion, or other protected categories, there should be no constitutional obstacles.

. . . As long as we refuse to pay for making a high risk of punishment highly certain for every offense, we must continue to pick the least worst alternative. Making a low risk of arrest highly certain for most offenses is an open invitation to every rational criminal. By keeping crooks guessing, we may have better luck at keeping them honest.

criminal process but also in reducing the amount of crime. (See MicroBits 1.1 on the allocation of scarce police resources to increase deterrence and thus decrease crime. Professor Sherman suggests that sometimes a slight outlay can bring significant results. Notice, too, how uncertainty can play a positive role in prevention.)

Some Other Examples of Microeconomic Models and Their Implications

Consider briefly two other examples of economic modeling and some of their implications.

What Do Consumers Optimize?

The typical answer of economists to the question of what consumers optimize is *satisfaction*: consumers try to make the best out of every situation. This very loose formulation will be specified more precisely in Chapter 3. For the moment, however, concede that it implies consumers would try to choose the least expensive of two equally suitable alternatives. But consider the following case to understand how failing to accept even such a simple assumption can lead to foolish consequences.

The Verrazano Narrows Bridge, which spans New York Harbor and is among the longest suspension bridges in the world, connects the New York City boroughs of Brooklyn and Staten Island. For good numbers of metropolitan New Yorkers, it is a fast and easy route to New Jersey and points south. An alternative route would involve crossing into Manhattan, taking one of two tunnels or the George Washington Bridge to New Jersey, and then proceeding south (see Figure 1.1). Prior to mid-1985, it cost $1.75 for a passenger car to cross the Verrazano in either direction, with no further charge to the driver who entered New Jersey via the Goethals

FIGURE 1.1

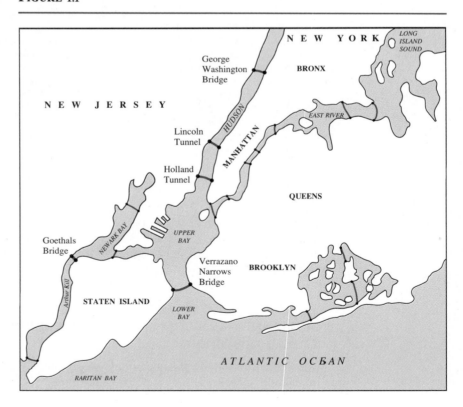

Bridge. On the return trip, the New Jersey–New York crossing (over the Goethals) cost $2.00, so that the round-trip cost $5.50 for an automobile. On the other hand, the Manhattan–New Jersey direct route was free outward and cost $2.00 return, for a $2.00 round-trip fee.

Many people drove into Manhattan from Brooklyn in order to save $3.50 in tolls. Others, including many coming from Manhattan, used the Verrazano for convenience, despite its higher round-trip cost.

The picture was significantly modified in 1985. In its infinite wisdom, Congress altered the toll structure on the Verrazano, making it free on the Staten Island–Brooklyn leg and double the price, $3.50, in the Brooklyn–Staten Island direction; the other toll structures remained unchanged. Think for a minute: How would you now react? Use Figure 1.1 to plan a trip from Brooklyn to New Jersey and back. Now do the same for a round-trip from Manhattan to New Jersey.

If you drive out via Manhattan and back via Staten Island your toll cost would be $2, no different from returning via Manhattan. This is a new option, available only because of the new, "wrong" one-way toll. On the other hand, if you pursued the old route, your outward Staten Island leg would cost you $3.50, and your inward leg would cost another $2.00. A double incentive has been created. On the one hand, the convenience of leaving via Staten Island now costs double, while the opportunity to return via that borough has fallen from $1.75 to zero. The option of avoiding tolls is open to Brooklyn drivers as long as they are willing to begin their trip south via Manhattan.

Of course, drivers changed their behavior. Indeed, not only did private passenger cars start shifting into the expected pattern—leaving via Manhattan and returning via Staten Island—but trucks, whose toll costs could reach $25 per trip, began to line up in Manhattan. Studies soon showed that traffic on feeder streets, which prior to the toll conversion had moved at the turtlelike speed of 7.7 miles an hour, now shuffled along at the snaillike pace of 2.8 miles an hour. Not startling, you say. Nor should you be surprised to learn that after the experiment had been on for two months, bridge toll revenue was down by $1 million.

The Verrazano Narrows Bridge wrong-way toll model teaches a simple lesson: People do optimize; they try to minimize expenses where they can. Similarly, business decision makers do seek to cut costs when they find an obvious opportunity to do so. The strict profit- or utility-maximization assumptions used by microeconomic models are often unrealistic and extreme, but their conclusions are quite useful in reality. Policymakers who ignore them do so at their own peril.

Allocating Scarce Hospital Resources

Hospitals all too often face a quandary known as triage. When two patients need a liver transplant and there's only one available liver, when the amount of available antityphus vaccine does not suffice for all those who have possibly been infected, when an ambulance brings in a patient with a heart attack but the coronary care unit is full, hospital personnel are forced to make heartrending decisions. Who gets the liver? Who is to be inoculated? Who, if anyone, is to be moved out of the coronary care unit? These medical concerns are also truly economic issues. In all cases of triage, scarce resources have to be allocated. As lamentable as the alternatives are, and as uncertain the outcomes are a choice must be made.

Consider three possible solutions: (1) first come, first served; (2) market; and (3) potential social benefit.

1. One might argue, as is often the case, that the first patient in is entitled to the first available, say, liver. Such a decision rule in a sense abdicates making a choice. Chance, not reason, rules.

2. A second solution might be that the liver goes to the highest bidder. Indeed, in many circumstances in our economy, the market does determine who acquires scarce objects. One certainly could advance the position that the families concerned should be permitted to bid for the one available liver, and the family whose need is most urgent, expressed by its willingness to outbid the others, merits the organ. Most people reject this alternative as appalling. Few on principle would deem it fair to assure the more affluent so directly a better chance of life and to relegate the poor to the bottom of the heap.

3. The third alternative would be to consider who could most benefit society from the transplant: the renowned physician or the coalminer, the 82-year-old or the 23-year-old, the star quarterback or the unemployed drug addict. Of course, in many and perhaps most cases the contrasts would be less glaring and the decisions far more difficult. Yet a decision is unavoidable; the question is how to reach the best decision.

To think as an economist, measuring the costs against the benefits, is certainly not the entire answer. But cost/benefit considerations should not be ignored either. At the very least, they help the decision maker evaluate the impact of the decision from a broader perspective.

Conclusion

The thrust of this chapter has been to disarm those critics of economic theory who assert, "It's all right in theory, but it won't work in practice." Such people fail to comprehend the purpose of theory—to simplify, a necessary act when brainpower is limited and relationships are complex—and the uses to which analysis can be put—to explain general interrelationships rather than every single facet of every single issue. You've seen that economics involves making decisions under conditions of scarcity, that microeconomic models are useful in setting up methods of attacking these problems, and that one can increase the sophistication of economic theory when it is useful to do so. Moreover, you now realize that economic issues are not limited to business-type problems. Whenever choice exists, resources are scarce, and decisions have to be made, microeconomic theory frequently offers a helping hand in reaching sensible decisions.

Chapter 2 analyzes the pricing mechanism in a market economy. While ethical or political considerations set the overall guidelines within which supply and demand operate, for the most part such issues are ignored in Chapter 2. Instead, the chapter focuses on cases in which the consensus suggests that economic considerations may be permitted to determine the outcomes.

Key Terms

Asymmetric information
Comparative statics
Dynamic model
Econometrics
Frictions
Long run
Microeconomics
Normative economics

Opportunity cost
Positive economics
Rational choice
Scarcity
Search costs
Self-interest
Short run

Review Questions

1. In what ways does economics differ from politics and religion on the one hand, and sociology and psychology on the other?
2. The chapter implies that Adam and Eve were spared from making economic decisions in the Garden of Eden. Do you agree? Why or why not?
3. Vernon L. Smith has written about the role of economic theory as follows: "Theory economizes on the statement of behavioral regularities. It is a shorthand way of summarizing more detailed and complex descriptions." Further, "Theory brings a coherence—an underlying pattern or rationale—that integrates otherwise diverse observations and phenomena into a single whole." Smith claims that another important function of theory is to "chart the path to new observations based upon predictions of phenomena or events for which there was previously no special motivation or search."[10] Are

Smith's statements consistent with this chapter?

4. *a.* List and briefly explain the four key assumptions of microeconomic theory.

 b. How might one's understanding of economic decision making be altered by dropping each of these assumptions?

5. Why do you think that the first Nobel Prize in economics was awarded for the formulation of econometrics?

6. *a.* Why might an individual choose a life of crime rather than engage in legal activities?

 b. How does economic theory explain recidivism?

 c. Using your understanding of economic theory, devise a program to deter crime.

7. A Michigan mechanic in 1988 opened an advisory service. For $19.95, the mechanic offered to diagnose a car's ailments over the phone, prescribe the needed remedies, and estimate the cost. How can the demand for such a service be related to asymmetric information?

Food for Thought

1. Economic theory suggests that when the demand for homes falls, housing prices will decline as well. The price decline should then encourage sales. Nevertheless, one often encounters For Sale signs that seem to have hung around for months. Is economic theory wrong, is the housing market an exception, or is there another explanation?

2. Efforts by U.S. authorities to control drug addiction have generally been directed at inhibiting supply. The notable lack of success of this policy has suggested to some that efforts aimed at limiting demand might be more effective. Underlying both these suggestions is an economic theory of drug addiction that considers both the demand for and the supply of narcotics. What might such a theory be?

3. Gary Becker of the University of Chicago has opined that love and marriage are amenable to economic analysis. In the dry language of theorists, Becker suggests that among the incentives for marriage is

that "persons in love can reduce the cost of frequent contact and of resource transfers between each other by sharing the same household."[11] What might be some of the elements that enter into a theory of marriage? How would you then formulate an economic theory of divorce?

4. Prior to a 1991 Supreme Court decision, many states prohibited those convicted of a crime from directly benefiting from the fruits of that crime. Under these laws, the profits from books such as those written by Joey or Sam, or from movies based on their lives, would be used to reimburse the victims for their losses rather than accrue to the criminal. You might want to consider the moral issues involved and also the impact of such laws on the economic theory of crime.

5. *a.* While taxpayer integrity underlies the U.S. tax collection mechanism, the U.S. Internal Revenue Service is not unaware of temptations to cheat. Cross-checking income statements (e.g., verifying taxpayer reports of

interest earned against interest payments to taxpayers filed by banks) is routine, as are sample audits to uncover the dishonest. Who will be audited, however, is never known in advance. How does uncertainty play a role both in taxpayer decisions to cheat and in IRS decisions about whom to audit?

b. Recently, the IRS requested an appropriation to finance additional agents, arguing that the cost of each agent is more than compensated for by the revenues collected by the agent. If you were a staff member of the congressional committee charged with evaluating the IRS's argument, what are some of the questions you might want to ask the commissioner of the IRS? Could you suggest alternatives to the IRS proposal?

6. Why does the public feed coins into parking meters, given that meter readers seldom come by and that even if they do the fine is usually minor?

Suggested Readings

Although it sometimes seems that no two economists agree on even the most straightforward policy advice, appearances belie reality. For a good taste of economic theory translated into consensus prescription, sample some chapters in Alan S. Blinder's *Hard Heads, Soft Hearts: Tough-Minded Economics for a Just Society* (Reading, Mass.: Addison-Wesley, 1987). In fact, if only policymakers would integrate into their thinking some fundamental microeconomic principles, the resulting policy would be far more effective, a point emphasized by a former economic adviser to the British government, Sir Alec Cairncross, in "Economics in Theory and Practice," *American Economic Review* 75, no. 2 (May 1985), pp. 1–14.

Economic methodology is a dry subject that generally repels students and attracts but few professional economists. Nevertheless, methodological disputes often underlie policy prescriptions, as will be evident from examining Mark Blaug's *The Methodology of Economics, or How Economists Explain* (Cambridge: Cambridge University Press, 1980). The crucial role of rationality in economic theory as viewed by economists and psychologists is reported in Robin M. Hogarth and Melvin W. Reder, eds., *Rational Choice: The Contrast between Economics and Psychology* (Chicago: University of Chicago Press, 1987). The place of altruism in economics can be sampled in Kenneth Boulding, *A Preface to Grants Economics: The Economy of Love and Fear* (New York: Praeger Publishers, 1981).

The economic theory of crime is examined in great detail in David J. Pyle, *The Economics of Crime and Law Enforcement* (New York: St. Martin's Press, 1983); Pyle's Chapter 4, "The Deterrent Effect of Capital Punishment," not only reviews the Ehrlich model but also considers later developments and criticisms. Although it is addressed to economists rather than to beginning students, you will still obtain a good taste of the issues involved even if you only skim through the chapter.

The series of essays by Jack Katz, *Seductions of Crime: Moral and Sensual Attractions in Doing Evil* (New York: Basic Books, 1988) offers an interesting sociological counterpoint to Pyle's work, while James Q. Wilson and Richard J. Herrnstein set forth an interdisciplinary model in Chapter 2, "A Theory of Criminal Behavior" in *Crime and Human Nature* (New York: Simon and Schuster, 1985). (Let me know whether you agree with the publisher's claim that this is "the definitive study of the causes of crime.")

Notes and Answers

1. Adapted from Bruce Jackson, *A Thief's Primer* (London: Macmillan, 1969), pp. 193–94, 212–13. Jackson interviewed Sam, a prisoner in a Texas penitentiary.

2. Joey (with Dave Fisher), *Killer: Autobiography of a Hit Man for the Mafia* (Chicago: Playboy Press, 1973), pp. 74, 76, 80–81, 98–99.

3. Lionel Robbins, *An Essay on the Nature and Significance of Economic Science* (London: Macmillan, 1952), p. 16.

4. Note that underlying this technique is the implicit assumption that when the demand curve shifts down initially, you'll end at the lower price equilibrium. The comparative static conclusion is perfectly acceptable for a good deal, but not all, of contemporary economic analysis.

5. Not-for-profit institutions were much concerned with provisions of the 1986 tax reform proposal that would have curtailed charitable deductions. Obviously, the heads of these gift-recipient organizations didn't believe that altruism alone was the driving force behind the donations they received.

6. In all fairness, it may not be the simplemindedness of legislators and regulators that lead to shortsighted policy actions. Especially in the case of legislators who are frequently up for reelection, shortsightedness and survival are often synonymous.

7. As Sam says, "They don't get *mad* at you for checks. I've never even been touched; I've never been forced to sign a confession with checks" (Jackson, *A Thief's Primer*, p. 78).

8. Isaac Ehrlich, "Participation in Illegitimate Activities: A Theoretical and Empirical Investigation," *Journal of Political Economy* 81, no. 3 (June 1973), pp. 521–64, reprinted with some revision and expansion in Gary S. Becker and William Landes, *Essays on the Economics of Crime and Punishment* (New York: Columbia University Press, 1974), pp. 68–134.

9. Ehrlich later used essentially similar methodology and techniques to study the effectiveness of the death penalty. He concluded that the death sentence had a significant deterrent effect on the number of crimes committed. States in which the death penalty for murder was imposed had lower murder rates than states that had either abolished or had not enforced the death penalty. Isaac Ehrlich, "The Deterrent Effect of Capital Punishment: A Question of Life and Death," *American Economic Review* 67, no. 3 (June 1977), pp. 452–58.

10. See Vernon L. Smith, "Microeconomic Systems as an Experimental Science," *American Economic Review* 76, no. 5 (December 1982), pp. 923–55.

11. Gary Becker, "A Theory of Marriage," *Journal of Political Economy* 51, no. 4 (July/August 1973), pp. 813–46.

CHAPTER

2

BASIC DEMAND AND SUPPLY

The pricing system—How is order produced from freedom of choice?—is a scientific mystery as deep, fundamental, and inspiring as that of the expanding universe or the forces that bind matter.
Vernon L. Smith, Economics Professor (1982)

An essential activity in any science is the systematic testing of theory against fact. Economics is no exception.
Harry H. Kelejian and Wallace E. Oates, Econometricians (1981)

Learning Objectives

After studying this chapter, you should be able to:

- Define demand and supply functions, and explain how demand and supply curves are derived from such functions.
- Distinguish between demand and quantity demanded, and supply and quantity supplied.
- Comprehend how the equilibrium price and quantity are determined when the market mechanism is free to operate.
- Explain how shifts in supply and demand affect market equilibrium in comparative static and dynamic cases.
- Understand the importance of the allocating and signaling functions of the price system.
- Follow the working of actual markets, both in situations where prices are free to respond to the forces of supply and demand and where they are controlled.
- Understand the consequences of intervention with the market mechanism.

Demand and Supply in the Gold Market

The Gold Market

In 1934, Congress passed the Gold Reserve Act, making it illegal for U.S. residents (with a few exceptions, such as dentists) to own gold. At the same time, Congress set the value of an ounce of gold at $35. That price remained fixed until 1968, when a free market in gold was permitted to emerge alongside the controlled one. In 1973, the link between the dollar and gold was severed, and nowadays the gold market is free to set price without official intervention. Figure 2.1 traces the dollar price of gold from 1934 through 1991. You can see that the price of gold was stable until 1967 and then became extremely mercurial, ranging from a low of $36 in 1970 to a peak of $614 in 1980.

This contrast between past price stability and current volatility should lead the curious to wonder:

1. How was the price of gold kept fixed at $35 for over 30 years?
2. How is the price of gold determined currently?

The Demand Function

The **demand function** relates the behavioral motives that underlie individual or group purchase decisions to the quantities of a specific good or service they wish to buy.

Let's work through a schematic simplification of the gold market, beginning with the demand for gold. One of the fundamental relationships economists seek to determine is the **demand function,** which links the motives that lead purchasers to acquire a specific item or service and the amounts of that commodity or service they wish to purchase. A few catchall categories are generally applicable to all demand functions— price, income, and taste—with other elements added where appropriate.

Price.   That the amount of gold people wish to buy depends on the price of gold is self-evident. Economists also include in the price category the prices of *substitutes*. Thus, the purchase decision depends on the *relative* price of gold: gold prices in comparison to the prices of substitutes.

Income.   That those in the upper-income strata are adorned in gold necklaces and are served from gold vessels while lower-income families make do at best with gold-plated jewelry and "silver"-ware suggests that the demand for gold is related to income.

Taste.   How strong a predilection we have for a particular item, which may be individually or culturally determined, influences our demand for that good or service. Thus, in the United States today it's not considered appealing to cap front teeth with gold crowns; somehow the gold smile never caught on here as it did in Eastern Europe.

FIGURE 2.1   Average Gold Prices, 1934–1989

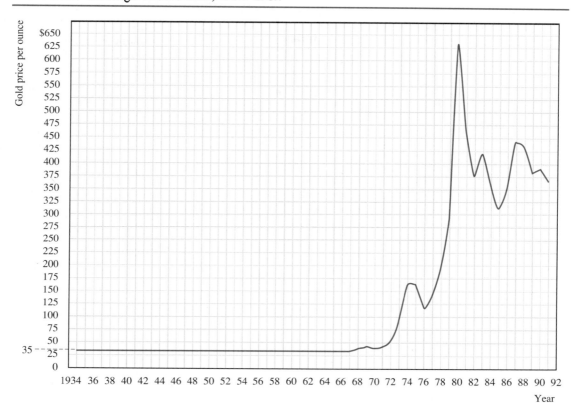

Other. Other economic motives play a role in the demand for gold. Gold has long been used as a store of wealth. The French peasant and the Indian merchant hoard gold, their traditional defense against the unknown. A speculative demand for gold has developed in the United States; some buyers acquire gold not for its usefulness or aesthetic qualities, but to sell later at a higher price. Gold is also used as a raw material in the space program, and better-quality electronic components use a thin gold wash to prevent corrosion of sensitive parts. All of these motives are germane to the demand for gold.

Population. The price, income, taste, and other categories apply to an individual's demand for gold. Often, however, economists focus on the entire market's demand, be it the total demand of a nation's residents and firms or even of the entire world. Thus, aggregation of the entire market requires an additional variable—population.

A **demand curve** is a pictorial representation of the relationship between price and the quantity desired by buyers per unit of time. A change in **quantity demanded** occurs if and only if more or less of a good or service is desired subsequent to a change in its price.

The Demand Curve.   The demand function is typically portrayed by using a **demand curve,** a pictorial representation of the relationship between the price of the item in question—the y-axis in Figure 2.2—and the quantity sought by purchasers—the x-axis.[1] Thus, the demand curve tells us that when the price per ounce is $900, buyers will want to acquire 1,000 tons annually (point *a*), but when the price is $600, they'll want to buy 1,600 tons per year (point *b*). A movement along a demand curve from *a* to *b* is normally referred to as a change in **quantity demanded.**

The other motivational factors that are included in the demand function appear behind the scenes in Figure 2.2. It is only because the public has earned a specific income and comes with a known set of tastes, and because the prices of substitute products are given, that we can set the demand curve precisely where it is.

This distinction can be driven home by asking a simple question: How do you think demanders as a group would respond if their incomes were increased (assuming nothing else has changed)? Draw the new demand curve on Figure 2.2.

FIGURE 2.2   The Demand for Gold

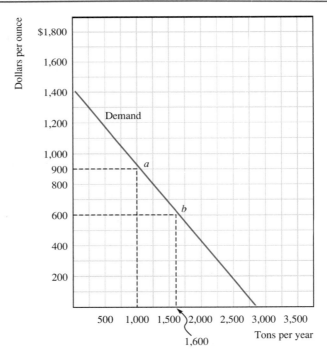

As the price per ounce falls, the quantity of gold demanded increases.

When any element
of the demand func-
tion *other than the
price of the good
itself* changes, a
shift in **demand** will
occur.

By sketching the new curve to the right of the original one, you have clearly indicated that more gold will be desired when income rises. You also would have shifted the demand curve if tastes or prices of substitutes had been altered or if anything *other than a change in the price of gold* had occurred. Not surprisingly, the appropriate terminology here is shift in **demand.**

Thus, any demand curve reveals the relationship between the price and the quantity of the good the public wishes. At the same time, the demand curve relegates to the background the other motivational elements comprising the demand function.

MICROQUERY   The price of platinum increases. Will this affect the *demand* or the *quantity demanded* of gold? _____.[2]

MICROBITS 2.1

Econometric Demand Curves

The quantitative dimension missing in theoretical demand functions and curves is spelled out by the econometric demand functions discussed in the appendix to this chapter. The econometrically derived demand curve for gold depicted at the right was based on the world gold market during the period 1977 to 1983.* Indeed, the illustrations of gold demand used in this section are based on the econometric demand curve's general shape but have been updated to more accurately represent quantities during the late 1980s.

* Source: International Gold Corp., *Gold: An Economic Analysis of Supply and Demand, 1972–1983* (New York: International Gold Corp., 1984), p. 30.

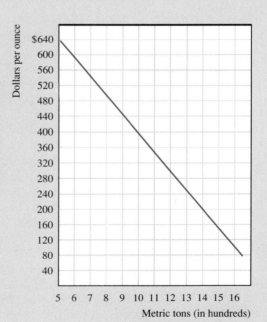

The Supply Function

The **supply function** relates the motives behind selling a specific item to the quantities of this good or service a producer and, by aggregation, all producers wish to sell.

Demand refers exclusively to the buyers of the product under discussion; supply, on the other hand, is used only to refer to the sellers of the product. In most other respects, the previous discussion concerning demand finds its analogue in supply. Just as there is a demand function, there's a **supply function,** which relates the determinants of the quantity of a product sellers wish to market to the multiplicity of forces that frame their decision. Profit is surely prominent: sellers will willingly produce more if they can increase their profits.[3] If costs per ounce of mining gold are relatively steady, then profits from gold sales will vary directly with the price per ounce.

The supply function encompasses the prices of substitutes in addition to the price of gold. Most producers have alternatives just as demanders do; they can use their capital, labor, and entrepreneurial skills to manufacture and sell other goods and services. They, too, will consider relative prices, for these indicate relative profitability. Technological innovations, too, can be an element in the supply decision; they alter the entire relationship between existing inputs and outputs. And although tastes of producers are not normally thought to play a role in supply decisions, certainly some products and services are deemed more socially acceptable than others. Also, of course, the amount supplied at each price depends on the number of firms producing and selling the item.

The Supply Curve.   The supply curve in Figure 2.3 relates the price of gold to the quantity produced. Note that the supply curve moves upward as it moves rightward; as price increases, *quantity supplied* rises, too. Why? _____

You understand that, with per unit cost of production stable and other things unchanged, a higher price implies an improved profit picture and thus induces more production. Less clear is the answer to another question: What happens if the costs of gold mining rise due to civil unrest in South Africa? Sketch the answer onto Figure 2.3.

You're right if you drew it to the left of the original supply curve. For any given price of gold, say $700, the increased cost of production has made it less profitable to mine gold and, not surprisingly, less gold will be hauled to the surface. That's equally true at the higher price of $800 and the lower price of $400.

MicroQuery   Would this properly be labeled a shift in supply or a change in quantity supplied? _____ .[4]

More difficult question: Shouldn't demand be included in the supply function, for if there were no demand, there would also be no supply? _____ because _____.[5]

FIGURE 2.3   The Supply of Gold

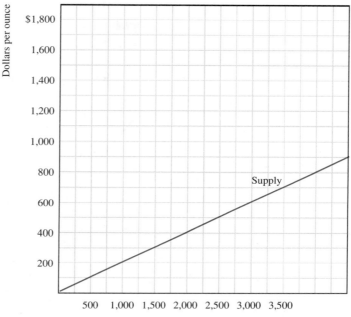

As the price per ounce rises, the quantity of gold supplied increases, too.

Supply and Demand Equilibrium

Figure 2.4 brings together the demand curve of Figure 2.2 and the supply curve of Figure 2.3. The demand curve expresses the quantities buyers are willing to purchase at various prices; the supply curve indicates the amounts sellers are willing to place on the market at various prices. The market mechanism now goes into operation.

Imagine an auctioneer who picks a price for gold out of a hat and shouts out that price. All those who are willing to buy at that price wave green flags; the number of flags would indicate how many tons gold buyers want to buy at that price. Sellers, on the other hand, are equipped with red flags, and they, too, wave their flags to show how much gold they're willing to supply at the stated price. But there's a dropout rule in this auction: When the quantities demanded and supplied are totaled and are found to be unequal, any buyer or seller can lower his or her flag. That forces the auctioneer to start over.

The auctioneer randomly picks a price of $600. Buyers wish to buy only 1,600 tons; it's a relatively high price and keeps many buyers on the

FIGURE 2.4   Demand and Supply Equilibrium in the Gold Market

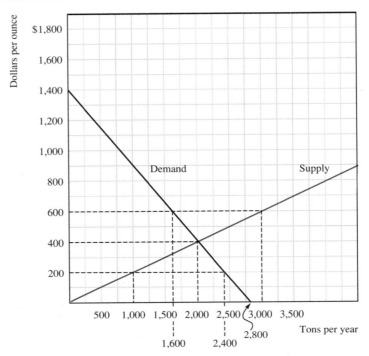

Equilibrium occurs at the price of $400 per ounce and the quantity of 2,000 tons per year, the intersection of the demand and supply curves.

A condition of **excess supply** exists when the quantity supplied at a given price exceeds the quantity demanded.

Excess demand refers to a situation when the quantity demanded at a given price exceeds the quantity supplied.

sidelines. On the other hand, such a high price attracts sellers, who would gladly supply 3,000 tons of gold per year. Buyers who notice all those sellers wanting to get rid of their gold would be foolish to keep their flags up; surely with so many willing sellers, the price would decline. In terms of Figure 2.4, the quantity supplied at the price of $600 is 3,000 tons per year and the quantity demanded is 1,600 tons, which leads to an **excess supply** of 1,400 tons. And so, on to the next round. The price picked is $500. More buyers raise their flags, but fewer sellers do. Still, if you look at Figure 2.4, gold remains in excess supply. Buyers still would be wise to keep out of the market.

The third round opens with a price of $200. Buyers are jolted out of their lethargy; a sea of green becomes visible. Indeed, it's overwhelming because few red flags are to be seen. Buyers have come out in force, but sellers have retreated. Instead of an excess supply, the market displays an **excess demand.**

MICROQUERY What is the excess demand at the price of $200? _____ tons per year.[6]

Equilibrium, or market balance, occurs at a price where the quantity supplied equals the quantity demanded. Excess supply = excess demand = 0.

The auctioneer picks again, this time coming up with a price of $400. The sellers' red flags, representing a quantity supplied of 2,000 tons, are precisely matched with the buyers' green flags. Lo and behold, **equilibrium.** No one withdraws, the price is determined, and all buyers and sellers who are willing participants in the market are matched. (In Figure 2.4, the intersection of the supply and demand curves is, of course, the equilibrium point.) Those sellers who were willing to accept at least the market price sold, and those buyers who were willing to pay at least the market price bought. To be sure, many buyers go home unsatisfied, as do many sellers. Sellers who wished to sell at a price higher than the $400 market price found no willing takers; buyers who were willing to buy only at a price less than $400 found no willing sellers.

Comparative Statics: Before and After

No market price is fixed forever. In many markets, prices change daily and often during the course of the day. (Think of the stock market.) In other markets, prices remain stable over periods of days, months, or even years (e.g., college tuition). The supply and demand apparatus is a convenient mechanism for explaining why and how prices change in response to shifts in the fundamental elements encapsulated in the supply and demand functions.

Demand Increases. You indicated in Figure 2.2 that an increase in income will lead to a rightward shift of the demand curve. So will a rise in the price of substitutes, a stronger preference for the product, and an increase in the number of demanders in the market. And, if speculators feel that the price will rise in the future, they too will increase their present demand. How does an increase in demand affect price?

Figure 2.5 reproduces Figure 2.4 but adds a stronger demand, D', for gold to the original demand curve. The increase in demand has raised the price of gold to $500 and resulted in a new equilibrium quantity of 2,500 tons. This, of course, is the comparative static result.

But the price of gold has not only risen over recent years; it has fallen, too. Can that be explained by the supply and demand technique?

Supply Increases. The gold market obtains its supply not only from newly mined gold but from already existing gold as well. Thus, suppliers can draw on inventories of gold to sell to buyers. Imagine the following scenario: Speculators who bought gold because they felt gold would rise

FIGURE 2.5   **An Increase in the Demand for Gold**

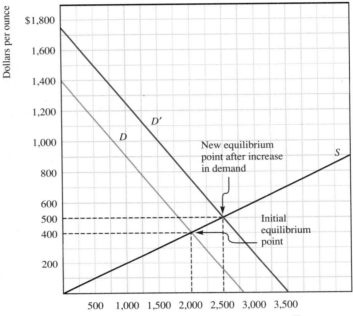

When the demand increases, the entire demand curve shifts rightward and intersects the given supply curve at a higher price and a larger quantity.

now believe that price has peaked and will soon fall. What happens on the market? _____

If you wrote that supply increases—at every existing price, suppliers are willing to place more gold on the market—and so the supply curve shifts rightward, you were right.

Figure 2.6 returns to the equilibrium of Figure 2.4 and adds a new supply curve, *S′*. The result: a new, lower equilibrium price, $300, and a higher equilibrium quantity, 2,200 tons. You should be able to explain why this comparative static result indicating a lower price and increased quantity is correct. Indeed, by now you should be able to demonstrate the impact of a decreased demand on price and equilibrium quantity as well as how price and quantity will be altered if supply is decreased. Try it to test yourself before continuing.

The Role of Market-Determined Prices and Quantities

Not every student of economics will find the pricing system as mysterious and inspiring as Professor Smith suggests in this chapter's opening quotation.

FIGURE 2.6 An Increase in the Supply of Gold

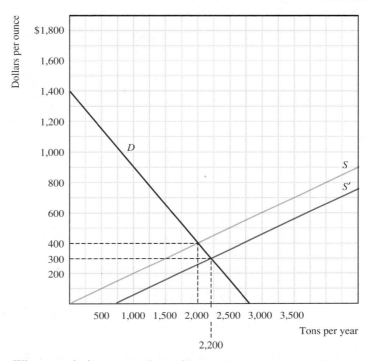

When supply increases, the entire supply curve shifts rightward and intersects the given demand curve at a lower price and a larger quantity.

When price functions as an **allocating mechanism,** it provides the available goods and services to those most willing to pay for them. Price serves as a **signaling mechanism** when it sends messages to producers to respond to the demands of the market.

Yet the pricing system is fundamental to a market economy because it serves two critical functions: it is both an **allocating mechanism** and a **signaling mechanism.**

The gold market described in the previous pages illustrates both the allocational and signaling functions of the price system. Only those individuals willing to pay at least the equilibrium price were *allocated* the available supply of gold. At the same time, the very presence of a demand for gold *signaled* suppliers that a market for their product existed. Moreover, when demand for gold increased, sellers were being signaled by the market mechanism to increase the quantity supplied.

The price system is an extremely efficient method for increasing the material wealth of an economy. It serves to minimize the impact of scarcity: scarce resources flow in the directions desired by the public. Only those goods and services, in those quantities that are demanded, will be produced. And only those who are willing to pay for the scarce resources will be able to buy them.

Clearly, however, minimizing scarcity may not be considered among society's highest priorities. Policy choices will have to be made when

MICROBITS 2.2

Confusing Demand and Quantity Demanded

The following statement appeared one day in *The Wall Street Journal*: "The coffee market is behaving the way the basic textbooks say a market behaves: Prices go up, demand falls, and prices come down." Do you agree?

Well, Professor William Poole of Brown University did not. Poole wrote, "When I taught economics the analysis went this way: 'If the supply curve shifts back, then the price will rise and the quantity sold will fall.

No further price change will occur unless there is another shift in either the supply curve or the demand curve.'" He ended, "Please don't confuse my students with the elementary fallacy of mixing up the amount demanded with the demand curve."

If the distinction between changes in demand and in quantity demanded wasn't clear before, is it now?

---

economic efficiency conflicts with other goals. Moreover, the price system may provide misleading or incorrect signals, so intervention may be necessary. Yet it is often possible to have the best of all worlds: use the price system to allocate scarce resources and send the proper signals while achieving other goals as well. And it is possible to have the worst of all worlds: diminish the efficacy of the market economy and still not achieve other high-priority objectives. Think about these points as you read the following applications.

Applications: Supply and Demand in Free and Regulated Markets

The gold market described in the preceding pages is one of many free markets for the world's commodities. The supply and demand curves sketched in the figures make reasonable sense and constitute a legitimate representation of the world gold market. The freedom of buyers and sellers to agree on a market price is also characteristic of the foreign exchange market, where the international price of the dollar is determined. In contrast, prices in the gold market before 1968, and in some loan markets even today, are subject to some degree of government control.

Free Markets

The Puzzling Behavior of the U.S. Dollar, 1973–1990.   Figure 2.7 plots the value of the U.S. dollar against an average of other foreign currencies

**FIGURE 2.7   Average Exchange Rate of the U.S. Dollar, 1973–1990
(March 1973 = 100)**

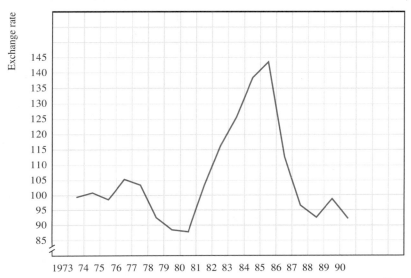

over a decade and a half. It has gone from an index value of 100 in mid-1973 to a low of almost 85 in mid-1980, to a high exceeding 150 in early 1985, and down to 95 by late 1989. Supply and demand analysis can both explain the dollar's volatility and provide a framework to investigate further the reasons for these fluctuations.

To simplify, consider a two-country world, with the United States as one country and Japan as the other. The exchange rate, then, is the value of $1 in terms of units of Japanese yen: How many yen will a dollar buy? In Figure 2.8, the exchange rate of the dollar—yen per dollar—is plotted on the vertical axis, and the quantity of dollars demanded and supplied per year on the horizontal scale. The Japanese, who earn yen in their domestic market, demand dollars to buy U.S. goods (e.g., beef); services (motion picture rentals); and assets (U.S. Treasury securities). But Americans want Japanese goods, services, and assets, too: Toyotas, flights on Japan Air Lines, and equity stakes in Japanese corporations. In order to acquire the yen to buy these Japanese products, U.S. residents must sell dollars; they are dollar suppliers.

It's reasonable to assume that both Japanese demand curves for dollars and U.S. supply curves for dollars are normally shaped.[7] The logic is straightforward. A dollar that costs a Japanese purchaser 200 yen is twice as expensive as a dollar costing only 100 yen. Consequently, any dollar-priced good is also twice as expensive: the Ford Taurus priced at $8,000 equals 1.6 million yen in the former instance, but only 800,000 yen in the

FIGURE 2.8   The Determination of the Dollar-Yen Exchange Rate

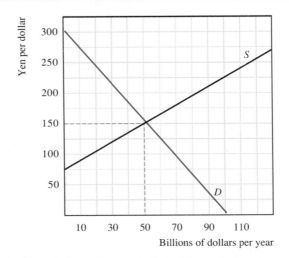

The number of yen a dollar will buy is found
at the foreign exchange rate where the
quantity of dollars demanded by the Japanese
is precisely matched by the dollars U.S.
residents wish to relinquish to acquire yen.

latter. Fewer Japanese will buy U.S. products, and thus demand fewer
dollars, when the yen price of the dollar is high than when the foreign
exchange rate of the dollar is low. Look at the demand curve in Figure
2.8; at 200 yen to the dollar, the Japanese wish to acquire only $33 billion,
while at 100 yen to the dollar, the quantity demanded increases to $67
billion.

The reverse is true from the viewpoint of American buyers of Japanese items. For them, the more yen the dollar buys, the cheaper Japanese
goods are. So, the Sony Watchman priced at 20,000 yen costs $100 when
the dollar equals 200 yen, but $200 when the dollar can be exchanged for
100 yen. These observations are implicit in the rising supply curve in
Figure 2.8.

The equilibrium exchange rate in Figure 2.8 comes at 150 yen per
dollar. But the foreign exchange market is in continual flux. It is these
exchange rate gyrations that economists seek to explain using supply and
demand analysis. In one sense that task is relatively simple; in another,
immensely difficult. Simplicity occurs at the surface level, for by now you
understand that the dollar rises in value whenever one of the following
occurs:

· Demand increases and supply remains unchanged.
· Supply falls and demand is fixed.

· The demand curve shifts rightward and the supply curve leftward.
· Both curves shift rightward, but the demand curve shifts further than does the supply curve. (Check out these statements by drawing the appropriate demand and supply curves onto Figure 2.8.)

Of course, the dollar's value will decline if these four relationships are reversed.

The analysis becomes more challenging when the economist is forced to select which of the options listed above is appropriate in each particular instance. To choose correctly, the economic analyst must delve beneath the supply and demand curves and ask what, precisely, caused them to shift. Economists today are hardly unanimous in explaining either the dollar's weakness in the periods 1973 to 1980 and 1985 to 1989 or its obvious strength during the period 1980 to 1985. Despite the absence of a consensus answer, the very fact that supply and demand analysis leads economists to ask the appropriate questions is useful, for in science, the search for the correct answer often hinges critically on asking the right questions.

A final comment. The free-market exchange rate performs its allocation and signaling functions. Dollars and yen flow to those whose demands are most intense, while signaling new opportunities for both demanders and suppliers.

Regulated Markets

The public's demand and the politician's frequent response to unexpected price gouging is price control. Often, producers invite government intervention to protect their profits. While interference is sometimes necessary and effective, rarely do political decision makers think through the consequences of their actions or the available alternatives. Keep this in mind while reviewing the following cases.

The Gold Market prior to 1968: Price-Fixing the Yellow Metal.   Monetary theory and, to some extent, U.S. practice during the first third of this century linked the rate of inflation and deflation to the price of gold. When the Great Depression of the 1930s raised the possibility that gold would flow out of this country and cause businesses to suffer further price deflation, the political authorities removed gold from monetary circulation and instituted a higher price of gold, to be fixed at $35 an ounce. Demand and supply analysis can explain how the price of gold was stabilized from 1934 through 1968.

It would stretch one's imagination to believe that the supply and demand curves never shifted during that entire 34-year interval or that the supply and demand shifts precisely offset each other with the same constant price result. (To test yourself, show how offsetting shifts in supply and demand would keep the price stable.) In fact, the price of gold was kept constant by the U.S. Treasury's willingness to buy all gold supplied at $35 an ounce and to sell gold to authorized dealers at that price. Figure 2.9 shows how such a policy works.

The supply and demand curves labeled *D* and *S* represent all of the participants in the gold market, except the U.S. Treasury, and intersect at $35 an ounce. *D'* indicates a stronger demand for gold, and in a free market would result in a price of $____.[8] At the fixed price of $35, however, the quantity demanded on *D'* exceeds the quantity supplied by five tons per year. That excess demand can be met by the Treasury supplying the missing five tons.

Or consider the alternative: an increase in supply resulting in a new supply curve. (Draw it onto Figure 2.9.) In the absence of Treasury intervention, this excess supply would cause the price of gold to fall. With the Treasury as a willing buyer, however, the price stays up. No supplier would be foolish enough to sell gold on the market for less than $35 as long as the Treasury will pay $35 the ounce. Thus, the supply curve of the

FIGURE 2.9   Fixing the Price of Gold

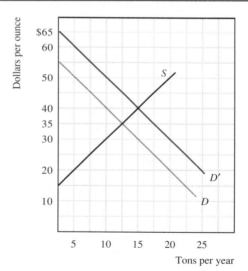

The supply and demand curves depicted here exclude the actions of the price fixer. As demand increases from *D* to *D'* price would rise. That increase is prevented by the policy of the Treasury, whose supply curve has to be provided by you.

entire market, the Treasury included, would be represented on Figure 2.9 by a horizontal line at $35.

What about the demand curve of the market, Treasury included? (Draw that onto Figure 2.9.) When you realize that no buyer would be willing to pay more than $35 an ounce for gold as long as the Treasury stood ready to sell it at that price, then the demand curve, too, becomes horizontal at $35. Is it surprising, then, that since the demand and supply curves overlap at $35 an ounce, the price of good remained at $35 an ounce?

Could this policy persist forever? Not if demand continued to rise, for then the Treasury at some point would run out of gold. Indeed, as the Treasury's gold stock nears depletion, speculators would anticipate the dismantling of the policy and a rise in the price of gold. Their demand for gold would put further pressure on the declining gold stock. Ultimately, the stabilization policy would cease and the price of gold would rise. That in a nutshell is the reason the Treasury abandoned its policy of gold price stabilization during the late 1960s.

Usury Laws: The Wrong Means to Noble Goals.   The major religions of the Western world forbid usury, that is, interest rate charges in excess of some accepted level. (In some instances, that level is zero, so any interest charge is by definition usurious.) In the United States, states that have passed usury laws have applied them to consumer rather than to business borrowing. The ostensible purpose for limiting the interest rate a lender may legally charge is a social concern: consumers, especially poorer ones, should not be forced to pay exorbitant interest charges. Figure 2.10a sketches out the background and the immediate impact of the law. With a normal demand curve (indicating that individuals will borrow more at lower interest rates) and a normal supply curve (demonstrating lenders' readiness to increase the quantity of loans supplied at higher interest rates), the market interest rate would be 10 percent, the price at which quantity supplied matches quantity demanded.

When the authorities impose a rate ceiling of, say, 8 percent, an excess demand is created. Lenders wish to lend only $90 billion per year, while borrowers seek to obtain $120 billion. In the absence of further change, this disequilibrium will persist. What are the consequences of such intervention in the loan market?

· *The market's allocative mechanism is disrupted.* First, notice that the size of the market is artificially expanded. An extra $20 billion is demanded by potential borrowers who would not have wanted to borrow at the 10 percent market interest rate but would pay at least 8 percent. Second, since price can no longer serve to distribute the limited loans to the demanding borrowers, some other rationing mechanism must be devised. Perhaps each borrower is given only a portion of the loan desired; perhaps first come, first served; perhaps friends are funded before stran-

FIGURE 2.10   **The Impact of a Usury Law**

a.   The Short-Run Impact

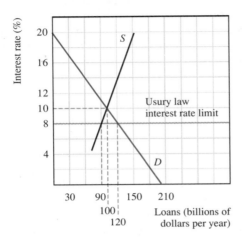

b.   A Long-Run Impact: The Creation of a Black Market

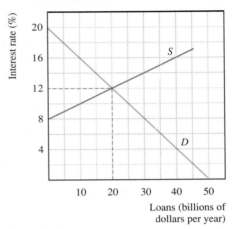

a.   When a usury law is imposed at 8 percent, an excess demand disequilibrium is created, leading to only $90 billion in loans and an excess demand of $30 billion.

b.   Both borrowers whose loan needs are not met and lenders who find the usury ceiling too low may develop an illegal loan market. On that market, the interest rate will be determined by the interplay of supply and demand.

gers, even if the latter had more urgent needs and would be willing to pay a higher rate. But all such alternatives defeat the allocating function of the market, which requires that those whose needs are most intense (as represented by their willingness to pay a higher price) obtain the scarce resources.[9]

• *The signaling function of the market is stymied.* Because the price of loans cannot rise above 8 percent, changes in demand and/or supply that would lead to higher interest rates cannot be indicated to market participants. In turn, capital resources will be misallocated. As you will see in Chapter 18, the interest rate is a key variable in making investment decisions. When interest rates are kept artificially low, capital will be used even though other resources are more abundant. Moreover, users of capital will not respond to changes in scarcity; there's no price shift to pass on the appropriate message.

• *The ostensible purpose is rarely achieved.* Perhaps one could be reconciled to inappropriate economic controls if they proved effective in attaining their goals. Unfortunately, price controls rarely accomplish their desired objectives. Thus, during the inflationary 1970s, when the difference between free-market interest rates and usury limits drifted evermore apart, bankers preferred to lend to prime corporate borrowers at higher market rates rather than channel funds at the ceiling rates to the targeted beneficiaries, single-family home buyers.

• *Market reaction in the long run.* Figure 2.10a represents the short-run impact of imposing usury laws But the market is a dynamic, and short-run constraints do have long-run consequences. Two are especially pertinent: (1) the development of a black market and (2) resource shifting.

1. *The black market.* The incentive to develop an illegal or **black market** is apparent: some borrowers who are willing to pay more than the usury rate will seek out lenders who wish to lend at a higher rate. Let's see how such a market could evolve and operate. First, assume that in the regulated market each borrower obtains only a portion of the loan sought, that portion being the difference between the available quantity supplied at the usury rate and the quantity demanded at that rate. Specifically, in Figure 2.10a the quantity demanded is $120 billion and the quantity supplied is only $90 billion. Thus, each borrower who is willing to pay at least 8 percent obtains three fourths of the desired amount legally. The demand curve in Figure 2.10b represents the unfulfilled fourth. So, at the rate of 10 percent, borrowers had wanted to obtain $100 billion; they actually received three fourths of that amount, or $75 billion, and would be willing to pay 10 percent for the missing $25 billion.[10] Similarly, the quantity demanded at 8 percent is $30 billion, the excess demand at that interest rate. The supply curve in Figure 2.10b is merely the supply curve of Figure 2.10a above 8 percent, after taking into account the $90 billion lent on the legal market. Thus, at an interest rate of 10 percent, the quantity supplied is $10 billion, the difference between the $100 supplied in the entire market and the $90 billion lent at the ceiling interest rate. Similarly at 14 percent, the quantity supplied equals the $120 billion of Figure 2.10a less $90 billion, or $30 billion.[11]

You understand that in this illegal market the equilibrium interest rate will be 12 percent.

But there's more to this tale. Some law-abiding lenders, who become aware of the higher rates available in the black market, will be enticed to shift their loanable funds from the legal market to the illegal one. How does that affect the supply curves in both markets? The demand curves? Draw the new supply and demand curves onto both parts of Figure 2.10.

You are perfectly correct if you shifted the supply curve leftward in Figure 2.10a, indicating fewer suppliers in the legal market, and rightward in Figure 2.10b, showing a compensating movement as lenders enter the black market. But as lenders move out of the legal market, the portion of the loan that demanders can satisfy from the legal market also falls, and they, too, have to shift into the illegal market. If this process continues, the illegal market will dominate and the market price will approach the unregulated market price. The usury rate mechanism will have been substantially, if not totally, circumvented.

Thus, the silver lining in the cloud of the illegal market is that the outcome approximates the free market and restores its allocational and signaling functions. But it does raise a disturbing question that policy-makers rarely address: If price controls are maintained for a sufficiently long period and unleash forces that reestablish the free-market outcome, why regulate prices in the first place?

2. *Resource shifting.* Black markets, however, do not always grow large; if they do, the authorities often crack down to reduce their scope. That does not imply that the long-run consequences of market interven-tion are those predicted by the regulators. At the very least, some suppli-ers shift production into other unregulated, more profitable markets, and some simply sell their product in regions that are not regulated. Such was the case with one major bank that switched its credit-card billing from New York, which had an unrealistically low usury rate, to a western state with no usury law. The presumed beneficiaries lose out whether suppliers abandon production entirely or shift out of the area. In terms of Figure 2.10a, the supply curve is displaced continuously leftward over time until all lenders have departed from the regulated market.

Wheat in the Desert. Most Americans' impressions of Saudi Arabia could be summarized as an immense desert floating on a sea of oil. In-deed, oil is that nation's major natural resource and predominant export; the country imports most of its consumer products, including staples of various sorts, as well as industrial goods and services. And yet, because of government intervention in the market, Saudi Arabia began to produce enough wheat to meet its own needs and by 1985 had a substantial sur-plus. But the cost is mind-boggling,[12] making the U.S. agricultural give-aways seem reasonable by comparison.

Consider the following: In 1983, the world price of wheat was in the neighborhood of $150 a ton. In Saudi Arabia, the cost of producing a ton of wheat was about $600. In order to induce wheat production, the Saudi marketing board offered to buy wheat from farmers for $1,000 per ton, guaranteeing the producers a profit of $400 per ton. It made admirable sense for a profit-oriented agriculturalist to drive a well a mile deep for water to irrigate sandy fields.

While the setting of minimum prices by the Saudi Arabian govern-ment in this instance is the reverse of the usury rate policy just discussed, its consequences are no less problematic. Figure 2.11 sketches the domes-tic Saudi wheat market. Wheat production is unprofitable whenever the price for wheat is below $600 per ton. Above that price, the supply curve takes its normal shape, starting at a hypothesized output of 400,000 tons per year and rising as prices increase. Domestic demanders, considering the price of wheat on the world market, would not be willing to pay more than $150 per ton, but would increase their quantity demanded at lower prices. Obviously, the supply and demand curve don't meet; the maxi-

---

MICROBITS 2.3

The Price Ceiling that Caused the Russian Revolution

Sometimes, the consequences of a price ceiling are far-reaching, changing the political constellation of the world, as the following episode illustrates.

Nicolas Slonimsky is one of those immigrants who have enriched the cultural life of America. During his long and multifaceted career—he was 92 in 1986—Slonimsky was a piano accompanist to Serge Koussevitsky and the Boston Symphony Orchestra and to several famous opera singers, a modern composer and conductor who championed a number of avant-garde composers and their works, a professor of Slavic languages at Harvard, and an author of numerous books on music. In 1916, Slonimsky was a draftee in the Czarist army and was in St. Petersburg for the start of the Russian Revolution. Here is his explanation of the events:

Actually, all of the trouble started because of a crazy rule about the electric trams. *Soldiers,* because of their service in the war, *were being allowed to ride free, but because of the way they tended to hog all the available space, preventing civilians from even getting on the trams,* the number of soldiers permitted on board a tram was limited to six at a time. If a

seventh soldier boarded, all seven were subject to immediate arrest, notwithstanding the manifest innocence of the first six. This led to increasing clashes between soldiers and military police, and one day in February [1917] some regular Army troops were called in to back up the military police, but they refused to act against their buddies. So then, in an effort to staunch the deteriorating situation, the most loyal imperial regiment, my own Preobrazhensky, was called in to quell the mutiny—only, we refused, too. And within hours came word that the Czar had abdicated. We'd had no idea! All over a silly, unenforceable regulation.* [italics added]

Read the italicized words again. What happens to the quantity demanded when the price ceiling is zero? When the supply of trollies did not adjust to the additional need for them, an alternative course of action had to be taken. How unpredictable and, at least according to Slonimsky, revolutionary was the result!

---

*Quoted in Lawrence Wechsler, "Boy Wonder," *The New Yorker,* November 17, 1986, p. 70.

---

mum price offered by buyers is far below the minimum price farmers need to grow wheat. And so, wheat would be imported, as was the case prior to the subsidization policy.

Introduce now the minimum wheat price of $1,000 per ton, represented by the horizontal line at the $1,000 level. That line crosses the supply curve at an output of 800,000 tons per year, which becomes the quantity produced. The marketing board pays out $800 million, and the farmers receive a subsidy worth $400 times 800,000 tons, or $320 million. When the marketing board sells the crop domestically at no more than $150 per ton, it recoups $120 million, for a net cost of $200 million per

FIGURE 2.11   **The Saudi Arabian Wheat Market**

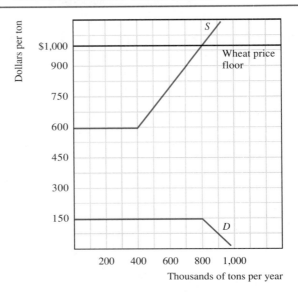

The $150 per ton world market price precludes domestic demanders from purchasing domestic wheat costing $600 per ton. Production takes place only because of a government-guaranteed price of $1,000 a ton.

year. The Saudi government might have provided such a substantial subsidy in order to guarantee itself a strategic wheat supply in case of war or blockade or some other adverse political event. But even to the oil-rich Saudis, such a degree of subsidization seemed profligate and led to modest reductions in the price floor.

By now you should understand how the Saudi Arabian agricultural policy wastes resources. It would be far cheaper to take advantage of efficient world producers and stockpile wheat than to grow it in the desert and deplete the country's scarce water supply.

The consequences of intervening in the price system in both the usury law and agricultural subsidy examples were quite clear. But that's not always the case. Consider this paradox: The U.S. government insists that each package of cigarettes carry a warning label designed to scare people away from smoking and thereby reduce the demand for cigarettes. At the same time, the government subsidizes tobacco production and thus increases supply. Will the net effect of these conflicting policies be an increase or a decline in tobacco consumption? Theory alone cannot answer this question. And even when economic theory can indicate the potential impact of the policy change, be it a private business decision or a public policy issue, sometimes that's just not enough. Decision makers would benefit from a quantitative estimate of the impact. To do that, we need to derive econometric supply and demand functions, the methods and qualifications for which may be found in the appendix to this chapter.

The Dynamics of Supply and Demand

Although comparative static models are frequently useful, they cannot be applied to all circumstances. In this final segment of the chapter, you'll read about a dynamic model, which considers explicitly the timing of supply-demand responses. The famous cobweb model also sets the stage for uncertainty. Once you concede that reactions in the market are not instantaneous, you realize that additional unknown actions can occur in the intervening period.

The Cobweb Model

The comparative static model of the gold market suggested that when the demand for gold increases, the price of gold will rise and, consequently, the quantity of gold supplied will increase as well. You must realize two things, however. First, gold mining and processing take time; producers can't immediately increase production and ship more gold to the market. Second, for output to increase, gold-mining firms either must be convinced that the higher price is going to last for a while or must somehow be able to lock in the higher price. Otherwise, they could be stuck with high-cost, low-profit inventories.

The cobweb model demonstrates what can happen to overanxious suppliers who react to market vagaries. It shows how the time element in production can lead to a cycle of actions and reactions. To achieve the cobweb outcome, asymmetric reactions by demanders and suppliers must be postulated. While demanders condition their purchases on current prices, suppliers determine their production of the basis of past prices. So, for example, if it takes a year to mine, process, and ship more gold from existing facilities, then the assumption requires suppliers to believe that 1995 prices will prevail in 1996, but demanders in 1996 will buy gold only on the basis of 1996 prices.

Figure 2.12 sketches a normal demand curve and a modified supply curve, with quantity supplied based on the prices of the previous period.[13] Thus, the point on the supply curve where price equals $200 per ounce and the quantity supplied equals 200 tons must be read as follows: When price *last year* was $200, then the quantity supplied *this year* will be 200 tons. (Of course, the point on the demand curve corresponding to $200—1,400 tons—refers to the quantity demanded this year.) The supply curve's designation contains a subscript, $t - 1$, to indicate that the quan-

FIGURE 2.12   The Cobweb

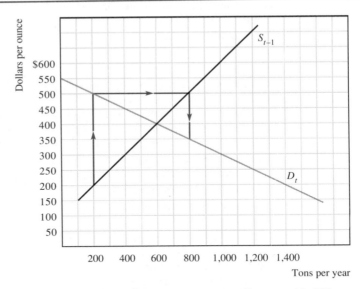

Starting at a price of $200 an ounce, suppliers provide 200 tons, which forces price up to $500 per ounce. That in turn induces suppliers to sell 800 tons, which forces price down to $350 per ounce.

tity supplied is based on the previous period's price. And, for symmetry, the subscript t is appended to the demand curve to show that the quantity demanded in any period depends on the price in that same period.

Now let's see what happens. Begin with a 1995 price of $200 per ounce, leading suppliers to bring only 200 tons to the market in 1996. What will the 1996 price be? _____

If you wrote in $500, that's perfect. Since 200 tons are available on the market, the demand curve shows that buyers would bid up the price to $500. At any lower price, there'd be too many demanders for the limited quantity of gold available on the market. (Notice in Figure 2.12 the vertical line drawn upward from S_{t-1} at the quantity 200, stopping at the demand curve.)

What happens next? Of course, the higher-than-anticipated 1996 price leads to seller reaction; sellers increase production, anticipating that in 1997, gold will sell for the 1996 price of $500 an ounce. How much will they expect to market in 1997? _____

The way to tell, of course, is to look at the 1996 price and find the corresponding quantity supplied on the supply curve—it's 800 tons—since 1997's expected sales depend on 1996's actual price.

But what actually happens in 1997? Since 800 tons were produced, that large quantity finds few demanders at high prices. Only when the price falls to $350 per ounce will sufficient buyers come into the market to purchase the available quantity supplied.

You should now be able to figure out the situation in 1998, after suppliers react to the 1997 gold price of $350. Do that by drawing the 1998, and for good measure the 1999, results onto Figure 2.12. (Check in the Notes and Answers section for the correct answers.[14]) If you've drawn it properly, you will understand why the model is dubbed a *cobweb.*

In successive rounds, a **converging cobweb** moves toward the supply-demand intersection, while an **exploding cobweb** moves away from that point.

One final note: Figure 2.12 is a **converging cobweb.** Were you to trace out the pattern forever, you'd ultimately find the cobweb comes to an end at the supply-demand intersection. But that outcome depends crucially on the relative slopes of the supply and demand curves. The cobweb "**explodes,**" or moves ever outward rather than inward, when the slope of the demand curve is larger (in absolute value) than the slope of the supply curve. Or, by drawing the slopes of both curves at precisely the same angle, you can parade endlessly around the perimeter of a square. Try it.

Protection against Uncertainty: Futures Markets

Virtually all suppliers face the problem implicit in the cobweb: a time lapse between the decision to produce and the actual completion of production. But producers can't wait. Farmers can't delay planting while the crop price is being established, nor can students forever change majors. True, producers not selling in competitive markets can control their prices and thus reduce the uncertainty deriving from fluctuating prices. But producers in competitive markets do not have this option.

When output is not perishable and the costs of storage are modest, producing for inventory becomes a viable alternative to either delaying production or selling in a weak market. The stored output can be sold when demand and prices strengthen. But for perishable products or those whose inventory costs are significant, storage is not a profitable method of reducing uncertainty.

A **futures market** is an organized mechanism for determining prices prior to the physical availability of the commodity in question. Prices for current delivery are determined on the **spot market**.

In many instances, **futures markets** have evolved to remove price uncertainty. In essence, sellers commit their future output at a fixed price determined months or even years in advance. Both sellers and buyers benefit—sellers because they know precisely how much they're going to collect per ton and buyers because they know exactly how much it's going to cost them. Thus, in late November 1986, when an ounce of gold was priced on the **spot market** at $388.20, the futures market price for delivery in August 1988, almost two years later, was $414.70. In other words, a gold seller in the futures market would be guaranteed by the purchaser of the futures contract a price of $414.70 for the gold the firm would bring to market in August 1988.

A **hedger** uses the futures market to guarantee future prices, passing on the risk to the **speculator.** The latter hopes to achieve a profit from a favorable discrepancy between the agreed-on futures price and the spot market price.

You realize, of course, that uncertainty has not disappeared; it's merely been shifted from the **hedgers** to the **speculators.**[15] In fact, in August 1988, the spot gold price was actually \$431.31 per ounce. Had the contract not been made, the seller could have earned a profit on each ounce of gold of more than 4 percent. But that's the price of insuring against uncertainty. After all, the price could have moved in the other direction as well, leading to significant real losses had the seller not hedged.

Although the term *speculator* is often used pejoratively, speculators perform a useful economic function. By absorbing risk from producers, speculators permit suppliers to produce more rather than withhold output, conditioned by their understandable reluctance to commit their own scarce resources to an unknown future. Thus, speculators help alleviate the scarcity that lies at the foundation of the economic problem.

A Concluding Thought

This chapter, focusing on the ability of the market system to limit the impact of scarcity, points out the importance of the price mechanism in both allocating scarce goods and signaling the types and quantities of products desired by the marketplace. It demonstrates how in a broad variety of markets and circumstances, the supply and demand mechanism can be used to understand real-life events. Moreover, the chapter notes that interference with the free interplay of supply and demand can lead to resource misallocations and the elimination of the very benefits the price system is uniquely qualified to achieve.

Nevertheless, many economists feel that a totally unregulated price system does not always benefit society. At times, the conditions for the free market are not satisfied even in the absence of government intervention, as when private monopolies dominate an economy and thus distort the operation of the market mechanism. At times, the market cannot appropriately allocate resources because the costs to

society of certain types of economic activity, though created by private producers, are not borne by them, as in the case of industrial air pollution. And one may, on ethical or social grounds, be dissatisfied with the distribution of income that is a consequence of the unregulated operation of the market system. These are issues that cannot be avoided.

Yet one lesson bursts forth from the examples of market regulation included in this chapter: The market is a vital, resilient force. Regulatory intervention must be accomplished by working through the system rather than by ignoring its existence.

Perhaps both the advantages of the pricing mechanism and the conflicts inherent in its use can best be illustrated by a final case: the baby market.

In 1978, Elisabeth M. Landes, a postdoctoral fellow at the University of Chicago's School of Business, and Richard A. Posner, then a professor of law at the university's Law School and now a federal appellate judge, wrote an article that raised the following question: Why are there so few white babies available for adoption?[16] Landes and Posner argued that the adoption agencies that dominate the legal market do not charge a market-clearing price, evidenced in part by an excess demand for white babies. As you would expect from the earlier discussion of usury laws, under such conditions a black market in white babies has arisen, with prices on that market far in excess of the regulated price.[17]

Landes and Posner's provocative solution: a free market in newborn infants, in which babies would be rationed among potential adoptive parents by price.[18] Landes and Posner believe that "the price system would do as good a job as, or a better job than, adoption agencies in finding homes for children that would maximize their satisfactions in life." Moreover, "willingness to pay money for a baby would seem on the whole a reassuring factor from the standpoint of child welfare." Among the positive side effects of their proposal, Landes and Posner note that a free market in babies would reduce the demand for abortion, since a mother could sell her newborn after carrying it to term rather than abort the fetus. Finally, they argue that the major resistence to the proposal comes from adoption agencies and their professional personnel who benefit most directly from the existing system.

Critics of the Landes-Posner plan abound. Some view a market for babies as intrinsically repugnant, others dispute the notion that ability to pay can be equated with care and concern, and still others fear turning children into commodities.[19] And what do you do if you're dissatisfied with your purchase? Do you return it to the natural parents? Undoubtedly, the Landes-Posner proposal, based on a supply and demand analysis of the baby market, remains a provocative solution to a serious social problem. It also indicates once again the distance economics has traveled in contemporary America.

Key Terms

Allocating mechanism	Quantity demanded
Black market	Quantity supplied
Converging cobweb	Shift in demand
Demand curve	Signaling mechanism
Demand function	Speculator
Equilibrium	Spot market
Excess demand	Supply
Excess supply	Supply curve
Exploding cobweb	Supply function
Futures market	Usury laws
Hedger	

Review Questions

1. *a.* Specify the demand and supply functions for the following:
    (1) Deodorants.
    (2) Pet food.
    (3) Arrows.
    (4) Gasoline.
    In each case, explain your choice of the variables included.
  b. Draw the demand and supply curves for each of the above.

2. *Given:* normally shaped demand and supply curves for spies, with the annual salary on the ordinate and the annual hours worked on the abscissa. *To do:* Fill in the table below, indicating whether the variable listed across the top will be increased, decreased, or left unchanged by the action listed on the left. (Treat each action as independent of previous ones.)

	Demand	Quantity Demanded	Price	Supply	Quantity Supplied
War tensions rise					
Penalties for spying are reduced					
A tax is imposed on spies					
Technical advances reduce the need for on-the-spot espionage					
A maximum salary that is less than current pay is imposed on spies					

3. Use supply and demand analysis to demonstrate how the dollar/yen exchange rate will be uniquely affected by:
  a. An increase in the Japanese rate of inflation.
  b. A quality improvement in U.S. automobiles.

4. *a.* How is a price ceiling maintained in the face of continued excess demand?
  b. Why is an illegal market likely to develop in such circumstances?
  c. What are the likely positive or negative consequences of such price controls?

5. *a.* How does price serve both as an allocation and a signaling mechanism in a free market?
  b. Why are these functions compromised in a market in which prices are regulated?

6. Draw and explain an exploding cobweb.

7. How does a future market serve to shift risk from producers to speculators?

8. Draw the supply and demand curves implicit in the proposal to substitute the free-market model for adoption agency placement. Explain why excess demand exists under present arrangements and why it would disappear under the Landes-Posner proposal.

Food for Thought

1. Use supply and demand analysis to map out the following real-life events:
   a. "Demand for Used Jets Sends Prices Soaring"
   b. "Orange Juice Prices Plunge as Weather Is Mild in Florida"
   c. "Advance in Copper Prices Is Attributed to Rising Demand, Declining Supply"
   d. "High Prices Induce New Oil Exploration/The Normal Lag between Discovery and Production Is Four Years"
   e. "Short Supply Causes Hotel Prices to Soar"
   f. "Suzuki Samurai's Sales Have Plunged since Consumers Union Called It Unsafe"

2. Scalpers who illegally sell tickets to sporting events at the stadium just prior to the game usually charge a significant premium over the ticket's stated price.
   a. Use supply and demand analysis to explain this phenomenon.
   b. Why do the prices often fall drastically as the time of the game approaches?
   c. Are scalpers performing a useful economic function?
   d. Can you provide a rationale for the official ticket window charging less for a ticket than the public is willing to pay?

3. In an article on the kiwi, a brown, egg-shaped fruit that hails from New Zealand, a newspaper wrote, "An expanding demand inevitably brought new suppliers into the market. . . . [Soon] the world was awash in kiwis, and the price dropped dramatically. . . ." Can you detect a confusion between demand and supply and quantity demanded and supplied?

4. Among the problems pointed out by critics of rent control, which sets limits on the rents landlords may charge tenants, is the deterioration of urban housing in cities where such controls are enforced.
   a. What is the connection between rent control and urban blight?
   b. Could you suggest an alternative plan that would not interfere with the price mechanism yet would protect tenants and permit landlords to earn a reasonable profit?

5. If enrollment in engineering schools depends on the current starting salaries of engineers, but the supply of new engineers comes into the job market four years after initial enrollment, can you explain why engineering school enrollment is subject to periodic fluctuations?

6. Some economic thinkers have proposed alleviating critical shortages of uncontaminated blood for transfusions; kidneys, livers, and lungs for transplants; and surrogate mothers to carry fertilized human ova by permitting a free market in blood, human organs, and surrogate motherhood. What would be the advantages and disadvantages of these proposals?

Suggested Readings

Contemporary U.S. gold mining, with both historical and human interest elements, is featured in John Seabrook, "Gold Mining," *The New Yorker,* April 24, 1989, pp. 45–80. Robert Solomon's *The International Monetary System, 1945–1976: An Insider's View* (New York: Harper and Row, 1977) provides a scholarly account of gold's role in U.S. policy before and after 1968.

A somewhat dated yet fundamentally sound review of U.S. agricultural subsidy programs may be found in Chapter 4, "Income Transfers to Agriculture" of the *Economic Report of the President, 1986* (Washington, D.C.: Government Printing Office, 1986). A more general critique of government involvement in economic activity is Hernando de Soto's *The Other Path: The Invisi-*

ble Revolution in the Third World (New York: Harper and Row, 1989).

Minor league baseball is the subject of a theoretical and empirical demand and supply study by John J. Siegfried and Jeff D. Eisenberg, "The Demand for Minor League Baseball," *Atlantic Economic Journal* 8, no. 2 (July 1980), pp. 59–69.

Notes and Answers

1. Note that the price of gold is measured in dollars per ounce, while the quantity is designated in tons per year. Specifying the price per quantity and the time dimension is crucial. It clearly makes a difference whether we're discussing dollars per ounce or per pound and demand for gold per week, per year, or per decade.

2. The correct answer is demand, since the price of substitutes is one of the elements kept constant when sketching the demand curve. Only a change in the price of gold would lead to a change in the quantity demanded.

3. In this elementary discussion, it will suffice to define profits as the difference between revenues (or earnings) and costs, and the per unit profit as the difference between price and cost per unit.

4. Because some element in the supply function other than price changed, this clearly represents a shift in supply.

5. However innocuous this statement appears, it masks a confusion many students encounter. By definition, the supply function encompasses only those causes that *directly* affect sellers. In the case of demand, the impact on suppliers is indirect, for demand registers its influence on sellers through price. If the demand for the product is weak, then suppliers would be unable to command a high price. Consequently, their profits would be low and so, too, would their production. Profits and prices are the direct causes, and they're already found in the supply function. Listing demand there would be redundant.

6. 1,400.

7. Advanced texts in international economics demonstrate the conditions under which this paragraph is technically correct.

8. 40.

9. Recent literature on the allocation of banking resources suggests that to some extent lenders may prefer a situation wherein they are faced by an excess demand. Because borrowers do not always pay off their loans and because lending is an art, bankers may prefer to have a larger selection of potential clients so that they can pick and choose. Nevertheless, most economists would distinguish between rational decisions made by lenders to better control their own allocation of resources and interest rate ceilings imposed upon them by statute or regulation.

10. Actually, this is a bit misleading, for an individual borrower might be willing to pay more than 10 percent, considering that she had already obtained three fourths of the loan at the unexpectedly low price of 8 percent. Introducing this consideration will only complicate the analysis without altering the thrust of the argument, so it's omitted here. Nevertheless, you might want to work out a more correct demand curve to verify this last statement.

11. This, too, is a bit of a simplification, for it doesn't take into account the lenders' risk of being caught and paying the penalties for violating the usury law or, alternatively, the cost of bribing the enforcers of the code. Thus, the actual supply curve in Figure 2.10b

will be somewhat to the left of that depicted here.

12. London's *The Economist* called it "the world's most successful and lunatic agricultural policy" (November 23, 1985), p. 70.

13. The relevant variable in the supply function is not the price of gold but the *expected* price of gold. In the case of the cobweb, this expectational relationship is very crude: the expected price of gold when it comes to market is assumed to equal this year's price.

14. For 1998, the quantity of gold supplied is 500 tons, which sells for a price of $425 per ounce. That leads to a 1999 outcome of 650 tons produced, which is sold at a price of $387.50 per ounce.

15. Here again an obvious expectational element enters into the demand curve. The speculator is concerned not with the current price of gold but with the price of gold when the futures contract matures.

16. Elisabeth M. Landes and Richard A. Posner, "The Economics of the Baby Shortage," *Journal of Legal Studies* 7, No. 2, (June 1978), pp. 323–48.

17. Landes and Posner believed that in the mid-1970s the maximum legal market costs were $3,000, while black-market prices were thought to lie in the $9,000–$40,000 range.

18. The authors were careful to note that they "do not suggest that parents should have the right to sell older children." Some parents, however, surely would disagree!

19. See the letters to the editor in *The Wall Street Journal*, August 19 and 22, 1986, that came in response to an article on Judge Posner and his "infant formula."

Appendix
From Theory to Empirical Estimation

How Econometricians Estimate Demand Functions

The relationship between theory and empirical estimation is close and direct. Theory sets up the overall pattern; the empirical tasks are then (a) to examine the facts for their consistency with the conceptual design and (b) to estimate the relative importance of the manifold causative forces. A theoretical skeleton shows the economist what to estimate. And quantitative estimates help the economist assess the validity of the analytic framework itself and the significance of the theory's various components. The scientific process typically finds the economist or econometrician first specifying, then fitting data, and finally evaluating test results.

Consider the demand function for gold presented at the beginning of this chapter. Theory suggests that the demand function contains the price of gold; the price of substitutes; the incomes of the public; a preference variable; and, for the entire market demand, a population variable.

The econometrician can formulate these components into a testable equation that might look like this:

$$Q_D = a + bP_G + cP_P + dY + eN + u$$

In words, the equation reads as follows:

Quantity demanded of gold = a, a constant (to be calculated) + b, a coefficient (to be calculated) $\times$ the price of gold + c, a second coefficient $\times$ the price of the appropriate substitute (say platinum) + d, a third coefficient $\times$ income + e, a fourth coefficient $\times$ population + u, a random variable.

The task of the econometrician, having formulated the appropriate equation, is to find the proper data to represent these **independent,** or causal, **variables** as well as the **dependent variable.** Then, the econometrician performs the techniques of the trade, which, in an age of computer technology, is normally the simplest task. The calculated equation might read as follows:

$$Q = 1{,}000 \text{ tons} - 50P_G + 67P_P + 1.4Y + 0.1N$$

where Q is in tons; the Ps are in dollars per ounce; the income variable, Y, is in units of $100 million; and N, the population variable, is in units of 200 million individuals.[1]

The equation then is interpreted as follows:

1. *The constant: 1,000 tons.* If all of the variables—P_G, P_P, Y, and N—were set at zero, the public's demand for gold would equal 1,000 tons. This obviously puzzling statement isn't to be taken literally; in essence it contributes to defining the end point of the demand curve on the quantity axis.

The causal or determining forces in an econometric equation are called the **independent variables,** while the variable to be determined is known as the **dependent variable.**

2. *The price of gold variable: −50P_G.* If the price of gold rises by $1 an ounce, the quantity of gold demanded would decline—note the minus sign—by 50 tons.

3. *The price of platinum: 67P_P.* On the other hand, if the price of platinum rises by $1 an ounce, the quantity of gold demanded would increase by 67 tons. (Why should there be a direct relationship between the price of platinum and the quantity of gold demanded? _____[2])

4. *The income variable: 1.4Y.* If the public's income increases by $100 million dollars, the quantity of gold demanded would increase by 1.4 tons.

5. *The population variable: 0.1N.* Finally, if the population expands by 200 million, the quantity of gold demanded would increase by 1/10 of a ton.

Having reached this far, the econometrician now evaluates the results by addressing the two questions raised earlier: (*a*) Is the theory consistent with the facts as portrayed by the econometric outcome? and (*b*) How important are the individual variables? If you've already taken a course in econometrics, you know that tests can be conducted to answer these questions. They are discussed in all elementary econometric textbooks.

Econometric Issues in Estimating Demand

This brief description of econometric technique has avoided mentioning the manifold problems faced in trying to derive numerical estimates of a demand curve. Today, econometrics is as much an art as it is a science. Its difficulties need to be mentioned in order for you to be able to evaluate the significance of the empirical results that will appear throughout the text. Indeed, some economists believe these problems to be so massive that they have little faith in econometric estimates.

a. Operationally Defining the Variables.   A number of obvious questions crop up when translating conceptual terms into measurable ones. For example what substitutes should be considered as important in determining the quantity of gold demanded? Given a variety of measures of income, which one should be used? And, how can you measure preferences? Another set of questions is addressed to the timing relationships: Is the quantity of gold demanded in this period related to the present period's income or perhaps to some combination of present and past periods' incomes?

b. Functional Forms.   Take a look again at Figure 2.2 (p. 32), which depicts the demand curve for gold. If you were to determine the mathematical relationship expressed in the curve, you would write:

$$Q_D = 2,800 - 2P_G.$$

Thus, for every increase in the price of gold by $1, the quantity demanded will decline by two tons. Technically, the slope of the demand curve is −2. This and all other demand and supply curves in the figures in this chapter were straight lines or linear. But if the true demand is curved while the econometrician assumes the demand curve is linear, he may derive an erroneous empirical demand curve. That could lead to inappropriate decisions.

c. Data Gathering.   The data-gathering stage is sometimes, though rarely, easy. The root of the problem lies in the fact that the econometrician normally works with data already assembled. The researcher rarely has the time or the resources to start data collection from scratch. But such data are usually not designed with econometric testing in mind, and so they are rarely suitable and certainly not optimal. (This is especially true in the derivation of supply curves, which are normally derived from cost data produced by accounting departments for their own needs.)

d. The Identification Problem.   The first three issues mentioned above apply to any type of econometric problem. Identification becomes an issue when the structure of the model is such that the separate relationships can't be untangled. To be specific, consider our demand for gold. Look at Figure 2A.1a, which replicates the diagram in MicroBits 2.1 but includes points that indicate the prices of gold and the quantities demanded for each year between 1977 and 1983. Can we construct a demand curve from these points? _____

The tempting answer is yes, because the points seem to fall along a downward-sloping line. Yet constructing a demand curve from the given points would violate the fundamental assumption of the demand curve, which shows the relationship between price and quantity demanded, *other elements remaining unchanged*. In fact, Figure 2A.1b draws in a single demand curve that encompasses the entire period (D) and a series of demand curves (d_1–d_4) that reflect an equally legitimate

FIGURE 2A.1   The Identification Problem

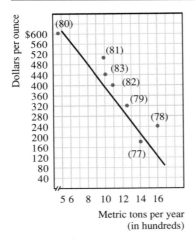 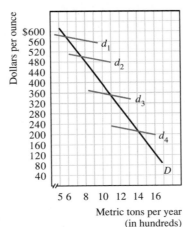 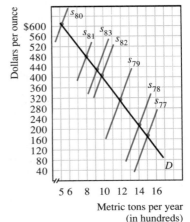

a.   Is this a demand curve?

b.   Which demand curve(s) is (are) the correct demand curve(s) for gold? Note that for any given change in price, quantity demanded changes more on the *d* curves than on the *D* curve.

c.   Identifying a demand curve by postulating shifting supply curves. Given the quantities sold in each year and the market prices, then if the supply curve has shifted, these shifts must trace out the equilibrium points along the demand curve *D*.

outcome. D and the d_1-d_4 tell two different stories about the demand for gold. In the case of d_1-d_4, a \$40 change in the price of gold leads to a much larger increase in the quantity of gold demanded than would be the case for an equivalent price change along D. Which is the correct one? How can you identify the true demand curve?

Figure 2A.1c suggests one way out. Note that the demand curve in the diagram is the D curve of Figure 2A.1b. Added to the figure here is a series of supply curves that have shifted over time. Each of the supply curves has a date attached to it. If you have reason to believe that the demand curve was stable and the supply curve shifted as is depicted here, you will have identified the demand curve. Why? Because the shifting supply curves and equilibrium points trace out only one possible demand curve, D. (One minor problem: If you've identified the demand curve, you cannot identify the supply curve. Why not?[3])

Those responsible for the gold study[4] believe the demand curve for fabricated gold (which includes gold sold in the form of official coins and medals, industrial gold, and karat jewelry) to be identified. The demand for gold remained stable, while the supply of gold fluctuated, tracing out Figure 2A.1a. While identification is not always so simple, sophisticated econometric techniques permit identification in more complicated instances.

Econometric testing is invaluable even if it's not always decisive. Quantitative estimates help assess the applicability of a purely theoretical formulation and evaluate the quantitative importance of the many forces influencing the dependent variables. At best, they enhance economists' understanding of existing relationships and enable them to predict the consequences of alternative policies. At worst, they force economists to face theory with the cold facts of reality and to grapple with such discrepancies that become evident.

Key Terms

Independent variable
Dependent variable

Notes and Answers

1. The u, being a random variable, has no consistent relationship to the quantity of gold demanded, and so falls out in the empirically estimated equation.
2. Since gold and platinum are substitutes, an increase in the price of platinum would lead buyers to replace platinum with gold.
3. You can't tell what the slope of the supply curve is, for any slope for the dated supply curves, as long as it passes through the appropriate point on the demand curve, is equally legitimate. Try it yourself.
4. See the reference in MicroBits 2.1.

PART

II CONSUMER DEMAND

Chapters 3, 4, and 5 address the intellectual foundation of consumer demand. In contrast to macroeconomics, where economists search for the motives behind aggregate spending and saving decisions, the microeconomic theory of consumer demand focuses on the composition of demand. What motivates individuals to buy certain goods rather than others? Both psychological and economic forces will play key roles as you examine in Chapters 3 and 4 how individual demanders behave when allowed to choose among products. Then, in Chapter 5, you'll turn your attention to the demand for a particular good, such as air travel, oil, and cigarettes.

Technical analysis is the bread and butter of microeconomic theory. But you should not lose sight of the objective even when you're focusing on the method. Always ask yourself: How can I apply the analysis to real-life issues? The problems may be as trivial as "Why do supermarkets periodically put rolls of toilet paper on sale?" to as crucial as "Would a heavier tax on alcoholic beverages save lives by reducing drunken driving?" These chapters will equip you with an approach to answering such questions, which has a far more lasting value than the answers provided.

3

CONSUMER CHOICE: OFTEN CONSUMERS REALLY DO BUY SMART

For there is no natural limit to wants and most people spend their lives trying to satisfy them.
Aristotle

[Economists] deal with man as he is; not with an abstract or "economic" man but a man of flesh and blood. They deal with a man who is largely influenced by egoistic motives in his business life . . . but who is neither above vanity and recklessness, nor below delight in doing his work well for its own sake.
Alfred Marshall (1890)

Learning Objectives

You should come away from this chapter with an understanding of:

- The meaning of indifference curves and indifference maps in general and in differing choice situations.
- The meaning of the budget line, its constraining impact on consumer decision making, and the interpretation of shifts in its location and slope.
- The conditions for consumer equilibrium, and how equilibrium changes when income or prices change.
- Some applications of indifference curve theory.
- How experiments with humans and animals confirm economists' views of the theory of choice.
- The consequences of dropping some of the rigid assumptions of simple indifference curve theory.

The Homeless and the Frightened

Consider a subject that has both positive and normative implications: how best to improve the condition of the urban poor, especially the homeless. Should the government make outright money payments to those deemed eligible for support, enabling them to find shelter but also permitting them to use the funds for other purchases? Or should such government outlays be specifically earmarked for rent? All of us are likely to have gut reactions to these alternatives, and indeed, Congress has implemented both types of programs. One purpose of this chapter is to demonstrate that the microeconomic theory of consumer choice can contribute significantly to public policy debates by analyzing issues and reaching conclusions that are not altogether apparent.

Consumer choice theory is obviously relevant on an individual level as well. For example, microeconomic analysis can assist potential investors in evaluating their options for allocating their funds among alternative investment vehicles. For the most part, Americans keep the bulk of their funds in banks, either in checking accounts or in various higher-earning savings accounts. Middle-class Americans also own securities in modest proportions, while more affluent U.S. residents hold a large share of their wealth in securities and relatively little in bank accounts. Since bank accounts pay little by way of interest and offer little opportunity for capital gains, while stockholders accrue dividends and capital gains, it's certainly legitimate to wonder, Do Americans fear being heavily involved in stock market activities? Alternatively, given the low returns, why does anyone keep his or her wealth in a bank account?

Choice characterizes much of our daily activities, and the weighing of benefits against costs is the common tie that binds both the social issue of housing policy and the personal one of savings allocation. Choice is the central topic of this chapter. A framework for understanding how consumers reach their decisions—the role of the elements intrinsic to Chapter 2's demand functions—is thus important to us as consumers. But such a framework is also important to producers and to social scientists, who want to understand consumer motivation, and to government policymakers, whose intervention in markets has repurcussions in consumer spending decisions.

The decision-making technique highlighted in this chapter is *indifference curve analysis*. It is a particularly robust method and deserves your concentrated attention because it crops up in a number of different contexts throughout this text. This chapter, like the previous one, begins with the simple theory and makes a number of useful assumptions in order to develop the essential points. Then, to demonstrate the flexibility of indifference curve analysis and its relevance to a number of the real-life examples, some of the more rigid assumptions are dropped. The results are often surprising.

*"We don't say you've been <u>bad.</u> You've just
made some bad <u>choices.</u>"*

SOURCE: *The New Yorker,* January 14, 1985, p.27.

Indifference Curve Analysis

It's trivial to claim that consumers prefer more to less. Yet this very lack of novelty turns out to be extremely useful when dealing with consumer choice. Satisfaction cannot be measured directly; no student has yet volunteered to have a probe inserted into his head for recording the brain impulses that occur as he makes choices. At best, satisfaction, or **utility,** can be mapped indirectly. By offering a series of choices and asking which set the consumer prefers—which is better or worse or equal—the investigator can infer **ordinal utility.** (By the way, this method stands in sharp contrast to **cardinal utility;** see MicroBits 3.1.)

Indifference curve analysis runs most smoothly by making three simplifying assumptions:

* *Consumers maximize utility.* Consumers strive for the best outcome for themselves; they do not make decisions that are inimical to their well-being.

* *Consumers are rational; they do not make contradictory choices.* Thus, if Joel prefers Porsches to Chevettes and Chevettes to public transportation, he will never prefer public transportation to Porsches. This principle is known as **transitivity.** It does *not* state that rational consumers will never take buses, but merely that they would prefer to drive Porsches.

Utility is the economist's synonym for satisfaction. When measuring **ordinal utility,** the researcher is concerned with the relative degree of satisfaction—more or less. **Cardinal utility** measures satisfaction numerically.

The **transitivity** condition assures the consumer will be *consistent* in making choices.

Vilfredo Pareto: The Father of Indifference Curves

Vilfredo Pareto (1848–1923), an Italian economist and sociologist, was originally trained as an engineer and, indeed, spent over a decade in that profession. He came to economics by chance, after exposure to the general equilibrium theory of Leon Walras, a giant among 19th-century economists. When Pareto and Walras met some years later, Pareto so impressed Walras that when the latter retired from his professorship at Lausanne University (Switzerland) in 1893, Pareto was appointed Walras's successor. Pareto's academic life, however, was short-lived. After inheriting a fortune from an uncle in 1898, he

moved to a small Swiss town, where he devoted the remainder of his life to his scientific studies. Pareto made important contributions in both economics and sociology.

Two of Pareto's most significant accomplishments are indifference curve theory and the definition of an optimum. Consumer demand theory prior to Pareto was based primarily on cardinal utility. Economists imagined that a consumer constructed a numerical scale against which he measured satisfaction, analogous to a thermometer that recorded temperature. Pareto, who coined a rather strange term, *total ophelimity*, to describe cardinal utility, argued that such measurement was neither possible nor necessary. His indifference curve analysis relies on ordinal utility. It reaches the same general conclusions without basing itself on unsubstantiable and patently absurd assumptions.

Pareto's name is most closely associated with the concept of Pareto optimality, an ideal accepted by economists the world over and a concept you'll meet in Chapter 19. Pareto defined an optimal situation as one in which it is impossible to improve the utility of one party without diminishing the utility of someone else. (If it were not so, the first could do better while the second lost nothing, or vice versa, so total utility would be greater.) This definition has major implications for economic policy; you can visualize its impact on redistributive taxation, for example.

Pareto's influence is widespread. Although few of his writings have been translated into English, Pareto's teachings have been absorbed and transmitted by the most important economists of the 20th century.

• *All decisions are made a certain world.* All the choice options, their costs, and their consequences are known at the time the decision is made.

Introduction: The Topographical Map Analogy

Figure 3.1a is a photograph of the Half-Dome, an unusual rock formation found in California's Yosemite National Park. One can reach the peak in any number of ways—hiking up the slopes or even scaling the face. Figure 3.1b is a topographical map of the Half-Dome. As you can see, it's a series of more or less concentric circles, each one with a number attached showing the altitude of that particular elevation above sea level.

MicroQuery   Are these numbers cardinal or ordinal? _____[1]

The map is a useful guide for the hiker who wishes to reach the peak in the least fatiguing manner or, for that matter, to plan out the optimal way to reach any particular elevation. Three paths have been drawn on

Figure 3.1

---

a. Yosemite's Half Dome

b. A Topographical Map of the Half Dome

the topographical map. The first, which starts at Lost Lake and proceeds directly to the peak, reaches ever higher elevations, as shown by the map numbers. The second, which starts at the foot of Mount Broderick, runs from left to right. At first, it moves upward. Then, after reaching its maximum at 6,800 feet, it descends until it returns to the bottom. The final path runs parallel to the second, but begins at a height of 6,400 feet. Obviously, path 3 reaches an altitude not achievable by someone hiking on path 2.

The Indifference Map: Accounting for Taste

All points on a single **indifference curve** represent identical levels of satisfaction.

Just as higher numbers on the topographical map indicate higher elevations, so do higher **indifference curves** represent greater levels of satisfaction. But in contrast to the cardinal measurements that are manifest on topographical maps, the numbers on the indifference map are ordinal. Moreover, different topographical maps of a particular area are identical because they describe an objective reality; indifference curves, applying to the preferences of individuals, will differ among persons.

Deriving an Indifference Curve. Andrea's indifference map between sweaters and videotapes can be derived by investigating her preferences. Take any arbitrary combination, such as *a* in Figure 3.2 with the coordinates 10 videotapes and four sweaters, as the reference point. Use that to divide the figure into four quadrants. Clearly, Andrea would prefer any combination of videotapes and sweaters in quadrant I (such as *s*) to *a*: the former contains more videotapes and more sweaters than *a*. Similarly, any combination in III would be less desirable. It's only in II and IV that Andrea will have to make her preferences known.

Inspect *b,* which at eight videotapes and seven sweaters provides Andrea with two fewer videotapes but three more sweaters. If Andrea prefers *b* to *a,* then she is obviously not indifferent between these two combinations. Try *c,* with eight videotapes and six sweaters. Should Andrea be ambivalent between *a* and *c,* then by definition both these combinations must be points on her indifference curve.

The amount of the *y* good that will be sacrificed in order to obtain one unit of the *x* good without increasing or decreasing the level of satisfaction is called the **marginal rate of substitution (MRS).**

The results of repeatedly trading off sweaters for videotapes at different coordinates in II ultimately yields the segment of Andrea's indifference curve labeled U_1 (*U* stands for *utility*), which defines a border between those combinations of tapes and sweaters that are preferred to points on U_1—those northeast—and those that are less desirable—those southwest. The southeastern segment of U_1 would be derived similarly, yielding an indifference curve that is convex to the origin.

The implicit trade-off along an indifference curve is called the **marginal rate of substitution (MRS).** The convexity of U_1 to the origin reflects the fact that the trade-off is not constant. At *c,* for example, where Andrea has six sweaters and eight videotapes, she's willing to trade off one sweater in order to acquire one more videotape; the MRS = 1.

FIGURE 3.2   Finding Andrea's Indifference Curve

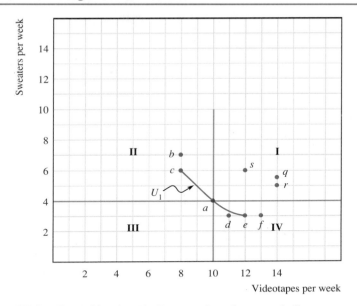

While all combinations in I are preferred to *a* and all combinations in III are less desired than *a*, some points in II and IV will be preferable to *a* and others will be less desired. Points *c, a,* and *e* lie on a single indifference curve, U_1.

You can demonstrate this by moving one unit rightward from *c*, so that Andrea will have nine videotapes, and then dropping down to U_1, which would indicate five sweaters, as is depicted in Figure 3.3. By moving to the right, you've increased Andrea's satisfaction, which is offset by returning her to the original indifference curve. This means that Andrea's gain of one videotape is just compensated for by her loss of one sweater. Were you to perform this same exercise at *a*, when Andrea's down to four sweaters, you'd discover that Andrea would have to be given two more videotapes in order to induce her to give up one sweater. Or, alternatively, each additional tape is worth not a whole sweater but merely half of one.

In fact, the MRS is the (inverse) slope of the indifference curve at the particular point in question:

$$\text{MRS} = \frac{\Delta y}{\Delta x}$$

where the deltas (Δ) stand for "change in."[2]

FIGURE 3.3   Andrea's Indifference Map

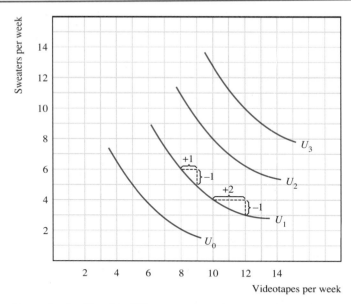

Note the family of indifference curves that constitute the indifference map. Also note the fact that each curve is convex to the origin, depicting a declining MRS.

The marginal rate of substitution of sweaters for videotapes declines as Andrea acquires more videotapes. It's probably true with few exceptions the more you have of any one thing, the less each individual item means to you. Conversely, the less you have of something, the more important is each one. So, as you obtain more videotapes, the **marginal utility,** or extra satisfaction, of each videotape is less, while the marginal utility of each sweater grows as you possess fewer. Consequently, the more videotapes and fewer sweaters you have, the fewer additional sweaters you'll be willing to forgo to acquire one more videotape.

Marginal utility is the *extra* satisfaction obtained from consuming an additional unit.

Drawing the Indifference Map.   Take one more look at Figure 3.2. Point *s* is preferred to *a* (Why?), but is *s* preferred to *q*? If *q* is preferred, try *r*. If Andrea is indifferent between *s* and *r* but both are preferred to *a,* then *s* and *r* must lie on a higher indifference curve than U_1.

Figure 3.3 sketches out Andrea's indifference map by including additional indifference curves, each one numbered with successively higher subscripts. Aside from the fact that the *U*s replace the elevation numbers and the curves are more concentric, the indifference map is not unlike the topographical map. Indeed, you can imagine the indifference curve map as a two-dimensional representation of a hill. As you move up the hill, reaching the higher numbered *U*s, you have more of both commodities and thus higher levels of satisfaction. On the other hand, moving along a given indifference curve keeps the satisfaction level constant despite the changes in the commodity bundle, just as moving along a topographical line keeps the elevation constant despite the change in scenery. (Micro-Bits 3.2 explains why indifference curves can't cross.)

Nonconvex Indifference Curves: Atypical but Reasonable Behavior Examined

Must indifference curves be convex? Economic theorists note at least two instances when the marginal rate of substitution does not decline: *(a)* the case of perfect complements and *(b)* the case of a nondesired good, or a "bad."

Perfect Complements.   Consider two goods that are normally used in combination (one right and one left sneaker) or that an individual uses in a precise mixture (one teaspoon of sugar per cup of coffee). Giving the consumer two left sneakers and one right one is no better than giving her one of each; the extra sneaker is, at least for the present, superfluous. In

---

MICROBITS 3.2

Why Indifference Curves Can't Cross

Crossed indifference curves violate the condition of transitivity noted on page 69. Glance at the accompanying figure, which shows two intersecting indifference curves.

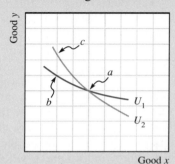

Look at the left side of the intersection. Point *a*, at the intersection, and point *b* both lie on indifference curve U_1 and by definition represent the same level of utility. Points *a* and *c* on U_2 are also indifferent. Now if both *b* and *c* are indifferent to *a*, they must be indifferent to each other.

But point *c* contains the same amount of commodity *x* and more of *y* than does *b*. Therefore, *c* must be preferred to *b*.

Obviously, *c* cannot at the same time be indifferent to and preferred to *b*. So, intersecting indifference curves must be rejected as a logical impossibility.

FIGURE 3.4   Nonconvex Indifference Curves

a.   An indifference map for perfect complements

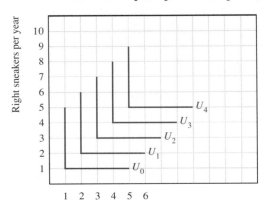

b.   Points on an indifference curve of a "bad"

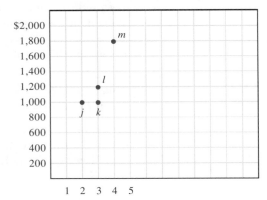

a.   While adding pairs of shoes moves the consumer to ever higher indifference curves, adding more right sneakers without simultaneously adding left sneakers leaves the consumer on the same indifference curve.

b.   Points *j*, *l*, and *m,* lie on an indifference curve and indicate that the consumer will take more of the bad and still remain indifferent only if compensated by receiving more of the good.

all such cases, the goods in question will be desired in fixed proportions, and obtaining additional units of either one or the other will not increase satisfaction. Some indifference curves for right and left sneakers are drawn in Figure 3.4a; their right angle, located at the 1 : 1 ratio, is maintained throughout. So, five right sneakers and one left sneaker are not preferred to one right and one left sneaker. On the other hand, five right sneakers and five left sneakers are preferred to the one right and one left combination.

MICROQUERY   The MRS can take on only three values. What are they? _____[3]

A "Bad."   Some people abhor certain commodities—meat, broccoli, plane trips. If these predilections are less than absolute, so that individuals can be bribed to overcome their abhorrence, you might discover the indifference curve points depicted in Figure 3.4b. Money is plotted on the y-axis, representing an individual's ability to acquire a whole array of commodities and services. Plotted on the x-axis are plane trips. Dick is afraid to fly, but with appropriate incentives, he could be induced to travel by plane. Now take a look at point *j*, representing a reference point of $1,000 and two flights. For Dick to fly once more—to move him from *j* to *k*—would by definition reduce his utility, for three flights are worse than two. But giving Dick another $200, moving him to point *l*, would find him just as satisfied as at the initial point. Points *j* and *l* must then be two points on Dick's indifference curve. But they're certainly not tracing out convexity to the origin. Similarly, *m,* representing more trips, would be on the same indifference curve only if a further money payment were made. If you connect the three points, you'll derive an upward-moving indifference curve, a strange apparition.

MicroQuery   In what two ways is the MRS in the case of a "bad" different from the normal case of convexity shown in Figure 3.3? _____

_____ 4

Notice that the indifference curves drawn to the right of the one you've constructed represent *lower* satisfaction levels. It's analogous to descending from the peak on the topographical map.

The Budget Constraint: Facing Reality

The indifference map depicts preferences. But preferences alone do not determine consumption. Budget limitations force consumers to make choices, and so onto the role of income and prices in the theory of consumer choice.

Return to Andrea, whose income this week is $500 and who must decide to either enliven her wardrobe or buy some videotapes. A number of assumptions will make life a bit easier at this point:

- Andrea can't spend more than $500. (We won't permit her to borrow.) Consequently, the more Andrea spends on clothing, the less she can spend on videotapes.
- Andrea can't save; she has to spend the $500 this week.
- Andrea can't buy anything other than sweaters and videotapes. (How tedious! Unfortunately, the two dimensions of a diagram limit us to two commodities.)
- A sweater costs $50, and a videotape costs $20.

The last two assumptions enable you to derive the maximum number of sweaters and the maximum number of videotapes Andrea can purchase. You can also calculate the possible combinations of sweaters and videotapes, all within the $500 spending limit. Andrea could spend all of her money on sweaters and buy 10 ($500/$50) sweaters this week. Or, she could acquire 25 ($500/$20) videotapes. Or 4 sweaters at $50, for $200, and

FIGURE 3.5   **Andrea's Budget Line**

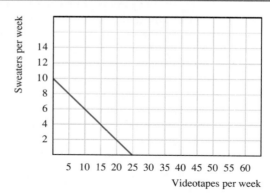

Given that Andrea has $500 to spend, the
price of a sweater is $50, and each videotape
sells for $20, the budget line depicts the
possible combinations of sweaters and
videotapes that Andrea could buy.

A **budget constraint,**
or **budget line,** plots
an individual's at-
tainable consump-
tion possibilities,
given income and
the prices of the
commodities in
question.

15 videotapes for the remaining $300. Figure 3.5 plots Andrea's **budget
constraint,** or **budget line,** which traces out all of these possibilities. (Note
that the axes are in units of sweaters and videotapes, not dollars. The
dollars are implicit.)

MICROQUERY

a. Can you calculate the dollars it would take to reach the combination of
two sweaters and 20 tapes? _____
b. Why can't you buy six sweaters and 12 tapes? (Try plotting these
coordinates on Figure 3.5.) _____[5]

Budget Lines and Income Changes.   What would happen if Andrea had
fewer or more dollars to spend? Clearly, Andrea's budget line would be
lower in the former case and higher in the latter. (Draw a budget line for
$600 onto Figure 3.5.[6])

Budget Lines and Price Changes.   What would happen to the budget line
if prices changed? Let's say the price of videotapes has doubled, so that
each one now costs $40. With the endpoints now at 10 (as before, since

the price of sweaters hasn't changed) and 12.5, the budget line has shifted inward and has become more steeply sloped. Figure 3.6 juxtaposes the old and the new budget lines. (Draw onto Figure 3.6 the budget line when the price of videotapes falls to $10 each. Is it flatter? If not, try it again.)

Consumer Equilibrium: Desire Confronts Financial Ability

To pull things together: The indifference map depicts individual preferences in the absence of any financial constraints, while the budget line portrays financial limits without being concerned with preferences. The time has come to see what happens when tastes and financial ability confront each other.

Andrea has $500 to spend this week, which she will exhaust on sweaters ($50 apiece) and videotapes ($20). Andrea's objective is to spend the $500 to maximize her satisfaction, or, in the language of indifference curves, to reach the highest possible indifference curve.

Let's start Andrea with 10 sweaters and ask her whether she'd be willing to trade off sweaters at the rate of 2.5 videotapes for each sweater given up. (Why 2.5? Because on the market, a sweater is 2.5 times as expensive as a videotape. She'd be foolish to take less than 2.5 videotapes for each sweater forgone.) In terms of Figure 3.7, Andrea begins on the budget line at 10, 0. Notice that she's on an indifference curve, too, the one labeled U_2. Could she do better? Surely. She could walk along the path, altering her mix of sweaters and videotapes. As she does so, she achieves ever higher indifference curves until she ascends to U_5, the highest she can reach, and winds up with 4 sweaters and 15 tapes. If she continued along the budget line, she'd start descending—the topography

FIGURE 3.6   Price Changes and the Budget Line

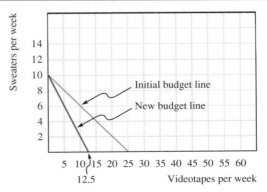

An increase in the price of videotapes shifts the budget line inward since fewer videotapes can be bought with the constant income.

FIGURE 3.7   **Consumer Equilibrium**

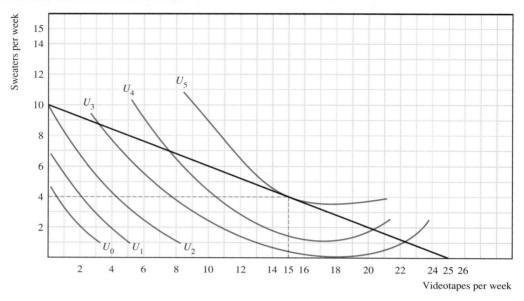

When Andrea reaches the four sweater, 15 videotape combination, she will have achieved the highest level of satisfaction for her given tastes, income, and prices.

analogy again—as indicated by the lower-numbered indifference curves lying to the right of U_5.

The geometry is quite clear. *Equilibrium is achieved when the budget line is tangent to an indifference curve.*

Notice something else. By starting with 10 sweaters and ending with 4, Andrea traded 6 sweaters to acquire 15 videotapes. That ratio of 1 : 2.5 is precisely the ratio of the price of videotapes to sweaters, as well as the slope of budget line and the value of the marginal rate of substitution. It is no coincidence that in equilibrium, the following equation is true:[7]

$$\text{MRS} = \frac{P_x}{P_y}$$

A good is classified as a **normal good** when more of it is consumed as income increases and less as income falls.

Income Changes.   If both sweaters and videotapes are **normal goods,** then Andrea should want to buy more of both as she earns more income. Recall that an increase in income shifts the entire budget line outward and parallel. Figure 3.8 plots two budget constraints together with Andrea's indifference curves. Clearly, she moves from an equilibrium of 4, 15 to 5, 17.5.[8]

Shifts in Relative Prices.   Not surprisingly, Andrea will buy fewer videotapes if the price of videotapes rises. Figure 3.9 takes the two budget lines

FIGURE 3.8   Equilibrium and Income Shifts

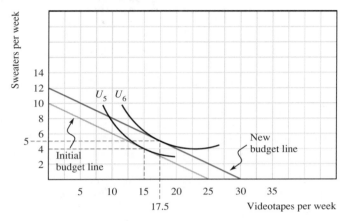

Andrea's income increase of $100 weekly enables her to buy more sweaters and more tapes. She achieves her new equilibrium at five sweaters and 17.5 videotapes.

FIGURE 3.9   Equilibrium and Price Changes

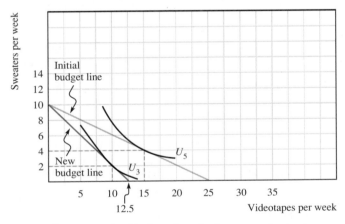

When videotapes double in price, Andrea reevaluates her consumption decision and buys fewer videotapes; in this instance, she also buys fewer sweaters.

of Figure 3.6 and juxtaposes them onto Andrea's indifference map. The initial equilibrium of 4, 15 is found on the original budget line. The new equilibrium at 2, 10 occurs at the tangency of the new budget line, when videotapes have doubled in price. The inward swing of the budget line makes the previous equilibrium unattainable; Andrea is constrained to a

MicroBits 3.3

Unusual Equilibria

The text dealt with two unusual types of goods (pp. 75–77). The main purpose of this box, consequently, is twofold: to explain *(a)* why sneakers are bought in pairs and *(b)* why people won't buy "bads." A third purpose of this box is to introduce corner equilibria, which will come in handy near the end of this chapter to explain why people prefer brand-name products.

The Shoe Box

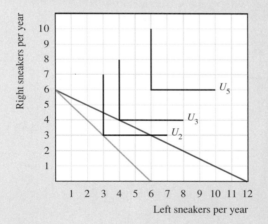

The figure here reproduces the right-angled indifference curves of Figure 3.4a and adds two budget lines. If the price of a right sneaker = the price of a left sneaker = $30 (on the reasonable assumption that the same amount of leather, labor, and machine use enters a right sneaker as it does a left sneaker), then the relevant budget line is the inner one, the one with the slope of 1. If the

individual has $180 to spend on sneakers, then the budget line is anchored at six right sneakers and six left sneakers. As you can see, optimum purchase requires a combination of three right and three left sneakers or, simply put, three pairs of sneakers.

What if, on a whim, shoe retailers hold a sale on left sneakers, cutting the price in half for a limited time only. Do you think consumers would charge in, stocking up on left sneakers? Surely most two-legged individuals would not. Take a look now at the outer budget line, anchored at 6 and 12. The tangency position is on a higher indifference curve because our buyer could now afford to buy another pair of sneakers. (The three pairs he usually buys now cost only $135 instead of $180; three right at $30 = $90, and three left at $15 = $45. A fourth right costs another $30, and a fourth left costs another $15, for a grand total of $180.) But given the right angle of the indifference curve, which merely indicates the unwillingness of the buyer to purchase anything other than pairs, the proportion of right to left sneakers remains the same: one right for each left.

Now if the overwhelming majority of buyers will only buy pairs, then sellers would be stupid to sell sneakers in any other way. That's why sneakers are sold in pairs.

Fear of Flying

The indifference curve constructed in Figure 3.4b assumed that Dick would fly only if he were compensated by an extra money payment. Since airlines don't pay passengers, Dick won't ever travel by plane.

MicroBits 3.3 continued

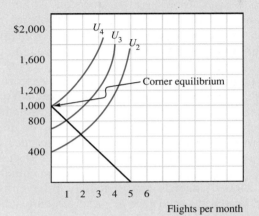

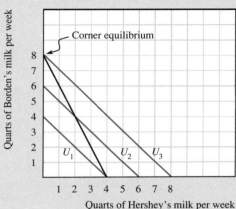

The equilibrium position for Dick is known as a corner solution: Dick ends up with money only and no flights. Let's say the fare costs $200 per trip and Dick has $1,000. With his budget line anchored at $1,000 and five flights, as you can see in the figure here, the highest indifference curve Dick can reach is U_4, which touches the y-axis at $1,000. (Note that in this case, the tangency condition is violated!) Any indifference curve to the right indicates a lower level of utility. (If you're not sure why, check back to the text reference for Figure 3.4b.)

Corner Equilibria

A more usual example of corner equilibrium occurs when two goods are perfect substitutes, both providing, unit for unit, an equal amount of satisfaction. Thus, most people are indifferent to whether they're buying a quart of fresh Borden's, Hershey's, Dairylea, or Acme milk. Consequently, the individual indifference curve is a straight line with a 1 : 1 trade-off: you'd be sufficiently compensated by having your lost quart of Borden's milk replaced by a quart of Hershey's to remain indifferent. It makes sense, then, to expect that the consumer will buy only the cheapest brand of milk. The figure's budget line implicitly postulates that Hershey's is twice as expensive as Borden's. Equilibrium is, as in the previous case, at the highest indifference curve, U_3, and mandates that the consumer buy eight quarts of Borden's milk weekly. (Show on the figure that if the price relationship was reversed, the consumer would buy only Hershey's.*)

Answer

* The budget line would be anchored at four quarts of Borden's and eight of Hershey's, enabling the consumer to reach U_3 only when eight quarts of Hershey's are bought.

point on the new, lower budget line. The tangency once again is the best she can do.

The reasoning is also straightforward. The doubling in the price of videotapes forces Andrea to reassess her previous decision. Although her preferences haven't changed, she now has to give up twice as many sweaters to acquire one videotape. Because it's not as worthwhile as before, Andrea will simply buy fewer videotapes.[9]

Recap. This is a good point to recapitulate. By now you've learned to determine the consumer's optimum combination of two goods. You can construct the budget constraint once you know the income available for spending and the relative prices of the goods in question. Given the consumer's indifference curves, you can find the highest indifference curve attainable without violating the budget constraint. You further realize that if either income changes or relative prices are altered, the old equilibrium becomes irrelevant and a new tangency emerges. (If you haven't mastered all of this, it would be wise to return to the point of confusion. The rest of this chapter assumes you're thoroughly familiar with the technique developed to this point.)

How Best to Subsidize Housing: An Application

Indifference curves can rarely be discerned. Consequently, the applications using indifference curve analysis tend to be based on reasoning rather than on specific evidence. This section returns to the chapter's opening and the issue of whether the urban poor would benefit most from a specific housing grant or a general welfare payment.[10]

Glance at the complicated-looking Figure 3.10, and then for analytic ease, accept the following assumptions:

- The government subsidy equals 50 percent of the rental paid by eligible families.
- The typical family earns $1,000 per month.
- A normal rental is $100 per room per month. (For example, a three-room apartment rents for $300 monthly.)

Consider a family that earns $1,000 and is not eligible for a rental subsidy. This family's situation is represented by the lowest budget line, anchored at $1,000 and 10 rooms (i.e., if it would spend all of its income on rent, the family could starve in a spacious 10-room apartment). The highest indifference curve the family can reach, U_1, suggests that it will maximize utility with a two-room apartment. The dwelling will cost the family $200 and leave $800 for the remaining monthly expenses.

FIGURE 3.10   Grants versus Earmarked Subsidies: The Case of Housing Benefits

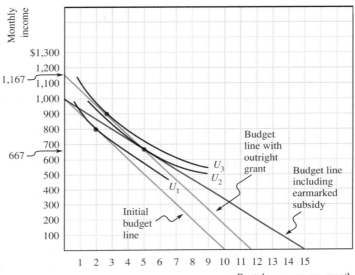

In this case, a subsidy that can be used only for housing turns out to put the beneficiary on a lower indifference curve than an identical money payment to be used at the consumer's discretion.

Now introduce the 50 percent subsidy, which means a decline in the price of housing to the subsidized family. The two-room apartment costs the family only $133—the government pays an additional half or $67 so that the landlord still receives $200—a three-room apartment would cost $200, and so on. Thus, the budget line swings outward, touching the x-axis at 15 instead of 10.

MICROQUERY   If the family spent all of its income on housing, how large an apartment could it rent? _____ . How much would the family pay from its own income? _____ How much would the landlord receive in rent, including the subsidy? _____[11]

The outward swivel of the budget line leads to a new equilibrium on U_2, which induces the family to rent a five-room apartment. A careful reading of the diagram will disclose the sources of the $500 that the landlord collects in rent. Glance at the tangency and locate its coordinates: $667 and five rooms. The $667 refers to the funds available for the family's other uses, implying that $333 ($1,000 − $667) must be spent on rent. The difference between the landlord's receipt of $500 and the $333 paid by the family, or $167, is the rental subsidy paid by the government. (Note that $167 is half of $333.)

Consider how the alternate proposal of granting this family an outright payment of $167, to be spent as it wishes. Of course, the rent subsidy program will simultaneously be revoked. On Figure 3.10, that case is indicated by the budget line anchored at $1,167 (family income plus grant) and 11⅔ rooms. (Because the rents are not subsidized, the budget line is parallel to the initial budget constraint.) Find the tangency at $900 and 2⅔ rooms; the family has opted for smaller quarters than under the rental subsidy program. It has decided to spend only $267 on rent rather than $333. That leaves $900 for alternative expenditures. But note, too, that the family has now reached a higher indifference curve than under the rental subsidy program, that is, U_3 rather than U_2.

You can now visualize the public policy debate. On the one hand, those who favor outright subsidies suggest that the poor should be permitted to make their own decisions. Forcing them to spend in ways that are not consistent with their own evaluation of benefits will lead to lower levels of well-being for them. In contrast, an earmarked rental subsidy, though certainly beneficial to the poor, gives the government less bang for its bucks. Moreover, an earmarked program is more expensive to administer than are outright grants.

Some counter with a paternalistic refusal to grant that the poor know what's best for themselves. Many middle- and upper-class Americans implicitly blame the poor for their own poverty. They contend that if the poor want benefits, they must accept conditions. Other critics reject such a simplistic appraisal of poverty, pointing to the number of very young children and very old adults who constitute the bulk of the poor. Moreover, very many poor people work full-time and still fail to achieve more than a low-level income. Nevertheless, many Americans still favor earmarked housing subsidies for the useful social purpose they serve. That's because they attach a special virtue to assuring adequate housing, believing that in addition to the benefit it provides directly, proper housing also entails numerous side benefits, including a healthier environment and family pride. Thus, the government's outlays should be used to further goals other than a narrowly focused one such as the immediate social welfare of the beneficiary of the grant.

These viewpoints differ on social as well as economic grounds, and economic analysis can do little more than to clarify the fundamental differences. But such clarification is crucial if intelligent policy decisions are to be made.

Approaching Real Utility Functions

Most empirical work in the consumption area has emphasized the demand for specific products. Relatively scant attention has been paid to indifference curves per se. Yet the little that has been reported is remarkably consistent with the previous analysis. Both humans and animals have been the subjects of indifference curve research; two studies are briefly surveyed here to give you a taste of experimental work in this area.

Human Indifference Curves

Perhaps the most ambitious experimental program to derive indifference curves was conducted in 1967 by Professors K. R. MacCrimmon and M. Toda.[12] Using seven UCLA undergraduates as subjects, MacCrimmon and Toda devised a money payment technique that motivated the students to reveal their true preferences. To keep the problem manageable, the students were asked to construct two sets of indifference curves: (1) between money and pens and (2) between money and pies. (In the latter case, they had to eat the pastries before receiving the payoff.)

Figure 3.11a reproduces a typical money versus pens indifference curve drawn by one of the subjects. The curves are negatively sloped and convex to the origin. The authors also note that the indifference curves do not intersect. Figure 3.11b depicts a typical money versus pie trade-off; the indifference curves here are akin to the "bads" of the fearful flyer. Indeed, because the pastries had to be consumed, the subjects had to be paid off to induce them to eat more than a small quantity. Thus, direct observations confirm the conclusions about the shapes of indifference curves.

Rats

Animal studies corroborate another aspect of indifference curve analysis: as the budget line is altered, more of the cheaper commodity will be consumed.

A group of economists studied how male albino rats would respond to changes in relative prices.[13] In one test, the rats were trained to depress levers that would deliver premeasured cups of either Tom Collins mix or root beer. (Don't try to account for the taste of rats!) Each time the appropriate lever was depressed, the rats would be exposed to one of the two beverages for five seconds, enough time to consume the drink. But the total number of presses was fixed initially at 300, and once the rat had used his allotted number, no further drink would be available.

The analogy to the budget line should be apparent. The maximum number of 300 depressions represents income, and the implicit relative

FIGURE 3.11   **Human Indifference Curves**

<table>
<tr>
<td>

a.   **Indifference curves for money versus pens for subject no. 4**

</td>
<td>

b.   **Indifference curves for money versus pastries for subject no. 5**

</td>
</tr>
</table>

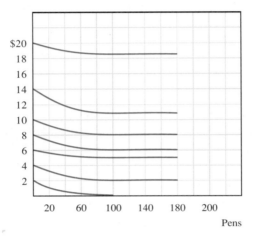

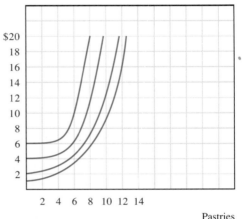

a.   Student 4 is willing to give up many pens to obtain dollars.

b.   Student 5 will eat more pastries only if compensated with additional dollars.

SOURCE: K. R. MacCrimmon and M. Toda, "The Experimental Determination of Indifference Curves," *Review of Economic Studies* 36 (1969), pp. 443, 445.

"price" is 1: for each cup of root beer ordered, one less cup of Tom Collins mix is available. The *A* lines in Figure 3.12 indicate that in a single day, each rat could consume either 15 milliliters of root beer, 15 milliliters of Tom Collins mix, or some combination of the two. The dots on the line indicated by *a* represent mean consumption patterns for each rat; both clearly prefer root beer to the mix.

The researchers then increased the relative price of root beer. They did this by decreasing the size of the cup that dispensed the root beer and cutting down on the amount of time the rat had to drink it, while simultaneously increasing the size of the cup with the Tom Collins mix and the time available to drink it. But the rats still had their 300 opportunities to depress the lever. The new budget line is labeled *B*, and the dots once again indicate the mean consumption. It's amazing to see how human the rats acted: they cut back on root beer consumption and increased their intake of Tom Collins mix. What's still more surprising is the rats' behavior when initial conditions were restored: the dots marked *a'* show a return to the initial consumption pattern. (It's clearly evident for the second rat, for whom the restoration is virtually total. But even the first rat returned almost to his initial position.)

FIGURE 3.12   Budget Lines for Two Rats

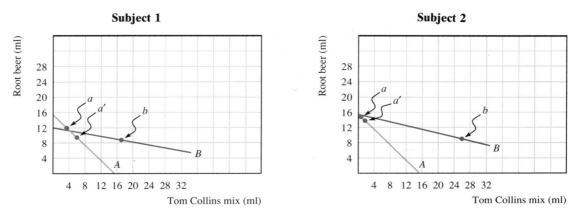

When the Tom Collins mix became cheaper, both rats increased their consumption of it. But they returned to nearly their initial consumption pattern when its price was later raised.

SOURCE: John H. Kagel, Howard Rachlin, Leonard Green, Raymond C. Buttalio, Robert L. Busmann, and W. R. Klemm, "Experimental Studies of Consumer Demand Behavior Using Laboratory Animals," *Economic Inquiry* 13 (March 1975), p. 27.

Relaxing Assumptions: Bringing Indifference Curve Analysis Closer to the Real World

The experiments involving both humans and animals suggest that indifference curve theory and its implications are grounded in reality. But the theory and its explanation so far have made some rather rigid assumptions. The final section of this chapter examines the consequences of removing some of these assumptions. You'll explore four issues: uncertainty, asymmetric information, changing tastes, and consumer irrationality.

Uncertainty and Savings: Portfolio Diversification

The opening discussion of savings options can be summarized as follows: Why do people diversify their portfolios rather than concentrate on the asset that yields the most? The answer hinges on risk. It is impossible to identify the securities that over time pay best while simultaneously protecting the asset holder against default or capital loss. Part of the problem has to do with the uncertain nature of the economy and interest rates: a company's fortunes vary with the overall economy, as well as with conditions in its own industry and the management of the firm itself. Diversification enables individuals who are **risk-averse** to obtain a lower but more assured yield instead of a possibly larger but less certain return.

An individual who is **risk-averse** prefers safety over risk taking.

FIGURE 3.13   **Why Investors Diversify**

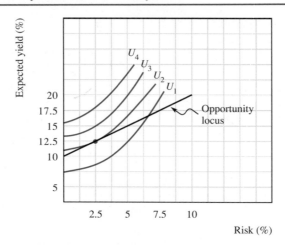

In a two-asset world where one is relatively
low yielding but secure and the second is
higher yielding but more risky, a risk-averse
investor will choose a diversified portfolio. A
combination of assets, even though it carries
some risk, provides greater utility than a
nondiversified portfolio.

However, risk-aversion is not likely to be absolute. Compensate people sufficiently for risk and they'll take a chance. In other words, yield is a
"good," risk is a "bad," and the two can be traded off in the now-familiar
upward-sloping indifference curves displayed in Figure 3.13. With yield
on the ordinate and risk on the abscissa, the investor is willing to take
additional risk and still remain indifferent if she's paid off in a promised
higher yield. Of course, higher yield and less risk are better; they'd put
her on indifference curves with successively higher numbers.

Let's further consider the two-asset choice set in Figure 3.13. One
asset, say a bank certificate of deposit, is insured by the FDIC (so there's
no credit risk), shows no price fluctuation, and offers an assured interest
return of 10 percent annually. A second asset, say an equivalent value of
corporate common stock, guarantees neither yield nor capital gain but
comes with a historical return of 20 percent annually and a 10 percent risk
of default.[14] In the worst-case scenario, the corporation will go broke,
which means not only that dividends will cease but also that the entire
investment will become worthless. In the best-case scenario, the yields
will exceed that of the CD over the life of the investment, while the risk
will never come to fruition.

What are the investor's choices? Table 3.1 suggests a sampling.

The first option says, "Put all your funds in the safe CD. You'll earn
only 10 percent, but you'll have no money at risk." Option 5 is the exact

TABLE 3.1   **A Menu of Investment Choices**

Option: CD/Stock (%)	Expected Yield (%)	Expected Risk (%)
1. 100/0	10	0
2. 75/25	12.5	2.5
3. 50/50	15	5
4. 25/75	17.5	7.5
5. 0/100	20	10

opposite: "Risk it all. You may be biting off a great deal of risk, but if you're lucky, you'll earn 20 percent." Options 2, 3, and 4 are intermediate positions, becoming ever more risky but proportionally more profitable as the relative weight of stock in the portfolio increases. The combinations are plotted in Figure 3.13; the straight-line **opportunity locus**, an analogue to the budget line, indicates possible alternatives.

The achievable combinations of risk and return are traced out by the **opportunity locus***.*

Since the indifference map indicates the investor's preferences and the opportunity locus specifies the available options, the investor's optimal portfolio yields 12.5 percent with a 2.5 percent risk, or option 2 in Table 3.1.

The principles of indifference curve analysis explain why neither an entirely riskless nor a totally speculative portfolio is optimal. Simply put, such portfolios would entail the investor's achieving a lower level of satisfaction than optimal portfolio 2. The investor is willing to trade off some risk for extra return; diversification permits the matching of preferences with opportunities.[15]

Choice, Asymmetric Information, and Habits

The simplifying assumption that consumers make informed choices based on full information must be revised when sellers possess substantially more expertise than do buyers. Asymmetric information normally characterizes such decisions as which used car to buy and which physician to select. Consumers will be forced to acquire knowledge, either from firms, through personal search, or from their own experience. Fortunately, however, indifference curve analysis can be suitably modified to deal with asymmetric information.

The cost of information acquisition is obvious when search services are supplied by a commercial firm (e.g., automobile diagnostic centers). Analytically, search expenditures increase the cost of the product to the buyer and so alter the slope of the budget line. That's equally true when a search is undertaken less formally. Researching by working through one's personal network or the library is time-consuming and entails the opportunity cost of the time spent on the search.

In contrast to expending funds or effort on search, buying based on habit economizes on search costs by allowing the buyer to rely on past experience. Essentially, habit converts the buyer from a searcher into a regular customer. You can understand, then, the importance to companies of brand names. If the consumer can be induced to try a brand-name product and is actually satisfied with it, habit will take over. Search costs then work for the product by increasing the cost of switching.[16]

Figure 3.14 points out an interesting consequence of habitual buying: the indifference curve shifts in favor of the known product and thus permits the producer to exercise some degree of control over the price of the product. In Figure 3.14a, Kleenex and Brand X tissues are compared and found to be physically identical, giving rise to an indifference map for perfect substitutes. (Recall the third figure in MicroBits 3.3.) The budget line shows Brand X to be cheaper. For the same $10, you can buy 20 boxes of Brand X at 50 cents a box or 12.5 boxes of Kleenex at 80 cents a box. The optimum consumption point lies at the corner where U_5 and the budget line meet. The consumer buys only Brand X. But if the consumer on the basis of past experience has become habituated to Kleenex, then the indifference map shifts in favor of Kleenex. Thus, in Figure 3.14b, the indifference curves are constructed so that the consumer is willing to give up two boxes of Brand X for one box of Kleenex. Now, with Kleenex still

FIGURE 3.14   Objectively Identical but Differently Perceived Goods

a.   Objectively determined indifference curves   **b.   Perceived differences**

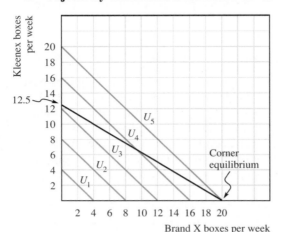
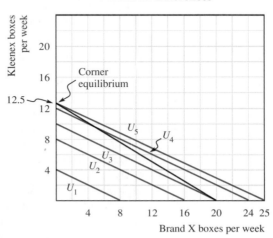

a.   Since Kleenex and Brand X are identical tissues, an objective evaluator would be willing to trade them off only on a one-to-one basis. Given that Kleenex is more expensive, this consumer buys only Brand X.

b.   Because the consumer habitually buys Kleenex tissues, being convinced that they are twice as good as Brand X, she is willing to pay more for Kleenex and buys brand-name tissues exclusively.

60 percent more expensive, the consumer buys only Kleenex. Moreover, if the price of Kleenex is increased to no more than $1 per box, the customer's purchase pattern will remain unaffected. (See what happens in Figure 3.14 if the relative price of Kleenex moves from 80 to 90 cents.)[17]

Developing Tastes: The Evolving Gourmet

The last example jettisons the earlier assumption that consumers are endowed with a clear but immutable set of preferences. Obviously, that isn't altogether realistic, as tastes do change over time. Taste changes are relatively easy to demonstrate using indifference curves, as you can see by studying Figure 3.15.

FIGURE 3.15   From Meat and Potatoes to Gourmet

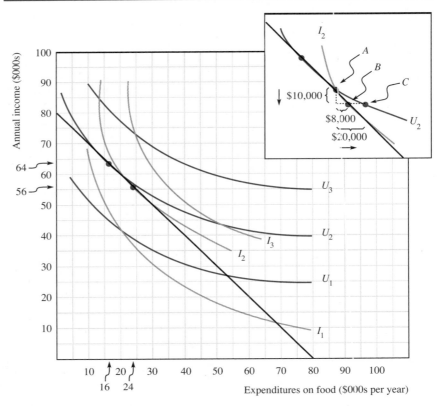

The flatter U curves indicate a greater willingness to trade off larger amounts of food for income than do the steeper I curves. Contrast the movement from A to B along I_2 and from A to C along U_2. Gourmet Mr. I will be willing to accept $10,000 less in general expenditures in order to acquire $8,000 more in food. Meat-and-potatoes Mr. U will require $20,000 more in food to compensate him for spending $10,000 less on other categories.

Consider Calvin, who used to eat to stay alive but now stays alive in order to feast.[18] Calvin's initial utility map, indicated by the U curves, shows that his eating preferences aren't particularly strong. Although Calvin enjoys his steak and potatoes, he isn't willing to trade off substantial amounts of income to obtain additional food. Consequently, for the given budget line, his spending on food is not atypical of that of most Americans—20 percent of his $80,000 annual income.

When Calvin moves into an environment that substitutes dining for eating and cuisine for food, the old indifference map becomes irrelevant. The new Calvin is willing to swap a good share of his income to satisfy his palate; the I curves replace the Us. It's hardly surprising that for the given budget line, the optimum consumption set shifts in the direction of more dining and less income left for other types of spending. (Calvin will now spend 30 percent of his income on food unless he becomes a food critic, in which case Nirvana!)

Are Consumers Rational?

Finally, it's time to scrutinize the key assumption of this entire chapter, consumer rationality. How can the belief that consumers always act to maximize their satisfaction be reconciled with such acts of gullibility as buying diamonds through the mail with a money-back provision, provided the package remains sealed? Or the thousands who sent their $2 in the mail to buy a guaranteed roach-killer, only to receive two blocks of wood and the curt instructions, "Place roach on Block A. Bang Block A with Block B."

SOURCE: *The Wall Street Journal*, December 15, 1986, p. 35. Reprinted from *The Wall Street Journal*; permission Cartoon Features Syndicate.

Consumers aren't always rational. Our behavior is far more complex than can be understood on the basis of narrow dollars-and-cents calculations. Indeed, the entire profession of marketing is premised on the denial of the rational consumer and the belief that we can be manipulated in a variety of ways. (See MicroBits 3.4 for a list of needs thought by marketing professionals to motivate consumer purchasing behavior.)

Economists have not been unaware of the criticism of the basic assumption of rationality. The quote that opens this chapter demonstrates that Alfred Marshall, the giant of English economists at the turn of the century, recognized it. Economists have dealt with this objection in two ways. First, the defensive: Economic theory, of necessity, simplifies; rational behavior is such a simplification; and theoretical conclusions must be modified when the assumption proves inappropriate or misleading. However, in many cases, even simplified and unrealistic assumptions do lead to useful results.

A more aggressive stance has been taken by Professor Jack Hirshleifer. He accepts economic imperialism, the fact that economics has conquered the other social sciences, as inevitable. Economics is, in Hirshleifer's view, "the universal grammar of social science." In economics, the central concepts of optimization on the individual level and equilibrium on the aggregate level may have to be modified by incorporating new observations from other disciplines, but they will remain at the core of the evolving, unified social science discipline.[19] And rationality is central to the optimizing concept.

Thus, you can deal with the validity of presumed consumer rationality either way. You can apply the theory of consumer choice only to those instances where consumers can be expected to behave rationally, which probably encompasses a broad expanse of their decision-making opportunities. Alternatively, you can assume that the model is applicable almost universally, its conclusions are extensively valid, and there is no better substitute presently available that will closer approximate real-life situations.

Consider as an alternative the psychological theory of cognitive dissonance, which essentially suggests that people modify their beliefs to cope with or even deny reality rather than accept and adjust to it. (For example, a coalminer will claim that black lung disease isn't really pervasive among miners and, in any case, won't affect him. He won't cut back on his exposure to coal dust.) Hirshleifer sets up the following challenge:

> Suppose a military commander learns that his left flank is dangerously weak. The economist, expecting a *rational* response, predicts that the general will reinforce his left. The cognitive-dissonance theorist rather expects a *rationalizing* response instead, in which the general chooses to believe that the enemy will not attack him on the left.

What do you think the general will do?

MICROBITS 3.4

Consumer Needs: The View from the Marketing Profession

Possible Needs Motivating a Person to Some Action

Physiological Needs

Food	Warmth	Activity
Drink	Coolness	Rest
Sex—tension release	Body elimination	Self-preservation
Sleep		

Psychological Needs

Abasement	Deference	Order
Acquisition	Distinctive	Personal fulfillment
Affiliation	Discriminating	Playing—competitive
Aggression	Discriminatory	Playing—relaxing
Beauty	Dominance	Power
Belonging	Emulation	Pride
Being constructive	Exhibition	Security
Being part of a group	Family preservation	Self-expression
Being responsible	Imitation	Self-identification
Being well thought of	Independence	Symmetry
Companionship	Individualism	Tenderness
Conserving	Love	Striving
Curiosity	Nurturing	Understanding (knowledge)
Discovery		

Desire For

Acceptance	Distance—"space"	Retaliation
Achievement	Distinctiveness	Satisfaction with self
Affection	Fame	Security
Affiliation	Happiness	Self-confidence
Appreciation	Identfication	Sensuous experiences
Comfort	Prestige	Sexual satisfaction
Contrariness	Recognition	Sociability
Dependence	Respect	Status
		Sympathy

Freedom From

Anxiety	Imitation
Depression	Loss of prestige
Discomfort	Pain
Fear	Pressure
Harm—psychological	Ridicule
Harm—physical	Sadness

Source: Adapted from E. Jerome McCarthy and William D. Perreault, Jr., *Essentials of Marketing,* 5th ed. (Homewood, Ill.: Richard D. Irwin, 1991), p. 133.

Conclusion

How is the optimum consumption pattern of an individual consumer found? Indifference curve analysis suggests that if the consumer's preferences, income, and range of price options are known—and if the products are "goods"—equilibrium will occur when an indifference curve and the budget constraint are tangent. No other combination will yield a higher level of satisfaction.

Of course, if income, price, or taste changes, a new equilibrium, with a different consumption pattern, will result. But that, too, will be the optimal one from the consumer's viewpoint.

This simple theory of consumer choice, which is borne out by experimental studies, yields powerful conclusions. In this chapter, indifference curve analysis was applied to both vital and trivial issues: housing subsidies, portfolio diversification, selling in pairs, brand names, and why those afraid but not terrified of flying still don't fly. The next chapter takes indifference curve analysis one step further as the foundation for demand curves.

Key Terms

Budget constraint (or budget line)
Cardinal utility
Indifference curve
Marginal rate of substitution (MRS)
Marginal utility
Normal goods

Opportunity locus
Ordinal utility
Risk-averse
Transitivity
Utility

Review Questions

1. *a.* Draw an indifference map for Alyssa, who must select breakfast from a menu limited to eggs and cereal.
   b. Find Alyssa's equilibrium meal given a $4 budget and the price of cereal $1 a bowl and eggs 50 cents each.

2. *a.* Draw an equilibrium position for Rebecca, consumer of two normal goods, ski boots and binoculars, specifying her income and the prices of the products.
   b. Show what happens to Rebecca's purchases if she loses her job, cutting her income by half.
   c. Rebecca is reemployed at her previous salary but discovers that the price of ski boots has doubled. Demonstrate her new set of purchases.

3. Why can't indifference curves cross?

4. *a.* Why are earrings sold in pairs?
   b. Using indifference curve analysis, demonstrate the impact of a new fad—

wearing mismatched earrings—on Ilana's purchases.

5. *a.* Under what conditions are indifference curves likely to be concave to the origin?

   b. Show that equilibrium in this case will occur in a corner.

6. Why doesn't Ted, a risk-averse consumer, invest all of his funds in safe, low-interest-earning Treasury securities?

7. *a.* Why do most consumers, having chosen a physician for the family, rarely switch to another?

   b. Why do some families change their family doctor?

8. What are the costs involved in finding the best professor for a specific course?

Food for Thought

1. Demonstrate how the possibility of consumer debt will affect the conclusions of the simple model of consumer equilibrium presented in this chapter.

2. How does the presence of a price ceiling affect the consumer's indifference map, budget constraint, and equilibrium?

3. Look at the accompanying diagram that relates to one child who participates in the school lunch program. Maryanne is provided with a heavily subsidized lunch each school day. The alternative to the lunch program is an income subsidy, ena-

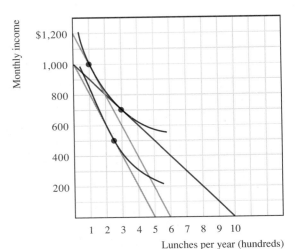

Lunches per year (hundreds)

bling Maryanne's parents to buy her lunch.

   a. What is the equilibrium position in the absence of any type of subsidy program? (Use the lowest budget line.) How many days will Maryanne eat school-provided lunches? How much income will the family spend on such lunches each year?

   b. After Maryanne becomes eligible for the subsidized lunch, the effective price drops to $1 per day. Now how many lunches will Maryanne eat in school, and how much will the family spend? What will be the cost to the government of this subsidy?

   c. Dropping the subsidies and providing Maryanne's parents with an income grant of $200 means that a family's budget line reaches $1,200. How many lunches will Maryanne eat in school, how much will the family spend, and how much will the government save under this alternative?

   d. Which, if any, is the best plan with regard to the family's welfare?

   e. What conclusions might be drawn about the cost-effectiveness of the two approaches to lunches? Consider not only the direct government costs but also any indirect costs and/or savings that might result.

4. The analysis in this chapter demonstrated that a direct income subsidy would increase consumer welfare more than a rent-subsidy program. Can you demonstrate the conditions that would reverse this conclusion?

5. *a.* Draw the indifference map of Jan, who, although she doesn't like the odor of cigarette smoke, when offered the last seat on a plane in the smoking section, accepts.

   b. Using Jan as an example, explain why nonsmokers can often be found in the smoking section.

6. Draw the equilibrium portfolio for the gambler, who is invigorated by risk.

7. *a.* What will be the impact of a successful advertising campaign for a specific brand of lip gloss on the typical consumer's indifference map and consumption pattern?

   b. Why do companies introducing new or "improved" consumer products tend to offer "cents-off" coupons for an initial period?

8. Demonstrate with indifference curve analysis how consumer search for information regarding watches will affect the consumer's equilibrium.

Suggested Readings

An interesting alternative to the indifference curve analysis discussed in this chapter is Kelvin Lancaster's *Consumer Demand: A New Approach* (New York: Columbia University Press, 1971).

   White male Carneaux pigeons rather than rats were the subject of an experiment reported in Raymond C. Battalio, John H. Kagel, Howard Rachlin, and Leonard Green, "Commodity-Choice Behavior with Pigeons as Subjects," *Journal of Political Economy* 84, no. 1 (February 1981), pp. 67–91.

   Why do the same people who insure, and thus indicate themselves as risk-averse, also gamble, which suggests they welcome risk? The classic treatment of this anomaly is found in Milton Friedman and L. J. Savage, "The Utility Analysis of Choices Involving Risk," *Journal of Political Economy* 56, no. 4 (August 1948), pp. 279–

304. A simpler exposition may be found in Donald N. McCloskey, *The Applied Theory of Price* (New York: Macmillan, 1985), Chapter 3.

   For some psychological insights into theories of consumer decision making, sample the articles on consumer behavior in Benjamin Gilad and Stanley Kaish, *Handbook of Behavioral Economics, Vol. A* (Greenwich, Conn.: JAI Press, 1986), pp. 63–148.

   George Akerlof is an economist who is positive about cognitive dissonance theory in general and suggests it as an alternative to the economic theory of crime mentioned in Chapter 1. See his *An Economic Theorist's Book of Tales: Essays that Entertain the Consequences of New Assumptions in Economic Theory* (Cambridge: Cambridge University Press, 1984), Chapter 7, "The Economic Consequences of Cognitive Dissonance."

Notes and Answers

1. Cardinal.
2. To be precise, we're dealing with the marginal rate of substitution of sweaters (y) for

video tapes (x) as video tapes (x) are substituted for sweaters (y). That means the number you'll derive for the MRS refers to how

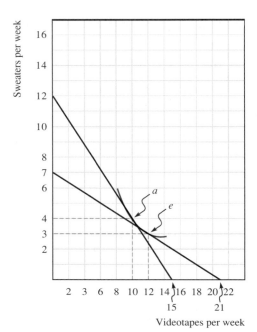

Sweaters per week

Videotapes per week

many sweaters (or parts thereof) you'll have to give up for each unit of videotape you gain in the process of adding to your videotape library. Technically, the MRS should take on a negative value in this case; economists have tended to ignore this point. To obtain the *precise MRS* for any point, draw a line tangent to the point and determine where it touches both the y- and the x-axes. Then, divide the *y* value by the *x* value. For example, in the accompanying figure at point *a*, the tangent drawn in touches the two axes at 12 and 15. Divide 12 by 15, for an MRS of 0.8. At *e*, the MRS = 7 ÷ 21 = 0.33. Obviously, as *x* increases, the MRS declines.

3. 0, 1, and infinity. The slope (Δy/Δx) of any point other than the right angle is either 0 or infinity, while the slope at the right angle is 1.

4. First, the MRS itself is *positive,* not negative. Instead of having to give up something to obtain another good, in this instance the consumer has to be bribed by giving him more *y* in order for him to be willing to take more of *x*. Second, as you move rightward on

the *x*-axis, the MRS rises; more *y* has to be given to the consumer in order to induce him to take equal increments of *x*.

5. *a.* $500. Indeed, you've just read that the budget line is derived on the basis of $500 available for spending.

   b. Have you plotted them? If so, you've discovered they lie beyond the budget line. Think of the budget line as a boundary between the attainable, all points lying on or within the budget line, and the unattainable, those plotted outside the boundary. Obviously, then, the 6, 12 combination is unachievable within the confines of the $500 budget.

6. You'll notice that the budget line will be a straight line parallel to the initial line. Since that will always be true for the cases in this chapter, you can take advantage of the fact that you need only two points in order to draw a straight line. Take the end points, in this case 12 and 30, and you'll always have the correct budget line.

7. Recall that the MRS is the slope of the indifference curve and equals Δy/Δx. Here the MRS is 10/25. The relative prices of the two commodities, P_y/P_x are $50/$20 (or 25/10), which is the inverse of the slope of the budget line. So, in equilibrium,

$$\text{MRS} = \frac{1}{\dfrac{P_y}{P_x}} = \frac{P_x}{P_y}$$

8. There's really no reason to assume that the indifference curves are parallel, and so combinations at different income levels need not contain the same proportions of sweaters to tapes.

9. Whether Andrea will also buy fewer sweaters or not is a topic to be examined in Chapter 5.

10. This issue is not limited to housing. Medicaid is targeted for the poor, who do not receive funds to pay for health services. Instead, payments are made directly to the providers.

11. 15; $1,000; $1,500.

12. "The Experimental Determination of Indifference Curves," *Review of Economic Studies* 36 (1969), pp. 433–51.

13. John H. Kagel, Howard Rachlin, Leonard

Green, Raymond C. Battalio, Robert L. Basmann, and W. R. Klemm, "Experimental Studies of Consumer Demand Behavior Using Laboratory Animals," *Economic Inquiry,* 13 (March 1975), pp. 22–38.

14. Students who have already taken a course in finance will realize that the riskiness of an investment is typically measured by the standard deviation of the yield or the beta. Tradition has here been traded off for simplicity.

15. Actually, diversification can lower overall risk as well, but to prove that requires additional development of this case. A simple presentation of the "efficient portfolio" theory can be found in Burton G. Malkiel, *A Random Walk down Wall Street* (New York: Norton, 1990); see Chapter 7, "How Good is Fundamental Analysis."

16. Habitual purchases tend to be concentrated on products where customer search costs are high relative to the prices of the products themselves (e.g., gasoline). On the other hand, habit hardly plays a role when contemplating expenditures involving large sums of money (e.g., a car).

17. The slope of the budget constraint will become shallower, but the same corner solution will result. Only if the slope exceeds 2, which will occur if Kleenex is priced at over $1 while Brand X remains at 50 cents, will the equilibrium switch to the opposite corner. Try it.

18. Read through Calvin Trillin's lively and humorous autobiographical articles on eating, assembled in his *American Fried: Adventures of a Happy Eater* (Garden City, N.Y.: Doubleday, 1974); or *Alice, Let's Eat: Further Adventures of a Happy Eater* (New York: Random House, 1978). You'll quickly discern how much Mr. Trillin will sacrifice for the good meal.

19. Jack Hirshleifer, "The Expanding Domain of Economics," *American Economic Review* 75, no. 5 (December 1985), pp. 53–68.

4

CONSUMER DEMAND: WE WANT WHAT WE WANT WHEN WE WANT IT

But economics is not, in the end, much interested in the behaviour of single individuals. Its concern is with the behaviour of groups.
Sir John R. Hicks (1946)

People buying top-of-the-line cars aren't buying transportation. They're buying dreams.
Beverly Hills Car Dealer (1987)

Learning Objectives

In this chapter you will discover:
- How to use indifference curves to derive an individual demand curve.
- The meaning and uses of the *income* and *substitution* effects.
- How to derive a demand curve for a product from the individual demands of potential purchasers.
- The concept of consumer surplus.
- How economists actually estimate market demand curves.
- Some exceptions to the simple theory of demand that stem from social pressures, asymmetric information, and price expectations.
- How demand analysis has been used for policy analysis.

The Pricing of Calculators

Table 4.1 lists the prices between 1972 and 1979 of the cheapest portable electronic calculators found in the Sears catalog.[1] The table illustrates a

TABLE 4.1   Prices of Portable Electronic Calculators, 1972–1979

Year	Price	Year	Price
1972	$99.50	1976	$7.99
1973	58.95	1977	*
1974	58.95	1978	6.85
1975	13.88	1979	5.86

* No inexpensive calculator appeared in the 1977 catalog.

phenomenon not uncommon after the introduction of a new piece of technology: Initial high prices are followed by a steep drop in price. Indeed, the table understates the drop in price. As calculators became so much more sophisticated, the same dollar outlay in 1979 bought a better calculator than it did in 1972. Not surprisingly in light of Chapter 3's analysis of consumer optimizing behavior, as price went down, the number of calculators sold steadily increased.

One of the purposes of this chapter is to link the relationship between individual consumer decisions, spelled out in Chapter 3, and the market for specific products that was discussed in Chapter 2. In addition, we'll examine an empirical demand function and consider some exceptions to the simple theory of the declining demand curve. The chapter concludes with two illustrations of how demand analysis is used in the private and public sectors of the U.S. economy.

From Indifference Curves to the Demand Curve

Deriving a Demand Curve: Chedley Takes Off

If you followed the basic argument of Chapter 3, you should be able to see the connection between an individual's indifference curve and her demand curve. Take a look again at Figure 3.9 (p. 81), in which Andrea's reaction to an increase in the price of videotapes is explored. Not surprisingly, Andrea's optimum combination of sweaters and videotapes changes, and she ends up by acquiring fewer videotapes. Wouldn't Andrea's demand curve for videotapes give you precisely that information?

Figure 4.1a simplifies the idea underlying Figure 3.9 by relabeling the ordinate in *dollars* to represent a specific amount of income. So, if we start Chedley off with an annual income of $100,000 and postulate that the price of a short commuter flight is $50 per trip, the relevant budget constraint is anchored at $100,000 on the ordinate and 2,000 flights per year on the abscissa. (The slope is $100,000/2,000, which, of course, equals the

FIGURE 4.1   **Deriving Chedley's Demand Curve**

a.   Chedley's travel planning guide

a. As the price of flights decreases, Chedley's optimum positions dictate she fly more often. The tangencies are connected by the price-consumption curve.

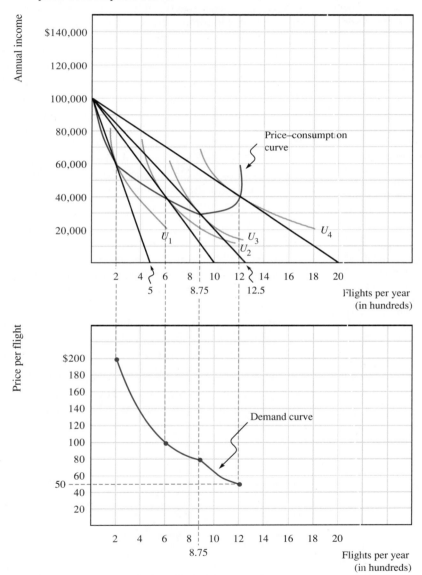

b.   Chedley's demand curve for air travel

b. As the price per flight declines, Chedley's demand curve indicates how many additional flights she'll take.

The **price-consumption curve** connects equilibrium consumption combinations derived by changing price.

$50 price.) Chedley's optimum consumption package, given the indifference map depicted in the diagram and the $50 price, is 1,200 trips. That leaves her with $40,000 to spend on other consumer goods and services.

Figure 4.1a, as you've probably noticed, contains a number of other budget lines. Each line represents an alternative price. The **price-consumption curve** is drawn on the Figure 4.1a to connect the equilibrium points. The last two columns in Table 4.2 list the optimum combinations of flights and income available for other expenditures implicit in the price-consumption curve. Figure 4.1b plots this information slightly differently, using only the first two columns. The result is Chedley's demand curve for air travel. The close relationship between Figure 4.1a and Figure 4.1b is highlighted by their construction. Note, however, that while the two diagrams share common abscissas, their ordinates differ. Consequently, price is measured differently in the two diagrams. In Figure 4.1a, price equals _____,[2] while in Figure 4.1b, you can read the price directly off the ordinate.

The increase or decrease in the quantity purchased that follows from *just* a change in relative prices is called the **substitution effect**. The change in the quantity bought that results from a change in the purchasing power of a given amount of income is known as the **income effect**. The total change in quantity demanded resulting from a price change constitutes the **price effect**.

Actually, we could leave well enough alone and stop here. Economic theorists, however, have pressed on a bit further by distinguishing between two plausible reasons why Chedley is willing to fly more often as the price goes down:

Motive number 1: A lower price induces Chedley to reorder her priorities. The reduced price of air travel upsets the existing relationship between the relative price of flying and other products. It's sensible to substitute some of the now lower-priced product for other goods that have become more expensive in comparison.

Motive number 2: The fall in airfare means that Chedley's income stretches further. She could travel as much as before, but because each trip costs less, Chedley will have funds left over. With that extra spending power, she could travel some more.

These explanations were first popularized by the British Nobel Prize–winning economist Sir John R. Hicks, who called them, respectively, the **substitution** and **income effects**. The combination of the income and substitution effects is called the **price effect**.

TABLE 4.2   Chedley's Optimum Consumption Packages

Price per Flight	Number of Flights	Dollars Remaining
$200	200	$60,000
100	600	40,000
80	875	30,000
50	1,200	40,000

Decomposing Price Changes: Income and Substitution Effects

Students often confuse the income effect of a price change with the impact of an income change. While the terms seem related, they in fact stem from different sources. In the case of the *income effect of a price change,* the fundamental source is the *price change.* When the price of chess sets decreases, it is *as if* the buyer had obtained additional income. Because Damon's existing income can stretch further, he can buy the same quantity of chess sets he previously desired and still have some of his fixed income left over to do with as he pleases. On the other hand, *a change in income* means precisely that: the consumer has more income and can buy more chess sets and other items even though existing prices have not changed.

If individuals spend less on a particular good or service as their income rises, that product is known as an **inferior good.**

One further point: It should be obvious that when airfares come down, people will fly more often. Air travel is a normal good (defined on p. 80). As you will see shortly, for a normal good, both the substitution and the income effects work to increase quantity demanded as price falls. Less apparent is that a price cut will increase the quantity demanded even for an **inferior good,** such as travel on intercity buses.

Income and Substitution Effects for a Normal Good.   Let's return now to Chedley's decision to take 400 additional flights when the fare is cut from $200 to $100 per flight. How can that price effect be decomposed into its respective substitution and income effects?

Let's deal first with the substitution effect, which requires that Chedley reorder her priorities among air travel and other purchases because the relative price of flying has fallen. We'd like to ask Chedley, "How many more flights would you buy only because the price cut changed relative prices?" To answer that question accurately, Chedley will have to abstract from the fact that the lower price also enabled her existing income to stretch further. Conceptually, she can eliminate the increase in purchasing power by remaining on her initial indifference curve, which represents the best Chedley could do with her given income.

Glance at Figure 4.2, which extracts from Figure 4.1a the two relevant budget lines and indifference curves for Chedley's decision. Chedley started off in equilibrium on U_1 with 200 flights per year and $60,000 left to spend on other products. Let's confine Chedley to U_1 and thus constrain Chedley's ability to buy more of everything. At the same time, let's vary airfares relative to other products from $200 per flight to $100. Geometrically, that would entail modifying the slope of B_1, the initial budget constraint in Figure 4.2, and swinging it along U_1 from the initial equilibrium to a new tangency on B_2 at $30,000 and 450. (Verify that the slope of the budget line equals $100 at the new tangency. You can do that either by calculating the slope from the endpoints or by noticing that the new line lies parallel to B_3.)

FIGURE 4.2   Price, Substitution, and Income Effects

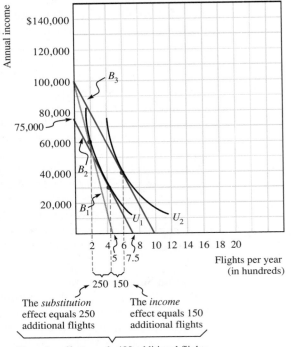

A decrease in the price of air travel induces a *price* effect, which combines both a substitution and income effect.

What does the new equilibrium mean? Simply that if Chedley had only been permitted to reorder her travel priorities in light of the new relative price, she would have flown 450 times instead of only 200. Because flights have become relatively cheaper, Chedley would have substituted 250 flights and spent $25,000 less on other products. So, *the substitution effect equals 250 flights*.

With the substitution effect isolated, it's a relatively simple matter to find the income effect. Since

The price effect = The income effect + The substitution effect

then

The income effect = The price effect − The substitution effect

We already know that the price effect equals 400 flights and the substitution effect is 250 trips; the income effect must equal 150 flights.

What's happened here is straightforward. The fact that Chedley reaches U_2 as a result of the price reduction is a result of both an *as if* increase in income and a shift in relative prices. The shift in relative prices has already been accounted for by a movement along U_1. The change from the U_1, B_2 tangency to the final U_2, B_3 tangency must be caused by the income effect. Diagramatically, shift B_2 parallel to itself—keeping relative prices constant—until it touches U_2. The result: an increase of another 150 flights demanded by Chedley.

MicroQuery   Has Chedley's income actually increased? _____ [3]

Can you demonstrate that flights are a normal good? Yes, just by looking at the upward shift of B_2 until it smothers B_3. Had an actual increase in income occurred—say, from \$75,000 to \$100,000—Chedley would have flown more often. And, if you've mastered this section, you will conclude that *for a normal good, a price cut will induce the consumer to purchase more of the cheaper good both because of its income and substitution effects.*

That conclusion, however, would not be precisely true for an inferior good. Read on to understand the distinction between the impact of a decline in the price of an inferior good as opposed to a normal good.

Income and Substitution Effects for an Inferior Good.   Rice is a staple in the diet of many Americans, especially those hailing from an Asian or a Mexican tradition. Of course, immigrants do over time tend to adapt to the more typical meat-and-potatoes American diet. So let's examine the behavior of Louis, a resident of San Antonio who entered the United States some decades ago and who consumes both rice and beef. How does Louis respond to a reduction in the price of rice?

Figure 4.3a looks much like Figure 4.2, except that bags of rice per week are substituted for flights, and, as will become clear, the income effect is negative. Inspect the diagram. An initial price of rice of \$10 per five-pound bag results in Louis's purchasing two bags weekly, the budget line–U_1 tangency. When the price decreases to \$5 per bag, Louis ups his rice purchases to three bags. Figure 4.3b reproduces this price effect in the form of two points on Louis's demand curve.

Just as in the case of Chedley, the substitution effect is derived by varying the slope representing the old price along the original indifference curve until it becomes equal to the new price. As you can see from the Figure 4.3a, the new equilibrium on U_1 occurs at four bags of rice weekly. So, the substitution effect equals two bags.

What is the income effect? _____

FIGURE 4.3   Louis's Rice Consumption

a.   Negative income effect versus a positive substitution effect

a.   A decrease in the price of rice induces a negative income effect since rice is an inferior good. In this case, however, the positive substitution effect caused by the price decline overwhelms the negative income effect. Consequently, the quantity of rice demanded increases.

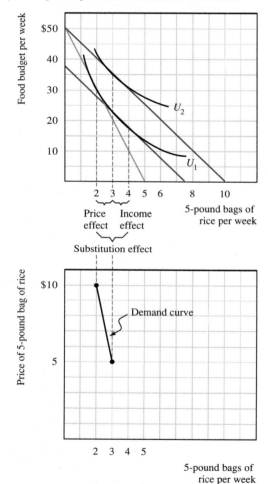

b.   Points on Louis's demand for rice curve

b.   Despite the negative income effect, the demand curve still shows the normal downward slope. More rice is demanded as price declines.

MicroBits 4.1

Sneakers and the Pure Income Effect

Income and Substitution Effects for Perfect Complements

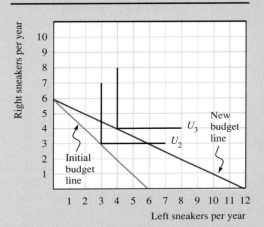

Take a look at the right-angled indifference curves of the figure here, reproduced from the first figure in MicroBits 3.3. Recall that equilibrium always occurs at the right angle and an equal number of right and left sneakers are bought. Now, cut the price of left sneakers in half; the budget constraint shifts outward. The consumer ends up with four pairs of sneakers instead of three. Why?

Examine first the income effect: With left sneakers half as expensive, the original three pairs now cost less than before. To recall the numbers already used on page 82, a price

cut from $30 per left sneaker to $15 means that three pairs cost only $135 instead of $180. With the $45 left over, the customer can buy another pair of sneakers. But if that's the case, there's nothing left to be explained by the substitution effect. Indeed, *in the case of perfect complements, the price effect and the income effect are identical.*

If you are skeptical, you can convince yourself by constructing a budget line parallel to the new price ratio that is also tangent to U_2. How many additional left sneakers does the substitution effect tell our consumer to buy? You're right if your construction led you to answer *none.* But if that's so, you must be convinced that the income effect and the price effect are equal.

Isn't that intuitively correct? Since the substitution effect works by requiring Jack to substitute the now less-expensive product for the more expensive one, it implicitly assumes that such substitution will not decrease his satisfaction, which is what happens as a consumer moves along a given indifference curve. But is that true if Jack is asked to substitute left sneakers for right ones? Would he remain on the same indifference curve as he substituted left for right sneakers? In short, in the case of perfect complements, there is no substitution effect, and the increase in purchases after a price decline will only result from the income effect.

Your inspection of Figure 4.3a should inform you that the income effect is *negative* one bag: were Louis's food budget actually to increase from \$37.50 to \$50 with the price set at \$5 per bag, he'd buy less rice. Combining the two—a plus 2 and a minus 1—yields the price effect: a net increase of one bag of rice weekly.

In short, *even in the case of an inferior good, a decrease in price will still lead to an increase in quantity demanded.* That's true because for most goods and services bought by the consumer, the income effect is likely to be small. After all, we tend to spend very little of our income on any one particular product, so that even if the price of one product falls, the impact on our total purchasing power is apt to be minute. On the other hand, any decrease in price induces us to switch to the now-cheaper product.[4] (Note that not all products must demonstrate both income and substitution effects. MicroBits 4.1 explores the case of perfect complements, in which there's only an income effect.)

The Position of the Demand Curve

By now it should be quite clear that for any given set of prices, initial income, and indifference map, the position and the overall shape of a person's demand curve is predetermined. Had either of these conditions been changed, the demand curve would also have been modified. Consider Melissa, whose indifference map is plotted in Figure 4.4a. This 24-year-old with a \$40,000 annual income as a computer programmer is definitely a yuppie. High among her leisure-time activities is skydiving. The array of budget lines radiating from \$40,000 reflects different prices for a day of skydiving, and the tangencies are reflected in the demand curve in Figure 4.4b.

When Melissa successfully interviews for a new position as systems analyst, she finds that her pay jumps to \$50,000. Draw Melissa's new equilibria onto Figure 4.4a, and on Figure 4.4b draw her new demand curve for skydiving days. Your construction should conform to your intuition: Melissa's demand curve is still downward sloping, but it lies to the right of the initial one.[5]

The ABCs of Market Demand: Or, the People Unite

Our individual demands for most of the goods and services we buy are conditioned primarily by our tastes (as represented by individual indifference maps), our incomes, and the prices of the products and their alternatives in consumption. Barring some exceptions discussed later in this chapter, the demand curve for a specific good or service can be derived by a simple process of summing the demand curves of individuals.

FIGURE 4.4   Positioning the Demand Curve

a.   Melissa's indifference map: income versus skydiving

a. As price per day of skydiving declines, Melissa indulges in this activity
more often. New tangencies, drawn to the right of the old ones, will be
generated if Melissa's income is increased to $50,000. Your job is to
draw in the new set of budget lines and indicate the new tangencies.

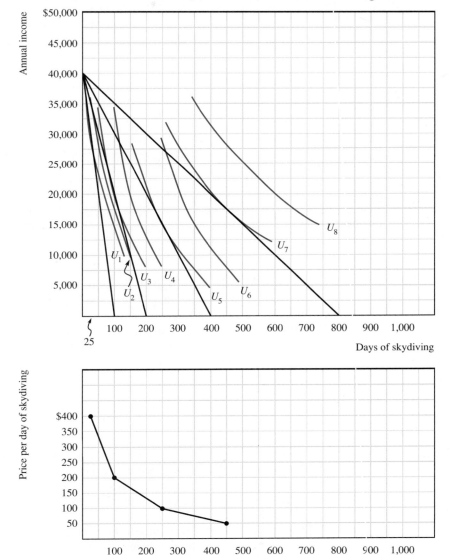

b.   Melissa's demand curve for skydiving.

b. Melissa's falling demand curve is provided, given her $40,000 income.
You'll find her new demand curve to the right of this one, representing
her $50,000 income.

FIGURE 4.5 The Market Demand for Tires as the Sum of Individual Demands

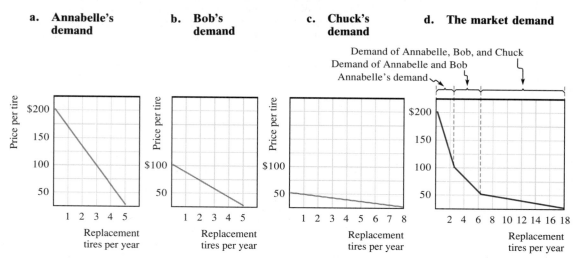

a. **Annabelle's demand**   b. **Bob's demand**   c. **Chuck's demand**   d. **The market demand**

The market demand curve is the sum of the individual demands of potential buyers. At prices of $100 or more, Annabelle is the sole interested purchaser. But at lower prices, first Bob and then Chuck enter the market.

Consider three college students in the market for replacement tires: Annabelle, Bob, and Chuck. Given the fact that tires wear down gradually and can be replaced at different use intervals, it's not improper to presume that the frequency of replacement will depend on individual preferences and incomes, as well as market prices. Figure 4.5 reproduces the individual demand curves of Annabelle, Bob, and Chuck.

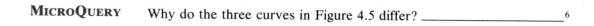

MICROQUERY   Why do the three curves in Figure 4.5 differ? _____ 6

The curves are summed horizontally in Figure 4.5d, so at any price of $100 or more, the market demand curve only reflects Annabelle; the two others are unwilling to replace tires at those prices. (That's why the points on the market demand curve until $100 in Figure 4.5d and those on Annabelle's demand curve in Figure 4.5a are identical.) As the price moves below $100 per tire, Bob enters the market, and at just below $50 Chuck decides it worthwhile to replace his tires.

At $80, Annabelle is willing to buy three tires yearly, and Bob one. Thus, the entire market demand equals four tires. At $25 per tire, all will replace their tires more frequently, and so the total quantity demanded is a bit more than 12.[7]

The preceding two paragraphs suggest that the market demand curve is downward sloping for two reasons:

- At lower prices, new buyers enter the market. (Bob moves in as the price falls below $100, while Chuck enters when the price falls below $50.)
- At lower prices, those already in the market are induced to buy more. (At $40, Annabelle buys four tires instead of three and Bob buys three rather than one.)

Obviously, these three people constitute only a small share of the replacement tire market. But the principle of market demand derived by summing the individual demands of all potential buyers holds true for the entire market.

Consumer Surplus

A hypothetical market demand curve for the U.S. consumer replacement tire market appears in Figure 4.6. The diagram is meant to focus your attention on an interesting implication of demand curve analysis that will come in handy later: Consumers as individuals and as a group gain by paying a uniform market price.

FIGURE 4.6   Consumer Surplus

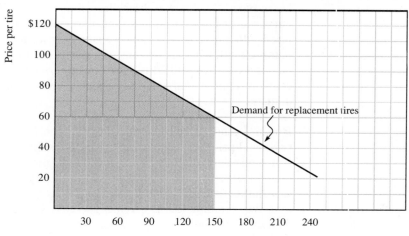

The difference between what consumers are willing to pay, which is represented by the area below the market demand curve, and the amount they actually pay—price per unit × the quantity purchased—represents a bonus called *consumer surplus*. Here it's the purple triangle.

To see why that's so, begin by assuming that the market price for a tire is $60 and that each year 150 million replacement tires are bought. The gray box in the diagram indicates total consumer expenditures on replacement tires, $60 × 150 million, or $9 billion.

Now focus on Harold, who bought the 60 millionth tire. Draw a line upward from the abscissa at 60 until you hit the demand curve, which will be at a price of $96. In other words, Harold would have been willing to pay $96, even though he actually paid $60. Harold implicity benefited to the tune of $36 dollars. The same principle applies to Maud, who bought the 120 millionth tire. Maud was prepared to pay $72 to acquire a tire; she actually paid $60. Indeed, any individual who was disposed to pay more than the actual market price, but did not have to, gained. The total value of that benefit is called **consumer surplus**, which is depicted by the light purple triangle in Figure 4.6.

Consumer surplus is the difference between the amount purchasers would be willing to pay for a good or service and the actual amount they do pay.

You understand that a lower price increases consumer surplus and a higher price reduces it. But you should also realize that a full discussion of the implications of consumer surplus must include supplier reactions as well. After all, if demand alone were considered, one might conclude that maximizing consumer surplus would require a zero price. Unfortunately, no free-market supplier would be willing to produce at a zero price. And if there's no supply, there will be no sales and so no surplus either.

What happens when the market demand curve shifts in response to an increase in consumer income, and what will be the impact on consumer surplus? If, independently, the parents of Annabelle, Bob, and Chuck increase the stipend sent monthly to their children, the students may well be induced to change their tires more often. The individual demand curves shift outward, and so must the market demand curve for tires. If prices do not change, then consumer surplus will rise. You can also comprehend why an increase in the price of gasoline will reduce the demand for tires and so reduce consumers surplus in the tire market. As each individual demand curve shifts inward, so, too, will the market demand curve.

Recap.   And so, in a sense, we've gone full circle. In Chapter 2 you reviewed price determination by juxtaposing demand and supply curves. But those demand curves were derived intuitively rather than by exploring consumer behavior and choice. In this chapter and in Chapter 3, you saw that consumer demand has a rationale of its own. By now, you realize that the demand for a specific good or service depends on individual demands; the market is a whole that is no more than the sum of its individual components. Clearly, then, anything that modifies the decisions of individuals will be reflected in the market, and, conversely, any change in the market must be mirrored in the actions of individual decision makers. (The role of advertising in affecting demand is briefly examined in MicroBits 4.2.)

MICROBITS 4.2

The Economist and the Advertiser

Although the per capita consumption of beef by U.S. residents takes third place to that in Argentina and Uruguay—Argentinians consume on the average more than one and a half times as much beef as Americans and the Uruguayans just a bit more—the meat-and-potatoes characterization of Americans is not a stereotype. Domestic beef producers, however, have found little consolation in this high world rank. They were disappointed because annual per capita beef consumption remained basically stable at 75 to 80 pounds over the early 1980s, despite continuous real income growth in the United States. Health concerns over the relatively high cholesterol content of beef and an overall change in domestic tastes to lighter foods and fewer calories were primarily responsible for the relative weakness in the beef market. Economists would say that the rising demand for meat that comes from the combination of income growth and beef's being a normal good was offset by changes in taste.

The Beef Industry Council in 1987 tried to reverse the trend away from beef. It initiated a $30 million advertising campaign consisting of television, radio, and print media ads, one of which is reproduced here.

Notice how the ad tries to allay concerns over beef's cholesterol and calories. Surely you understand that a successful advertising campaign will influence individual families, and through them, the demand curve for the entire industry. At worst, the demand curve

SOURCE: Courtesy Leo Burnett U.S.A.

will slowly move to the right, while a more pleasant scenario (for the Beef Industry Council) would see it shift strongly rightward. But in either case, increased sales is clearly the objective.

The Market for Calculators

We're now ready to return to the electronic calculator market that opened this chapter. Certainly preferences, incomes, and prices all played and still play a role in calculator purchase decisions. No one can doubt the utility of those hand-held or desk-size marvels. Surely they are goods, not bads, and we'd be willing to give up income in order to acquire them. Undoubtedly, too, the average U.S. individual income, even adjusted for inflation, increased between the early 1970s, when calculators first were introduced, to 1979. In fact, U.S. per capita disposable income in 1972 dollars rose from $3,860 in 1972 to $4,512 in 1979. As the last section suggested, the increase in income, along with the plausible assumption that calculators are not inferior goods, implies that individual demand curves were shifting rightward over time. And so the market demand curve must have moved rightward as well.

But something else was happening simultaneously. As consumers went shopping for calculators, they discovered that over the years, prices were falling. Advances in microchip technology had brought down costs of producing calculators; competition among manufacturers and between distributors such as Sears forced retail prices down. So, not only were we better able to afford calculators because of our higher incomes, we were also induced to buy them because of the lower price. That is, we moved to a lower point in our shifting individual demand curves. The net result was that many people owned a number of calculators. In the calculator market, individuals responded as indifference curve theory would project.

You may be able confirm another conclusion on the basis of your own experience. Many individuals did not buy calculators in the early years; even though the price was falling and their income was rising, they still felt that the price was too high to justify spending some of their hard-earned income on a calculator. But as prices continued to come down, more and more consumers took the initial plunge, buying their first calculator. In short, the market demand for calculators expanded for the two reasons mentioned earlier: (1) additional purchases by those already in the market and (2) first-time buyers. Both indicated that the market demand for calculators should show a downward-sloping demand curve.

Estimated Demand Curves: An Oily Example*

Economic theory contributes to a clearer understanding of consumer behavior by pointing out the underlying sources of consumer decisions.

---

* This section may be skipped without affecting continuity. Those students who do read this section might find it worthwhile to refresh their memories about the methods used and the problems encountered in estimating demand curves by turning back to the appendix to Chapter 2.

Theoretical analysis leads to implications that have important consequences both in terms of public policy and individual business decisions; you've seen that in earlier chapters and will recognize its validity again in the pages to come. But often the greater precision provided by quantitative estimates is more useful than the qualitative responses of theory. Decision makers both in the private and public sectors can conduct themselves more intelligently when they take into account not only the directional impact of their actions but also its magnitude. That requires empirically estimating demand functions, the subject of this section.

By way of introduction, virtually all empirical studies of demand reject the convenient straight-line demand curves used by most textbook writers. Instead, curved demand curves that turn out to be linear in their logarithms seem to fit the data best. This holds true for the following example as well.

The Demand for Oil

The relationship between the quantity demanded of oil and its price should entail few surprises. The higher the price of oil, the greater the number of individuals who will be induced to economize on its use, and consequently, the lower the quantity demanded in the market. In contrast to this inverse relationship of quantity demanded to price, we would expect the demand for oil to rise with income. Finally, although individual consumers may find it difficult to substitute other fuels for oil, fuel-intensive businesses such as electric utilities will react to higher oil prices by switching over time to alternative energy sources. For them, too, high past prices will reduce current demand, so that current demand will depend on past as well as current prices.

Professor Dermot Gately derived a demand curve for oil using current price, current income, and the past year's sales to take into account the impact of previous years' prices.[8] The resulting demand function, expressed in terms of logarithms is:[9]

$$\ln(\text{Demand}_t) = \text{constant} + a[\ln(\text{Income}_t)] + b[\ln(\text{Price}_t)] + k[\ln(\text{Demand}_{t-1})]$$

Gately discovered that this general equation fits well the data covering 1950 to 1982 for the United States, Japan, and four European countries. Take one example, the demand for oil in the United Kingdom. The actual equation that Gately calculated was as follows:

$$\ln(\text{Demand}_t) = -3.83 + 0.81[\ln(\text{Income}_t)] - 0.15[\ln(\text{Price}_t)] + 0.72[\ln(\text{Demand}_{t-1})]$$

The empirical results conform to our theoretical expectations. Income is positively related to oil demand, while the sign of the price variable is appropriately negative.[10] (Such empirical equations can be used not only for explaining past oil market behavior but also for predicting future oil demand. See the appendix to this chapter for a forecasting application.)

Although most markets that economists study are as well-behaved as the oil market, exceptions do surface. Three such phenomena are considered in the next section.

Dropping Assumptions: Introducing Social Pressures, Asymmetric Information, and Expectations into Demand Analysis

In 1946, Sir John Hicks wrote, "The simple law of demand—the downward slope of the demand curve—turns out to be almost infallible in its working. Exceptions to it are rare and unimportant." Perhaps Hicks was right. But the cases in this section suggest that what he believed true for postwar Britain might not be so in the United States as it approaches the 21st century.

Two types of exceptions are developed in the next pages:

- Cases where either the individual or the market demand curves formulated earlier are no longer appropriate: market demand curves may not be the sum of individual demand curves, or they may rise rather than fall.
- Instances where the relationship between demand and current price is at best tenuous.

Social Pressures and Demand: Dumpsters as Status Symbols

The **bandwagon** (or **demonstration**) **effect** is at work when an individual's consumption is conditioned by the consumption of others.

Keeping up with the Joneses seems to be a fundamental force in the spending behavior of many American consumers. Known as the **bandwagon effect** in the literature of microeconomics or the **demonstration effect** in the writings of development economists, the central ideal is that our demands for certain goods or services depend not only on their usefulness, but also—and perhaps primarily—because the pacesetters in the community consume them. By acquiring such products or services, we are identifying ourselves also as trendsetters. Price, then, enters as a secondary and perhaps even a minor consideration.

The **Veblen effect** explains why the higher the price carried by a product, the *larger* the quantity demanded will be.

To take this point a step further, consumers may well purchase certain goods and services primarily in order to instill envy in others who are less able to afford these products. In fact, in the case of **Veblen effect** goods (named after Thorstein Veblen; see MicroBits 4.3), unless price is sufficiently high to put the product out of the reach of the bulk of the community—like the silver cutlery displayed by a California shop at $1,799 per *place setting!*—it will hardly serve its purpose. The assumptions that underlie standard demand theory are violated in all such cases.

MicroBits 4.3

Thorstein Veblen, an Economic Rebel (1857–1929)

Thorstein Veblen made enemies easily. His pen was sharp, his tongue sharper. As a lecturer, he was deadly boring. Veblen had no interest in his students; it was rumored that his office hours extended from 4:00 to 4:02 P.M. and 3:00 to 3:50 A.M. This individualist who cared little for the gentility of academia tolerated his colleagues no better. Nor was his domestic life a model one; scandals involving women were not uncharacteristic of Veblen. Not surprisingly, Veblen became an academic migrant, teaching at the University of Chicago, Stanford, the University of Missouri, and the New School for Social Research.

Veblen's powerful intellect and brilliant pen are well exemplified by his scathing indictment of American society, *The Theory of the Leisure Class* (1899). The tome reflects an alienated individual, a farm boy raised in rural Wisconsin to a poor Norwegian immigrant family. But the book transcends that personal bitterness, containing a good deal of truthful provocation and a most original manner of examining society.

Central to Veblen's thinking was a theory of institutional evolution: Society moves from a peaceful "barbarian" phase to a preindustrial stage to an industrial state, forming in the process institutions that are appropriate to each stage. But at each phase of the evolution, the forces for progress clash with those championing the status quo. The latter are epitomized by the leisure class.

The leisure class is characterized both by conspicuous leisure and conspicuous consumption. Doing little if any productive work and spending for the sake of showing off are

Source: The Bettmann Archive

the hallmarks of this class, which also retard social and economic development. It was Veblen's focus on conspicuous consumption that lent his name to goods whose primary purpose is to distinguish between the superrich and the merely wealthy.

Consequently, the demand curve that describes the demand for band-wagon or Veblen effect goods will differ as well.

The Bandwagon Effect.   The social dimension of our consumption of certain goods or services is obvious. It's not surprising to see a wave of renovation flow through a neighborhood as one family adds on a deck in the back, another builds a den, and a third constructs an entire new floor. Indeed, for those who can't afford to renovate, parking a dumpster outside the house and filling it with debris may suffice to impress.[11] Thus, the bandwagon effect.

It's not difficult to handle the bandwagon effect theoretically once you realize that the market demand is no longer the sum of individual demands as was understood until now. For example, the demand for vacations can be visualized as consisting of two parts: (1) the quantity and quality of vacations an individual would select in the absence of social pressure, and (2) the additional quantity and/or quality taken because a person's friends try to one-up him or her. In a sense, then, Figure 4.7 depicts a situation where the market demand curve is greater than the sum of the individual demand curves.

Consider first the demand curve labeled with the lower-case *d*. It represents the sum of individual demands for vacation days in the absence of a bandwagon effect and is contrasted to the shallower *D* curve, which

FIGURE 4.7   The Bandwagon Effect

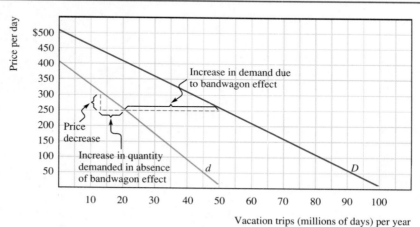

In the absence of bandwagon effects, *d* is the appropriate demand curve, so that a price cut does increase quantity demanded, but only slightly. Introducing ''keeping up with the Joneses'' considerations replaces *d* by *D* and leads to a larger impact on vacation days for any given price reduction.

includes the presence of the bandwagon effect. Clearly, if price per day falls from $300 to $250, quantity demanded will increase not only by 7.5 million vacation days (from 12.5 million to 20 million) because of independently acting consumers, but also by an additional 30 million days because of the interdependence of individuals.

The Veblen Effect.   While the bandwagon effect reflects the fact that the whole sometimes is greater than the sum of its parts, it does not change the direction of the demand curve. That is left to the Veblen effect.

The Veblen effect is also easy to handle conceptually. In essence, for the select few, the higher the price of a product, the more desirable it is: the demand curve for those individuals who prize exclusivity *rises* from left to right instead of falling. Just think about it: if a Rolls Royce were available for a mere few thousand dollars instead of a minimum exceeding $100,000, then why would the superrich want it? In that case, the lower price would reduce quantity demanded, as Figure 4.8 shows, rather than increase it.

But hold on. Wouldn't the lower price bring these objects of conspicuous consumption into the reach of those who could now afford them and give rise to a bandwagon effect? That reasoning is true, but short-lived. After a while, even those who could now afford to emulate the affluent would stop buying the product: if it's no longer good enough for the superrich, the merely rich won't want it either.

FIGURE 4.8   The Veblen Effect

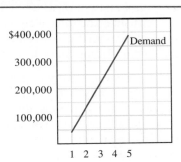

Rolls Royce sales
per year (000s)

As the price of a Rolls falls, it serves less its purpose of conspicuous consumption. The superrich will buy *less,* finding alternative vehicles to satisfy the need to show off.

Asymmetric Information: What Does Price Imply about Quality?

The negatively sloping demand curve may also prove inappropriate when market frictions such as asymmetric information are perceived to exist. Consumers may alter their purchase attitudes if information is imprecise, costly to obtain, or believed unreliable. Price may then be used as a signal for quality.

Consider markets where quality can be altered without the consumer's being aware of the change or without his understanding its nature. For instance, few drivers know the difference between gasoline with an 87 octane rating and that with a 92 rating. Moreover, even the technically proficient consumer cannot tell whether the more expensive gasoline is really being pumped into her tank.[12]

Surely some vendors will capitalize on consumer ignorance. They might drop the price of premium octane gasoline but simultaneously pump out a lower octane fuel. Consumers, being uninformed, suspicious, and uncertain, interpret price changes as a signal that quality has been altered even when it hasn't. They may react to the price decline by *decreasing* quantity demanded.

Actual Prices versus Expected Prices

An entirely new dimension is added to standard demand theory upon introducing expectational elements into consumer behavior. Typically, demand analysis has shied away from expectations, especially price expectations, even though real consumer buying behavior is predicated on an implicit, if not explicit, set of expectations.[13] The consequences of expectationally motivated actions are complex and not well understood.

Consider the following possible reactions to an announcement that in light of heavy dealer inventories, automobile manufacturers are offering significant discounts to buyers.

1. If enough individuals view the discounts as a harbinger of further price cuts, they will abstain from buying. This absence of buyers will depress price and thus justify demander expectations. At this second stage, however, buyers reenter the market. In this scenario, falling prices lead to momentary reductions in demand, but ultimately the demand shifts back to its original position and quantity demanded increases.

2. Alternatively, the actual direction of the market may well induce buyers to persistently revise their expectations downward. They reason that since price has continued to fall, it will fall still further. Demand then becomes dependent on *expected* and not actual prices.

Figure 4.9 depicts two market demand curves. They both are typical demand curves, but the outer one, *D,* assumes that a change in price will

FIGURE 4.9   Demand and Price Expectations

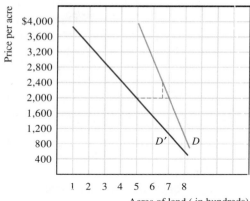

When price declines from $2,400 to $2,000
and the public expects further price declines,
then the demand curve shifts inward. Instead
of quantity demanded increasing to 700, it
actually falls to 500.

not generate expectations of further price modifications. But what if a
price cut from, say, $2,400 to $2,000 for an acre of residentially zoned
suburban land generates expectations of further price declines? Demanders of land do not respond to the dictates of the *D* curve and buy 700
acres. Rather, the expectation of further price decreases induces buyers
to shift to a new, inner demand curve, *D'*. The end result: Only 500 acres
are demanded at the $2,000 price.

MICROQUERY   If the inner-city area closest to the suburbs experiences an influx of low-
income families, leading to emigration from the central city, how might *D'*
for suburban property appear on Figure 4.9? _____ [14]

In all of these instances, demand is affected by elements not normally
considered by demand theory but nevertheless important. Social influences do affect our buying patterns, as does the presence or absence of
such frictions as information costs and expectations of price changes. But
with appropriate modifications, the economist can reach meaningful conclusions even in these situations.

They Have Their Designs on You

You can judge for yourself the truth of the saying "Someone has designs on you" by trying to make some sense out of designer labeling. The appeal of designer products is to a large extent contrived. It's not so much the quality of the merchandise or even the style that induces demand as it is the fact that the product smacks of exclusivity and expense. Surely those who buy designer clothing or jewelry for pets are obviously declaring, "We've made it. Just look at us and you can tell." And since goods and services meant for conspicuous consumption must be recognizable as such, the designer labels or brand names must be prominently displayed. Moreover, it's critical that designer clothes or fancy restaurants be more expensive than similar consumables that lack the exclusiveness element. Otherwise, what kind of statement is being made?

Yet designer products face an inherent paradox. Although in principle they are meant to be Veblen effect goods, they are produced in immense quantities and must be sold by appealing to a mass market. Ralph Lauren or RayBan products must exude exclusiveness and yet be within the reach of significant numbers of customers. Pricing such goods surely must be an art, for the demand curve may well look like that in Figure 4.10, with both rising and falling segments. At very high prices, the market will be limited because few people are willing to pay a steep price for the

FIGURE 4.10   The Market for Designer Jeans

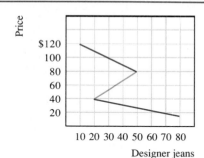

As price is reduced from $120 to $80 on designer jeans, more buyers enter the market. But if price is reduced to below $80, the loss of exclusivity leads many purchasers to drop out of the market. Below $40, the label becomes meaningless, and the jeans now are bought only because of their functional utility.

designer's cachet. As price comes down, more demanders enter the market, demonstrated by the falling segment between $120 and $80. At $80, the market is sufficiently impressed by the label and the expense, so that any further price reductions will lead to a loss of exclusivity, and buyers drop out of the market. Thus, between $80 and $40, the demand curve shows that as price declines, quantity demanded declines as well. However, as price continues to fall, the designer aspect becomes meaningless; the product competes with nondesigner goods on a competitive basis and so attracts more customers as the price falls.

MicroQuery   If you were asked to set a price for this item based only on the information provided by Figure 4.10, where would you set it? _____ [15]

Applying Demand Theory

Airline Pricing[16], or Why Two Passengers Sitting next to Each Other Probably Paid Different Prices

Few economists working for businesses and for governments doubt the value of understanding consumer demand theory. Without it, many decisions would be taken haphazardly rather than rationally. In its pricing of seats, the airline industry has been among the most effective practitioners of demand theory. In practicing "yield management," the art of squeezing the maximum revenue from each seat, the airlines are in essence searching for the points on the demand curves of particular groups of flyers.

American Airlines' staff of 90 yield managers has a simple objective: to sell the most seats at the highest possible fares while simultaneously assuring the flights leave with the fewest possible empty seats. Yet achieving a goal is a tough challenge. Not only does AA run over 1,500 flights a day, but the yield managers are responsible for over half a million future flights, which will carry 50 million passengers. Moreover, the multiplicity of fares on each flight means yield managers must decide how many seats to allot to each fare category.

Almost a year before the departure of AA flight 332, the yield managers will examine the flight's historic profile. Does it leave on a Friday afternoon, in which case it's likely to have attracted sizable numbers of full-fare-paying business travelers, or on a Wednesday, when fewer business people fly? The managers will parcel out the seats among fare classes based on this profile, modifying it as the weeks move on and more information becomes available. AA's computers are programmed to alert the yield managers if any unexpected change—such as a particularly heavy demand for the seats in a particular price category—occurs. The managers may then decide to expand the seat allotment of this class and decrease the seats available to a lower-priced category.

With AA 332 now a half-year prior to departure, the yield managers reexamine the demand picture. They adjust seat allotments in line with their perception of market demand. The managers may limit the number of spaces available for special discount fares and keep open seats designated for more expensive tickets. But as AA 332's flight time approaches and seats remain unsold, the pressure mounts on the managers to offer more discount seats. Indeed, it's not unusual for all special bargain seats to be fully booked only to become available a few days later as the yield managers adjust to the absence of demand that was expected to materialize in the interim.

Both overbooking by the airlines and no-shows by customers have to be taken into account. The historic profile will have indicated the volume of overbooking and no-shows on previous flights, but the past is at best only indicative of the future. So, even as late as two hours before the flight, the yield managers will be jockeying AA 332's seating allocations. They'll offer more discount seats if it appears that the flight will not be fully booked, assuming that lower fares attract customers. In general, this belief in a negatively sloped demand curve has paid off. According to one AA spokesperson, the yield management system is worth hundreds of millions of dollars to the airline.

Once the doors are closed and AA 332 proceeds on its way, the yield managers can forget about the flight—that is, until a few weeks hence, when they begin their planning for next year's AA 332. By then, the seating pattern of this year's AA 332 will be reflected in the profile that the yield managers call up on their computer monitors.

The Demand for Public Transportation[17]

Governments, too, turn to demand theory for answers, as the following case suggests.

That New Yorkers are taking the bus less often is obvious from Figure 4.11a. That fares have also been rising is clear from Figure 4.11b. And that the two are related is surely consistent with demand theory. In that case, what's the problem?

Actually, the conundrum of bus ridership is a dual one. On the one hand, subway fares have risen as well, yet subway ridership seems to have stabilized at about 1 billion rides per year despite the fact that subway fares are identical to bus fares. On the other hand, the quality of the bus fleet has improved as newer, more modern buses have replaced many antiquated vehicles and as older buses have been restored to higher stan-

FIGURE 4.11   New York City Bus Ridership and Fares

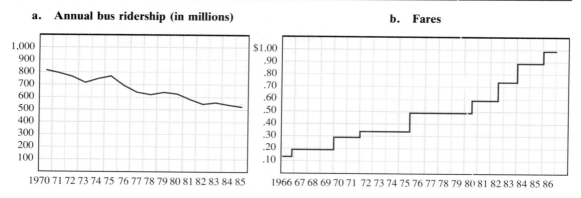

a.   **Annual bus ridership (in millions)**   b.   **Fares**

SOURCE: *The New York Times*, November 3, 1986, p. B1.

dards of performance and comfort. And bus speed improved from 7.7 miles an hour in 1970 to 8.2 miles an hour in 1980.

Since the relative price of bus travel has remained constant compared to subway fares, there should not have been a movement up the bus travel demand curve. And since the quality of bus service has not deteriorated, the demand curve for bus rides should not have shifted leftward. Why, then, did ridership fall?

New York City transit authorities believe that the city bus demand function is more complex than is apparent at first blush. Both population density and a broader specification of bus substitutes should be included. Authorities suggest that population shifted within the city, making bus routes in population-losing neighborhoods redundant while more heavily populated neighborhoods lack adequate bus service. And taxis, not only subways, are substitutes for buses.

Indeed, taxi rates have not increased as much as bus and subway fares have, which may account for some diversion of ridership. Whether changes in population density could have been responsible for the decline in bus travel is being investigated. Clearly, increasing ridership depends heavily on the outcome of the investigation, for if population shifts moved the demand curve inward, a relatively simple solution is at hand: Reroute the buses to capture the lost neighborhood riders.

Unfortunately, simple and logical solutions devised by economists may conflict with political considerations, which will have the decisive voice in a system where the government owns and operates buses and subways. It has been known to take 40 years to change a bus route in New York City! Quite clearly, demand theory may lead the official horse to water, but it can't make it drink.

The lesson of this section is clear: The question Is demand theory useful for anyone other than economic theorists? must be answered with an emphatic yes. The cases of demand for airline seats and urban bus travel represent the kind of exercise that economists are often called upon to do for their employers, public or private.

Economists, however, have economized on presenting the results of their studies by referring to a concept that is the subject of Chapter 5, elasticity. But before leaving Chapter 4, how about a puzzle?

In all of the cases and examples used in this chapter, the person who buys the product being discussed makes the purchase decision based on his or her own preferences. Even when social influences play a role, the consumer decides how to react to those external forces. But in many instances, the individual who makes the purchase decision is not the person who actually buys the product. Two examples spring readily to mind:

- Who decided what textbook would be used for this microeconomics course? Who bought this book?
- Does the physician who prescribes a medicine for a patient actually buy the medicine?

Surely you can think of other examples in which the order and the purchase are performed by unrelated individuals. So the question that naturally comes to the fore is, How would you describe the individual and the market demand curves in such cases? For example, how would you handle the case where the physician is either unaware of the drug prices or unconcerned about the buyer's ability to afford the prescribed drug? We'll come back to this question in Chapter 5 after you've mastered the idea of elasticity.

Summary

In this chapter you've discovered how indifference curve analysis forms the basis for an individual's demand curve for a specific product and how individual demand curves can be summed up to derive the market demand for a good or service. The negatively sloped demand curve reflects both substitution and income effects. Substitution effects always lead to a larger quantity demanded when price is cut. But the income effect of a price decline induces an increase or a decrease in quantity demanded depending on whether the product in question is a normal or inferior good. In most cases, however, the principle of the downward-sloping demand curve holds.

This chapter also noted some exceptions to the conclusions of elementary demand theory. When consumption decisions are colored by social pressures—the bandwagon effect—then mere aggregation of individual demand curves may underestimate the total market demand. And the negative slope of the demand curve may not be sacrosanct for Veblen effect goods or for goods whose quality is thought to be associated with price.

Finally, economists not only apply the theory of demand on the job but also invest major resources in translating the abstract demand function into empirical counterparts. Economists' recommendations are far more meaningful when they can accurately project the quantitative as well as the qualitative consequences of their proposed actions.

Key Terms

Bandwagon (or demonstration) effect
Consumer surplus
Income effect
Inferior good

Price-consumption curve
Price effect
Substitution effect
Veblen effect

Review Questions

1. *a.* Show how the demand curve is derived from a price-consumption curve.
    b. Explain how the substitution and income effects demonstrate that quantity demanded increases when the price of a normal good falls.
2. Sketch the substitution and income effects of a price *increase* for both a normal and an inferior good.
3. *a.* What is consumer surplus?
    b. Explain and sketch the impact on consumer surplus when a competitive market is taken over by a monopolist who raises price and reduces the quantity sold.
    c. Suppose the government forces the monopolist to restore the original price. What happens to consumer surplus?

4. Cellular telephones that first sold at $3,000 per unit have come down to the $200 to $300 price range. At the same time, the market, which had few subscribers before 1984, exploded to over 3 million by 1989. Explain the relationship between the price and quantity trends.
5. Draw and explain the market demand curves for each of the following quotations from *The Wall Street Journal:*
    a. "I noticed the price increase but I got it anyway. People like it because it's statusy." (March 12, 1987, p. 35).
    b. "While many [baby boomers] might help fuel the initial success of a new ice cream or fashion, many stop buying when one of these products becomes too commonplace. (March 13, 1987, p. 27).

6. Manufacturers of a Veblen good increase their supply. What happens to price and quantity sold?
7. *a.* Draw the demand curve for meat loaf when consumers have confidence in the integrity of their butchers and be-lieve that higher-priced chopped meat contains a smaller portion of fat.
   b. Draw the demand curve when consumers are uncertain whether to trust their butchers.

Food for Thought

1. Use indifference curve and demand analysis to explain the objective of the Beef Industry Council's advertising campaign discussed in MicroBits 4.2 (You might want to refer back to Figure 3.15, p. 93.)
2. Refer to the last figure in MicroBits 3.3 (p. 83). What are the substitution, income, and price effects of a change in the relative price of the two milks from the given ratio of 2 to a new ratio of ¾?
3. "College officials say that students and their parents—not always accurately—tend to identify a good education with high tuition." (*The New York Times,* May 14, 1987, p. B13). How would you, as a college financial officer, use this information to set tuition?
4. How would you use demand theory to price a new perfume, tentatively named Skunk, the Odor You Won't Forget?
5. Governments often stabilize the exchange rate of their currency at a fixed price above its free-market value. This intervention keeps import prices down but also leads to unsustainable balance-of-payments deficits. Ultimately, the inability to finance the deficit puts pressure on the government to devalue, that is, lower the exchange rate. How can the role of expectations in the theory of demand help explain why the authorities keep such devaluation deliberations top secret?
6. Can you explain the rationale behind pricing cross-continental flights at fares comparable to those of flights that cover a third of the distance?

Suggested Readings

The original exposition of the income and substitution effects can be found in J. R. Hicks's now classic *Value and Capital: An Inquiry into Some Fundamental Principles of Economic Theory* (Oxford: Clarendon, 1946); see Chapter 2, "The Law of Consumer's Demand."

You might want to follow the indifference curve analysis of rats, discussed in Chapter 4, by reading John H. Kagel, Raymond C. Battalio, Howard Rachlin, and Leonard Green, "Demand Curves for Animal Consumers," *Quarterly Jour-nal of Economics* 96, no. 1 (February 1981), pp. 1–15.

Harvey Leibenstein—in "Bandwagon, Snob, and Veblen Effects in the Theory of Consumers' Demand," *Quarterly Journal of Economics* 65, no. 2 (May 1950), pp. 183–207—distinguished between these three effects. You're urged to consult this stimulating yet not technically demanding article for a definitive elucidation of the middle category, which is not discussed in this chapter.

Notes and Answers

1. The cheap models disappear from the catalog after 1979, when Sears switched to more sophisticated calculators and computers.
2. The slope of the budget line.
3. No. Her income has always equaled $100,000.
4. That is not to claim that a price reduction will always lead to an increase in quantity demanded. Some exceptions are discussed later in this chapter.
5. The equilibria are obtained by anchoring a new set of budget lines at $50,000. For the same prices as before, the tangencies are approximately at $25,000, 62.5; $20,000, 150; $15,000, 350; and $22,500, 550, respectively. The demand curve will be shifted rightward, reflecting the following relationships:

Price	$400	$200	$100	$50
Quantity	62.5	150	350	550

6. Although the prices faced by Annabelle, Bob, and Chuck are identical, we need not assume the three have identical incomes or preferences.
7. The equations for the demand curves for Annabelle, Bob, and Chuck, respectively are: $Q = 5 - .025P$; $Q = 5 - .05P$; and $Q = 8 - .16P$. Substituting 25 for P in each equation and summing yields $4.375 + 3.75 + 4 = 12.125$.
8. Dermot Gately, "Lessons from the 1986 Oil Price Collapse," *Brookings Papers on Economic Activity* 2 (1986), pp. 237–71.
9. While the logarithmic form may seem complex, it really isn't. Converting the original data into logarithmic form is readily handled by the computer. Also note that the t subscripts stand for the current year and the $t - 1$ refers to the prior year. Finally, in terms of the actual calculations, the econometrician enters data on current income, oil prices, and previous years' sales into a regression program, which generates the value of the constant and the coefficients a, b, and k.

10. The sign of the final variable is less intuitively obvious, but for econometric reasons it must be positive. See, for example, Robert S. Pindyk and Daniel L. Rubinfeld, *Econometric Models and Economic Forecasts* (New York: McGraw-Hill, 1991), pp. 204–206. Students who are familiar with statistics might be pleased to learn that the R^2 of this equation was 0.984.
11. In the years when few automobiles were equipped with air conditioning because it was so expensive, stories were told of drivers who kept their windows closed in the midst of the summer heat merely to convey to others that they owned a car AC unit. Similarly, in the early days of TV, when a set really chewed up a large portion of the typical family's monthly income, many just installed a roof antenna to indicate their ostensible TV ownership.
12. Airplane gasoline is color-coded to prevent mistakes, but as a side effect this maintains vendor honesty. Automotive gasoline users are not provided with such protection.
13. Supplier expectations were discussed in the cobweb example of Chapter 2.
14. The new curve would lie to the *right* of D, because a higher current price for land leads to expectations of further price increases. Thus, the initial price increase would induce a greater current demand than suggested by D.
15. $80. You would be earning the most revenues at that price: $80 times 50 million units sold. Try any other combination.
16. This example is adapted from Eric Schmitt, "The Art of Devising Air Fares," *The New York Times,* March 4, 1987, pp. D1--D2. In 1992, American simplified its pricing policy, making life far simpler for its pricing staff.
17. Adapted from Richard Levine, "Fewer Riders Take City Buses, and Officials Aren't Sure Why," *The New York Times,* November 3, 1986, p. B1.

FORECASTING OIL DEMAND

Empirical models of demand functions that prove accurate in understanding the past may also prove useful in predicting the future. This appendix examines how economists use empirical demand functions to forecast. But it also suggests some of the pitfalls in economic forecasting.

Begin with the British oil demand equation by Professor Gately, described on page 119. It's 1997 now, and we want to forecast oil demand in 1998. Recall that the last variable in the equation was the prior year's oil sales; for 1998, that number would be 1997's sales. The forecaster first would have to obtain the most recent information, presumably 1996's sales and perhaps some data about oil sales in earlier parts of 1997. The forecaster would then have to make an educated guess, perhaps by extrapolation of the past, as to 1997's total oil sales.

The second variable, current income, is even more difficult to obtain, for a very simple reason: current income for 1998 will not be known until 1998 is over. Yet we're now in 1997. So, current income for 1998, too, has to be predicted. How is that done?

Income forecasting is an art, not a science, and so no single method is universally accepted by economists. Some rely on subjective forecasts within the framework of the national income and product accounts. Others utilize more formal econometric methods, building sophisticated models of the economy and its industries. Still others are satisfied with judgmental methods, favoring back-of-the-envelope calculations or using business cycle indicators. This multiplicity of methods leads to a variety of forecasts. Although for the most part, economic forecasters agree on the direction of income change, few concur on its magnitude. Nevertheless, for each forecaster, the bottom line is a quantitative estimate of income that will be used with the demand equation.

Having estimated 1997 oil sales and 1998 income, the rest of the process is mechanical. All the forecaster does is plug these two numbers into the equation, vary possible 1998 prices, and write down the outcomes.

Let's say, for example, the British demand for oil in 1997 is 1.6 million barrels per day and predicted income for 1998 is £360 billion. Plugging these numbers into the original estimating equation

$$\ln(\text{Demand}_t) = -3.83 + 0.81[\ln(\text{Income}_t)] - 0.15[\ln(\text{Price}_t)] + 0.72[\ln(\text{Demand}_{t-1})]$$

yields:[1]

$$\ln(\text{Demand}_{1998}) = -3.83 + 0.81[\ln(360)] - 0.15[\ln(\text{Price}_{1998})] + 0.72[\ln(1.6)]$$

Finding the logarithms of the numbers in the parentheses, multiplying them out by their respective coefficients, and consolidating the numbers gives you:

$$\ln(\text{Demand}_{1998}) = 1.276 - 0.15[\ln(\text{Price}_{1998})]$$

Finally, plug in some likely 1998 prices, look up the natural logs, multiply out by 0.15, subtract that from 1.276 (the estimated constant), and obtain the ln of current demand. If you remember your logarithms, you can now derive the anti-logarithms either from a logarithm table or from a good pocket calculator. Alternatively, you can plot the logarithms directly into double logarithmic paper to derive the demand curve sketched out in Figure 4A.1.

A word of caution needs to be raised here concerning the reliability of this demand curve and the forecasts based on it. You understand that this predicted demand curve depends critically on two assumptions: (1) that the future replicates the past and (2) that the forecasts used in setting up the last equation are correct. If, for example, solar and geothermal energy had won a significant share of the fuel market since the original equation had been estimated, the original demand curve would lose relevance. A prediction based on an outdated equation is highly suspect. And, of course, if the present oil sales or income forecasts are wrong, then even if the equation is fundamentally sound, the resulting demand curve for 1998 will not be accurate.

Thus, it is not surprising that economists in the forecasting business are a cautious lot. As one wag has commented, "It's not a bad idea to predict direction, nor is it a bad idea to predict timing. Just never do the two together!"

FIGURE 4A.1   The British Demand for Oil, 1998

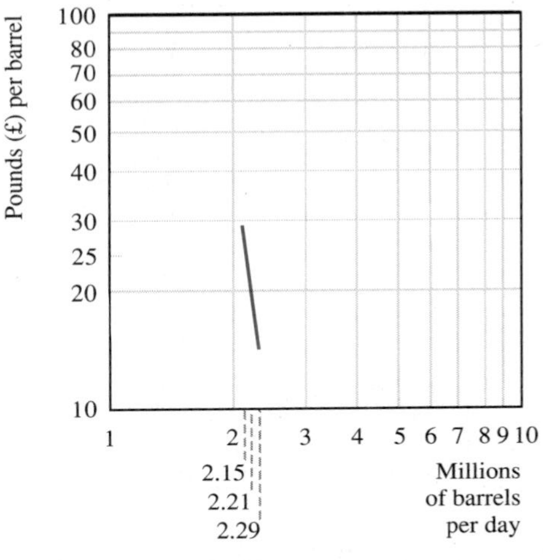

Notice that on double logarithmic scales, the oil demand curve is a straight line.

Notes and Answers

1. Income is in billion of pounds and the actual demand as well as the past sales of oil are in millions of barrels per day. The calculations omit the zeros.

5

ALL YOU EVER WANTED TO KNOW ABOUT ELASTICITY AND PERHAPS MORE

Can one desire too much of a good thing?
Shakespeare

Our old men have lost the elasticity of youth.
Benjamin Jowett, British Classicist (1817–1893)

Learning Objectives

After studying this chapter, you should be able to:
- Explain the meaning and relevance of elasticity.
- Measure price elasticity of demand and supply using two methods.
- Understand the relationship between price elasticity and total revenue.
- Apply price elasticity concepts to real situations in the business and public sectors.
- Explain and apply income and cross elasticity.

Drug Prices and Beer Taxes

Despite intense research efforts, a broad-based cure for AIDS has yet to emerge. In early 1987, the Federal Drug Administration approved azidothymidine (AZT), a drug that could prolong the life of certain types of

137

AIDS patients. However, AZT came with two critical catches: potentially fatal side effects and an unbelievable price. The annual dosage of AZT initially cost $8,300 wholesale and $10,000 retail, and although its price has come down, it remains an incredibly expensive drug.

When an Oregon congressman queried AZT's manufacturer, "How did you arrive at a price of $10,000? Why didn't you set it at $100,000?" he was told that the research effort "involved a significant amount of risk. . . . Because the full usefulness of AZT and the efficacy and speed of introduction of competitive products are unknown, our financial returns are uncertain."[1]

Some might wonder whether it's moral to exploit the weak and sick. A true believer in the market might respond that the market itself works to eliminate such exploitation. As you know from Chapter 4, rational consumers shy away when the price of a product or service is set too high.

Yet there's a crucial difference between the demand for a life-saving drug and the typical consumer product. Because the alternative to the use of AZT is dying sooner, it's absurd to compare the demand for AZT and that for acne medicine, surfboards, diet 7UP, or eyeglasses. The economist distinguishes between these two cases very simply by stating that the demand curve for AZT has zero elasticity, while the demand curves for most everything else have elasticities greater than zero. The meaning of this shorthand expression and the reason for the general popularity of the concept of elasticity throughout the economic literature are the themes of this chapter.

Elasticity plays a role in less dramatic instances as well. Just consider a government strategy to diminish beer-induced drunken driving. If the government raises the tax on beer and thus price rises, less beer will be consumed, fewer people will be intoxicated, and drunken driving will be diminished. The crucial question is, How large a tax should the government impose? Obviously, it could initiate such a stiff tax that no one would buy beer, and thus prevent all beer-induced accidents. But such a draconian policy would inspire a wave of protests by social beer drinkers. After all, most people who drink beer don't get drunk, and not all of those who lose their sobriety drive. Why penalize all for the sins of a minority? Some compromise will have to be devised; elasticity will be important in achieving that compromise.

Actually, elasticity is a very general concept, and in this chapter you'll be exposed to price elasticity for both demand and supply, income elasticity, and cross elasticity. Once again, however, the purpose of mastering the general concept is to learn how to use it. So this chapter has multiple goals: not only to show you what elasticity is and how to compute it, but also to demonstrate how elasticity is used in practice.

The Meaning and Measurement of Price Elasticity

Elasticity Defined

Elasticity is the percentage change of one variable in terms of another.

Elasticity has become the preferred measure of the impact of one variable, say price, on another, say quantity demanded. Its primary virtue lies in that it's expressed in percentage terms, which facilitates comparison among products. Unlike slope, elasticity is independent of the scale in which the good is expressed.[2]

Price elasticity of demand is the percentage change in quantity demanded divided by the percentage change in price. When that percentage is *greater than one*, demand is **elastic**; when it's *less than one*, it's **inelastic**; and when it *equals one,* there is **unitary elasticity**.

More specifically, **price elasticity of demand** deals with the responsiveness of quantities demanded to alterations in price. It answers the question "If price is changed by, say, 1 percent, by what percentage will quantity demanded be altered?"

Economists distinguish between three broad categories of price elasticity: elastic, inelastic, and unitary. When quantity demanded is very responsive, so that a small price change (in either direction) brings a disproportionate reaction in quantity demanded, then demand is **elastic**. Conversely, demand is **inelastic** when the price change brings a relatively small response in quantity demanded. And when the percentage change in price is precisely matched by the percentage change in quantity demanded, then you've come across the unique case of **unitary elasticity**.

Return now to the AZT example. A change in price won't change the quantity demanded; demand is perfectly inelastic. Given the inconceivable alternative, patients who would be helped by the drug are hardly likely to say, "The price is too high; I'd rather die instead." The quantity demanded is always the same, so that the percentage change in quantity demanded for any given price change is zero. (Draw a demand curve for a product with a perfectly inelastic demand. It will be a vertical line.)

Such cases are rare. But zero elasticity might also apply to one of the cases mentioned at the end of Chapter 4. The doctor who prescribes a drug is totally uninterested in, and therefore unresponsive to, price, while the patient who must buy the medicine prescribed is not likely to ask for a smaller dosage or fewer pills because of an apparently excessive price.

The demand curves shown in earlier chapters almost always were characterized by negative slopes, so their elasticity was greater than zero.[3] Figure 5.1 is a typical straight-line demand curve relating price and quantity of TV sets sold per year. What is its elasticity?

Measuring Elasticity

First, a crucial point: Do not confuse elasticity with slope. A negative slope can be elastic, inelastic, or both. Indeed, you'll see that points on the demand curve in Figure 5.1 run the gamut from very elastic to very inelastic, with unitary thrown in for good measure.

FIGURE 5.1   **Price Elasticity of Demand**

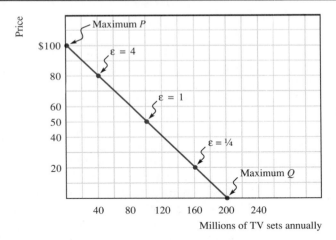

To calculate price elasticity, multiply the slope ($\Delta Q/\Delta P = Q$ maximum/P maximum; here = 2) by the P/Q ratio at each point. Thus, where $P = \$80$ and $Q = 40$, $P/Q = 2$, and $(\Delta Q/\Delta P)\, P/Q = 2 \times 2 = 4$.

The Arithmetic Method.   The difference between elasticity and slope becomes clear once you've learned how to calculate elasticity. The general formula is as follows:

$$\varepsilon_p = \frac{\text{Percentage change in quantity demanded}}{\text{Percentage change in price}} = \frac{\dfrac{\Delta Q}{Q}}{\dfrac{\Delta P}{P}} = \frac{\Delta Q}{\Delta P} \times \frac{P}{Q}$$

The price elasticity of demand, symbolized by ε_p, is defined in the first fraction. The middle fraction tells you how to obtain the percentage change: You take the absolute change (symbolized by Δ) and divide it by the appropriate number. (Thus, if you bought your home for \$100,000 and sell it later for \$120,000, you've gained 20 percent—\$20,000/\$100,000— over the purchase price.) The final fraction simplifies the calculation by replacing a four-component fraction with two simple fractions that have to be multiplied by each other.

If you now examine the two components of the last fraction you'll notice that the first one is the (inverse) slope of the demand curve. So, elasticity is the slope *times* another fraction, price divided by quantity. Quite obviously, then, slope and elasticity are not the same.

Turn again to Figure 5.1. The slope for any straight-line curve is always constant; here it's 2.[4] To find elasticity, you'll have to take P and divide it into Q. But which P? The answer is, any P and its companion Q. But if that's true, every point on the demand curve will have a different elasticity! That indeed is the case.

Take any point, say $P = 80$, $Q = 40$. Elasticity at that point equals:

$$2 \times \frac{80}{40} = 4$$

Or another point, $P = 20$, $Q = 160$. Elasticity $= 2 \times 20/160 = 1/4$. Finally, calculate elasticity at $P = 50$, $Q = 100$: __ $\times$ __/__ = __.

A few lessons need to be driven home here:

- At least for a linear demand curve, one should not talk about the elasticity of the entire curve. You can only discuss the elasticity of demand at a certain price.
- Notice that as price moves down, elasticity does, too. As P decreases, Q increases and therefore P/Q falls. When you multiply a smaller P/Q by a constant slope, elasticity must decline.
- If you look carefully, you'll notice that elasticity equals 1 at a very specific point. More on that shortly.

The Geometric Method.   An even simpler method of calculating elasticity can be used if you are given a demand curve. Instead of bothering to calculate the slope and then multiplying it by P/Q, an equivalent method can be proven geometrically. It boils down to a simple fraction:

$$\varepsilon_p = \frac{P}{P - P_{max}}$$

where P is the price at the point on the demand curve whose elasticity you wish to find and P_{max} is the intercept of the demand curve with the price axis. To calculate price elasticity of demand, then, you need to know only two points, the price and the y-intercept of the demand curve. Look carefully at the point on the demand curve adjacent to $P = 80$ in Figure 5.2. The elasticity calculation is performed at the side; it precisely equals the elasticity calculated for $P = 80$ in Figure 5.1. Finish off the rest of the elasticity calculations; they must also be identical to the other points in the earlier figure. Once again, you see that slope and elasticity are not the same. Note, too, that the midpoint of the demand curve, where $P = 50$, will also be a point of unitary elasticity. *Indeed, for any linear demand curve, elasticity always equals 1 at the midpoint.* You should be able to see why that is so using the $P/(P - P_{max})$ for formula.[5] (MicroBits 5.1 tests your new understanding of the distinction between slope and elasticity.)

Curvilinear Demand Curves.   Demand curves, of course, need not be straight lines. When they are not, as in Figure 5.3, the definitions remain the same, as do the methods. However, the slopes at every point on a

FIGURE 5.2   Geometric Derivation of Price Elasticity of Demand

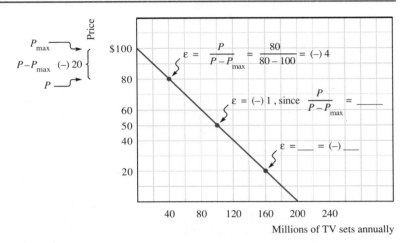

Using the geometric method requires just having the demand curve and the values on the price scale. Fill in the missing blanks on your own.

FIGURE 5.3   Elasticity and Curvilinear Demand Curves

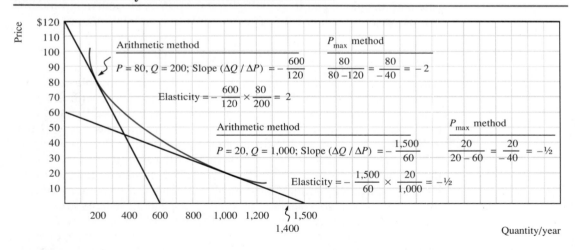

curvilinear demand curve differ, and so you may have to take the extra step of calculating the slope. The simplest noncalculus way to find the slope, $\Delta Q / \Delta P$, involves drawing a tangent to the curve at the point in question and reading off the Q and P intercepts. Multiply that by Q/P and you've obtained the elasticity. Alternatively, once you've drawn in the

---

An Exercise in Elasticity

Take a look at the pairs of points (a, a^*; b, b^*; and c, c^*) in the two figures here. For each diagram, state which point in each pair is more elastic. Then, calculate elasticity to verify your assertions. The answers appear below.

Quite obviously, the outer demand curve in the left figure has a steeper slope; its maximum quantity lies to the right of the inner curve. However, and this is the crucial point, the y-intercepts of both curves are identical. Therefore, using the P_{max} formula will force you to conclude that the elasticities on both curves for the same price are *identical*. In short, the slopes differ but the elasticities are the same.

That is not true for the curves in the right-hand figure. The demand curves are parallel, so the slopes are identical. But for every given price, the equivalent Q on the outer curve is greater, and thus P/Q must be smaller. Consequently, for every price, the point on the outer demand curve is *less elastic*. The slopes are the same; the elasticities differ. So, the motto of this exercise is, *You can't tell elasticity by looking at the slope.*

The specific elasticity calculations are as follows:

1. In the left figure, $\varepsilon_a = \varepsilon_{a^*} = 1.5$; $\varepsilon_b = \varepsilon_{b^*} = 1$; $\varepsilon_c = \varepsilon_{c^*} = 1/4$.
2. In the right figure, $\varepsilon_a = 3$, $\varepsilon_{a^*} = 1.5$; $\varepsilon_b = 1.67$, $\varepsilon_{b^*} = 1$; $\varepsilon_c = 1/3$, $\varepsilon_{c^*} = 1/4$.

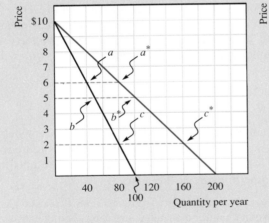

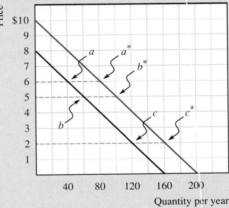

---

slope, you can use the P_{max} method to calculate elasticity. Both alternatives are demonstrated in Figure 5.3 for two points on the demand curve.

A special and important subset of curvilinear demand curves is the category of *constant elasticity*. Figure 5.4a sketches in two such curves, one in which the elasticity is 1 throughout and a second in which elasticity

FIGURE 5.4 **Constant Elasticity Demand Curves**

a.   Arithmetic scale

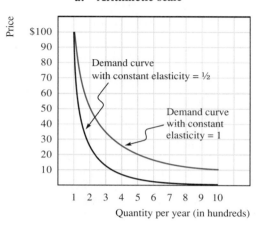

b.   Full logarithmic scales (log-log)

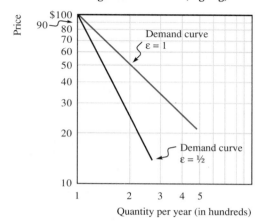

a.   Both demand curves are curvilinear and
their elasticities are constant, but they
differ in the values of the elasticities.

b.   A curvilinear demand curve will be
linear in logarithms. Its constant
elasticity appears as a straight line.

is ½ for the entire range of the demand curve. Figure 5.4b presents these
same curves on double-logarithmic paper. Note that constant elasticity
demand curves turn out to be linear in logarithms. This property is an
appealing one in many empirical studies of demand curves, as you will see
shortly.

Elasticity and Total Revenue

By now you've probably had enough method and want to know what it all
means. One important implication of elasticity deals with its relationship
to **total revenue**. If you were to verbalize the meaning of an elastic demand, you might say something along these lines:

Total revenue
equals price times
quantity.

> If we cut price by 1 percent and elasticity is greater than 1, that means that
> the percentage increase in quantity demanded is greater than the percentage
> cut in price. So, we'll earn a bit less on each item sold, but we'll sell propor-
> tionately more goods. Total revenue, then, must rise.

The converse is true for an inelastic demand, in which case the quantity response to a price cut is disproportionately small. Although sales do
increase—that must be true if the demand curve is negatively sloped—the
sales increment is less than proportionate to the price reduction, and total
revenue will fall.

Verify this by returning to Figure 5.1. Remember that any point on the demand curve above its midpoint is elastic. Now, total revenue at $80 per TV set equals $80 × 60 million TV sets annually, or $4.8 billion. Cut price down to, say, $50, and total revenue will equal $5 billion. Hence, in the region of elastic demand, a price cut leads to an increase in revenue.

Proceed to cut the price of a TV set to $20, moving into the inelastic region. What happens to total revenue? As you should expect, it falls, becoming $3.2 billion.

MICROQUERY   At what point on the demand curve is total revenue maximized?
_____ 6

Try to intuit now what happens to total revenue on a curvilinear, constant elasticity demand curve. You're right if you deduce that total revenue remains constant if the constant equals one, declines if the constant is less than one and you decrease price, and rises if the constant is greater than one and you cut price. You can verify this by multiplying price times quantity on the two curves in Figure 5.4a.

Last question: What happens to total revenue, if, instead of cutting price, you raise price? Try to work out the answer yourself.

*Elasticity and Indifference Curves**

You can cap off your mastery by relating elasticity to the price-consumption curve, discussed in Chapter 4. Turn back to Figure 4.1 (p. 105), but start with Chedley's demand curve in Figure 4.1b. Because this demand curve is curvilinear, you'll have to imagine tangencies at each of the dotted points on the demand curve and determine whether the points lie above or below the midpoint. In fact, all prices at $80 or above are in elastic regions, while the $50 point is in the inelastic region.

Now look at Figure 4.1a. What you will be searching for is some relationship between the price-consumption curve, which connects the optimum consumption points, and the elasticity conditions just established from Figure 4.1b. If you look carefully, you'll notice that the price-consumption curve falls until the quantity of flights equals 875, and rises thereafter. Indeed, that is the clue. *Elasticity is greater than 1 when the price-consumption curve falls, and it is less than 1 when the price-consumption curve rises.* Why?

You'll need to put together a few strands of information you've already absorbed. First, check again the ordinate; it's Chedley's annual

---

* This section is of above-average difficulty and may be skipped with no loss of continuity.

income. Recall, too, that an equilibrium point represents the optimum combination of income and purchases of a specific product, which, in Chedley's case, is flights. Now, the difference between Chedley's initial income and her income remaining after spending some on flights must equal Chedley's dollar spending on flights. Thus, looking at the $60,000, 200 flight equilibrium, it must be true that Chedley would spend $40,000 in order to buy those 200 flights. But look at her spending from the airlines' point of view; that $40,000 is the airlines' revenue from this one customer.

Look now at the tangency on U_2 ($40,000 and 600 flights) following a price reduction from $200 to $100 per flight. The new equilibrium implies that Chedley is willing to spend $60,000 when price has fallen, which means that the airlines' sales have risen by $20,000. But doesn't that suggest that at these points demand must be elastic? After all, price has fallen and total revenue has increased.

On the other hand, when price falls again from $80 to $50 per flight and Chedley moves from the $30,000, 875 equilibrium to the $40,000, 1,200 equilibrium, Chedley's spending on flights falls from $70,000 to $60,000. From the airlines' point of view, price has been cut but revenue has declined; that's indicative of an inelastic demand. And so it is.

Table 5.1 summarizes the relationship between elasticity, price changes, total revenue, and the price-consumption curve.

Elasticity and Oil

The oil demand curve for Great Britain highlighted in Chapter 4 (p. 119) was converted into a hypothetical forecasting equation in the appendix to Chapter 4. That equation, $\ln(\text{Demand}_{1998}) = 1.276 - 0.15 \ln(\text{Price}_{1998})$, is

TABLE 5.1   Elasticity and Total Revenue

	Total Revenue	Direction of Price-Consumption Curve
When price is reduced and elasticity is		
Greater than 1	Increases	Downward
Equal to 1	No change	Horizontal
Less than 1	Decreases	Upward
When price is increased and elasticity is		
Greater than 1	Decreases	Upward
Equal to 1	No change	Horizontal
Less than 1	Increases	Downward

NOTE: This summary, which ties together all the possible connections between price changes, elasticity, and total revenue, should not be memorized. Use it instead to test yourself against its conclusions. Do you understand why each consequence follows from the conditions?

linear in logarithms. Now recall the assertion made just a few pages back that a linear logarithmic curve has constant elasticity. That constant is the *coefficient of price,* namely 0.15.

Just what does that mean? First, because the elasticity is less than 1, British oil demand is inelastic. Specifically, were price to rise by, say, 10 percent, quantity demanded would fall by only 1.5 percent. Consumers of oil would not be able to cut back in any significant way. That information would be crucial to a hypothetical oil monopoly. The monopolist would be able to raise prices without much of a decline in sales. And, as you understand from Table 5.1, when demand is inelastic and prices rise, revenue increases. How lovely to be a supplier faced by an inelastic demand: the more you raise your prices, the greater your total income will be!

British oil consumers are not the exception. Professor Gately's calculations for other industrialized countries range from an elasticity of 0.05 percent for the United States to 0.22 percent for Italy. But then, realizing our dependence on oil, the inelastic nature of demand should not be surprising. Oil, in its raw state or manifold processed forms, lies at the foundation of the American way of life.

"This doesn't have anything to do with the falling price of oil, does it?"

But cheer up; econometric equations are not chiseled in stone. All econometric equations are based on history and just can't deal with episodes that are well beyond the range of past experience. Although we were shocked out of complacency in the 1970s when the OPEC cartel quadrupled oil prices in a few years, we might react much differently if oil prices were multiplied tenfold. Moreover, price depends on supply as well as on demand. And, as prices rise, the incentive for new producers to enter the market intensifies, making it more difficult for existing suppliers to maintain high prices. Indeed, as you will see in Chapter 11, that's precisely what happened as the 1970s turned into the 1980s. The attempt to preserve extraordinarily high oil prices simply didn't work.

Using Elasticity: Beer Taxes and "Sales"

Taxing Beer: Paying More but Worrying Less

Clearly, one does not have to earn a Ph.D. in economics to realize that the government can use tax measures to cut down consumption on the taxed good or service. Indeed, tax policy can be an effective alternative to outright prohibition of sales of a specific good or service. (Thus, some economists have advocated placing a tax on marijuana rather than declaring it illegal.) The effectiveness of a given tax policy in dissuading purchases or, alternately, the size of the tax bite needed to achieve the desired reduction in consumption critically depends on elasticity. If demand is highly inelastic—say 0.25 percent—price will have to be quadrupled in order to reduce consumption by a mere 1 percent. On the other hand, for a very elastic demand—say 500 percent—a 1 percent tax hike will reduce consumption by 5 percent.

Michael Grossman and his associates investigated the impact of a stiffer beer tax on teenage drinking and thus on deaths from drunken driving.[7] The research of these economists is not trivial. Government tax policy has inadvertently increased the number of deaths from drunken driving, because inflation eroded the real burden of the federal excise tax on alcoholic beverages.

Grossman and his associates began with a demand function for beer drinkers, ages 16 to 21, that consisted of the typical independent variables—the price of beer and of other alcoholic beverages, and family income—as well as other causes likely to account for drinking (e.g., legal and religious). Using refined econometric techniques, they found that an increase in the real price of beer by 1 percent would reduce drinking of frequent drinkers (4 to 7 times a week) by 1.18 percent, and of fairly frequent drinkers (1 to 3 times weekly) by 0.59 percent.

That fewer drunken-driving deaths would be caused by a stiffer tax policy is clear. But the precise quantitative relationship had to be discovered. This Grossman and his associates did by formulating and testing another econometric equation. They concluded that a tax policy that set the beer tax equal to the tax on liquor and protected against its erosion by inflation would have reduced the mortality rate among youths in the years they studied (1975 to 1981) by an eye-catching 54 percent, from 51 per 100,000 to 28.[8]

Is the death-reducing consequences of a significant increase in the price of beer worth it? After all, to achieve such a substantial reduction in alcohol-induced fatalities, beer taxes would have to rise (in 1984 prices) by 13 times, or by about 35 cents per 12-ounce can. That's a decision that the political authorities, who decide on tax rates, and indirectly you yourself, who elect the politicians, will have to make. Demand and elasticity analysis can point out the different options, along with the benefits and costs of each; the ultimate action, however, rests with others.

Retail "Sales" and Elasticity

You watch a shopper approach the checkout counter with 24 rolls of toilet paper and you wonder about the bug that's infected that family. But then you notice the sign, "Toilet Tissue—Three Rolls for $1," and you understand.

What does this have to do with elasticity? The economist would answer that sales and elasticity are intimately related. Sales are designed to change the elasticity of demand in either of two ways:

1. They alter the time patterns of purchases.
2. They shift customers among firms.

The Time Pattern of Purchases.   Figure 5.5 deals with the first of these phenomena. Stella, for example, need not buy a new diving mask in March when she's planning her summer vacation in Bonaire; she can do that any time within the next few months. So, while the annual demand for scuba masks is represented by $Demand_{yearly}$ in Figure 5.5, the demand curve for scuba masks in March might be very different, as represented by $Demand_{March}$. Notice that if the price is cut from $25 to $20, quantity demanded on the annual demand curve will increase by 50,000 units. But if the price is cut by the same $5 in March, the quantity demanded on the March curve rises by 75,000 units. Why? Because a number of purchasers simply alter the timing of their purchases.

Which demand curve is more elastic in the $25 to $20 range? Clearly, the March one is more elastic: the same percentage change in price brings a larger percentage increase in quantity demanded along the inner curve than along the outer one. (Test yourself: calculate elasticity at $20 and $25.) And so it is with the purchaser of toilet paper. The total amount of toilet paper purchased per family per year is very probably not very price

FIGURE 5.5   How a Sale Affects the Timing of Purchases: The Demand for Diving Masks

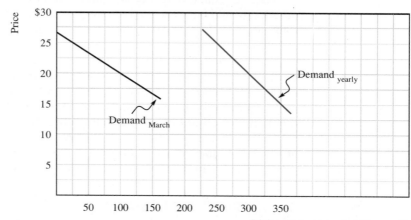

While a decrease in price by 20 percent—from $25 to $20—raises annual mask demand by 20 percent—from 250,000 to 300,000—it increases the quantity demanded in March by 300 percent—from 25,000 to 100,000.

elastic. Nevertheless, because they can stock up on toilet paper, consumers buy a disproportionate amount during periods when the paper is on sale and cut back their purchases when the price returns to its nonsale level. In such circumstances, the seller of the product is not increasing the firm's total annual revenues from the sale item but rather affecting the distribution of sales over time.

"Sales" to Attract Customers from Rivals.   That's not the case when the intent of the sale is to shift customers around. Here, there's definitely an opportunity to increase the firm's revenues. But there's a catch. Consider the double-edged effect of a sale. On the one hand, a sale attracts new customers, presumably away from vendors who are not reducing their prices at the same time. Clearly, these new buyers increase the seller's total revenue. On the other hand, existing customers may also take advantage of the lower sale price. So some of the revenue normally generated from the old customers is lost. Price elasticity of demand is crucial in determining whether the firm is a net gainer or loser.

Take a look at the curve labeled Demand$_{market}$ in Figure 5.6, the normally sloped demand for portable TVs in a midsize U.S. city. At $75 per unit, 100,000 TVs are sold annually. Typically, Crazy Freddie holds 5 percent of the market, selling 5,000 sets. But if Crazy Freddie runs a sale, cutting the price to $50 for President's Week only, customers might flock to Freddie, abandoning such well-known competitors as Geriatric Gerry or Schizophrenic Suzie. Crazy Freddie might then increase sales significantly. Demand is elastic between $75 and $50, so Freddie's total revenues increase. But if the price-cutting strategy doesn't bring in substantial numbers of customers—if demand is relatively inelastic—then total revenue decreases. The curve labeled Demand~Crazy Freddie~ is elastic in the relevant region. (Don't be confused by the slope; remember slope and elasticity aren't the same). Check it out, and to test your understanding, draw a demand curve for Crazy Freddie that's inelastic between $75 and $50.

In brief, the ability of a sale to increase revenue depends critically on the price elasticity of demand. *The more elastic demand is, the more revenue a sale will bring in.*

One caution: The focus in this section has been always on revenue, not profit. Increasing revenue is not necessarily the same as increasing profit, since revenue is only one element in the profit calculus. Costs, too, must be considered when assessing profitability. Despite this caveat, it remains true that elasticity has a critical role to play when firms determine prices and when government authorities consider changing tax rates.

FIGURE 5.6   The Demand for Portable TVs: The Market as a Whole and Crazy Freddie's

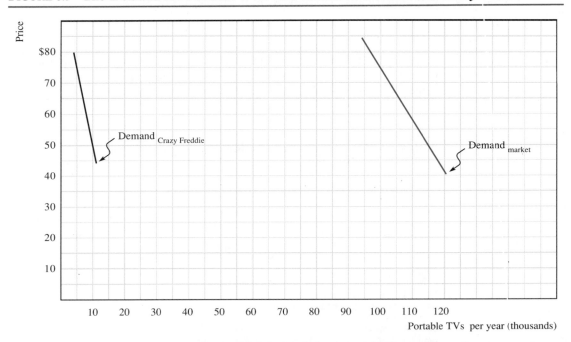

While a price cut might not increase quantity demanded very much, the reaction of consumers to a price reduction by a single seller might suggest an elastic demand for that seller.

Other Elasticities: Income, Cross, and Supply

Income Elasticity

Income elasticity refers to the percentage change in quantity demanded for a given percentage change in *income*.

The idea of quantity responsiveness to changes in price can easily be applied to variables such as income as well. One useful elasticity concept related to the demand function is **income elasticity.** Income elasticity refers to the responsiveness of quantity demanded to income changes. To calculate income elasticity, substitute the term *income (Y)* for *price* in the price elasticity of demand formula presented on page 140. Thus:

$$\varepsilon_Y = \frac{\Delta Q}{\Delta Y} \times \frac{Y}{Q}$$

Cross-elasticity of demand refers to the percentage change in the quantity demanded of a specific good or service in response to a change in the price of *some other good or service*.

Now, it should be apparent that some goods respond positively to income; they are the normal goods that you ran across in Chapter 3. Thus, the sign of the elasticity coefficient will be positive. (A positive income elasticity shifts the demand curve rightward when income increases, and vice versa for a fall in income.) Conversely, inferior goods, for which demand falls as income rises, will show a negative sign for their income elasticity. Table 5.2 lists some income elasticity coefficients calculated econometrically. Do they seem plausible to you?

Substitutes are goods used instead of each other; **complements** are goods normally used in conjunction with each other.

Cross-Elasticity

Cross-elasticity relates to the impact of the price change on one good to the sales of a second. It serves to define another set of products: **substitutes** and **complements.** Consider Geri at the beach: She can protect her-

TABLE 5.2   **Income Elasticity Estimates**

Product	Income Elasticity
Fruits and berries	0.70
Cigarettes	0.50
Coffee	0.29
Margarine	−0.20
Flour	−0.36

SOURCE: H. Wold and C. E. V. Leser, "Commodity Group Expenditure Functions for the United Kingdom, 1948–1957," *Econometrica* (January 1961); S. M. Sackrin "Factors Affecting the Demand for Cigarettes," *Agricultural Economics Research* (July 1962); J. J. Hughes, "Note on the U.S. Demand for Coffee," *American Journal of Agricultural Economics* (November 1969). [Cited in Martin Bronfenbrenner, Werner Sichel, and Wayland Gardner *Economics* (Boston: Houghton Mifflin, 1987), p. 441.]

self from the sun either by using a sunscreen lotion or an umbrella. Presumably, if the price of sunscreens were to rise, Geri would be more likely to rent an umbrella. If so, an increase in the price of sunscreens leads to an increase in the demand for umbrellas. Umbrellas and sunscreen lotions are substitutes. That would be reflected in their cross-elasticities, which are defined along the same line as price or income elasticity:

$$\varepsilon_c = \frac{\Delta Q_x}{\Delta P_y} \times \frac{P_y}{Q_x}$$

where *x* refers to umbrellas and *y* to sunscreens. *When products are substitutes, then the value of cross-elasticity is positive.*

On the other hand, consider sunscreens and towels at poolside: If the price of sunscreens rise, Geri would use less sunscreen and stay out of the sun instead. She'll sweat less and need fewer towels. So, the higher price of sunscreens, *y*, reduces Geri's demand for towels, *x*. *The elasticity coefficient is negative when products are complements.*

The impact of cross-elasticity on the demand curve is shown in Figure 5.7. Figure 5.7a depicts the market demand for sunscreen lotions; Figure 5.7b, the demand for umbrellas; and Figure 5.7c, the demand for rental

FIGURE 5.7   Cross-Elasticity at the Beach

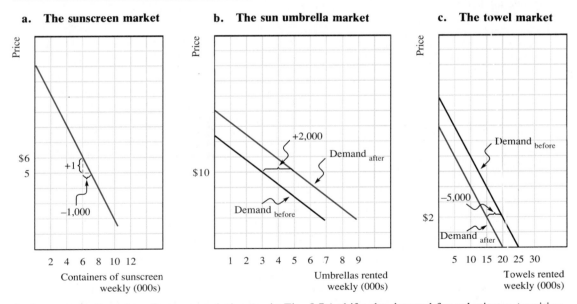

a.   **The sunscreen market**   b.   **The sun umbrella market**   c.   **The towel market**

An increase in the price of sunscreen lotion (as in Fig. 5.7a) shifts the demand for substitutes (positive cross-elasticity goods) outward (as in Fig. 5.7b) and for complements (negative cross-elasticity goods) inward (as in Fig. 5.7c).

MICROBITS 5.2

Du Pont Saved by Cross-Elasticity

How does one decide whether two products compete with each other? For a company accused of violating the antitrust laws, the right answer to that question can save the accused corporation substantial sums of money and sometimes its very existence. If the company can prove the presence of viable competitors, the monopolizing charge will be much harder to support. Obviously, every product has some other product competing with it. The transportation industry, for example, is characterized in the diagram as consisting of a slew of wheeled sources of locomotion. Planes, trains, and passenger cars obviously compete for passenger traffic over both long and short distances. Most individuals, however, would not consider airplanes and roller skates to be competitors. The critical question is, Where do you draw the dividing line?

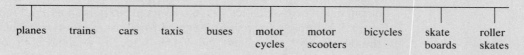

| planes | trains | cars | taxis | buses | motor cycles | motor scooters | bicycles | skate boards | roller skates |

In 1947, the U.S. Department of Justice accused Du Pont of monopolizing the cellophane market. On the surface, the allegation was justified: Du Pont produced 75 percent of the cellophane sold in the United States. Du Pont countered that the government had failed to consider the availability to purchasers of substitutes. The case proceeded through the federal judiciary with typical haste. Nine years later, the Supreme Court rendered its decision in a hefty 192-page opinion, with supplements covering another 140 pages (*United States* v. *E. I. du Pont de Nemours & Co.,* 351 U.S. 377 [1956]).

The cross-elasticity was clearly the crux of the case. Justice Reed, delivering the opinion upholding Du Pont, noted:

An element for consideration as to cross-elasticity of demand between products is the responsiveness of the sales of one product to price changes of the other. If a slight decrease in the price of cellophane causes a considerable number of customers of other flexible packaging materials to switch to cellophane, it would be an indication that a high cross-elasticity of demand exists between them; that the products compete in the same market. The court below held that the "[g]reat sensitivity of customers in the flexible packaging markets to price or quality changes" prevented Du Pont from possessing monopoly control over price. . . . The record sustains these findings.

towels. All are normal, negatively sloping demand curves. In Figures 5.7b and 5.7c, the demand curves identified as "before" are based on an initial price of $5 per 14-ounce container of sunscreen. Assume that a day's rental of an umbrella and a towel is $10 and $2, respectively, so that 3,000 umbrellas and 20,000 towels are rented each week. Now, let the price of sunscreen rise to $6. Because umbrellas are substitutes, the demand for umbrellas shifts rightward. At the same price of $10 per daily rental, the demand for umbrellas rises to 5,000. (Calculate ε_c. Be sure to pay attention to the sign: $\Delta Q_x =$ _____; $\Delta P_y =$ _____; using initial values, $P_y =$ _____; $Q_x =$ _____; so that $\varepsilon_c = ($ _____/_____$) \times$ _____/_____ $=$ _____ .[9]) At the same time, the demand for towels shifts inward; at $2 per towel, demand falls to 15,000. Thus, the cross-elasticity must equal -1.25. (Is that calculation correct? Verify it.[10])

As apparently arcane a subject as cross-elasticity can have some important policy implications, as MicroBits 5.2 suggests.

Supply Elasticity

Elasticity is not limited to the demand function. The **price elasticity of supply** refers to the degree of responsiveness of the quantity supplied to changes in price. The formula is identical to that of demand,[11] namely,

$$\varepsilon_s = \frac{\Delta Q}{\Delta P} \times \frac{P}{Q}$$

Once again, when supply is elastic, a relatively small change in price will have a magnified or disproporationate impact on quantity supplied. On the other hand, when supply is inelastic, a given percentage change in price will have only a modest impact on quantity supplied. And if elasticity is 1, a given percentage change in price will affect quantity supplied precisely proportionally.

Calculating Elasticity of Supply.   As in the case of demand elasticity, the elasticity of supply can be calculated arithmetically by obtaining the (inverse) slope $\Delta Q/\Delta P$ and multiplying its value by P/Q. Alternatively, a geometric method can be used. Both methods are described in Micro-Bits 5.3.

Supply Elasticity and Time.   While a vertical demand curve is unusual, a vertical supply curve—one that has an elasticity of zero—is more plausible. Consider the fishing boats that leave Gloucester, Massachusetts, each evening and return early the next morning with their holds full of fish. Customers wait eagerly for the catch, each one with his or her particular demand function. But the supply is limited to whatever was brought into port that morning. A higher price will not increase the quantity of fish supplied, leading to the supply curve S_{today} in Figure 5.8.

Clearly, if prices were to remain high for some time, fishermen would have additional incentive to increase their catch. On the other hand, a run of low prices may induce some fishermen to ship out for fewer hours or perhaps stay home altogether. The resulting supply curve, S_{month}, will be more responsive to price, in other words, more elastic. Indeed, if prices

---

MicroBits 5.3

Calculating the Elasticity of Supply

The Arithmetic Method

Examine the three straight-line supply curves indicated in the figure: S_1, S_2, and S_3. Each has the same slope, calculated by taking any two prices and their respective quantities, and dividing the change in quantity by the change in price. Thus, on S_2, when $P = \$8$, $Q = 40$ and when $P = \$6$, $Q = 30$. The change

Calculating the Price Elasticity of Supply

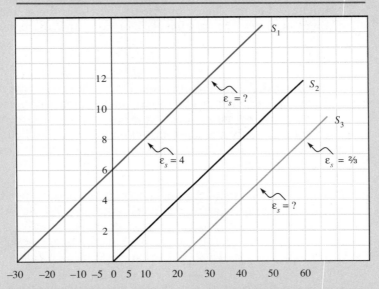

The three supply curves have identical slopes, equal to 5. Elasticity, however, differs. Elasticity for S_1 exceeds 1; for S_3, it is less than 1, and for S_2, it equals 1 for each point on the different supply curves.

remain encouraging for prolonged periods, the size of the fishing fleet may increase. Conversely, if prices stay low, fishing boat owners may decide to devote themselves to sports fishing rather than commercial ventures, or they may move their operations elsewhere. In either case, S_{year} represents this longer adjustment time and is the most elastic of the supply curves.

MicroBits 5.3 continued

in $Q = 10$, the change in $P = 2$, and thus the former divided by the latter equals 5. The price elasticity of supply at the first set of coordinates equals $(\Delta Q/\Delta P)(P/Q) = 5 \times$ $^8/_{40} = 1$. Calculate the elasticity at $P = \$6$, $Q = 30$.

Lo and behold, it also equals 1. In fact, you may posit a general statement: *Whenever the supply curve passes through the origin, price elasticity of supply will always be unitary.*

Calculate elasticity for the two indicated sets of coordinates on S_1 and S_3. You'll notice another regularity: *Whenever the supply curve intersects the price axis, price elasticity of supply will always be greater than 1. And when the supply curve intersects the quantity axis, the curve will always demonstrate an inelastic supply.*[*] If you are skeptical, work it out for some other points. Or, to be convinced, consider the geometric method.

The Geometric Method

The geometric method for calculating the price elasticity of supply is similar to the

---

[*] As you can see, for the supply curve as well as the demand curve, slope and elasticity are not the same. However, because of the relationship of the supply curve to the quantity axis, you can tell just by looking whether the elasticity of supply for any given supply curve is greater than, equal to, or less than 1.

method for determining elasticity of demand in that the former, too, uses a ratio. But instead of dealing with the price axis, it will be simpler to focus on the quantity axis.[§]

You need two values to calculate the price elasticity of supply: (1) the quantity that corresponds to the point whose elasticity is to be determined, Q, and (2) the quantity at which the supply curve touches the quantity axis, that is, the quantity intercept (Q_{int}). The formula is as follows:

$$\varepsilon_s = \frac{Q - Q_{int}}{Q}$$

Refer to the figure and consider a point on each of the three given supply curves. Take $Q = 60$ on S_3 with its corresponding $Q_{int} = 20$. Then price elasticity of supply equals $(60 - 20)/60$ or $2/3$. Or, consider $Q = 10$ on S_1 with the value for $Q_{int} = -30$. Then, $\varepsilon_s = [10 - (-30)]/10 = 40/10 = 4$. The price elasticity of any curve passing through the origin must be 1: Since the $Q_{int} = 0$, the fraction boils down to Q/Q.

Note, finally, that curvilinear supply curves are handled just like curvilinear demand curves. Find the tangent to the point you wish to examine, then use either the arithmetic or geometric method to calculate elasticity at that point.

[§] You could also calculate demand elasticity from the quantity axis and supply elasticity from the price axis.

Of course, in some instances, supply can never be increased and the supply curve remains permanently vertical. However, such cases are more rare than would first appear. It's true that in the case of the creations of dead painters, sculptors, and craftspersons, the elasticity of supply remains zero. But land and natural resources, which are typically used as examples of items in fixed supply, are not actually fixed. With prices

FIGURE 5.8   Supply Elasticity and Time

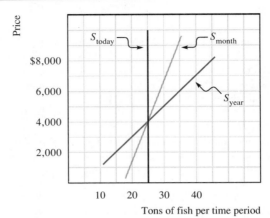

The more time producers have to react to price changes, the greater the price elasticity of supply.

"I'll have whatever is in bountiful supply."

sufficiently inviting, land can be reclaimed and mineral resources can be sought and exploited.

Before you move on to some more applications, why not take a stab at MicroBits 5.4.

Supply Elasticities à la Russell Baker

In the following article, Russell Baker of *The New York Times* comments on the judgment in the Baby M case, in which a couple paid a woman for her egg (fertilized by the husband's sperm) and for rental of her uterus during pregnancy. The child upon birth was to belong to the couple. The woman reneged on the contract after the birth, and after a lengthy and emotional court case in New Jersey, Baby M was awarded to the couple.

Bring Back the Stork

Here are some money figures that have been in the news lately:

$50 million—That is roughly the amount various bidders paid for the Duchess of Windsor's jewelry.

$39.9 million—This is the sum paid for a Van Gogh sunflower by somebody who doesn't want to be identified.

SOURCE: National Gallery of London

$11.75 million—This is the minimum payment guaranteed Marvin Hagler for appearing in a boxing match last night with Sugar Ray Leonard.

$11 million—This is the minimum payment guaranteed Mr. Leonard.

$8 million—This is the amount, according to the Rev. Oral Roberts, that God said the Reverend's flock had better come across with if they wanted Mr. Roberts to live to see another April. The money was paid; Oral Roberts lives.

$17,500—This is the amount William Stern contracted to pay Mary Beth Whitehead and the Infertility Clinic for services that produced the person widely known as Baby M.

What is striking about these figures is the wide disparity between the amounts spent on frivolity, triviality and grossness and the piffling sum spent on creating a human being.

At a cost of $17,500 per human being, the $50 million spent by the buyers of the Duchess's jewels could have produced 2,857 brand new human beings. The $33.9 million spent by the mystery buyer of the Van Gogh could have produced 2,280.

I am not saying it was wrong for them to spend their millions on canvas and baubles. Surviving in this world requires a lot of ego support. Some people can get it from owning famous gewgaws. And anyhow, they might say, what about the population explosion?

MicroBits 5.4 continued

Isn't it better to have our $89.9 million spent on sterile, inanimate objects than to have it churning out 5,137 new human beings?

The argument is not so easy as regards the $8 million spent on the Rev. Oral Roberts, which could have produced 457 new lives had it not been earmarked for keeping Mr. Roberts from being "taken home" by God.

Here, it seems to me, we are treading very close to philosophical quicksand. Wouldn't a good Christian gladly choose to go "home" if he knew that doing so would bring 457 new souls into the world?

The question is beyond my scope. My only interest here is in the curiously low value placed on new human beings, especially at a time when childless parents are desperate to expand their families.

The explanation may be that until now big-time entrepreneurs have been too delicate to cash in on the demand for babies by bringing the full power of American industrial know-how to bear on the baby-supply problem.

Judge Harvey R. Sorkow's decision in the Baby M case, however, now makes such delicacy look quaintly old-fashioned. In saying that a contract to produce a baby for pay is no more assailable than any other contract, he gives legal blessing to baby-making as business.

Legislatures or appeals courts may cancel this invitation for free enterprise to do its worst, but if they don't, better order your baby fast because that $17,500 price will soon be as gone as the 1936 Ford.

Prices in the baby market can easily be hoisted by skillful use of hype. You can see a good example of it at work in the multimillion-dollar payday Messrs. Hagler and Leonard enjoyed last night in Las Vegas because a lot of people had been persuaded that matching the two was like matching Jack Dempsey and Muhammad Ali.

Legitimizing a baby industry opens the door for marketing experts to hype the quality of its tiny merchandise by hyping the production record of its manufacturers. It's disgusting to imagine the catalogue descriptions of the company's producers:

"Has already produced five perfect little beauties . . . World-famous pediatrician says, 'Her knack for turning out stunningly flawless little darlings who look exactly like their fathers is absolutely uncanny' . . . Her last three were accepted by Yale before leaving the obstetrics floor . . . If perfection is what you demand in your child, act immediately to sign this classic child-bearer while she is still between engagements . . . Price? If you have to ask, you can't afford her."

There will be plenty of customers willing to pay through the nose once hype sets its hook in the marketplace. Look at all the people in the world competing with each other to shell out millions for jewels and paintings. You can be sure there are plenty among them ready to pay several million for the right to boast not only that they got a perfect specimen, but also that they paid a record price to the woman who made it.

Questions to Consider

1. Using the concept of supply elasticity, explain the high prices of the Duchess of Windsor's jewelry, the Van Gogh sunflower painting, and the guaranteed minimum incomes to Messers. Hagler and Leonard versus the "curiously low value placed on new human beings"?
2. The marketing experts quoted near the end of the article wish to modify the elasticity of supply

MicroBits 5.4 continued

of individual "baby producers." How and why? (Hint: What is this sentence trying to convey: "Price? If you have to ask, you can't afford her.")

Answers

1. Because the first four items Baker mentions are unique, they should be represented by perfectly inelastic (vertical) supply curves. The late Duchess of Windsor, for whom King Edward VIII of England abdicated the throne in 1936, owned only a limited amount of jewelry. Only a handful of Van Gogh paintings remain, among which *Sunflowers* holds a special place. There are very few highly skilled middleweight boxers. Thus, demanders bid up the price to astronomical figures.

However, surrogate mothers willing to carry a child for a fee are not rare and will become even more abundant as time goes by. Their supply curve is upward sloping; its elasticity is greater than zero. So a stronger demand will encourage an increase in quantity supplied and help restrain the price increase.

2. The marketing experts would try to convince buyers that each surrogate mother is unique, thereby changing their clients' supply curves to zero elasticity. Parents presumably would pay far more for a guaranteed high-quality baby than for one of an unknown quality, much as spectators are willing to pay more to watch a title boxing match than to sit through two unknowns slugging it out. Thus, each "baby producer" would constitute a market to itself with no competing substitutes. The bidding for the services of such a mother is likely to be heated and the price high, as the hint suggests.

Source: Copyright © by the New York Times Company. Reprinted by permission.

Using Elasticity: Cigarettes and Cars

The Pricing of Canadian Cigarettes

A *Wall Street Journal* headline in November 1985 read, "Canadian Cigarette Makers Slash Prices on Some Brands to Counter Sales Drop." The article relates that in May 1985, the Canadian government increased the tobacco tax by 25 cents, raising it to 82 cents per pack. This brought up the average price of a pack of 25 cigarettes to $2.54 (about 10 cents per cigarette), in contrast with the then typical U.S. price of $1.04 per 20-cigarette pack (about 5 cents per cigarette). Canadian cigarette consumption fell in the first nine months of 1985 by 4.3 percent, suggesting an elasticity of demand of approximately 0.4.[12] Surely you're not surprised that a product used habitually shows a demand that is relatively inelastic.

Although consumer expenditures on cigarettes increased, Canadian cigarette manufacturers didn't share in these higher outlays. The increase went to the tax collector. Indeed, producer income fell, as the revenues per pack had not risen and quantity demanded had fallen. So, the producers thought about recouping some of their lost revenues.

One manufacturer, Rothman's, responded by, in effect, cutting prices. It introduced a 30-unit pack at the price of a 25-unit one. Rothman's management reasoned that although the demand for cigarettes in general was inelastic, they could attract customers from other producers by holding a sale. The price cut along with the implied elastic nature of the Rothman brand would bring in more income.

This entire case can be clarified with the aid of Figure 5.9. Assume (1) that cigarette market demand and supply can be represented by the Demand$_{market}$ and Supply$_{net [of taxes]}$ and (2) that the equilibrium price equals $2.29 per pack of 25 cigarettes. Quantity sold equals 45 billion cigarettes yearly. Impose now the new 25-cent tax. Sellers will provide the same quantity they did before only if they would receive the same net proceeds

FIGURE 5.9   The Impact of a Tax Hike on Canadian Cigarette Prices and the Reaction of One Supplier

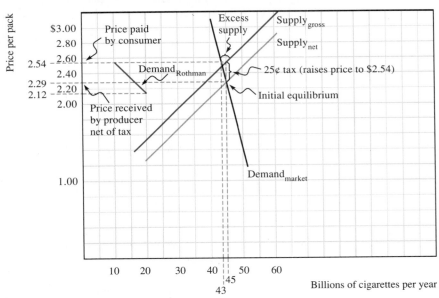

The imposition of a 25-cent per pack tax on cigarettes forces prices to rise initially by 25 cents, from $2.29 to $2.54. Consumers react by cutting back on purchases from 45 billion cigarettes to 43 billion. That leads to reduced producer revenue. Rothman reacts by reducing prices by 17 percent, to $2.12, believing that sales will increase substantially. Although Rothman's management concedes demand for cigarettes in general is inelastic, they believe demand for their particular brand in existing circumstances is elastic.

as they did before, namely $2.29 per pack. But to do that, they would have to jack up the price by 25 cents. They would pass on the tax hike to the consumer by charging $2.54 per pack. The upper supply curve, Supply$_{\text{gross [of taxes]}}$ traces out the price per pack they'd have to gross (that is, receive from the customer) in order to earn their targeted net, which is 25 cents per pack less than the gross. This new supply curve replaces the earlier one. (If you're not clear about that, just think about the price that would be needed in order to induce the cigarette manufacturers to supply 45 billion cigarettes: Isn't it $2.54?)

To be sure, cigarette producers will try to pass the full burden of the tax to the consuming public. The real question is, Will consumers continue to buy 45 billion cigarettes at a price of $2.54? The demand curve says no! They will buy only 43 billion cigarettes.

Take a look now at Table 5.3. Before the 25-cent tax was imposed, the producers sold 45 billion cigarettes, or 1.8 billion packs at $2.29 per pack. Their total revenue came to $4.12 billion. After the tax was imposed and passed on to the consumers, sales fell to 1.72 billion packs.[13] Revenue declined by $190 million. Of course, the government gained; its receipts from this tax boost increased by $430 million. Together, then, consumer expenditures on cigarettes rose to $4.36 billion ($3.93 + $0.43 billion), as could be anticipated whenever elasticity is less than 1 and price increases.

Rothman's reaction was surely typical of producers; they wanted to raise their revenues. Rothman's management must have assumed a demand curve depicted by Demand$_{\text{Rothman's}}$, which is far more elastic than the demand for cigarettes in general. By increasing the number of cigarettes in each pack by five, Rothman's reduced the effective price per equivalent 25-unit pack to $2.12. If the demand curve is correctly represented in Figure 5.9, then the 17 percent decrease in price would have led to a 100 percent increase in sales, significantly fortifying Rothman's revenues.

The story, however, must conclude on a sad note, at least as far as Rothman's was concerned. Their pricing policy implicitly relied on the

---

TABLE 5.3   The Impact of the 25-Cent Cigarette Tax on Producer and Government Revenues

	Price		*Quantity Sold (billion cigarettes)*	Total Revenue ($ billions)	
	Paid by Consumers	*Received by Producers*		*Producers*	*Government*
Prior to new tax	$2.29	$2.29	45	$4.12*	$0
After tax	2.54	2.29	43	3.93	0.43

* When packaged 25 per pack, 45 billion cigarettes equal 1.8 billion packs; when multiplied by $2.29 a pack, the total is $4.12 billion.

belief that other cigarette manufacturers would not respond to the Rothman price cut. Rothman's competitors, however, were not so accomodating. They lowered their prices, too, thus nullifying Rothman's advantage. The price war that Rothman's began was welcomed by smokers, who benefited from the cheaper prices, and by the government, whose tax revenues increased as sales moved up again, but not by the Canadian cigarette industry, whose profits fell. Such is life north of the border. (And, at times, south of it as well.)

Forecasting Automobile Demand: The Role of Income Elasticity

The automobile industry spends a good deal of money and attention on forecasting the demand for its products. These forecasts are quite sophisticated. The companies predict not only overall automobile sales but also sales for each particular model being produced. These forecasts are also confidential. Obviously, no firm wishes to provide important pricing and marketing information to its competitors. However, Table 5.4 will give you a sense of what economists working in Detroit do.

Table 5.4 summarizes elasticity estimates economists obtained when they analyzed the automobile industry. That the estimates differ is not surprising. The periods reviewed were not identical, nor were the proxies used to represent each element in the demand function. What is amazing is the narrow range of differences in the elasticity estimates, given the diversity of approaches. The bulk of the price elasticity estimates differ by no more than 0.3. Although the variation in income elasticity is wider, the studies are unanimous in pointing out a substantial degree of income elasticity. No one would suggest that new automobiles are an inferior good! They conclude that a 1 percent increase in income will increase sales by 2.5 to 4.2 percent.

What does that mean in Detroit? When planning next year's production, management must have some idea whether they should tool up for a 10 million car year or only a 7 million year. They'll begin by forecasting

TABLE 5.4   Elasticity Estimates for New Automobile Sales

Study	Price Elasticity	Income Elasticity
Suits, original	−0.6	+4.2
Suits, revised	−1.2	+3.9
Chow	−1.2	+3.0
Roos & von Szeliski	−1.5	+2.5
Atkinson	−1.4	+2.5

Source: U.S. Senate, Committee on the Judiciary, Subcommittee on Antitrust and Monopoly, *Administered Prices: Automobiles, Report* (Washington, D.C.: Government Printing Office, 1958), Chap. 6.

next year's income, a critical element in the demand for new cars. (Refer back to the appendix to Chapter 4, which mentions some of the methods used to predict income.) Let's say that the staff economists project an increase in income of 3.5 percent for the following year. If we arbitrarily select Chow's income elasticity estimate of 3.0, the inevitable conclusion is that, other things being equal, new car demand in the next year should rise by 10.5 percent.

Turn to MicroBits 5.5 for a curious example of supply elasticity.

MICROBITS 5.5

India and the Supply of Skeletons

The article reproduced here deals with a policy shift by the Indian government to prohibit the export of human skeletons. As you read the article, keep the following points in mind:

- See if you understand why the supply curve of Indian skeletons before the change in policy was characterized by an elasticity of more than zero, but as a result of the new rules, the curve became totally inelastic.
- If you understand that, you'll also be able to comprehend why the price of "used" skeletons rose.
- Explain also the positive cross-elasticity of *supply*. Note the relationship between the increased price of authentic skeletons and the sales of substitutes.
- Finally, consider how higher prices influence the development of alternative sources. Does that conform to your expectations about the elasticity of supply given more time to adjust to the rise in prices?

Skeleton Dealers Get Jitters as They Find Nothing in the Closet

It is talked about only discreetly.

"We've got a few odd bones lying about, that's it," confides a London dealer, preferring to say no more. "It's a delicate situation."

"I'm sorry, I can't say much about it," another middleman says, "This is a political hot potato."

These are not happy times in the skeleton business. Customers, mainly medical and dental schools, want human bones for anatomy instruction. Dealers want to accommodate them. But India, the skeleton mother lode, has cut off the supply.

The result is that despite stockpiles, some medical students are already going without a study set of bones. Unless the shortage eases, teachers say, the quality of medical instruction may suffer.

"I wouldn't go so far as to say you shouldn't break your leg," says Adrian Bowers of Liverpool University's medical school. "But there will be an impact."

Joint Ventures Until recently, India supplied the world with between 10,000 and

15,000 full skeletons a year and an extra 50,000 skulls, exported by 13 Calcutta companies that the Indian government allowed to buy unclaimed bodies from morgues, hospitals and the police. Last August, all that trade stopped; the Indian government banned it.

In places where anatomy students are expected to buy their own skeletons, prices of old bones are rising like the Dow Jones Industrial Average. At some British medical schools, older students are reselling the traditional half-skeleton set to first-year students for the equivalent of $200, up from $100 a year ago.

That's if there are any for sale. At St. Bartholomew's Hospital medical school in London, "the No. 1 problem is that at the beginning of the academic year last October, our students couldn't buy their own skeletons," says Alan Aldritch, chief technician.

Not everyone likes talking about it. "We do not wish to be quoted in the press," says an official at Adam Rouilly & Sons, a British biological supplier that recently cut skeletons from its catalog and is pushing plastic replicas.

"You're not going to get much help on this one," adds a doctor who teaches at a large medical school. "People prefer not to discuss where these things come from."

Stiff Opposition   People also prefer not to producing them. And that, as much as anything else, explains why skeletons should be in short supply while the basic raw materials are so abundant.

The well-off countries that buy skeletons prefer to leave the business to others. In the past, India has been willing to oblige, but it has never been happy about its role as the world's boneyard.

"The trade is repulsive and distasteful," says P. R. Chakravarty, spokesman for the Indian Embassy in London. "That's why an opposition lobby has been able to put pressure on the government and have it banned."

Twice before India stopped skeleton exports, only to restore them in the quest for hard currency. The last time it cut off supplies, in 1976, its commerce minister said that "the prestige of the country is worth more than the export earnings." A year later, a different Indian government revived the trade.

Behind the embargo this time were rumors of skulduggery. There were allegations that some traders were robbing burial grounds and buying bodies illegally from those too poor to afford a funeral pyre. A legislator charged that one trader had smuggled out the bodies of thousands of children. After a sharp debate in Parliament, the government reimposed the ban.

Since then, sales of plastic substitutes have grown, and one British entrepreneur is offering a three-dimensional paper model. But no one makes a skeleton like the Grim Reaper.

Proxy skeletons lack subtle detail, such as contours where muscles were attached. And unlike the die-cast pretenders, authentic skeletons come in all shapes and sizes, giving students a proper appreciation of human variety. "Teaching on a plastic skeleton is just hopeless" says Dr. Bowers of Liverpool. "There are all sorts of delicate bones in the sinus and other passages, layers and holes, which plastic doesn't replicate very well."

MicroBits 5.5 continued

Finding alternative sources isn't easy. Almost all Western body-donor programs require returning remains for burial or assuring families that the remains will be interred. In skeleton-processing (like sausage-making, best left undescribed), no remains remain.

The legacy of a pair of 19th-century Scots also complicates the situation. William Burke and William Hare, Edinburgh hoteliers, ran a sideline business of smothering guests and selling the cadavers to a local doctor for dissection. Ever since the ensuing scandal, "The need of physicians, in subtle ways, has been to distance themselves as much as possible from the supply of human materials," says David Gunner, the coordinator of anatomical gifts at Harvard Medical School.

During India's last embargo, sources developed from spots remote to Western teaching centers, including Borneo and Bangladesh. This time, dealers in human dry goods aren't saying where they're shopping.

"There's a possibility of another country coming through, but I really can't say who it is," says a British skeleton salesman, insisting that he, too, be anonymous. At Carolina Biological Supply Co., one of the biggest bone dealers in the U.S., product manager Richard Lovesy says, "What we have in stock isn't pertinent to your story."

Carolina's 1,104-page catalog gives an impression of plenty. It lists 39 real and plastic skeleton models: male and female, adult and child, painted and unpainted, with stand and without, stitched in the joints and loose. There are hundreds of fragment products, including skeletal hands, femurs, tibias, shoulder joints, vertebral sets, take-apart skulls and ear bones.

Carolina's top-of-the-line skeleton is a hanging model with the joints stitched together, a spring-loaded jaw, a full set of teeth and a slide-out steel cabinet for storage, sticker-priced at $807. The company will sell you a basic set of bones for $216.85, no strings attached.

As previously reported, Carolina made it big during the U.S. frog shortage with its line of pickled and exotic amphibians, while federal education money kept raising demand from high-school biology classes. But the skeleton shortage may not be such a boon. Full skeleton sets are said to be nearly gone at Carolina. Although Mr. Lovesy won't tell, he does say that he is "not very hopeful" about supplies. "There is no other known source."

Even if one can be found, the days of cheap skeletons may be over. Harvard's Mr. Gunner says India was particularly efficient at the delicate task of stringing the bones together. "It's quite an art, actually," he says. "And India's articulation work is incredible."

If the bones aren't strung, he explains, they don't hang naturally for study. With needle and thread, Indian artisans can make sure the hip bone's connected to the thigh bone and the thigh bone's connected to the knee bone.

Summary

Certain general statements about the price elasticity of demand and supply emerge from this chapter.

1. *Price elasticity of demand depends on income.*
   a. For normal goods, as income increases, elasticity declines.
   b. For inferior goods, an increase in income leads to a rise in elasticity.
2. *Price elasticity of both demand and supply depends on the existence and nature of substitute goods.* When the price of a good or service that has close substitutes in demand rises, sales will decline more than if only poor substitutes are available. (That, of course, will be reflected in the product's cross-elasticity.) Similarly, if the product had close substitutes in production, an increase in its price would induce more suppliers to produce the good or service.
3. *Price elasticity of both supply and demand is dependent on time.* The more time suppliers or demanders have to adjust to price changes, the more significant their reaction will be.
4. *When the demand curve is linear, price elasticity depends on price.* The lower the price is, the more inelastic demand is.

Perhaps you really have learned more than you ever want to know about elasticity. On the other hand, by now you should appreciate its importance to anyone who is concerned with demand or supply. Public officials, when devising policies that will influence consumer or producer income or spending, can ill afford to ignore the reactions that are summarized in the notion of elasticity. Business profits often depend critically on the values of various elasticities: price elasticity of demand and supply, income elasticity, and cross-elasticity. While it is not easy to calculate elasticity in the real world, the businessperson can ignore it only at his or her own peril.

Business profits depend on demand. In the absence of buyers, profits are zero. But profits are obviously related to costs as well. The next two chapters present the ideas and techniques microeconomists use to analyze costs.

Key Terms

Complements
Cross elasticity
Elastic
Elasticity
Income elasticity
Inelastic

Price elasticity of demand
Price elasticity of supply
Substitutes
Total revenue
Unitary elasticity

Review Questions

1. *a.* Define price elasticity.
   b. Explain how a business firm would change its pricing if at the existing price structure:
      (1) Demand is elastic.
      (2) Demand is inelastic.
   (Assume costs would not be affected by the resulting changes in quantity demanded.)

2. Air travel is a normal good.
   a. What would happen to the price elasticity of demand should the traveling public's income increase?

   b. How could you, as an airline economist, use this information to suggest fare modifications?

3. *a.* Calculate elasticity for each of the points on the straight-line demand curve in the figure below.
   b. Do the same for the points on the curvilinear demand curve in the diagram.
   c. Calculate the elasticity for each of the points in the supply curve.

4. Do you agree with the following statement? "As long as the demand curve is perfectly inelastic, the elasticity of the

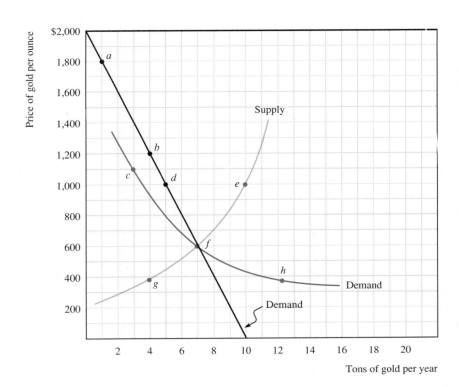

supply curve is irrelevant to the economist.''

5. Indicate whether the income elasticities of the following products are positive or negative. Explain your reasoning for each.
   a. Public transportation.
   b. Household help.
   c. College education.
   d. Foreign vacation travel.
   e. Fine china.
   f. Used textbooks.
6. a. Use elasticity to explain why automobile dealers reduce the prices of cars in their inventories shortly before new models come into their showrooms.
   b. Why are turkeys always on sale before Thanksgiving?
7. a. Give examples of two products that are complements in demand and a substitute for one of them.
   b. Assume that the demand for one of the goods rises. What happens to the demand and price of the other two? Why?

8. What do the following statements suggest about the price elasticity of demand?
   a. "A growing number of fliers are responding to higher ticket prices [by] . . . canceling travel plans." *The Wall Street Journal*, October 17, 1990, p. B1.
   b. "I don't think the public can be fooled, and if they don't want to buy a book, they won't, regardless of the price." *The Wall Street Journal*, March 29, 1988, p. 36.
9. As Bolivia's crackdown on drug trafficking began to show results in 1990, the price Bolivian farmers received for 100 pounds of raw coca leaves dropped from $400–$500 to $5–$7. The farmers cut back on coca production and used their lands to plant fruits and other food crops.
   a. Is the price elasticity of supply for coca leaves negative, zero, or positive? Why?
   b. Which of the supply curves depicted in Figure 5.8 best describes the situation in Bolivia? Why?

Food for Thought

1. a. Why do stores holding sales frequently limit the quantity of sale items an individual buyer may purchase? Is this related to elasticity?
   b. Use elasticity to explain postseason sales, for example, of bathing suits after July 4 and of ski equipment in April.
2. Phrase the following situation in terms of elasticity: "RJR Nabisco plans to introduce its new Sterling budget cigarettes with ads that compare Sterling's low price with the cost of rivals' full-priced smokes. The catch is that RJR runs the risk of having smokers trade down from *its* full-priced brands." (*The Wall Street Journal*, September 6, 1990, p. 272.)
3. Compare the assumptions about price elasticity of demand held by the pricing decision makers of the two football teams mentioned in the following: "Fans of national champion San Francisco '49ers hand over $30—20 percent more than last season [for tickets]. . . . With only one win last year, the Dallas Cowboys keep tickets at $25 and $19." (*The Wall Street Journal*, August 30, 1990, p. A1.)

4. When the patent on Inderal, a heart drug, expired in 1985 and cheaper generic substitutes emerged, Inderal sales began to decline. The producer responded by increasing Inderal's price by 20 percent, leading to revenues in 1985 that equaled those of 1984. However, when it raised its price by 16 percent in 1986, revenues fell by 60 percent. Draw the demand curve for Inderal and indicate how price elasticity can help explain the relationship between Inderal's pricing policy and sales.

5. Auto-fleet managers responding to a survey concerning air bags provided the following data:

Price:	$250	$200	$150	$100	$50
Percentage who would buy:		13	20	39	72	100

a. Calculate the elasticities implied by these responses.
b. Why do these calculations represent "implied" rather than true elasticities?

6. People with total health-care insurance incur about 50 percent more medical expenses than do those who first have to pay substantial out-of-pocket costs before their coverage takes effect.

a. What does this statement suggest about the elasticity of medical services demanded were the cost of total medical coverage insurance to be substantially reduced?
b. What does it imply for both private and public health insurance providers?

7. When the Berlin Wall first came down in late 1989, some entrepreneurs began to sell souvenier pieces of the wall from a 50-pound chunk that was purportedly flown in from Berlin. Within two hours of setting up a table on New York's Fifth Avenue, the vendors sold $3,000 worth of wall at prices ranging from $5 for a chip to $20 for a chunk.

a. Draw the supply curve of wall pieces as it stood on the first day of sale. What is its elasticity of supply?
b. What do you expect to happen to the supply elasticity over the month? What would then happen to price?

8. Although a study mentioned in this chapter demonstrated that a tax on beer would reduce drunken driving, the opposite impact is conceivable. People might respond to a higher beer tax by switching to a more potent intoxicant such as whiskey.

a. How could you use cross-elasticity to determine which of these effects is more likely?
b. Should beer and whiskey be shown to be substitutes, what policy would you recommend to reduce drunken driving?

9. What would be the effect on the elasticity of supply of surrogate mothers should such a form of childbearing become socially acceptable?

10. The sale is not the only instrument used by business to change the elasticity of demand facing the firm. Suggest others.

Notes and Answers

1. Cited in Marilyn Chase, "AIDS Drug Comes to a Market Worried about Its Cost," *The Wall Street Journal*, March 23, 1987, p. 6.

2. If you measured the demand, say, for grapes in terms of tons and in terms of pounds, the slope of the latter would be 2,000 times the slope of the former.
3. The sloppiness about plus and minus signs that has typified economists in connection with elasticity has by now become a convention. The jargon of economists focuses on the absolute value of the elasticity number. So, demand is elastic if its absolute value is greater than 1 and inelastic if its absolute value is less than 1.
4. To refresh your memory and make life easy, to find the (inverse) slope of any linear demand curve, take the endpoints, labeled maximum Q and maximum P in Figure 5.1, and divide the latter into the former.
5. At the midpoint, P will always equal $P - P_{max}$.
6. The midpoint. It stands to reason that where elasticity equals 1, total revenue is maximized. For in the elastic region, price cuts increase revenue and in the inelastic region, price cuts decrease revenue. So total revenue must be maximized where elasticity moves from greater than 1 to less than 1 or where it just equals 1.
7. Douglas Coate and Michael Grossman, "Effects of Alcoholic Beverage Prices and Legal Drinking Ages on Youth Alcohol Use," *Journal of Law and Economics* 31, no. 1 (April 1988), pp. 145–71. See also Henry Saffer and Michael Grossman, "Beer Taxes, the Legal Drinking Age, and Youth Motor Vehicle Fatalities," *Journal of Legal Studies* 16 (June 1987), pp. 351–74.
8. Saffer and Grossman, "Beer Taxes," p. 372.

Incidentally, Grossman and his associates believe that young drinkers demonstrate a more elastic demand than do adults because (1) the latter are more likely to have become habituated to alcoholic beverages, (2) the income effect of a price change is stronger for young people, because they are likely to spend a larger share of their total income on drink than are adults, and (3) the bandwagon effect is more important for young drinkers than for adults (take a look at Figure 4.7, p. 122). See Coate and Grossman, "Effects of Alcoholic Beverage Prices," pp. 149–50.

9. 2,000; 1; 5; 3,000; $(2,000/1) \times 5/3,000 = 3.33$
10. $\Delta Q_x = -5,000$; $\Delta P_y = 1$; $P_y = 5$; $Q_x = 20,000$, so that $\varepsilon_c = (-5,000/1)(5/20,000) = -25,000/20,000 = -1.25$.
11. The difference between the price elasticity of demand and of supply lies in the sign. If it's negative, then it's demand; if it's positive, then it's supply. Alternatively—and for economists who ignore signs—you just have to remember whether you're dealing with the supply or the demand function.
12. The tax increase of 25 cents brought the price up to $2.54, so that the original average price was $2.29. Price rose by 10.9 percent, inducing a quantity decline of roughly 4.3 percent; $.043/.109 = .039$
13. The situation depicted here, in which the entire tax is passed on to the demanders, is inconsistent with demand-supply equilibrium. (Notice the presence of excess supply at $2.54.) The mechanics of tax shifting will be discussed in Chapter 8, where a distinction is made between short-run and long-run consequences of a tax boost.

III

PRODUCTION COSTS

Although you're now going to shift your attention from consumers to producers, you'll find that production theory has much in common with the theory of consumer choice. Tastes are psychological—not economic—phenomena, yet they underpin consumer demand theory. Similarly, technology—not economics—provides the foundation for production theory. But just as consumers use economic criteria to select among products, so too do producers use economic variables to choose among alternative inputs into production.

Inputs are not free, and so using inputs efficiently keeps production costs down. Chapters 6 and 7 develop a method of efficient input usage for both the firm that's starting from scratch and the one that has already been engaged in production.

These chapters also set the stage for moving in two divergent directions. On the one hand, each firm demands the inputs from factor suppliers, the subject of Part VI. On the other hand, each firm employs inputs to produce its outputs, so that factor costs are crucial to decisions concerning how much output to produce and how to price that output. This path is pursued in Part IV.

6

PRODUCTION THEORY: BUILDING A BETTER MOUSETRAP

All twelve violins were playing identical notes. This seems unnecessary duplication and the staff of the section should be drastically cut.

No useful purpose is served by repeating with horns the passage that has already been handled by the strings. If all such redundant passages were eliminated, the concert could be reduced from two hours to twenty minutes. If Schubert had attended to these matters, he would probably have been able to finish his symphony after all.

Excerpt from a review by an efficiency expert of Schubert's *Unfinished Symphony;* Attributed to Lord Barneston, *The London Observer*

You probably won't die of hard work, but why take the chance?
Anonymous Bumper Sticker

Learning Objectives

By the time you'll have mastered this chapter you will understand how:
- Inputs and outputs are related in the production function.
- The production function provides the basis for and an understanding of business output decisions.
- The production function can be sliced to yield physical product curves.
- Production choices are illustrated by an isoquant map.
- To distinguish between the concepts of diminishing returns and returns to scale.
- Economists have estimated production functions.
- To use estimated production functions with caution.

Mining by Hand and Machine

Take a close look at the photographs. The first shows some of the 400,000 Brazilians who took apart a mountain in northern Brazil; over 40 tons of gold were removed here between 1980 and 1987. Notice the absence of earth-moving machinery; the mountain was gouged out using dynamite and picks, and ore was brought to the top on the backs of porters (see the two men carrying sacks in the lower right-hand corner of the picture). The second photograph is a close-up of dirt carriers mounting a hillside on wooden ladders, each man with his sack of dirt. Such scenes are not uncommon in Southeast Asia or Africa, where hordes of unskilled laborers undertake backbreaking construction tasks.

In sharp contrast is the method of open-pit coal mining in the United States. As the third photograph shows, immense shovels the size of 10-story buildings gouge out the landscape. Then giant trucks, with wheels as wide as Magic Johnson is tall, haul the earth to coal-extracting plants.

A moment's thought will suggest to you why different production techniques are used in Brazil and the United States. Two considerations play a major role:

- The productivity of alternative techniques.
- The costs of using different production methods.

As a student of economics, you realize how critical it is for a production manager to be aware of the different types of available production technology. A business executive could not come to a rational decision without being able to weigh the alternatives. Once given that choice, however, it's not at all intuitive that the manager might refrain from selecting the most advanced method. Yet it may well be that it's more cost-effective to utilize a less up-to-date production technique. Clearly, the Brazilian gold-

SOURCE: © Sebastiao Salgad/Magnum

SOURCE: © Sebastiao Salgad/Magnum

SOURCE: © James Shaffer

mining corporation prefers the technologically primitive digging operation to the use of heavy equipment.

This chapter will deal only with the first aspect of the complex problem of input selection. It examines the theoretical and empirical relationships between output and the resources used to generate that product. Chapter 7 will come to grips with how to combine the various resources to minimize input costs. There, too, you will explore how to evaluate the costs of producing at different output levels. Chapter 8 then combines costs with revenues to discuss profit optimization criteria. (An encouraging note for those of you who mastered indifference curve analysis: The next two chapters will use the tools you've already become familiar with, although in a different context. Half the battle has already been won, and perhaps more than that.)

But first a few words on the types of business firms that normally underlie models of production theory. Although major corporations dominate the American business scene in terms of assets, revenues, sales, and number of employees, most businesses in the United States are owned either by an individual or by partners. The stereotypic firm in microeconomic theory in general, and in the next few chapters in particular, more nearly resembles the individually owned and managed enterprise—the family farm, the small manufacturing operation, the local retail shop—than the multifaceted corporate giant. One or a few owners assume comprehensive, hands-on decision-making responsibilities. This simplification enables economists to focus on production decisions and ignore problems that stem from the many levels of authority characteristic of the giant business firm. Also, we need not worry about conflicts between the stockholder-owners and the company's professional managers.

The First Foot in the Door: The Production Function

Only God can violate the law of the conservation of matter (i.e., that matter can neither be created nor destroyed). Producers must acquire inputs and combine them appropriately in order to fabricate a good or provide a service. To be sure, they must operate within the confines of existing technology. No one can make sophisticated optical instruments without specialized lens-grinding equipment. Nor can you send rockets to the planets without powerful thrust-generating propellants. Economists take such technological constraints as givens. Instead, they focus their attention on the relationship between inputs and outputs, the so-called **production function**. It is the production function that lies at the foundation of decision making whenever producers decide which resources to employ and in which combinations.

The **production function** relates the technologically feasible maximum amount of output for all given quantities of inputs.

Imagine a car wash. Labor and washing machinery are the two primary inputs and "washed cars" is the product. The car wash production function relates the various combinations of machinery and labor needed to process a given number of vehicles. The three-dimensional view in Figure 6.1a represents part of a hypothetical car wash production function and is derived from plotting an input on each axis—in this case, machine hours (capital input, or K) and labor hours (L)—and the consequent number of cars that can be washed daily. It's not surprising that the longer the car wash is open, the more vehicles that can be washed.

The production function actually quantifies the relationship between inputs and output. As is apparent from Figure 6.1a, using two machine hours ($2K$) per day with three labor hours ($3L$) leads to 184 cars cleaned, while employing $5K$ and $4L$ permits processing 335 vehicles. (This figure is not unlike Figure 3.1a, the mountain analogue of utility.)

Figure 6.1b reproduces Figure 6.1a in two dimensions. The axes are still machine hours and labor hours, but the inside of the box now lists the

FIGURE 6.1a   The Car Wash Production Function

a.   A 3-dimensional view

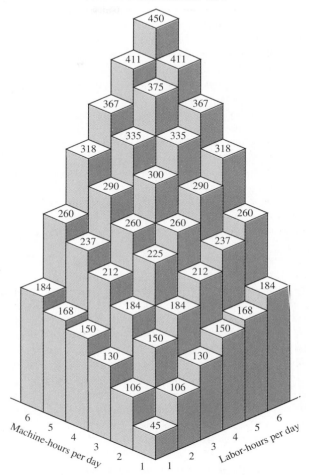

The more labor-hours and/or machine-hours
employed each day, the more cars are washed.

output in grid form. At each intersection of a quantity of capital and labor, the grid permits you to ascertain the number of vehicles washed. (Ignore for the moment the lighter numbers in between the grid coordinates.) Check out $2K$ and $3L$, and $5K$ and $4L$; you should read off 184 and 335, respectively. Again, it is important to emphasize that these numbers are technically determined; no economic decision prescribed these outputs.

FIGURE 6.1b   The Car Wash Production Function

b.   The production function grid

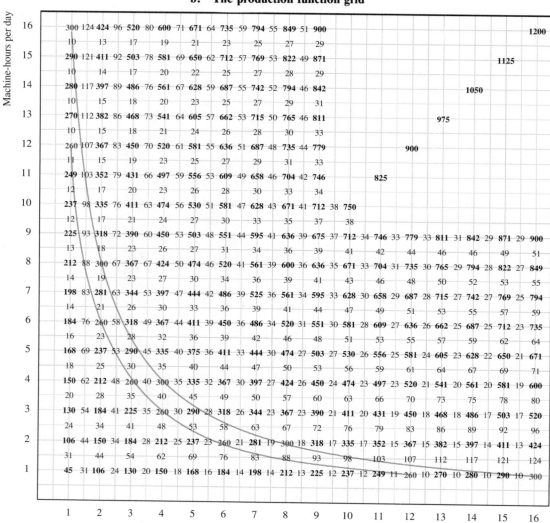

For any combination of machine time and labor time, the grid coordinates express the number of cars washed.

The same would be true for an agricultural production function that related rainfall and fertilizer usage on a given acreage of farmland to the resulting bushels of corn produced. The production function merely tells you how much output any given amount of inputs are naturally capable of producing.

MicroQuery What happens if the manager of the car wash, having employed three labor hours and two machine hours, discovers that only 150 cars had been washed? _____

Something is obviously wrong. If the production function was specified correctly, then the operation was being run inefficiently. The manager should either be using less input for the output obtained or getting more output for the amount of input used.

Slicing the Production Function

Figure 3.1b (p. 71) sliced a mountain to provide you with a two-dimensional topographical map. In the next few pages, you'll discover how the production function looks when it is sliced. You'll notice how similar it is to the indifference curve map when it's cut through horizontally. But first discover what happens when you slice the mountain vertically. It's like looking up the sides of the Grand Canyon while you're standing at the base.

The Side View: Total Product Curves.   Begin by fixing a value on the *y*-axis, say two machine hours per day, and increase the quantity of labor used at the car wash. In Figure 6.1b, you reach successively higher numbers of vehicles washed:

Labor used Hours per day	1	2	3	4	5	6	7	8	9	10	11	12	13	14	15	16
Cars washed Number per day	106	150	184	212	237	260	281	300	318	335	352	367	382	397	411	424

The **total physical product (TPP)** curve depicts the relationship between physical output (e.g., no. of cars washed) and a varying input (e.g., labor), *holding other inputs (e.g., capital) constant.*

Figure 6.2a plots these values on a continuously rising **total physical product (TPP)** curve. The curve clearly indicates that the more labor hours people put in at the car wash, *even when holding the quantity of machine time constant,* the more vehicles are cleaned.

What happens if you perform the same exercise but increase machine time to three hours daily? Fill in the missing numbers of cars washed and sketch the new TPP curve in Figure 6.2a.

FIGURE 6.2   **The Family of Physical Product Curves**

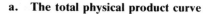

a.   **The total physical product curve**

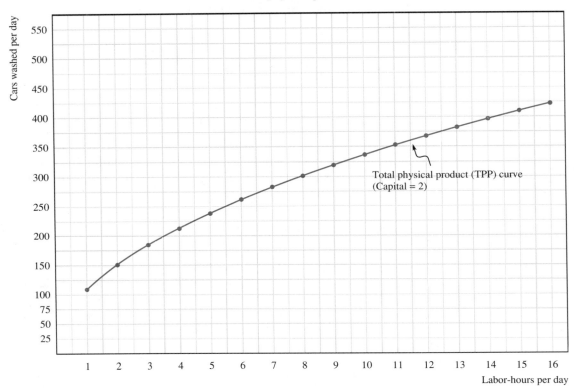

a.   Holding capital constant at 2 and varying labor leads to a total physical product curve that rises, but (in this case) does so at a decreasing rate.

Labor used																
Hours per day	1	2	3	4	5	6	7	8	9	10	11	12	13	14	15	16
Cars washed																
Number per day	—	—	—	—	—	—	—	—	—	—	—	—	—	—	—	—[1]

The conclusion: Labor is more productive if it can work with more machinery.

In short, moving along a single TPP curve indicates that more can be produced by using more labor for a given amount of capital. Shifting to a higher TPP curve as more capital is used indicates that more can be produced for every given hourly labor input.

b.   The average physical product and marginal physical product curves

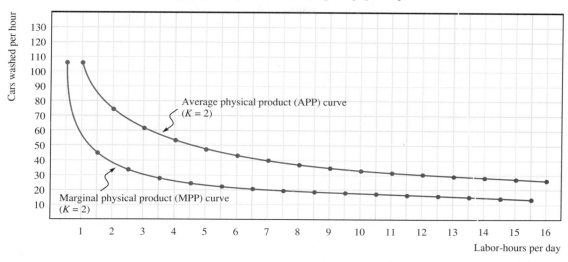

b.   When the TPP curve rises at a decreasing rate, both the APP and MPP curves will fall, with the MPP curve lying below the APP curve.

Average physical product (APP) equals total physical product divided by the variable input. **Marginal physical product (MPP)** equals the *change* in total output divided by the *change* in the variable input.

Average and Marginal Physical Product.   Sometimes it is useful to work with concepts that are mathematically derived from TPP, namely, **average physical product (APP)** and **marginal physical product (MPP)**. When you measure average physical product, you answer the following question: What happens to *output per unit* as different quantities of variable inputs are combined with a fixed amount of a second input? To calculate the APP in the car wash example when you used two hours of capital daily but varied labor hours, you'd divide the TPP by the variable input. Fill in the missing numbers below:

Labor used																
Hours per day	1	2	3	4	5	6	7	8	9	10	11	12	13	14	15	16
Average cars washed																
Number per hour	106	75	61	53	—	—	—	—	—	—	—	—	—	28	27	26.5^2

As you can see, using three labor hours daily, 61 cars are washed each *hour*, or 183 for the three-hour day. But with four labor hours daily, only 53 cars are washed per hour, even though together 212 cars are washed. In other words, as more worker hours are employed, average productivity declines. The APP curve in Figure 6.2b plots these values; its falling nature is apparent.

Why should the average product fall? The answer once again is not economic but arithmetic. Given the technical nature of the production function that specifies the relationship of labor input to output, the APP is predetermined. It falls in this example, but it could just as well rise or change direction.

Marginal physical product answers a slightly different question: How does output *change* when a variable input *changes,* given a constant amount of fixed input? For MPP, we want to know how many *more* cars will be cleaned if we *increase* labor input by one hour, but keep machine usage constant. To calculate the MPP, we need four bits of information: before and after input, and before and after output. Thus, the MPP for a fourth labor hour daily equals 28 cars:

$$\frac{\text{TPP}_{\text{cars (@4 hrs. L)}}}{\text{Labor}_{4\text{ hrs.}}} - \frac{\text{TPP}_{\text{cars (@3 hrs. L)}}}{\text{Labor}_{3\text{ hrs.}}} = \frac{212 - 184}{4 - 3} = 28.$$

The curve labeled MPP in Figure 6.2b is derived by performing these calculations for each two values in the grid. (The MPP values are plotted in between the appropriate labor inputs.) In fact, the lightly lettered numbers on the grid in Figure 6.1b are the marginal physical products.

Return to Figure 6.1b and notice that the marginal physical product

- Is different for different quantities of variable input, given a quantity of fixed input.
- May have different values for the same change of variable input if the fixed input has been changed (move along a line other than $K = 2$).
- Can be calculated either by fixing machine time and varying labor hours or by fixing labor time and varying hours of capital usage (keep L constant at 3 and vary K).

In this particular example, the MPP falls for any given fixed input as the variable input increases.

The **law of diminishing returns** postulates that when one or more inputs are held constant and a variable input is increased, then total output (TPP) will increase, but it will do so at a diminishing rate; the MPP will fall.

The falling marginal physical product is synonymous with the famous **law of diminishing returns,** which merely verbalizes the downward path of the MPP. Diminishing returns are also evident in the ever more slowly rising shape of the TPP in Figure 6.2a. Implicit in both these statements is an important point: The law of diminishing returns is not an economic phenomenon. It is the arithmetic consequence of the technological, biological, or engineering relationships that are imbedded in the production function. Consequently, the law of diminishing returns need not have a logical explanation.

Despite the noneconomic nature of the law of diminishing returns, its inevitability has become one of the accepted dogmas of economics. At some point, all production functions will be characterized by diminishing returns.

SOURCE: Drawing by Dana Fraden; © 1976 The New Yorker Magazine.

Generalized Physical Product Curves

Increasing returns occur when, with one or more inputs fixed, the marginal physical product increases with increasing amounts of the variable input employed. **Negative returns** occur when increasing the variable input leads to output *reductions*.

The car wash example's TPP curve and its derived APP and MPP curves are specific examples of a more generalized set of relationships. Such a production function will show either **increasing returns** or **negative returns** in addition to the diminishing returns of the car wash function. As in the case of diminishing returns, increasing and negative returns refer to the direction or value of the marginal product as the variable input increases. Increasing returns occur when total physical product rises at an *increasing* rate, so that the marginal physical product rises. (See Region I in both parts of Figure 6.3.) On the other hand, negative returns emerge when you increase the variable input and production actually declines, so that marginal physical product becomes negative. Region III in each part of Figure 6.3 depicts negative returns.

The production function implicit in Figure 6.3 suggests that there is some optimum relationship between the fixed and the variable inputs. Using too little of the variable factor relative to the fixed input underutilizes the latter. Using more of the variable input diminishes the efficiency of the input combination. And, using so much of the variable factor that it overwhelms the fixed factor actually impairs production.

Think of an assembly line that was designed for 100 workers. Use only 25 workers and you'll have to slow down the line. Each worker needs time to put down one set of tools, move over to the next work station, and pick up the second set of tools. Now add another 25 workers. The number of times each worker takes to perform a given step in the assembly process is more than cut in half; not only does each have to pick up fewer tools, but he has to move over less often. Thus, the addition of

FIGURE 6.3 The Generalized Physical Product Curves

a. Total physical product

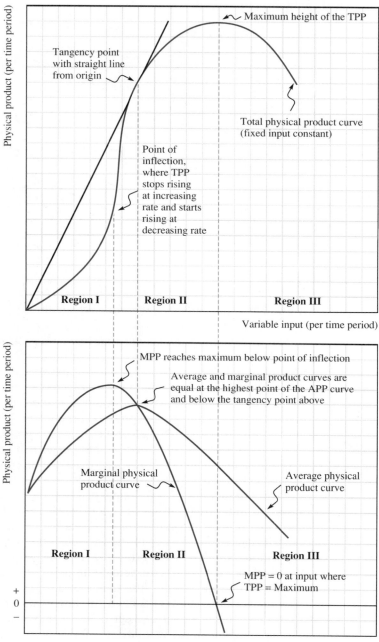

b. **Average and marginal physical product**

188

25 more workers—a 100 percent increase—permits output to increase by more than 100 percent: Increasing returns!

When you reach 100 workers on the assembly line, you've achieved the design optimum. Adding more workers will permit you to speed up the line. But you've reached Region II, the area of diminishing returns: TPP increases, but at a diminished rate, and MPP falls.

Finally, consider adding 500 workers to an assembly line designed for 100. The workers don't have adequate space to move, they get in each other's way, and output actually decreases: Negative returns!

You understand that production will not take place in the region of negative returns. No employer would want to hire so many workers that production is impeded. But no employer will want to operate in the region of increasing returns either. This counterintuitive outcome will be clarified in Chapter 16.

The Second Foot: Isoquant Analysis

Points on a production function that indicate equal amounts of output despite differing input combinations lie on a single **isoquant**.

A fruitful method of examining choice in production is to generate an **isoquant** map, the production analogue to the indifference map.[3] Return to Figure 6.1a, but slice it horizontally. Notice the two isoquants drawn in Figure 6.1b: One connects 260 cars washed; the other, 300 cars. (Draw in isoquants for 335, 450, and 520.)

Indifference Curves and Isoquants: Fraternal, Not Identical, Twins

How They're Alike

• Both represent equal levels of something—satisfaction for indifference curves, output for isoquants.

• The slopes of both have similar names and interpretations: the marginal rate of substitution for indifference curves and the **marginal rate of technical substitution (MRTS)** for isoquants. The insertion of the word *technical* in the latter term emphasizes the fact that the trade-off between inputs is technologically or naturally determined. Normally, the curves are convex to the origin, representing diminishing MRS or MRTS. In the case of the indifference curve, a falling MRS indicates (1) that one good can be traded off for another good, but (2) as the consumer acquires more and more of one good, he or she will be ever less willing to give up the other commodity. For isoquants, the declining MRTS implies that one input can be substituted for another. But as more and more of any one input is substituted for another, it will take ever greater increments of the first to compensate for further reductions in the second.

The **marginal rate of technical substitution (MRTS)** is the slope of the isoquant. It represents the number of units of one input that must be substituted for a second input in order to maintain constant output.

Take a look at Figure 6.1b again. With 16 hours of machine time and 1 hour of labor, output equals 300. Give up 8 hours of machine time and you'll still remain at 300 output if you merely add 1 more hour of labor (so that you'll reach 8 machine hours and 2 labor hours). The MRTS = $\Delta K / \Delta L = (16 - 8)/(1 - 2) = -8$. But if you move further to the right on the isoquant, say at $4K$ and $4L$, the MRTS = $(8 - 4)/(2 - 4) = -2$. In other words, at first, 1 unit of labor can do the same job as 8 units of capital. But as more and more labor replaces capital, the substitutability of labor for capital diminishes. At the second point, one unit of labor can only do the job of two units of capital. The reason is that labor and capital, although substitutes, are not perfect substitutes.

MICROBITS 6.1

Production by Formula

Input substitution is not always possible, especially in types of manufacturing that adhere to specific formulas. For instance, every bottle of Coke produced anywhere in the world begins with a proprietary syrup manufactured to specifications by the Coca-Cola Company in Atlanta and sold to its bottlers throughout the world. The chemical ingredients of drugs must be combined in precise proportions; deviations or substitutions can have fatal consequences. Similarly, many brand-name consumer products—Gleem toothpaste, Efferdent denture cleanser, Enfamil baby formula, Revlon hot pink nail polish, and Lotus 1-2-3 spreadsheet software—all adhere to precise specifications in production, which is one reason you can be sure that as you repeatedly purchase a brand-name product, you'll obtain the same product quality again and again.

The figure here suggests the absence of choice in combining resources in the making of photographic film. Black-and-white film essentially consists of a cellulose or acetate base, an intermediate "antihalo" layer to prevent reflections, and a light-sensitive coating that is a mixture of 40 percent silver bromide crystals and 60 percent gelatin and water. Adding more gelatin at the expense of silver weakens the quality of the film, as does substituting silver for gelatin. Thus, 2 tons of

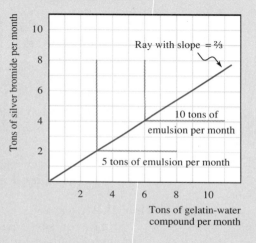

silver bromide combined with 3 tons of gelatin and water will provide 5 tons of emulsion; 4 tons of silver bromide and 6 tons of gelatin and water will provide 10 tons of film coating, and so on. But 2 tons of silver and 6 tons of the gelatin-water liquid will still only provide 5 tons of the surface layer; the remaining 3 tons of gelatin-water cannot be used. In the figure, the ray running from the origin through the right angles of successive isoquants indicates that silver bromide and gelatin-water must be used in a 2:3 ratio; any other combination simply wastes either the silver compound or the gelatin-water mix.

When two inputs must be used in constant proportions and cannot be substituted for each other in production, the production function reflects **fixed input coefficients.** But when substitution among inputs exists, the production function is characterized by **variable input coefficients.**

At times, right-angle indifference curves or isoquants may occur. In such instances, either substitution in consumption (e.g., right and left sneakers) or substitution in production (e.g., hydrogen for oxygen in the production of water by electrolysis) is impossible. In the latter case, the production function is characterized by **fixed input coefficients** (see Micro-Bits 6.1 for an example). This stands in contrast to **variable input coefficients.**

Neither indifference curves nor isoquants can cross. (The reasoning for isoquants is identical to that for indifference curves as described in Chapter 3, p. 75.)

Isoquants can be circular, as can indifference curves (see Figure 6.4). However, production will never take place along chord *EBC* on the lowest isoquant since for any point there you could find another point on chord *EAC* that yields the same output but requires fewer inputs. Thus, both *A* and *B* yield an output of 100 million bars of soap weekly, but *A* uses 100 machine hours (*K*) and 550 labor hours (*L*), while *B* requires 325*K* and 1,300*L*. Obviously, *B* is never an economical point of production. Similarly, *C* is a possible production point, while *D* is not, since both utilize 75 machine hours. But *C* requires 100 fewer labor hours per week

FIGURE 6.4   Circular Isoquants

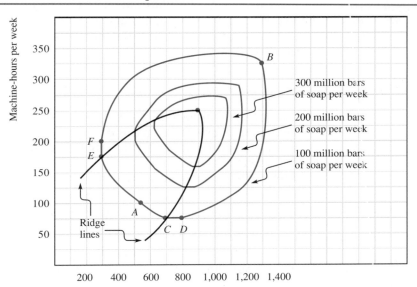

Production will only occur within the ridge lines. For any point outside the ridge lines, resources will be wasted, since the same output could be attained with fewer inputs by operating within the ridge lines.

than does *D*. (You should be able to explain why *E* is practicable but *F* is not.)

In short, even for circular isoquants, operation will take place only on the convex portion of an isoquant, defined as the region from where an isoquant becomes vertical (e.g., *E*) to the point where it becomes horizontal (e.g., *C*). These boundaries are marked by **ridge lines.**

On an isoquant map, **ridge lines** demarcate the region within which production will take place.

How They Differ

· A key difference between indifference curves and isoquants involves ordinal versus cardinal numbering. Indifference curves can only be ordered ordinally (i.e., higher and lower, or first, second, etc.), because utility is not measurable. But output is a measurable quantity. The numbers attached to isoquants are output quantities, not imaginary values.

Back to Brazilian Gold

The distinct mining techniques mentioned in the opening paragraphs of this chapter imply that the mining production function permits factor substitution. **Labor-intensive** mining methods compete with **capital-intensive** methods. The resulting isoquant map will show the combinations of labor and machine time needed to move say 100 cubic meters of earth, running the gamut from heavy reliance on labor with little machine time to extensive use of machines and relatively minimal labor contributions. The Brazilians could have mined gold using less labor and more capital. That they didn't does not reflect the technological options but rather production costs.

Production methods that use relatively more labor than capital are called **labor-intensive,** while methods that rely more heavily on capital than labor are called **capital-intensive.**

Weapons Delivery Systems

The production function and the trade-off implicit in isoquants need not be limited to business applications. It can be used wherever outputs and inputs can be quantified and related to each other. Consider the idea of a defensive first strike that advocates overwhelming the enemy quickly and decisively the moment it becomes evident that the aggressor is set to attack.

· Your mission: Obliterate designated military and industrial sites in the enemy's territory.
· Your means: Missile delivery systems.
· Your choice: Missile-carrying aircraft or missile submarines.

Consider the alternatives: Bombers are more vulnerable to antiaircraft devices, but can move closer to the target and deliver the missiles more accurately. Moreover, because of their speed, aircraft can be quickly reallocated to alternate targets and be rearmed once the initial payload has been delivered. Submarine-deployed missiles must be fired from a body of water, which limits both the range and the accuracy of the individual shot. Submarines are slow-moving delivery platforms, but they are more difficult to detect. Clearly, trade-offs do exist; they are depicted in Table 6.1. Use the table to construct isoquants in the space provided in Figure 6.5.

TABLE 6.1   A First-Strike Scenario

Thousands of Tons of TNT Delivered	*Number of*	
	Bombers	*Submarines*
1,500	400	250
1,500	333	300
1,500	250	400
1,500	100	1,000
2,000	500	250
2,000	375	333
2,000	250	500
2,000	125	1,000
2,500	500	520
2,500	400	650
2,500	260	1,000

FIGURE 6.5   Alternative Missile Delivery Options: Tactical Choices

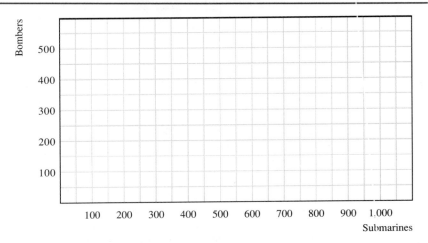

The isoquants constructed offer alternative means of delivering a given amount of destructive power.

Isoquants and the Scale of Production

What happens to output when all inputs are increased? Return to the car wash grid, but instead of adding only additional labor time, add more machine time as well. Will diminishing returns occur? _____

Under **increasing returns to scale** (or **economies of scale**), equiproportionate increases in *all* inputs lead to more than proportionate increments in output. When **decreasing returns to scale** (or **diseconomies of scale**) occur, proportional increases in *all* inputs lead to less than proportional increments in output. Under **constant returns to scale,** equiproportionate increments in *all* inputs result in equiproportionate increases in output.

The answer is no, because the law of diminishing returns applies only when some factors of production are held constant, not when all inputs are varied. Economists use the term *returns to scale* to describe relationships between inputs and outputs when *all* factors of production vary.

Three possibilities present themselves: **increasing, decreasing,** or **constant returns to scale.** (The first two terms are also called **economies of scale** and **diseconomies of scale**.) Once again, the returns to scale relationships are imbedded in the physical nature of the production function.

- *Constant returns to scale* characterize the car wash production function. If you double inputs from 2*K*, 2*L* to 4*K*, 4*L*, output doubles from 150 cars washed per day to 300.
- *Economies of scale* are shown in Figure 6.6, which reproduces the isoquant map of Figure 6.1b, but renumbers the isoquants. When inputs double from 2*K,* 2*L* to 4*K*, 4*L*, output moves from 150 to 375, a 250 percent increase. And similarly, a 50 percent increase from 4, 4 to 6, 6 leads to an increase in output from 375 to 600, or 60 percent.
- *Decreasing returns to scale* can be shown in Figure 6.6 by a similar renumbering. Why not try it yourself?

FIGURE 6.6   Economies of Scale

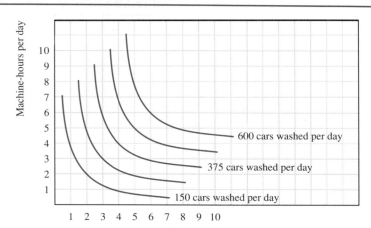

Increasing simultaneously both inputs leads in the case of increasing returns to scale to a more than proportionate increase in output.

Why might a production function exhibit returns to scale? Think for a moment of the relationship between airplane size and passenger miles flown. Transporting passengers requires capital in the form of the plane, and fuel and labor in the form of a crew. If you increase the physical size of the plane by 10 percent, put in 10 percent more aviation gasoline, and similarly supplement the crew size, will you be able to increase the number of passenger miles flown by 10 percent? Perhaps. But can you keep on increasing these capital and labor inputs and expect to obtain constant returns to scale? Definitely not. Boeing's jumbo 747, carrying three times the payload of the 727 for greater distances, is not merely a larger airplane but a differently constructed vehicle. Physical constraints in the form of *decreasing returns to scale* limit the ability of airplane designers to replicate precisely the smaller plane on a larger scale.

A word to the wise: Avoid later confusion by having clear in your mind the distinction between diminishing returns and decreasing returns to scale. The former occurs when at least one input is fixed, the latter when all inputs are variable.

Examining an Oily Production Function

The distinction between varying some factors and varying all factors carries over in the empirical study of production functions. You'll see that clearly in the following case study of oil pipelines.

Pipelines

Pipelines are a common mode of transporting oil from the southwestern U.S. oilfields to user concentrations in other parts of the nation. The pipes themselves come in a variety of diameters, and the "throughput" (the volume of fuel carried per time period) rises with the size of the pipe. But throughput can also be increased by pumping; the more horsepower used, the greater the throughput. Obviously, then, a given throughput can be achieved by some combination of pipe size and pumping power. (Is this production function represented by fixed or variable input coefficients? _____[4])

Figure 6.7a is based on an engineering production function calculated by Leslie Cookenboo, Jr., with the inside diameter of the pipelines on the ordinate, horsepower on the abcissa, and throughput in terms of barrels per day.[5] Notice the convex shape of the isoquants, indicating a declining MRTS. Now, take a ruler and place it horizontally at diameter of 26 inches. Read off the throughput as you follow it rightward, increasing the horsepower. The values you'll derive constitute total product, with pipeline size the constant input and horsepower the variable input. The resulting TPP curve is plotted alongside as Figure 6.7b. Does it indicate increas-

FIGURE 6.7   **Isoquants and a Total Physical Product Curve for Pipeline Throughput**

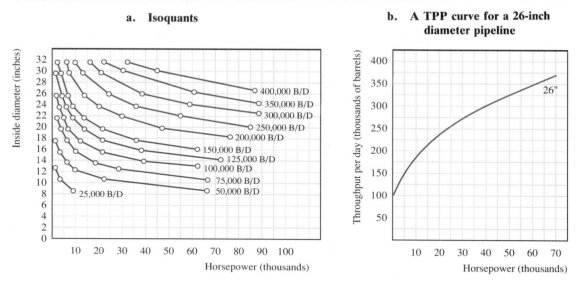

a. **Isoquants**

b. **A TPP curve for a 26-inch diameter pipeline**

SOURCE: Leslie Cookenboo, Jr., *Crude Oil PipeLines and Competition in the Oil Industry* (Cambridge: Harvard University Press, 1955), pp. 15, 16.

ing, diminishing, or negative returns? (Try plotting another TPP curve, say pipeline diameter of 22 inches. It should lie below the 26-inch curve and should also demonstrate diminishing returns.)

What does this production function say about returns to scale? What happens to throughput if both pipeline diameter and pumping power are increased? Try it by choosing some arbitrary starting point, say $D = 8$ and $H = 10$, with throughput equal to 25,000 barrels per day. Double that to $D = 16$ and $H = 20$; throughput rises to 100,000 barrels per day. A doubling of both inputs leads to a quadrupling of output, certainly increasing returns to scale.

What does all this mean to an economist working for Exxon? Clearly, the production function provides the staff economist with options. It enables him to cost out alternatives for any given level of throughput. And focusing on the returns to scale aspect permits the economist to weigh the desirability of proposing a large-scale venture instead of advocating multiple small-scale projects.

Let's assume that the O. B. Noxious pipeline company is considering constructing a 10-mile project that will provide the market with a daily supply of 300,000 barrels of fuel. This quantity of oil could be delivered through one pipeline designed to carry 300,000 barrels daily, through two lines running parallel, each capable of carrying 150,000 barrels per day, or through three lines with a combined 300,000 barrel daily capacity. The isoquant map provides unequivocal advice: Build one pipeline, not many.

The O. B. Noxious economist may then use the production function in reaching another decision. The firm must still consider the appropriate combination of diameter and horsepower in the single pipeline it's decided to construct. The isoquant map permits the economist to map out the following alternatives, each of them capable of delivering the desired throughput:

Diameter (inches)	32	30	26	24	22
Horsepower (thousands)	16	21	39	58	88

To be sure, this menu of alternatives only provides the foundation for a decision. Cost elements, which are introduced in Chapter 7, will have a significant role to play. Nevertheless, this listing of alternatives is the necessary first step.

MicroBits 6.2 contains a discussion of the Cobb-Douglas production function, which has long been popular among empirical economists. It also provides quantitative estimates for some manufacturing production functions.

The Validity of Empirical Production Functions

A continuous theme of this chapter has been the production function as a technological or natural relationship between inputs and outputs. It tells you precisely the maximum amount of output that can be obtained for each combination of inputs. This theoretical conception was just clothed with empirical content in the pipeline and manufacturing examples. The following questions are dealt with in the next few paragraphs: How accurate are empirical estimates of production functions in general, especially when labor is one of the measured inputs? Similarly, what role does the presence of waste play in interpreting empirical production functions? The answers to these two questions suggest that economists and business executives must treat estimated production relationships with a degree of caution.

The Human Element in Production.   Production functions can be highly accurate when they are derived from inanimate inputs. That is clearly true, for example, when pipeline dimensions and horsepower are related to throughput. When it comes to relationships involving people, however, the concept of a specifiable and certainly a rigid input-output connection must be doubted. The car wash example can readily be accepted on the theoretical plane. But it's not plausbile to treat labor hours as a uniform

Returns to Scale in Manufacturing

In a 1928 article, Professors A. W. Cobb and Paul Douglas (the latter was to become a prominent U.S. senator) estimated an empirical production function for the United States for 1900–1922:

$$P = 1.10L^{.75}C^{.25}$$

where P = total annual production, L = labor input, and C = capital input. Virtually all work in production functions since then has stemmed from this pioneering function.

The Cobb-Douglas function has three interesting properties. First, the exponents of labor and capital individually indicate whether the function is characterized by increasing (>1) or diminishing (<1) returns for that input. (The car wash example is a Cobb-Douglas function based on the following equation: Cars washed = $100L^{.5}K^{.5}$. You can see why both labor hours and machine hours show diminishing returns.) Second, you can tell by summing the exponents whether the function is characterized by increasing (>1), constant ($=1$), or decreasing (<1) returns to scale. (The original Cobb-Douglas function showed constant returns to scale; $0.75 + 0.25 = 1$. What is the nature of the returns to scale in the car wash production function used in this chapter?*) Third, the Cobb-Douglas function can be estimated by regression techniques in a straightforward manner because it is linear in logarithms. (The original Cobb-Douglas equation can be rewritten as follows: $\log P = \log 1.10 + 0.75 \log L + 0.25 \log C$.§)

It was not long before economists began to explore individual industries using Cobb-Douglas functions. For example, Moroney‖, in searching for economies of scale in U.S. manufacturing, calculated Cobb-Douglas production functions for a number of industries using the following form:

$$\log V = \log \Gamma + b_1 \log X_1 + b_2 \log X_2 + b_3 \log X_3 + e$$

where V is an output measure, Γ and the bs are coefficients to be estimated, X_1 is capital, X_2 and X_3 are inputs of production and nonproduction workers, respectively, and e is a random variable. For 18 major industrial classifications, Moroney found that the sums of the b coefficients ranged from 0.947 (petroleum and coal) to 1.109 (furniture). After further testing, he concluded that 13 of the 18 industries were characterized by constant returns to scale.

As econometric methods became more sophisticated, investigators began to fit production functions to other functional forms. Nowadays the estimation of production functions has become a subspecialty of econometrics.

---

* See what happens to the Cobb-Douglas function when you double L and K:

$$= 1.10\,(2L)^{.75}\,(2C)^{.25}$$
$$= 1.10\,(2^{.75})(L^{.75})(2^{.25})(C^{.25})$$
$$= 1.10\,(2^{.75+.25})(L^{.75})(C^{.25})$$
$$= 1.10\,(2^{1})(L^{.75})(C^{.25})$$
$$= 2\,(1.10\ L^{.75}\ C^{.25}).$$

In other words, doubling L and K leads to double output. The same is true for the car wash production function.

§ Remember that exponents can be converted into log form; the multiplicative relations then change to additive ones. The estimation of log-linear functions was discussed in connection with the empirical oil demand curves in Chapter 4. The same technique applies to production functions.

‖ John R. Moroney, "Cobb-Douglas Production Functions and Returns to Scale in U.S. Manufacturing Industry," *Western Economic Journal* 6, no. 1 (December 1967), pp. 39–51.

input analogous to machine hours. People are not robots who share identical qualities and can be programmed to perform a specific task repeatedly with uniform consistency. Moreover, even if one could conceive of equal quality labor, the social dynamics of people working together affect their output in irregular and unpredictable ways. At best, simplifying the nature of labor and human productivity in empirical studies provides the economist with a first approximation. But when implications are drawn for public or private policy decisions, such quantitative information must be applied with care.

With this in mind, it becomes more apparent why producers often favor capital-intensive over labor-intensive methods even when the latter appear to be more productive. Labor input may not really be more productive if the data have not dealt properly with the human element. Machines don't talk back, machines don't call in sick, machines don't go on strike, machines don't get injured on the job. Nor does a piece of capital equipment have personal problems that affect its ability to perform. Taking all of that into account increases the actual productivity of the inanimate machine relative to labor.

Trimming the Fat.   Empirical production functions are based on actual numbers derived from operating businesses. This, too, should raise warning flags.

Profitable firms tend to be sloppy. They have little incentive to control costs. Managers often ignore the presence of superfluous or nonproductive workers, buy the latest technology even though it isn't really needed, disregard material wastage, and/or permit product quality to deteriorate. This **x-inefficiency** leads to lower output than the maximum achievable with given inputs or requires more inputs for a given output than the minimum necessary. It's only when profits turn down and those in top management begin to worry about their jobs that the executive suite begins to scrutinize operations for cost-cutting economies. Only then is the fat trimmed, which allows the true relationship between inputs and outputs to emerge.

X-inefficiency refers to waste that stems from excessive use of productive resources.

What does waste have to do with empirical production functions? Clearly, when a company operates inefficiently, it does not achieve the maximum possible output from its production inputs. Thus, the actual production function that emerges from measuring the inputs and the resulting output underestimates the true input-output relationship. The production function probably is biased as well. But because we have no way of measuring the degree of underestimation or bias, the empirical estimate is merely an approximation of the authentic production function. Thus, a policymaker would be served better by a cautious economist. The recommendation that stems from an appreciation of the fuzziness of the empirical production function is surely more credible than advice based on a precision that is illusory.

Summary

Joan Kimberlane, senior vice president for Omni Enterprises, has a difficult but not insuperable task. She is charged with combining the many resources—labor of various grades, machinery of different functions, and inventories of raw materials—needed to produce the firm's output of miniature paper umbrellas in the most profitable manner. To come to any kind of decision, Joan must first know the paper umbrella production function (PUPF), the basic relationship between assorted inputs and output that was the subject of this chapter. Of course, if the PUPF allowed for no factor substitution, if the isoquants were right-angled, then at least part of the decision would be easy; Joan would be bound to use the factors in the proportions specified by technology. But PUPF permits factor substitution; the isoquants are convex to the origin, as is the case when the input coefficients are variable. So, Joan will have to decide the optimum factor proportions.

Joan will know something else: at what point she will face the law of diminishing returns if she decides to increase one of the factors of production while holding the others constant. Joan will have learned to read this off the production function, either by looking at the total physical product (TPP) curve and discerning where its rate of increase begins to decline or by glancing at the marginal physical product (MPP) curve and noting where it starts to turn down. (If the PUPF is described by a Cobb-Douglas production function, then she will know whether diminishing returns begin right away merely by looking at the exponent of the variable factor of production.) Joan also realizes of course that the entire TPP and MPP curves will shift if she decides to vary one of the factors that she had previously held constant.

Joan will tell by observing the production function whether it is characterized by increasing, decreasing, or constant returns to scale. That is, the PUPF will not only indicate the rate at which one factor can be substituted for another—the marginal rate of technical substitution (MRTS)—but also if all the factors are increased simultaneously, whether output will increase more than proportionally, less than proportionally, or by the same percentage. (Again, if the PUPF is a Cobb-Douglas one, then Joan will know this by summing up the exponents.)

Actually, Joan should treat the production functions produced by her economists with some caution. That is especially true when dealing with labor inputs, because motivation and social interactions may not have been adequately considered when Omni's economists calculated the PUPF. But it is also important to realize that the data used to relate input to output probably contained some waste. So, if she properly motivates her work force, Joan will probably do better than the estimated PUPF indicates.

Finally, Joan knows that her task has only begun. She knows production functions and isoquants are analogous to menus. They inform Joan what's available and permit her to compare options. But just as Joan wouldn't choose from a menu without seeing the prices of each dish, so, too, would she not select a set of inputs without having additional information about their costs. Introducing costs and then making input decisions is the task of Chapter 7.

Key Terms

Average physical product (APP)
Capital-intensive methods
Constant returns to scale
Decreasing returns to scale (or diseconomies of scale)
Fixed input coefficients
Increasing returns
Increasing returns to scale (or economies of scale)
Isoquant
Labor-intensive methods

Law of diminishing returns
Marginal physical product (MPP)
Marginal rate of technical substitution (MRTS)
Negative returns
Production function
Ridge lines
Total physical product (TPP)
Variable input coefficients
X-inefficiency

Review Questions

1. *a*. Draw a generalized total physical product curve and indicate on it the regions of increasing, diminishing, and negative returns. Explain the meaning of each region.
   b. Do the same using average physical product and marginal physical product curves.

2. The grid on the next page relates hay and fish meal as sources of nourishment to the weight cattle gain from their diet (pounds per month).
   a. Is this production function characterized by increasing and/or diminishing returns? How do you know?
   b. What type of returns to scale are represented by this grid?
   c. Sketch onto the grid at least two isoquants.

3. "Diminishing returns are more a characteristic of agricultural production functions than of manufacturing production functions." Do you agree? Why or why not?

4. Coconut growers in Thailand have begun an experiment in which the men who pick the coconuts are replaced by monkeys. Draw the isoquant map that illustrates the coconut-picking production function.

5. In what ways are isoquants similar and dissimilar to indifference curves?

6. *a*. What is the marginal rate of technical substitution?
   b. What is the relationship between the MRTS and the convex shape of the isoquant?

7. Why will production take place only within the ridge lines?

8. Why should empirical production functions be applied with caution?

9. Professor Heady and his colleagues at Iowa State University varied the proportions of grain (*G*) and hay (*H*) in the diet of 36 cows and measured the resulting milk output. They also took into account the inherent genetic differences in the cows (*A*). The estimated Cobb-Douglas production function they obtained was as follows:

$$\text{Milk} = 15.749 H^{.1213} G^{.2758} A^{.3659}$$

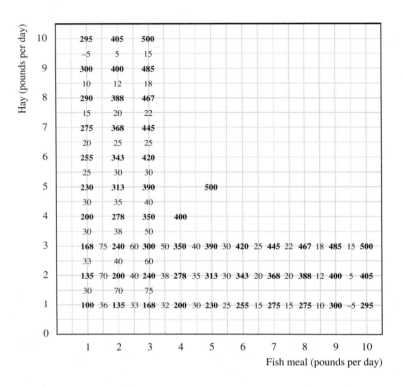

a. Does this function show diminishing, increasing, or constant returns to hay? to grain? to genetics?

b. Is this production function character-ized by decreasing, increasing, or constant returns to scale?

c. Is there any economic explanation for these results?

Food for Thought

1. How can you use the production function to explain the automation of many production processes such as robotics in factories and word processors in offices?

2. How would the production function of coffins, which are traditionally made of wood or metal, be affected by the introduction of fiberglass caskets?

3. Some companies have turned to a lighter weight paper to save on mailing costs. Draw schematic "before" and "after" curves to demonstrate the impact of such a move on a firm's physical product, average physical product, and marginal physical product curves. (Use total weight mailed as the output and labor time as the variable input.)

4. What is the MRTS for a production function that is characterized by fixed input coefficients?

5. South Korea imposed quota limits on imports of Chinese chopsticks. At the same time, U.S. exports of chopsticks to Japan have increased. What might these

two facts combined with your general knowledge of production methods in the United States and China indicate about the nature of the chopstick production function?

6. Use production theory to suggest why some industries are characterized by small firms (e.g., dairy farming), others by large firms (e.g., automobiles), and still others by a variety of firm sizes (e.g., retailing).

7. Some firms are reluctant to fire workers even in slack periods both because the employees have been trained to meet the firm's needs and also because the supervisors are familiar with the workers' performance. What impact will such practices have on empirical production functions?

8. When firms invest in more capital, worker productivity increases.
   a. Demonstrate the truth of this statement.
   b. How might this provoke labor-management disagreements?

Suggested Readings

The literature of empirical production functions requires skills that are beyond the typical experience of the undergraduate. Nevertheless, you might want to peek at one or another of the classic, if dated, surveys of empirical production functions: A. A. Walters, "Production and Cost Functions: An Econometric Survey," *Econometrica* 31, nos. 1–2 (January-April 1963), pp. 1–66; or Earl O. Heady and John L. Dillon, *Agricultural Production Functions* (Ames, Iowa: Iowa State University Press, 1961).

Among the first economists to call attention to the interrelationship between human behavior and business organization was Harvard's Harvey Leibenstein, whose x-inefficiency upset the simple neat relationship between inputs and output. See his seminal "Allocative Efficiency vs. 'X-Efficiency,' " *American Economic Review* 56, no. 3 (June 1966), pp. 392–415. Much of the empirical

work on x-efficiency since Leibenstein's pathbreaking article is summarized in Roger S. Frantz, "X-Efficiency in Behavioral Economics," in *Handbook of Behavioral Economics: Behavioral Microeconomics*, ed. Benjamin Gilad and Stanley Kaish (Greenwich, Conn.: JAI Press, 1986), pp. 307–23.

You might be amused by Barbara Toohey's "Sexual Revolution Wrecks U.S. Productivity," *The Wall Street Journal*, May 8, 1981, p. 26. She attributes the decline in U.S. productivity to weakening of the work ethic, a direct consequence of the sexual revolution's offering new options. Toohey claims that "the greatest percentage of the world's work is done by unhappily married people—those dedicated workers who flee to office, factory or shop . . . in order to escape their intolerable home situations."

Notes and Answers

1. The correct answers are obtained by reading along the machine-hours = 3 line in Figure 6.1b, viz.: 130, 184, 225, 260, 290, 318, 344, 367, 390, 411, 431, 450, 468, 486, 503, 520. Plotting these points will yield a curve lying above the original TPP curve.
2. 47, 43, 40, 37.5, 35, 33.5, 32, 30.5, 29.
3. It's called isoquant because it connects points on the production function where output ("quant"[ity]) is equal ("iso").
4. Variable, since input substitution is possible.
5. See Leslie Cookenboo, Jr., *Crude Oil Pipe Lines and Competition in the Oil Industry* (Cambridge: Harvard University Press, 1955), pp. 14–24.

PRODUCTION COSTS: BUILDING A BETTER AND CHEAPER MOUSETRAP

In the long run, we're all dead.
Lord Keynes (1936)

Learning Objectives

In this chapter you'll learn:

- About a plethora of cost concepts—fixed, variable, short-run, long-run, total, average, and marginal—and when to use them.
- How firms can use isoquants and input prices to keep costs down.
- How changing input costs affect production decisions.
- How decreasing and increasing costs as well as economies and diseconomies of scale are related to short-run and long-run cost curves, respectively.
- The shape of actual cost curves in a variety of industries.
- Some applications of isoquant analysis.
- How uncertainty affects production costs.

Flying to Bankruptcy

Continental Airlines pioneered the application of cost analysis to airline decision making. The following two examples are based on actual cases that occurred during the early 1960s:[1]

- Continental regularly schedules a flight to leave Colorado Springs at 11:11 P.M. for Denver and to return at 5:20 A.M. Although some cargo is carried on the return flight, rarely is there a passenger on board. Is flying empty as stupid as it sounds?

· Should Continental flight 625 from Rottenboro to Smellyhollow be canceled given the following financial information?

Total cost of flight	$84,500
Total revenue	$55,000
Net loss	$29,500

Chapter 6 outlined production options in a variety of settings. In this chapter, you'll learn how to choose among those options. You are already familiar with the fundamental analysis, which is similar to Chapter 3's consumer choice theory and the budget line–indifference curve tangency. You know that isoquants are the producer analogue of indifference curves. You'll see in this chapter that for producers, relative input costs play the same role as relative prices in the theory of consumer choice.

Nevertheless, there are some important differences between consumption and production theory:

· While the consumer's budget was assumed fixed, it's unrealistic to so constrain producers. Because they can decide to produce more or less, producers can also opt to vary their spending on inputs.

· Producers often have less flexibility in decision making. It's normal for entrepreneurs to make commitments to factor suppliers (e.g., in 1987, Continental Airlines signed a 25-year lease for space at Newark Airport). Economists have analyzed separately those instances where firms have locked themselves into prior commitments and those in which the producer starts totally unencumbered.

· Cost is a term that is open to more interpretations than is price. Indeed, the following section is a brief dictionary of costs.

Once you understand the various meanings of costs, you can begin to resolve the input choice problem. That is the task of the third section of this chapter, where you'll see how a firm can produce a given output with minimum resource costs. Once that is accomplished, you can quickly move on to the next stage, the derivation of cost curves. In a sense, cost curves are the key new concepts of this chapter. They are not only important in themselves but also play a critical role in determining a firm's optimum profit position. They are also the basis for the firm's supply curve.

The shape of cost curves in the real world is also addressed in this chapter. Following some applications—from why there's unemployment in labor-rich countries to how best to collect garbage—the chapter concludes with a discussion of the impact of uncertainty on production.

The Many Meanings of *Cost*

As consumers we use the word *cost* synonymously with *price*. When we ask, "How much does that pair of jeans cost?" we mean "What's the price of that pair of jeans?" As we navigate now in the production stream, it becomes necessary to distinguish between cost and price. *Cost* is used to indicate the value of the resources employed to produce a good or service, such as labor costs or capital costs. *Price,* on the other hand, is reserved for the price at which the product is sold.

Money Outlays versus Opportunity Costs

It is often important to distinguish between money outlays and opportunity costs. Clearly, the money costs of production are the expenditures the producer lays out in assembling the factors of production and producing the product. While money outlays are important, in many contexts the idea of opportunity cost overshadows the actual financial outlays. In the next few chapters, we shall be generally working with monetary expenditures, but you must realize that opportunity costs often lurk in the background.

Short Run versus Long Run

The firm is not committed to any outlays in the **long run.** The situation changes to the **short run** once a commitment to some factor of production has been undertaken.

Blake is seriously contemplating opening up a detective agency. She's spotted the right location, knows where she can get some used but serviceable office equipment, has friends who'll be available when required, and has lined up suppliers for the few odds and ends she'll need. But she's made no commitments to anyone. That defines this case as **long run.** As long as all the options are open, Blake can back out without any outlays other than wasted time and punctured dreams.

But if Blake takes the initial step and rents the office, the case becomes a **short-run** situation. Having undertaken payments to the landlord for six months, she now faces a different type of decision. Should Blake suddenly get cold feet and decide not to open the agency, those rental costs are still going to have to be paid.

MicroQuery   Six months are up and Blake has to decide whether to renew the lease. No other commitments have been made. Is signing the lease again a short-run or long-run decision? _____ [2]

Fixed versus Variable Costs

Fixed costs are independent of the volume of production, while **variable costs** vary with output.

The distinction between the long run and the short run is particularly germane to a second set of terms: fixed and variable costs. In the short run, some costs are **fixed.** The moment Blake signs the six-month lease at $500 per month, she has undertaken a fixed cost of $3,000.

But, of course, Blake will encounter additional costs once her detective agency gets underway. She'll have to pay free-lancers $20 an hour. Blake's labor costs will rise in direct proportion to the number of hours she employs her investigators. All those costs that are directly related to production are called **variable costs.** *Thus, the short run is characterized by both fixed and variable costs.*

In *the long run, all costs are variable,* since all costs depend on the volume of output. So, if Blake decides at a later point not to renew her lease, she will not have to make any payments.

MicroQuery

Maria has decided to convert her existing beauty salon into a specialist nail boutique. What are some of her fixed and some of her variable costs?
                                                                                                    3

Average versus Marginal Costs

Average costs equal total costs divided by output, while **marginal costs** equal the *change* in total costs divided by the *change* in output.

In Chapter 6, you learned to distinguish between average and marginal physical product. The same kind of calculations can be performed to find **average** and **marginal costs.** For the former, divide total costs by output; for the latter, divide the change in total costs by the change in output. The question answered by average costs is, If it costs Blake $25,000 a month to cover the expenses for eight divorce investigations that she's supervising, how much does it cost for each investigation? The answer of course is $25,000/8, or $3,125. On the other hand, if you ask, How much does it cost Blake to take another case if she is already monitoring eight? the answer would be, Since it costs $25,000 for eight and $26,225 for nine, the marginal cost of the ninth case is $1,225.

This is an appropriate place to draw some conclusions from this list of cost definitions. In the short run, the firm faces both fixed and variable costs. But as the firm alters its output, only the variable costs change. (Why? _____ [4])
Thus, the marginal costs that the firm experiences as it expands output from given fixed resources are entirely due to its variable costs. Or, to put it differently, the opportunity cost of using fixed resources is zero. That leads to a major conclusion in the theory of the firm: *Decisions about output are based entirely on marginal costs; fixed costs are totally irrelevant to any output decision.*

Continental Airlines' Cost Analysis

With these concepts in mind, we can return to the two cases involving Continental Airlines that opened this chapter. First, let's look at the empty 5:20 A.M. return flight. Chris F. Whalen, vice president in charge of economic planning, relied on the concept of opportunity cost to justify flying empty from Colorado Springs to Denver. Had the flight remained at Colorado Springs, Continental would have had to pay for hangar space. The cost of flying back even without passengers was less than the cost for overnight storage.

In the second case, marginal analysis led to retaining Continental flight 625. The total costs of a flight include both fixed and variable costs. Thus, staff accountants included in the cost of a flight not only the cost of the fuel, crew, food, beverages, paper products, and all the sundries that flying entails, but also a share of the **overhead costs**—rental of facilities, all noncrew staff costs (including the accountants doing the calculations), insurance, advertising, and so on—that any going company encounters. But the overhead costs are fixed costs; they'll be incurred by Continental whether 625 flies or not, so they are irrelevant when dealing with the decision to cancel the flight.

Overhead costs are those not directly associated with production.

A calculation based on economic reasoning runs as follows:

Total variable cost of flight 625	$48,500
Total revenue	$55,000
Total *net* revenue from flight	$ 6,500

Consider only the additional or marginal costs that would be incurred if the flight were run. In this case, the expenses directly attributable to flight 625 were $48,500 in variable costs. Since the flight earned $6,500 more than it cost, Mr. Whalen would have been foolish to cancel it.

The moral of these examples is clear: To make rational economic decisions you must begin by applying the relevant cost concept.

The Third Foot: Keeping Costs Down with Isoquant Analysis

Remember Joan, whom we left hanging with her paper umbrellas at the end of Chapter 6. Like most managers, Joan wants to hold down her expenses as much as possible. In one sense, that means eliminating all possible waste. Or, in the language of Chapter 6, Joan wants to be as sure as possible that she's actually operating on the paper umbrella production function and avoiding x-inefficiency.

An additional way for Joan to keep costs down is to use a method based on isoquants. Let's assume that Joan hires two different types of labor: skilled and unskilled. The fundamental question she asks herself is,

"Can I maintain my volume of production at the present level and still cut my costs further by substituting some unskilled labor for skilled employees?" Alternatively, "Should I hire additional skilled labor and use fewer unskilled ones to bring my costs down?"

Joan sits down at her PC and begins to examine the choices presented by her isoquant map. Say weekly production of 500,000 umbrellas is achieved by combining 30 trained workers and 16 unskilled workers on an eight-hour shift, five-days-a-week basis. A second point on the 500,000 isoquant is 34 skilled umbrella makers and 10 less-skilled workers. Which is better? Joan does some simple calculations: Since a skilled worker costs $300 per week, while each unskilled employee runs only $150 weekly, her present operation costs come to $300 × 30 + $150 × 16, or $11,400. If Joan were to cut back on the unskilled to 10 employees and add four more trained workers, her total costs would rise to $11,700. Obviously, Joan is better off to continue as she is.

However, Joan might cut her skilled labor force to 28 and use 19 unskilled employees, a production combination that would also yield the half-million weekly umbrella volume. Why not cost this out?

The $11,250 expenses suggest that Joan could gain by substituting less trained personnel for higher quality labor. In fact, Joan would keep on switching until further changes in input mix no longer reduce costs. She would be making her already lean operation even more efficient.

The lesson of Joan's trading off is clear: Economizing on production costs depends on (1) the technological possibilities of switching one input for another as implicit in the isoquant map, and (2) the costs associated with each of the inputs.

Isocost Lines

Return to the car wash example of Chapter 6. The two inputs that were needed to run the car wash were labor and machine time. The employer could use more or fewer work hours as well as more or fewer machine hours as specified in the production function of Figure 6.1 (see p. 181). How much of each input will be used depends on its costs. Let's say Brad wishes to consider initially spending no more on variable costs than $96 per day and that the cost of operating the car wash machinery is calculated to be $6 per hour, while labor runs at $8 per hour. Quite obviously, Brad could spend the entire $96 on machine time, running his machines for 16 hours. Alternatively, he could spend the entire sum on labor, obtaining 12 hours of labor time. Brad has intermediate options as well: 8 hours of machine time ($48) + 6 hours of labor ($48), or 4 hours of machine time ($24) + 9 hours of labor ($72), or 10 hours of machine time

FIGURE 7.1   A Family of Isocost Lines

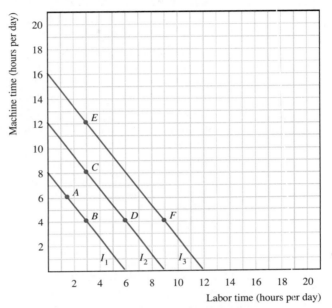

When machine time costs $6 per hour and labor costs $8 per hour, each isocost line will have a slope equal to ⅓, but will have a different position depending on the desired expenditures on inputs. Each point on an isocost line, of course, represents an identical outlay. Thus, outlays on *A* = expenditures on *B*, *C* = *D*, and *E* = *F*, but expenditures on *E*(= *F*) > *C*(= *D*) > *A*(= *B*).

All points on a single **isocost line** represent combinations of inputs that cost the same.

($60) + 4.5 hours of labor ($36). These are all plotted out on the **isocost line,** I_3, in Figure 7.1; they are all points on a linear equation:

$$I_3 = (\$6)q_K + (\$8)q_L,$$

where the *q*s are the quantity of machine time (*K*, for capital) and labor hours (*L* for labor), respectively, on the given isocost curve, I_3.

Keep the following considerations in mind when examining the isocosts in Figure 7.1. (You might want to refresh your memory by looking at the budget line in Figure 3.5 on p. 78.)

- The axes represent *quantities* of inputs. In this instance, the *y*-axis measures hours of machine time per day while the *x*-axis counts labor hours per day.
- The endpoints of each isocost line indicate the maximum amount of that factor available for a given outlay; on I_3, for $96, the pro-

ducer can acquire either 16 hours of machine time *or* 12 hours of labor time.

- The slope, $\Delta Y/\Delta X$, or 4/3, represents the trade-off between machine and labor time for a given outlay. Thus, were the producer to decide to use four hours less machine time, for a savings of $24, he could use the $24 to acquire three hours of labor time. Since the input prices are kept constant, all of the isocost curves in Figure 7.1 have the same slope.
- Notice that the slope of the isocost line equals the relative price of labor time to machine time ($8/$6, or 4/3). *The slope of the isocost line ($\Delta Y/\Delta X$) equals the inverse of the price ratios of the inputs in question ($1/p_y/p_x$).*[5]
- Isocost lines differ in their total expenditures on the variable inputs: For I_1, outlays = $48; for I_2, outlays = $72; and for I_3, outlays = $96.

Isoquant-Isocost Equilibrium

Surely it's reasonable to presume that any producer wishes to obtain the maximum output for any given dollar outlay. The producer's optimization problem is thus analogous to that of the consumer who strives for maximum satisfaction from a given income (see Figure 3.7, p. 80). It follows that just as the tangency position of the indifference curve and the budget line maximizes the consumer's utility, so, too, does the tangency of the isoquant and the isocost provide the producer with the maximum product for a given expenditure.

Study Figure 7.2, which combines the isoquants derived in Figure 6.1b with the isocost lines of Figure 7.1. Start at any intercept, say, the point where machine hours = 16 and labor hours = 0. Move your eyes along the line as you decrease machine time and increase labor time: you reach ever higher isoquants until you come to the tangency, which occurs on the isoquant representing 520 car washes per day. That is, spending $96 a day on labor and capital will enable the car wash owner to service, at most, 520 cars.

What would happen if you were to move further along I_3? The same expenditure would move you to lower isoquants, meaning fewer cars would be washed for the same outlay. Thus, maximum efficiency in the allocation of resources is given at the tangency, where the slope of the isoquant (the MRTS) and the isocost line is equal. Stated formally: In equilibrium, MRTS = $\Delta q_y/\Delta q_x$.

The logic of isoquant-isocost tangency says, "You've come to the point where any further changes in input composition would reduce production. So, stop switching." Indeed, that's precisely the mental exercise your mind should have been performing as your eyes were following I_3.

**FIGURE 7.2   Optimum Resource Combinations:
The Isoquant-Isocost Tangency**

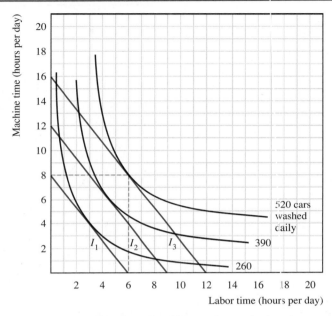

For any given dollar outlay, the producer obtains the
maximum production at the isoquant-isocost tangency.
The actual amounts of the resources employed are given
by the coordinates of the tangency. Thus, for an outlay
of $96 per day, the producer is on I_3, washes 520
vehicles, and employs eight hours of machine time and
six hours of labor.

Return now to Figure 7.2. How much capital and how much labor
time should the car wash manager utilize? _____ . If you read off
the coordinates of the tangency, you'd see that Brad's operation could
wash those 520 vehicles by using eight hours of machine time and six
hours of labor time. No other combination of inputs could yield more
washes. (How much would the manager have to spend on variable costs?
_____[6])

Shifting Factor Prices and Cost Curves.   Just as the rational consumer
reacts to a price change by buying more of the cheaper good and less of
the more expensive good, so, too, will a producer adjust by using less of
the more expensive resource and more of the cheaper one.

For the producer, however, the input price change affects not a single
equilibrium, but a host of them. Figure 7.3 reproduces the isoquant map

FIGURE 7.3   Isoquant-Isocost Equilibrium When Input Prices Change

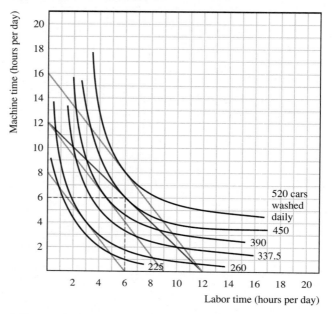

When capital time becomes more expensive, producers
shift the composition of input to use less of the more
expensive input. However, the cost increase also reduces
the output attainable for a given outlay.

of Figure 7.2, retaining the original isocost lines (light purple). Assume
now that the cost of an hour's use of capital has increased to $8. A single
new isocost curve is drawn in on the assumption that Brad still wants to
spend no more than $96 on his variable costs. Note that the new isocost
curve is now anchored at 12 and 12, rather than 16 and 12. In other words,
the higher cost of machine time means that if Brad spends the entire sum
on machine usage, he will obtain no more than 12 hours, rather than the
prior usage of 16.

Look now at the resulting equilibrium of the isocost curve and the
isoquant to which it is tangent.

- The old tangency of 520 is no longer achievable; Brad's $96 won't
stretch far enough to buy the resources needed to wash 520 vehicles daily. The best he can do now is 450 washes per day.
- As expected, the optimum proportion of capital and labor has
changed. Whereas previously Brad used more machine time than
labor time, the increased price of capital usage induces him to
reduce capital time and increase labor time. The new tangency

indicates six hours of each, a 1:1 proportion rather than the earlier 4:3 proportion.

Of course, Brad is not restricted to the $96 isocost line. He can draw in a series of isocost lines on Figure 7.3. Why not pencil them in? When you do so, you'll confirm the conclusions of the last paragraph: For each outlay, fewer cars will be washed and the equilibrium composition of inputs will shift in the direction of 1:1. Do check it out.

Mining Techniques in the United States and Brazil: An Issue Resolved

By marrying isocost lines and isoquants, you can better understand the difference between Brazilian labor-intensive mining techniques and U.S. firms' capital-intensive practices. Since the mining production function is the same in both countries, then whether the firm chooses labor- or capital-intensive techniques rests entirely on the relative prices of capital and labor. If labor is the more expensive input, then profit-seeking firms will use more capital-intensive methods. Should labor prove less expensive, then the business will select the more labor-intensive procedure.

Unskilled labor is relatively cheap in a poor, heavily populated country such as Brazil. The opposite is true in the United States. So, in Figure 7.4, a schematic isoquant for mining appears along with two isocost lines.

FIGURE 7.4   Capital-Intensive versus Labor-Intensive Operations

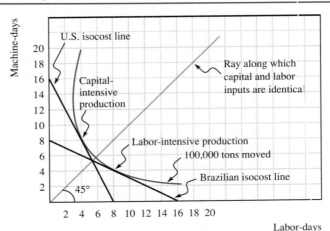

When the price of capital to labor is low, as it is in the United States, capital-intensive techniques are employed. When, however, capital is relatively expensive in comparison with labor, as is true for Brazil, labor-intensive methods are utilized.

The steeper line is that of the United States; the shallower one, that of Brazil. (Why are they drawn that way? _____[7])
If a ray radiating from the origin at a 45° angle represents equal capital-labor inputs, then tangency to the right of the line indicates labor-intensive methods. That's where Brazil's tangency is found. The U.S. position is on the left-hand side of the ray, demonstrating that capital-intensive mining methods are used.

Short-Run Costs

Brad and Spike at the Car Wash

It's summer, and Brad has promised his nephew, Spike, two hours' work per day for the next week. Although Brad is not at all certain how many cars are going to appear each day at the car wash, he is committed to paying Spike $16 a day at least for this week. Spike is to Brad a fixed cost. On the other hand, Brad's machine-operating time and thus machine costs are not subject to any constraints. He can shut the equipment off entirely. Then, his daily cost will consist of only the $16 he pays Spike. Alternatively, Brad can operate the machines for varying amounts of time, in which instance variable capital costs will be encountered.

Table 7.1 records Brad's variable equipment expenses, while Figure 7.5 portrays them graphically. The first two columns in Table 7.1 reproduce the relationship between machine hours per day and cars washed, with labor time held constant at two hours per day. These numbers are identical to Figure 6.2a's total physical product curve. The focus of this chapter, however, is not on total product curves, but on cost curves. So the third column simply translates the capital inputs into costs: at $8 an hour, the more time the machinery operates, the greater the capital costs are. If you just examine columns (1) and (3), you can see that the data relate the equipment costs of cleaning various quantities of vehicles to the number of cars washed.

The **total variable cost (TVC)** curve relates total variable costs to output.

Figure 7.5a plots the data of columns (1) and (3), deriving the **total variable cost (TVC)** curve. Notice the upward sweep of the TVC curve, indicating the not surprising conclusion that the more cars are washed, the more capital time will have to be employed and thus the greater the total costs are of washing the cars. Notice also that the curve is rising at an increasing rate: as more cars are washed, each additional car costs more than the car before it. (You can verify that by looking at the last column in Table 7.1, which calculates the marginal costs of car washing at different output levels, or at the MC curve in Figure 7.5b). This last observation is not self-evident and therefore needs some elaboration.

TABLE 7.1   Variable Costs in a Car Wash

Output (1)	Capital Input (2)	Total Variable (Capital) Costs (3) = (2) × $8	Average Variable Costs (4) = (3)/(1)	Marginal Costs (5) = Δ(3)/Δ(1)
0	0	$ 0	$0.00	$0.00
106	1	8	.09	.08
150	2	16	.11	.18
184	3	24	.13	.24
212	4	32	.15	.29
237	5	40	.17	.32
260	6	48	.19	.35
281	7	56	.20	.38
300	8	64	.21	.42
318	9	72	.23	.44
335	10	80	.24	.47
352	11	88	.25	.47
367	12	96	.26	.53
382	13	108	.27	.53
397	14	112	.28	.53
411	15	120	.29	.57
424	16	128	.30	.61

Increasing costs refers to the rising marginal costs that occur when more and more variable resources are combined with a fixed resource.

Increasing and Decreasing Costs.   Actually, you've already come across the rising slope of the TVC curve and the rising MC curve in another guise: the principle of diminishing returns. Diminishing returns are really the alter ego of **increasing costs,** the name used to connote the rising rate of growth of the TVC curve or the upward movement of the MC curve. Recall that in Chapter 6 the car wash production function was characterized by diminishing returns from the start. That implies increasing costs as you can see by glancing at Table 7.1. Start with five machine hours employed daily: variable costs are $40, and 237 cars are washed. Adding a sixth hour increases output to 260 cars washed: the extra machine hour increases output by 23 cars at an additional cost of $8. Now add another hour, bringing output to 281. But this seventh hour of equipment time increases the number of cars washed by 21—diminishing returns—at the same $8 cost as the extra 23 washed during the sixth machine hour. So, the additional cost of the 23 vehicles serviced during the sixth hour = $8/23, or 35 cents, while the additional cost of the 21 serviced during the seventh hour = $8/21, or 38 cents.

Increasing costs are evident throughout column 5 of Table 7.1, as they are by the rising marginal cost (MC) curve of Figure 7.5b (once again, plotting the value of the MCs at their respective midpoints). The table and the lower panel of Figure 7.5 also show the rising average variable cost (AVC) curve, calculated by dividing output into total variable costs.

FIGURE 7.5   Variable Cost Curves for a Car Wash

a.   Total variable costs

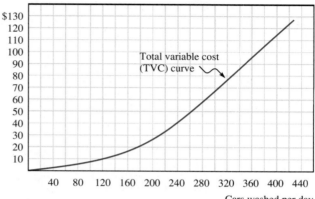

a. As more cars are serviced, requiring more variable inputs, TVC rises. The rising slope of the TVC curve indicates that costs rise more rapidly than output as output increases.

b.   Average and marginal costs

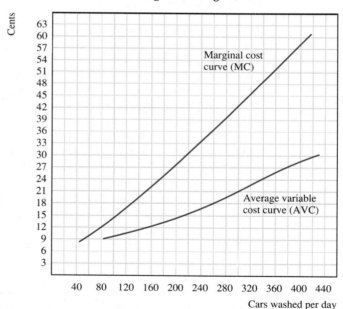

b. The more cars washed, the greater is the marginal cost of each car. The rising MC pulls up average variable costs as well in this example of increasing costs.

A Generalized Cost Function

Decreasing costs exist when the MC falls as increasing amounts of variable inputs are combined with a fixed resource.

You realize, of course, that increasing costs need not set in right from the start. Other production functions can lead to different forms of cost curves, such as those considered in MicroBits 7.1. A more generalized cost curve allows both for **decreasing** and increasing costs. (Students of microeconomic theory have found this generalized version easier to manage. It will serve us well in the chapters that follow.)

MICROBITS 7.1

Cost Curves of Various Shapes

A hypothetical set of cost-output data for bicycle production is set out in the table.

Cost-Output Data for Bicycle Production

Output	TVC	AVC	MC
A			
0	$ 0	$ 0	$ 0
1	10,000	10,000	10,000
2	15,000	7,500	5,000
3	17,500	5,500	2,500
4	19,000	4,750	1,500
5	20,000	4,000	1,000
B			
6	20,500	3,417	500
7	21,000	3,000	500
8	21,500	2,688	500
9	22,000	2,444	500
10	22,500	2,250	500
20	27,500	1,375	500
30	32,500	1,083	500
40	37,500	938	500
C			
45	40,000	889	500
46	45,000	978	5,000
47	55,000	1,170	10,000
48	70,000	1,458	15,000
49	90,000	1,837	20,000

Decreasing (Marginal) Costs

Begin by focusing on the relationship specified by the data in Section A of the table. As output increases, costs rise, too. But they do not rise as quickly as output, so that both AVC and MC fall. The intensified use of the inputs as production rises permits economies of production that are the analog of increasing returns mentioned in Chapter 6. The upper set of figures plots the TVC, AVC, and MC curves: the TVC rises at a diminishing rate, corresponding to a declining MC in the left-hand diagram. The AVC falls for an arithmetic reason: whenever the additional sum to be averaged is less than the previous average, the average falls.*

---

* It's also true that when the additional sum to be averaged is greater than the previous average, the average rises. Only when the marginal addition equals the previous average will the average neither rise nor fall. These cryptic statements deserve modest elaboration. Take the following example. The times of the first three milers in an NCAA race were 3.8, 4.0, and 4.2 minutes. Their average speed would be calculated by summing up the three numbers and dividing by 3 for an average speed of 4 minutes per mile.

footnote continued, p. 221

Decreasing Costs

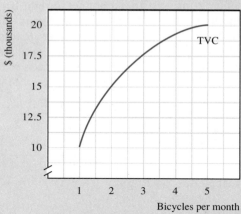

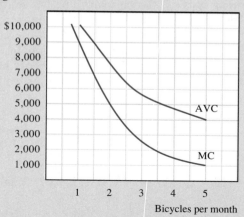

Constant Costs

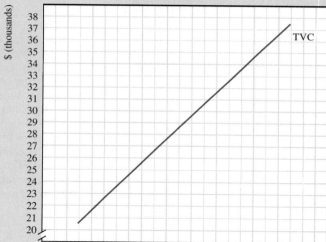

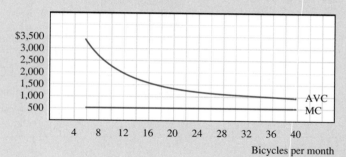

MicroBits 7.1 continued

Constant (Marginal) Costs

Section B of the table suggests that neither decreasing nor increasing costs occur. Instead, over the 6 to 40 assembly range, output increases but marginal costs remain constant, as is evident both from the table and the two lower figures showing constant marginal costs. (Can you explain why AVC still falls, even though MC is steady? _____ §)

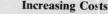
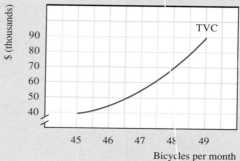

Increasing Costs

Increasing (Marginal) Costs

Section C of the table, like Table 7.1, takes the opposite tack: instead of TVC rising at a diminishing rate, it rises at an increasing rate. MC is increasing, as is AVC, being pulled up by the higher MC. The figures to the right portray these relationships.

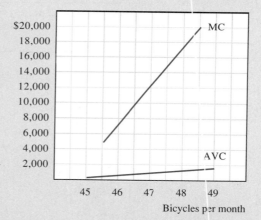

Now add the time of fourth miler across the line, who was clocked in at 4.6, a marginal number that is larger than the average. Recompute the average; it's gone up to 4.15. On the other hand, had we added a number that was smaller than the average, say, the first three runners and the speed of a horse who did the mile at 2.0 minutes, the average, 14/4 = 3.5, would fall. Finally, add the time of a biker, who is clocked precisely at 3.5 minutes, to the array of numbers. The total rises to 17.5, and the average, 17.5/5 = 3.5. In short, if the marginal is more than the average, the average will rise; if the marginal is less than the average, the average will fall; and if the marginal equals the average, the average will neither rise nor fall.

§ In line with the preceding footnote, as long as the marginal lies below the average, the average will fall.

Diminishing, Constant, and Increasing Marginal Costs: Fitting the Parts Together

The figures on page 222 combine the three sections of the table into a single, comprehensive set of cost curves. The TVC rises first at a diminishing rate, then at a constant rate, then at an increasing rate. In other words, production first becomes more efficient, driving down marginal and average costs. As output increases, efficiency remains constant, keeping marginal costs constant. Finally, further production increases

MicroBits 7.1 continued

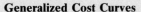

Generalized Cost Curves

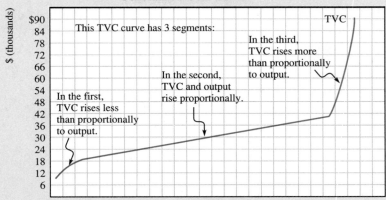

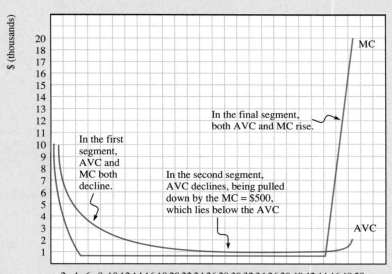

lead to reduced efficiency, forcing up both marginal and average costs.

What does all of this mean to the firm? Of course, the cost relationships in each individual firm depend on the particular structure of the resources used by the firm, the technology available to it, and the costs of the inputs. Nevertheless, it's quite likely that the final figure describes a broad array of cost-output relationships. After all, the shape of

MicroBits 7.1 continued

the figure does say something about the economics of operations. To take the constant cost section of the table first, it's plausible to assume that many manufacturing techniques exhibit some flexibility in operation. Thus, the speed of the bicycle assembly line may depend on the number of employees used in the assembly process. Having fewer workers means a slower line; having more employees permits the line to be speeded up sufficiently to compensate for the increased labor costs. Marginal costs would then remain the same.

But there may well be an initial section of diminishing costs. It's clear that if the demands on the firm are for 5 and not 20 bicycles daily, the assembly line will not be used very efficiently. It might be slowed up somewhat and a worker or two might be laid off. But it's unlikely that the 50 percent output reduction will lead to cost reductions of 50 percent when the firm is already down to a skeletal crew. And the reverse is true: As production picks up, the assembly line can swing back into capacity operation by speeding up slightly and hiring back the laid-off workers. The additional costs will be small: declining marginal costs.

The fact that some factor is fixed means that ultimately production efficiency will be inhibited. There is a limit to how fast the assembly line can be run without affecting the output, no matter how many additional workers can be added. In the extreme, you simply run out of physical space to fit people along the line. But even before that, the firm will experience diminishing returns and increased costs.

Thus, a cost curve that shows decreasing, constant, and increasing costs has conceptual validity. Whether it's also empirically true is a matter for discussion later in this chapter.

Table 7.2 and Figure 7.6a eliminate the constant MC segment of the final figure in MicroBits 7.1, leaving only the curve's initial segment, with costs rising less than proportionally to output, and the final segment, in which costs rise more rapidly than output.

A second important change is also introduced: since we're observing the short run, fixed costs have been included. Both Table 7.2 and Figure

TABLE 7.2   The Family of Total Cost Curves

Output (1)	TFC (2)	TVC (3)	TC (4) = (3) + (1)	MC (5)	AFC (6)	AVC (7)	ATC (8) = (6) + (7)
0	$1,000	$ 0	$ 1,000	$ 0	$ α	$	$ α
10	1,000	6,500	7,500	650	100	—	750
20	1,000	—	13,000	—	50	600	—
22	1,000	13,244	14,244	622	45.45	602	647.45
25	1,000	15,312.50	16,312.50	690	40	612.50	652.50
30	—	—	20,500	—	—	—	—
40	1,000	32,000	33,000	1,250	25	800	825

FIGURE 7.6   The Family of Total Cost Curves: A Generalization

a.   The total cost curve

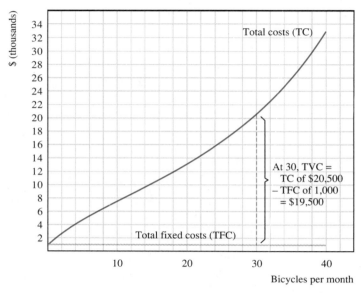

a. This smooth TC curve contains a segment of diminishing
costs and another of increasing costs. The TC itself is a
constant TFC plus a rising TVC.

b.   Average and marginal cost curves

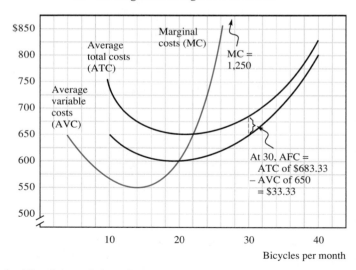

b. The shape of the TC curve above results in U-shaped ATC,
AVC, and MC curves, with the MC cutting both the AVC
and the ATC at their respective minima.

Total fixed costs (TFC) are the costs associated with the fixed factor of production. **Total costs (TC)** = TFC + TVC. **Average fixed costs (AFC)** equal total fixed costs divided by output. **Average total costs (ATC)** = TC/Q = AFC + AVC.

7.6 add **total fixed costs (TFC)** of $1,000 (Col. 2 in Table 7.2 and Figure 7.6a). **Total costs (TC),** the sum of fixed and variable costs, now appear as Column 4 in the table and the rising curve in Figure 7.6a. The MC remains as it was in MicroBits 7.1, since marginal costs are related to variable, not fixed, costs. Columns 6, 7, and 8 list some derived costs—**average fixed costs (AFC),** average variable costs, and the sum of the two, **average total costs (ATC).** (Some entries in Table 7.2 have been left blank for you to complete. See the Notes and Answers section for the correct answers.[8]) The corresponding ATC, AVC, and MC curves are traced out in Figure 7.6b.[9]

The differences between Figure 7.6 and Figure 7.5 are worth specifying:

- Whereas Figure 7.5a's curve is labeled TVC, Figure 7.6a labels the curve Total costs (TC). The TC curve, of course, is the sum of the labeled Total fixed cost line (TFC) and the implicit TVC curve. (You can calculate TVC by subtracting TFC from TC; one such TVC is indicated on the diagram.)
- The presence of fixed costs means that even when the firm is not producing any bicycles, costs are $1,000. So, the TC begins at $1,000, unlike the TVC, which begins at $0.
- The distinction between total costs and total variable costs in the upper diagram implies a corresponding difference in the lower between ATC and AVC. By definition, that difference is average fixed costs, which take a very specific shape. (See MicroBits 7.2.)
- While, as just noted, TVC is only implicit in Figure 7.6a, it is the AFC that is implied in Figure 7.6b. Notice the narrowing of the ATC and AVC curves as output increases. But the distance between the ATC and the AVC is nothing more than the AFC. (Again, an AFC point is noted in the figure.)
- The MC curve represents first decreasing and then increasing costs; it is neither always rising as in Figure 7.5b nor showing a constant returns segment as in the final figure in MicroBits 7.1.
- *The MC cuts the AVC at the lowest point of the AVC curve.*[10] A geometrical explanation for this is provided in MicroBits 7.3.
- *The MC also cuts the ATC at the minimum point of the ATC curve.* The reasoning is identical to that underlying the relationship between the MC and the AVC.
- However, the minimum point of the ATC occurs at a larger output and so lies to the right of the minimum value of the AVC. That's because at least for some units of output, the rising AVC is offset by a falling AFC. As output continues to increase, the impact of the declining AFC gets ever weaker and soon is overwhelmed by the rising AVC. That ultimately forces up the ATC.

MicroBits 7.2

Average Fixed Costs

The relationship of AFC to output—notice how the numbers in Table 7.2's Column 6 always diminish as output increases—should be understood, for it has economic meaning beyond mere arithmetic. (The arithmetic reason lies in the definition of AFC: since TFC, the numerator, is constant, and output, the denominator, is continually increasing, AFC must continuously fall.*) The economic interpretation can be summed up in the term *spreading the overhead*.

Consider the bicycle manufacturer's $1,000 rent, which is due whether the assembly line is operating or not. If only a single bike is assembled, the entire $1,000 is allo-

---

* The exact shape of the AFC is a rectangular hyperbola, based on the definition: $AFC = TFC/Q$. An interesting property of the rectangular hyperbola occurs when you multiply any two coordinates; the product of any multiplication always equals the same number. In this case, of course, multiply any AFC by its coordinate Q, and the result will be the constant TFC.

Bicycles per month

cated to that bicycle. However, if the company assembles 25 bicycles, then the $1,000 overhead is shared among the 25, with each one contributing $40 toward the rent. With 40 units produced, the share of each is only $25. So, the larger the volume produced, the broader the overhead can be spread. The figure here plots AFC: the larger the output, the smaller the AFC.

For a variety of reasons, it is neater to work with the U-shaped cost curves in the chapters that follow. The U shape also has some theoretical validity. Microtheorists believe that the presence of fixed resources in the short run ultimately forces marginal costs upward. These increased costs have their counterpart in decreasing costs at low levels of output, where the fixed resources are in a sense underutilized. At some level of production, the variable inputs will mesh perfectly with the fixed input. That combination of fixed and variable costs will yield the lowest possible costs of production. That's the bottom of the U-shaped average total cost curve.

Note that the constraint imposed by fixed costs disappears in the long run, to which we now turn.

The Geometry of Marginal and Average Costs

Examine the dark purple total variable cost curve in the figure here and calculate the AVC at $Q = 30$. (Divide TVC = 19,500 by 30, which equals 650.) To reach the identical result geometrically, construct a right-angled triangle, where one side is 19,500, the other

The Geometry of AVC and MC Curves

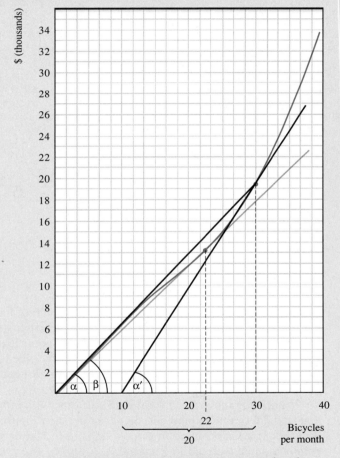

The AVC of any point is calculated by computing the value of the tangent of a line connecting the origin with the TVC (e.g., $\tan \alpha$). The MC of any point is derived by drawing a tangent to the TVC at that point and calculating the tangent of that tangent (e.g., $\tan \alpha'$).

MicroBits 7.3 continued

side is 30, and the hypotenuse connects the origin with 19,500. Since the tangent of an angle equals the opposite over the adjacent, then tan α = 19,500/30, which is the AVC. To generalize, the tangent of any angle drawn from the origin to a point on the TVC curve equals the AVC.

The MC is the slope of the TVC. To find the slope geometrically, draw a line that is tangent to the point on the TVC curve whose slope you want to determine and calculate the tangent of the tangent. Angle α' in the figure is obtained by drawing the tangent at TVC = 19,500. The tangent of angle α' = 19,500/20 = 975. At Q = 30, the MC is greater than the AVC.

Now take a look at β (light purple), which is the angle obtained by drawing a line from the origin that is tangent to the TVC. What can you conclude about this construction?

You should be able to see that angle β tells us two things simultaneously: Because the line forming β connects the TVC with the origin, tan β = AVC. But because that line is also tangent to the TVC, tan β = MC. So at Q = 22, MC = AVC.

If you were to construct other angles on this diagram, you'd discover that at points on the TVC to the right of Q = 22 (such as Q = 30), the AVC is greater than the AVC at 22. Similarly, points to the left of Q = 22 also will show that the AVC is greater than the AVC at 22. So this AVC curve must be U-shaped, bottoming out at Q = 22. And that's exactly the point that the AVC = the MC. Obviously, the MC cuts the AVC at its lowest point.

Long-Run Costs

Economies of Scale

Recall that the long run is defined by the absence of fixed costs; all costs are variable. That being the case, the isoquant-isocost technique used in connection with the car wash earlier in this chapter is appropriate for the long run. In the long run, Brad is not stuck with Spike for two hours daily. He can send Spike home or require him to work longer hours. In the long run, Brad finds both capital and labor variable.

What happens to Brad's costs as he varies both inputs? If you assume that both labor and capital cost $8 per hour, then Figure 7.7 returns you to Figure 7.3; your penciled-in isocost lines in the latter should be identical with the ones depicted in Figure 7.7.

An **expansion path** connects the isoquant-isocost tangency points for any given set of prices. It relates the quantity—and implicitly, the cost—of inputs to output as production increases.

Table 7.3 takes some of the tangency points that lie along the **expansion path** in Figure 7.7 and inserts the appropriate numbers in Columns 1, 2, and 3. Column 4 calculates the total costs of using the specified number of inputs at $8 an hour. The average and marginal cost values are derived by methods now familiar to you. (If you're not quite sure, check back to Table 7.1. As a self-test, fill in the blanks in this table.[11])

FIGURE 7.7   The Expansion Path

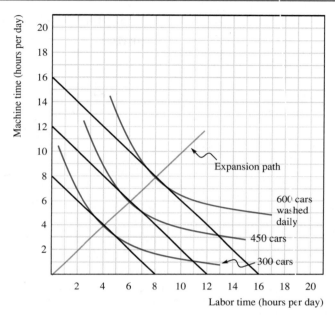

For any given set of relative prices, shifting outlays will generate new tangencies. The locus of these tangencies is the expansion path, which indicates the relationship of output to simultaneous changes in all productive factors.

You recall from Chapter 6 that the car wash production function was a Cobb-Douglas production function exhibiting constant returns to scale: equiproportionate increases in all inputs led to equiproportionate increments in output. The long-run total cost curve analogue is represented by Figure 7.8a, while the ATC and MC curves, which are horizontal and

TABLE 7.3   Output and Long-Run Costs in a Car Wash

Labor Input (1)	Capital Input (2)	Output (3)	Total Costs (4)	Average Costs (5)	Marginal Costs (6)
1	1	45	$16	$.21	$ 0
2	2	150	32	.21	.21
3	3	225	—	—	.21
4	4	—	64	—	.21
5	5	—	—	—	—
6	6	450	96	.21	.21

FIGURE 7.8   Long-Run Car Wash Costs

a.   Total costs in the long run

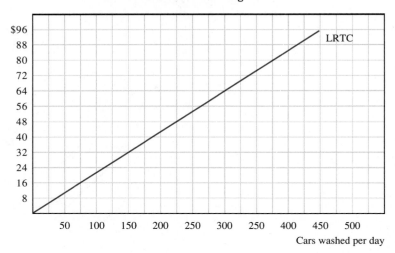

a.   A long-run total cost curve that exhibits constant returns to scale will increase at a constant rate.

b.   Average and marginal costs in the long run

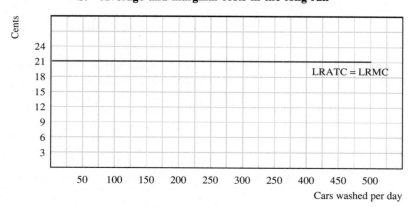

b.   Under constant returns to scale the LRATC and the LRMC will be constant and equal. Greater production facilities have no advantage over smaller ones.

FIGURE 7.9   Long-Run and Short-Run Costs: The Envelope Curve

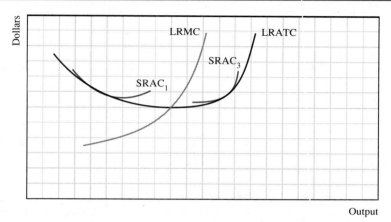

The lowest production cost for any given output occurs at the
tangency of the short-run and long-run average cost curves.

equal, are found in Figure 7.8b. (The "LR" attached to the curves signifies "long run.")

Of course, production functions need not exhibit constant returns to scale; they may show either increasing or decreasing returns to scale. The corresponding long-run average cost curves will then either be continuously decreasing or increasing. It is equally possible to construct long-run cost curves characterized by both economies and diseconomies of scale, in which case the long-run average cost curve will appear as in Figure 7.9. (Disregard for the moment the other curves in the diagram.) MicroBits 7.4 suggests why the long-run average cost curve turns upward.

MICROBITS 7.4

Economies and Diseconomies of Scale

Is there an underlying logic for economies and diseconomies of scale? The reasoning must differ from that of increasing and diminishing costs, which hinge upon the constraints fixed inputs impose upon cooperating variable factors. But why should a producer, having discovered the optimum scale of production, not simply repeat that scale over and over again and so never encounter diseconomies of scale?

To answer this question requires us first to distinguish two types of scale effects: plant and firm.

Economies at the Plant Level

Let's deal with the plant first. It is certainly legitimate to wonder whether operating costs change as the size of a factory or store changes. Is a larger factory more efficient in the production of a given type of output—be it tires, records, soft drinks, or shotgun pellets—than a smaller one? The accepted answer is, Yes, but not forever. Economies of scale do exist, but they cannot always be exploited. Similarly, diseconomies of scale can arise at the plant level.

Economies of Scale.   As plant size increases, average costs fall for one or more of the following reasons:

• *Specialization.* A larger plant permits the utilization of job-specific workers and machinery. That reduces costs either because by repetition employees become more adept at their particular task or because management can better allocate employees with different skills to jobs more suited to their individual qualities. Similarly, machines that are designed for one task tend to be both cheaper to acquire and operate than more flexible capital equipment.

• *Technology.* Only in plants capable of handling a large scale of production will it make economic sense to use modern high-speed machinery.

• *Physical relationships.* Double the diameter of an oil pipeline or the walls of a warehouse: What happens to throughput or storage space? You understand that both expand more than proportionally merely because of the nature of the

laws of physics. (Engineers use the ".6 rule" for calculating cost increases as capacity expands: A piece of equipment such as a storage tank that is twice as large as a smaller one costs only .6 more.)

• *Input integration.* Say one machine can optimally produce 30,000 containers a day, while a second machine can stuff tennis balls into 50,000 containers a day. You'll need two container-making machines to keep the packaging machine working full-time, but you'll then waste some of the capability of the former. On the other hand, if you were to produce 150,000 tennis balls, you could integrate the two types of capital: Use five container assemblers and three ball stuffers.

Economies of scale even at the plant level cannot always be achieved. The producer would be foolish to take advantage of the possible technical economies of scale when the market is too small to digest the output of even a single optimum-sized plant.

Decreasing Returns to Scale.   At the plant level, long-run average costs rise for a very simple reason: When you continuously increase the size of a plant while increasing correspondingly other cooperating inputs, you run into costs related to physical size. The simultaneous assembly of many giant cargo or passenger planes, for example, typically occurs under one roof, even though each plane is put together at a fixed site within the plant. Consequently, all parts have to be brought to the plane, from wing components to toilet seats. As the size of the plant expands, the parts have to travel farther and farther within the plant, requiring time and labor merely to move them to the proper site. In other words, at some point in at least some types of production, as plant size expands,

MicroBits 7.4 continued

costs related to the very size of the plant rise. Smaller plants minimize these distance problems.

Scale and the Firm

Why not resolve plant diseconomies of scale by building many small-size plants at a number of different sites? (Assemble aircraft in two plants, each with a 20-plane capacity, rather than in one plant with a capacity of 40 planes.) This possibility leads to the second issue: scale in the multiplant firm. Can firm size increase without engendering additional costs? Or, to put it differently, what is the most efficient *firm* size?

The plethora of multiplant firms suggests that economies of scale at the firm level do exist. Even though plant economies may be exhausted, the cloning of plants combined with a central management would appear to be cost-effective in many instances.

Yet the optimal size of the firm, like that of the plant, is limited. Many economists be-

lieve that plant reproduction cannot proceed indefinitely. They point out that the larger the firm becomes, the more difficult it is to manage. Multiplant firms require a layer of management at the plant level and a second layer of central management to ensure coordinated policies. Moreover, managers must spend time integrating operations at the various sites. And the more layers of management that have to approve decisions, the more time it will take for such decisions to be made. Decision making also suffers because those who establish overall policy and those who implement it at the plant level may be operating on different wavelengths. Slower and more inefficient decisions may well be the result. Thus, firms, too, suffer from diseconomies of scale.

Economies of Scale in the United States

While it is difficult to generalize about the shape of the long-run cost curve that would hold true across all industries, it is neverthe-

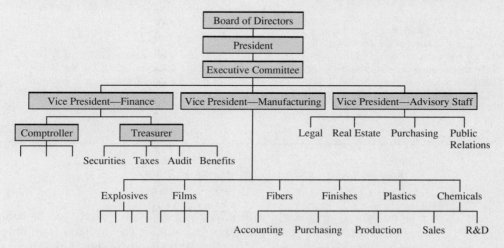

SOURCE: Adapted from Alfred D. Chandler, Jr., *The Visible Hand* (Boston: Harvard University Press, 1977), p. 458.

less inviting to speculate. Consider the frequency of the multiplant firm in the United States, be it in industries such as basic materials and household appliances or in services such as supermarket chains or branch bank systems. At the least, one can argue that management sees some value to operating a number of plants rather than building sufficiently large factories or shops to house all operations under one roof.

This argument is suggestive but hardly conclusive. The reasons corporate leaders opt for multiplant firms may be unrelated to diseconomies of scale. Even though the many plants are more costly to operate, the firm may still decide on the multiplant route because it saves in other ways, such as through risk diversification or minimizing transport costs.

At the firm level, diseconomies of scale may at least be partly responsible for the multidivisional structure, or M-form, that characterizes large U.S. corporations.* In contrast to the functionally organized and centralized unitary structure of corporate governance, or U-form, the M-form decentralizes decision making by dividing the firm into separate divisions. As is evident in the accompanying organization chart of a chemical corporation, the manufacturing end of the company is partitioned into divisions—chemicals, explosives, and so on—each one of which is responsible for developing, manufacturing, and selling its products. Each division, as far as operations are concerned, is virtually a separate company with managers exercising a great deal of autonomy on decisions that affect only their division's activities. On the other hand, functions that involve a number of divisions and hence require companywide coordination (such as securities, employee benefit programs, corporate public relations, or legal matters) are relegated to a higher level in the hierarchy. Thus, the M-form, by decentralizing where possible, seeks to avoid the coordination costs associated with immensity. Whether it accomplishes this goal remains unproven.§

---

* Alfred D. Chandler, Jr., in *Strategy and Structure: Chapters in the History of the Industrial Enterprise* (Cambridge, Mass.: MIT Press, 1972), first pointed out the importance of this management innovation in this book on the historical development of the M-form in the United States.

§ See Henry O. Armour and David J. Teece, "Organization Structure and Economic Performance: A Test of the Multidivisional Hypothesis," *Bell Journal of Economics* 9, no. 1 (Spring 1978), pp. 106–22.

The Relationship between Short-Run and Long-Run Cost Curves*

The firm always starts with a long-run decision: What type of commitments should the entrepreneurs undertake? The horizon is infinite, so when Brad initially plans labor and capital inputs for his car wash, he does

---

* This section is of above-average difficulty and may be skipped with no loss of continuity.

so without any constraints. That, as you have seen, gives rise to the family of long-run curves, which are also called **planning curves**. It certainly seems reasonable to presume that Brad has some sense of how many cars are going to be run through the wash daily, and so he can identify the relevant isoquant. And, given the costs of the inputs at $8 an hour for both labor and machine time, Brad can plan to operate on a specific tangency point on the isoquant. Assume that he believes that the daily volume will be 300 vehicles, leading him to plan using four hours each of machine and labor time each day, an equilibrium point in Figure 7.7. This is also consistent with a point on his long-run total, average, and marginal cost curves in Figure 7.8, which is reproduced in Figure 7.10.

So far so good. Now, imagine that Brad has been either too optimistic or too cautious, and actual demand for car washes is less or more. Since Brad has leased car wash equipment on a four-hour-per-day basis, he has locked himself into fixed costs of $32 daily. Brad can, however, vary labor time, using either less labor should fewer than 300 cars come to the wash or more labor should he face a stronger demand.

Doesn't the decision to expand or decrease output when some costs are committed move the firm into the short-run mode? The car wash production function grid on page 181 permits you to trace out the relationship between fixed machine time at four hours and the output derived from that fixed input as labor time is varied. The first two rows of Table 7.4 are based on that grid; the remaining lines calculate the short-run costs associated with the different numbers of cars washed as the $8 per hour labor input is increased.

A set of short-run cost curves is derived from this table and plotted in Figure 7.10 (SRTC, SRAC, SRMC). Note that at every point except one, the short-run total and average cost curves lie above the respective long-run cost curves. The only point at which the short- and long-run curves touch is at an output of 300 cars washed, for a total cost of $64.

This relationship between the short-run and long-run cost curves is not coincidental and is steeped with economic meaning. Let's say you

TABLE 7.4   **Short-Run Costs in a Car Wash**

Labor input	1	2	3	4	5	6	7	8	9	10
Cars washed	150	212	260	300	335	367	397	424	450	474
Labor costs	$ 8	$ 16	$ 24	$ 32	$ 40	$ 48	$ 56	$ 64	$ 72	$ 80
Fixed costs	$ 32	$ 32	$ 32	$ 32	$ 32	$ 32	$ 32	$ 32	$ 32	$ 32
Total costs	$ 40	$ 48	$ 56	$ 64	$ 72	$ 80	$ 88	$ 96	$104	$112
MC (cents)	5.3	12.9	16.6	20	22.8	25	26.6	29.6	30.7	33.3
AVC (cents)	5.3	7.5	9.2	10.4	11.9	13	14.1	15	16	16.8
AFC (cents)	21.3	15	12.3	10.6	9.5	8.7	8	7.5	7.1	6.7
ATC (cents)	26.6	22.5	21.5	21	21.4	21.7	22.1	22.5	23.1	23.5

FIGURE 7.10 Car Wash Costs in the Short and Long Run

a. Total costs

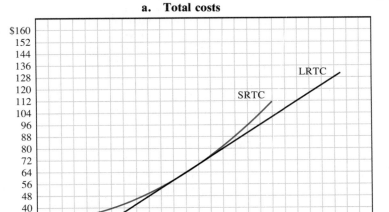

a. Because of fixed costs, the short-run total cost curve is higher than the long-run total cost curve except at the point where output = 300. So, although the short-run total cost curve represents efficient operation given existing fixed commitments, it is usually possible to reduce costs further once those commitments are no longer binding.

b. Average and marginal costs

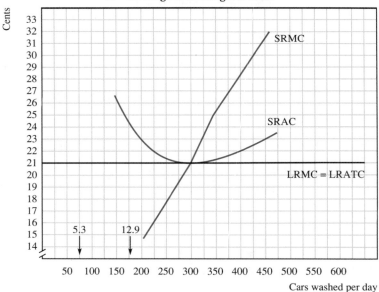

b. The short-run average cost curve exceeds the long-run average cost curve except at output = 300 for the same reason that the short-run total cost curve is greater than the long-run total cost curve.

236

decide that Brad really anticipates only 150 cars passing through his car wash daily. Would you recommend that Brad employ four hours of machine time and one hour of labor time, as Column 1 in Table 7.4 suggests is possible? Certainly not, for the $40 cost per day indicated by the short-run total cost curve in Figure 7.10a, or 27 cents average cost per car apparent on the *SRAC* curve in Figure 7.10b, is not the cheapest way to wash 150 cars. You can see in both parts of the diagram that the long-run cost curve lies below the $40 and 26.6 cent respective costs. Indeed, you could drive down total costs to $32 and average costs to 21 cents by changing your combination of inputs: use two hours of labor time and two hours of machine time instead of the four capital, one labor combination.

Why, then, if only 150 cars begin to show up daily, doesn't Brad switch? The answer, of course, is that he's already committed to use four machine hours; the $32 is a fixed cost. Calculate for yourself how much it would cost Brad if he were to cut back his machine time to two hours and use two hours labor time instead of the four-K, one-L combination he now uses. _____ 12

In short, if you can start anew, the planning curve tells you the cheapest possible production cost for any given output. For, in the long run, you can combine your factors of production to minimize your input costs. But once you've undertaken fixed costs, the long-run options are no longer relevant. You must now work with these commitments and focus on how best to operate in the short run. Now it is the short-run cost curves that indicate how to minimize costs for a given output level.

You understand of course that an infinite number of short-run cost curves exists, each curve depending on the extent of fixed costs. Just to convince yourself of the truth of this proposition and to bring home once again the lessons of the preceding paragraph, calculate the short-run costs for Brad's operation assuming that he has contracted for only two hours of machine time rather than four. Reproduce Table 7.4 and plot the points on Figure 7.10. Your diagram should clearly show that short-run costs are higher than long-run costs except at the output of 150 cars washed. See also if you can explain the relationships between your presently constructed set of cost curves and the short-run curves that already exist in the diagram. The revised table and diagram appear in the Notes and Answers section[13] at the end of the chapter.

Recap

Economists remain enamored with both U-shaped long-run and short-run average and marginal cost curves. Refer back to Figure 7.9, which plots a set of short-run average cost (SRAC) curves against a pair of long-run average cost (LRATC) and long-run marginal cost (LRMC) curves. Notice how the short-run curves snuggle into the long-run curves, or, in the less picturesque jargon of the profession, are enveloped by the LRATC curve. At one point, the two curves are identical, but at all other points, short-run costs lie higher. Note, too, that the relationship between ATC and MC holds: The LRMC cuts the LRATC curve at the bottom of the LRATC. (Draw in the SRATC$_2$ curve that meets the LRMC = LRATC intersection.)

But, as you've read, theory does not mandate that either long-run or short-run cost curves be U-shaped. Short-run curves can be characterized throughout by diminishing, constant, or increasing costs, while long-run curves can exhibit economies or diseconomies of scale exclusively. The precise shape of the cost curves needs to be discovered by examining firms and industries, a taste of which is provided in the next section.

Demystifying Empirical Cost Curves

Should the courts have demolished AT&T's telephone monopoly? Should the government permit IBM to continue dominating the computer market? Can small banks survive without government regulations that prevent large banks from swallowing smaller ones? To a very important extent, the answers to these normative economic queries depend on the cost structure of the industry, as you will discover in the next few chapters. But it is not the theoretical cost curves developed so far that matter. Those who make public policy need to know the specific cost curves in the particular industry under discussion.

In principle, estimating cost curves is no different from attempting to calculate demand curves or production functions. In practice, however, econometricians have their work cut out for them. The purposes of this section are (1) to introduce you to some of the results obtained from applying econometric techniques to cost-output relationships and (2) to make you aware of the problems faced by the researchers in seeking to estimate both short- and long-run cost curves.

Is there an alternative to econometrics? Most researchers in cost studies would say no. But MicroBits 7.5 reports the results of a survey that suggest otherwise.

Short-Run Cost Curves

Joel Dean, the father of the empirical study of cost curves, began his seminal studies in the 1930s. They remain a symbol of clarity, although the degree of sophistication of such studies has progressed substantially in the past half century. Dean also possessed the foresight to work with products that lent themselves to empirical estimation; the next case is just one example.

The Belt Factory.[14]   A less complicated production setting than a belt factory is hard to find, especially if you're dealing only with finished strips

The Shape of the Average Total Cost Curve as Seen by Businesspersons

Back in the early 1950s, University of Michigan Professor William J. Eiteman and G. E. Guthrie, a graduate student there, suggested that engineers designed factories so that they could operate at minimum cost when used to capacity, capacity being defined as the "greatest physical output possible."* At operation levels of less than capacity, costs per unit would rise and might be considerably higher at very low operating levels. Eiteman and Guthrie tested their hypotheses by sending out to businesspersons a sheet with the eight short-run cost curves that appear below, asking them to select the curve they thought best described their firm's average cost curve.

Examine each curve. The first and the second show the ATC rising right from the start, although the rates of increase differ. The third through the sixth are U-shaped, differing basically in the location of the point of minimum ATC. (Costs turn up more quickly as capacity is approached in the fifth figure than in the sixth.) The seventh figure portrays decreasing costs throughout, while the last demonstrates decreasing costs initially, followed by constant costs for most of the operating levels.

What did the survey show? Consider the following breakdown of the 334 respondents:

Figure number	1	2	3	4	5	6	7	8
Number of respondents	0	0	1	3	14	113	203	0

Clearly, the vast majority felt that decreasing costs were pervasive either throughout the entire operation or through most of it. Eiteman and Guthrie's hypothesis was apparently borne out by the results of their survey.

* "The Shape of the Average Cost Curve," *American Economic Review* 42, no. 5 (December 1952), pp. 832–38.

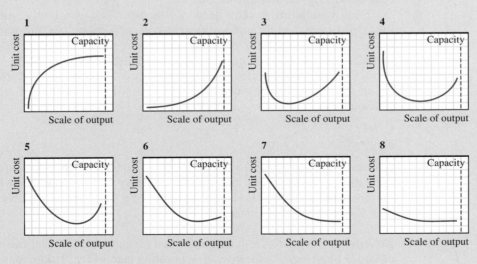

of leather without the buckle. Dean was able to calculate a simple regression equation that described the relationship between costs, number of belts, and belt weight:

$$TC = -60{,}178 + 0.77Q + 70{,}181.30W$$

where Q stands for the quantity of belts and W for their average weight. The linear relationship between output (Q) and total costs is both evident from the equation and from Figure 7.11, which depicts one of Dean's cost curve sets. Notice that average costs decline as quantity produced increases. Johnston, studying the generation of electricity, also found constant marginal costs and falling ATC[15], a result not uncommon in short-run cost studies.

MicroQuery   Given the constant MC in the lower panel, (a) what is the AVC? and (b) why is the ATC falling continuously? (a) _____ (b) _____

[16]

Costs and Cobb-Douglas Production Functions.   A substantially different cost curve shape is implicit in the Cobb-Douglas production functions mentioned in Chapter 6. The diminishing returns to horsepower in the oil pipeline case and to capital and labor in both the original Cobb-Douglas study and Moroney's survey all point to increasing costs right from the start. These cost functions are identical in shape to the short-run car wash cost curves developed in this chapter.

Such conflicting results need not be troubling. Certainly, different industries may operate under different cost conditions, so that no single pattern need be true for every case. Yet a good number of economists are troubled by the lack of consensus. They base their skepticism on the serious empirical issues faced in estimating cost curves. But before moving to the problems, first consider some empirical estimates of long-run cost curves.

Long-Run Cost Curves

Studies of economies and diseconomies of scale are often based on examining different plants or firms of different sizes and determining whether the costs of operating the larger ones are less than, equal to, or greater than those of smaller businesses.

Electricity.   Johnston's study mentioned earlier also looked at the impact of larger plant size on the cost of generating electricity. Taking data from

FIGURE 7.11   Partial Regressions of Total, Average, and Marginal Combined Cost on Output: Leather Belt Shop

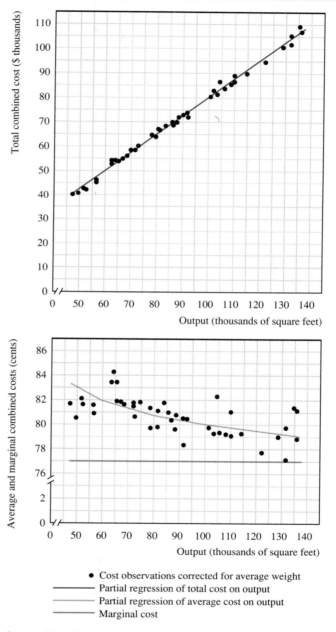

● Cost observations corrected for average weight
——— Partial regression of total cost on output
……… Partial regression of average cost on output
——— Marginal cost

SOURCE: Dean, *Relation of Cost to Output for a Leather Belt Shop*, p. 27.

73 coal-using British generating plants, Johnston estimated a long-run total cost curve whose shape is described as follows:

$$TC = 132.3 + 2.6387Q$$

where TC is in thousands of dollars and Q is in millions of kilowatts. The long-run average cost curve that results from this equation is reproduced in Figure 7.12.

Actually, the L-shaped LRATC curve is not surprising in electrical generation; production of electricity is subject to the "physical relationships" reason for economies of scale noted in MicroBits 7.4. Increasing the capacity of an electrical production plant normally involves using larger generators. And the nature of generating technology is such that bigger generators produce more kilowatts per hour than smaller generators at a less-than-proportionate increase in construction and operating costs.

Banking.   Commercial banking in the United States is composed of a small number of multinational giants, a second layer of large institutions that are important either nationally or regionally, and a very broad base of

FIGURE 7.12   Long-Run Average Costs in the British Electrical Generating Industry

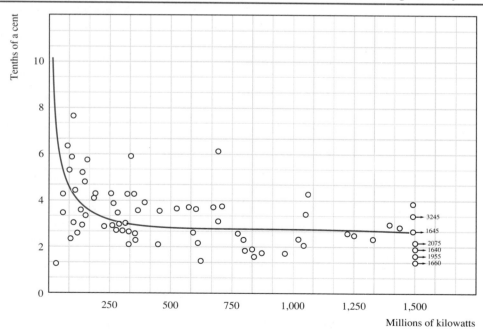

SOURCE: J. Johnston, *Statistical Cost Analysis* (New York: McGraw-Hill, 1960), p. 70.

small, localized institutions. Studies of economies of scale in banking seek to discover whether the larger banks run their operations more efficiently than the smaller institutions do. In general, studies conducted between the 1950s and 1970s reported that the LRATC curve declines as bank size increases up to the $25 to $50 million deposit range and remains steady thereafter. However, rarely was there sufficient data to reach any conclusion about the banking giants. Using more powerful econometric techniques, some investigators in the 1980s confirm the older studies. Others suggest that a U-shaped LRATC would be more appropriate. Unlike electrical generation, however, none of the theoretical reasons mentioned in MicroBits 7.4 can convincingly explain why a larger bank is likely to be more efficient than a smaller one.[17]

Problems in Empirical Studies of Cost Curves

The division of opinion about economies of scale in banking arises partly from problems particular to banking and similar industries and partly to general empirical issues. You can well understand how banking differs from all previous examples. A belt is a belt and a kilowatt hour is a kilowatt hour. But what does a bank produce? Simply defining the output of a bank is contentious. Think about it. Does a bank produce loans, deposit services, paper flows? Does it do all of these things and more? Moreover, a bank is undeniably a multiservice operation. When comparing different multiservice or multiproduct firms, you want to be sure to identify only cost differences that are based on size rather than on differences in product mix. Unfortunately, that's easier said than done.

Yet even for the single product firm, empirical cost estimation is an uncertain business. The data provided by firms are rarely gathered for cost analysis reasons. (Normally, cost data are needed by the firm's accountants for tax and other financial purposes.) Econometric modelers are particularly vexed by the treatment of depreciation and joint costs. Accountants rarely relate depreciation to actual plant and equipment usage. And the allocation of joint costs that are attributable to a number of products (such as general overhead costs and management) is infrequently done on the basis of economic rationale. Yet the econometrician estimating cost functions for a particular product must know the actual input costs of that product. Recall, too, that economies of scale are defined for given prices and a given production function. Yet over time input prices are not constant, nor does technology remain static. The vital issue boils down to one question: Can the econometrician clean up the data to reveal a meaningful cost curve?

Conclusion

Do these empirical problems and the mixed results force economists to discard the U-shaped cost curve? Here's the conclusion reached by Professor A. A. Walters after a thoroughgoing survey of empirical production and cost functions:

> [While] the U-shaped hypothesis does not inspire great confidence . . . , this is *not* because it has been refuted by direct empirical evidence. . . . [T]here is no large body of data which convincingly contradicts the hypothesis of a U-shaped long run [average] cost curve and the fruitful results which depend on it.[18]

In short, the student of the firm will be wise to keep his or her mind open and avoid generalizations. The best course appears to be to treat each situation individually.

Keeping Down Costs: Some Applications

Cost curves play a critical role in the chapters that follow. So in this section, the examples used relate only to isoquant analysis. Three issues are introduced: why there's significant unemployment in less developed countries (LDCs), how new methods of production affect resource use, and how users of oil reacted to the decline in petroleum prices during the 1980s.

Western Technology and LDC Unemployment

It seems almost paradoxical that in less developed economies, a number of industries use capital-intensive methods rather than labor-intensive processes. After all, most LDCs are characterized by large populations, implying at least that labor should be the less expensive resource. Surely, then, businesses should opt for labor-intensive methods, as suggested by Figure 7.4 in connection with gold mining in Brazil.

An interesting hypothesis was proposed by Professor Richard S. Eckaus.[19] He argued that the technology used in LDCs stems primarily from the developed world and was designed for the economic conditions prevailing there. Consequently, when entrepreneurs in LDCs seek to improve productivity in their own spheres, they are faced with the capital-intensive methods developed in the West.

Take a look at the isoquant appearing in Figure 7.13; it's right-angled, as was the film isoquant in MicroBits 6.1 (p. 190). But its ray also lies on the capital-intensive side. (Check back to Figure 7.4 if you're not sure.) Now look at the isocost line. Even if it's very shallow, representing a low price of labor, tangency will still occur at the right angle, leaving you with a capital-intensive output. Thus, employers use little labor relative to capital even if capital is expensive and labor cheap.

Actually, the Eckaus hypothesis is plausible in such heavy industries as petroleum extraction and refining, steel making, automobile manufac-

FIGURE 7.13   **Fixed Input Isoquants and Unemployment in LDCs**

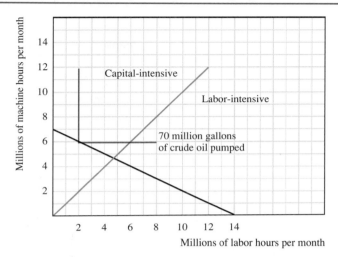

Even though an hour of capital is twice as expensive as an hour of labor, in equilibrium, the firm employs three times as many hours of capital as it does labor.

ture, and shipbuilding. Whether right-angled isoquants generally characterize LDC production choices is more debatable.

The paradox of high unemployment in LDCs can be resolved even if the isoquants retain their normal convexity by asserting that even in the third world labor is not cheap.

Two complementary reasons suggest why labor is expensive. First, the abundance of humans is not synonymous with cheap labor if the word *labor* implies a modicum of stable labor force behavior, a minimum degree of literacy, and a basic set of technical skills. If in fact the number of people possessing the necessary qualities and skills is limited and their wages reflect their scarcity, then labor may be more expensive than capital. Consequently, capital-intensive methods may be less costly production technologies even in the LDCs.

A second reason for labor being expensive stems from government policies that subsidize capital or that artificially raise labor costs. The cost of labor must include government-mandated fringe benefits and compensation for job loss. While such generosity benefits some workers, it simultaneously raises labor costs and discourages employment in the first place.

See for yourself. Figure 7.14 sketches out an isoquant for the production of bicycle gears that is convex, not right-angled. Draw in an isocost curve reflecting relatively more expensive labor costs, and indicate the

FIGURE 7.14   Variable Factor Proportions and Unemployment

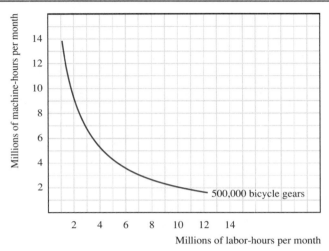

Draw in an isocost line with labor more expensive than capital. Would more labor time or machine time be utilized?

amount of labor and capital hours that would be used to produce 500,000 bicycle gears.[20]

Technological Change: The Modern Way to Pick Up Garbage

A **neutral technical change** occurs when the same inputs are used in the same proportions but output is larger.

Figure 7.15 deals with a case of **neutral technical change**, where the input proportions remain the same but the same quantity of input produces a larger quantity of output. Production continues along the initial ray, but instead of four acres and two tons of fertilizer producing 200 tons of avocados, the genetically modified trees yield 400 tons of avocados.

Neutral technical change is probably the exception. In most instances, not only will output increase, but technology will modify factor proportions as well. Technical change will then either be **capital-saving** or **labor-saving.**

When technical change is **capital-saving**, the new production method not only increases output but also uses relatively less capital to do so. On the other hand, when technical change is **labor-saving**, output increases and relatively less labor is employed.

Much of recent U.S. technology is labor-saving. The rise of containerization, where large containers, filled at the factory, are lifted aboard a ship rather than being loaded at the pier by stevedores, means that extra capital is spent on containers and on container-handling equipment. But the costs saved by not using expensive dockside workers more than compensate for the capital outlays. Similarly, more refined navigation equipment in modern airplanes has replaced the expensive human navigator.

Let's build on Figure 7.13, but modify it for the experience in the developed world. Garbage collection is typically a labor-intensive occupation, as indicated by the lower ray in Figure 7.16. Obviously, employers

FIGURE 7.15   Neutral Technical Change

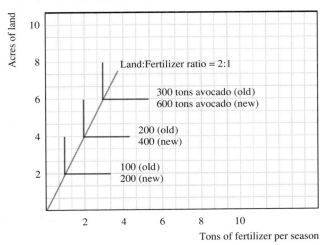

With neutral technical change, each isoquant takes on a higher value but the factor proportions remain the same.

FIGURE 7.16   Labor-Saving Technology in Garbage Collection

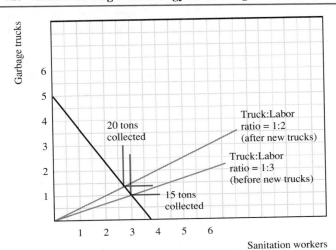

The introduction of new garbage trucks reduces the labor input relative to capital and also collects more trash for the same dollar outlay.

have a strong incentive to seek alternative production technologies that will reduce their reliance on expensive labor.

The challenge: to pick up more garbage, which seems to be expanding exponentially, while cutting back on labor.

The response: the two-person garbage truck. This more expensive piece of collecting equipment has a stronger compactor and a larger container, enabling two sanitation workers to do the work of three. Thus, a second ray that is less labor-intensive can be added to Figure 7.16, enabling the garbage-collection firm not only to obtain more output than before, but also to use less labor per unit of capital than before.[21] (On the same isocost line, more garbage is collected at the same cost.)

Oil to Gas: A Do-It-Yourself Problem

Most of the electricity generated in the United States comes from thermal plants that convert some fuel—coal, natural gas, oil, nuclear power—into electricity. Since about 10 percent of this electricity-generating capacity can use either gas or oil, a convex isoquant for electricity is appropriate. One such isoquant is sketched out in Figure 7.17. Table 7.5 lists the price of each fuel in millions of Btus (British thermal units, which is the amount of heat required to raise the temperature of one pound of water by one degree, and is the fundamental measure of energy) for 1970, three years before the first oil shock, and 1979, the year of the second oil shock. Draw two isocost lines on Figure 7.17, and then complete the quantity columns of Table 7.5 (Hint: Start the 1970 isocost line at 16 gas and the 1979 isocost line at 17.5 gas.)

The 1970 isocost curve has an inverse slope of 1.46, and so stretches from 16 gas to 11 petroleum, coming to tangency with the isoquant at about 8 gas and 5.5 oil. The 1979 isocost line is steeper, since the relative price of oil has increased. It stretches from 17.5 to 10, and the tangency occurs at about 10 gas and 4.3 oil. Clearly, as the relative price of oil rose, electric companies shifted from oil to gas.

TABLE 7.5   Generating Electricity

Year	Price of Oil*	Oil Consumption§	Price of Gas*	Gas Consumption§
1970	$0.41	—	$0.28	—
1979	$3.05	—	$1.74	—

* Price per billion Btus taken from the U.S. Energy Information Administration, *Annual Energy Review 1985*, p. 25.
§ In quadrillion (=1^{15}) Btus

FIGURE 7.17   Gas and Oil Usage in Electricity Production

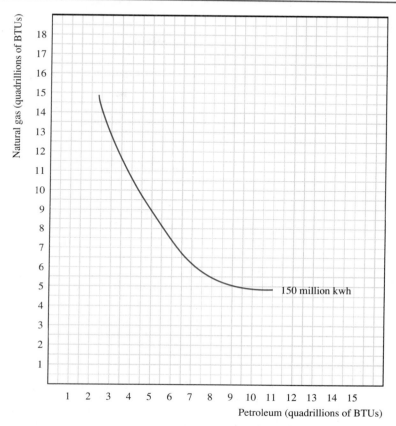

The use of gas and oil depends on the relative technical qualities of the fuels as given by the shape of the isoquant and their relative prices. Prices are given in Table 7.5. Your task: to find the optimal mix of gas and oil for 1970 and 1979.

Indeed, that's what happened. Before the two oil price shocks drove the price of oil skyward, utilities used more of the cheaper fuel, oil. Then as gas prices became relatively less expensive, the utilities increased their relative use of the now-cheaper natural gas and cut back on petroleum usage.

This scenario, like many in economics, is intuitive. Nevertheless, it's comforting to have intuition and analysis confirmed by real-life events. Doesn't this give you a little more confidence in microeconomic theory?

Uncertainty in Production: Flexible versus Dedicated Machinery

Until now, this chapter has assumed certainty. Management knew about the nature of the production function and relative prices, and thus the cost curves at all levels of production. Managers could identify the exact point where average costs are lowest, the bottom of the U-shaped ATC curve.

In reality, of course, such things are often murky. Knowledge about sales is also likely to be incomplete, so that production planning is equally uncertain. Yet long-run commitments have to be made despite uncertainty about the future.

Flexibility in production is one way of contending with uncertainty. By paying into an unemployment insurance fund that compensates laid-off workers, employers face less resistance when they have to temporarily cut down their work force. At the same time, they maintain a continuing link with their regular labor force without paying employees their full pay or keeping them on the job producing goods that cannot be sold.

Flexibility applies to capital as well. Figure 7.18 shows two average cost curves for hosiery knitting. One, labeled $ATC_{\text{Inflexible Ingo}}$, permits Inflexible Ingo to achieve an average cost level of 30 cents at an output of 2,750 dozen pairs of medium-size, medium-weight panty hose. Ingo is able to do that because his factory is equipped with highly specialized knitting machinery that is relatively inexpensive because it is unadapt-

FIGURE 7.18   Uncertainty and Plant Design

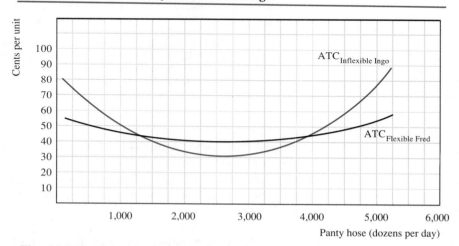

The rigidity of Ingo's equipment enables him to produce at a lower cost in the 1,250–4,000 range. Anywhere else, Fred's flexible machinery keeps costs down.

able. On the other hand, the inflexibility of the knitting machines means that large deviations from its preprogrammed rate of production would raise average costs sharply.

Flexible Fred's factory stands in sharp contrast. Fred has acquired machinery that can be adjusted to various sizes and gauges. Such machinery is more expensive, and its flexibility is wasted if all Fred produces is medium-size, medium-weight panty hose. Fred's ATC does not fall to the depth of that of Inflexible Ingo; 40 cents is as low as Fred can go. But Fred's flexibility allows him to handle alternative outputs at a relatively slight cost increment.

Which method is superior? Obviously, the answer depends on how often Ingo is on target. If Ingo, for example, can avoid uncertainty by operating on a made-to-order basis only and have his customers wait until he has sufficient orders to run his plant in the range of 1,250 to 4,000 dozen pairs daily, he's going to come in at lower costs than Fred. But if neither of these conditions is possible, it's probable that, over time, Fred's costs will be lower.

Virtually all business firms hedge against uncertainty. Factories keep spare parts on hand to make sure that equipment breakdowns are quickly repaired. The hoarding of specialized labor is not uncommon either. Some firms keep redundant employees on their payrolls just in case their skills may be needed in the future.

In essence, hedging against uncertainty is like buying insurance. The payments are not explicit, but rather they are opportunity costs of capital tied up in parts and labor inventories. And like insurance, it's a cost whose cash benefits may never be collected. Nevertheless, the presence of uncertainty as a cost of production cannot be ignored by economists dealing with the business firm.

Summary

When we last saw Joan Kimberlane, at the beginning of this chapter, she'd mastered the dictionary of cost concepts. She could distinguish between money outlays and opportunity costs, between short-run and long-run costs, between fixed and variable costs, and between average and marginal costs. Then Joan mastered the concept of isoquant-isocost equilibrium, so that the trade-off represented by her paper umbrella production function could be equated to the relative prices of her skilled and unskilled labor inputs ($MRTS = P_x/P_y$). Of course, should the skilled umbrella makers demand higher wages and the firm accede to these demands, Joan would have to review her present equilibrium ratio. She could restrict the impact of the wage boost on production costs by using more of the less expensive unskilled personnel and less of the more costly skilled employees.

By now Joan has mastered the family of short-run cost curves. Senior management has encumbered the firm with a number of overhead, or fixed, costs. Since labor is paid on a weekly basis, raw materials are purchased as the need occurs, and utilities are in line with operations, Joan has to contend with variable costs as well. A staff member familiar with econometrics has devised a small model of the firm. It turns out that for both the long and the short run, the paper umbrella average cost curves are conveniently U-shaped, with the marginal cost curve cutting through the bottom of the U. In other words, given the firm's fixed costs, the short run is characterized by

diminishing costs and then increased costs, while the long run shows first economies of scale and then diseconomies.

Joan's task is still incomplete. While Joan knows how costs vary as output changes, she has yet to decide how much to produce. For that, she has to know more than costs alone. Joan must have an idea how much income will the firm earn at various output levels. It is to the revenue side of the firm that we now turn.

Key Terms

Average costs
Average fixed costs (AFC)
Average total costs (ATC)
Capital-saving technical change
Decreasing costs
Expansion path
Fixed costs
Increasing costs
Isocost line
Labor-saving technical change

Long run
Marginal costs
Overhead costs
Planning curves
Short run
Total costs (TC)
Total fixed costs (TFC)
Total variable costs (TVC)
Variable costs

Review Questions

1. Categorize the following items as either fixed or variable costs:
   a. Energy to run equipment.
   b. Raw materials.
   c. Office temporaries.
   d. Machine shop tools.
   e. Fire insurance.
   f. Inventory of finished goods.
   g. Leased vehicles.
   h. Payroll taxes.
2. a. Explain what happens to the equilibrium combination of inputs in Figure 7.3 when the cost of a machine hour falls from $6 to $4.
   b. Once again starting at equilibrium,

   what happens when the hourly wage rises to $10?
3. (Refer back to Chapter 6, review question 4.) Demonstrate the conditions needed to assure that Thai growers will replace men with monkeys.
4. Draw AVC and MC curves for each of the following situations:
   a. The TPP exhibits increasing returns and the TVC shows decreasing costs.
   b. The TPP shows neither increasing nor decreasing returns and the TVC indicates constant costs.
   c. The TPP operates in the diminishing returns region and the TVC demonstrates increasing costs.

5. Why can a cost function that is characterized by diminishing returns also demonstrate economies of scale?

6. What causes diseconomies of scale at both the plant and firm levels?

7. After drawing a U-shaped LRATC curve, add to the diagram at least two short-run average cost curves. Explain the economic significance of the fact that the short-run curves touch the LRATC curve at only a single point.

8. Would an economic strategist recommend constructing a single electrical generating plant to meet an anticipated demand of 1,500 million kilowatts or 2 plants, each capable of delivering 750 million kilowats. Your answer should be based on Figure 7.12 (p. 242).

9. A calculated Cobb-Douglas production function turns out to be:

$$\text{Paper clips} = 6.94 M^{.7} L^{.5}$$

where M is metal and L is labor. What can you say about the shape of the short-run and long-run cost curves?

10. Demonstrate the isoquant equilibrium that would validate the following quotation from "A Survey of India," *The Economist* of May 9, 1987:

Because labour is bolshie, immovable and low on skills, it is relatively expensive compared with subsidized capital, which to the industrialist can be almost cost free. This is why Indian factories, with their infinite supply of labour, employ less than 1 percent of the population and are becoming increasingly capital-intensive. (p. 12).

11. "No matter whether the AVC curve falls or rises, the AFC will always decline. Therefore, the MC will also decline continuously." Do you agree or disagree with either or both statements? Explain.

Food for Thought

1. What happens to the expansion path and the TVC curve when both capital and labor prices fall by 50 percent? (Refer to Figure 7.2, p. 213.)

2. Draw and explain an isoquant-isocost equilibrium for traffic control, which can be accomplished either through traffic signals or people.

3. Why might industries with limited domestic markets be interested in exporting?

4. Facsimile (fax) machines send letters instantaneously cross-continent for a fraction of the cost of overnight express delivery services.

   a. Use isoquant analysis to explain why faxing has become so prevalent among U.S. businesses.

   b. Why, then, do many individuals and firms still use express delivery services?

5. Use isoquant analysis to explain why the piggyback trailer—one cab towing two trailers—has become a common sight on U.S. highways.

6. How will an increase in fixed costs affect the total cost, average total cost, average variable cost, and marginal cost curves?

7. *a.* What is the optimum size plant output in Figure 7.9 (p. 231)?

b. Draw some short-run MC curves onto Figure 7.9. What is the economic interpretation of the relationship between the MC, ATC intersection for plant 1 and the SRAC, LRATC tangency?

8. Why will producers not necessarily introduce a labor-saving innovation? Draw and explain.

9. Regulators normally permit price increases when the rate of return on capital invested in public utilities is less than the target rate of return. Use isoquant analysis to demonstrate that this type of policy leads utility management to overinvest in capital. (This is known as the Averch-Johnson effect.)

10. Does the figure at the right represent a long-run average cost curve? Explain.

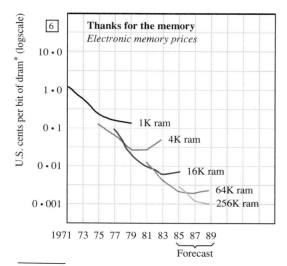

* Dynamic random access memory.

SOURCE: "The Other Dimension: Technology and the City, A Survey," *The Economist,* July 6, 1985, p. 12. © 1985, *The Economist,* Newspaper Ltd. Reprinted with permission.

Suggested Readings

An extensive treatment of scale economies, including a wealth of bibliographic detail, may be found in F. M. Scherer and David Ross, *Industrial Market Structure and Economic Performance* (Boston: Houghton-Mifflin, 1990), pp. 97–141. See also Bela Gold, "Changing Perspectives of Size, Scale, and Returns: An Interpretive Survey," *Journal of Economic Literature* 19, no. 1 (March 1981), pp. 5–33. Dennis D. Miller, in

"Economics of Scale," *Challenge* (May-June 1990), pp. 58–61, suggests that diseconomies of scale may account for the shorter longevity of taller people.

An excellent advanced discussion of production and cost theory may be found in William J. Baumol, *Economic Theory and Operations Analysis* (Englewood Cliffs, N.J.: Prentice-Hall, 1977), Chapter 11.

Notes and Answers

1. Adapted from "Airline Takes the Marginal Bone," *Business Week,* April 20, 1963, pp. 111–14.

2. Long-run, because once again all Blake's options are open.

3. Since she's already in the shop, presumably she's already leased the space, so rent is a fixed cost. Similarly, Maria has probably

borrowed money for the beauty parlor equipment, some of which can be converted to the new business, so the interest charges she pays each month are fixed costs. Quite likely, she has some type of liability insurance should any customer be injured on the premises: that's a fixed cost, too. On the other hand, because she pays her manicurists on an hourly basis, buys her supplies of emery boards and false nails in line with her needs, pays her utilities to a large extent on the basis of usage, these are all variable costs.

4. Because, by definition, fixed costs do not vary with output changes while variable costs do.

5. The equation for any isocost line is $I = p_x q_x + p_y q_y$, where I is the constant expenditure represented by any given isocost, the ps are the prices of the two inputs and the qs are their respective quantities. For any given I, q_y/q_x (the slope of the isocost line) $= p_x/p_y$. In terms of I_3, $I_1 = \$96$, $p_x = \$8$ and $p_y = \$6$. The intercept on the y-axis is found by setting q_x to 0 and solving for q_y. Thus,

$$I_3 = p_y q_y \qquad \text{and} \qquad q_y = I_3/P_y$$
$$\$96 = (\$6)(q_y) \qquad\qquad 16 = \$96/\$6$$

(Use this method to prove that the x-intercept equals 12.) To find any q_y given the isocost line, the relative prices of the inputs, and the quantity of x, solve the first equation in this footnote for q_y:

$$q_y = \frac{I}{p_y} - \frac{p_x}{p_y} \times q_x$$

and substitute the known values. Try it for $I_1 = \$48$, the relative prices as given, for $q_x = 6, 3,$ and 1.

6. Of course, $96. If you're not sure, calculate

it. More important, understand that since 520 is a point on I_3, which was predicated on a $96 outlay, it must represent precisely that sum.

7. Since labor is relatively more expensive in the U.S., for the same dollar outlay, the firm will be able to acquire less labor than capital. The opposite is true for Brazil.

8. Answers to omissions in Table 7.2 by rows: Row 2: 650; Row 3: 12,000; 550; 650; Row 5: 40; Row 6: 1,000; 19,500; 837.50; 33.33; 650; 683.33.

9. The equations for the curves are as follows:

$$TC = 1000 + 800Q - 20Q^2 + 1/2\ Q^3$$
$$ATC = TC/Q$$
$$= 1000/Q + 800 - 20Q + 1/2\ Q^2$$
$$MC = \Delta TC/\Delta Q = 800 - 40Q + 3/2\ Q^2$$

10. That is consistent with the first footnote in MicroBits 7.2: If the MC is below the AVC, it pulls the AVC down; if it's above the AVC, it pulls the AVC up. Only at the minimum point of the AVC, where the AVC = the MC is the AVC being pulled neither up nor down.

11. Answers to omissions in Table 7.2 by rows: Row 3: 48; .21; Row 4: 300, .21; Row 5: 375, 80, .21, .21.

12. Instead of $40, Brad would still pay the $32 fixed cost but would have to pay labor $16, for a total cost of $48.

13. Revised Table 7.4 and new diagram are as follows:

When Machine Time Is Constant at Two Hours

Labor input	1	2	3	4	5	6	7	8	9	10
Cars washed	106	150	184	212	237	260	281	300	318	335
Labor costs	$ 8	16	24	32	40	48	56	64	72	80
Fixed costs	$ 16	16	16	16	16	16	16	16	16	16
Total costs	$ 24	32	40	48	56	64	72	80	88	96
MC (cents)	7.5	18.2	23.5	28.5	32	34.8	38.1	42.1	44.4	47.1
AVC (cents)	7.5	10.7	13	15.1	16.9	18.5	19.9	21.3	22.6	23.9
AFC (cents)	15.1	10.7	8.7	7.5	6.8	6.2	5.7	5.3	5.0	4.8
ATC (cents)	22.6	21.3	21.7	22.6	23.7	24.7	25.6	26.6	27.6	28.7

a. Total costs

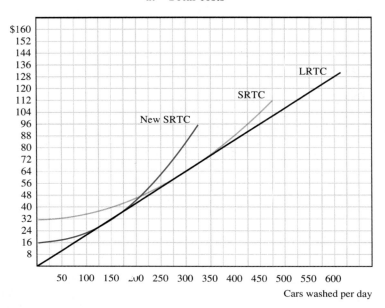

b. Average and marginal costs

Points on New SRMC

Cents	Cars Washed
7.5	53
18.2	128
23.5	167
28.5	198
32	225

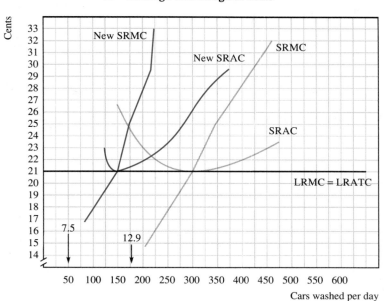

14. Joel Dean, *The Relation of Cost to Output for a Leather Belt Shop* (New York: National Bureau of Economic Research, 1941), and *Managerial Economics* (Englewood Cliffs, N.J.: Prentice-Hall, 1951), Chapter 5.

15. J. Johnston, *Statistical Cost Analysis* (New York: McGraw-Hill, 1960), Chapter 4, section 1.

16. When the MC is constant, the AVC = the MC. The reason for the declining ATC then must be the falling AFC. Check back to Figure 7.8 (Remember that in the long run, ATC = AVC) for the first part of the answer. The figure in MicroBits 7.2 shows the shape of the AFC.

17. The introduction of computer technology may have given an edge to larger banks in the beginning years of computerization, but whatever advantage that provided was quickly dissipated with the advent of small, high-powered computers. Today, even the smallest bank can computerize at a relatively low cost.

18. A. A. Walters, "Production and Cost Functions: An Econometric Survey," *Econometrica* 31 (January-April 1963), pp. 1–66; citation on p. 52. A more recent study concluded cynically: "On my reading of both theory and the evidence, statistical cost and engineering studies teach us precious little about even the relationship between business size and cost. If he likes, an optimist can await the day when we will have learned a lot about costs. I think he will have a long wait." See John S. McGee, "Efficiency and Economies of Size," in *Industrial Concentration: The New Learning,* Harvey J. Goldschmid et al., (eds.) (Boston: Little, Brown, 1974), pp. 55–97; citation on p. 88.

19. "The Factor Proportions Problem in Underdeveloped Areas," *American Economic Review* 45, no. 4 (September 1955), pp. 539–65.

20. Any isocost line that was more steeply sloped than a 1 : 1 capital : labor ratio is appropriate. It will be tangent to the isoquant to the left of an imaginary 45° ray.

21. In 1983, it took 2,900 sanitation workers in New York City, working in three-man crews, to collect 3.3 million tons of garbage. In 1986, the year in which the two-man crews working with more advanced collection vehicles were introduced, 2,620 workers collected 3.5 million tons.

PART

IV

THE PERFECTLY COMPETITIVE FIRM

Part IV pulls together the chapters on demand with the chapters on costs in the least complicated—if admittedly the least realistic—market. In the first two chapters (8 and 9) that constitute this wonderful world of make-believe, you'll discover a survival manual for the competitive firm subject to the unsympathetic jungle of the market. Because the market sets the product price, the firm survives by fine-tuning its output. But the firm must be ever-vigilant, for its competitors stand poised to copy its production techniques and improve them. Naturally, these competitors are always on the prowl to win over the firm's customers. Consumers are the primary beneficiaries of this competitive marketplace that keeps producers on their toes as the market becomes ever more efficient. That will become clear by the end of Chapter 9.

An implicit policy recommendation emerges from these chapters: A hands-off government microeconomic policy is best. Why fix something that isn't broke? Chapter 10 sounds a dissonant note, as it examines two broad situations where the competitive marketplace doesn't deliver. Consequently, it also introduces the conceptual basis for government intervention in microeconomic affairs.

8

THE PERFECTLY COMPETITIVE MARKET: SHORT-RUN ANALYSIS

What profit does man have for all his labor that he toils under the sun?
Ecclesiastes (1:3)

We shut down as soon as shutdown costs are less than operating losses. Our plants can only operate if they don't build inventory.
Lumber Company Spokesman (1981)

Learning Objectives

After studying this chapter, you'll be able to understand:

- Firms' multifaceted objectives and the key role of the profit-maximization hypothesis.
- Economists' specific interpretation of perfect competition.
- The MR = MC rule for profit maximization (or loss minimization).
- How the competitive firm determines its optimum output and calculates its profits.
- The relationship between a firm's production decisions and its supply curve.
- Why domestic firms seek protection from imports and why such actions impose economic costs on the economy.
- The impact of taxes on the short-run profitability of the firm.
- Why firms may be better off with less information than with more.
- How uncertainty influences business decision making.

Price Making and Price Taking

You enter the neighborhood 7-Eleven to buy a six-pack of 7UP. The price is marked on the cans. To wax Shakespearean: To buy or not to buy? You face a similar decision at an auction: To bid or not to bid? In the first case, the store manager exercises discretion over price and lets the customers decide how much to buy. In the auction scenario, the seller decides how much she wishes to sell and the buyers decide at what prices. But whatever technique is used, one thing is clear. The seller can control only one variable—price or quantity sold. If the seller is a **price maker** and sets the price, the market determines the volume sold. If the seller decides on the sales volume, the market fixes the price, turning the seller into a **price taker.**

While a **price maker** exercises discretion over the price to charge customers, the **price taker** has no such control.

This chapter deals with price takers and how they determine output. Such decisions are typical of competitive markets found in many branches of agriculture and mining as well as in some types of manufacturing. To be sure, markets that are considered competitive in the real world only approximate the model of perfect competition portrayed in this chapter. Nevertheless, the principles developed here are applicable to a variety of market structures and to public as well as to business decisions. Indeed, the mode of analysis used in this chapter remains at the core of modern microeconomic thinking.

The chapter opens with a brief discussion of producer objectives. We shall adhere to the general view of economists that profit maximization is a very useful assumption when analyzing the goals of profit-oriented businesses. We proceed then to examine the meaning economists apply to "perfect competition," which sets the stage for the key section of this chapter: output determination under perfect competition. The model of the competitive firm is then shown to be the basis for the familiar supply curve. The following applications subsection uses the competitive model to examine the impact of quotas that restrict imports and elaborates on the tax-shifting cigarette case introduced in Chapter 5.

How are business decisions affected when information is neither readily available nor costless? How are production decisions modified in the presence of uncertainty? These questions form the core of the final pages of this chapter, as we try to reconcile the theory of the firm with the complex world beyond the textbook.

Firm Objectives

The Owner-Operated Enterprise

It is not difficult to posit objectives of the firm when the firm is a small, family-run enterprise. Financial security, if not outright affluence, surely ranks high among the goals of entrepreneurs. Yet we should not insist that the owner-operater pursues profits single-mindedly. The lives of business-people are multifaceted. At a minimum, they must have the leisure time to enjoy the fruits of their activities. So, for owner-managers, profit-maximization can be broadened to encompass "utility-maximization." In terms of Chapter 3's utility map, an owner-manager strives to attain the highest indifference curve in the trade-off between profits and other joys of living.

Figure 8.1 depicts the indifference map of Spruce Bruce, the owner-manager of Spruce Bruce's Ornaments. The ordinate indicates the company's dividends while the abscissa measures total expenditures on a variety of fringe benefits such as leisure time, first-class travel, health club membership, and so on. The dividends are Bruce's money income; because Bruce is the sole owner, all profits accrue to him. And, insofar as Bruce decides to spend some of the firm's revenues on fringe benefits, his profits will decline by the identical dollar amount paid out on fringes. Thus, the budget line has a slope of 1; the trade-off between income and

FIGURE 8.1   Money Income versus Fringe Benefits

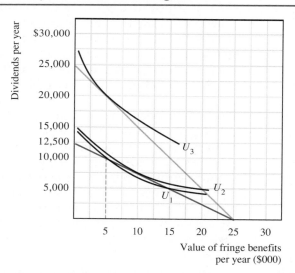

When Bruce is the sole proprietor of Spruce Bruce's, his decision about the distribution of income between money dividends and fringe benefits will only be influenced by his preferences. But when he has to share profits with others, theory suggests that he'll lean more toward fringe benefits than to money income.

SOURCE: This diagram is adapted from the pathbreaking article by Michael Jensen and William Meckling, "Theory of the Firm: Managerial Behavior, Agency Costs, and Ownership Structure," *Journal of Financial Economics* 3 (1976), pp. 305–60.

fringe benefits is one for one. The indifference map outlines Bruce's preferences between money income and fringe benefits.

How will Bruce decide to divide his profits, equal to $25,000 for the year, between dividend payments and fringe benefits? The tangency of the budget line anchored at $25,000; $25,000 with the indifference curve U_3 indicates that Bruce takes $20,000 in cash income and $5,000 in fringe benefits.

The Separation of Management from Ownership

Although profit or utility maximization is a sensible goal in describing the behavior of the owner-operated firm, does it also make sense for immense publicly held corporations? The typical stockholder-owner is not involved in the running of the firm, where professional management makes virtually all the important decisions. Are the objectives of the managers and those of the owners consistent or not?

Consider Bruce's behavior soon after selling a 50 percent stake in Spruce Bruce's to a group of business associates. Now, if the firm were to continue to earn $25,000 and pay that amount out in dividends, Bruce would only receive $12,500, his half-share of the profits. On the other hand, if Bruce as CEO were to reward himself generously with fringe benefits, he would be the sole beneficiary. In the extreme, Bruce could manage the business so that dividend payments fell to zero, and he would appropriate the entire bundle of profits in the form of fringe benefits. These new options are represented by the lower budget line, anchored at $12,500 and $25,000. What does the slope of ½ indicate? _____

_____[1]

The indifference curve–budget line tangency shouts out, ''Bruce—take out $7,500 in dividends (an equal amount will be received by Bruce's partners) and treat yourself to $10,000 in fringes!''[2]

Does this inconsistency between owners and managers mean that economists have to reject the assumption of profit maximization in firms that are not owner-managed? MicroBits 8.1 presents some alternatives to profit maximization that have been applied to more complex business organizations. But more recent work on the **principal–agency** relationship suggests that the conflict between owners and management is less intense than previously imagined.

An **agent** is any person or entity employed by the **principal** to implement the objectives of the principal.

Put yourself in the place of a major stockholder who has to rely on Bruce to operate the corporation. How might you reconcile the conflict between what's best for Bruce, the agent, and what's best for you, a principal?

Two obvious ways to limit management's self-interest can be found within the framework of profit maximization.

You and your partners might hold down Bruce's fringe benefits to say $5,000. Figure 8.1 has a dashed line rising at $5,000, indicat-

---

What Does the Business Firm Try to Achieve?

Do firms run by professional managers really aim to maximize profits when those profits go to the stockholders rather than to the managers? That question is probably as old as the separation of ownership and management, and has led a host of economists to postulate alternatives to the profit-maximization assumption. Here, we outline three such alternatives.

1. *The desire for secure profits.* In 1947, the Austrian economist K. W. Rothschild* proposed that firms strive to maintain a secure position in their industry. Such security motives may be consistent at times with profit maximization, but they may also be inconsistent. For example, the quest to increase the firm's market share may well induce it to charge prices that are lower than those likely to yield maximum profits. (U.S. firms have so accused the Japanese.) Secure profits might also explain why firms consistently build excess capacity. Their ability to supply buyers on short notice, although unprofitable, may enable them to cement the buyers' allegiance.

2. *Satisficing.* Nobel laureate Herbert A. Simon has suggested that firms seek a satisfactory rate of profit rather than maximum profits.§ While it is not easy to define the satisfactory rate, it is clear that "satisficing" can often conflict with profit maximization. Thus, if the satisfactory rate of profit is 25 percent, management may not be interested in pursuing risky ventures that might boost the profit rate to 50 percent but also might reduce overall profitability to 15 percent. After all, if such ventures succeed, the rewards accrue to the stockholders. But if they fail, senior managers may well find themselves job hunting. Satisficing also suggests that operational inefficiency might well be ignored as long as the target rate of profit is achieved.

3. *Sales maximization.* One of the world's eminent microtheorists, New York University's William J. Baumol, suggested a third alternative: Management pursues maximum sales as long as it attains some minimum acceptable rate of profit.‖ Size then becomes an objective. Yet size and profitability need not run hand in hand. Decisions that are taken to increase sales may come at the expense of the firm's rate of return.

---

§ Herbert A. Simon, "Theories of Decision-Making in Economics and Behavioral Science, *American Economic Review* 49, no. 3 (June 1959), pp. 253–283.

‖ William J. Baumol, *Business Behavior, Value, and Growth* (New York: Harcourt Brace Jovanovich, 1967), Chapter 6.

---

* K. W. Rothschild, "Price Theory and Oligopoly," *Economic Journal* 47 (1947), pp. 299–320.

---

ing that maximum. Bruce has no choice but to operate at the $10,000, $5,000 point on the budget line. To be sure, that puts him on a lower indifference curve, U_1, and in a nontangency position. But it does limit Bruce's discretion and improves the principals' return.

- You could introduce an incentive scheme. Induce Bruce to put his best efforts into earning profits for the firm by offering him a share of the profits. (That would shift Bruce's budget line. Which way? _____[3])

Principals impose on themselves **agency costs** to assure that their agents will act in the best interests of the principals.

Whatever means you use to control Bruce's self-interest, you'll encounter **agency costs.** In the former case, the principals will have to monitor Bruce's compliance with their instructions. And, obviously, motivating Bruce by profit sharing means lower profits per share for you and your partners.

How useful, then, is the assumption of profit maximization? Surely in the owner-managed firm, profit or utility maximization appropriately describes the firm's objective. Even where owners and managers have different goals, successful resolution of the principal–agency conflict puts owners and managers on parallel, if not identical, tracks. Moreover, as you'll see, viewing all firms as profit maximizers, even if not fully realistic, is extremely fruitful. Finally, under perfect competition, to which we now turn, the profit-maximization assumption is sensible. Any firm that sacrifices profitable opportunities for other goals may well find itself at the mercy of competitors who are more profit-driven.

How Economists Define *Perfect* Competition

The perfectly competitive model used by microeconomists is predicated on four key assumptions:

1. The inability of any market participant to control price.
2. Product homogeneity.
3. Free entry and exit.
4. Perfect knowledge.

Each of these concepts merits a brief explanation.

1. *No control over price.* The perfect competitor is left to the mercy of the impersonal market. Typically, the market comprises a large number of buyers and sellers, with each participant too insignificant to exert any impact on market price. The individual firm cannot defy the market by pricing its output higher than the prevailing price because it would simply fail to attract any buyers. All of its potential customers would gravitate to competing producers who were charging the lower market price.

Ah, you say, but isn't each firm unique? Wouldn't some buyers maintain their allegiance even if they have to pay more? The answer comes in the second assumption.

2. *Product homogeneity.* If products are identical, there's no reason to patronize one firm over another. Product homogeneity rules out any differences—be it in the form of service, quality, convenience, or whatever—that would lead customers to favor one competitor over another.

3. *Free entry and exit.* Perfect competition retains a high degree of vitality by postulating that anyone can enter the market or leave it as he or she pleases. It assumes no impediments to entry such as high capital requirements or a recognizable brand name.

4. *Perfect knowledge.* To make the competitive mechanism work, both the buyers and sellers must be aware of their options. Clearly, if Helen doesn't know that the identical hiking boots are cheaper at Michael's Trailware than at Bonnie's Bootique, she won't shop at the lower-priced competitor. Similarly, if Marty is unaware of the latest in testing equipment for use in his medical laboratory, he stands to lose out to his better-informed competitors.

These four assumptions are crucial for explaining how the perfectly competitive market operates. One corollary of the first two assumptions helps define the demand facing the perfectly competitive firm.

Demand: The Market and the Firm

A **product** or **industry demand curve** refers to the demand curve for a particular product or for the output of a particular industry.

The demand curves that were explored in earlier chapters typically demonstrated negative slopes. Because those demand curves represent the demand for a particular product—gold, wheat, flights, apartments—they are called **product** or **industry demand curves.**

In contrast, the demand curve facing the individual firm participating in a perfectly competitive market is *horizontal* as depicted in Figure 8.2.

FIGURE 8.2   The Demand Curve Facing the Firm Operating in a Perfectly Competitive Market

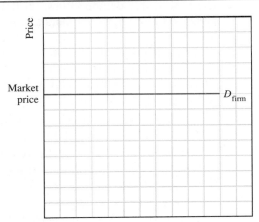

As long as the perfect competitor charges the market price, the firm will be able to sell all it wishes. If, however, the firm charges more than the market place, sales drop to zero.

(Technically, the elasticity of the demand curve facing the perfectly competitive firm is infinite.[4]) The interpretation is straightforward: Because the individual firm cannot control price, it must be satisfied with the reigning market price. At that price, the competitor can sell as much as the firm produces. No purchaser would be willing to pay more than the market price to buy a homogeneous product from the firm. If the seller should insist on charging more, the quantity demanded falls to zero. Of course, the firm would be unwilling to sell at a lower price: If it can sell as much as it wishes at the market price, why cut price below that?

Pedaling to Short-Run Profit Maximization

The stage is set and the actors have been assembled, so we can start the performance. You learned about firms' short-run cost curves in Chapter 7; you just read about competitive firms' demand curves; and you accept that profit maximization is the goal of the firm. How are these disparate elements assembled into a meaningful presentation of firm decision making?

Really Making It: The Excess Profit Case

Figure 8.3 reproduces from Figure 7.6 (p. 224) the cost curves of Pedal Pushers, our bicycle manufacturer. Figure 8.3a shows total costs, while Figure 8.3b displays the average total and marginal cost curves. In addition, the firm's demand curve at the presumed market price of $725 appears in Figure 8.3b. Its analogue in Figure 8.3a is the total revenue (TR) line.[5]

For the moment, we'll define profit (π) as the difference between total revenue and total cost. To maximize profit, Pedal Pushers must merely select the output at which this difference is the greatest. Management may use any of three methods:

- *Trial and error.* Find the revenues and costs at each output level, subtract each cost datum from its corresponding revenue number, and identify the largest profit position.
- *Mathematical.* Discover the equations that describe each of the two curves, subtract one from the other to obtain the profit equation, and use calculus to elicit the maximum point.
- *Geometrical.* As in Figure 8.3a, draw a line parallel to the TR curve that is also tangent to the TC curve. The output that corresponds to the tangency is the one at which profits are maximized.

Any of these methods leads to a conclusion that the maximum-profit output equals 25 bicycles per month. By reading on the vertical scale that

FIGURE 8.3   Excess Profits for Pedal Pushers

a.   Profit maximization using TR = TC method

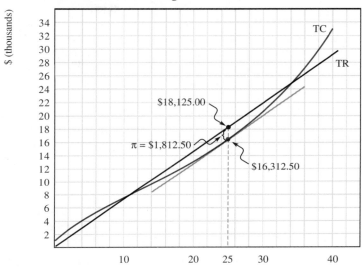

a.   As the TR rises above the TC, profits become positive. At the output at which the line parallel to TR becomes tangent to the TC, profits reach their maximum.

b.   Profit maximization using the MR = MC method.

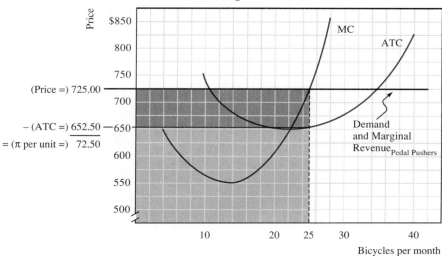

b.   Profits are maximized at an output of 25 bicycles, the output at which MR = MC. Total profits = $(P \times Q) - (ATC \times Q)$; in this instance: ($725 \times 25$) − ($652.50 \times 25$) = $1,812.50.

total revenue = \$18,125 and total costs = \$16,312.50, you'll see that profits at 25 bicycles per month equal \$1,812.50. (Use Table 7.2, p. 223, for TC and calculate TR by $P \times Q$. Convince yourself that profits would be lower at any other output.)

Marginal revenue (MR) is the revenue earned by producing an additional unit of output. It equals the change in total revenue divided by the change in output (ΔTR/ΔQ).

You'll find Figure 8.3b far more useful, if a bit more complicated. But first, commit to memory a new term: **marginal revenue.** For a horizontal demand curve, marginal revenue is constant and equal to price. (Check it out: If 10 units are sold at \$725 each for a total revenue of \$7,250, and 11 bicycles are sold at 11 × \$725, or \$7,975, then the additional or marginal revenue generated by the 11th bicycle is precisely \$725.)

Now notice in Figure 8.3b where the MR line cuts the MC line. Profits are maximized when production equals 25 bicycles, the output at which *marginal revenue = marginal cost*. It's clearly not accidental that this is precisely the same output we found in Figure 8.3a.[6] Nevertheless, this rule is not immediately obvious, and MicroBits 8.2 provides a brief explanation.

MicroBits 8.2

Total Profits versus the Profit Margin

Can the profit margin (or profits per unit sold) decline and total profits rise? Although your first impulse might be to answer no, the correct response is yes. Read on to see why.

Recall first that marginal revenue is the revenue earned from selling another unit of output, while marginal cost is the cost of producing another unit of output. What happens to the profit position of Pedal Pushers if the revenues generated from selling another bicycle exceed the costs of producing it? Clearly, total profits must rise. Indeed, as long as marginal revenue is greater than marginal costs, total profits will increase no matter what happens to the difference between price and average cost.

Take a look at Figure 8.3b again. The average cost of an individual bicycle when 22 bicycles are produced is \$647.45. Since price equals \$725, the profit margin on each bicycle equals \$77.55, and total profits are \$1,706.10. Now increase output to 25 bicycles. Total costs rise to \$16,312.50, according to Table

7.2, and average costs move up to \$652.50. With the price still at \$725, the profit margin *drops* to \$32.50. But what happens to total profits? Total revenues are now 25 × \$725, or \$18,125. With total costs equal to \$16,312.50, total profits rise to \$1,812.50!

Once again, as long as the additional costs are less than the additional revenues gained from increasing production, total profits will rise. Only where MR = MC is it no longer possible to boost profits by producing more. (Take another look: What is the relationship between MR and MC at an output greater than 25, say 27.5? Why would it not be profitable to expand production beyond 25? _____
_____*)

---

* For any additional unit beyond 25, MC > MR. Production there reduces total profits, because on each additional unit, the revenue generated is less than the cost of that unit. Thus, bicycle number 27.5 costs \$825 to produce but sells for only \$725.

Now calculate π = TR − TC. We know that

$$TR = P \times Q = \$725 \times 25 = \$18,125$$

We also know that ATC = TC/Q, so that if[7]

$$TC = ATC \times Q = \$652.50 \times 25 = \$16,312.50$$

then

$$\pi = TR - TC = (P - ATC)Q = \$1,812.50$$

In terms of Figure 8.3b, 725×25 is the area of the entire grey rectangle; 652.50×25 is the area of the lower light grey rectangle; and the difference between the two, the upper dark grey rectangle, is total profits.[8]

Barely Making It: The Zero Profit Case

The rule that profits are maximized when MR = MC applies no matter what the price may be. Visualize a fall in the price to $647.45, perhaps because demand has fallen, perhaps because new firms have entered the market. Pedal Pushers must respond to the new price in the only way it can: because it is locked in to the market price, it must adjust output. (Why won't it continue to produce at the old output of 25? _____

_____
                                                                 9

Pedal Pushers restores its output to its optimum, according to Figure 8.4, at a quantity of 22 bicycles. Calculate π:

$$TR = P \times Q = \$_____$$
$$TC = ATC \times Q = \$_____$$
$$\pi = TR - TC = \$_____$$

If you've computed properly, you'll discover that $\pi = 0$; the TR rectangle and the TC rectangle coincide.

Does that imply that Pedal Pushers should go out of business? Here's where accountants and economists might part ways. Accountants abhor zero profits the way nature abhors a vacuum. Economists, however, would want to examine this situation a bit further. If Pedal Pushers had properly learned microeconomics, its owners would have included in their calculations of total costs all relevant opportunity costs, including the returns expected from alternative employment. In other words, *the zero profits case represents the firm's ability to cover all outlays and repay its owners their opportunity costs.* Economists call this **normal profits**. (By extension, then, profits in the previous case represent **excess profits**.)

In short, operations would continue in a zero profits or a normal profits situation. But a price less than $647.45 would bring the firm into the red. How would Pedal Pushers react to a price of $600? Read on!

Normal profits are the minimum profits needed to induce the owners of a firm to remain in business. **Excess profits** are those earnings that exceed both the firm's money expenditures and the normal profits that owners receive to cover their opportunity costs.

FIGURE 8.4   The Zero Profits Case

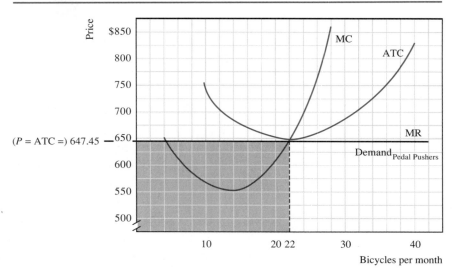

MR = MC at 22 units of output. But at that output, ATC = $647.45, which is also the selling price. Excess profits then disappear.

Uh-Oh! The Loss Case

A $600 price poses two challenges to Pedal Pushers' management:

1. Should they stay open and continue production in the hope that the price fall is very temporary? Or should they shut down for a few weeks or months, clinging to the belief that price will ultimately rise?[10]

2. If management decides to remain open, what is the firm's appropriate output?

The second question is the easiest to answer, for you already know the optimum production rule: MR = MC. However, now the rule enables the firm to minimize losses rather than to maximize profits. Glance at Figure 8.5. Optimum production is at an output of 20 bicycles per month, the output at which MR = MC. (See for yourself that if the firm produces even one more bicycle, then MC > MR. The additional bicycle increases losses. Similarly, if the firm had produced only 19 bicycles, MR > MC, and so losses could have been reduced by producing another bicycle.)

Now calculate the loss from producing 20 bicycles. The point on the ATC curve above 20 shows that cost per unit is $650. Thus, total costs = $13,000. Sales income equals $600 × 20, so total revenue = $12,000. Thus, total loss = $1,000. In other words, by continuing to produce, the firm will lose $1,000 each month.

You can see this in Figure 8.5 by computing the rectangles. In this instance, however, the cost rectangle ($650 × 20) will be larger than the revenue rectangle ($600 × 20). The upper (dark grey) rectangle, which equals $50 × 20, or $1,000, is the total loss.

Notice something else. If you turn back to Table 7.2 (p. 223), you'll observe that total fixed costs (TFC) were also equal to $1,000. TFC, the firm's overhead, must be paid whether the firm remains open or not. So, at P = $600 per bicycle, it's really immaterial whether the firm stays open or shuts down. Pedal Pushers loses $1,000 a month either way.

Implicitly, then, you've answered the first question: Should Pedal Pushers shut down or stay open at P = $600? From the profit point of view, it doesn't really matter.

Test yourself: How should management react to a decline in price below $600? Why?_____

If you answered, "Shut down because the continued production will lead to a loss that is larger than TFC," you're in good shape. In fact, you can see that from Figure 8.5.

Take a look at the relationship between P and AVC, the operating cost per unit. (Remember, AVC doesn't include the firm's overhead.) If the price collected by Pedal Pushers covers at least its average operating costs, then the firm's losses do not increase by staying open. That's the

FIGURE 8.5   Shut Down the Shop?

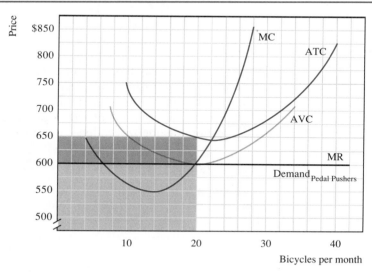

By staying open, the firm covers its variable costs, but revenues do not suffice to cover fixed costs. By shutting down, the firm also loses a sum equal to fixed costs. It's a toss-up whether to stay open or shut down.

case in Figure 8.5: The operating cost of each bicycle is $600 (AVC above 20), and the price of each bicycle is also $600, so operating costs are covered and fixed costs are not.[11] But if price were to fall below $600, then not only would fixed costs be uncovered by revenues, but so would some share of the operating costs. Clearly, it would be better to lose only fixed costs than a larger sum. In short,

- If $P >$ AVC, the firm not only covers its operating expenses, but also can use part of its revenues to pay off some of its fixed costs. The decision should be: Keep operating.
- If $P =$ AVC, it doesn't matter whether the firm stays open or shuts down; in either case, the loss = TFC.
- If $P <$ AVC, staying open increases the loss beyond TFC; the sensible course of action is to shut down.

The **shutdown point** is the lowest point on the AVC. If the product's price is less than the minimum AVC, the firm will cease production.

For that reason, the minimum point of the AVC is called the **shutdown point.** It distinguishes between the lowest price at which production would continue and even lower prices at which the firm would be wise to close down completely.

Short-Run Market Demand and Supply

The Short-Run Supply Curve

The time has come to weave together the separate strands of the previous pages. You've discovered that as the market price of bicycles changes, Pedal Pushers reacts by modifying output in line with the MR = MC rule. Table 8.1 summarizes these results. At a price less than the $600 shutdown price, Pedal Pushers will temporarily suspend production. At $600, losses equal $1,000, which would also be incurred by remaining closed. So, it's the minimum price at which production will take place. Should Pedal Pushers decide to produce, output will equal 20 bicycles. At the

TABLE 8.1   Marginal Cost and Supply

Price	Marginal Cost	Quantity Supplied
$575	$575	0
600	600	20
647.45	647.45	22
725	725	25
825	———	—

$647.45 price, the firm breaks even if it produces 22 units. At $725, the firm actually earns excess profits by producing 25 bicycles.

Now look at the first and the last columns, Price and Quantity Supplied. Isn't that the underlying relationship for the *supply curve*? (See Figure 8.6b.)[12] This lesson is crucial: *The rising supply curve is based on and derived from the principles of profit maximization.* Why do firms operating under perfectly competitive conditions supply the output they do?

- Competitive firms are price takers. They can't adjust their prices to bolster profits. They react only by changing production.
- Competitive firms produce the quantity consistent with their optimum profit position.

You can now fill in the last line in Table 8.1 by referring to Figure 8.6a. Confirm that you've correctly inserted the quantity supplied by looking at the supply curve in Figure 8.6a at $P = $825.

FIGURE 8.6   The Interaction between the Bicycle Firm and the Bicycle Market: Perfect Competition

a. Pedal Pushers

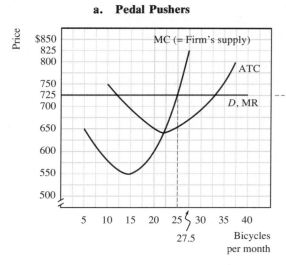

b. The bicycle market

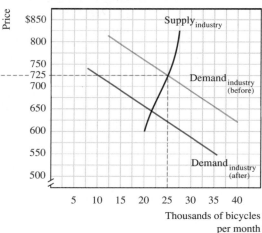

a. For Pedal Pushers, price is fixed at $725, so the firm finds its optimum profit position, MR = MC, at 25 units produced monthly.

b. The market supply, derived by summing the individual MC = supply curves of the 1,000 suppliers, is juxtaposed to the market demand curve of bike buyers. The competitive market mechanism equates quantity supplied and quantity demanded to determine P and Q simultaneously.

Market Price–Supply Interactions

Figure 8.6 points out the interrelationship between the market price and the firm's quantity supplied. The monthly demand for bicycles is represented in Figure 8.6b by Demand$_{industry(before)}$, while the supply is indicated by Supply$_{industry}$. The equilibrium market price is $725 and the equilibrium quantity equals 25,000 bicycles monthly. Figure 8.6a reproduces Figure 8.3b; Pedal Pushers' cost structure at a price of $725 induces it to assemble 25 bicycles.

Now if industry demand falls to Demand$_{industry(after)}$, you understand that price declines as well. The new market price = $\_\_\_\_\_$, the new $Q =$ _____, and Pedal Pushers now produces _____ units.[13]

You can play around with the slope of the supply curve, so that changes in demand cause different price reactions. But in all cases, the elasticity of supply hinges on the underlying marginal cost curves (which, in turn, depend on the production functions and input prices, as was spelled out in Chapters 6 and 7). Furthermore, all price changes lead to reactions by firms, as they adjust their quantity supplied to the new market price.

Recap

In a sense then, you've gone full circle from Chapter 2's discussion of supply-demand interactions. By now you understand that the demand for a particular good or service depends on underlying psychological relationships captured in consumers' indifference curves as well as the prices consumers face and their incomes. And, as you've just learned, the supply of any commodity or service in a competitive market depends upon the cost structure of the individual firms, their striving for maximum profits, and the number of firms in the industry. Shifts in either supply or demand curves affect the market price, which causes both demanders and suppliers to react. If equilibrium is upset by, say, a change in consumer tastes from bicycling to recreational swimming, buyers are affected directly. But so, too, are producers and sellers of both bicycles and swimsuits. Bicycle manufacturers, faced by a fall in price, reduce the quantity of bicycles supplied; swimsuit producers, faced with an increase in price, raise the quantity of swimsuits supplied.

Producer Surplus

You recall that consumer surplus is the difference between what buyers would have been willing to pay for some good or service and the amount they actually spent on it. It arises because some consumers have stronger demands than others and so would have been ready to pay more than the market price for their purchases. The analogue on the suppliers' side is

Producer surplus is the difference between the price necessary to induce suppliers to produce a given level of output and the actual price of that output.

producer surplus. A market price that just covers the costs of the less-efficient producers grants a bonus to lower-cost suppliers. And just as consumer surplus is measured by the area between the demand curve and the market price, producer surplus is measured by the area between the supply curve and the market price. Both consumer and producer surplus indicate a gain to some without a loss to others. Thus, the larger the combined total, the greater the benefit to the community.

Look back to Figure 8.6b. The cost of the 22,000th bicycle was $647.45. Yet, given the initial demand curve, it sold for $725. On that unit, producer surplus was $76.55. Producer surplus for the entire industry is merely the sum of the surplus for each bicycle sold.

Why does producers' surplus rise if demand for bicycles increases?

Two answers come to mind. First, producer surplus is larger for each unit sold previously, since the marginal cost curve remains the same while price increases. Second, more units are sold, and, except for the last unit, there'll be some producer surplus accompanying each of the new sales.

It's equally true that if prices decline, producer surplus will fall. And if the market is rigged so that suppliers can't sell as much as they would like and buyers can't purchase as much as they wish, both producer and consumer surplus will decline. That makes both groups worse off. The next section demonstrates the truth of this proposition.

Taxes and More Taxes: Applications

Stealing the Shirt off Our Backs: Import Quotas

Before you look at the label on the shirt or blouse you're wearing, would you be willing to bet that it's an import? Many of the textiles purchased in the United States come from foreign manufacturers. Indeed, consumption of domestically produced textiles would be further reduced if not for the quotas imposed on imports.

Turn to Figure 8.7. Begin with a closed U.S. market, so that price is determined by the domestic supply and the market demand. Figure 8.7b shows that at a price of $25 per shirt, Americans buy 80 million dozens annually. Figure 8.7a indicates how the $25 price affects a typical U.S. shirt manufacturer: MR = MC at an output of 50 million shirts. Since $P >$ ATC, the firm earns excess profits. (If you're not certain why that's so, check back to Figure 8.3b and the explanation there. To test yourself, calculate profits in Figure 8.7a at Q = 50 million; ATC = $21.)

Permitting foreign producers to enter the market raises the supply curve to the one in Figure 8.7b labeled "Supply: Domestic + Imports," and drives the market price down to $15 per shirt. But look at the impact

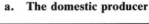

FIGURE 8.7   **Import Quotas: Protecting Domestic Firms from Foreign Competition**

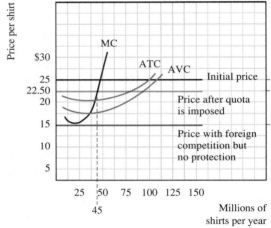

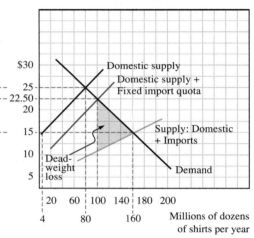

a. Without protection, foreign competition drives the price below the firm's shutdown point. With protection, the price rises to $22.50, enabling domestic firms to operate at a profit.

b. The domestic price of $25 comes down to $15 in the face of foreign competition. Imposing a quota of 40 million dozens reduces supply and boosts price to $22.50.

on the domestic firm in Figure 8.7a. Price has dropped below AVC; the firm is not covering its operating costs. The wisest course for this manufacturer is to shut down.

Not all domestic firms need to be such high-cost producers. Some will compete successfully with foreign merchandise. (Draw the cost curves of such a firm in Figure 8.7a.[14]) But notice how the total market is divided between domestic production and imports. Total quantity supplied equals 160 million dozen shirts, of which domestic supply is only 4 million dozen, or 2.5 percent of the entire market that once was totally dominated by U.S. producers.

MICROQUERY   What happens to the domestic shirt industry if all U.S. producers' cost structures are identical to the firm depicted in Figure 8.7a?

[15]

Firms threatened with sharp reductions in profits, and even bankruptcy, and workers who stand to lose their jobs are unlikely to remain complacent. Indeed, all who have an economic stake in the survival of the industry now move from the economic to the political arena. Their demand and the typical political inclination is some sort of protection against the foreign invasion.

Import quotas were imposed to shelter the textile industry. Figure 8.7b shows that the supply curve shifts leftward when the quota is set at 40 million dozen shirts per year. The curve labeled "Domestic supply + Fixed import quota" is merely the domestic supply curve plus the constant 40 million dozen quota. That leads to an equilibrium price of $22.50 and a quantity of 100 million dozen. Of that total quantity supplied, imports constitute the fixed 40 million dozen, while domestic producers supply 60 million dozen. So, domestic manufacturers increase their share of the domestic market from 2.5 percent to 60 percent.

The new price is certainly not as profitable to the firm as was the $25 initial price. Nevertheless, it's much better than the $15 price of the free market. You should be able to calculate the impact of the import quotas on the domestic firm of Figure 8.7a.

Price facing the firm: _____

Profit-maximizing quantity: _____

Total firm revenues: _____

Total firm costs (ATC = $20.50): _____

Total firm profits: _____[16]

The Deadweight Loss of Trade Restrictions.   Who loses when trade is restricted? We can identify two groups who lose and, correspondingly, two types of losses. First are the buyers of the 100 million dozen shirts, who paid $22.50 rather than $15, the competitive price. They implicitly lost $7 × 1.2 billion, or $8.4 billion. (In terms of Figure 8.7b, that's represented by the rectangle whose ordinate is $15–$22.50 and whose abscissa is 100 million.) But clearly their loss is compensated by the sellers' gain. There's a redistribution of wealth but no net loss.

That statement, however, cannot be made about the second group; for these consumers and producers, who have been closed out of the market, there's a net loss. Huck and Jim are part of the public who would have bought the 1.92 billion shirts had they been priced at $15. But with the quota-induced price of $22.50, only 1.2 billion are sold, and Huck and his friends, those potential buyers of the 720 million shirts, were locked out of the market. Their loss is uncompensated by anyone's gain. This uncaptured consumer surplus is the upper part of the light purple triangle (i.e., above $15) in Figure 8.7b.

A **deadweight loss** is a loss of production or consumption to some members of the economy without a corresponding gain by others.

Producers also lose. The quota forces some producers out of the market. These lost sales diminish producer surplus, the lower light purple triangle in Figure 8.7b. The combination of this lost consumer and producer surplus is called the **deadweight loss** of the quota policy.

Perhaps it now makes sense to you why, ever since the late 18th century, economists have opposed constraints on free trade. Imposing either tariffs or quotas prevents consumers from obtaining the goods and services they desire at the lowest prices. Moreover, if a commodity could be produced abroad more cheaply than domestically, why not take advantage of foreign efficiencies and thereby increase the world's production capabilities? But it should be equally clear that protected industries benefit from impediments to free trade.[17] So the battle lines between consumers and importers versus domestic producers are sharply drawn. How astonishing is it, then, when a protected industry asks that tariff barriers be removed? One such rare example is described in MicroBits 8.3.

MicroBits 8.3

"We Don't Need Any More Help"

"Harley Asks End to Tariff Aid," read an inner headline of *The New York Times* (March 18, 1987, pp. D1,25). The article reported that the only U.S. manufacturer of motorcycles, Harley Davidson, had asked the federal government to remove tariffs protecting the company. These import taxes had been imposed only four years earlier when Harley Davidson was facing an onslaught from Japanese motorcycle manufacturers. But Chairman Vaughn L. Beals said, "We're profitable again. We're recapitalized. We're diversified. We don't need any more help."

The motorcycle industry, founded in the early years of the 20th century, had once included over 150 U.S. manufacturers. But more recently, Japanese companies had so successfully penetrated the market that Harley Davidson remained the sole survivor. By 1982, overproduction led the Japanese to cut prices drastically on motorcycles sold in the United States. Harley protested and soon operated under an umbrella of tariff protection.

Harley began to increase its operating efficiency, improve its quality control, and redesign its bikes. By 1986, Harley had come out of the red for the first time since 1981. Its market share had risen from a record low of 12.5 percent in 1983 to 19.4 percent in 1986. Thus, Mr. Beals declared that tariff relief was no longer necessary: "We're sending a strong message out to the international industrial community: U.S. workers, given a respite from predatory import practices, can become competitive in world markets." What a "masterful stroke of public relations," noted the *Times*.

Yet the article also dispensed a dose of cynicism. A management consultant was quoted as saying, "Tariff protection was vital to Harley. But it was inducing Kawasaki and Honda to build big bikes in America to compete with them." In other words, maintaining the tariff in place would no longer defend Harley exclusively from competition but would also give an advantage to Harley's U.S.-based Japanese competitors. The decision may well have been the lesser of two evils rather than a purely public-spirited move. But in any case, it was a newsworthy exception to the general hold-on-forever attitude of producers protected by tariffs or quotas.

A dose of the real world of international business will be your parting gift. It is naive to believe that foreign exporters and domestic importers will passively accept trade restraints. Their business instincts will lead them to seek methods to circumvent if not to evade the controls. Smuggling to overcome import prohibitions has been a way of life the world over; the international trade in drugs is merely the most blatant example today. Less evident are lawful means to avoid trade barriers. Savor MicroBits 8.4 for two examples of legal avoidance rather than illegal evasion. You realize, of course, that the greater the evasion or avoidance, the less inimical the presumed adverse consequences. (That's one of the conclusions reached in Chapter 2's discussion of black markets.) Not that the loss disappears entirely; the resources that are used in evading and/or avoiding have to be compensated for, as does the uncertainty that normally prevails when the law is being skirted. Just remember that the consequences of economic policies are rarely as straightforward as they appear.

MICROBITS 8.4

Beating the Textile Quotas

Much ingenuity has been expended in circumventing quotas on textile imports. This box features two methods used successfully, at least for a time. The first involves redefining the product so that it no longer fits the legal meaning of a regulated category. The second deals with shifting import sources.

Note also the regulatory dynamic. As the mouse escapes the cat's paws, the cat tries to close the loophole. That only induces the mouse to search for a new loophole, which causes the cat to react. And so the game is played, if not forever, then for quite a while.

The Customs Fashion

This marvelously brief yet telling excerpt comes from a long article on the U.S. clothing industry featured in *The New Yorker* in 1988.

In the early 1980s, some companies began making jackets with zip-on sleeves. "The only reason for this was quota," an import-export lawyer explained to me. "That way, the garments could be called vests instead of outerwear, and vests fall into what's called the basket category—other garments." Quota on jackets was tight at the time, and there were no quotas on vests or sleeves. So people were bringing in vests with half-zippers on the armholes and sep-

arately shipping the sleeves with the other half of the zippers, and the stores would zip the sleeves and the vests together, or the customer would do it. This was actually an important fashion item while it lasted, and it lasted until Customs broadened the definition of outerwear to include vests with attachments for sleeves. The same people said, "O.K., let's take the zippers off and just leave the armholes open, and the sleeves can be sewn on after they get to the United States." That worked for a while, until Customs said, "No, we aren't going to treat as a vest anything that in its imported condition is not commercially viable as a vest. We don't think it's a finished vest; we think it's an unfinished jacket." So then importers actually went to the trouble of putting a commercial fin-

MicroBits 8.4 continued

ish on the armholes, and, after the vests got into the country, removing the finish and adding sleeves. Well, Customs finally put an end to *that* one by saying, "If you bring in a part of a jacket, we're going to make you use jacket quota, and that means if you bring in two sleeves we want *two* jackets' worth of quota." A lot of things you see in the stores are being generated by quota requirements rather than by some designer's great idea. U.S. Customs is the designer, you might say.*

Island Hopping

The second entry is extracted from a 1985 article in *The Wall Street Journal:*

U.S. apparel import rules have forced retailers and clothing importers to perfect the survival technique of island-hopping.

The theory is simple: To avoid U.S. limits on clothing imports and to bypass rising prices in the most popular overseas markets, retailers continually scout for factories in places with low-cost labor, opportunistic investment poli-

cies, and no significant history of doing business with the U.S. [and thus no quota constraints.] . . .

The process has put some unlikely locales on the apparel manufacturing map that otherwise wouldn't rate much attention from U.S. buyers. For example, Mauritius—an island speck 1,000 miles off the east African coast—shipped more than 665,000 men's wool sweaters and nearly two million woven cotton shirts to the U.S. last year. . . .

Yet each success in developing new sources carries a penalty—new import limits, in the form of negotiated or imposed quotas. [That, in turn, forces] retailers, their agents, and manufacturers to search unceasingly for the next virgin port of call.

"Each year, we find a new market, a new source for merchandize," says Vicky C. Davies, director and general manager of Dodwell Exports North America, Ltd., a Hong Kong buying office. Bangladesh was the hot find of 1984, and Sri Lanka the discovery of 1983, she says. "We're all just running a step ahead of the U.S. government before they put on quotas."§

* James Lardner, "The Global Clothing Industry," *The New Yorker,* January 11, 1988, p. 58.

§ Steve Weiner, "Rules Force Retailers, Importers into Survival by Island-Hopping," *The Wall Street Journal,* May 9, 1985, p. 6

Tax-Shifting: Who Pays the Tax?

Federal excise taxes are levied on a small number of goods or services such as alcoholic beverages, cigarettes, gasoline, and telephone calls. In some cases, the tax is added to the buyer's bill at the point of sale. In others, the tax is paid by the producer. But you've already seen in Rothman's cigarette case of Chapter 5 that, given normal supply and demand curves, buyers do not passively endure price increases passed on by sellers.

The discussion here carries this episode beyond the impact of the tax boost on the market demand and supply curves. Now that you understand the interrelationship of the competitive firm and the industry, you'll discover how taxation affects the firm as well as the industry in the short run. (We'll explore the long-run consequences in Chapter 9.)

Figure 8.8 is similar to Figures 8.7 and 8.6. Figure 8.8a is almost identical to Figure 5.9 (p. 162), which depicts an assumed competitive cigarette industry. The cost curves of Burns & Koff appear in Figure 8.8a. The initial industry supply and demand curves cross at a price of $2.29 per pack of cigarettes, enabling Burns & Koff to earn normal but not excess profits. Total industry production is 45 billion cigarettes per year; Burns & Koff manufacture 4.5 billion of them yearly.

The government now imposes a 25-cent tax. This raises the industry supply curve in Figure 8.8b to Supply$_{gross}$, a line 25 cents higher at each point than the original Supply$_{net}$ line. All that means, of course, is that for the firms in the industry to continue supplying as before, they would have to receive an extra 25 cents a pack from purchasers. After they pass their tax collections onto the government, their net proceeds per pack would then be just as they were prior to the imposition of the tax. So, they try to shift the tax onto the buyers. But their effort must fail. At $2.54 per pack,

FIGURE 8.8   The Impact of a Tax on the Firm and Industry in the Short Run

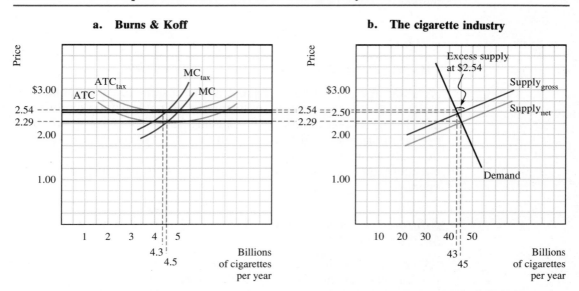

a.   The upward shift of the ATC and MC after the imposition of the 25-cent per pack tax means that if price does not rise from $2.29 to $2.54, Burns & Koff will operate at a loss. At $2.50, profit-maximizing output equals 4.3 billion, but $P < ATC$.

b.   When a 25-cent tax per pack is imposed, suppliers try to shift it fully to consumers. However, $2.54 is not an equilibrium price, so price is forced down to $2.50.

quantity demanded is less than quantity supplied. Price in the market gravitates to $2.50, the new short-run equilibrium.

How is this reflected in Burns & Koff? Look at Figure 8.8a. The original, pretax ATC curve bottoms out at $2.29, where MC crosses ATC. For the market price of $2.29, MR = MC at an output of 4.5 billion cigarettes annually. Now, with the 25-cent tax added on, both the ATC and MC curves shift upward by 25 cents. ATC_{tax} and MC_{tax} depict the new situation from the manufacturer's point of view. The tax imposed on the firm is no different from any other change that raises its operating costs.

That of course leads to Burns & Koff's dilemma: to cover the increased 25-cent cost, price has to rise by 25 cents. A $2.54 per pack charge would restore the firm to its zero profits position. But that price is unsustainable in a market over which the competitive firm has no control. Yet at the market price of $2.50 per pack, you can easily see that Burns & Koff find themselves in a loss position; price is below ATC. And while the firm can continue to operate as long as average variable costs are covered, Burns & Koff stockholders will not be pleased with continued losses.

We'll leave Burns & Koff's management to puzzle with this problem for the moment. We have discovered, however, that a tax that is not fully passed on will lower profits for some firms and induce losses for others. You'll see in Chapter 9 that this situation is unsustainable in a competitive market.

Uninformed and Uncertain Competitors

As usual, the analysis to this point in the chapter has been conducted under a number of simplifying assumptions. But at least two suppositions used in this chapter deserve to be examined a bit more closely. Although perfect information underlies much of the analysis, rarely does information correspond to this ideal. Moreover, avoiding uncertainty and its implications ignores the uncertain environment under which most firms operate.

Information: What You Don't Know May Well Harm You, but So May What You Do Know!

As mentioned earlier in this chapter, perfect knowledge means that every participant in the market—both on the buyers' side and the sellers' side—knows all there is to know. The buyer is never deceived by appearances. Similarly, the seller is fully cognizant of competitors' prices and quality, is privy to the most efficient methods of production, and is aware of the prices and quality of the inputs the firm buys.

Surely, no one knows everything. Just as consumers adjust to incomplete information, so, too, do producers spend time searching for and assessing information. But information is not a free good and thus must be programmed into the cost structure of the firm.

Information Costs and Benefits

How much information should a competitor seek? The marginal revenue–marginal cost analysis developed in this chapter suggests that the firm construct a marginal-cost-of-information (MC) curve and a marginal-benefit-from-information (MB) curve. The shape of both the MC and the MB curve will depend on a variety of considerations. Figure 8.9a assumes that MB is a declining function of time. Every additional hour spent gathering information is less valuable than each previous hour. The figure also assumes a rising MC curve, reflecting ever greater marginal expenditures for each additional hour spent searching. The equilibrium, MB = MC, point tells the firm to spend no more than 40 hours a month on information search. Beyond that, the return from information is inadequate to compensate for additional costs. On the other hand, spending less than 40 hours means that the firm isn't taking sufficient advantage of its information-gathering options.

Using MB = MC analysis suggests an important conclusion that may at first appear strange: *It is neither wise nor profitable for the firm to obtain as much information as possible.* Instead, management must weigh the benefits of additional information against the costs involved. Figure 8.9a shows that although spending 50 hours will provide the firm with more market knowledge, the extra search is excessively costly. For example, while the benefit of spending just the 50th hour in search is $46, the cost is $58, which makes for a loss of $12.

In short, by searching more and spending more, you can obtain more information. But if the benefits from the additional information obtained are not worth the marginal costs, the firm is better-off with less information.

Costly information forces us to revise some of our earlier analysis. We'll now have to adjust the firm's total and average cost curves to reflect information costs and benefits.

Figure 8.9b shows two sets of cost curves. One includes information costs; the other includes only the costs of production. We assume initially that as output expands, the benefits of information rise faster than do the costs. So, production costs adjusted for information decline between the 625 and 4,500 monthly output range. Beyond 4,500, however, additional information costs swamp benefits, so that the ATC$_\text{with information}$ lies above its ATC$_\text{without information}$ counterpart. Notice the new minimum ATC point.

FIGURE 8.9   Information Search

a.   Optimal search

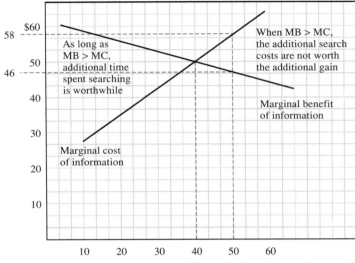

a.   The more time spent on seeking information, the greater the cost of each additional hour spent, but the smaller the marginal benefit of each search hour. Equilibrium occurs when the marginal benefit of search = its marginal cost.

b.   Information and the firm

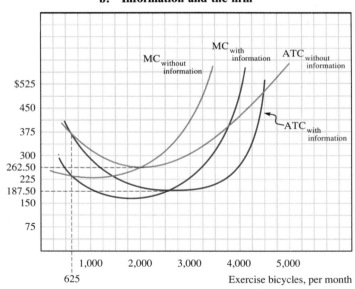

b.   Without seeking additional information, average production costs are minimized at 2,000 bicycles. Spending money on information alters the ATC and MC curves. By linking information outlays to production, the firm discovers its ATC dropping below ATC$_{without information}$ in the 625–4,500 production range, because in that range the marginal benefits of search are greater than the MC of search. That reduces the minimum cost point of the firm from $262.50 to $187.50.

More important, the MC has shifted rightward. That leads to a shift in both the firm's and the industry's supply curve. (Which way? _____[18]) and if supply moves, so does price. Thus, introducing information into the supply side of the market has broad implications.

One final note: Information is a spongy commodity; the knowledge you acquire is not always reliable. To put it differently, information, especially regarding future events, involves some degree of uncertainty. Indeed, many of a firm's choices, such as whether to remain in business in the face of declining prices, are based on guesses about the future.

Uncertainty and Bankruptcy

As price declines and profits turn into losses, the firm's managers must decide whether to continue operations or not. The $P \geq$ AVC rule developed in this chapter assumes the continuation of fixed costs. It ignores another option: **bankruptcy.**

One type of bankruptcy entails closing the business. The bankruptcy court turns over the firm's assets to a court-appointed trustee, and relieves the owners of all obligations, including fixed costs.

Another type, **Chapter 11 bankruptcy,** permits the firm a temporary respite from its creditors. With the consent of the bankruptcy court, the firm presents a course of action that will enable it to continue functioning. Often that action involves renegotiating the firm's commitments to its creditors, leading to reductions in costs and outstanding debts.[19] In this instance, the firm will remain in business even if price is less than current average variable costs, provided the outlook is promising.

The decision to go into bankruptcy, however, is not without its disadvantages. It costs money for lawyers and court fees, as well as management time, energy, and nerves. Moreover, the creditworthiness of the firm is clearly tarnished. Consequently, the management of a business in the red must weigh the benefits of bankruptcy against its costs.

Uncertainty and International Commodity Agreements

Uncertainty makes life difficult for everyone, but it especially threatens the viability of the competitive firm. After all, competition squeezes profits and leaves the firm with little margin for error. One source of uncertainty stems from unstable prices. Even if price, on the average, suffices to keep the industry profitable, price volatility complicates year-to-year decision making.

An **international commodity agreement (ICA)** is one attempt to reduce price fluctuations. Because both the buyers and the sellers of, say, coffee or tin gain from stabilizing prices, they agree to establish an ICA to meet their joint needs. ICAs have been formed between consuming and producing countries for coffee, cocoa, natural rubber, sugar, and tin.

Bankruptcy is a legal procedure under which a court, having found an individual or a firm's liabilities to exceed its assets, arranges for the orderly distribution of the remaining assets to the bankrupt's creditors.

Under a **Chapter 11 bankruptcy,** the firm is permitted to continue its operations while delaying paying its creditors.

An **international commodity agreement (ICA)** between consuming and producing nations seeks to stabilize the world price of a specific output, typically a raw material.

However, they do not all function with the same degree of success, and some no longer operate at all. How they work and why they sometimes don't will become evident as you read on.

Consider the following sequence of expected natural rubber prices (per ton) in each of five successive years: $1,500; $595; $865; $1,065; and $975. A buyer of raw rubber for the Goodyear tire company would have to spend time and resources on planning an optimal purchasing sequence. But, you ask, why not stock up a four-year supply when the price is the lowest in the second year? That seemingly obvious response ignores the realities of decision making in an uncertain world. The $595 is only a projected price and may be way off base. Remember also that the buyer must program into his calculations future inventory costs, which themselves are subject to uncertainty. Will he look like a complete fool if the price of synthetic rubber declines, so that his competitors now undercut Goodyear's prices by using the cheaper latex while he's stuck with a stock of natural rubber? Similar considerations affect sellers. They must continuously reevaluate production and inventory decisions, worry about layoffs when prices are low and the availability of appropriately trained personnel when prices are high, and consider whether to increase or decrease capacity, all in an environment of uncertainty.

International commodity agreements represent the alternative: Stabilize prices at the five-year average price of $1,000. Price uncertainty is eliminated, so that both buyers and sellers can base future decisions on the fixed price.

Figure 8.10 examines the impact on the individual firm of both price fluctuations and price stability. Consider first how the firm reacts to two demand curves, Demand$_{high}$ and Demand$_{low}$ in Figure 8.10b. For the given supply curve, price is high for the former demand curve and low for the latter. At $P = $1,250 and ATC = $1,050 per ton, the firm in Figure 8.10a sets production at 7,000 tons and earns $1.4 million in excess profits. On the other hand, when $P = $750, production and resource use are cut back. If the firm produces at the MR = MC output with ATC = $1,075, profits are a negative $1.3 million. Indeed, since price is less than AVC, this particular firm will shut down production altogether. In fact, costs are even higher, because the firm must develop strategies to deal with uncertainty.

The firm would be far better-off with Demand$_{average}$ and a fixed price of $1,000. As Figure 8.10a indicates, the firm earns normal profits. Moreover, in the absence of uncertainty, its production decisions are boringly repetitive but less costly.

One important question remains: How is the price stabilized? Neither purity of soul nor international agreement will suffice to keep the price at $1,000 per ton. Instead, producers and consumers of rubber agree to establish a **buffer stock agency (BSA).**

Back now to Figure 8.10b. In years of low demand, when production

A **buffer stock agency (BSA)** is charged by the ICA with the mechanics of stabilizing the price of the commodity.

at the average price (8 million tons) exceeds the quantity demanded at $1,000 (3 million tons), the BSA buys up and stores the surplus 5 million tons. On the other hand, when demand is high and quantity demanded at the average price is greater than quantity supplied, the 5 million ton buffer stock is sold. If the calculations of the buffer stock administration are correct, then the years of overstock should be matched by years of depletion, and on the average, the buffer stock equals zero.

How simple an idea, yet how complex the reality. You can well understand that if the price trend is not flat, the commodity arrangement may collapse. If prices are continuously rising, then the buffer stock agency, continuously responding to excess demand by selling from its commodity inventory, must ultimately run out of the stored commodity. Moreover, rising prices encourage the suppliers to seek an end to the agreement, since they obviously benefit from the upward price trend. On the other hand, a falling price trend demands that the BSA continuously buy the surplus commodity. Unless it has very deep pockets, funds for purchasing the surplus would ultimately run out. Moreover, secularly falling prices would induce the demanders to pull out of the agreement, since it is they who benefit from that trend.

FIGURE 8.10   International Commodity Agreements

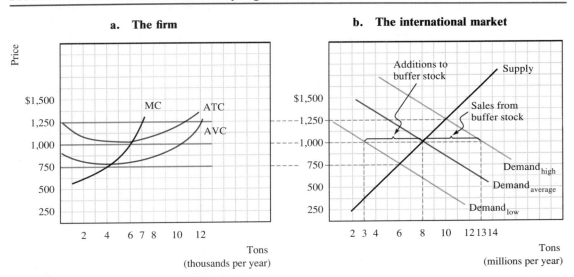

a.   With $P = \$1,250$, MR $=$ MC at 7,000 tons, and since $P >$ ATC, the firm obtains excess profits. On the other hand, when $P = \$750$, $P <$ AVC and the firm shuts down. At the stabilized price of $1,000, MR $=$ MC at 6,000 tons, $P =$ ATC and normal profits are earned.

b.   Without an international commodity agreement, price $= \$1,250$ when demand is high and $750 when demand is low. With an ICA and a $1,000 price, when demand is low, the agency buys 5 million tons—the difference between quantity demanded and supplied at $1,000. On the other hand, when demand is high, the buffer stock agency sells 5 million tons to keep price at $1,000.

Summary

Return to Joan's umbrella operation. In Chapter 7, we saw her master both short-run and long-run cost curves, and find them to be U-shaped. Joan had learned how to use her inputs with maximum efficiency, so that the cost curves represented the minimum costs for any given level of output. She had yet to discover the optimum level of output—how much to produce. If paper umbrellas are sold on a competitive market, then Joan's mastery of this chapter should have taught her how to set the output level in the short run: she will find the quantity at which *marginal revenue equals marginal cost (MR = MC)*.

To be sure, the stylized conditions of perfect competition—no single firm can control price, product homogeneity, unrestricted entry and exit, and perfect knowledge—and the assumption of profit maximization may not be characteristic of Joan's situation. Nevertheless, the more these conditions describe the paper umbrella industry, the more applicable their implications in the real world.

In a perfectly competitive market, MR equals price and is determined by the market. Joan will not charge less than the market price. Nor will she be able to survive by charging a price greater than the market price. (This condition makes the demand curve for the competitive firm perfectly elastic.) Since MC varies with output, Joan's task is to discern the output of paper umbrellas at which MC equals price.

Now, the MR = MC condition need not assure Joan of profits. The firm's profitability hinges on the relationship between price and average costs. As long as price exceeds average costs, the firm earns excess profits. That's because total revenue (= $P \times Q$) will be greater than total costs (= ATC $\times Q$). Normal profits will be earned if the market price only just covers average costs. On the other hand, should price lie below average costs, Joan would be wise to inspect the relationship between *price* and *average variable costs*. Only if $P >$ AVC, so that operating contributes to covering some share of total fixed costs, should Joan recommend continued operation. If, however, AVC is greater than price, the firm will become better off by shutting down. It will then only lose its total fixed costs.

The relationship between a changing market price and the MC curve of the firm permits Joan to calculate her firm's supply curve, which is identical to the MC curve above the shutdown point. An industry analyst could sum the MC curves of Joan and her fellow competitors to determine the market supply curve. The actual market price can then be found by juxtaposing the market supply curve with the market demand curve.

To be sure, this analysis is highly simplified. The existence of such frictions as information deficiencies that must be remedied by expending additional resources force some revision of the simple conclusions. So, too, does the presence of uncertainty. And the very nature of a competitive market leads producers to seek ways to reduce the tensions of competition. Nevertheless, the competitive model's fundamental conclusion of equating MR with MC is one of the key lessons of microeconomics: *Modern economic analysis revolves around the weighing of marginal benefits against marginal costs.* This principle perhaps more than any other serves to distinguish economists today from practitioners of other professions.

This chapter has focused on the marginalist principle in the short-run theory of the firm. Clearly, however, the principle can be applied to the long run as well, with most interesting consequences. Chapter 9 analyzes long-run decisions of the firm; it should lead you to understand why economists are so enamored with the competitive model.

Key Terms

Agency costs
Agent
Bankruptcy
Buffer stock agency (BSA)
Chapter 11 bankruptcy
Deadweight loss
Excess profits
International commodity agreement (ICA)

Marginal revenue
Normal profits
Price maker
Price taker
Principal
Producers' surplus
Product (or industry) demand curve
Shutdown point

Review Questions

1. *a.* How can a principal either force or encourage an agent to comply to the principal's wishes?
   b. Use Figure 8.1 to show that unless the principal limits the agent's fringe benefits to less than $10,000, the constraint will be meaningless.
2. List and explain the conditions of perfect competition.
3. Is it strange that although the industry demand curve in a perfectly competitive industry has a negative slope, the demand curve facing the competitive firm is flat?
4. Use Figure 8.3a to depict the impact of a decline in price to $647.45 on equilibrium output and profits.
5. Show, using Figure 8.5, the impact on Pedal Pushers of a market price of $625.

Calculate profits or losses, and explain why the firm should not close down.
6. "A firm should continue to operate as long as its revenues cover its fixed costs." Do you agree? Explain.
7. Explain the identity of the competitive firm's supply curve and marginal cost curve (above the shutdown point).
8. *a.* Would you favor a doubling of the quota on shirts? Explain using Figure 8.7b.
   b. Would the domestic manufacturer depicted in Figure 8.7a agree? Show why or why not.
9. Why might management prefer less to more information?
10. Show how a buffer stock agency (BSA) stabilizes price in the face of fluctuating demands for an ICA commodity.

Food for Thought

1. *a.* Which is better for minimizing the principal–agent conflict—limiting fringe benefits or providing profit-sharing incentives? Explain using Figure 8.1.
   b. Sketch out on Figure 8.1 and explain the impact of a profit-sharing arrange-

ment that provides Spruce Bruce with 25 percent of the firm's profits.
2. *a.* In early February 1987 Health-Tex, Inc., a manufacturer of children's clothing, planned to close down plants in Maine and Virginia and lay off over

1,000 workers. The reason given: The plants were old and small, with high overhead costs. Consequently, the firm was unable to compete with both other domestic and foreign clothing manufacturers. Do you agree with the Health-Tex decision?

b. Is the second quotation opening this chapter consistent with the shutdown rule suggested in the text?

3. a. Show that a tariff on textiles would produce the same results as an import quota.

b. Why, then, have economists preferred tariffs to quotas?

4. "Strategic trade policy" advocates using tariffs as a weapon of economic policy when the bulk of the costs fall upon foreigners. What elasticity conditions would be consistent with such a policy?

5. a. Show the deadweight loss that stems from the decision to raise cigarette taxes in Figure 8.8b.

b. Would the loss be greater or smaller if the demand were more elastic? If the supply were more elastic?

c. Could you justify the contention that the loss in consumer welfare in this specific case ought not to be measured by the loss in consumer surplus? (Hint: Is there a distinction between shirts and cigarettes?)

6. a. Show the redistributive impact and the deadweight loss of a gasoline monopolist, who sets price higher than it would have been had the market been perfectly competitive. (Assume normally sloped supply and demand curves.)

b. Would taxing away the monopolist's excess profits resolve the detrimental impact of monopoly power?

7. a. Demonstrate the impact on a BSA of a trend of decreasing commodity demand.

b. What are the salient differences between the agricultural subsidy program mentioned in Chapter 2 and the ICA of this chapter? Discuss both objectives and techniques.

Suggested Readings

Those interested in ICAs might read Christopher L. Gilbert, "International Commodity Agreements: Design and Performance," and Alasdair Macbean and Ductin Nguyen, "International Commodity Agreements: Shadow and Substance," *World Development* 15, no. 5 (1987), pp. 591–616 and pp. 575–90, respectively.

Notes and Answers

1. For every dollar in dividends Bruce is willing to give up, he can obtain $2 worth of fringe benefits.

2. Don't feel sorry for Bruce, for despite the budget line having moved inward, that only represents Bruce's options from Spruce Bruce's Ornaments. Remember, though, that Bruce received a lump-sum payment for his half of the firm, which can be invested for additional income.

3. Increase the slope from ½ in the direction of 1.

4. Recall from Chapter 5 that elasticity is defined as $(\Delta Q/\Delta P)P/Q$. Since $\Delta P = 0$, the

entire denominator equals 0, and anything divided by 0 = α.

5. The TR curve is a straight line, since it is derived by multiplying a constant—price—by a variable—quantity. Prove to yourself that this statement is correct.

6. That shouldn't be surprising, since the slope of the TR curve (= $\Delta TR / \Delta Q$) is the MR, while the slope of the TC curve is the MC. By finding that point on the TC curve whose slope is identical to the slope of the TR curve, we are simply equating MR and MC.

7. $652.50 comes either from Figure 8.3b or from Table 7.2.

8. Note that profit in Figure 8.3a is indicated by a linear distance between TR and TC, while in Figure 8.3b, profit is demonstrated by a rectangle. Similarly, TR and TC are points in the upper panel but rectangles in the lower panel.

9. At 25, MC now exceeds the reduced MR. Whenever that happens, profits are less than optimal.

10. Temporary shutdowns are not uncommon in American industry. Automobile manufacturers often cut back on production as seasonal demand slows and then cease production for a while to permit their inventories to shrink. Going bankrupt is an option explored later in the chapter.

11. You can see that in the diagram as well. Remember that ATC − AVC = AFC. At 20, AFC = $650 − $600 = $50 and TFC = $50 × 20 = $1,000.

12. Note that the abscissa = thousands of bicycles per month, not units. The supply curve drawn here represents an industry of 1,000 firms identical in every respect to Pedal Pushers. Consequently, the supply curve of Pedal Pushers has the same shape but is only 1/1,000th of the amount indicated on the abcissa.

13. $647.45; 22,000; 22.

14. The correct picture will show that the lowest point of the ATC of the effective competitor will at least be tangent to the $15 price. That will enable the surviving domestic firm to earn at least normal profits.

15. They all close down, ceding the entire domestic market to imports.

16. $22.50; 45 million; $1,012.5 million; $922 million; $90 million.

17. The political appeal of protectionist measures becomes stronger as the producer surplus accruing to foreign suppliers becomes greater.

18. The supply curve shifts rightward.

19. Creditors will agree only if they believe they stand to gain more by the firm's remaining operational.

THE PERFECTLY COMPETITIVE FIRM IN THE LONG RUN

Peter Martin, who in 1964 founded the New Yorker Bookshop, . . . that closed for economic reasons in 1982, died of emphysema in San Francisco last Thursday.
Obituary, *The New York Times* (March 8, 1988)

The best competitor is a dead competitor.
Anonymous

Learning Objectives

By the time you master this chapter, you'll understand:

- The conditions for long-run equilibrium in a perfectly competitive market.
- The role played by perfect knowledge and freedom of entry in bringing about long-run equilibrium.
- Why economies of scale and a competitive long-run equilibrium are incompatible.
- How long-run equilibrium analysis can be used for policy purposes.
- Why economists still are captivated by the model and implications of perfectly competitive markets.

Airlines and Banking

Although neither the airline industry nor the banking industry fulfills the conditions for perfect competition, they nevertheless can shed a good deal of light on the workings of the competitive marketplace.

Airlines

Who decides how much an airline can charge and where it can fly? Until a decade and a half ago, rates and routes were proposed by the airlines and approved or rejected by federal regulators. The Civil Aviation Board (CAB) opposed price competition and so initiated a vicious cycle. Since the airlines couldn't compete using price, they substituted "service" competition, including more frequent flights. Flying more often meant averaging fewer passengers per flight, thereby raising average costs. The CAB allowed the airlines to raise prices to forestall losses, but that led to a decline in quantity demanded and a further fall in passenger load.[1] Declining demand in turn justified the CAB's policy of restricting entry into the national air carrier market. The CAB felt that a free-for-all entry policy could lead to losses among existing carriers.

Radical change occurred in the post-1978 era, when deregulation and price competition became the names of the game. Not surprisingly, the average price of flying fell as discounts of one sort or another became common.[2] At the same time, the structure of the industry changed. Entry became more open, alternative pricing strategies became possible, and discount airlines blossomed.

Yet if you examine the airline picture today, you'll see less competition, not more. The discount airlines have fallen on rough times, some of the larger carriers are bankrupt, and others have merged to become airline giants. In fact, already by 1986 the six largest air carriers controlled 84 percent of the market, whereas the big six only ruled over 73 percent in 1978. What happened to competition?

Banking

Over 10,000 banks dot the United States. They come in all sizes, from the tiny Union National Bank in Temple, Oklahoma, with only $793,000 in assets in 1991 to New York's giant Citibank, the flagship of Citicorp whose assets exceed $200 billion. Some bankers operate out of a single office, while others supervise a network of hundreds of branches. Yet, big or small, concentrated or dispersed, all banks provide pretty much the same types of services. Bankers compete for our patronage in a variety of ways, including the interest rates and fees they charge on loans, the interest rates they pay on deposits, and the convenience they offer in terms of location and hours of service.

The banking industry in the United States today is undergoing dramatic change. Banks failed in record numbers during the 1980s, although depositor losses were negligible because virtually all banks are federally insured. Sometimes, failed banks were closed and depositors paid off. In many cases, however, the insurance authorities arranged for failing banks to be taken over by healthier institutions. A decline in the number of banks and an increase in the number of branch banks were the inevitable outcome.

Clearly, competition in the area served by the merged banks must suffer. Yet, insofar as larger banks are more efficient than smaller ones, the merger policy reduces operating costs, which can lead to improved services and lower prices to bank clients. Whether the outcome of regulatory mergers is beneficial or detrimental depends to a large extent on the degree of competition prevailing after the takeovers. If competition remains strong, then the market will ensure that cost savings are passed on to bank customers. If not, then depositors and borrowers will lose out.

The next section of this chapter explains, on theoretical grounds, why firms operating in a competitive industry will be unable to extract excess profits from the public. Unfortunately, such general proofs can only point regulatory policy into the right direction. The regulators must grapple with specifics rather than apply general principles. In each particular case, they must ask:

- Is the industry in question perfectly competitive (or approximately so)?
- Are there economies of scale that can be appropriated?

These questions are empirical, not theoretical. The third section of this chapter combines the implications of long-run equilibrium with the facts of the airline and banking industries. Additional applications of the long-run consequences of competition are discussed in the fourth section. This chapter concludes with some general comments on the implications and usefulness of the competitive model.

Economic Darwinism: Long-Run Equilibrium in Perfectly Competitive Markets

Long-run equilibrium exists when economic conditions are such that no existing firms leave the industry and no new firms enter.

Long-run equilibrium can hold true in any market, whether perfectly competitive or imperfectly so. After all, equilibrium means only that stability has been achieved and, unless buffeted by outside forces, the position of the firm and industry will remain the same over time. For a *perfectly competitive market* to be in long-run equilibrium, two further conditions must be met:

A firm is **optimally sized** when it operates at the lowest point of the long-run average cost curve.

1. Firms must not be subject to persistent economies of scale; long-run average costs (LRATC) must not be allowed always to fall.
2. The market must be large enough to accommodate sufficient **optimally sized firms** to preserve vigorous competition.

These two conditions guarantee that when the competitive battle is finally over and no additional firms enter the industry nor do existing firms leave, sufficient numbers of firms remain so that none can control the price of the product. Why these conditions must be met and why they are related to the LRATC will become apparent as you read on.

The Firm and the Industry

Return to the Pedal Pushers example in Chapter 8. When we left them on page 276, Pedal Pushers had faced a profitable price of $725 per bike, but a fall in industry demand had brought the price down to $647.45. At the lower price, the firm would break even at an output of 22 units. Now take a look at Figure 9.1, with the industry demand and supply curves in Figure 9.1b and Pedal Pushers' short-run average total cost (SRAC) and

FIGURE 9.1   Long-Run Equilibrium in a Perfectly Competitive Market

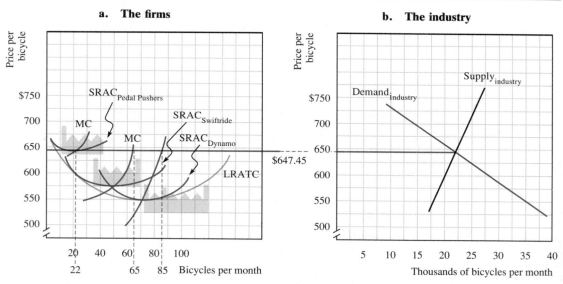

a.   **The firms**

b.   **The industry**

a. Although Pedal Pushers can survive at a market price of $647.45 per bike, it could not remain in business at a lower price. Yet, both SwiftRide and Dynamo could produce at lower costs because their plants are larger. New entrants, coming in at Dynamo's lowest SRAC, would force price down to $550. In long-run equilibrium, only Dynamo-sized plants could survive.

b. While price in the short run is determined by the existing industry supply and demand curves, as new entrants begin producing, supply rises and price comes down. Only at $550 will the supply curve stop shifting.

marginal cost (MC) in Figure 9.1a. The break-even price and output are consistent with Figure 8.4. Notice, however, that Pedal Pushers is only one of the individual firms represented in Figure 9.1. The cost curves of two more firms—SwiftRide and Dynamo—also appear. And so does the long-run average cost (LRAC) curve. (Figure 9.1a is virtually identical to Figure 7.9, p. 231).

Examine Figure 9.1a carefully. You'll quickly see that the larger the plant or firm (sketched in the background), the lower the average cost of each plant. That is reflected not only in the individual short-run curves, but in the left-hand segment of the LRATC as well. Economies of scale exist up to 70 bicycles per month. Thus, while it costs Pedal Pushers $647.45 to manufacture each of 22 bicycles, the same 22 units can be produced in SwiftRide's larger plant for $600. But economies of scale extend still further. If Dynamo decided to produce 50 bikes (i.e., the output at which SwiftRide's SRAC bottoms out), it could do so more cheaply than can either Pedal Pushers or SwiftRide. In fact, Dynamo could produce 70 bicycles per month at a cost of $550 per bike.

What would happen to average costs if a bicycle manufacturer decided to build a factory that was even larger than Dynamo's? _____

Average costs would rise, as the new firm would operate on the rising segment of the LRATC. In this case, too large is more costly.

A Digression.   "Too large is too costly" is true in two senses. You've just read the first. The second applies when a firm produces well below capacity. Would it be cheaper for SwiftRide or for Dynamo to produce 22 bicycles? Figure 9.1a suggests SwiftRide; Dynamo is too big.

That's a lesson the Ford Motor Company learned the hard way. In 1971, Ford built a modern engine block factory in Flat Rock, Michigan. The four-story plant, large enough to enclose 72 football fields, cost Ford around $200 million. It was one of Ford's largest and most economical facilities, and was designed to produce 500,000 tons of V-8 iron engine blocks yearly. Unfortunately, as demand for the gas-guzzling V-8's dwindled, Flat Rock could no longer be fully utilized. With low volume, the average cost of engine production went sky-high. In 1981, Ford closed the plant, laying off 2,500 production line workers. In the words of one observer: "Its closing is a lesson in mass production. Sometimes you really can be too big."

Long-Run Equilibrium.   What does all this mean to Pedal Pushers? As long as the price per bike remains at $647.45, Pedal Pushers can survive. But at that price, both SwiftRide and Dynamo earn excess profits. (How much is a bit complicated, but you should be able to figure it out. For SwiftRide, MR = MC at an output of 65 units, for total revenues of $42,084.25. At 65 bikes, ATC = $585 and total costs come to $38,025.

Therefore, π equals \$4,059.25. For Dynamo, maximum profit occurs at
____ bikes, total revenue = \$_____, total costs = \$_____, and
π = _____.[3])

Is this situation consistent with long-run equilibrium in a perfectly
competitive market? The answer is no. The status quo will be upset
because of forces set into motion by two crucial assumptions of perfect
competition: *perfect knowledge* and *freedom of entry*. Potential entrants
into the bicycle market are aware of the excess profits that both SwiftRide
and Dynamo are raking in. These new competitors enter the bicycle industry by setting up plants that emulate the most profitable firm, Dynamo.
When the plants come on line, the supply curve shifts rightward. Given
the same demand curve, price falls.

How far does price fall? If you've followed the reasoning so far, you
understand that price will settle at \$550 per bike. At any higher price, new
entrants will still profit from entry. Some part of their ATCs, being identical to Dynamo, will lie beneath the market price. Only at \$550 does the
incentive to enter evaporate.[4] (Now draw in the new supply curve in

"Don't worry about me. I'm a survivor."

SOURCE: Drawing by Handelsman; © 1988 *The New Yorker* Magazine.

Figure 9.1b.) In long-run equilibrium, the market supply will be 35,000 bikes per month at a price of $550. Each optimum-sized producer will supply 70 bicycles, a measly 2 percent of the market.

In short, *competitive long-run equilibrium is achieved (1) when P = minimum LRATC and (2) when sufficient numbers of firms inhabit the industry*. Only when price falls to the lowest point of the LRATC will entry neither be stimulated nor exit encouraged.

Adapt or Perish.   Clearly, Pedal Pushers cannot continue to operate at its present level of relative inefficiency. But, must Pedal Pushers become a victim to the rigors of competition? Or can it survive? Actually, Pedal Pushers does have a long-run alternative to producing at a loss: adapt. Pedal Pushers can expand its plant to Dynamo's size and thereby reduce its operating costs. Such a reaction would once again enable Pedal Pushers to earn normal profits.

In a sense, then, there's a Darwinian survival-of-the-fittest process working in the competitive market. Adapt or disappear are the nasty options for the competitive firm. If a firm *can be undercut* by a cheaper-cost producer, the rules of the competitive marketplace suggest that it *will be undercut*. Of course, that implies that the industry is characterized by ease of entry and exit, by readily available information so that firms can take the appropriate action, and by sufficient firms to be competitive. Implicitly, perfect competition assumes either a U-shaped LRATC curve with the U rising at a relatively small share of the entire market, or an L-shaped LRATC curve. The importance of the latter presumption is the subject of MicroBits 9.1.

Some Practical Realities.   While survival of the fittest is a key element in the competitive marketplace, who will be the fittest is not predetermined. Moreover, the working out of long-run equilibrium takes time, so that at any moment, efficient and inefficient firms will coexist. Let's consider each of these points in turn.

First, who will survive—the old firms or the newcomers? Certainly, existing firms can adjust their operations to meet the newcomers on an even footing. (See MicroBits 9.2, on the textile industry.) Indeed, the old firms may have some advantages not available to new firms, such as reputation, customer contacts, and experience in production and marketing. On the other hand, old firms may be set in their ways and unwilling to adapt. They may also be locked into obsolete production facilities that should be junked but aren't or into contractual agreements with employees and suppliers that cannot be renegotiated. Thus, it is not apparent whether the survivors will be existing firms, newcomers, or some of each.

MicroBits 9.1

Economies of Scale and the Death of Perfect Competition

For long-run equilibrium to be compatible with the competitive market, the latter must be sufficiently large to permit a sufficient number of optimally sized firms to survive. Here, we will demonstrate the converse: if economies of scale characterize the market, then only one firm will survive and competition will be replaced by monopoly.

The figure on the next page reproduces the left hand side of the U in Figure 7.9, but adds some additional short-run cost curves. Focus on $SRAC_{Cheery}$ and $SRAC_{Dreary}$. Each curve represents one of two egg producers: Dreary Eggs and Cheery Eggs. At a production level of 100,000 eggs per month, the costs per egg are 5 cents for Cheery and 6 cents for Dreary. Since eggs are eggs and since both Cheery and Dreary are price takers, Cheery has a 1-cent cost advantage per egg.

What must happen to Dreary in a competitive market? _____

Clearly, if the market price is 6 cents, Cheery earns a penny of eggcess profits per egg or $1,000 per month, while Dreary breaks even. And if the market price is 5 cents, then Cheery breaks even, while Dreary ultimately must leave the market. In either case, Cheery, the larger egg producer, is better-off than the smaller Dreary.

But the figure implies that another egg producer, Rosy, can open a plant that's even larger than that of either Cheery or Dreary and produce lower-cost eggs. Indeed, Rosy's hens can lay 200,000 eggs per month, equal to the combined output of her competitors, at an average cost of 4 cents. By undercutting Cheery and Dreary, pricing the eggs at 4.5 cents, Rosy can capture their market share and still earn excess profits.

As a matter of fact, Rosy can do better. Because Rosy's SRAC is still falling to the right of 200,000 eggs, Rosy can cut costs further. Rosy can produce at the minimum point

---

Second, consider the time element. It's quite clear from the previous chapter that firms will not drop out of the industry immediately when price falls below their average total costs; their fixed commitments act as a drag on their actions. The entry of new competitors also takes time. In the real world, information is not disseminated immediately, and when it is, it is often incomplete. Clearly, entry decisions by entrepreneurs are rarely hastily taken. Often, capital has to be borrowed, location decisions have to be made, and a labor force has to be assembled and trained.

Consequently, competitive industries are normally in flux.[5] If you were to view the industry as a motion picture, you'd observe the turmoil as some firms expire and others are born. On the other hand, if you were to halt the film at any point, you'd observe efficient firms operating side by side with inefficient ones. But time does not stop, and the conclusion is inevitable: Only low-cost producers will survive in the long-run competitive equilibrium.

MicroBits 9.1 continued

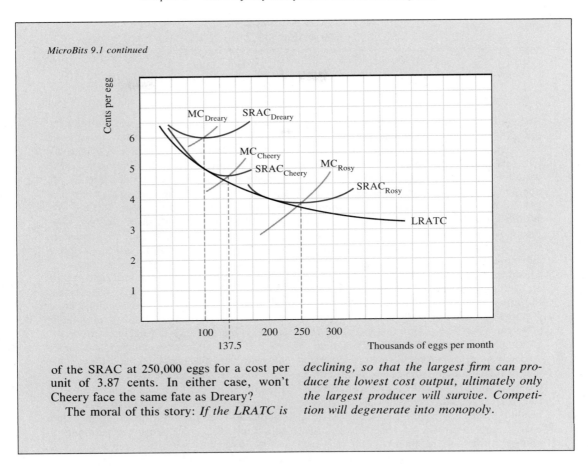

of the SRAC at 250,000 eggs for a cost per unit of 3.87 cents. In either case, won't Cheery face the same fate as Dreary?

The moral of this story: *If the LRATC is declining, so that the largest firm can produce the lowest cost output, ultimately only the largest producer will survive. Competition will degenerate into monopoly.*

Innovation and Perfect Competition

That to survive in the long run producers must remain competitive can be driven home by examining the impact of a technological innovation in the competitive marketplace. A new invention or a new method of production either permits more of a good or service to be produced at the same costs or the same amount to be produced at lower costs.[6]

Figure 9.2 on page 306 reproduces the final equilibrium position of Figure 9.1, labeling the relevant curves as "old." Price per bicycle has now settled at $550, each producer sells 70 per month (Figure 9.2a), while total production and consumption equals 35,000 per month (Figure 9.2b). A new method of inventory control enables production costs to be cut by 5 percent, so that average costs fall for those firms using the new technique. The cost curves labeled "new" in Figure 9.2a describe the lower-cost option.

MicroBits 9.2

Survivors

Ricke Knitting Mills, on Flushing Avenue in the Maspeth section of Queens, is a one-story red brick structure that was built in 1955 and looks its age. It's the sort of factory a person wouldn't mind living next to, and quite a few people do live next to it, in two-story clapboard houses with aluminum awnings. Within a few blocks' range are a florist's, a neighborhood bar, and a V.F.W. post, and Ricke seems at home and in scale with these surroundings. A pedestrian heading down Flushing Avenue between Fifty-eighth Road and Fifth-eighth Drive might not even notice the jump from residential to industrial use, although it would be hard to miss the three identical red Chevy Corvettes sitting in the parking lot in front of the factory building.

The Corvettes belong to Richard, Joseph, and Bruce Goldman, who have been running the place since their father, Milton, retired a few years ago. All three cars and all three brothers were on the premises when I arrived one afternoon in July of 1986. Bruce, the youngest, was in the back of the factory, working with the electronic knitting machines, in which Ricke has invested heavily;

Joseph, the middle brother, was on the production floor, watching over the progress of an order; and Richard, the oldest, was at his desk in the front office, fielding phone calls, periodically checking to see who had set off the bell that signals arrivals and departures through the factory's front door (which is just outside the office), and, in the intervals between these activities, giving me a sweatermaker's perspective on the subject of international trade.

I repeated an observation I had heard from several fashion-company executives: that American knitwear factories didn't have the patience to deal with small or complicated orders and took a grudging attitude toward the job of making samples. "A lot of mills are run by older men, and they don't want to make samples," Richard said, "We *do* make them, and we make them fast. Liz Claiborne, for instance, needs at least three samples of each garment. It used to be that a mill could pick and choose the garments it wanted to make. My father had a group of core people he could depend on. In January or February, his accounts would call him into

---

What happens in a perfectly competitive market?

The producers who adopt the cost-cutting technology earn excess profits at the old competitive market price. The perfect information assumption implies that all interested parties know not only about the innovation but also about the higher profits captured by the firms who introduced it. So, others in the industry—and new entrants, too—emulate the innovators, bringing an increase in supply and a fall in price. Supply continues to increase until it stabilizes at Supply$_{new}$ in Figure 9.2b. The new equilibrium price, of course, is $522.50, the price consistent with the minimum point of the new LRATC.

MicroBits 9.2 continued

the city, and they'd sit down and plan their orders for the whole year. We can't operate like that anymore. If a customer says 'Jump,' we say 'How high?'"

"Liz Claiborne makes goods all over the world. Calvin Klein, London Fog—they're the same way. We've demonstrated to them that we're willing to drop whatever we're doing to satisfy them, as long as they give us the same lead time they do overseas. In the last eighteen months, we've spent a million dollars on electronic knitting machines. It was an all-or-nothing gamble. We have big notes to pay. Things are very, very tight. But we can cover every base now. We might not have tremendous volume, but we have triple-lock machines in four-cut, five-cut, six-cut, seven-cut, eight-cut, and ten-cut. Also, we're a cab ride away from the garment district. The buyers and the designers can be here in fifteen minutes."

"A lot of the mills are run by older people who really don't have the vision," Joseph Goldman said, "They're so set in their ways—"

"Right," Richard broke in. "My father used to work on the old flat machines and circular machines, and as we started to become more and more electronic he stopped

going into the knitting department. Even though the stitch configurations were the same and the basics of knitting were the same, the programming was so alien to him that he gave up on it. A lot of the older mill-owners are trying to upgrade their machinery, but they're not upgrading their thinking to go along with it. Running a knitting machine is not only running it for the orders. The beauty of having the computer controls is that we can interrupt an order, make some samples, get back into production, and satisfy two people at the same time.

I asked Richard how he thought his sweaters compared in quality with those from the Far East.

"People will tell you the quality is better overseas—that's nonsense," he said. "They buy machines from the same people we do. Knitting is knitting, whether we do it or they do it or Joe Schmo does it—whether it's done in Taiwan or on Mars. There's only four different things you can do: you can knit, you can tuck, you can miss, you can transfer. That's it."

Back to the Future: Competition in the Airlines and Banking Industries

Airlines

You should not be surprised by the airline market as you reexamine the situation there using the framework of long-run competitive equilibrium. When deregulation occurred in 1978, the expected competitive process began to germinate. New entrants, anticipating profitable opportunities,

**FIGURE 9.2   The Impact of a Cost-Saving Innovation on Long-Run Equilibrium in a Perfectly
Competitive Market**

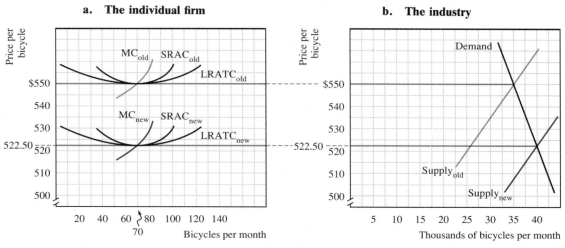

a.   **The individual firm**   b.   **The industry**

a.   A cost-cutting innovation lowers the LRATC.
If only some of the old firms adopt the
technology and earn excess profits,
newcomers will imitate the most efficient
firms, their supply will drive the market price
down, and force the old-timers either to adapt
or exit. The new equilibrium for the
individual firm is at $522.50 per bicycle and
an output of 70 bikes per month.

b.   The inflow of new firms shifts the industry
supply curve outward. Only at $522.50,
where the efficient firm breaks even, will
entry stop and the supply curve cease its
rightward movement.

began providing passenger service. (The total of interstate carriers rose
from about 36 in 1978 to 125 by 1984.) They attracted customers by
offering lower prices. Since flying is basically a homogeneous service—
getting you from here to there—and cost studies showed no significant
economies of scale in the airline industry, the newer carriers began to take
market share from existing lines. The older firms reacted by cutting their
prices to match the upstarts, putting pressure on everyone's profit picture. Some carriers could not withstand the competition and so had to
drop out of the industry. (By 1986, less than 100 airlines operated interstate.) That flow and ebb is surely consistent with competition.

Actually, this stylized portrait is somewhat misleading. First, deregulation has not been total. Regulations still favor the older firms over the
new. For example, existing airlines have locked-in airport terminal gates
and departure time slots, giving them a decided advantage over newcomers.[7]

Second, though the immediate consequence of more competition was increased efficiency, that paradoxically led to less competition. That same competition that forced the formerly protected national carriers to seek lower costs led to the less competitive hub-and-spoke system. Under the hub-and-spoke concept, a national carrier concentrates flights on a few urban centers. (United, for example, has hubs at Chicago, Denver, and San Francisco.) The airline routes passengers to these hubs from the outer rim along the spokes, using either its own planes or joining forces with small commuter airlines. The traffic flow generated at the hub increases passenger loads, enabling larger, more efficient jets to fly the longer trips while smaller planes, which are more efficient for small numbers of passengers and shorter hauls, are used to feed the hubs. In fact, the integration of plane use not only cuts costs to the air carrier, but also enables the hub airline to provide more frequent connecting flights.[8] The flip side of the lower cost and better service is that competitors find it more difficult to challenge any airline already dominating the hub. (How likely are competitors to try to penetrate Minneapolis, where Northwest controls 80 percent of the traffic, or St. Louis, where TWA has captured 85 percent?)

Banking

Let's return now to the competitive situation in banking. First, What does the LRATC curve in banking say about the potentiality for effective competition? Chapter 7 cited conflicting conclusions about the LRATC. Some empirical studies found that economies of scale characterize commercial banks until the $25 to $50 million range, after which the LRATC curve turns flat. Other studies demonstrated a U-shaped LRATC curve, with the U bottoming out at a relatively small bank size. What do these studies imply?

The L-Shaped LRATC Curve.   Figure 9.3 sketches out the first alternative: economies of scale to, say, $50 million, and no economies or diseconomies thereafter. This LRATC curve suggests that

- Banks that are smaller than $50 million are too small; they cannot take full advantage of the cost economies that larger banks can.
- No cost advantage accrues to banks larger than $50 million, whether they are as small as $75 million, as medium-size as $250 million, or as large as $500 million.

Now, consider a banking market such as California, which epitomizes an L-shaped LRATC curve. California has permitted commercial banks to set themselves up as either single-office units or branch networks. And both types of banks have flourished in that state, including the Bank of America, among the nation's largest. The survival of banks of different

FIGURE 9.3   Long-Run Average Costs in Banking

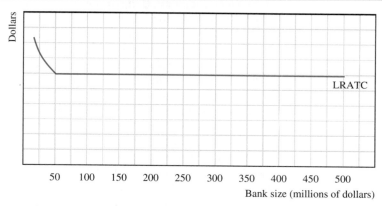

As banks grow to the $50 million size, their average costs decline. Once they've reached $50 million, however, further growth does not bring average costs down.

sizes is consistent with the presumption that big banks have no particular cost advantage over their smaller rivals. (You can verify this statement by drawing a series of SRAC curves onto Figure 9.3.)[9]

A clear policy recommendation to the regulators follows from this observation. Because the market is competitive, merging failing banks in California will be beneficial for two reasons:

· Merging small banks (less than $50 million) will reduce costs, while merging larger banks will not increase costs.

· Bank customers benefit. Where a merger leads to reduced costs, competition assures that the cost savings will be passed on to bank customers. But even where no cost savings are likely, as when two $150 million banks are merged, clients of the acquiring bank will not lose out, while customers of the failing institution will continue to be served by banking facilities.

The U-Shaped Alternative.   The regulatory decision is far more complex when the LRATC is U-shaped, as in Figure 9.1. The Goldilocks dilemma emerges: as she discovered, some porridge was too hot and some too cold; only one was just right. Similarly, banks that are too small and those that are too large are inefficient. True, the market is competitive. But that's hardly useful if mergers will generate cost inefficiencies instead of lower costs.

The regulators then face a different set of options. Clearly, merging a failing bank into another institution so that the resulting bank lies in the $25–50 million size range makes good economic sense. Economies of scale are gained and passed on. But would you unequivocally recommend merging two institutions that are on the right side of the U? Why not?

You're correct if you wrote that such an action would only increase costs. The failing bank is preserved, but both the new and the old banks' clients pay for that decision in less efficient banking services and presumably higher charges. It's not clear that the availability of banking facilities to the customers of the failing bank offsets the higher costs imposed on the surviving bank's clients. It might make more economic sense to close down the failing bank instead of merging it with a solid institution.

Taxation and Pollution: Two Applications

The competitive long-run outcome has some interesting, indeed startling, implications. In this section, you'll learn why taxes are always ultimately paid by the consumer and why it makes sense to pollute.

Tax-Shifting II: Why the Consumer Always Pays the Tax Bill

In Chapter 8, we left Burns & Koff facing a Hobson's choice (p. 283). If the firm decided to pass on the 25-cent cigarette tax in full, the new price of its cigarettes would be higher than the market price. Burns & Koff could anticipate a substantial loss of business to its competitors who did not raise prices as much. Alternatively, Burns & Koff could limit its price increase to the new market price and absorb that part of the tax not covered by the price hike. That's actually the scene in Figure 8.8 (p. 283). At the $2.50 market price (Fig. 8.8b), Burns & Koff is not covering its costs. (In Figure 8.8a, the $2.50 price horizontal lies below the ATC_{tax}, the curve that includes both production costs and taxes.) Burns & Koff's short-run position may have been viable, but its long-run outlook was rather bleak.

What happens in the long run? We may presume the Burns & Koff situation is typical of all cigarette firms operating in a perfectly competitive market. Since costs are not being covered, some of them must drop out. To be sure, exit may not happen immediately, but it's inevitable whenever some firms' fixed-cost commitments expire.[10] What happens to industry supply then? Won't it decline? Draw in the long-run equilibrium supply curve on Figure 8.8b and fill in here the following blanks:

Long-run equilibrium price _____

Quantity supplied and demanded for the industry _____

Output supplied by Burns & Koff (a survivor) _____

Excess profits of Burns & Koff _____[11]

Realize what has come to pass. Prices prior to the imposition of the 25-cent tax were $2.29 a pack. Now, in long-run competitive equilibrium, prices have risen to $2.54. Who pays the tax? Clearly, the smoker.

Pollution Pays: A Hard-Nosed Business View

Dirty Dick and Snow White run competing chemical firms located on the Moon River. Snow White, an environmental purist, has installed a series of purifiers in her plant to make sure that no harmful chemicals will be spewed into the river. Dirty Dick views the Moon as God's gift to chemical manufacturers; he certainly isn't going to spend on purification equipment. Figure 9.4a shows the cost curves of both Snow White and Dirty Dick, while Figure 9.4b depicts supply and demand curves and a price that covers Snow White's higher average total costs. Clearly, then, Dirty Dick earns excess profits. Doesn't it pay to pollute?

Actually, the scenario so far guarantees Snow White normal profits. But that situation is likely to be short-lived. You understand that the excess profits earned by Dirty Dick will generate new entrants who can earn excess profits only by emulating Dick's production techniques. So, supply increases and price comes down until all excess profits are wiped out. (By now, you surely can draw in the long-run equilibrium supply

FIGURE 9.4   Pollution Pays

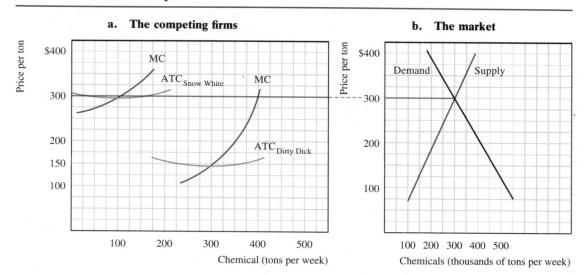

a. At a price of $300 per ton, Snow White breaks even, while Dirty Dick earns excess profits. New entrants will force price down so that Dirty Dick breaks even and Snow White shuts down permanently.

b. New entrants force supply upward and price down to achieve a new, lower-cost equilibrium.

curve and discover the long-run equilibrium price.[12]) In long-run equilibrium, Dirty Dick and his imitators survive; Snow White returns to Fairyland.[13]

Use of long-run equilibrium is not limited to public policy. Business planners can also use it well, as MicroBits 9.3 demonstrates.

Why Economists Love the Perfectly Competitive Model

The benefits of the competitive marketplace, implicit in much of this chapter and Chapter 8, explain the love affair that economists have had with perfect competition. It's time to consider these advantages explicitly.

The Efficiency and Welfare Implications of the Competitive Model

Return to the central issue of microeconomics: How can we, both in our individual lives and together as members of a society, squeeze the most out of the scarce resources at our disposal? One answer is, of course, don't waste them: *Make sure that every scarce input is devoted to its most desired use*. That statement implies:

- Don't use more resources than are needed to produce any particular good or service.
- Set priorities, so that the goods produced and the quantities placed on the market coincide with the priorities of the users of the goods.

Minimizing Scarcity.   Let's elaborate. Can bananas be grown in Alaska? Sure—in greenhouses with artificial weather set at tropiclike temperatures and humidity. Would you recommend that Alaskan growers enter the banana market? Surely not. They cannot compete with the free sunshine of Florida, Honduras, and the Philippines. Those Alaskans who ignored economic realities would soon enough discover their folly. Competition ensures that only those producers who take advantage of the most abundantly available resources and who minimize the use of scarce resources survive.

The absurdity of this example does drive home two points: (1) Low-cost production uses fewer scarce resources than does high-cost production, and (2) low-cost producers prevail over high-cost producers in a competitive market.

MicroBits 9.3

Break-Even Analysis

Juicy Jane markets a variety of fruit-based soft drinks in a local market. Although the soft-drink market is not perfectly competitive, Jane feels that she has little control over price. But, of course, production decisions are hers alone. Consequently, Juicy Jane's total revenue curve takes on the shape familiar to you from Figure 8.3 (p. 269). The TR curve, rising at a constant $4 per gallon as depicted in the diagram on the next page, is the product of the given price times the quantity produced.

If the industry's long-run cost curve is characterized by constant returns to scale, then the long-run total cost curve will also be a rising straight line and the long-run average cost curve will be horizontal. (They will look like the curves in Figure 7.8 on p. 230.) That information is useful to Jane, for it opens up a range of alternatives if she wishes to invest in a second plant. Jane knows that starting small will not cost her more per gallon of soft drink than opening up a larger plant.

Break-even analysis offers Jane a simple decision-making technique to determine how large a plant to build. Consider three of Jane's alternatives: small, medium, or large. The short-run TC curves sketched onto the accompanying figure represent these options.

Look carefully at the diagram and notice that each of the TC curves crosses the TR curve at least at one point. Those intersections are break-even points. Where they cross, TR = TC and (excess) profits are zero. In the case of TC_{small}, the break-even point occurs at an output of 100,000 gallons per week; for TC_{medium}, at 200,000 gallons; and for TC_{large}, at 300,000 gallons.

Jane merely has to ask herself, How much can we sell from our new plant? If Jane believes that she'll only be able to sell 275,000 gallons monthly, then certainly constructing the largest plant would be foolish. Her sales estimates are below the 300,000 gallons needed to cover all costs. On the other hand, she'd shy away from the smallest plant, too. As drawn in the diagram, costs for the lowest are optimal at 200,000 gallons, the tangency with the LRTC curve. Beyond 245,000 gallons (where $TC_{small} = TC_{medium}$), the medium-size plant produces soft drinks at lower total costs. So, break-even analysis suggests that Jane's optimal choice is to operate the medium-size plant.

Of course, break-even analysis is merely a crude approximation of reality. Linearity makes for simplicity but not necessarily accuracy. Furthermore, break-even analysis re-

---

The contrast between high-cost producers and low-cost producers for most goods and services is rarely as vivid as the banana example. But the same principle applies and the same conclusion follows. The cheaper producer uses fewer resources and so survives in the competitive marketplace.

The innovation example of this chapter carries this point further. A lower-cost method of bicycle production was not adopted throughout the competitive industry because producers were particularly interested in

MicroBits 9.3 continued

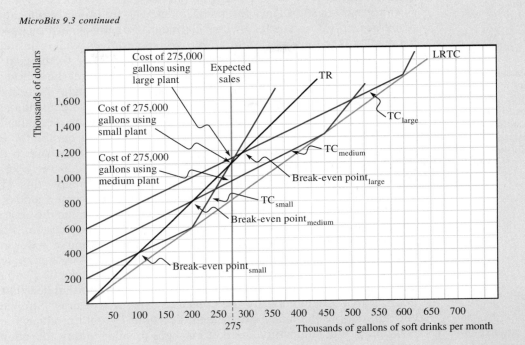

lates both prices and costs to output without considering such influences as changing demand or technology that will shift both cost and revenue curves. More complications enter if the firm produces multiple outputs.

Yet do not discard break-even analysis en-tirely. Sometimes, approximations are useful. Back-of-the-envelope calculations are certainly cheaper and quicker than more complicated studies and may provide an initial indication of the fruitfulness of further investigation.

being technologically advanced. Rather they were compelled to adapt because the market is a cruel taskmaster. Existing bicycle producers who prefer the status quo are undercut by innovation-adopting competitors; the obsolete won't survive.

In short, competition forces low-cost production in the marketplace. And low-cost production, by using up the least possible quantity of scarce resources to produce a given output, minimizes scarcity and so maximizes efficiency.

Consumer sovereignty means that the production sector of the economy responds to the decisions of the consuming public.

Allocational efficiency refers to the optimal distribution of resources among industries so that the resulting output corresponds to the demands of the decision-makers.

Setting Priorities.   But how much output should be produced? The answer to this question aims to minimize scarcity by properly allocating resources. It is best handled by considering first what we mean by devoting resources to their most *desired* use. Who determines what is desired?

Most contemporary societies give at least lip service to the goal of **consumer sovereignty,** although they do not always agree how best to achieve that objective. In a market economy, consumers themselves make myriad individual decisions that are translated into demands and relayed to the productive sectors by the price mechanism. Technically, consumer desires are expressed by the market demand curves for the various goods and services they wish to purchase. So, the point in the bicycle demand curve at 35,000 bicycles at a price of $550 per bike in Figure 9.1b, for example, must mean that the buyers believe this $550 spent on bicycles is better than $550 spent on other consumer goods.

In short, in a free-market economy, consumers determine the desired use of the economy's resources by their willingness to buy certain products and not others. It follows, then, that efficient allocation of goods in a free-market system requires that just the right amount of each good and service to meet the public's demands is produced. Production should neither be so abundant that output is wasted nor so shorthanded that it doesn't appropriately satisfy the consuming public's desires. Strangely enough, despite the many independent decisions by both producers and consumers, the competitive market manages to achieve this **allocational efficiency.** Let's see how.

Efficient Allocation.   Turn back to Figure 9.1b, compare the $647.45 initial equilibrium price with the $550 long-run equilibrium price, and ask yourself a simple question: Where are consumers better-off?

Clearly, all consumers would prefer to pay the lower price and buy more bicycles rather than pay more and purchase fewer bikes. Each buyer would be on a higher indifference curve with the lower price. Is that result also consistent with allocational efficiency? In this particular case, the answer is yes. The reasoning runs along the following lines.

Focus on Dynamo and assume that the firm produces 70 bikes per month when the market demand is 22,000 units monthly.[14] Because the market price is $647.45, Dynamo's managers rightly conclude that the firm should expand production. Let them expand production by one bike. How much would that marginal unit cost? Slightly more than $_____.

If you wrote $550, you're right; it's profitable to expand production because Dynamo's MC is less than its MR. But that's not the critical point in this connection. We're not concerned with Dynamo's profitability as much as with allocational efficiency for society as a whole. So, shifting focus ever so slightly, ask, What is the total cost of resources used to produce that extra bike? You'd have to give the identical answer, slightly more than $550. That's because the MC simultaneously measures two types of costs: How much more Dynamo would have to spend to produce an additional unit, and how much more would have to be spent to attract resources to the bicycle manufacturing industry.

Now return to the consumer and ask, How much satisfaction does a consumer obtain from an additional bike? The answer would have to be slightly less than $_____.

That's right: $647.45. To induce another customer to enter the market, the price would have to be cut.

Now put together these two points. The 22,001th bicycle costs the economy (say) $551, but it benefits the one consumer who bought the bike by (say) $642. Is the benefit greater than the cost? If so, wouldn't the community as a whole benefit from having another bike per month produced? Indeed, as long as the benefit is greater than the cost—that is, as long as $P >$ MC—then there's a net gain from increased production. Resources will move to bicycle production from areas where they are less desired in order to increase the net satisfaction of consumers. So, allocation efficiency is improved by producing more as long as $P >$ MC.

If you understand this conclusion, you also realize that once the long-run equilibrium of 35,000 bicycles costing $550 each had been reached, reducing the price to, say, $525 and increasing output further is not an allocationally efficient move. Why? Wouldn't the public be able to buy more bicycles at a lower cost, and thus increase its benefit? _____

The answer is "Yes, but. . . ." The question focused only on the benefits of the price cut, but not on its costs. If all firms were identical to Dynamo and all were producing the 35,000 bicycles at minimum cost long-run equilibrium, then producing extra output would cost more than $550. Does the economy obtain a net benefit from producing extra bicycles? The benefit to consumers is evaluated at $525 per bike, but each bike costs extra resources that exceed $550. Surely you would not recommend moving resources from other industries into bicycle production under these circumstances.

So, allocational efficiency is achieved when the resource costs of producing an extra unit of output are neither greater nor less than the benefits measured by consumers' willingness to pay for the goods or services in question. In summary:

- When $P >$ MC, then the benefits derived from extra production are greater than its costs, and so society will benefit from increased output.
- When $P <$ MC, then resource costs exceed the public's benefits, and output should be cut back.
- When $P =$ MC, then resources are being optimally allocated, because the marginal satisfaction of the public is precisely equal to the resource costs of producing that output.

Now for the finale. *In the long-run equilibrium of a perfectly competitive market, P = MC. Thus, perfect competition guarantees optimal resource use.*

In short, economists' crush on perfect competition is based on the consequences of the long-run competitive equilibrium:

- Production occurs at the lowest possible cost.
- Resources are allocated in the most efficient manner.
- The consumers' will is done, if not in heaven, at least in the competitive marketplace.

One final remark: The compatibility of the efficiency result of perfect competition and consumer sovereignty is a positive statement, not a normative one.[15] It posits that the free will of consumers sets the standard for judging efficiency. It is the market's response to their demands or lack of demand that dictates production. It follows that a decision to cut back on Bible purchases and buy X-rated videos instead is as valid from the allocational efficiency viewpoint as the converse. And while economists as individuals may have strong personal feelings about the desirability of self-improvement courses versus time spent in front of the tube, those opinions are scientifically irrelevant in judging the efficiency of the market mechanism. Simply put, the only relevant question in judging efficiency is, Do people get what they want at the price they are willing to pay and at a marginal resource cost that equals the price?

Why Is There So Little Perfect Competition?

Perfect competition never existed in the production marketplace; it is the figment of the theorist's creativity.[16] Several reasons for this gap between theory and reality come to mind:

- The general rarefied air of economic theory.
- The costs of competition.
- The anticompetitive role of government.

Theory and Reality

The nature of theory is to abstract from the real world, so it's not surprising that microeconomic theorists have described a system that cannot exist. True, some of the conditions of perfect competition mentioned in Chapter 8—the inability of any individual market participant to control price, product homogeneity, and freedom of entry and exit—do occur in some markets. After all, an egg is a homogeneous product, it's not difficult to enter or exit from the egg production industry, and no single producer controls a large enough share of the industry to dominate egg pricing. The same is true in many other agricultural markets, in certain types of natural resources such as coal, and even in some manufactured items.

But one condition for perfect competition—perfect information—can, by its very nature, never be realized. As mentioned in Chapter 8, because information is expensive, it does not always pay to obtain all attainable knowledge. But even if knowledge were free, some information would be intrinsically unavailable. The future, for example, is uncertain. That fact will dampen entry, since a potential entrant wonders, Will the industry's glowing profit projection continue after I've begun production? When information is proprietory—such as trade secrets and specific firm cost and profit conditions—the chances are small that they'll be discovered by potential competitors. This absence of *perfect* information means that reality will always fall short of the perfect competitive ideal.

The Costs of Competition

But there's another reason why competition fails to achieve an importance presence in the real world: Competitors don't like it! As Adam Smith pointed out in 1776:

> People of the same trade seldom meet together, even for merriment and diversion, but the conversation ends in a conspiracy against the public, or in some contrivance to raise price.[17]

Competition mandates that goods manufacturers and service providers cut their prices, improve their services, minimize inefficiencies, stay abreast of all cost-cutting advances—for what reason? To benefit the consumers! What's in it for the sellers? Actually very little. Moreover, the profits of a competitive firm that gains a head start on its rivals will soon be dissipated as its competitors catch up.

So, competition is unstable; it sows the seeds of its own dissolution. To be sure, government rules such as antitrust laws frequently prevent collusion among producers. Yet, the pressure to collude despite the antitrust laws, or to discover ways to cooperate within the confines of these statutes, is very real. Even more to the point is the fact that government actions often work against competition.

The Role of Anticompetitive Government

Although antitrust laws place government on the side of competition, a more usual role is for the government to protect competitors from competition. Thus, the government-sponsored agricultural subsidy programs analyzed in Chapter 2, the import quotas discussed in Chapter 8, or the restrictions on entry in the airline industry mentioned in this chapter substitute government-sanctioned anticompetitive acts for the freedom of the competitive market. More blatant examples such as resale price maintenance laws, whereby the producer dictates the minimum price chargeable by a seller, have now been largely removed from the statutes. But they are part of 20th-century U.S. history.

The Deadweight Losses of Government Intervention

The cost to the economy of anticompetitive practices can be calculated initially by measuring the deadweight loss of the policy. You've already seen that in Chapter 8's analysis of an import quota. It is directly evident in the following case study of the price-support mechanism for milk operated by the U.S. Department of Agriculture.

Milking the Consumer.   Federal legislation forces the Department of Agriculture to buy at a fixed price all milk products not sold on the private market. In 1986, for example, that minimum was 11.6 cents per pound, and cost taxpayers about $2 billion. We also paid the storage costs on the surplus dairy products bought by the government. And, as consumers of dairy products, we were forced to pay an inflated price instead of the estimated competitive market price of 9 cents. That this is hardly a sensible policy will be evident from analyzing Figure 9.5.

Take a look at the demand and supply curves of Figure 9.5. The competitive equilibrium of 9 cents per pound and 138 billions pounds produced is irrelevant at the price floor of 11.6 cents. At the higher price, consumers buy only 130 of the 145 billion pounds produced by the industry. The government buys the difference at the floor price for a total cost of $1.74 billion (which equals the area of the entire shaded rectangle).

To calculate the deadweight loss of the floor-price policy, we need to discover both the consumer and producer surpluses. On the consumer side, consumer surplus is the area under the demand curve between the 11.6-cent floor price and 9-cent equilibrium price for the 138 billion pounds that would have been demanded at the market clearing price. That consists of two areas: (1) a rectangle of 130 billion × 2.6 cents, or $3.3 billion, and (2) the triangle—labeled I—whose area equals (½)(8 billion)(2.6 cents), or $104 million.

Producer surplus is the area *above* the supply curve between the floor and equilibrium prices for the entire quantity sold. That, too, consists of two areas: (1) the same $3.3 billion rectangle calculated for the demanders and (2) two triangles—labeled I and II—whose area together equals $299 million.[18]

If the milk support program were not costly to the taxpayer, the deadweight loss would actually turn into a net gain. After all, the $3.3 billion represents a transfer from consumers to producers, and the $104 million loss of consumers' surplus (triangle I) is more than compensated for by a producers' surplus of $299 million (triangles I plus II). The net

FIGURE 9.5   The Economic Costs of the Milk Price Support Program

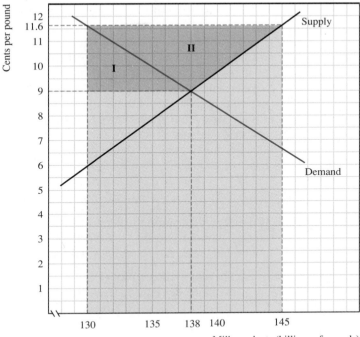

The milk products' support price of 11.6 cents per pound rather than the 9 cents per pound market price benefits producers, but costs even more to consumers and taxpayers. Though the producer surplus (I and II) is greater than the deadweight loss to consumers (I), the taxpayers must pay for the 15 billion pounds of milk product not purchased by demanders at a price of 11.6 cents (the entire shaded rectangle).

gain would be triangle II. But you just can't ignore the transfer of the $1.74 billion from taxpayers to producers. The taxes imposed on the public to finance the producer subsidy engender additional deadweight losses.[19]

A less costly alternative program is implicit in the diagram. Why not remove the price floor and pay $299 million net gain straight to the milk suppliers? The actual cost to the consumers will be only $195 million. For revoking the support program will restore to consumers the deadweight loss. Surely paying triangle II is better than paying the entire shaded rectangle.

The Political Economy of Intervention.   The reason why governments are more apt to protect producers than consumers is not hard to find.

Competitors frequently organize lobbies; the amorphous public, who loses from anticompetitive practices, is politically impotent. Moreover, each producer stands to gain substantially from government-supported anticompetitive practices, while each consumer is likely to lose just a bit.

Think about it in the context of the milk subsidy program. How much would you save per year if the subsidy program were eliminated entirely or if it were changed from a price support to a direct subsidy program? $10! As much as it pays for the milk lobby to press for a few more cents per hundredweight, it makes absolutely no sense for an individual consumer, or even a good number of them, to spend time and money to resist the price-raising program.

In short, even in those markets where perfect competition can be most expected, it often fails either to emerge or to be sustained.

Why, Then, Study Perfect Competition?

If the perfectly competitive model is perfectly unreal, students may legitimately wonder whether it's worth studying. The vast majority of economists who believe it is valuable do so for two reasons:

- The competitive model sets a standard and thus permits us to evaluate deviations from that standard.
- Standards, in turn, permit the fashioning and evaluating of public policy measures.

If you'd never worked for a major bank and turned up for a job interview in a green plaid sports jacket, a pink shirt, a pair of jeans, and white sweat socks under your trendy sneakers, you might wonder why they never called you back for a second interview. Just as it is useful to have a dress standard for evaluating a job applicant, so, too, is it useful to have a standard for evaluating an economic system.[20] Economists judge markets that are not perfectly competitive in terms of how closely they approximate the perfect competition standard. They presume that the more markets emulate perfect competition, the more beneficial they will be. (You'll see examples of that in future chapters dealing with monopoly, oligopoly, and monopolistic competition.) Similarly, those who wish to objectively prescribe policy measures need a target. And the very fact that economists write critically about restraints of trade and collusive business practices and support antitrust legislation presupposes a model of something better. So, we study the perfectly competitive model if only to show you how the economic system could be improved. We may never replicate it, but at least we know in which direction to head.

In **contestable markets,** firms can enter or leave the industry without being subject to any constraints.

If you're still not convinced, you might find solace in the views of some economists who claim that the stringent conditions postulated by the competitive model are really not necessary. This theory of **contestable markets,** summarized in MicroBits 9.4, achieves the same conclusions of the competitive model by focusing on freedom of entry and exit.

MICROBITS 9.4

Contestable Markets*

The theory of contestable markets is the brainchild of William J. Baumol of New York and Princeton Universities, and John C. Panzar and Robert D. Willig, then associated with Bell Laboratories, the research arm of the American Telephone and Telegraph Company.

In its strictest sense, contestable markets are those where existing firms hold no cost advantage over newcomers and where exit is absolutely costless. A firm that is not now in a particular market will be able to enter the market with ease, and, if conditions turn out to be uninviting, to leave it with equal facility. (You might imagine that a firm can enter the taxi market by leasing cabs and hiring drivers on a month-to-month basis. Thus, if profits are not as high as expected after a month or two, the company simply doesn't renew its leases on either its cabs or its drivers.)

Quite clearly, profits in contestable markets can never be excessive in the long run. If they are, new firms enter to reap excess profits. Similarly, existing firms can't be inefficient. If they were, more-efficient newcomers would be induced to enter and force the inefficient to adjust or drop out. For these same reasons, contestable markets are typically characterized by $P = $ MC.

Thus, the major welfare attributes of perfect competition can be obtained with less rigid assumptions. Mobility into and out of the industry, even in the absence of perfect knowledge, can lead to efficiency, proper resource allocation, and consumer sovereignty.

Indeed, the elimination of the CAB and the deregulation of the airline industry was prompted to some extent by the idea of contestable markets. That industry seemed particularly suited to applying contestable market theory, because entry and exit from particular routes and into and out of the industry in general was thought to be relatively easy. Aircraft, the major capital outlay of the airlines, and ground facilities can typically be leased. So, newcomers should have been able to penetrate the most profitable routes and leave them just as easily. The congestion of airport facilities and the hub-and-spoke system mentioned earlier suggest entry is not as simple as was thought. This is hardly a weakness in the theory of contestable markets. It's just that in retrospect, the contestable markets theory is not as applicable to the airlines industry as initially conceived.

Of course, the assumption of free entry and exit that characterizes perfectly contestable markets is rather rigid; no significant market in a real economy is likely to meet these conditions. Nevertheless, the conclusions of the contestable markets model and those of the perfectly competitive model run along the same track. They both suggest that the competitive marketplace is an ideal to strive for.

---

* This box is based on Professor Baumol's 1981 presidential address to the American Economics Association, reprinted in the *American Economic Review* 72, no. 1 (March 1982), pp. 1–15.

Summary

Back to Joan Kimberlane and her paper umbrella manufacturing plant. We last saw her find her optimum operating output at MR = MC. While that enabled Joan's firm to earn excess profits, she understands that this surplus is short-lived. The nature of perfect competition in her industry leads Joan to expect new competitors. These newcomers will replicate the most efficient firm in the industry, and, as their output hits the market, will force prices down until the long-run competitive equilibrium is reached. Although this will not happen immediately, ultimately *P = minimum LRATC* and all excess profits will have been squeezed out. Further market penetration will be discouraged.

What happens if someone discovers that a thinner, less expensive paper will satisfy customer needs just as well? Joan, having mastered this chapter, knows that ignoring this new development is the recipe for disaster. Adaptation is the name of the game, and the sooner the better. Joan has learned by experience that the competitive marketplace is a harsh taskmaster. The producer who does not compete does not survive.

Of course, neither consumers nor economists share Joan's viewpoint. For them, competition is wonderful. The consumer obtains the product at the cheapest price possible. Moreover, buyers benefit directly from any reductions in the cost of producing the product.

It is true that increased costs—perhaps due to a sudden scarcity of a critical input—are also passed on to the consumer, a fact that most buyers could do without. Nevertheless, economists, being concerned with efficient usage of scarce resources, welcome this symmetry. Just as efficiency is enhanced when more abundant resources are used more intensively, so, too, are resources better allocated if less abundant inputs are used less intensively. Allocational efficiency is improved when demanders are forced to pay more for products that use up resources that have become more scarce. Indeed, Joan understands that the competitive marketplace, by assuring that *P = MC*, optimizes resource allocation. It's just that while Joan has nothing personal against competition—indeed, she sees virtue in competition among her suppliers—her life would be far more relaxed if competition for her output were less perfect. How heavenly it would be if all the other paper umbrella manufacturers went out of business! Alternatively, wouldn't it be marvelous if the government could preserve industry prices and profits?

We'll leave Joan to her dreams for the moment. Chapter 10 picks up and expands on a theme touched upon in this chapter in the pollution example, which showed that on occasion the perfectly competitive market doesn't produce efficient results. What happens then?

Key Terms

Allocational efficiency
Consumer sovereignty
Contestable markets

Long-run equilibrium
Optimally sized firms

Review Questions

1. Explain why long-run competitive equilibrium occurs at the lowest point of the LRATC curve.
2. Explain the meaning of "closed for economic reasons" in the chapter's opening quotation, assuming that the retail market for books is perfectly competitive.
3. *a.* Use a diagram to demonstrate the two meanings of "too big is too costly."
   b. Explain why the use of smaller planes to service the spokes is consistent with "too big is too costly."
4. What is the optimum size of the firm if the long-run average cost curve is (*a*) consistently falling and (*b*) horizontal?
5. *a.* Since the benefits of cost-reducing innovations do not stay with the competitive firm, why would a firm ever adopt such innovations?

   b. What are the efficiency implications of your answer?
6. Demonstrate and explain why, in the long-run, the burden of a tax will be borne solely by the consumer, even if demand is not perfectly inelastic.
7. Why does the equality of price and marginal cost guarantee allocational efficiency?
8. *a.* Show the deadweight loss of a policy that limits the interest rates lenders can charge. (Use Figure 2.10a, p. 46).
   b. Calculate the deadweight loss resulting from the tax on cigarettes of Figure 8.8b (p. 283).
9. Why is a perfectly competitive market necessarily contestable but a contestable market not necessarily perfectly competitive?

Food for Thought

1. *a.* Show how rising fuel prices that increase the cost of transportation will affect the long-run equilibrium of the trucking industry as well as the individual trucking firm.
   b. Would you favor or oppose the government offering trucking firms modest subsidies on their gasoline costs to offset this price rise? Explain.
2. A caption on a cartoon in which a storeowner is shown talking to his partner, reads: "Given the downward slope of our demand curve and the ease with which other firms can enter the industry, we can strengthen our profit position only by equating marginal costs and marginal revenue. Order more jelly beans."

   a. Are the conditions mentioned in the first phrase relevant to the conclusion reached in the second?
   b. Is the word *only* used correctly, if indeed the first phrase correctly describes the case?
   c. Was the cartoonist a good microeconomic theorist?
3. *a.* How do impediments to exit such as political constraints on plant closings affect long-run competitive equilibrium?
   b. Would you favor repealing such constraints?
4. In an article in *The Wall Street Journal* (September 18, 1981) dealing with the demise of funeral casket manufacturers,

the author describes the industry as comprised mostly of small, family-owned businesses. The industry had shrunk from 650 to 400 companies between 1965 and 1981, with further shrinkage anticipated. The causes were both supply-related (a lack of skilled craftsmen and the rising cost of hardwood) and demand-driven (the fall in the U.S. death rate and a rise in cremation). Within the casket industry itself, metal was replacing hardwood, because metal caskets are easier to make and can be mass-produced.

a. Draw the LRATC curve of the casket industry.

b. What do you think will happen to competition in the casket industry if the downward demand trend continues?

5. Some U.S. newspapers began printing on a lower-quality paper after the price of newsprint rose in 1989.

a. Could the decision to use the cheaper newsprint only after the price increase represent an x-inefficiency? Explain.

b. Based on your understanding of the newspaper market, would you predict that this practice would become widespread?

6. How could you use break-even analysis to evaluate two projects with the following cost curves:

$$A: TC = \$500 + \$3Q$$

$$B: TC = \$100 + \$23Q$$

7. *a.* Demonstrate that the deadweight loss of a floor-price policy will depend on the elasticity of supply and demand.

b. What elasticity conditions will minimize the deadweight loss?

Suggested Readings

An excellent survey of airline regulation and deregulation may be found in Chapter 6 of the *Economic Report of the President, 1988,* while agricultural transfer programs are reviewed and their economic costs analyzed in the 1986 issue of this annual.

Although the most comprehensive version of contestable markets theory will be found in William J. Baumol, John C. Panzar, and Robert D.

Willig, *Contestable Markets and the Theory of Industry Structure* (San Diego: Harcourt Brace Jovanovich, 1982), it is beyond the reach of most students at this stage of their education. However, Elizabeth's Bailey's introduction describing the birth of contestable markets theory is wonderful reading for those who wish to understand how economic theories are born and developed.

Notes and Answers

1. T. E. Keeler, "Airline Regulation and Market Performance," *Bell Journal of Economics* 3 (Autumn 1972), pp. 339–434, compared intrastate air prices of carriers not subject to CAB price regulation with similar routes for airlines subject to CAB controls. He found that fares on the latter ranged 20 to 95 percent above those of the unregulated airlines.

2. Paul W. Bauer, "'Don't Panic': A Primer on Airline Deregulation," Federal Reserve Bank of Cleveland, *Economic Review* (Fourth quarter, 1986), p. 19.

3. 85; $55,033.25; $47,600; $7,433.25.

4. If too many firms enter, the market price will be driven below $550. All of the optimally sized firms will lose, leading some to drop out. Supply falls until price rises back to $550.

5. If demand is changing simultaneously or the industry is subject to supply shocks, the picture gets even more murky. But the essential conclusions hold true.
6. Recall the technological change/garbage collection analysis of Chapter 7.
7. Airlines virtually own the rights to use specific airport gates and departure times. The shortage of gates and prime-time departure times, a consequence of the slow growth of airport facilities and the rapid increase in passenger travel demand, forces new competitors into most unsatisfactory positions. Some economists have proposed replacing the existing allocation procedure with a competitive method, requiring that all the airlines bid for gates and time slots.
8. The hub-and-spoke system is a marvelous example of the input integration source of economies of scale for the firm (p. 232). Take three feeder planes, each one with 150-passenger capacity, and collect travelers along different points of the rim. Deliver them to the waiting jumbo with its 450 seat capacity. Obviously, the air carrier that can schedule its flights so that the three feeders meet the jumbo allocates its scarce resources more efficiently and so has a cost advantage over a carrier that either has no feeders or uses the jumbo as both the short-haul and the long-distance carrier. But it's also true that the more efficient carrier is also going to be bigger.
9. Note that the coexistence of banks of various sizes does not *prove* that the LRATC is horizontal over a significant range. Remember the point made earlier: if you stopped the motion of a competitive marketplace at one moment of time, you'd discover the presence of banks of different sizes. That would be true even if the LRATC curve were U-shaped. You'd then observe some temporary survivors who will be eliminated in the long run. In addition, there's a practical issue. Neither exit nor entry is free; banks are born and die only upon regulatory approval. So, the existing structure in California might reflect less ue true workings of the competitive marketplace than the decisions of bank regulators.

If you're interested in banking competition, you might want to glance through Chapters 8 and 9 of Jonas Prager, *Fundamentals of Money, Banking, and Financial Institutions* (New York: Harper and Row, 1987).
10. Rothman's announced in June 1989 that it would close down its Montreal cigarette manufacturing plant because of " 'excessive taxation' [that] is driving down tobacco consumption. It said it expects sales to drop further as new taxes are introduced. . . ." *The Wall Street Journal,* June 20, 1989.
11. The new supply curve crosses the demand curve at a price of $2.54, which is the long-run equilibrium price. At that price, the industry meets customer demands for about 42 billion cigarettes yearly. Burns & Koff supplies 4.5 billion cigarettes, in line with $MR = MC_{tax}$. But at that price, $P = ATC_{tax}$, so that excess profits are zero and the firm is earning only normal profits.
12. The supply curve crosses the demand curve at $P = \$150$.
13. If these results trouble your sense of fairness, be patient. Chapter 10 deals with policy measures to resolve cases in which the market results differ from those that are deemed socially desirable.
14. Actually at $P = \$647.45$, Dynamo's output would be found at the point where $MR = MC$. But that's not important here.
15. For the definition of these terms, see page 16.
16. Markets such as the stock exchange, where goods or services are not produced but merely exchanged, do exhibit many of the characteristics of perfect competition.
17. Adam Smith, *The Wealth of Nations* (New York: Modern Library, 1937), p. 128.
18. Change the two triangles into a rectangle and a triangle and calculate the areas of each. The former, 8 billion times 2.6 cents, equals $208 million, while the latter, (½)(7 billion) (2.6 cents), equals $91 million.
19. You can see that by calculating the deadweight loss of the cigarette tax in Figure 8.8b.
20. But while the dress standard may be arbitrary, the standards for judging an economic system are grounded in reason.

APPENDIX

INCREASING, DECREASING, AND CONSTANT COST INDUSTRIES

This chapter operated with an implicit assumption: the growth of the industry does not affect the cost structure of the firm. That is, the LRATC of the individual firm remains the same whether the industry consists of 2 firms or 2,000.

What would happen to the analysis if the cost structure of the firm *is* affected by the size of the industry? This appendix allows you gluttons for punishment to consider two such options:

In an **increasing cost industry,** the LRATC of the firm rises as the size of the industry increases. In a **decreasing cost industry,** the LRATC falls as more firms comprise the industry. An LRATC that is independent of industry size *is* characteristic of a **constant cost industry.**

· **Increasing cost industries**—as the industry grows, each firm finds it *more* expensive to operate.

· **Decreasing cost industries**—as the industry grows, each firm finds operating *less* expensive.

Clearly, the missing option is the **constant cost industry,** where changes in the industry size do not affect the operating costs of the firm. (Constant costs were implicit in the chapter.)

Before we analyze the adjustments need to account for the impact of industry size on the firm, consider first why industry size might affect the costs of the individual firms. Two reasons are often advanced:

· Internal economies or diseconomies of suppliers.
· External economies or diseconomies.

The first reason focuses on the cost structure of firms that supply inputs to the producer. For example, in Chapter 7 you learned that electricity production is characterized by economies of scale. Now consider a manufacturer of knitwear, who uses a host of electricity-driven machinery to produce sweaters. When the industry is small, so that the electric utility is operating well below capacity, each knitting mill will have to pay for the utility's high generating cost. But as more sweater makers use the utility, the electricity supplier moves further along its falling LRATC curve. As the costs of electrical generation decline, each knitwear producer benefits from lower electric input costs.

Of course, the opposite reaction is equally plausible. The industry uses a resource that is produced under diseconomies of scale. In that case, the input producer finds its cost rising as the industry grows and requires more inputs. These higher costs are then passed on to the resource user.

External economies or diseconomies refer to sources of decreased or increased cost to the industry that are unrelated to suppliers' economies or diseconomies of scale. Think of a newly discovered oil field with 500 billion barrels of oil stored underground. At the rate of 100,000 barrels pumped per day, the field will be depleted in 37.5 years. Now, if four other oil companies sink wells into the field, not only will all the oil be brought to the surface in about seven years, but each well will have to be sunk to a lower depth sooner. Since the deeper down you drill, the more expensive per foot it is, the presence of more drilling rigs raises the cost to *each* oil extracting firm.

On the other hand, consider on-the-job training or apprenticeship programs. By their very nature, such programs are costs to the firm doing the training. So, a garage may hire a woman straight out of high school and train her to repair transmissions. Normally, she'll be paid during her apprenticeship, though at a scale well below that of a master mechanic. However, as the industry becomes important in the region, the local high school may offer a vocational program in automotive repair. That relieves the individual garage of some of its training outlays. Thus, it's not surprising to encounter publicly supported agricultural schools in farm communities or maritime training in seaboard localities.

Increasing Cost Industries

Figure 9A.1 examines the case of increasing cost industries. In Figure 9A.1a, Straight and Deep Oil Drillers is in equilibrium at a price of $20 per barrel oil and an output of 100,000 barrels. The oil industry is depicted in Figure 9A.1b, with

FIGURE 9A.1   An Increasing Cost Industry

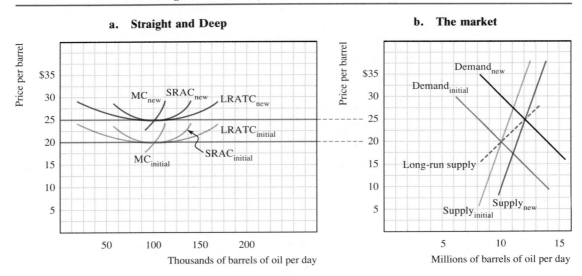

a.   As industry production rises, Straight and Deep's drilling costs rise, forcing up the family of cost curves. But while costs rise, long-run equilibrium requires that price rises sufficiently to make sure that the firm earns no more nor less than normal profits.

b.   The increase in industry demand initially drives price up (Supply$_{initial}$ and Demand$_{new}$) inducing entry. Firms continue to enter as long as excess profits can be earned. When Supply$_{new}$ is reached, P = $25, and no further suppliers enter. The LRS connects the 2 equilibrium points. In the increasing cost case, LRS has a positive slope.

quantity supplied equaling quantity demanded at $20. This is assumed to be the long-run equilibrium, so that no firm is earning excess profits and firms are neither entering nor departing the industry.

Now, demand for oil rises, raising the price per barrel, and leading to excess profits for existing firms. That, of course, induces entry and shifts the supply curve rightward. How far? If this industry were *not* an increasing cost industry, then price would decline until the initial long-run equilibrium was restored. But the case examined here does involve increasing costs. As new firms enter and so expand industry size, the average costs of each firm rise. Straight and Deep's LRATC moves upward. So, the new equilibrium price must be higher than $20, say $25. (Whether the new price is $25 or $27.81 or $53.99 depends on the precise relationship between industry size and the individual firm's costs. The important point is that the price must be higher than $20.) As you see in Figure 9A.1b, the supply curve crosses the demand curve at $25, while in Figure 9A.1a, Straight and Deep is back into zero profits position. But this must be the long-run equilibrium of the firm and the industry. (Why? _____
_____[1])

FIGURE 9A.2   A Decreasing Cost Industry

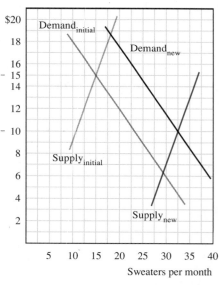

a.   Nifty Nitwear

b.   The market

a.   New entrants drive down costs to all firms, so the "initial" cost curves of Nifty Nitwear are replaced by the lower "new" curves. But because price also falls by $5, the normal profits earned before are not increased. Nifty breaks even at a lower price.

b.   Although the new demand initially drives prices up, the entry of new suppliers shifts supply upward and price down. Because new supply drives costs down, the new long-run equilibrium price lies below the starting equilibrium price.

FIGURE 9A.3   A Constant Cost Industry: A "Do It Yourself" Exercise

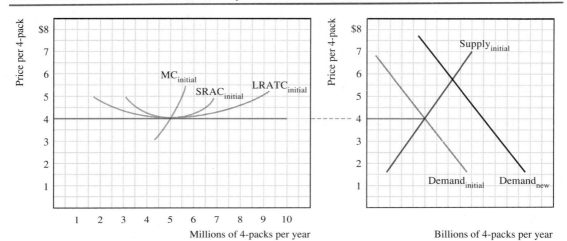

Millions of 4-packs per year

Billions of 4-packs per year

A **long-run supply (LRS)** curve joins long-run equilibrium supply-demand intersections for different industry sizes.

When you connect the two equilibrium points, you generate a **long-run supply (LRS)** curve. The LRS curve will always be positively sloped for an increasing cost industry. It tells you that as the industry grows larger, it can provide additional output only by paying more for its inputs.

Decreasing Cost Industries

Exactly the opposite situation occurs for a decreasing cost industry. In Figure 9A.2, with the initial long-run equilibrium at $15 a sweater and an increase in demand, price initially rises. The resulting excess profits induces an influx of knitwear manufacturers. But because the additional entrants reduce costs for all, our representative firm, Nifty Nitwear, finds its costs falling. Consequently, the new long-run equilibrium will have to be at a price below $15. Draw the LRS curve onto Figure 9A.2.[2]

Constant Cost Industries

This one is for you. Use Figure 9A.3 to draw in the new equilibrium price, the final equilibrium LRATC of the firm, and the LRS. You'll find the answer in Note 3.

Key Terms

Constant cost industry
Decreasing cost industry
Increasing cost industry

Notes and Answers

1. Straight and Deep and its identical-twin competitors are operating at the minimum point of the LRATC. Because price is just covering LRATC and no one is earning excess profits, no additional firms will enter nor will existing firms leave.

2. It should connect the two supply-demand intersections in Figure 9A.2b and thus be negatively sloped.

3. The new equilibrium price is identical to the old, $4, so the firm's equilibrium remains unchanged. The LRS is a straight line that connects the old supply–demand intersection with the new one, whose new supply curve crosses the new demand curve at $4.

WHEN THE PERFECTLY COMPETITIVE MARKET FAILS: EXTERNALITIES AND PUBLIC GOODS

A pollution-free society is unattainable, both physically and economically. To think otherwise is not to think.
Alan S. Blinder (1987)

No good deed ever goes unpunished.
Claire Booth Luce

Learning Objectives

By the time you have digested this chapter, you will:

- Understand the concept of externalities.
- Realize the incompatibility of the competitive marketplace and the prevention of such external diseconomies as pollution.
- Comprehend how the apparent conflict between environmental issues and economic constraints can be reconciled.
- Be convinced of the critical importance of social cost/benefit analysis despite the real difficulties of employing it in an uncertain world.
- Come to grips with the "free-rider" issue and its importance in explaining why the competitive market will either not supply or supply too few "public" goods.
- Understand the distinction between pure and impure public goods, and discover whether the competitive market can play a role in providing the latter.

331

· In general find that some rather obvious and highly touted solutions to pressing contemporary public issues may not be the best or even very good.

When the Earth Is Clean and the Air Is Free

Empty soda bottles and cans are not notable health hazards. Nevertheless, they offend our aesthetic sensibilities when they spoil an otherwise pacific landscape. How disturbing it is to hike through a quiet, apparently virgin forest, enjoying both company and nature, only to discover through the trashy signs of incivility that you're not pioneers.

That people are occasionally inconsiderate is not news. That they are even more uncaring about strangers is even less surprising. So, leaving empty cans at a campsite or littering highways represents consistent, even rational, behavior. Proper disposal involves some effort, if only to find a garbage can; littering is a thoughtless, effortless procedure. So, the rational egoist will litter.

Yet the community as a whole finds litter repulsive and expends effort and funds to clean up our highways, forests, and city streets. In effect, the litterbug imposes the costs of cleanliness on the community in general. And since the economic system provides no incentive for the despoiler to restrain himself, some weird sort of equilibrium prevails: The litterer litters and the community uses scarce resources to clean up.

Littering is a relatively innocuous case. Far more serious situations are reflected by the appalling headlines that shout at us:

"The Ozone Layer Is Rapidly Dissipating; Skin Cancer Rates on the Rise"

"Urban Air Pollution Reduces Life Expectancy"

"Water, Water Everywhere but Nary a Drop to Drink"

The earth seems to be deteriorating before our very eyes, and even if our future seems tolerable, we have to wonder about the legacy we'll be leaving our children.

OK, you say, the environment is a serious issue. But what does all this have to do with microeconomics? Isn't the physical world the province of the natural scientists and the environmentalists? Certainly scientists and environmentalists make critical contributions to our understanding of the fundamental issue. But that should not exclude a prominent role for economists, whose intimate involvement stems from their professional concern over how best to use scarce resources.

There's a second and perhaps more compelling reason for involving microeconomics in the study of pollution. One can make an excellent case for attributing environmental pollution to the workings of the economy.

By Strategic Use of Postcards, Thoreau Manages to Keep Walden Pond Unspoiled.

SOURCE: Drawing by Ed Fisher; © 1987 by *The New Yorker* Magazine, Inc.

As you saw in the last chapter, the competitive nature of the marketplace may at times clash with preserving the purity of the natural environment. If polluting is costless but pollution control is not, then the do-gooder who insists on employing pollution abatement techniques may well price himself out of the market.

Finally, the economist is concerned with designing antipollution measures. Who better can advise on efficient pollution reduction policies?

Garbology.   Did you know that the average family in the United States disposes of about a ton of garbage each year? Typically, garbage is picked up by municipal sanitation department employees. We, as law-abiding citizens, dutifully take the garbage out. The alternative, letting the garbage decompose in the yard, is illegal in most urban areas. Ponder this seemingly foolish question: Why not offer free choice? Why shouldn't those of us who want our garbage picked up be able to contract with garbage collectors, while those of us who relish the sight of decomposing matter be allowed to use our yards as dumps? Why do government authorities take such decisions out of our hands?

One of the purposes of this chapter is to consider pollution and the public provision of certain goods and services as instances of **market failure**, the inadequacy of the competitive marketplace and its incentive structure to achieve socially desired goals. Second, if public policy is the vehicle for community improvement, we want to consider whether such goals can be attained without jeopardizing the benefits of the market. The answers to these questions are not always obvious, as you'll discover by turning to the first issue: environmental purity.

> **Market failure** occurs when competition does not provide either the efficiency or the welfare benefits that are the anticipated consequences of the competitive process.

"We Have Seen the Enemy and They Are Us."

The Issue

Environmental contamination is a particular example of a more pervasive economic concept: **externalities,** whose benefits or costs are not fully obtained or borne by the initiating parties. Externalities can be **negative**, as in the pollution example. All those who drink the contaminated water or breathe the poisonous air suffer, even though neither group was responsible for the pollution. Yet there's no economic motive for the polluter to desist; the polluting firm is not bearing any of the costs it imposes on others.

Externalities can be **positive** as well. When electric utilities bury transmission lines to reduce repair costs from storm-caused damage, they simultaneously diminish the danger of downed lines electrocuting the unwary.

> **Externalities** occur when an economic act spills over to third parties who are not directly involved in the action. A **negative externality** adversely affects the bystanders; a **positive spillover** benefits the third parties.

The common element in all these cases can be easily summarized: *The cost/benefit calculations of the individual differ from the broader cost/benefit calculations of the general community.* The firm's production decisions are based on a narrow cost/benefit framework. The firm's managers ask, ''What is most profitable for us?'' not, ''What is best for the community?'' Yet optimal allocation of resources requires that someone consider the third-party consequences.

Figure 10.1 highlights the issue. The public's demand curve is juxtaposed on the private industry's supply curve, which is the sum of the marginal cost curves of the industry's firms. This supply curve is based only on their production cost; the firms are not responsible for the negative spillovers they impose. Consequently, the market price is $150 per ton, and the equilibrium sales amount is 450 tons. That equilibrium, however, would not hold if firms were charged for the externalities they inflict on the public. If they were required to install pollution abatement equipment, their combined production and prevention costs would generate the

FIGURE 10.1

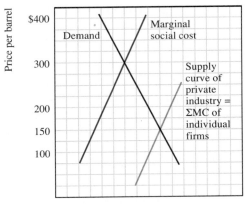

Firms that pollute understate the true costs of production, because their operating costs exclude the cleanup costs imposed on others. The marginal social cost curve encompasses all these costs. The competitive market outcome, with weekly production at 450,000 tons, does not include the negative externalities and so overallocates resources to chemical production. If all costs were taken into account, how many tons of chemicals should be manufactured?

marginal social cost curve. Equilibrium price is higher and quantity is lower. Fewer chemicals would be demanded by the public if the price were to reflect the full costs of chemical production.

That is the general reasoning underlying *government intervention.* Since the market mechanism fails to achieve the optimum distribution of resources, the alternative mechanism—community action—needs to be introduced.[1]

The Wrong and Right Ways of Resolving the Private/Public Discrepancy

The Outright Ban.   Perhaps the most popular method of dealing with negative externalities is the outright ban. The government declares, "Thou shalt not pollute!" The logic behind the prohibition is that if pollution is harmful, stop it at the source. Moreover, the ban imposes the costs of pollution on those responsible. The firm that contaminates the river or the air will simply have to absorb the prevention costs. What's wrong, then, with banning pollution? If you think it through, you'll realize that to

    ban nuclear power and so avoid another Chernobyl,

    ban oil-based power and so avoid oil spills and air pollution,

    ban power based on coal and so avoid both unsightly and unsafe
    land areas as well as air pollution,

    ban hydroelectric power to avoid interfering with marine life, and

    ban gas- and wood-based energy to avoid gas transmission lines
    that interfere with the natural habitats of wildlife and woodcutting
    that is synonymous with destroying forests

would mean that you will have to dispense with virtually all of the energy sources that power modern life. As Professor Blinder suggests in the chapter's opening quotation, you obtain absurd results if you carry the pure environmental position to its natural conclusion. Few are foolish enough to do that.

Tolerant Nature.   Fortunately, the clash between the comfortable life and the clean environment can often be resolved. A single smokestack in an otherwise nonindustrial environment does not threaten air quality. The relatively small amount of polluting gases will be naturally dissipated without adversely affecting the environment. Similarly, a clean lake can absorb some pollutants without harming the ecology of the waters or its safety as a source of drinking water. Banning polluting activities in such instances makes no sense. Indeed, using the term *pollution* is altogether inappropriate.

When Economics and Environmental Issues Conflict.   Nevertheless, at times polluting activities surpass the limits of safe absorption. In that case, environmental damage can be identified with a deterioration in the public's quality of life and often health. The infamous Los Angeles smog or the notorious Denver brown cloud are not just unsightly or the butt of jokes; they are real health hazards. The stench and the diseased fish that come out of Tacoma's Commencement Bay are more than inconveniences. What should be done?

Surprisingly, economists would not necessarily recommend that pollution be halted and the environment be restored to its pristine state. The health and other benefits of a particular antipollution program may be insubstantial compared to its costs. That's the case, for example, with a specific benzene standard that was estimated to save no more than a third of a life per year at an annual cost in excess of $100 million. Indeed, the same type of marginal cost/marginal benefit analysis used in connection with the firm's quest for information is appropriate in the environmental area (refer back to Figure 8.9a, p. 286).

Consider the following not unrealistic scenario: A lake has become so polluted that it is not fit for drinking, swimming, or fishing. The residents with lakefront properties decide that the water quality must be improved, and their hired consultant suggests the following alternatives:

Degree of Cleanup	*Consequence*
60 percent	Water will be fit for drinking
90 percent	Water will be suitable for drinking and swimming
100 percent	Water will be clean enough for drinking, swimming, and fishing

The 100 families that comprise the community are then asked how much they would be willing to pay for a cleanup that would provide them with (1) drinking water only, (2) drinking water and safe swimming as well, and (3) all three uses. Their responses are:

	Average per Family Daily Benefit	*Total Benefit*	*Marginal Benefit*
Left as is		0	0
Drinking only	$20	$2,000	$2,000
Drinking and swimming	30	3,000	1,000
Drinking, swimming, and fishing	35	3,500	500

The marginal benefit (MB) step curve in Figure 10.2 plots the marginal benefits of the varying degrees of cleanup.

**FIGURE 10.2   Marginal Benefits and Costs of Alternative Degrees of
Water Purification**

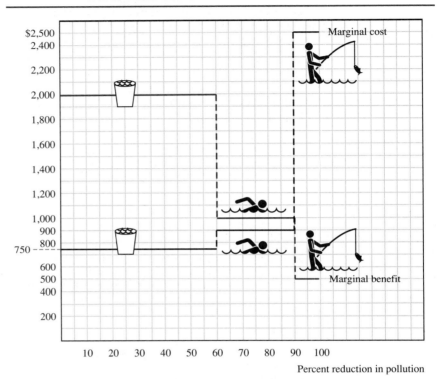

Percent reduction in pollution

As long as the marginal benefits of cleaning up the polluted lake exceed the
marginal cleanup costs—as they do both for drinking and swimming
purposes—the community's net benefits are positive and recommend
purification. However, when the MC > MB, then further purification is
inefficient. The MB obtained from making the lake fishable is just not worth
the MC.

Economic decisions, of course, cannot rest on benefits alone; costs
must be considered. In general, marginal costs of pollution prevention or
abatement rise. The greater the extent of cleanup, the greater the cost for
each additional percent of relief. The marginal cost (MC) step curve in
Figure 10.2 shows marginal costs of $750 per day for sufficient purification
to provide the residents with drinking water only, $900 per day for clean-
ing up the lake for both drinking and swimming purposes, and $2,500 per
day for sufficient cleanup to turn the lake into an angler's paradise.

How much should the community now spend on environmental
cleanup? Figure 10.2 leads you to conclude that the appropriate degree is
90 percent, the point at which MB = MC. Further cleanup is just not

worthwhile when the extra benefits to the fishers ($500 daily) are compared with the extra costs to the community ($2,500). On the other hand, cleaning the lake so that only drinking water is provided is not economically sensible either. The extra costs of cleanup from 60 to 90 percent are only $900 daily, while the residents measure their extra benefits as $1,000 daily.

In short, pollution is a "bad" and environmental purity is a "good." But since obtaining goods is costly, the economist insists that decisions be made only after considering both the cost and the benefit consequences of any decision. In most cases, the eradication of all pollutants will be so expensive that it will not make any economic sense. (Need it make eco-

---

MicroBits 10.1

Congressional Confusion on the Pollution Front

Congress appears to be ambivalent if not inconsistent when it comes to considering the costs of a cleaner environment. The Clean Air Act as amended in 1970 reads in part:

> Any national secondary ambient air quality standard . . . shall specify a level of air quality the attainment and maintenance of which . . . is requisite to protect the public welfare from any known or anticipated adverse effects associated with the presence of such air pollutant in the ambient air. (42 U.S. Code 7409, 1.b.2)

In a case involving the standards for lead emitted from gasoline-fueled automobiles, the Lead Industries Association asserted that the Clean Air Act called for the Environmental Protection Agency to consider the economic costs and technological feasibility of achieving the mandated standards. The District of Columbia Appeals Court, in a decision left standing by the U.S. Supreme Court, wrote:

> The legislative history of the Act also shows the [EPA] *may not consider economic and technological feasibility* in setting air quality standards; the absence of any provision requiring consideration of these factors . . . was the

result of a deliberate decision by Congress to subordinate such concerns to the achievement of health goals. (10 *Environmental Law Reporter* 20652, pp. 8–80; italics added)

Clearly, the EPA is not allowed to consider economic costs.

In contrast, consider the words of the Federal Insecticide, Fungicide, and Rodenticide Act of 1972, the legislation that regulates pesticide use:

> The Administrator [of the EPA] shall register a pesticide [for use] if he determines that . . . it will perform its intended function without *unreasonable adverse effects on the environment*. (7 U.S. Code 136a, 5, italics added)

The same act defines the italicized words to mean "any unreasonable risk to man or the environment, taking into account the economic, social, and environmental costs and benefits of the use of any pesticide" (7 U.S. Code 136bb). Consequently, the EPA can approve a pesticide if the economic costs of banning a pesticide are so substantial as to outweigh the environmental benefits. Any comments?

nomic sense? See MicroBits 10.1 for two different approaches used in the U.S. antipollution laws.)

Pollution Controls: Restraints and Taxes.   All well and good, you say. But surely not everyone in the community is responsible for polluting the lake. Why should they have to pay for cleaning it up? Or, in a broader context, how do you get the individual polluter to consider marginal costs to the environment? This question is especially critical in light of the analysis in Chapter 9. The good citizen, Snow White, would through her altruistic actions be put out of business, while her polluting rival, Dirty Dick, would survive and profit.

Since altruism won't motivate Dirty Dick, coercion may be needed to enforce the community's antipollution program. The community can insist that Dick's plant limit its emissions by forcing it to cut back on its output. Figure 10.3 reproduces Chapter 9's Figure 9.4a, with Snow White's self-imposed higher costs. Since Snow White's output is pure, the authorities will leave her alone. She'll continue to produce 100 tons weekly. But Dirty Dick will be told that his firm has to reduce production to 100 tons. See what happens to Dick's costs, revenues, and profits: average costs rise to $____, and with price still at $300, profits fall to $____.[2] He's now no better-off than Snow White.

There is an alternative method that may prove more effective. It works with Dick's economic interests rather than against them. Consider a tax of $55 per 100 tons of output. Draw onto Figure 10.3 the impact of the tax on Dirty Dick's average and marginal costs, using the technique of Figure 8.8a (p. 283). If you drew it properly, Dick's cost curves should be slightly above Snow White's. Indeed, under these tax conditions, Dick would be wise to install the same antipollution devices that Snow White did and cut his costs down to her level. Pollution will be reduced, and the polluters—Snow White and Dirty Dick—rather than the community will bear the costs. Efficiency and equity are both served; the externality is effectively internalized. And, as already shown in Figure 10.1, the social marginal cost curve replaces the old supply curve, leading to a more appropriate allocation of scarce resources.

Efficiency versus Equity.   But such a congruence as described above does not always occur. Consider a more complex yet typical pollution situation, in which differing types of plants all contribute to the deterioration in the area's environmental quality. A steel plant, a chemical factory, and an electrical generating facility all discharge their wastes. Yet not only are their impacts on the environmental quality unique, but their costs for pollution control are also usually distinct.

Figure 10.4 reproduces two diagrams from a study of pollution control costs. Figure 10.4a is the marginal cost curve of improving the air quality by reducing discharges from a petroleum plant, while Figure 10.4b

FIGURE 10.3   Cleaning Up Dirty Dick

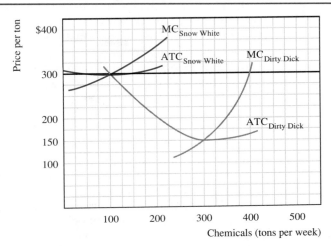

Quantitative emission controls imposed on Dirty Dick will cut his output to 100 tons weekly, and thus curtail pollution. Alternatively, a $55 tax per 100 tons produced will raise Dirty Dick's ATC and MC curves, inducing him to install emission control equipment that is less costly than the tax.

FIGURE 10.4   Marginal Costs for Pollution Reduction in Petroleum and Beet-Sugar Refining

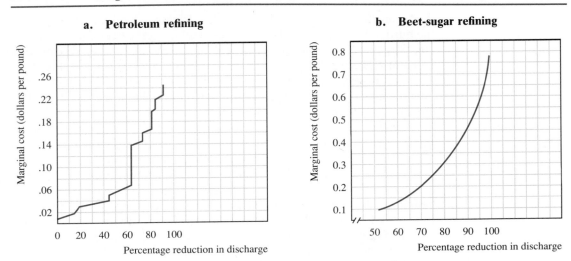

a.   Petroleum refining

b.   Beet-sugar refining

SOURCE: William J. Baumol and Wallace E. Oates, *Economics Environmental Policy and the Quality of Life* (Englewood Cliffs, N.J.: Prentice Hall, 1979), pp. 213, 214.

is the MC/clean air relationship from a beet-sugar refinery. Put yourself in the position of the environmental control officer in charge of the region. Both plants have already cut down pollution to 60 percent, but you've concluded that pollution must be reduced further. Your first reaction might be to order each plant manager to cut down pollution by, say, 10 percent. Does that make economic sense?

Think about it. On the surface, it seems fair and effective. But it is *not* an efficient way to reduce pollution. As you move from 60 to 70 percent, every percentage reduction in petroleum refinery pollution costs between 6.5 and 14 cents per pound of discharge, while an identical reduction in beet-factory-induced contamination costs between 14 and 22 cents per pound. Cutting down petroleum refining pollution by 20 percentage points—going from 60 to 80 percent reduction in discharge—costs from 6 to 16.5 cents per pound.

The unmistakable conclusion may not be fair, but it's straightforward: Impose the entire burden of pollution reduction on the petroleum refinery! From an efficiency point of view, the air will be equally clean but the costs to industry overall will be smaller than if you divide the burden equally. Naturally, the petroleum refiners will scream bloody murder, and from an equity point of view they may be right. But not from an economic point of view.

You can see this clearly if you just imagined that a single company owned both the petroleum-refining and beet-processing plants. How would management decide to allocate the cutback if costs were the only consideration? Clearly, the entire burden would be borne by the petroleum division of the combined company.

A Reconciliation: The Sale of Pollution Rights.   Inequitable shifting of the burden inevitably meets resistance, including the use of political muscle. So, there is some value in seeking a resolution that will be both efficient and equitable. Economists have written much about establishing a market in pollution rights, although the very notion of "rights" to pollute seems anathema to many people. To its credit, Congress in its 1990 amendments to the Clean Air Act introduced such a mechanism for sulfur dioxide (SO_2) emissions, a cause of acid rain. The first transaction under this act, in which the Tennessee Valley Authority bought the right to emit 10,000 tons of SO_2 from Wisconsin Power and Light for an estimated price of $2.5 to $3 million, occurred in May 1992, and more are likely to follow.

The scheme would work as follows. Using marginal cost/marginal benefit analysis, the authorities would decide how much of a particular type of pollution would be appropriate per day or month (e.g., 100 cubic feet of polluted water per day). They would then divide this amount by some number (say, 100) to obtain the quantity of available rights. These 100 rights, entitling each possesser to dispose of one cubic foot of water daily, would be auctioned off on a periodic basis.[3] The pollution right thus becomes a license to pollute. Polluting without a license would not only be illegal, but also subject to heavy fines.

Who would demand the rights? Of course, polluters would. But their demand for a permit would be related to its price. Too high a price would induce them to seek alternatives such as emission controls. Now consider two polluters. For one, the marginal cost of preventing an outflow of a given volume of polluted water daily ranges from $5 to $15 per cubic foot. For the second, prevention costs would run from $25 to $50 per cubic foot. Surely, the first polluter would not be willing to pay more than $15 per right; the second would go as high as $50.

Let's say the bidding drives the price up to $20 per right. The first polluter would not be interested in acquiring rights and would install emission controls instead. The second, of course, would buy rights, since the cost of the license is less than the alternative of cleaning up.

Why is the pollution rights solution better than imposing the entire burden on the polluter who has the lower prevention costs such as the petroleum refiner in the earlier case? Think about it for a moment. Who will voluntarily prevent pollution? Won't it be the petroleum plant? And wouldn't the beet-sugar refiner continue to pollute? So, we've achieved a low-cost reduction in pollution voluntarily, working through the market system by permitting each producer to choose that option must profitable to it.[4] Both equity and efficiency are attained. (MicroBits 10.2 suggests another solution that can work in some cases.)

Lawyers and Scavengers. Pollution licenses have entered the decision-making system through at least two back doors: pollution damage suits and container deposit laws. Litigious Larry, whose home is being blackened by the soot of a neighboring carpet plant, can request the local court to enjoin further emissions. That's the equivalent of a ban. However, injunctions are rarely granted; Larry stands a better chance of winning a suit for damages. Damage awards force the polluter to analyze its economic alternatives. The firm can pay the damages and continue to pollute, the analogue of a pollution license fee. Or, the firm can install pollution abatement equipment and save itself the costs of litigation and damage awards. In essence, the decision whether or not to pollute—and if yes, how much to pollute—hinges on the relative costs of pollution and its abatement, much as is the result of a pollution fee scheme.[5]

Container deposit charges, too, resemble pollution licenses. The potential polluter pays a refundable fee. Litter is reduced if the can is returned. But even if the can is discarded, someone is likely to retrieve the container to collect the deposit. This system is quite efficient. The individual who tosses away his finished soda can obviously considers the cost of the time and effort involved in returning the container to be worth less than the loss of the deposit charge. On the other hand, the individual who picks up the can feels that the refund is worth more than his time and

MICROBITS 10.2

Logging Rights and the Sale of Public Forest Land

The United States owns immense acres of timberland in the Northwest. Domestic timber companies would like no less than to chop down the vast forests for lumber. Environmentalists vehemently oppose any logging, citing wildlife conservation as well as public recreational use as reasons to keep axes out. The U.S. Department of the Interior has compromised by permitting limited lumbering in public forest land. Some economists have suggested that instead of leasing tracts for their timber rights while retaining public ownership, the Department of the Interior would better preserve the forest by selling forest land outright to the lumber companies.

This recommendation seems strange. After all, leasing land means that the land would be left for the public benefit after the timber companies were finished, which would not be the case if the land were owned privately. But if you mull it over some more, you might have second thoughts. If the companies don't own the land, they could not benefit from conserving the forest. Instead, they'll cut down a wide swath of woods and then select only those felled trees suitable for further processing. The remaining trees will be left to rot. So, when the lumberjacks are finished, a forest will have been turned into a wasteland.

But if the land is sold to the lumber companies, a new set of considerations enters the picture. Trees too small to be felled today are left to grow larger over time. They can be cut down next year or a decade from now. Because the lumber company owns the land and thus the trees, it considers long-term criteria rather than shortsighted ones. In fact, the lumber companies will plant trees to replace the ones they've cut down, for when the saplings mature, they, too, can be used for lumber.

This particular example is representative of a broad set of situations where common ownership leads to overutilization. Something that's owned by no one is also preserved by no one. "Exploit now" becomes the motto, for if the firm waits too long, someone else may beat it to the punch. So, the blue whale faces extinction because no one owns either the seas or the whale population. The quicker and more total is the harvest of any one whaling ship, the more profitable it has to be.

The resolution of the problem seems straightforward. If overutilization derives from the lack of individual property rights, remedy it where possible by establishing property rights. Such rights cannot always be set up. There's no technical way to exert ownership over seagoing whales or air. But in many instances, the environment can be preserved by selling off the property to users, whose self-interest dictates that they conserve rather than waste. Can you think of any other examples?

effort. The deposit fee system thus enables each individual to specialize—some throw away, others pick up. It's similar to the pollution prevention performed by the refiner with the lower marginal costs.

Uncertainty and the Environment

To this point, we have assumed that the costs of pollution and its prevention can be accurately assessed. Yet smog is not merely a characteristic of certain urban environments. Even scientists' basic understanding of environmental dangers is hazy. The gap in our knowledge about the consequences of meddling with nature substantially complicates decisions that involve cost/benefit analysis. For how can we discuss in any meaningful way the marginal benefit of pollution reduction if we haven't a good notion of the damage of environmental contamination? Decisions that are reasonably simple when information is complete become horribly complex when we realize how beclouded we are by the surrounding uncertainty.

Even where documentation exists—smoking and lung cancer, for example—problems still arise in quantifying the benefit of reducing pollutants by varying degrees. What are the marginal benefits of eliminating smoking in public places entirely as opposed to permitting nonsmoking and smoking sections of differing proportions? How much benefit accrues to our friends around the lake if the lake is partially cleaned up, not in the world of the textbook, but in reality?

Some environmentalists deal with this uncertainty in a very simple way: Since we don't know the risk, why take the chance? Economists, however, have made some headway in measuring the benefits of a cleaner

environment. Indeed, the lake example suggests one way: ask those likely
to be affected how much they would pay in order to clean up the environment in varying degrees.[6]

But even these methods will not yield accurate results. Consequently,
it's an exaggeration to draw marginal cost/marginal benefit curves with
the precision of those in Figure 10.2. Instead, it makes more sense to
indicate a range, as in Figure 10.5, which implicitly offers a breadth of
choices. Persons who are risk-averse by nature will want to minimize the
chances of making errors. They will more heavily weight the benefits of
pollution reduction and work with the right border of the marginal benefit
curve. They'll also minimize the costs of pollution control and focus on
the right border of the MC curve. For them, Figure 10.5 shows MB = MC
at the 60 percent level of pollution reduction. Others, however, are less
concerned with the consequences of wrong environmental decisions.
They may minimize the benefits of a cleaner environment and anticipate
higher cleanup costs, leading them to the far-left borders and only a 25

FIGURE 10.5   Cost/Benefit Analysis in an Uncertain World

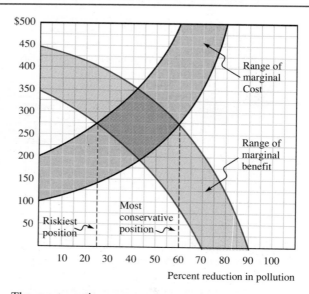

The most cautious approach to environmental
cleanup weighs the benefits from pollution
reduction most and costs least, leading to a 60
percent reduction in pollution (but not 100
percent!). The least cautious approach does the
reverse—minimizes benefits and maximizes the
likely costs, so that pollution should be cut back
only 25 percent.

percent reduction in pollution. Still others may take intermediate positions. In terms of this scenario, no one option is more compelling than another; they all are defensible in light of the fuzziness of the facts. Nevertheless, one conclusion emerges even in this case of uncertainty: *Neither the information nor the uncertainty is likely to justify a 100 percent reduction in pollution.*

Recap

Environmental pollution is a specific case of market failure, where the competitive market system does not yield an efficient solution. Because third parties suffer and the social cost/benefit calculations differ from private cost/benefit criteria, a legitimate case can be made for community action instead of competitive market decisions. Though outright bans of pollutants rarely command economists' approval, reducing pollution to the point where marginal social cost equals marginal social benefit is defensible. Further pollution is neither environmentally nor economically justifiable. Realize, however, that we lack accurate information both on the benefits and the costs of pollution reduction. This uncertainty suggests that there's room for debate about the appropriate degree of pollution reduction.

Pollution reduction can be achieved in a number of ways, among which are emission controls, emission taxes, and the sale of pollution rights. While the former two will internalize the externalities by imposing the costs of pollution on the source, these policies may not always reduce pollution in the cheapest way. *Most efficient pollution reduction is obtained by equating the MCs of all pollution sources,* that is, by reducing pollution first from the least-costly sources of pollution reduction.

Any good or service that is desired by the community but would not be adequately provided if it were left to the working of the market is called a **public good.**

Private Affluence and Public Poverty

Environmental pollution is merely one example of market failure. That the competitive mechanism does not always provide efficient solutions is applicable to other issues as well. In this half of the chapter you'll encounter a broad category of goods and services collectively called **public goods.**

The Free-Rider Problem and Market Failure

The family which takes its mauve and cerise, air-conditioned, power-steered, and power-braked automobile out for a tour passes through cities that are badly paved, made hideous by litter, blighted buildings, billboards and posts for wires that should long since have been put underground. They pass on into a countryside that has been rendered largely invisible by commercial art. . . . They picnic on exquisitely packaged food from a portable icebox by a polluted stream and go on to spend the night at a park which is a menace to public health and morals. Just before dozing off on an air mattress, beneath a nylon tent, amid the stench of decaying refuse, they may reflect vaguely on the curious unevenness of their blessings. Is this, indeed, the American genius?[7]

By contrasting the plethora of private goods and the dearth of public goods, Professor John Kenneth Galbraith points out a fundamental weakness of the market mechanism. We are willing to pay for those services that we consume as individuals, even if they are trivial. Yet we are unwilling to support an adequate amount of services that are supplied communally even though we view them as critical for our individual well-being. Why?

A **free-rider** is an individual who can obtain a service without paying for it.

Economists have suggested that one answer lies in the problem of the **free-rider:** If someone else will pay for the service, why not take advantage of her generosity? Here's a real-life example; only the name has been changed to protect the self-centered. In one urban neighborhood whose residents were frustrated by the police force's inability to cope with property crime, the homeowners' association hired a private security agency to patrol the streets in marked cars. Each homeowner was assessed $100 for the first year. Now consider this service from the point of view of Pete. Since the patrol car meanders quite visibly through the neighborhood and presumably deters burglars, Pete's home is protected as well. So why should Pete pay the assessment? He can obtain the benefit without bearing the cost as long as he is sure that enough of his neighbors do want the patrol and are willing to pay for it.

The patrol ran on a daily, 24-hour basis for the first year. But then Pete's neighbors woke up to his attitude. They, being equally rational, soon held back their contributions to the security service. The inevitable consequence followed. Patrol hours were cut back so that by the third year only one eight-hour shift was financed. In short, although each homeowner wanted the extra protection, each relied on his neighbors to pay for it. The result: a less-than-desired amount of service.

Two characteristics of a public good are evident in this example:

- The "You can eat your cake and I can have it" quality. The free rider's benefit does not reduce the benefit to others, because the marginal cost of an additional user benefiting from the good or service is zero.
- The "You can't stop me from eating the cake" quality. It is either impossible or extremely expensive to exclude any user from consuming the good or service. (Can you imagine a patrol car winding its way through the neighborhood towing a giant sign: "Burglars take note: We protect only the following residences . . ."?)[8]

And the consequences are evident, too: the plethora of free riders led to a substantial reduction and ultimately could lead to the elimination of the service.

Cooperative Solutions

The fact that no user can be excluded from the service effectively removes the profit incentive from the market. Why should any entrepreneur attempt to set up a private patrol service when few, if any, householders are likely to subscribe? This contrasts sharply with uniformed security personnel in retail shops to deter shoplifting and guards in banks to prevent holdups. These "private" services, limited to and paid for by the firm, benefit almost exclusively the payer.

You understand the dilemma. On the one hand, we do want certain public goods, but we wouldn't buy them if they were offered on the market. We'd wait for our neighbors to pay the price, and ride along on their coattails. Since both our neighbors and suppliers think likewise, the services are never offered in the market.

We would, however, agree to a nonmarket resolution: community action. Let's all decide to tax ourselves for the service, jointly enforce the collection of the tax, and individually benefit. Stated this way, the problem and the solution are self-evident. *Public goods will be provided publicly.*

It's Not Always That Simple

Unfortunately, few real-life instances fit the strict public-goods definition. Much more prevalent are goods that yield their benefits to some without reducing the benefits of others but from which free-riders can be excluded. Similarly, you can discover cases where you cannot prevent free riders from benefiting but where the marginal cost of an additional beneficiary is more than zero. What do you do then?

Correcting a Misconception. It may be best to begin by pointing out a common error: While it is frequently true that a public good is provided by a public authority, the converse need not hold. *Merely because some service is provided by a public authority does not necessarily prove that the good or service in question is a public good.* (Read the previous two sentences again. You'll save yourself a lot of trouble if they are clear in your mind.)

Is the mail service provided by the post office a public good? If you examine this question using the two characteristics mentioned above, you'd have to say no. At the least, the cost of delivering the mail to an additional user is not zero.

No less important is the second condition. Can the post office prevent an individual from using its services? Mailing a letter or package is surely no different from using the telephone; the mailer, like the caller, is easily identified and charged for the service. In fact, the package delivery services of United Parcel Service and the growth of such private mail and parcel delivery companies as Federal Express demonstrate convincingly that mail services are not public goods.

MicroQuery | Here's one for you to think about: Are highways—such as the interstate highway system—public goods? Why or why not?

_____

_____.9

In fact, in 17th- and early 18th-century America, privately owned turnpikes were not uncommon; the owners profited by charging tolls for using the roadway. Indeed, as a precursor of the future, a private highway was constructed outside of Washington, D.C., not long ago.

Pure public goods share two characteristics: (1) the cost to the marginal user is zero and (2) the marginal user cannot be excluded from participating in the goods' use.

Pure Public Goods.   What, then, are some **pure public goods** that meet the conditions of zero marginal cost for an additional user as well as the nonexcludability of the marginal user? A common example of a pure public good is national defense. No one believes that the defense budget must be augmented because of the many babies born each year. These marginal additions to the population receive the same protection at no extra cost to the existing population. Yet imagine General Withers storming into the delivery room to present the newborn Jill with a bill for the day's wages of six marines. Jill's understandable refusal to react to the bill may frustrate the general. But he can in no way deny Jill marine protection. (That stands in sharp contrast to the hospital services she's using and is surely willing to pay for.) The same arguments can be made about police services. The existence of uniformed patrol personnel deters crime at zero marginal cost for the individual, yet it's impossible to identify the specific individual who would be mugged if the police officer were not there. The classic example of the pure public good is the lighthouse, its beacon warning all passing ships of the dangerous shoals nearby. As long as the light shines, all the ships benefit. Yet the marginal cost of another ship's using the light is zero, and the light cannot be selectively shone to exclude those ships unwilling to pay the fee.[10]

Impure public goods are those for which either (1) the cost to the marginal user is not zero but there's no easy way to exclude free riders or (2) the user can be charged even though the marginal cost for that user is zero.

The "Impure" Public Good.   One soon runs out of examples of pure public goods. Nevertheless, the fundamental idea of a public good remains even in the case of **impure public goods,** which fail to meet the stringent purity conditions.

The Beach.   Consider the zero cost of having additional people lying in the sun and swimming in the water. After all, Tom's tan is not at all lighter because Tamara absorbs the ultraviolet rays in propinquity to Tom. Yet beach access can be controlled and thus charged for by simply erecting fences.[11] Private ownership becomes possible; the existence of private beach clubs is evidence that the demand for such facilities exists. So, the beach is an impure public good. Although the marginal cost of an additional sunworshipper is zero, he can be excluded if he is unwilling to pay the entrance fee.

Are resources allocated efficiently if access to the beach is limited? Many economists would argue that they are not. Figure 10.6 shows that a $5 entrance fee would cause a discrepancy between the zero marginal cost and the demand curve that measures marginal social benefit. The deadweight loss would be eliminated only by letting everyone in free. So that even in an instance where it's possible to charge, allocational efficiency dictates that no fees be imposed.

Garbage.   What about the converse situation? Costs do exist and they can be attributed to specific individuals, but it's impossible to impose them on the free riders. Consider garbage collection as an impure public good. Removing garbage from the neighborhood eliminates a public

FIGURE 10.6   Paying for the Sun

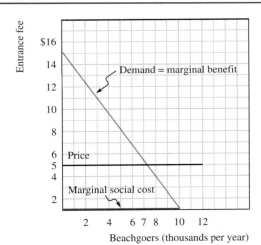

Although the MSC for a beachgoer is zero, a $5 admission fee will dissuade more than 3,000 people from enjoying the beach. Optimal resource allocation mandates that admission be free, so that MB = MSB.

health hazard and improves the appearance and fragrance of the community, a benefit for all residents. Clearly, too, the costs of the garbage pickups can be calculated for each site with reasonable accuracy. Yet in the absence of coercion, free riding is possible. Sloppy Sol could simply plead, "I enjoy the sight and smell of debris piling up in my yard. You can pick up your garbage, but leave mine alone."

If the community fails to coerce recalcitrant members to pay, free riding will increase until little garbage is picked up. Health hazards will persist even for those who dispose of their garbage properly. After all, the rats that thrive on Sloppy Sol's garbage could just as well infest his neighbor Neat Nadine's house and children. Which means, of course, that

MICROBITS 10.3

Public–Private Sector Cooperation: The Linowes Commission Report

There are essentially three techniques for the privatization of service delivery. The first method is simply selling the government's assets. . . . The second technique is contracting out, whereby the government enters into contracts with private firms to provide goods and services used by the government or demanded by the public. Contracting usually results in cost savings because the process is opened to competition among vendors. . . .

Contracting out in the United States has been employed most widely at the state and local levels. From coast to coast, government bodies, principally in response to pressures from taxpayers for greater efficiency, have been relying increasingly on the private sector to get the job done.

Since 1932 San Francisco has franchised garbage collection to private companies. Today, drivers own their trucks and are responsible for collections. In 1975, a study showed that San Franciscans were paying $40 a year for the private service, whereas New Yorkers in two comparable neighborhoods were paying $297 for municipal collection.

In 1977, Little Rock, Arkansas, contracted out its city hall janitorial services and achieved a 50 percent cost savings. . . . Orange County, California, reduced costs about 33 percent by contracting out its electronic data processing requirements. . . .

Innovative privatization efforts such as these are under way in numerous state and local governments throughout the country. Privatization is growing because it delivers major savings or improved service quality, or both, to local taxpayers.

Recommendation

The federal government should rely on the private sector for provision of commercially available goods and services. Because contracting provides a means to procure the same level of service at reduced cost, it is not in the public interest for government to perform functions in competition with the private sector.

Source: [Linowes Commission], *Privatization toward More Effective Government: Report of the President's Commission on Privatization* (Urbana: University of Illinois Press, 1988), pp. 1–3, 130–31.

if Neat Nadine is rational, she should refuse to pay for garbage collection, too. It's an "all or no one" proposition. And so, throughout the world, municipalities impose rules about garbage collection and disposal.

A Final Thought: Privatization

The idea of having private concerns competing for the right to provide public goods is appealing. Could the federal or local governments use the market system to supply public goods? Could a municipality insist that the garbage be disposed of properly but leave the particular manner to the competitive market? Could the criminal justice system decide who is to be incarcerated but leave the running of the prisons to the private sector? These questions are far from hypothetical. In many municipalities, garbage collection is mandated by government order but is handled by private firms. Elsewhere, fire fighting, hospital services, and even prisons are in the hands of private companies. **Privatization,** in fact, is a concept that became popular during the 1980s, leading to the appointment by President Reagan of the President's Commission on Privatization. A brief excerpt from the commission's report appears in MicroBits 10.3.

Privatization involves using the private sector to supply goods and services previously produced by the government sector.

Summary

Both environmental issues and public goods share a common feature: The competitive market fails to concern itself either with reducing pollution or providing an adequate amount of public goods. This jarring fact holds true even though the individuals who constitute society agree that pollution in general should be reduced and more and better public goods should be made available. This chapter sought to explain why the market fails in these two cases, and to point out how at least in principle community action can reduce environmental contamination and alleviate the shortage of public goods within the framework of a market economy.

Externalities that bring about a discrepancy between the private and public cost/benefit calculations lead to a suboptimal environmental outcome when environmental policy is left to the market. The individual firm will exploit the environment as long as nature is a free good. That others may have to foot the bill for the firm's actions is basically irrelevant to the firm's decision makers. One resolution is to internalize the externality, to make the firm pay the full costs of its actions. This principle underlies most government environmental policy and seems both plausible and fair. However, such a solution is not always efficient. A more appropriate principle is to reduce pollution from those sources that can do so at the least cost, the rule being to clean up more where the marginal cost is lowest and less where the MC is highest.

Of course, given the current uncertainty of both the benefits of various degrees of decontamination and the corresponding costs, it's too much to expect either environmentalists or economists to provide precise answers. Yet to accept the status quo or to insist on environmental purity each appears to be an equally inappropriate response in light of even rough estimates of the marginal benefits and marginal costs of various policy options.

Public goods represent a slightly different problem. Because free riding is possible, private entrepreneurs have no incentive to market such goods or services. That is especially true for pure public goods—from such critical ones as national defense to such trivial ones as watching fireworks—where the addition of another user does not increase the cost of supplying the good and there is no way to charge the marginal user. Only by joint community action will the public good be provided.

Pure public goods, however, are few. In many instances, the impure public good provides its services to an additional user at no cost to the existing users, but charges can be levied upon those who wish to benefit (the beach example). Alternatively, instances exist (the garbage pickup is one such case) where the marginal costs for providing the goods and services to additional users are not zero. But because some can avoid using the service, they thereby eliminate the benefit for those who are willing to pay. Again, the solution lies in joint action. In the case of beaches and the like, communities often decide to provide the service for everyone without access charges and cover expenses through taxes. For garbage pickup, communities insist that waste be properly disposed of, but practice varies. Some localities collect the garbage with community-owned and -operated facilities, while others obtain the service from the private sector. Privatization is an attempt to overcome another problem: government failure. The sad fact is that theoretical justifications for government intervention do not always give rise to efficient practical solutions. The combination of coercive government regulations with private sector implementation is an attempt to achieve the best of all possible worlds.

Market failure is not limited to externalities and the provision of public goods. The appendix to this chapter examines a situation where the market fails because of excessive competition. More often, however, market failure can be attributed to the formation of monopolies, the subject of Chapter 11.

Key Terms

Externalities
Free rider
Impure public good
Market failure
Negative externality

Positive externality
Privatization
Public good
Pure public good

Review Questions

1. Why does the competitive market "fail" in the case of (*a*) the environment and (*b*) public goods?
2. Characterize each of the following as a positive (P) or negative (N) spillover:

    a. Honeybees, while gathering nectar, fertilize a fruit orchard.
    b. Coyote hunters reduce the number of cattle-attacking predators.
    c. Consumers use chlorofluorocarbon-

based deodorants, which destroy the earth's ozone layer.

d. Motorists' scenic views are blocked by billboards erected alongside highways.

e. Offshore mining destroys lobster beds.

f. The failure of a bank causes a run on other banks.

g. Cigarette smoking in a closed area causes nonsmokers to inhale cigarette smoke.

3. a. Use a diagram to demonstrate that resources would be *underutilized* in an industry characterized by positive externalities.

b. What type of action could be taken to improve resource allocation in this case?

4. Why would an economist be likely to

a. Oppose banning all automobiles in a polluted urban center?

b. Favor unequal treatment of polluters, even though they may all be equally responsible?

5. Characterize each of the following as private (P), pure public (PP), or impure public (IP) goods, and in each case, justify your characterization:

a. Antiflu innoculation.

b. Destruction of mosquito breeding grounds.

c. Municipal bus service.

d. Home fire insurance.

e. A privately sponsored fourth of July fireworks display.

f. City streets.

g. National parks.

h. A professor's microtheory lecture.

i. Hospital services.

6. How would you respond to the following argument? "The city administration is justified in charging entrance fees to the beaches since it costs money to clean them up and to pay for the lifeguards and other staff."

7. a. Would privatization eliminate the problems associated with free riding? Explain.

b. How would privatization increase the efficiency of public goods delivery?

Food for Thought

1. Use the equimarginal principle developed in connection with pollution abatement to explain how a firm's management would allocate production between two manufacturing plants that produce, say, lightbulbs.

2. a. Demonstrate how differing marginal costs of pollution abatement would determine a firm's demand curve for pollution rights. (Assume a two-firm industry.)

b. Given a fixed supply of pollution rights, show how the price of a right is determined.

c. How many rights will each firm buy?

3. How is uncertainty likely to affect the pollution rights auction scheme mentioned in the chapter?

4. a. Use isoquant analysis to demonstrate that if a 12-ounce bottle costs more than a 12-ounce can, a soft drink bottler will use only cans.

b. What incentive or penalty would be needed to persuade the bottler to switch to refillable bottles rather than disposable cans?

5. a. How might pollution control schemes influence the location of industry?

b. Would relocations caused by government-imposed abatement outlays increase or decrease allocational efficiency? Explain.

6. What type of control mechanism might reduce the acid rain, generated by U.S. industrial plants, that pollutes Canada?

7. Did you know that early in this century the automobile was hailed for its environment-preserving qualities, replacing the polluting horse? What generalization could be drawn from this observation?

8. HBO scrambles its programs so that non-subscribers are unable to use their cable connections or satellite dishes to receive HBO broadcasts. Would public policy be better served if HBO were prevented from scrambling?

9. In many areas, private beaches compete with public beaches. What economic rationale might explain why some people are willing to pay for an apparently free alternative?

Suggested Readings

William J. Baumol and Wallace E. Oates, *Economics, Environmental Policy, and the Quality of Life* (Englewood Cliffs, N.J.: Prentice-Hall, 1979) is a highly readable and comprehensive textbook on environmental economics. A recent review is Maureen L. Cropper and Wallace E. Oates, "Environmental Economics: A Survey," *Journal of Economic Literature* 30 (June 1992), pp. 675–740. A more popular approach may be found in Alan S. Blinder, *Hard Heads, Soft Hearts: Tough-Minded Economics for a Just Society* (Reading, Mass.: Addison-Wesley, 1987), Chapter 5. Blinder contends that governmental environmental policy could be made significantly more efficient at relatively little cost. Steven Kelman, in *What Price Incentives? Economists and the Environment* (Boston: Auburn House, 1981), argues against using cost benefit analysis and economic incentives for pollution control.

Ronald H. Coase's "The Problem of Social Cost," *Journal of Law and Economics* 3 (October 1960), pp. 1–44, is the classic article on property rights and the control of damages, and is easily understandable by undergraduate students.

A good source of further breadth and depth on public goods are public finance textbooks. See, for example, Harvey S. Rosen, *Public Finance*, 3rd ed. (Homewood, Ill.: Richard D. Irwin, 1991), Chapter 6; or Joseph E. Stiglitz, *Economics of the Public Sector* (New York: Norton, 1986), Chapter 5.

Notes and Answers

1. Two points should be made in this connection. First, government action does not imply federal or even formal government decisions. Economic theory merely suggests that in instances of market failure, the remedy involves cooperative rather than individual decisions. Second, not all government intervention stems from market failure. Indeed, you've already seen a number of examples of "government failure," where intervention in the market mechanism leads to results that are worse than inefficient market solutions.

2. 300, 0.

3. The Clean Air Act issues pollution rights free to existing polluters rather than charging for the rights.

4. Antipollution groups could express their preference by buying rights and simply not using them. That would comply with their pollution-reducing agenda.

5. The courts have internalized the costs of the externality by upholding damage awards against polluters even when the environmental authorities have approved the pollution

source. Such was the case here, which is based on *Galaxy Carpet Mills, Inc.* v. *Massengill*, 338 S.E. 2d 428 (Ga. 1986). Galaxy was liable for damages even though it had received the approval of the state environmental agency. By the way, potential lawyers take note. This is just one area where microeconomics and law overlap.

6. Using the survey technique is discussed by A. Myrick Freeman III, *The Benefits of Environmental Improvement: Theory and Practice* (Baltimore: Resources for the Future, 1979), Chapter 5. An alternative method can be equally applied to the lake example. Since people should pay more to live in a less polluted region, the difference in real estate values will give us some handle on the benefit attributable to pollution control. Freeman notes (Chapter 6) that most empirical studies have shown residential property values and air pollution to be inversely correlated. He also points out (Chapter 7) that wages differ between healthier and less healthy environments, and constitute another method for measuring the benefits of a purer environment.

7. John K. Galbraith, *The Affluent Society*, rev. ed. (Boston: Houghton Mifflin, 1984) p. 192.

8. In the public choice literature, the former principle is known as "nonrivalry," and the latter as "nonexcludability." Public goods stand in contrast to private goods, which are both rival and excludable. (Real pastry is rival; once Peter finishes the slice it's no longer available to Paul. Pastry is also excludable. The baker won't let Peter have a piece if Peter won't pay.)

9. While many contend they are, strictly defined they're not. The fact that each car traveling over the highway weakens it and necessitates road maintenance means that the marginal cost of each user is not zero. Moreover, since entry onto the highway is limited to specific entry stations, the driver who wishes to use the highway can be charged.

10. Instead of the lighthouse, today's technology relies on radio signals that can be scrambled to exclude the free rider. Yet the cost of providing a marginal user with the benefit remains zero.

11. The radio beam sent to ships is analogous. Whether one ship or a thousand home in on the beam does not affect its cost; jamming is the equivalent of putting up a fence to prevent free riders from taking advantage.

APPENDIX
TV BROADCASTING AND PROPERTY RIGHTS

The Air Waves

Environmental issues and the provision of public services are examples of market failure caused by externalities or free riding. This appendix deals with market failure stemming from an excess of competition.

TV transmission technology precludes a competitive TV broadcasting industry. Think of such a mundane task as turning on the TV and watching a live performance. At the studio, TV cameras translate the visual images and sound into electrical energy that is broadcast through the air or via cable to your home. Your TV set reverses the process.

Do you ever wonder why the TV waves emanating from different channels don't bump into each other in the sky and deliver a jumble instead of distinct pictures? The answer is that the waves are unique carriers; it's as if each channel were carried by a separate wire. However, clarity mandates that each channel be separated from its neighbor by a discrete space or band. If two channels are inadequately spaced, they interfere with each other and neither comes in clear. (That's why you just get static in between radio stations.)

Visualize now a competitive market for TV channels. Since the air waves are free and since Tedious Ted has as much a right to them as does Notorious Ned, what's to stop either from broadcasting? But as more and more broadcasting firms enter the market, the distance between any two channels narrows. At some point, newcomer Friendly Fred interferes with the quality of the broadcasts by Ted and Ned; all suffer. But for Fred, access to some channel, even if it's not the best, is better than none. Moreover, Fred's very presence brings the quality of Ned's and Ted's broadcasts down to his level, and so removes the competitive edge that a better quality picture and sound would have given Ted and Ned. If you carry this scenario forward and visualize additional competitors and a further narrowing of the distance between channels, ultimately you approach the point where all the viewer obtains is snow and noise. The end result is a free market in television broadcasting but nothing for the viewer to see.

Figure 10A.1 poses this market failure problem graphically. In each panel, the light purple vertical line represents the height of the TV transmitters, which is technologically determined. In this example, all transmitters are equal. Similarly, in each panel the viewing audience is arrayed along the horizontal, each interval representing 1,000 families in this 12,000-family community. The diagonal arms emanating from the transmitters represent the dissipating strength of the TV signal. The further away from the transmitter, the weaker the signal. Make one further assumption: profitable operation requires at least a 2,000-family audience; otherwise advertisers will not fund programs.

FIGURE 10A.1   Market Failure in Broadcasting

a. The first entrant	b. The TV market shared by two channels	c. Five broadcasters compete	d. Too much competition

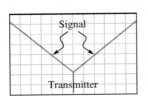 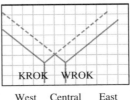 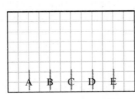 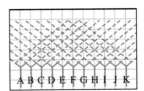

Viewers
(Each grid width = 1,000 families)

a. The first entrant captures the entire market and so serves 12,000 family viewers.

b. Because WROK's signal is stronger in the east, it dominates the 6,000 eastern viewers. Similarly, KROK is the sole programming source for the 4,000 western families. The 2,000 central families are evenly divided.

c. Solve market shares for yourself. [You might peek at Figure 10A.1d for the method.]

d. The large number of competitors leads to broadcast interference and a market share for each that is too small for long-term profitability. Channels B–J each cater to only 1,000 families, while A and K serve only 1,500.

Figure 10A.1a depicts the initial phase of the market. WROK is the only station, reaches all 12,000 families, and is highly profitable. You know by now the next step in the dynamics of the competitive process: profitability induces entry. Figure 10A.1b shows the first stages of entry. KROK sets up its transmitter near WROK. The diagram indicates the consequences of the new entrant. The 6,000 families to the east (right) of WROK are still served by WROK; its signal is stronger—closer to the ground—and is indicated by a solid line. The dashed line indicates the weaker signal of KROK. On the other hand, the 4,000 families to the west of KROK are captured by the new channel, the solid line to the left. The intermediate families are split, so that each captures half. The result: WROK serves 7,000 families, while KROK has a viewing audience of 5,000. Clearly, both are profitable, and so the competitive process continues.

Figure 10A.1c is left for you to complete. Five competitors are now in the market, each with a transmitter at the marked location. Draw the transmission strengths onto the figure, and identify the market shares of the five channels here: A: _____, B: _____, C: _____, D: _____, E: _____.[1]

The market remains profitable for all five, although only marginally so for three of the channels. So, further entry occurs, and Figure 10A.1d depicts the case where 11 competitors fill the air waves with their TV signals. As the signals of each station flow into the air, they soon bump into signals emanating from other sources. Each channel's clear zone lies only close to its transmitter. The result:

Except for the end stations, each channel reaches a viewing audience of 1,000, and even the outer channels cannot achieve an audience of more than 1,500. Competition has drowned out the profit from broadcasting despite the fact that the air is free.

The nonmarket solution to this problem takes different forms in different countries. In many nations, the government takes over ownership both of the air waves and access to them; broadcasting facilities lie exclusively in the government's hands. In the United States, the federal government licenses private broadcasting stations. In essence, the government sells to each broadcaster a property right to a specific segment of the wave spectrum for its exclusive use. The government defends that property right by limiting access to the air waves to others and by regulating the number of licenses per community. Presumably, the government could auction off such licenses to the highest bidder, and in that way capture for the public treasury the benefit of the TV or radio franchise. Instead, policy in the U.S. has been to grant licenses through an administrative rather than a pricing process. The quid pro quo demanded of the stations for the exclusive jurisdiction are such benefits as a minimum number of hours of public interest broadcasting.

Notes and Answers

1. The numbers are 3,000 for A and E and 2,000 for each of the others.

PART

V

IMPERFECT COMPETITION

The perfection implied by the competitive model breaks down in reality, when imperfect people and institutions cope in an imperfect world. Yet, we all believe perfection is worth striving for, and if we can't ever achieve it—barring some of us, who are clearly perfect—at least we struggle in that direction. The chapters that constitute Part V deal with market structures that are as far from the competitive ideal as monopoly and others that approach it more closely. We want to understand not only how these markets deviate from the perfect competitive yardstick but also the dimensions and consequences of such deviations. Finally, we want to examine some of the policy issues that emerge from the models as well as some of the policies actually implemented in the United States.

11 MONOPOLY IS MORE THAN A BOARD GAME

The principle can be applied generally: the way to make money is to get, if you can, a monopoly for yourself.
Aristotle

Diamonds are a gal's best friend.
Anita Loos

Learning Objectives

After reading this chapter, you'll understand:
- Three different reasons for the existence of monopoly.
- How a monopolist determines optimum price, quantity, and profits.
- Why it pays for a monopolist to discriminate if it can do so.
- How cartels function and why they typically are temporary.
- How monopolies reduce uncertainty.

Fly Fishing and Oil

Homer Davenport's 1902 cartoon, reproduced here, falls solidly within the American tradition. The monopolist is depicted as an insensitive giant, unconcerned with the lot of others less fortunate than he. If the monopolist's opponents are the proverbial widows and orphans, so much the better, for their impotence facilitates the monopolist's sybaritic life.

We picture the monopolist in control of a critical industry, be it transportation, a basic mineral, or some crucial consumer good. Yet a

365

monopolist need not be an ogre, and the industry need not be important.
Monopoly, after all, is merely exclusive control of an industry by one
firm. Begin by reading about a most unstereotypical case.

All for the Buck: Monopoly in the Fly-Feather Market[1]

Buck Metz is hardly the type of person you'd picture as a monopolist. Yet
he is. Buck totally dominates his market. He sets prices and decides
which orders to fill and which to ignore.

You have to know something about trout fishing to understand Buck's
niche market. Ardent fly fishers cast handmade lures made of chicken-
neck feathers to entice unsuspecting trout. They'll pay handsomely for
the right feather color and texture. Fortunately for Buck, feathers from
chickens raised for meat or eggs don't attract trout. Buck's feathers are
just the right kind.

The primary business of Metz Hatchery, like that of many other
family-owned breeders, was selling day-old chicks to growers. They in
turn raised the chicks until the birds were large enough for slaughter. But
after Buck began to take fly-fishing earnestly, he decided to raise a few
chickens and supply feathers for himself and some friends. Buck parlayed
that small, noncommercial venture into a highly profitable business that in
a decade grew into a flock of 5,000 chickens cross-bred for color and
quality.

How profitable feather selling is remains a family secret. Buck admits
that the average revenue from a feather bird is $15, compared to the $1.50

or so a grower gets from a chicken for slaughter. His $1 million investment was recouped much sooner than the eight- to nine-year wait for investment in the hatchery's traditional business. Moreover, while chick selling is a volatile enterprise, with growers exerting little control over prices and subject to fluctuating costs, Buck's monopoly control has brought stability to his profits. In fact, recently, his 45,000 necks couldn't meet demand, and so he plans to expand even further.

OPEC: The Oil Cartel

In a **cartel,** or **collusive monopoly,** competing producers work together as if they were a single firm.

In sharp contrast to Buck's monopoly is the **cartel,** or **collusive monopoly,** formed by the Organization of Petroleum Exporting Countries (OPEC). OPEC's impact was driven home to Americans during the 1970s with the dramatic hike in the prices of oil and its derivatives. A gallon of gasoline that sold for 35 cents in 1973 cost $1.22 in 1980.

Figure 11.1, which traces movements in the official price of oil as established by OPEC, attempts to put the energy crisis in perspective. After many years of oil price stability—from 1952 to early 1973, Saudi Arabian crude rose only from $1.75 to $2.59 a barrel[2] or 48 percent in 20 years[2]—OPEC quadrupled prices in late 1973/early 1974, as you can see from Figure 11.1. OPEC prices held reasonably steady during the next six years, but tripled between 1979 and 1981. So, the $2.59 barrel cost $34 by the end of 1981, a 1,313 percent increase in less than a decade. The trend came to a halt in 1981, and official prices fell. Nevertheless, oil prices still remained 10 times as high as they had some 13 years earlier. By the time the 1990 Iraq crisis erupted, the official price for a barrel of oil was $21.

Obviously, the strong demand for oil and its derivatives plays some role in explaining the events of the 1970s and 1980s. Yet oil demand was only a minor contributor to the skyrocketing oil-price trend. A much greater role must be assigned to the pricing policy of the oil cartel. The nations that constituted OPEC—primarily the Arab oil states plus Ecuador, Gabon, Indonesia, Iran, Nigeria, and Venezuela—jointly controlled about half of the world's oil production in 1970 and, still more important, owned two thirds of the world's then-known oil reserves. Banding together instead of competing against each other would best further their mutual interests. The cartel they formed would (1) fix a price for oil, (2) enforce that price by limiting overall supply, and (3) allocate the limited supply among OPEC members. It seems to have worked reasonably well for OPEC members, whose extraordinary profits came out of the pockets of the oil-importing nations.

As you see, monopolies come in all sizes and in all sorts. They may be profitable, break-even, or even losers, yet they do share certain analytic similarities. Furthermore, the microeconomic models of monopoly imply some negative consumer welfare and efficiency consequences, and so invite normative policy responses.

FIGURE 11.1   OPEC Oil Prices, 1971–1990

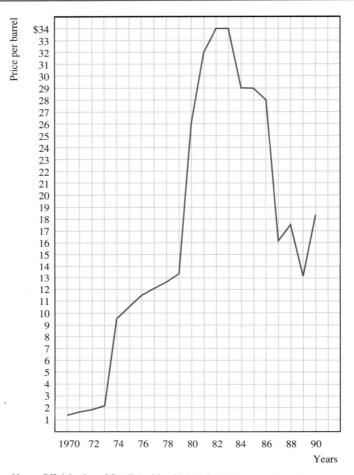

NOTE: Official price of Saudi Arabian Light-34° API, January of each year.

SOURCE: U.S. Department of Energy. *Annual Energy Review, 1989* (Washington, D.C.: Government Printing Office), p. 255.

This chapter deals with monopoly and its ramifications, beginning with why monopolies exist. Its key analytic section focuses on the static analysis of monopoly. From there it's just a short step to the analysis of various forms of monopolistic market segmentation and cartels. The final section examines one advantage of monopoly: reducing price uncertainty. Chapter 12 explores some policy implications of this chapter's analysis, including whether, and under what circumstances, monopoly should be controlled, and if so, how best to control it.

Realize at the outset, however, that monopoly today is not a major issue in the U.S. economy. The success of government antimonopoly policy, justified if not encouraged to a large extent by economic analysis, has significantly reduced the dimension of the monopoly problem. Nevertheless, the study of monopoly is important for two reasons. First, monopoly and perfect competition stand on the extremes of the theoretical spectrum of market structures. The sharp contrast between the two types of market structure help you better understand each one. Second, those interested in the origins and contemporary applications of antitrust policy—after all, both legal and illegal monopolists still exist—must ground themselves thoroughly in the theory of monopoly and its implications.

Why Monopolies Exist

The persistence of monopolies can be captured by a single phrase: barriers to entry. Other firms can't penetrate the monopolist's market. Among the most important reasons for monopoly are:

- Efficiency.
- Artificial entry barriers.
- Government sanctions.

Efficiency

In some instances, monopoly is simply the cheapest manner of producing the particular good or service. Recall the implications of the falling long-run average cost curve in Chapter 9. The larger the scale of operation, the lower the average cost of production. Even if the market began as a perfectly competitive one, the dynamics of the competitive process would lead to ever larger firms, until only one firm—the lowest-cost producer—would survive. (That's the conclusion of MicroBits 9.1, Economies of Scale and the Death of Perfect Competition.)

A **natural monopoly** occurs when the industry is characterized by economies of scale or when monopoly would eliminate costly and unnecessary duplication of resources.

Thus, one reason underlying **natural monopoly** is the efficiency that accompanies high-volume operation. A second type of natural monopoly occurs to avoid costly and inconvenient duplication. Imagine competing telephone companies, each of which would supply the user with a telephone. Visualize a mail-order company, with clerks seated at a desk covered by telephones, ready to take orders when the bell rings. Picture the mad scramble for the right phone as the clerk tries to answer it before the customer's patience wears out.[3]

When efficiency is the root cause of monopoly, then it's not so much that competitors are barred by some anticompetitive policy as much as the market functions more efficiently without competition.

Artificial Entry Barriers

The quote in Chapter 9 (p. 317) from Adam Smith's *The Wealth of Nations* pointed out that competitors don't really like competition. Thus, sellers have the incentive to form a cartel or to merge with or buy out competitors.

Control over technology or a critical natural resource is another way of artificially restraining entry. If the chip that IBM uses in its new series of computers cannot be easily copied or if a vital input source were in the hands of a single manufacturer,[4] then other firms are barred from competing.

MicroBits 11.1

Through the Looking Glass Unclearly

The following editorial appeared in *The New York Times* of May 16, 1988, on p. A16.

Q: What's the difference between $60 reading glasses prescribed by an optometrist in New York and a $12 pair from Woolworth's in New Jersey?
A: $48.

Most people eventually need reading glasses, and many can meet their needs with mass-produced eyewear from a five-and-dime counter display. Forty-eight states permit the sale of simple magnifying glasses without a prescription. Only New York and Rhode Island deny access to cheap, safe eyewear. The $48 question is whether Albany can be nudged to reform.

Natural aging of the eye makes it difficult for most people over 50 to read newspaper-size print. The problem can generally be remedied with magnifying lenses. Do-it-yourself fitting works for people without complicated vision impairment.

According to Dr. Calvin Roberts, associate professor of ophthalmology at Cornell Medical College, the only loss from a misfitting is the purchase price: the wrong lenses won't damage the eyes. Why, then, does New York bar sales without a prescription from a physician or optometrist?

The prescription eyeglass lobby argues, lamely, that the prohibition forces those afflicted with reading problems to have eye exams. That makes it possible for doctors to catch glaucoma and other degenerative eye diseases before sight is irreparably damaged.

In fact, there is no evidence that the ban has made New Yorkers more conscientious about eye care than residents of other states. By the same logic, aspirin would only be dispensed by prescription because anyone who feels a pain might benefit from seeing a physician.

The optician's lobby packs a solid financial punch in Albany. Senator Joseph Bruno and Assemblyman Richard Gottfried, sponsors of the repeal bill, deserve the help of every citizen who can see the larger public interest more clearly.

Government Sanctions

At times, either for political or economic reasons, the government sanctions and may even promote monopolies or monopoly practices. Competitors often use the political process to eliminate price competition. Agricultural price supports truncate the competitive market process, fashioning a cartel that will not sell below the support price. Tariffs and quotas protect domestic producers from the competition of foreign products. In banking and transportation, government regulations have in the past directly barred potential competitors from entering the market, often preserving local monopolies. In fact, the more you look, the more cases of government-approved monopolies you'll find. (See MicroBits 11.1 for another example.)

Patents and copyrights fall into this category as well. Here, the government provides the inventor or creator with an exclusive right over the patented or copyrighted material. To be sure, many believe that the stimulation of inventions and literary, artistic, or musical creation legitimatizes patent/copyright protection. Nevertheless, the holder of the patent or copyright is a monopolist.

Raising an Eyebrow: Monopoly Analyzed

Monopoly Demand and the Marginal Revenue Curve

The perfect competitive firm finds its equilibrium by adjusting its output to the market price. The profit-maximizing monopolist, on the other hand, faces a more daunting task. Since the monopolist's price cannot be challenged by competitors, the monopolist must determine the product's selling price. In fact, the monopolist might be able to compartmentalize the overall market and set different prices for different demanders. Multiple pricing strategies will be investigated in the next section. It's analytically simplest to examine first the monopolist who sets one price for all potential customers, and to discover that profit-maximizing price.

The analysis of monopoly pricing begins with a statement about the monopolist's demand curve. Since by definition the monopolist is the only firm in the market, the entire demand for the product—the market or industry demand—is the demand facing the monopolist. With a falling demand curve, it's quite evident that the monopolist can sell more only by cutting price. The implications of this statement are spelled out in Table 11.1.

The first two columns of Table 11.1 portray a highly stylized demand-curve relationship for designer eyebrow tweezers. At $10 per unit, they're just too expensive for anyone. But at $9 per tweezer, 100,000 would be

TABLE 11.1　Tweezing Out the Revenues and Costs for a Monopolist

Price	Quantity (000s)	Total Revenue (000s)	Marginal Revenue	Average Total Costs	Total Costs (000s)	Marginal Costs
$10	0	$ 0		$ —	$ 200	
			$9			$ 1.50
9	100	900		3.50	350	
			7			2.50
8	200	1,600		3.00	600	
			5			3.50
7	300	2,100		3.15	950	
			3			4.50
6	400	2,400		3.50	1,400	
			1			5.50
5	500	2,500		3.90	1,950	
			−1			6.50
4	600	2,400		4.50	2,600	
			−3			7.50
3	700	2,100		4.79	3,350	
			−5			8.50
2	800	1,600		5.25	4,200	
			−7			9.50
1	900	900		5.72	5,150	
			−9			10.50
0	1,000	0		6.20	6,200	

sold per month. That would bring the Highbrow Tweezer Corp. monthly revenues of $900,000.

Look now at the Total Revenue column. Whereas in a perfectly competitive market, the more sold, the larger the firm's revenues, that's just not so in the monopoly market. Revenues rise at first, reach their maximum at $2.5 million, and then fall. (You might want to plot out Highbrow's total revenue curve, which will turn out to be an upside-down U, peaking at $2.5 million.) Why?

The answer lies in the presumption that the monopolist must charge the same price to all purchasers. So, when price is cut to attract larger sales, the lower price also applies to all those demanders who were willing to pay the higher price. Take a look at the $P = 5 in comparison with $P = 6. At the latter price, the monopolist could sell 400,000 and earn $2.4 million. But if Highbrow wished to sell another 100,000 units and cut its price to $5, a double consequence would follow. First, the extra sales would add $500,000 to the firm's revenues. Second, the reduction in price from $6 to $5 on the first 400,000 units would diminish revenues on those units by $400,000. The net effect is to increase revenues by only $100,000, or a dollar per tweezer.[5]

That dual reaction holds true everywhere on the table. Verify it by filling in the blanks for a change from $P = \$3$, $Q = 700,000$ to $P = \$2$, $Q = 800,000$.

Revenue from new units sold _____

Revenue loss from reducing price on earlier units _____

Net change in total revenue _____

Net change in total revenue per additional unit _____ [6]

Take a careful look now at the Marginal Revenue column in Table 11.1. You'll find that MR lists, for each change, the net consequence of these two opposing movements on a per unit (rather than per 1,000) basis. And, not surprisingly, MR, which begins as a positive number, ultimately becomes negative, for at some point the impact of the price cut on existing quantity demanded overwhelms the influence of the additional sales brought in by the lower price.

MICROQUERY   How does the monopolist's marginal revenue differ from that of the perfect competitor? _____ [7]

Figure 11.2 plots the demand curve implicit in the first two columns of Table 11.1 and adds the marginal revenue curve as well. (To drive home the fact that the demand curve for the monopolist is the demand curve for the industry, the curve is identified as $Demand_{monopolist} = Demand_{industry}$.) Notice that not only does the marginal revenue curve slope negatively, but it does so far more sharply than does the demand curve.[8]

One final observation: Clearly, Highbrow Tweezers would not charge less than \$5. Selling more while earning less revenue is hardly a rational practice!

Marginal Revenue, Price, and Elasticity.   Because marginal revenue and elasticity are individually related to the demand curve, they must be related to each other.[9]

$$MR = P(1 + 1/\varepsilon).$$

Thus, when elasticity (ε) is -1 at the midpoint of the demand curve, MR is zero. For any point with a higher absolute elasticity, MR will be positive, and for any lower absolute elasticity, MR will be negative. Check this out in Figure 11.2.

Monopoly Equilibrium

Would Highbrow then charge \$5, the revenue-maximizing price? The answer has to "No." Highbrow's managers are interested in maximizing *profits,* not income. That means management has to consider its cost

FIGURE 11.2 Monopoly Equilibrium

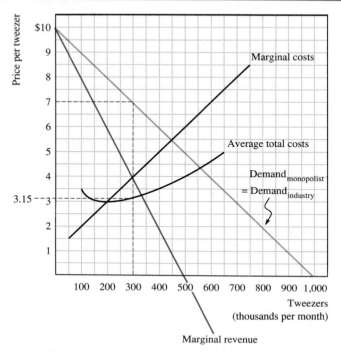

Highbrow Tweezers maximizes profits by finding the output that equates MR and MC. That occurs at 300,000 units per month for the given demand and cost curves. In order that precisely 300,000 tweezers be sold, Highbrow must set the unit price at $7. Profits can then be calculated by finding TR (= $P \times Q$), subtracting TC (= ATC $\times Q$).

structure in addition to its revenues. Table 11.1 lists costs, too, and both ATC and MC are plotted in Figure 11.2. (You might plot Highbrow's total cost curve on the same diagram you used to plot its total revenue curve. See if you can find the output that corresponds to maximum profits.)

MR = MC. The optimum profit rule, MR = MC, is identical for all market structures. For Highbrow, as Figure 11.2 shows, MR = MC at an output of 300,000 units.

Is 300,000 really the most profitable position? Determine what Highbrow's profits would be if it produced only 200,000 tweezers. From the diagram, you can readily see that the $6 MR would exceed the $3 MC. Thus, a move to 200,001 would add $3 to the firm's profit for the 200,001st unit. Producing the 250,000th unit would have increased profit for that unit by $1.50, since MR = $5 and MC = $3.50. Indeed, as long as MR > MC, expanded production would increase profits.

You can complete this demonstration by assuming the managers of Highbrow opted to produce 400,000 units per month. Explain here why that position is less profitable than the 300,000 output.

_____

_____

_____ 10

Calculating Profits.   The principle of profit calculation is identical with that mastered earlier. Find total revenue by multiplying price times quantity, find total costs by multiplying average total costs by quantity, and subtract total costs from total revenues. The only complication here is the absence of a given market price, since it is the prerogative of the monopolist to set its own selling price.

Finding the optimal price is not really a problem. The managers of Highbrow Tweezers know that they would maximize profits by selling 300,000 units a month, so they merely have to find the price that will generate sales of 300,000. Isn't that information contained in the demand curve, which tells the producer how much will be demanded by consumers at various prices? So, Highbrow's management merely has to find the price that corresponds to 300,000. Figure 11.2 shows it to be $7, the point on the demand curve directly above the MR = MC intersection.

(A word of caution: Students are all too often tempted to draw a horizontal line from the MR = MC intersection to the price axis. That clearly is mistaken. If you were to do that in Figure 11.2, you would find $P = \$4$. But at $4, the quantity demanded is 600,000 units, not the optimal 300,000.)

Let's now calculate Highbrow Tweezer's monthly profits:

$$\begin{aligned} TR &= \$7.00 \times 300,000 &= \$2,100,000 \\ -TC &= \$3.15 \times 300,000 &= \underline{945,000} \\ = \pi &= \$3.85 \times 300,000 &= \$1,555,000 \end{aligned}$$

A Pricing Shortcut.   Rarely will a monopolist have the information necessary to detect its MC = MR optimum. Management, however, may have some fragmentary information or some sense of the firm's elasticity of demand as well as its marginal costs. When that's the case, they can take advantage of MR = $P(1 + 1/\varepsilon)$ for pricing.

Begin by substituting MC for MR, since in equilibrium, MC = MR. Then, divide both sides by $(1 + 1/\varepsilon)$ to obtain:

$$P = MC/(1 + 1/\varepsilon)$$

In the Highbrow case, $\varepsilon = -7/3$ and MC = 4. Substituting into the equation yields:

$$P = 4/[1 + (-3/7)] = 4/(4/7) = 28/4 = 7.$$

In short, a monopolist prices its product by finding the profit-maximizing output in contrast to the perfect competitive firm, which sets its output to correspond to the market price.

Feathers and Salamanders

Flying Feathers

We're now ready to analyze the feather monopoly. Since Mr. Metz dominates the market for fly-fishing feathers and thus controls price, his challenge is simply to find the profit-maximizing output and then set his price. Figure 11.3 suggests a possible demand curve for the Metz Hatchery, the corresponding MR curve, and likely MC, AVC, and ATC curves. MR = MC at the actual output of 45,000 chicks fixes the actual average price at $15 a bird and generates $675,000 in income. Mr. Metz's variable costs are presumed to be $6 per bird, while fixed costs are estimated at $45,000. Thus, ATC at the optimum output comes to $7 per chick and total costs are $315,000. The $360,000 annual profits constitutes a profit rate exceeding 50 percent of revenue, so it's not surprising that Mr. Metz is reluctant to disclose his profits. How better to preserve his monopoly?

The Salamander King

The Metz success story obviously does not apply to Carl Lowrance, the salamander monopolist who went bankrupt. Read his story in MicroBits 11.2 before you proceed.

Whether the monopoly went to Mr. Lowrance's head, so that he priced himself out of the market by continuously boosting prices, or whether cost increases forced Mr. Lowrance to jack up prices is not quite clear from the article. Figure 11.4 examines both possibilities. In either case, it's evident that monopoly does not provide immunity from losses.

The Salamander King Outsmarts Himself.   Figure 11.4a begins with the normal set of demand and cost curves and sets an initial price at 25 cents per salamander. MicroBits 11.2 suggests that at 25 cents, Mr. Lowrance was subsidizing the scientists who relied on his salamanders. As you can see, producing 32 million amphibians and charging 25 cents was a losing proposition. MC (= $4) > MR (= 20 cents)[11] and P (= 25 cents) < ATC (81.25 cents). So Mr. Lowrance raised his price to $1 per salamander,

FIGURE 11.3   Feathers for Fly Fishers: Pricing and Profits at the Metz Hatchery

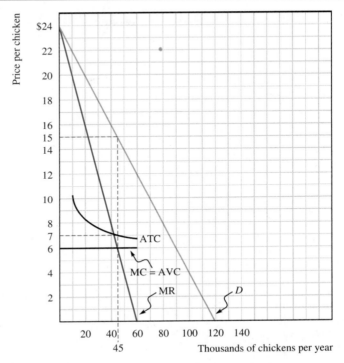

At the profit-maximizing output of $15, Metz sells 45,000 chickens, earning total revenues of $675,000. With ATC assumed to be $7 per bird and thus TC = $315,000, profits to the hatchery equal $360,000 annually.

surely a steep increase, but one that equated MR and MC. Moreover, it enabled him to operate at a profit. Calculate his profit at 2 million units: $P = \$$_____; ATC = _____ cents; π per unit = _____ cents, and $\pi = \$$_____.[12]

The scenario in Figure 11.4a suggests that Mr. Lowrance latched on to a wonderful discovery: raise price and raise profits. So he repeated his experiment, this time quintupling his price instead of merely quadrupling it. The result is evident by comparing both the MR and MC curves and the P and AVC curves.

While MC is greater than MR at an output of 0.33 million salamanders annually, note that if Mr. Lowrance were to increase production, he could bring down his MC below his MR and so increase profits. He could do that until MC once again equaled MR.[13]

MICROBITS 11.2

Some Say Supplier of Slimy Salamanders Shouldn't Stop Sales

Carl Lowrance is the one and only breeder of tiger salamanders, and he is thinking of going out of business.

That might be a blow to bass fishermen who use the slimy, beady-eyed amphibians as fish bait, but to hear some people tell it, it would be a positive disaster for medical science. Mr. Lowrance is the sole supplier of these salamanders to eye researchers seeking a better understanding of how the retina turns light into electrical signals to the human brain. Their animal studies might someday lead to a cure for certain kinds of blindness.

Edward Pugh, a psychology professor at the University of Pennsylvania, says that without the Lowrance salamanders, "we would all be up a tree." Carter Cornwall, an associate professor of physiology at Boston University, agrees: "I have substantial doubt that I could continue my research. I would be in serious trouble."

Researchers prefer the tiger salamander, which at 8 to 12 inches in length is one of the largest of 126 species of salamanders, because the creature's retinal cells are five to six times larger than mammalian cells. They are appreciably easier to isolate and study. Scientists from Palto Alto, Calif., to Cambridge, England, have grown dependent on Mr. Lowrance's salamanders, which he breeds by the thousand in ponds hereabouts.

An Unreliable Supply

Before Mr. Lowrance, researchers got salamanders on a catch as catch can basis. Their supply of animals caught in the wild was uneven in quality and often diseased. A Purdue University researcher once found himself with 70 blind salamanders. Blindness is a condition common among certain salamanders but not to be wished for in this research.

Frank Werblin, a professor of electrical engineering at the University of California in Berkeley, claims to be one of the first to use tiger salamanders. After several years of getting them where he could, he heard about Mr. Lowrance's breeding operation. In 1980, he started receiving batches [from Mr. Lowrence that were] of reliable genetic stock, were available year-round and were relatively inexpensive. Soon, more than 20 U.S.

In any case, with $Q = .33$, P is _____ than ATC, meaning that __

[14]

The Salamander King Meets the Market.   Figure 11.4b plays out a second scenario. Here, Mr. Lowrance really acted rationally as a profit maximizer. He raised prices only when MC increased. But as MC moves from MC_1 to MC_2 to MC_3, the ATC curves shift upward as well. With demand remaining the same, a profitable business at 25 cents per salamander—

MicroBits 11.2 continued

researchers and two in England had become regular customers.

Unfortunately, however, Mr. Lowrance has had his ups and downs. Two years ago, effluent from a Kansas City, Kan., slaughterhouse permanently ruined the breeding ponds Mr. Lowrance operated nearby. He recalls waking up one morning to find thousands of his breeders floating dead.

More Congenial Waters

To keep Mr. Lowrance's business from going belly up, too, Mr. Pugh persuaded the National Science Foundation and the National Institutes of Health to put up $50,000 in grant money to relocate Mr. Lowrance's operations to safe waters in Tulsa. . . .

The new arrangement, however, brought fresh complications. Because Mr. Lowrance had agreed to suspend his bait business and to raise his salamanders exclusively for research purposes for the duration of Prof. Pugh's grant, he raised his price, first to $1 per salamander, and then, last April, to $5. "I can't afford to keep subsidizing these guys," he says, referring to his friends, the scientists.

Mr. Lowrance says that he has invested $400,000 in his salamander-breeding business over the years and that the effort has been unprofitable. He has kept at it because he believed in it, he says, but he wants out now. A man of many ideas, he doesn't intend to just walk away, however. . . .

As things stand, Mr. Lowrance has been able to find no suitable successor to take over his business. Recently, he made the trip to Checkerboard Square in St. Louis, hoping to interest Ralston Purina in marketing salamanders as bait, pets or even as food.

Mr. Lowrance spoke to an assistant to the company's director of special chows. He says that Damon Shelton, whose own title is technical manager of special business groups, was interested in his salamander proposition and promised to try to sell the idea to his boss. "I knew it would take time," Mr. Lowrance says. Large corporations like Ralston Purina "are like a giant. It takes a while to move a toe, then a knee, then a leg."

Alas, the giant seems not to have taken Mr. Lowrance seriously. Brad J. Kerbs, the special-chows director, was told of the salamander proposal, but, says Mr. Kerbs with a chuckle, he shot it down.

Source: Robert Perez, "Some Say Supplier of Slimy Salamanders Shouldn't Stop Sales," Reprinted by permission of *The Wall Street Journal*, © 1985 Dow Jones & Company, Inc. All Rights Reserved Worldwide.

notice that at MR = MC at 32 million units and $P > $ ATC—degenerates into a losing proposition at $1 or even at $5 per lizard. (In both these instances, where MR = MC, ATC $> P$.) Mr. Lowrance should leave the business.

Would you want to buy it from him? You understand that this decision depends not only on your aptitude for salamander farming but also on which scenario more approximates the true picture. (Which alternative did Mr. Kerbs of Ralston Purina find more credible?)

FIGURE 11.4 The Salamander King

a. The salamander king outsmarts himself

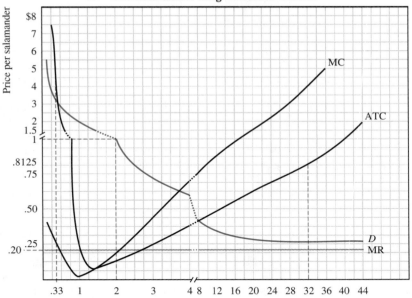

a. At $P = .25$, MC $>$ MR and ATC $> P$. Production is excessive and price is too low. On the other hand, at $P = \$5$, ATC $> P$ and additional output would reduce MC. Only at $P = \$1$ does MR $=$ MC and $P >$ ATC, permitting the salamander king to reap monopoly profits.

b. The market sabotages the salamander king's monopoly

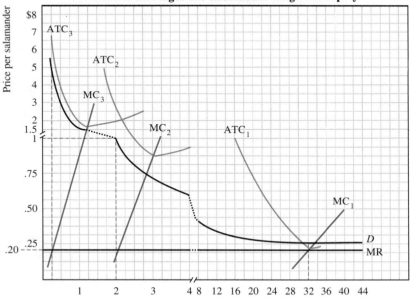

b. As the tale begins, the salamander monopoly is profitable. MR $=$ MC_1 at $Q = 32$ million and $P >$ ATC_1. But over time, costs rise to MC_2 and ATC_2. MR $=$ MC_2 at $Q = 2$ million, but the corresponding ATC_2 of $\$2.50$ per salamander is less than the $\$1$ price. As more time passes, costs rise further—to MC_3 and ATC_3—and even a boost to $\$5$ per salamander, the optimum profit position now, still leaves $ATC_3 > P$.

Discriminatory Monopoly

A **discriminating monopolist** is one who is able to charge different prices to different demanders.

Have you ever tried to get into a sold-out Springsteen concert or a Super Bowl game on the day of the game? If you have, you're probably familiar with the ticket scalpers who frequent these events. That scalper is likely to be a **discriminating monopolist.** So, too, is the sole supplier of well-drilling equipment in a locality where the municipal water supply has been contaminated. Unlike the nondiscriminating monopolist who sells the product at a single price, discriminating monopolists can distinguish among demanders and charge them unique prices.

First-Degree Discrimination

In **first-degree,** or **perfect price, discrimination,** a monopolist charges demanders the maximum price each is willing to pay.

In **first-degree discrimination** (also called **perfect price discrimination**), the monopolist is essentially able to creep into the brain of every buyer and charge each one the maximum he or she is willing to pay. Ticket scalpers, for example, control a supply of scarce tickets and let buyers bid for entry to the event. The highest bidders get first choice, the next highest, second choice, and so on until the supply is exhausted. By bidding, the demanders reveal the maximum price they're willing to pay, and the scalper takes advantage of this information to extract the highest possible prices.[15] (Scalper prices for a $75 Super Bowl XXI, 1987, seat were rumored to range from $1,500 to $2,000.)

Figure 11.5 reproduces Figure 11.2, with but one obvious alteration—the absence of a separate MR curve. Here, the demand curve and the MR curve are identical. What's the secret?

You'll recall that the MR curve for the nondiscriminating monopolist in Figure 11.2 falls more rapidly than the demand curve because in order to sell more, the monopolist had to reduce the price on previous units offered for sale. (Go back to the discussion of Table 11.1 if this statement is not entirely clear.) But that's not true for the first-degree discriminating monopolist. She can sell more by cutting the price to purchasers lower down on the demand curve without reducing the price to those buyers who sit higher up on the demand curve. Thus, when price is cut from $9 to $8, the first 100,000 sold at the higher price are still sold at that price and it's only the next 100,000 that are charged the lower price. If so, total revenues that equal $900,000 for 100,000 units now equal $1.7 million ($900,000 + $800,000) for 200,000. The added revenue equals $800,000 for the additional 100,000 units, or $8 per unit. But $8 is the price, so P = MR.

Optimum Profit.   Using the MR = MC rule, profit is maximized at an output of 450,000 units, the quantity at which the D = MR curve crosses the MC curve.

FIGURE 11.5   First-Degree Discriminating Monopolist

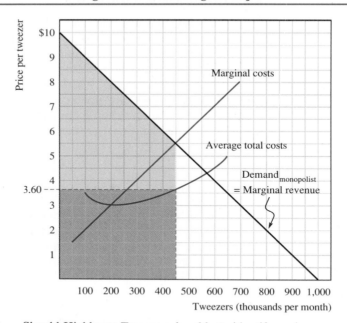

Should Highbrow Tweezers be able to identify each customer's highest price and be able to charge each one that maximum price, then HT's demand curve will also be its MR curve. MR = MC at 450,000 units, and TR will equal the entire area shaded. TC will equal the darker shaded area, so that π equals the lighter shaded area. Compare the profits area in this figure to Figure 11.2. Which is larger?

Calculating Profit.   Profit calculation is a bit more complicated, since P is not a uniform price. Instead, each unit (up to 450,000) is sold at a unique price. Thus, the first buyer pays just a smidgen less than $10 to obtain the first unit, the second one a little less than that; the 100,000th, $9; the 200,000th, $8; up to the 450,000th, who is the only buyer who pays the lowest price of $5.50. Total revenue, then, is the sum of all these units sold at the different prices. In geometric terms, it's the entire area under the demand curve from the origin to 450,000. That turns out to equal $3,487,500.[16]

Total cost is calculated the normal way: ATC (= $3.60 × 450,000) = $1.62 million and so are profits: TR − TC. Here π = $1,867,500. Visually, the total purple shaded area equals total revenue, the lower darker shaded area is total costs, and the upper lighter shaded area equals profits. Comparing Figures 11.5 and 11.2 shows you how much better off the first-degree discriminating monopolist is, an unsurprising conclusion. The monopolist has indeed extracted all the consumer surplus from the public!

Second-Degree Discrimination

Under **second-degree discrimination,** or **block pricing,** the same customer pays different rates for different quantities of the product purchased.

Rarely can a monopolist practice perfect price discrimination. More typical is **second-degree discrimination,** or **block pricing,** which is best represented by quantity discounts. Check your most recent telephone bill and you'll see second-degree discrimination in action. The first minute of each call may cost you 25 cents, with additional minutes priced at only a dime each. Similarly, the first 250 kilowatt-hours (kwh) of electricity used may cost 12 cents per kwh per month, but the next 250 may cost you only 11 cents. Analytically, second-degree discrimination is little different from first-degree discrimination. It is discussed more fully in connection with utility pricing in Chapter 12.

Third-Degree Discrimination

Third-degree discrimination requires that identifiable groups of buyers, each sharing a common characteristic, are charged different prices.

Rarely can demanders be individually segregated. Sellers, however, often can distinguish broad groups of purchasers and charge different prices to each group, giving rise to **third-degree discrimination.** That's why airlines charge more for business travelers than for vacationers. The latter can plan out their trips in advance and search out the best deals, while business travelers often fly in response to a sudden need.

Here's your chance to help out Penguin Airlines (whose motto is "It may take a bit longer, but our personnel are always dressed formally!"). Peter Albert Penguin, the senior vice president responsible for fare setting, must choose among two pricing policies: a single price for all seats versus a two-price system. Pa Penguin, as he's called by the staff, knows that business travelers have a less elastic demand than do vacationers. But he doesn't know which policy will be more profitable to the family airline.

Figure 11.6 reproduces the annual demand curves for both business travelers and vacationing patrons of Penguin Airlines, and sums up these demand curves horizontally to obtain the overall demand for Penguin.[17] A horizontal AVC = MC curve is drawn in on the assumption that each additional passenger requires just about the same service—a dinner, say, and two soft drinks—and the passenger's additional personal and baggage weight requires a proportional increase in fuel. On the other hand, the $12.5 million in fixed costs give rise to the falling ATC curve in Figure 11.6c.

The MR curve warrants clarification. The left-hand segment of the MR curve in Figure 11.6c, running from 0 to 125,000 passengers, corresponds to the left-hand segment of the demand curve and is identical to the MR curve in Figure 11.6a. The right-hand segment of the MR curve,

FIGURE 11.6   **Pa Penguin as a Third-Degree Discriminating Monopolist**

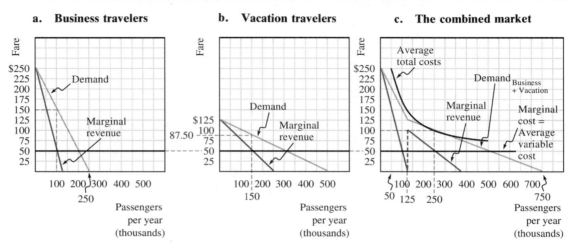

| a. **Business travelers** | b. **Vacation travelers** | c. **The combined market** |

If the monopolist could not discriminate, Figure 11.6c shows MR = MC at Q = 250,000, P = $100 but since ATC for 250,000 also = $100, π = 0. By discriminating, the monopolist distinguishes between the business traveler, who is willing to pay more, and the vacationer, who is unwilling to spend quite as liberally. The monopolist, after distinguishing the separate demand and MR curves (panels a & b) equates each market's MR with the overall MC. The result: sell 100,000 business-class tickets at $150 each and 150,000 tourist-class fares at $87.50 each. Profits now sum to $3,125,000.

from 125,000 onward, corresponds to the right-hand segment of the demand curve; at 125,000, MR = 100.[18] So, the left-hand part of the rapidly declining MR curve is resurrected (shown by the dashed line) and then falls somewhat more slowly. (The segment where MR < 0 has been omitted.)

Now to help out Pa Penguin. Figure 11.6c shows that a uniform, profit-maximizing (MR = MC) price would be $100, with 250,000 flights sold per year. Unfortunately for Penguin Air, average total costs for 250,000 trips also equal $100, so no excess profits will be earned.

But consider the alternative. Fly 250,000 passengers as determined by the equality of marginal revenue and marginal cost, but institute a two-price policy. Allocate seats between business and vacation fliers so that all 250,000 seats are sold. The only issue to be resolved is how much to charge each group. Now, we already know that the marginal cost of each passenger is $50 and that the marginal revenue of each group differs. So, let's apply the profit-maximizing MC = MR rule to each individually. Technically, you project the optimal MC point ($50) back to each of the respective groups to find in each market the point where it hits the MR curve. In Figure 11.6a, that occurs at 100,000 flights and mandates a $150 fare, while in Figure 11.6b, MC meets MR above 150,000 flights for a fare of $87.50.[19]

The result is enlightening, and will please Pa Penguin: 100,000 fares at $150 plus 150,000 fares at $87.50 equals total revenues of $28,125,000, for excess profits of $3,125,000. Discrimination works!

Just a final word about discriminatory monopoly. The monopolized product or service cannot be resalable, either by its very nature or because the monopolist can enjoin resale. Were this not the case, middlemen could buy the monopolized product in the cheaper market and resell it in the more expensive one. Discrimination would cease, because ultimately purchasers would only pay the lowest price.

Are scalping and air travel exceptions? No. In both of these cases, there's normally not enough time left before the game or trip to buy in order to resell. In the case of airline discrimination between first- and tourist-class fliers, each ticket designates location, preventing the latter from occupying a first-class seat. However, attempts at discrimination do fail. Consider entertainment events that do not play to full houses. Many people buy the cheapest seats and then, after the house has been darkened or the game underway, sneak up front.

Cartels: One for All and All for One

The world of the monopolist is relatively uncomplicated, at least in contrast to the cartel. As the term implies, collusive monopoly requires cooperation. All the members of the cartel must coordinate their pricing policies and subsume individual interests to those of the group.

The Analytics of Cartels

The collusive monopoly is easy to understand in principle, but it becomes more complex as the model more closely approximates reality. Price in the cartel model is set by formal agreement among the cartel's participants. Figure 11.7a shows the basic cartel model, which is identical to the monopoly model. Since the colluding firms act as a monopolist would, the MR = MC intersection in Figure 11.7a indicates that oil output should be set at 25 million barrels per day (bpd) and price should be $18 per barrel.

In contrast with monopoly, however, a second decision has to be made: Allocating the fixed output among the members. This issue stems from a paradox that can best be understood by examining Figure 11.7b. Once the price is fixed at $18 per barrel, then for each member, MR = P, because each additional unit can be sold at the same (agreed-on) price as each prior unit. Thus, the demand curve for each of the colluders is the P = MR curve.

Assume now that each of, say, three firms has an identical MC curve (MC$_{Olly}$). Then the profit maximizing output for each firm equals _____

FIGURE 11.7   **Cartel Pricing**

a.   The cartel as a whole

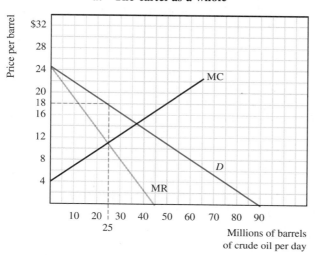

b.   The firm within the cartel

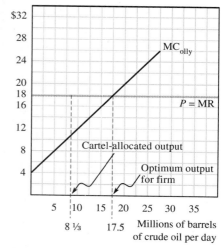

a.   Acting jointly, the cartel members become a monopoly, and using their combined MC curve in conjunction with the markets D and MR curves, set output below the MR = MC intersection. The output of 25 million bpd enables the cartel to set a price of $18 per barrel.

b.   For the individual cartel member, the $18 cartel price becomes a given, so MR = P. For this firm, optimum profit occurs at 17.5 million bpd, which exceeds the cartel-allocated output of 8⅓ million bpd.

million bpd, and the combined total for all three oligopolists is _____[20] million bpd.

The paradox is obvious. The optimum output for the colluding firms acting jointly equals 25 million bpd, while the optimum output for the entire industry when, at the $18 price, each examines its own profit position is 52.5 bpd! Clearly something has to give.

The typical solution is for the members to cut back on production until the combined amount marketed equals the agreed-on quantity. (In this case, each would agree to sell only 8.33 million bpd.) Yet, the paradox doesn't disappear, and each oligopolist has a strong incentive to sell more than its allocated quota. (MicroBits 11.3 reports on an experiment that indicates the overwhelming power of the incentive to cheat.) Yet cheating, by bringing a larger supply on the market, undercuts the agreed-on price and leads to the dissolution of the cartel. In a nutshell, impermanence is the history of most cartels.

The cartel theory outlined here can be used to understand OPEC pricing policy during the 1970s. But it also evokes a question: Why hasn't cheating led to OPEC's demise? A related issue that needs to be understood is the fall in crude prices from 1981 to 1990. Why wasn't the oil cartel strong enough to maintain price?

The Rise and Fall of OPEC, 1973–1990

Prior to 1973, the major oil-exporting nations thought themselves to be suffering from an excess of competition. In fact, U.S. and European oil refiners and marketers dominated the crude oil market, pretty much dictating prices to the oil extractors and playing off one against the other.[21] OPEC realized that the path to economic power lay through unity. Once they formed the cartel, they would act as a monopoly; Figure 11.7a pretty much describes their pricing policy during the 1970s.

The consequences of the oil price shocks of the 1970s, however, were poorly understood by OPEC. True, OPEC's price umbrella shielded its members in the short run. But OPEC failed to visualize the long-run demand and supply effects of its actions.

Demand. On the demand side, the higher price initially brought reductions in quantity demanded as, for example, pleasure driving and thus gasoline consumption were curtailed. Yet these cutbacks were modest; as you can see from the equation on p. 119, the demand for oil is rather price inelastic in the short run. The picture changed radically, however, over the long run, as the oil price shock led to inward shifts of the demand curve. The operative terms were conservation and energy efficiency. Smaller cars, more efficient electric appliances, and the substitution of other fuels for oil reduced the demand for oil at the OPEC-set prices.

The effect of these market reactions are highlighted in Table 11.2. Notice how world oil consumption, which had been rising in the early 1970s started falling in 1974 and 1975 and then again after the second oil shock in 1979–80.[22] And the switch to alternative energy sources, evident in the middle column of the table, shows a similar pattern, falling continuously in the 1980s. Go back to Figure 11.7a and sketch in a drop in demand. What happens to price even in a cartelized market?

Supply. Supply reactions were no less impressive. The OPEC price umbrella made profitable many existing oil wells that had been capped under earlier prices. Oil fields that remained underexploited because of overly expensive transportation costs now became viable. And, most of all, the umbrella sheltered an oil exploration boom that led to the discovery and exploitation of wells in the Gulf of Mexico, off the U.S. continental shelf, and in the North Sea. One consequence: OPEC's share of world oil output declined from 50.7 percent in 1971 to 36.6 percent in 1989.

OPEC's Survival. Both supply and demand reactions lead to the conclusion that oil prices would have to fall, as they did after 1981. In fact, spot

MicroBits 11.3

"All for One . . . One for All"? Don't Bet on It

A group of Texas A & M University students have acquired, to their chagrin, a special insight into the difficulties of the Organization of Petroleum Exporting Countries—or any other cartel—in fixing prices.

The 27 students take the introductory course Economics 203H, and they volunteered recently to be the subjects for an experiment conducted for The Wall Street Journal by Prof. Raymond Battalio.

The experiment explores what economists call the "free-rider problem" : In almost any effort in which a goal can be achieved only by common action, someone pays lip service to the agreement while quietly cheating for his own gain at the expense of neighbors. The experiment was devised by economists Charles Plott of California Institute of Technology, Mark Isaac of the University of Arizona and James Walker of Indiana University.

Each student in the experiment receives a mimeographed sheet showing 30 sets of figures. (See chart.) Each includes two dollar amounts.

"Each of you will write down on a slip of paper either '1' or '0,'" Prof. Battalio instructs them. The "1" votes will determine which set of figures will be used. One number in that set shows how much money Prof. Battalio will pay each student who voted "1"; the other shows how much will be paid each "0" voter.

The students are warned not to talk to each other. Without further comment a vote is taken. There are six votes for "1" and 21 for "0." The chart shows that those who voted "1" will receive 24 cents each while those who voted "0" get 74 cents each.

Obviously, voting "0" gives a bigger individual payoff than voting "1." A second vote yields only three votes for "1." The chart determines that those three each receive 12 cents while the 24 students who voted "0" each get 62 cents.

Suddenly, it dawns on the students that the figures are rigged: Students who vote "0" will always get 50 cents more than those who vote "1," but the fewer "1" votes, the less money everyone gets. "Let's all put down '1,' and nobody cheat," blurts out one student, not unlike a business owner—say, an oil exporter—who tries to induce his competitors all to sell at the same price. But the conspiracy suggestion succeeds only partially. Eleven vote "1" (for 44 cents each) and 16 vote "0" (for 94 cents each).

There is a buzz of consternation among the students. "OK, if you want to talk about it, go ahead," Prof. Battalio says, lifting the rule against collusion.

"Look," says the ringleader, "if we all vote '1' we will each get $1.08." "But," retorts another student, "if 26 of us vote '1' we'll get $1.04 and the one guy who votes '0' will get $1.54." Further discussion suggests

---

or current oil prices have consistently been below OPEC's official price since 1982, frustrating OPEC members who were counting on oil profits for covering government budgetary deficits.[23] They shored up their revenues by exceeding their quotas. Yet OPEC did not collapse in the face of substantial cheating, the prediction of the cartel model notwithstanding.

MicroBits 11.3 continued

that the only fair thing is for all to vote "1." That way, the class as a whole will end up $29.16 richer—the best possible collective result.

But again the conspiracy only partially succeeds; for the fourth ballot, 14 students vote "1"; for the fifth ballot, only six do so. The class gears up for a final try, all agreeing that the common good requires a unanimous vote for "1."

After explicit agreement by all to vote "1," the final vote is taken: Four vote "1" (for 16 cents each) and 23 vote "0" (for 66 cents each).

A smiling Prof. Battalio reaches into his pocket and counts out this round's payout— $15.82, or $13.34 less than if the conspiracy had been successful. "I'll never trust anyone again as long as I live," mutters the conspiracy leader. And how did he vote? "Oh, I voted '0,'" he replies.

No. of People Picking No. 1	Payout for Choice of Picking		No. of People Picking No. 1	Payout for Choice of Picking	
	1	0		1	0
1	$0.04	$0.54	16	0.64	1.14
2	0.08	0.58	17	0.68	1.18
3	0.12	0.62	18	0.72	1.22
4	0.16	0.66	19	0.76	1.26
5	0.20	0.70	20	0.80	1.30
6	0.24	0.74	21	0.84	1.34
7	0.28	0.78	22	0.88	1.38
8	0.32	0.82	23	0.92	1.42
9	0.36	0.86	24	0.96	1.46
10	0.40	0.90	25	1.00	1.50
11	0.44	0.94	26	1.04	1.54
12	0.48	0.98	27	1.08	1.58
13	0.52	1.02	28	1.12	1.62
14	0.56	1.06	29	1.16	1.66
15	0.60	1.10	30	1.20	1.70

The key to this puzzle lies with the production policy of Saudi Arabia, a sparsely populated nation that floats on oil. The Saudis played the role of swing producer, cutting back on their own output to compensate for the quota-ignoring actions of their OPEC partners. (Notice the swings in Saudi production in the last column of Table 11.2.)

TABLE 11.2 Oil Consumption Production, 1971–1989

Year	World Oil Consumption (Millions bpd)	Share of Oil in Energy Use (Percent)	Saudi Arabian Production, (% of OPEC Production)
1971	49.2	44.8	17.8
1972	52.8	46.1	21.2
1973	57.1	47.4	23.8
1974	56.4	46.4	26.8
1975	55.7	45.8	25.3
1976	59.1	46.1	27.4
1977	61.2	46.1	29.1
1978	63.1	46.1	27.4
1979	64.1	45.0	30.2
1980	61.6	43.5	36.3
1981	59.9	42.3	42.7
1982	58.4	41.2	33.5
1983	58.0	40.3	28.2
1984	58.9	39.5	25.5
1985*	59.1	39.4	20.7
1986	60.8	39.6	26.4
1987	61.8	39.0	23.0
1988	63.6	38.9	24.9
1989	64.7	38.7	22.7

* The data prior to and after 1984 are not fully comparable due to the shift in sources. However, they correctly reflect the trend.
SOURCE: 1971–1984: John Evans, *OPEC, Its Member States and the World Energy Market* (Harlow, England: Longman Group, 1986), pp. 360 ff. 1985–1989: *BP Statistical Review of World Energy,* various issues.

Return once again to Figure 11.7. Figure 11.7b indicates that the 25 million bpd had been allocated among the three oligopolists evenly, 8.33 million bpd each. Let's visualize two cheaters, each expanding output to 10 million bpd. If Olly keeps on producing 8.33 million bpd, total output will rise to 28.33 million, forcing the market price down to $16.44 (Figure 11.7a). The $18 price can be preserved only if Olly voluntary cuts production down to 5 million bpd, thus maintaining total cartel output at 25 million. It was Saudi Arabia's willingness to absorb its OPEC partners' quota overruns by restraining its own output that kept OPEC functioning. Indeed, once the Saudis relinquished their swing producer role in mid-1984, OPEC fell into disarray, and prices plunged.[24]

Uncertainty in Monopoly Markets

The downside of monopoly has run below the surface in this chapter and will be spelled out in the next. Yet, at least one redeeming feature of monopoly deserves to be mentioned. Monopoly can exert a stabilizing influence on the market, and so reduce uncertainty.

"Diamonds Are a Gal's Best Friend"

The Anita Loos song title "Diamonds Are a Gal's Best Friend," should lead you to wonder, Why? Though cut and polished diamonds are beautiful to behold, good imitation diamonds made out of zircon will deceive all but the expert. Beauty alone cannot account for their fascination. Aren't diamonds treasured because they are valuable and become even more valuable the longer they remain in one's safe? But why is that so?

A good part of the answer derives from the fact that the Syndicate, as the De Beers Central Selling Organization is known in the diamond industry, totally dominates the market. It controls the distribution of 80 percent of the world's supply of uncut diamonds, and does so in a unique way. Some 10 times a year, the Syndicate invites selected dealers to a "sight," where each is given a box of uncut diamonds to inspect. The dealer either accepts or rejects the entire box at a price set by De Beers. Refusal is rare, for future sight invitations hinge on the dealer's purchases. So, De Beers is assured both sales volume and price.

De Beer's pricing strategy is to continuously increase the value of diamonds. It will withhold quantity from the market if it fears economic conditions threaten to drive prices down, only to increase supply at a more propitious moment. De Beers acts as the commodity marketing boards discussed in Chapter 8 were supposed to behave. (Take another look at Figure 8.10b, p. 289, and draw the De Beers analog in Figure 11.8. Show how price and quantity change when (a) the monopoly reacts to a fall in demand by cutting price and (b) the monopoly preserves price.)

In fact, De Beers's control over supply is supplemented by its manipulating demand. Its marketing success in Japan, for example, is reflected by the rising proportion of Japanese who bought diamond engagement rings, increasing from only 6 percent in the 1960s to 67 percent by the late 1980s. The ever rightward shift of the demand curve supported by De Beers's near stranglehold over supply leads to an occasionally interrupted but basically upward trend of diamond prices.

Clearly, De Beers benefits from its market manipulation. But so does the individual diamond owner. The Syndicate has provided us with an asset whose value is assured to appreciate over time, which reduces the uncertainty connected with asset values in personal investment portfolios.[25]

Monopoly Output as Input

The same reasoning applies when a monopolized product is an input in the production process. Say you're a purchasing agent for a PC manufac-

FIGURE 11.8   Curbing Downside Risk: The Syndicate Adjusts to Declining Demand

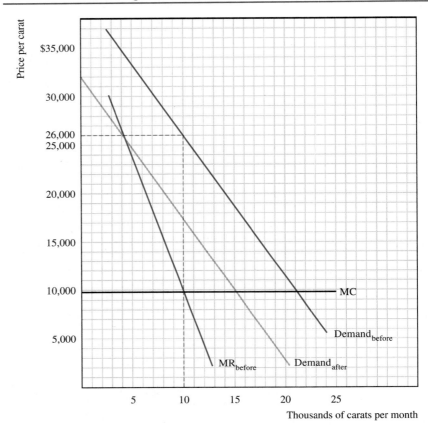

Before demand fell the Syndicate had set the per carat price at $26,000 and sold 10,000 carats. When demand is represented by the new Demand$_{after}$ curve, it can either lower price or maintain it. Your task is to (*a*) find the new quantity if the Syndicate retains the $26,000 price and (*b*) discover the new price and quantity if the Syndicate opts to adjust price. (Hint: for the latter, you'll have to insert the MR$_{after}$ curve).

turer, and you periodically buy computer memory chips. Consider now two scenarios:

1. Prices of chips fluctuate from $20 to $80 apiece and average $50. If a substantial order were to come in when the chips are priced at the maximum, your profit margin would be eroded. But you stand to reap a significant advantage should you be able to acquire the chips at the low end of the price range.

2. Chips are always priced at $50. You stand neither to gain nor to lose from fluctuating chip prices, since chips prices don't budge.

Which do you prefer? Notice that the average price in both cases is $50. The scenarios differ only in the degree of uncertainty.

Since most individuals are thought to be risk-averse, it's quite likely that purchasing agents like you would prefer input price stability. That's certainly the message conveyed by those opposed to floating exchange rates. Many manufacturers who use imported inputs in their products prefer the certainty of fixed exchange rates, which enables them to plan more accurately, to the potential·gains from buying imports when the fluctuating exchange rate turns in their favor. Similarly, that's the lesson from international commodity agreements. The buyers of the commodity prefer stability to instability.

Clearly, then, a monopolist who controls a vital input and keeps its price stable performs a useful service to the risk-averse user. When the stabilized price is also an artificially inflated one, the buyer must weigh the advantages of stability against the disadvantages of the high price. Can anyone be sure whether the net advantage is positive or negative?

In short, a monopolist's control over price can reduce downside price risk, a statement that cannot be made for a perfectly competitive market. And if reducing uncertainty is desirable, then monopoly can serve a useful public function. How important this benefit is compared to the harm monopoly causes remains to be seen in Chapter 12.

Summary

Although monopoly—in the strict sense of an industry totally dominated by a single firm or a group of sellers acting in concert—is rare in the United States, it is not entirely absent. At times, monopoly is more efficient than competition, as in the case of natural monopolies. More frequently, firms or entire industries can hide behind legally sanctioned entry barriers such as patents or quotas. We know the least about those monopolies that set up artificial entry barriers or collude to fix prices. Because they are subject to antitrust prosecution, such monopolists keep their lips sealed.

Analytically, the key difference between a monopoly market and a perfectly competitive one lies in the downward-sloping demand curve that faces the monopolist in contrast with the horizontal demand curve facing the competitive firm. Because the monopolist can sell more only by cutting price, the marginal revenue curve is also negatively sloped. But the profit-optimization rule, MR = MC, remains the same, as does the calculation of total revenue, total costs, and total profits. Typically, an industry characterized by monopoly will earn excess profits that can be sustained over time. However, no monopolist is immune to shifts in demand and costs.

The monopolist's profit position is enhanced if the market can be segmented. By making finer distinctions among its customers, the monopoly can extract higher prices from those willing to pay more while not abandoning those who would buy the product only at a lower price. (Of course, the lower price would have to cover marginal cost.)

In contrast to the individual monopolist who controls the industry, a cartel such as OPEC represents a coalition of firms that have joined forces to raise prices and restrict output. Such collusive monopolies tend to be short-lived, because the condition that each member adhere to its allocated quota clashes with its incentive to cheat. OPEC is a notable exception, overproduction by some members having been offset by Saudi Arabia's willingness to underproduce.

Reducing uncertainty by stabilizing prices is one possible advantage of monopoly. Whether that alone constitutes grounds for promoting monopoly, whether other redeeming features of monopoly support a promonopoly policy, and whether monopoly ought either to be prevented or regulated are the topics of Chapter 12.

Key Terms

Cartel (or collusive monopoly)
Discriminating monopolist
First-degree discrimination (or perfect price discrimination)
Monopoly

Natural monopoly
Second-degree discrimination (or block pricing)
Third-degree discrimination

Review Questions

1. *a.* List the entry barriers that set the stage for monopoly.
   b. Why are they so crucial to the monopolist?

2. Use Figure 11.2 to explain why a monopolist does not charge the highest possible price.

3. *a.* Compare the pricing policies of 2 monopolists, one selling a product whose demand is extremely inelastic, the other marketing a good whose demand is highly elastic.
   b. Explain why profitability and demand elasticity are closely related.

4. Although two brands of lipstick are identical, the public assumes that one is better than the other. Demonstrate how the manufacturer will price each of the brands to take advantage of the public's different elasticities.

5. Must a discriminating monopolist be profitable? Explain.

6. Show that the ticket prices in Figure 11.6 are identical to those derived from $P = MC/(1 + 1/\varepsilon)$.

7. Show that cheating is an intrinsic characteristic of cartels.

8. Why might airlines prefer an oil cartel to a free market in fuel?

Food for Thought

1. Demonstrate that under first degree discrimination, the deadweight loss will be lower and resources will be more efficiently allocated than under nondiscriminating monopoly.

2. Why doesn't ballpark management drive scalpers out of business by adjusting prices in line with market demand?

3. *a.* What economic rationale motivates some retail merchants and transportation companies to offer discounts to senior citizens?

   b. Why are such discount policies often constrained (e.g., no Saturday shopping, no rush-hour travel)?

4. Theater owners set fixed prices to take advantage of their monopolies of specific entertainment with limited runs. Nevertheless, some theaters sell tickets to students at a fraction of their list price a few hours before each performance.

   a. Explain the rationale of the students who buy earlier at full price as well as those who buy discount tickets at the last moment.

   b. Explain the theater owners' rationale.

   c. Construct a diagram that supports your argument.

5. Univanille, the vanilla pod cartel, consists only of Madagascar, Reunion, and the Comoros Islands, but controls 75 percent of the natural vanilla used to flavor such foods as vanilla ice cream. The 1987 price of a kilo of vanilla essence, which is extracted from the pods, was set at $3,000 per kilogram (= 2.2 pounds), while top-quality pods themselves sold for $72 per kilo. The latter was far above Indonesia's $15 per kilo price for somewhat lower-quality pods.

   a. Why has Univanille lasted for decades, defying the experience of most cartels?

   b. What advantage does Indonesia obtain by remaining outside the cartel? Demonstrate it diagrammatically.

   c. Scientists have recently developed an artificial vanilla that is almost identical in taste to the natural product, and they predict a price of $150 for a kilo of essence. What impact will that have on Univanille's future? Sketch it out.

Suggested Readings

You might want to contrast the classical analysis of monopoly—see E. A. G. Robinson, *Monopoly* (Cambridge: Cambridge University Press, 1941)—with the more contemporary views by F. M. Scherer and David Ross, *Industrial Market Structure and Economic Performance* (Boston: Houghton-Mifflin, 1990) and Dennis W. Carlton and Jeffrey M. Perloff, *Modern Industrial Organization* (Scott, Foresman/Little, Brown, 1990).

For an interesting yet simple survey of auction theory, see Loretta J. Mester, "Going, Going, Gone: Setting Prices with Auctions," *Federal Reserve Bank of Philadelphia Business Review* (March/April 1988), pp. 3–13.

Notes and Answers

1. This case is adapted from Sanford L. Jacobs, "Hatchery's Profitable Sideline Taps Long-Neglected Market," *The Wall Street Journal*, October 31, 1983, p. B1.

2. A barrel is 42 gallons, so the wellhead price rose from 4 to 6 cents per gallon over these two decades.

3. To be sure, this problem would be obviated were each of the competing phone companies to devise a unique sound. But isn't it simpler to have one phone company that provides us with one line over which we receive all of our calls? Natural monopolies are discussed in the next chapter.

4. For instance, the government contended in *United States* v. *Aluminum Company of America* [148 F.2d 416(2d Cir. 1945)] that Alcoa overstocked bauxite, the raw material out of which aluminum is made, primarily to keep it out of the hands of competitors.

5. Algebraically, the net effect combines the first change, $\Delta TR = P(\Delta Q)$, and the second, $\Delta TR = Q(\Delta P)$, so that $\Delta TR = P(\Delta Q) + Q(\Delta P)$.

6. $200,000; $700,000; −$500,000; −$5.

7. While the monopolist's MR falls and is always less than P, in a perfectly competitive market, $P = MR = $ constant.

8. Actually, for a linear demand curve, the slope of the MR curve equals twice the slope of the demand curve. This can be proven by calculating the slopes ($\Delta P/\Delta Q$) in Figure 11.2. More generally, when

$$Q_D = a - bP,$$

where Q_D is quantity demanded, P is price, and a and b ($= \Delta P/\Delta Q$) are constants, then

$$TR = PQ = P(Q_D) = aP - bP^2$$
$$MR = \Delta(PQ)/\Delta P = a - 2bP.$$

9. The negative sign of ε is critical here. The algebraic proof is as follows:

From note 5 we know that: $\Delta TR = P(\Delta Q) + Q(\Delta P)$

For a unit change in Q, divide by ΔQ to obtain: $\dfrac{\Delta TR}{\Delta Q} = \dfrac{P(\Delta Q) + Q(\Delta P)}{\Delta Q}$

Since $\Delta TR/\Delta Q = $ MR, consolidate and rewrite as: $MR = P + Q(\Delta P/\Delta Q)$

Multiply the last term by P/P: $MR = P + \dfrac{(Q)(\Delta P)P}{(P)(\Delta Q)}$

Factor out P: $MR = P \left[1 + \dfrac{(Q)(\Delta P)]}{(P)(\Delta Q)]}\right.$

Since the last term is the inverse of elasticity, obtain: $MR = P(1 + 1/\varepsilon)$

10. Any unit that exceeds 300,000 adds more to costs than it does to revenues because its $MC > MR$. Thus, the extra production must cut into the profits earned on previous units and diminish total profits.

11. The demand curve is $Q_D = 0.2 - 8/5Q$, giving rise to a MR curve that is constant at $0.20.

12. 1; 12.5; 87.5; 1,750,000.

13. There's a new lesson here: The $MR = MC$ equilibrium condition requires that MC cut MR from below.

14. P is less than ATC, meaning that Mr. Lowrance is running at a loss. If Mr. Lowrance persists in this policy, he would eventually be forced to leave the business.

15. This statement is a bit misleading, for in a typical auction, the winner is the one who is willing to pay more than the next-to-last remaining bidder. For all we know, the winner might have been willing to pay even more than the actual price paid. A "Dutch auction," in which the auctioneer starts from a high price, and if no one bites at the opening bid, gradually lowers the price, would resolve that discrepancy. In a Dutch auction, the seller actually does capture the maximum price the buyer is willing to pay.

16. The area of this half-house can be calculated by breaking it into a triangle and a rectangle. The base of the triangle equals 450,000 and its height equals $4.50 ($10 − $5.50), so that its area equals $1,012,500. The area of the remaining rectangle, whose width and height are 450 and $5.50, equals $2,475,000.

17. The kinked shaped of the combined demand curve is the result of this summation. For example, at $P = $75, business demanders want 175,000 flights while vacation travelers

demand 200,000 flights. The 375,000 total at the $75 price is a point on the combined demand curve.

18. If you were to project the right section of the demand curve all the way to the price axis and then draw a MR that falls twice as rapidly as the demand curve, you'd link up to the right MR section precisely above 125,000.

19. You'll get the same results using $P = MC/(1 + 1/\varepsilon)$ for each market.

20. 17.5; 52.5.

21. The market power of buyers vis-à-vis sellers is discussed in Chapter 17.

22. Of course, price alone does not determine consumption. In 1974 and 1975, for example, the price shock was augmented by a world recession that also drove down the demand for oil, while the expansion of the world economy during the 1980s brought the demand up. Notice, however, that it took until the end of the 1980s for oil demand to reach the level of a decade earlier.

23. Spot prices on Saudi Arabian crude fell from $28.75 in early 1984 to below $10 per barrel in the fall of 1986. While prices rose in response to strengthening demand, they hovered in the midteens until 1989. They skyrocketed again after an oil shortage panic generated by Iraq's invasion of Kuwait in 1990.

24. Nothing in this analysis is meant to downplay the political issues that faced OPEC, especially the Iran-Iraq war that began in 1979. The survival of OPEC is even more amazing when such noneconomic issues are considered.

25. Be aware of three pitfalls when purchasing diamonds as investments. First, prices do occasionally fall. Second, the retail markup runs around 100 percent of the wholesale price. Individuals, who generally buy at retail but sell at wholesale, must anticipate prices doubling merely to break even. Finally, the buyer is critically dependent on the integrity of the seller, since only an expert can evaluate the quality of a gemstone.

12

CONTROLLING MONOPOLY

*We once adored you, Valentine
But now you've made us sore—
With numbers like six-one-five-nine-
Four-two-eight-six-three-four;
We feel that we've been led astray,
You've treated us sloppily;
But that's the price we have to pay
When using a monopoly.*

"A Valentine to the Bell Telephone Company." Reprinted with permission from the April 1965 issue of *Mad Magazine* (no. 94), © 1965 by E. C. Publications, Inc.

[Agreements by physicians to reduce medical competition] can be hazardous to your personal freedom. You can go to jail.
U.S. Assistant Attorney General Charles R. Rule (1988)

Learning Objectives

After reading this chapter, you'll understand:
- How the static monopoly and perfect competitive models differ in terms of price, quantity, deadweight loss, efficiency, and resource distribution.
- The impact of alternative tax schemes on monopoly output and profits.
- The arguments for and against antitrust policy.
- Why natural monopolies are regulated.
- The rationale for various pricing schemes used for public utilities.
- How much monopoly has cost the U.S. economy.

Civil Antitrust Suits

Monopoly is presumed by most people to be harmful, but that's not always true. In some instances, the public would be best served by preserving a monopoly but controlling its policies to retain the good while restraining the bad. On the other hand, if the benefit of monopoly is minimal and its negative impact substantial, then eliminating monopoly power through antitrust policies, for example, would best secure public policy objectives. However, serving the public interest need not imply direct government intervention. The following case illustrates how private action can be mobilized to achieve public goals.

Hanover Drops the Shoe

Although the headlines have more often featured criminal prosecutions of U.S. monopolists, occasionally we do hear of civil law monopoly suits. Criminal penalties for antitrust violations convey a message: "Don't violate the antimonopoly laws. For if you do, you are subject to stiff fines and may even face a prison sentence." Civil antitrust suits, on the other hand, compensate victims for damages suffered because of the monopolist's actions. Such was the case in a 1955 civil antitrust action brought by Hanover Shoe, Inc., a manufacturer of shoes, against United Shoe Machinery, a supplier of shoe-making equipment.[1] Hanover contended that United Shoe had refused to sell it certain machinery, forcing Hanover to lease the equipment from United Shoe. Hamilton sought and ultimately won damages for overpayments in the neighborhood of $1 million.

But the U.S. civil law takes a further step. Victims are entitled to *triple* damages. Indeed, the actual amount United Shoe paid Hamilton, including trebling, interest, and court costs, approached $5 million.

It's not altogether obvious why a winning plaintiff is entitled to an award three times the amount of damage. It becomes even more perplexing if you acknowledge that the public at large loses when a competitive market is transformed into a monopoly. Why shouldn't the public, as represented by the government, be entitled to share the award?

Before resolving this question, it's important to investigate the underlying belief that monopoly is anathema. The chapter opens with a contrast of the static models of perfect competition and monopoly. The competitive marketplace wins the contest hands down and so provides the underpinning for antimonopolist sentiments. Such sentiments lead to antimonopoly policy, among which taxing away monopoly profits is one option, antitrust another. Both are evaluated in the following sections. However, antitrust policy is not without problems of its own, and they, too, are discussed.

The theme common to tax and antitrust policy is that the economy is better-off without monopoly. That presumption, however, does not apply to natural monopolies. Therefore, the chapter explores the methods and pitfalls of regulating local telephone or electric companies. There are both interesting analytic and practical issues to examine. The chapter concludes with a section on measuring the costs of monopoly.

Monopoly Versus Perfect Competition

The Highbrow Tweezer scenario of Chapter 11 is a stylized representation of monopoly pricing. It suggests why even nondiscriminating monopolists enjoy their state. Price is set above average costs so that excess profits are earned. And because monopolists hide behind barriers of entry of one sort or another, they need not contend with the swarm of competitors who imitate their product or production techniques, who flood the market with competing goods, and who drive the prices down for all until excess profits are eliminated. Monopoly insures that excess profits are preserved.

The presence of excess profits is merely one reason—and perhaps not even the most important reason—why economists oppose monopoly. When you contrast the results of the Chapter 9's competitive model with the implications of monopoly, you'll discover a variety of differences that weigh heavily in favor of the competitive model: more consumer satisfaction, greater efficiency, and a better distribution of resources. Let's take each of these points in turn.

The Price Front

Figure 12.1 can be used to contrast monopoly and competitive pricing. Consider the long-run equilibrium of the manufacturer of Peel-A-Way, a device that peels fruits and vegetables in one piece. To make life a bit simpler, assume that long-run average and marginal costs are constant. Given the demand, marginal revenue, long-run average cost, and long-run marginal cost curves, price is set at $6.50 per peeler. If competition were permitted, each producer could make the peeler at the same low $3 per unit cost as does Peel-A-Way, and each competitive firm would reach its minimum ATC point at an output of 50,000 units. On the left in Figure 12.1 are three such identical firms; their joint output totals 150,000 peelers. Another two are on the right, the last one sited at 700,000. So, the competitive industry consists of 14 manufacturers, each one producing 50,000 units monthly, and each selling peelers at $3 a piece.

What is the shape of the competitive industry's long-run average (LRATC) and long-run marginal cost (LRMC) curves? _____

The horizontal line at $3 represents not only the long-run cost curves for the monopoly, but also both the LRATC and the LRMC for the competitive firms.[2] It's also the competitive equilibrium price. For each

FIGURE 12.1   **Monopoly and Perfect Competition: Some Contrasts**

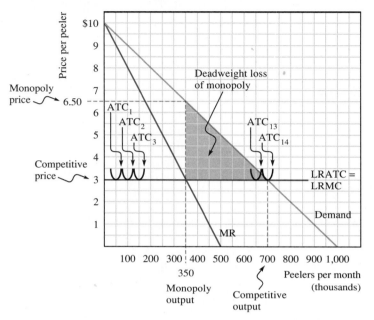

The monopolist limits production to 350,000 and charges $6.50 per peeler. A competitive firm could have produced an identical peeler at the same $3 cost, as indicated by the string of ATC curves along the LRATC = LRMC curve. Since competition forces price down to minimum LRATC, the competitive price would have been $3 (not $6.50) and quantity sold would have been 700,000 (not 350,000). The unproduced and thus unsold 350,000 peelers represent a deadweight loss, as indicated by the shaded grey area.

firm, MR = MC at a price of $3, so it's optimal; and because no excess profits will be earned at $3, it's also stable.

The contrast in price, then, is evident: $6.50 for the monopolist's customers and $3 for those buying on the competitive marketplace.

The Quantity Front

Figure 12.1 shows another contrast. The quantity sold on the competitive market is larger than under monopoly. In this case, consumers buy 700,000 peelers monthly; the monopoly output is only 350,000.

This, of course, is hardly worth an apple peel. The monopolist maintains a high price by keeping output limited. The monopolist contrives scarcity.

SOURCE: Reprinted by permission: Tribune Media Services.

So, not only do demanders pay higher prices under monopoly, but they also find their consumption restricted. Monopoly engenders a deadweight loss identical to that discussed in Chapter 8's analysis of quotas.

The Deadweight Loss of Monopoly

How much is the deadweight loss? You should be able to calculate it as $612,500 a month, a triangle labeled "Deadweight loss of monopoly" in Figure 12.1. This represents the lost consumer surplus.[3]

Efficiency Loss

Monopoly fails another test when compared to the perfectly competitive model. It is less efficient both in the short run and in the long run. While competition forces each firm to be efficient and operate at a cost consistent with minimum average cost, that is not true for a monopolist. There's no competitor to coerce the monopolist to become more efficient. Thus, as you saw in the short-run situation depicted in Figure 11.2 (p. 374), Highbrow's optimum profit point occurs at a per unit cost of $3.15, not at its $3 average-cost minimum.[4] Similarly, the pressure to adapt to cost-reducing innovations is less intense for the monopolist than for its competitive counterpart.

Resource Maldistribution

You know that resources are properly allocated when output expands to the point where marginal social benefit equals marginal social cost. In the absence of externalities, marginal social benefit is equated with the consumer's willingness to pay for the good, as represented by the individual's position on the market demand curve. Marginal social cost, on the other hand, is equated with the marginal cost of production.

In competitive equilibrium, MSB = MSC because in equilibrium P = MC. In other words, production expands to the point where the consumer who is willing to pay the market price just covers the resource costs associated with production. Any further output could be sold only if price were to be reduced. But in that case, the marginal purchaser would be paying less for the good than it costs to produce the product, a clear waste of resources. Resources would also be misallocated if a buyer who was willing to pay the MSC would be deprived of the product. Look again at Figure 12.1. It costs $3 to produce a peeler on a competitive market (MC = MSC = $3). Each of 700,000 purchasers, all of them willing to pay at least $3, can acquire one.

That's not the story in a market dominated by a monopolist. Peel-A-Way produces only 350,000 units; the marginal social benefit to the user is $6.50. But for the 400,000th unit, Peel-A-Way's cost is only $3. A consumer who is willing to pay $6 can't buy the peeler even though the resources devoted to peeler production cost substantially less than $6. In this case, resources that should be used for peeler production aren't.

Clearly, the competitive outcome is superior to the monopoly result on all counts—price, production, efficiency, and resource allocation.

Controlling Monopoly: Taxation

Given the lopsided contrast between the consequences of monopoly and perfect competition, it's no surprise that economists have traditionally advocated controlling monopoly. We will now consider taxation, the first of two mechanisms designed to curb monopoly exploitation.

Chapter 9's analysis of a tax imposed on a competitive industry demonstrated that the tax is ultimately shifted onto consumers. If that's true for monopoly as well, there's little to be gained by taxing a monopoly. However, it is theoretically possible to tax a monopolist in such a way that tax shifting will not occur. The case that immediately follows demonstrates shifting, while the second shows a rational monopolist forced to bear the entire burden of the tax.

Per Unit Taxes

Back to Highbrow Tweezer and the question, Will Highbrow receive its just punishment for its monopolistic extortion? Figure 12.2 deals with two types of taxes the government could impose on Highbrow: a variable cost levy such as an excise tax (Figure 12.2a) and a fixed-cost tax such as a franchise fee (Figure 12.2b). Both figures begin with Highbrow's initial set of average and marginal cost curves, and demand and marginal revenue curves. Consequently, output, price, and the profit rectangle are identical to those in Figure 11.2 (p. 374).

FIGURE 12.2   **Taxing Monopoly Profits**

a.   A per unit tax   **b.   A fixed-sum tax**

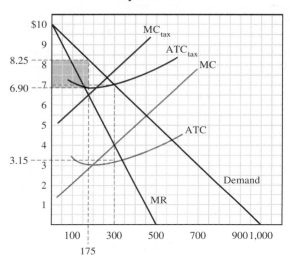   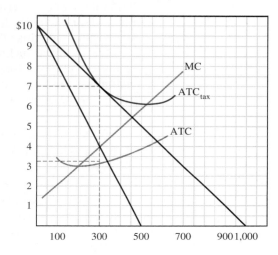

a.   When a per unit tax of $3.85 is levied on the monopolist, both ATC and MC shift. A new equilibrium emerges (MR = MC$_{tax}$ at 175,000), and price rises to $8.25. Profits, while diminished, remain positive, as indicated by the shaded area.

b.   When a fixed-cost tax is imposed, ATC rises but MC remains the same. Thus, the MR = MC equilibrium remains at 300,000 units and price remains at $7. But the profits of $1,155,000 are now absorbed by the taxing authority.

The sequence in Figure 12.2a runs as follows: A per unit tax of $3.85—the exact value of the profits per unit since P = $7 and ATC = $3.15—is imposed. By its very nature, this per unit tax increases variable costs, and so both the ATC and the MC curve rise by $3.85 at every point. Thus, the curves labeled ATC$_{tax}$ and MC$_{tax}$ are parallel to the initial curves but $3.85 higher.

Find the new monopoly equilibrium:

Output   _____

Price   _____

Total tax paid _____

Total profit   _____ [5]

Clearly, while Highbrow has been forced to absorb part of the tax—price has not increased as much as the per unit cost of the tax—it has managed to shift the bulk of the tax onto its customers. Moreover, the imposition of the tax has led to a reduction in output, certainly not an objective of a properly designed antimonopoly policy.

Fixed-Cost Taxes

Let's consider an alternative tax policy: a lump-sum imposition of $1,155,000. The government authorities may insist that Highbrow pay that sum in exchange for a license to operate. If Highbrow refuses, the government will close the firm.

One's natural inclination is to wonder whether this is any different from the previous case. Won't Highbrow pass this fixed-sum tax onto its customers, too? As you answer the questions that follow, you'll see that, at least in the conceptual world we're now inhabiting, Highbrow won't.

Will a fixed-sum tax increase fixed or variable costs?   _____

If it affects only fixed costs, will it change marginal costs?   _____

If a fixed-sum tax does not alter MC, will it change the MC = MR intersection?   _____

If the MC = MR intersection remains unchanged, will output be altered?   _____

If output remains the same, will price be changed?   _____

If neither output nor price is changed, is the tax passed on?   _____ 6

In short, Highbrow alone bears the full burden of the fixed-sum tax. It will now earn only the normal profits implicit in its average costs, but not any monopoly profits. Nor will output be changed. So the lump-sum tax imposition has redistributed the monopoly profits from Highbrow into the pockets of the government. Neat?

This analysis is borne out in Figure 12.2b. Since the addition of a fixed-sum tax increases average fixed and thus average total costs, the ATC curve in Figure 12.2b shifts upward. (The increase equals $1,155,000 divided by the quantity produced at each output.) But since variable costs are not affected, the MC curve doesn't budge. It continues to cut MR at $Q = 300,000$, requiring that $P = \$7$. Notice that the ATC_{tax} is tangent to the demand curve at those coordinates, so that production costs plus taxes exhaust the entire revenue. Notice also that the monopolist would be worse off at any other output. Everywhere else, the ATC curve lies above the demand curve. Instead of zero excess profits, production elsewhere would engender losses.

In short, static monopoly theory suggests that a policy designed to tax away monopoly profits should focus on fixed taxes, such as license fees, rather than such per unit levies as excise taxes. However, economists are not really enamored with the tax solution, for although it extracts the monopolist's excess profits, it fails to address monopoly's deadweight loss, inefficiency, and inappropriate resource distribution.

Antitrust: The Weapon of Choice

In contrast to taxation, antitrust legislation tries to undo all of the ills of monopoly. We return to the civil antitrust case, which seems to be similar to the taxing away of monopoly profits. Penalty payments such as triple damages, however, radically alter that similarity.

Hamilton versus United Shoe

Let's assume that in the case of Hamilton versus United Shoe, had there been no monopoly, the equipment rental charged by a manufacturer in competition with United would have been $5,000 per machine per year. At the $7,500 lease charged by United, Hamilton opts to use only 80 machines. In price-fixing cases, the courts have ruled that damage equals the difference between the actual price ($7,500) and the competitive price ($5,000) times the actual quantity bought or sold (80 machines per year). In terms of Figure 12.3, that's the shaded rectangle labeled ''Damages,'' which is equal to the excess costs of $200,000 (= $2,500 × 80) a year that

FIGURE 12.3   Calculating the Damages in Price-Fixing Antitrust Cases

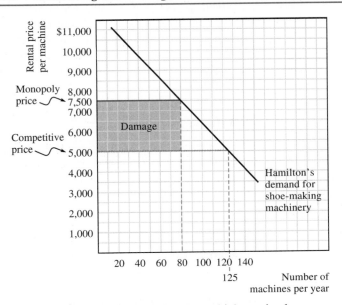

The defendant who is forced to pay a higher price because of monopoly is damaged by the price difference times the actual quantity purchased at the higher price. Of course, this disregards the fact that customers would have bought more had the price been the lower competitive one.

Hamilton paid and the excess profits United earned. The damage award redistributes income from the monopolist to its victim much as a tax takes excess profits away from the monopolist and adds it to the public purse.

The award of damages does not address the deadweight loss that results from the monopolist's artificially restricting supply. You can see from Figure 12.3 that had the rent been $5,000, Hamilton would have employed 125 machines a year and abstracted additional consumer surplus. (Label the consumer surplus area in Figure 12.3.)

That's where the imposition of triple damages comes in. The monopolist is charged more than the actual damage to compensate for the deadweight loss.

There's a second justification for penalties in excess of damage. Triple damages deter. Recall Chapter 1's economic theory of criminal behavior. Rational criminals take into account the penalty for the crime and the probability of being apprehended. If the cost to the monopolist were only the damage actually incurred by the plaintiff, then a rational monopolist would overcharge as long as she believes the probability of being discovered and successfully prosecuted is slight. The threat of triple damages radically alters that calculation.[7] Moreover, the plaintiff's incentive to sue should increase directly with its potential gains, and so should the monopolist's probability of being sued. The monopolist facing this potential cost may well decide that it's just not worthwhile to demonstrate its power.

You understand now why the penalties are awarded to the plaintiff: not to reward but to induce. Moreover, such penalties are not really meant to be an incentive to the plaintiff but a disincentive to the monopolist. Effective antitrust laws induce monopolists to pursue competitive pricing policies.[8]

Dissolving Monopoly

U.S. antitrust policy offers another option. The courts may break up illegal monopolies. In 1984, AT&T was split into seven smaller regional telephone companies. In such cases, dissolution not only eliminates the evils of monopoly, but simultaneously introduces the benefits of competition.

If an ounce of prevention is worth a pound of cure, then preventing monopoly formation must be superior to breaking up an already existing monopoly. Don't let the competitive marketplace deteriorate into a monopoly. This one sentence, in fact, lies at the foundation of prophylactic antitrust policy. The Justice Department or the Federal Trade Commission may oppose mergers or other combinations that would substantially lessen competition in an industry.

Thus, the static analysis of competitive versus monopolistic behavior suggests that whenever competition can be maintained or restored, price will be lower, output will be higher, the deadweight loss will be eliminated, low-cost operation will be guaranteed, and resources kept away by the contrived scarcity policy of the monopolist will flow to the industry. MicroBits 12.1 examines two antitrust cases that reached the U.S. Supreme Court. Which of the desired outcomes were important in the cases and which were attained?

Anti-Antitrust

Although antitrust laws appear to benefit society, some economists have objected to them as costly and unnecessary.

The Costs of Antitrust.   Antitrust policy is not costless. Resources are needed to identify firms that defy the antitrust laws, to prosecute violaters, and to monitor compliance with penalties imposed or agreements reached. Some antitrust cases have dragged on for years as the defendants litigated their way through the judiciary. For a long time, the only apparent beneficiaries were the attorneys and those who supplied the paper for all the briefs filed.

Monopoly and Substitute Goods.   Some economists have contended that antitrust policy is superfluous and can do more harm than good. They believe that the static analysis of monopoly inadequately describes the constraints imposed on monopoly in a dynamic economy. First, no product in a modern economy is so unique that there are no substitutes for it. To be sure, the cross-elasticity of demand will be larger for some than for others. But rarely will there be a product with absolutely no substitutes. Remember the Du Pont antitrust decision in MicroBits 5.2 (p. 154). Similarly, although Polaroid won a suit for Kodak's infringing upon its instant photography patents,[9] recent advances in photo developing technology—evident from the ubiquitous one-hour developing shops—suggest that Polaroid's monopoly is not absolute.

Second, a profitable product, even if monopolized, will encourage competitors. Burroughs-Wellcome's protected anti-AIDS medicine, AZT, faced competitive drugs within a few years. IBM patents did not protect the firm from imitators, who marketed high-quality, low-price clones. Disregarding the law is not unknown. Even the government's monopoly on postage stamps has been undermined by individuals who bleach out the cancellation marks on the stamps and sell them for new at two thirds of their face value.

Third, recent experience in the United States has demonstrated the potency of foreign competition. Even assuming that a single producer dominated the entire domestic market, imports can weaken the monopolist's grip.

Figure 12.4 shows how the exclusive franchisee of D'amaged Clothes, a Paris designer, can be driven out of business in the long run.

MicroBits 12.1

Attorneys and Baseball Players

U.S. antitrust law has been equivocal. While the law and the courts have most often opposed monopolistic practices, in some instances they have promoted monopoly.

The Licensed Professions

Professional ethics frequently serve to mask monopoly pricing practices. Physicians, pharmacists, and attorneys had successfully shielded their price setting from antitrust prosecution until the early 1970s. Since then, professional organizations have either been prosecuted or threatened by the antitrust authorities for such practices. The Goldfarb case set the precedent.*

In 1971, the Goldfarbs needed a title examination to complete buying their house in Fairfax, Virginia. They sought the cheapest attorney, since only a member of the Virginia Bar Association could provide this service. To their chagrin, every lawyer quoted the same price, based on a minimum fee schedule published by the Fairfax County Bar Association.

That turned out not to be surprising, since the State Bar Committee on Legal Ethics had ruled that if a lawyer "purely for his own advancement, intentionally and regularly bills less than the customary charges of the bar for similar services . . . it is a violation of Canon 7, which forbids the efforts of one law-

---

* Goldfarb v. *Virginia State Bar* 421 U.S. 258 (1972).

yer to encroach upon the employment of another." Indeed, "evidence that an attorney *habitually* charges less than the suggested minimum fee schedule . . . raises a presumption that such a lawyer is guilty of misconduct."

So the Goldfarbs sued the Virginia Bar Association in a case that ultimately reached the Supreme Court. There, Chief Justice Burger, in finding for the Goldfarbs, wrote, "Here a fixed, rigid price floor . . . was enforced through the prospect of professional discipline from the State Bar . . . [and] . . . reinforced by the assurance that other lawyers would not compete by underbidding. . . . These factors coalesced to create a pricing system that consumers could not realistically escape. On the record, respondents' activities constitute a classic illustration of price fixing."

The Monopoly that Is Our National Pastime

When Kurt Flood, the star centerfielder of the Cincinnati Reds for 12 seasons, was traded to the Philadelphia Phillies in 1969 without even being consulted, he requested that the commissioner of baseball declare him a free agent, able to negotiate with any major league team. Upon denial of that request, Flood filed a complex lawsuit against a slew of baseball officials and owners. One complaint argued that the "reserve clause," which binds a player permanently to the team he initially contracts with, violated the antitrust laws. While the team can trade the player on its initiative, it could prevent him from contracting with any other team even if the player refused to sign with his own team.

The Flood case made its way to the Supreme Court,§ which ruled that the antitrust laws did not apply to baseball. The opinion is startling for two reasons. First, the court deferred to precedent, a Supreme Court baseball antitrust case that was decided in 1922. Writing then for a unanimous court but interpreting the issue quite narrowly, Justice Oliver Wendell Holmes found that baseball was not interstate commerce, and thus not subject to federal antitrust laws. Some 30 years later, despite the fact that both location and TV and radio coverage had made baseball truly national in scope, the court upheld its precedent. Justice Blackmun, writing for the majority, although admitting that "professional baseball is a business and it is engaged in interstate commerce," nevertheless would not overrule the court's antitrust exemption for baseball.

Second, baseball is an anomaly. The courts have ruled that boxing, football, basketball, hockey, and golf are not exempt from the antitrust laws. Even Justice Blackmun commented, "If there is any inconsistency or illogic in all this, it is an inconsistency and illogic of long standing" that Congress should remedy.

Although over the years individual legislators tried to apply the antitrust laws uniformly to all professional sports, Congress invariably failed to act.‖ But the market did act. In 1975, Dave McNally and Andy Messersmith, pitchers for the Montreal Expos and the Los Angeles Dodgers, respectively, requested free-agent status. An arbitrator's ruling in December 1975 sided with the pitchers, and ultimately led to a contract compromise that revamped the entire player-club relationship. At present, players are reserved to their teams for a limited number of years. Thereafter they have the right to demand a trade; to veto a proposed trade; or, under certain conditions, to become a free agent. Baseball is still different but less so than it used to be.

‖ In the July 1958 hearings before the Senate Subcommittee on Antitrust and Monopoly, the following conversation took place between a senator and the "eloquent" manager of the New York Yankees, Casey Stengal:

Senator Langer: I want to know whether you intend to keep on monopolizing the world's championship in New York City?

Mr. Stengal: Well, I will tell you, I got a little concerned yesterday in the first 3 innings when I say the 3 players I had gotten rid of and I said when I lost 9 what am I going to do and when I had a couple of my players. I thought so great of that did not do so good up to the sixth inning I was more confused but I finally had to go and call on a young man in Baltimore that we don't own and the Yankees don't own him, and he is doing pretty good, and I would actually have to tell you that I think we are more the Greta Garbo type now from success.

Honestly, that's what Casey answered! You can check it out yourself.

---

§ *Flood* v. *Kuhn,* 407 U.S. 258 (1971).

FIGURE 12.4   The Loser: Declining Demand Drives the Monopolist out of Business

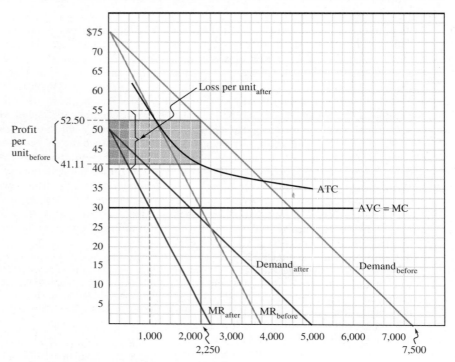

Life was rosy with the initial demand curve. The monopolist optimized by producing 2,250 units monthly, sold them at a price of $52.50 each and earned excess profits of $25,627.50 each month [=($52.50 − $41.11)(2,250)]. But with the fall in demand, the optimum profit position is at 1,000 units per month at $40 each. True, the $40 covers the AVC of $30, but not the ATC of $55. So, in the long run, the monopolist will shut down.

Initially, the monopolist prices the fashionable D'amaged blouse at $52.50; sells 2,250 blouses each month; and, given the ATC curve, earns a monthly profit of $25,627.50. But monopoly power disintegrates as copies flood the market, forcing demand leftward from Demand$_{before}$ to Demand$_{after}$. The profit-maximizing price and output on the new demand curve are $40 and 1,000 blouses, respectively. But at that quantity, ATC = $55, so that the profit-maximizing price has fallen below average costs. If this condition persists, then the rational monopolist will ultimately close up shop.

Some economists therefore conclude that antitrust isn't really necessary. The market itself is sufficiently vigilant to undo the adverse impact of monopoly.

Anti-Anti-Antitrust

Not all economists find these arguments convincing. They point out that an intelligent, forward-looking monopolist can survive. Moreover, even if monopolies perish in the long run, they may well have deleterious short-run effects that themselves have unfavorable long-run consequences.

Limit Pricing.   Consider again Burroughs-Wellcome, the manufacturer of AZT. This corporation can pursue at least two diametrically opposed pricing policies. It can go for broke in the short run, charging as much as the market can bear. With a perfectly inelastic demand, buyers have no choice but to pay the thousands of dollars needed annually. That, of course, will not only enrich the company in the short run, but will also stimulate the competitive hormones of other drug manufacturers. The higher the price, the more competitors will salivate at the fat profits.

A firm practicing **limit pricing** sets prices low enough to discourage potential competitors but high enough to earn excess profits.

But there's an alternative: use a **limit pricing** techniques. Charge a price higher than costs and earn some excess profits, but don't go overboard. Limit pricing simultaneously enriches the manufacturer and discourages competitors. Other drug manufacturers will have to consider whether potential profits warrant spending money on research and development of a substitute and then pricing their product competitively with the expensive but not exorbitant monopoly price. So, by not fully exploiting its monopoly power in the short run, the monopolist can maintain control and profits over a longer time horizon.

These contrasting policies are sketched out in Figure 12.5. The profit-maximizing price of a pair of roller blades is $75, with 200,000 units produced monthly. Since AVC is $50, the $5 million covers the assumed fixed costs of $1 million and leaves the $4 million in profits to attract competitors to the market.

But what if the monopoly prices the skates at $62.50 and sells 300,000 monthly? The $12.50 difference times 300,000 equals $3.75 million, and after subtracting the $1 million in fixed costs, sets monthly profits at $2.75 million. Surely, these reduced profits are less attractive to the potential market invader.

Which policy should the monopolist pursue? The answer depends on the particular circumstance in the specific industry. But the general point is that the monopolist may well survive over the long run and maintain the undesired consequences of monopoly during that interval.

Monopoly and Innovation.   A second criticism against waiting until the market responds has to do with monopoly control over investment and new technology. At least two motives can justify a monopolist's pursuing a go-slow policy when faced with new products or new production techniques. First, a monopolist would prevent the introduction of any innovation that would threaten its control over the industry. You can well under-

FIGURE 12.5   Preserving Monopoly over the Long Run: Limit Pricing

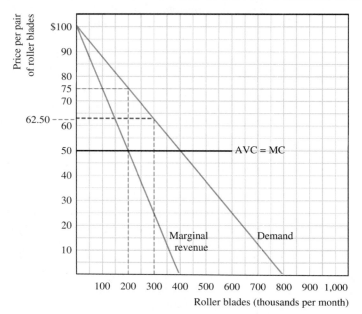

At the short-run profit-maximizing output of 300,000 price = $75, and profit (excluding fixed cost) = ($75 − $50) (200,000) = $5 million per month.

The incentive provided to competitors by this substantial profit can be diminished by charging $62.50 per unit, selling 300,000, and netting (again excluding fixed cost) $3,750,000. Although at 300,000 MC > MR, the smaller profit, by discouraging entry or the development of substitutes, may be more profitable to the monopolist over the long haul.

stand why IBM, which dominated the mainframe computer market, initially resisted the personal computer. Second, the monopolist might find it more profitable to delay introducing new techniques until existing fixed commitments were concluded. A monopolist might be inclined to wait until the leases on existing machinery expired before committing itself to acquiring more advanced machinery.

Could such delays occur in the competitive marketplace? Not likely. First, the absence of excess profits limits the funds available to the perfect competitor. More compelling, why should any single firm defend the industry from new products? Since the individual competitor commands only a tiny share of the market, its intervention would only raise its own costs while permitting its competitors to free-ride. And, insofar as fixed costs are concerned, the fact that one firm is encumbered by fixed commitments will not prevent a competitor from introducing a more efficient production method.

In short, the monopolist who controls the industry may also control the pace of technological change in the industry, whereas such dilatory tactics are not expected in the competitive marketplace.

When all is said and done, the effectiveness of antitrust versus market forces depends not on general principles—they can be argued in either direction—but rather on the characteristics of particular markets and the time frame contemplated. Benevolent monopolies may well exist, and even monopolies that are exploitive may ultimately wither away. Economists continue to disagree whether the benefits from waiting for the market to respond are substantial enough to compensate for the costs imposed on society by monopoly.

Natural Monopolies: The Bigger, the Better

The conflict between monopoly and perfect competition takes on a different dimension in the case of natural monopolies.

Characteristics of Natural Monopolies

Chapter 11 pointed out that natural monopolies occur when either one of the following conditions exist:

- The long-run average cost curve slopes downward over the relevant range of demand.
- Duplication of production facilities is wasteful.

Few examples of industries that combine large economies of scale with limited demand occur in an economy such as the United States, with its large and affluent industrial and consumer base. But certainly in less populated and poorer economies, demand for most products will be lower and often can be satisfied by one optimally sized firm. Yet even in developed economies, certain industries are characterized by massive overhead expenses and relatively insignificant variable costs. It is expensive to acquire the durable equipment needed to start a telephone company; to deliver water, gas, and electricity to homes and business establishments; or to initiate a railroad line. In these cases, initial outlays are substantial but maintenance costs are small. These high fixed costs exert a significant burden if output is low, but they are moderate when output is high.

Take the case of nuclear-generated electricity. A modern nuclear power plant, capable of producing 1 million kilowatts daily, costs around $2 billion to build. On the other hand, it can be operated by a handful of technicians and has few material input requirements. Since one such power plant can provide all the needs of a city the size of Baltimore, it would be expensive, wasteful, and thus foolish to operate the plant at less than capacity in order to make way for some competition. Moreover, it makes absolutely no sense to duplicate for each electric company the power lines that deliver the electricity to the user sites. Welcome to the realm of **public utility** pricing.

A **public utility** is an enterprise operating in a market in which demand is too limited to exhaust the firm's economies of scale, thereby subjecting the firm to public regulation.

The Dilemma of Public Utility Pricing

Figure 12.6 sets the scene for the dilemma of natural monopolies, represented here by a nuclear power plant. Given a falling average cost curve—and for simplicity a fixed AVC curve—the larger production is, the lower the per unit cost.

FIGURE 12.6   Public Utility Pricing

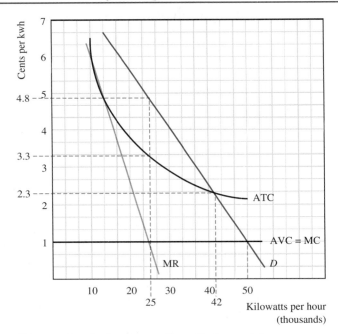

If unregulated, the monopolist will charge 4.8 cents per kilowatt hour and produce only 25,000 kilowatts per hour. Under *marginal cost pricing*, regulators will set P = MC = 1 cent per kilowatt hour. But, unless the utility is subsidized, it will ultimately shut down, since P < ATC. Under *average cost pricing*, the regulators set P = ATC = 2.3 cents per kilowatt hour, enabling the utility to break even at an output of 42,000 kilowatts per hour.

Recall that proper resource allocation requires that MSC = MSB, which, in the absence of externalities, is achieved when P = MC. That point in Figure 12.6 occurs at 50,000 kilowatts per hour (kwh). So, the preferred market structure is the one that will most closely achieve the MSB = MSC target.

Monopoly won't even approximate that goal. The P = MC criterion is suboptimal for a profit-maximizing monopolist, who seeks MR = MC. At the optimum monopoly output of 25,000 kwh, price will be set at 4.8 cents per kwh, and, with average total costs at 3.3 cents per kwh, profits per kwh are 1.5 cents.

Unfortunately, insisting on a competitive market structure is no better. A competitive outcome would raise costs and lower efficiency. If a regulatory policy would create five competitive firms, with each generating 10,000 kwh, the cost per kwh for each firm would be 6 cents, the point on the ATC above 10,000 kwh. That's almost triple the per kwh cost of a single firm producing 50,000 kwh, hence the dilemma. Both monopoly and competition would lead to high costs and low efficiency.

Public Utility Regulation

It is precisely for this reason that the public utility solution has become so popular. Whether the government itself owns the nuclear facility as is true in Western Europe or permits private ownership and merely controls price as is the case in the United States, government intervention aims at achieving the best of all possible worlds. By insisting that the public utility charge a low price, the government removes the utility's incentive to limit production. So, the public is able to consume more and resources are more appropriately allocated.

In **marginal-cost pricing,** price is set to equal marginal cost.

Single-Price Options.   One possible pricing policy is to impose a uniform price, which raises the question, What price should the regulators set? **Marginal-cost pricing,** setting P = MC, is an option favored by economic theorists. A price of 1 cent per kwh meets the condition for optimal resource allocation. There's just one problem with marginal-cost pricing. Figure 12.6 indicates that at P = MC, ATC > P, so that firm is losing more than a cent for each kilowatt-hour produced. Certainly that's not viable over the long run unless the government is willing to subsidize the utility.

In **average-cost pricing,** price is set to equal average total cost.

The alternative solution is **average-cost pricing,** which enables the utility to break even. In Figure 12.6, P = ATC at 2.3 cents per kwh and output will be 42,000 kwh. The public utility will cover its costs and earn a normal return without a government subsidy. (See MicroBits 12.2 for how this type of policy led to a strange anomaly during the years of the oil crisis.)

MicroBits 12.2

No Matter How You Play It, You Lose

The energy crisis of the 1970s that saw oil prices quadruple fathered a general movement toward conservation. The public was urged to cut back on energy consumption, including the use of electricity, which depended heavily on oil-powered generating plants. Such patriotic action, which was hailed as beneficial to each citizen, was doomed to backfire. Take a look at the scenario as shown in the figure below.

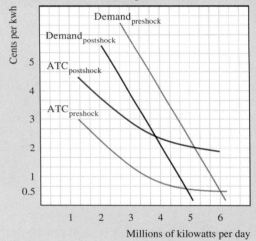

Millions of kilowatts per day

Prior to the rise in oil prices, average-cost pricing set the charge as 0.5 cents per kwh and consumption amounted to 6 million kwh daily (Demand$_{preshock}$ and ATC$_{preshock}$). With the quadrupling in oil prices—ATC$_{postshock}$ replaces the preshock cost structure—the authorities permit prices to rise to 2 cents per kwh. That by itself would have reduced the quantity demanded and raised price on the preshock demand curve.

But the public's sympathetic response to conservation pleas shifted the demand curve inward, leading to a new intersection of Demand$_{postshock}$ and postshock ATC. Economies of scale now work against the consumer, for as demand declines, average costs rise. Regulators, responding to pleas for higher prices to cover higher costs, permit price per kwh to rise to 2.4 cents, an additional 20 percent increase.

How paradoxical. By supporting the national energy conservation policy and conserving oil, we compounded the price increase. The increase in costs due to lower consumption was passed on to the very consumers who were urged to save in order to reduce costs!

Multiple-Pricing Options.   Utilities have been permitted to use more complex pricing schemes than the single-price option just analyzed. There's a common objective for all these alternatives: improving resource allocation while permitting the utilities to earn normal profits without subsidization. We turn first to second-degree discrimination, mentioned in Chapter 11.

Block Pricing.   As you recall, under second-degree discrimination the same consumer pays different prices for different quantities. Such block pricing is common in public utilities, where an individual or a business pays one rate for a "block" of, say, telephone message units and a lower rate for additional calls.

Return to Figure 12.6. Assume that all of the consumers' demand curves are identical, so that we can use the x-axis to represent either the demand of a single consumer or all demanders combined. So, for Everett, the abscissa reads "kilowatts per hour" and for the entire market, "thousands of kilowatts per hour." Let the utility now offer a two-price plan to Everett. Use up to 37 kwh and pay 3 cents per kwh; use more and pay 1 cent for each additional kwh.

How many kwh would Ev use? Clearly, 50. True, Ev would be happier paying 1 cent per kwh for each of the 50 kwh he demands. Nevertheless, his demand curve shows that he's willing to pay 3 cents for the first 37 kwh, and he's equally ready to pay at least a cent for another 13 kwh. And since everyone's demand curve is identical to Everett's, total quantity demanded will be 50,000 kwh. Production occurs at the optimum point of MB = MSC.

Calculate now the utility's profit. Since consumers pay $1,110 for the first 37,000 kilowatts and $130 for the remainder, TR = $1,240. With the utility's total cost for the 50,000 kwh equalling $1,100, the utility covers its cost and nets $140. The success of the block pricing scheme lies in the utility's capture of some of the consumer surplus. The outcome: The utility operates without a subsidy and still produces at the social optimum.

Peak-Load Pricing.   Decision makers can adjust prices to take advantage of demand fluctuating over time. You're familiar with the **peak-load pricing** techniques used by the telephone companies. Rates are highest during the busy daytime hours, fall in the evening, and are the lowest at night. Electric utilities in the northern United States often differentiate between higher rates in the summer, when air conditioning puts additional pressure on the electricity network, and lower rates in the winter, when demand is less intense.

Under **peak-load pricing,** buyers pay more per unit during periods of heavy demand and less when demand tapers off.

Figure 12.7 reproduces Figure 12.6 but adds a second demand curve and shoots up the MC curve at 50,000 kilowatts per hour. The two demand curves depict winter and summer demands. The perfectly inelastic segment of the MC curve indicates absolute capacity. The power plant simply cannot produce more than 50,000 kilowatts per hour.[10]

During the winter, all demand would be satisfied even with marginal-cost pricing. That would permit low-cost, efficient production and optimal resource allocation. But the plant would operate at a loss. During the summer, however, neither goals would be achieved and consumers would probably not be pleased. Quantity demanded at 1 cent per kwh would equal 68,000 kwh, well in excess of the plant's capacity, leading to blackouts and brownouts.

FIGURE 12.7   Peak-Load Pricing

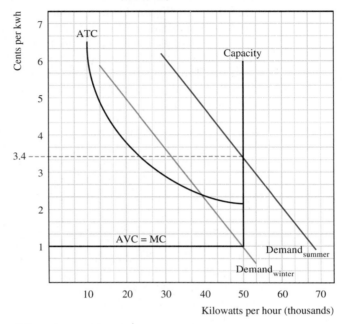

When demand is weaker, the utility charges 1 cent per
kilowatt, so that P = MC and MB = MSC. During the
period of strong summer demand, the utility charges 3.4
cents per kilowatt, again equating P and MC and MB and
MSC. In both instances, available capacity is fully utilized.
Also, the profits earned during the summer cover the
losses incurred during the winter.

The alternative is to raise the kwh rate to 3.4 cents per hour. That
would ration the available supply to demanders willing to pay the MC.
Productive efficiency would be attained, and given the capacity limita-
tion, resources would again be efficiently allocated. Moreover, the utility
would be profitable during the summer. Indeed, if the summer and winter
months balanced out, the utility would earn sufficient revenues over the
year to cover all of its costs. Again, resources are efficiently allocated
without a subsidy.

There's a second advantage to peak-load pricing: capital savings. You
understand why the telephone company charges less during nighttime,
when business use has fallen off. The telephone company needs more
equipment when its traffic flow is jagged and it must accommodate the
peaks, and less if the peaks are toned down. Look again at Figure 12.7.
With Demand$_{summer}$, any price below 3.4 cents per kwh leads to a quantity

demanded greater than 50,000 kilowatts per hour. Regulators may then insist that the utility company expand its capacity to meet the extra demand. But that additional investment would be idle during the other half of the year, hardly a cost-effective investment policy. Thus, the higher summer rates enable the utility to fully utilize existing capacity year round.

Peak-load pricing is a broadly applicable technique that can be employed whenever a firm's demand differs over time in a relatively predictable way. Thus, movie theaters typically charge more during the evenings and weekends, while hotels devoted to the business traveler are less expensive during weekends. They're all trying to even out their demand, use their existing facilities to capacity, and simultaneously reduce the need for additional investment.

Some Practical Issues of Utility Pricing

While most economists are comfortable with the general analysis of public utility regulation, they differ when it comes to applying theory to reality. Both economic and political issues have to be faced in public utility regulation. On the economic front, marginal- and average-cost pricing are inconsistent with a more dynamic efficiency approach. For example, why should a regulated utility's management bother to introduce cost-reducing technology when that merely encourages the regulators to cut the utility's prices? Thus, the pace of innovation will be slowed down. Conversely, why should the utility's decision makers be concerned with controlling costs and avoiding x-inefficiencies? Cost increases can be recouped by filing for price adjustments. The Federal Communications Commission responded to this criticism in 1989 by revising its pricing regulations over AT&T's long-distance telephone rates. The FCC replaced its fixed return on investment mechanism with a price range within which AT&T is free to set rates. Now when AT&T cuts costs, it will not be forced to cut its rate schedule. AT&T keeps any additional profits generated by this cost saving.

Inadequate or delayed price increases, even when justified, and conflicts of interest are two of the problems that surface on the political front. Fear of political repercussions makes regulators reluctant to approve cost-based price increases of such basic necessities as electricity or telephone service. On the other hand, some have argued that regulators are captives of the industry they presumably regulate, defending the interests of the few rather than the public. Regulators are accused of failing to exercise independent judgment, either because they're currying favor with prospective employers or because they came from the regulated utility and will return there when their term in the regulatory agency expires. The notion is compounded by the complexity of modern public utility pricing. Few outsiders can evaluate objectively the appropriateness of a given request for increased rates.

The practical issues of public utility regulation have led some economists to advocate a hands-off policy even in the public utility area. They contend that unregulated utility pricing will in the long run lead to more economically optimal results than will regulation. After all, even a public utility is subject to competition in a technologically advancing society. Certainly, the revolution in communication technology that is making the national network of telephone wires obsolete or the elimination of passenger train traffic by air transport lends some credence to their views. Clearly, however, regulation cannot simply be dismissed. Exposing the weaknesses of a policy does not necessarily justify its abandonment. Like much in economic policy, the issues are complex, and simple theoretical conclusions cannot be transferred naively into the public-policy arena. But then, theory cannot be ignored either.

Estimating the Costs of Monopoly

How significant are the costs of monopoly? Unfortunately, as far as the United States is concerned, the answer is far from clear. The divergence of opinion stems partly from measurement problems but mostly from disagreements about the true nature of monopoly costs.

Measuring the Deadweight Loss

Begin with the simplest analysis of monopoly's costs to the economy, the deadweight loss of Figure 12.1. To compute the deadweight loss for any industry, you must know the LRMC of the nonexistent competitive counterpart market as well as the industry demand curve. Clearly, a higher competitive cost structure or a more elastic demand for the product would reduce the deadweight loss. (Try playing around with the slope of the demand curve in Figure 12.1 and see for yourself.)

Arnold Harberger's pioneering study of monopoly's deadweight loss in the United States is simply an attempt to put numbers to Figure 12.1 for the entire U.S. economy.[11] Harberger assumed that all industries are characterized by long-run constant costs, giving him flat cost curves. Harberger then asserted that any industry's profits above the national average must have been caused by monopoly pricing practices. He further assumed unitary elasticity of demand throughout the U.S. economy.

The latter assumption makes the calculation possible. Let's reduce a monopolist's prices so that the industry earned only average profits. Unitary elasticity of demand guarantees that total revenues would remain the same, since the percentage decline in prices would be precisely offset by the percentage increase in quantity demanded. Look again at Figure 12.1 and at the following relationships that stem from the diagram:

Price	Quantity	Total Revenue	Total Costs	Profits
$6	400,000	$2.4 million	$1.2 million	$1.2 million
$4	600,000	$2.4 million	$1.8 million	$600,000

In this particular range, profits decline by 50 percent after the 50 percent price cut.[12] That's because revenue remained the same but the increased production brought total costs up.

All this implies that if a monopoly were replaced by a competitive market so that profits would fall to the all-industry average, you could calculate the corresponding increase in output. Now the increase in production is the base of the deadweight loss triangle, while the decrease in price is the height. And the missing hypotenuse is right in front of our eyes, since the elasiticity of the demand curve is assumed to be unitary.

Harberger's calculations led him to a startling conclusion in light of the historical fervor of antitrust in the United States. The deadweight loss for the U.S. consumer during the late 1920s, the period covered by his data, approximated $1.50 to $2 per capita. Other studies, using more recent data and different assumptions, have derived both larger and smaller estimates, but for the most part, the studies cannot find any significant deadweight monopoly losses.

Other Costs of Monopoly

But the deadweight loss is not the only cost associated with monopoly. Richard Posner has argued that if a monopoly is profitable, its costs will be artificially inflated by advertisements of its benevolence, payments for political support, and lobbying and other expenses designed to preserve monopoly profits.[13] Such expenditures would be redundant in a competitive economy. Posner is especially critical of government-regulated and thus protected industries, where such excessive costs are not subject to any market competition. He estimated, for example, that during the period of airline price regulation, the industry spent some 20 percent of its sales revenue on such nonproductive costs. In other words, monopoly causes x-inefficiency, which is not measured by simple deadweight loss calculations.

The empirical study of monopoly costs still remains a vast and unexplored territory. On the one hand, present estimates may be too low; on the other, they may be too high. Because econometric studies fail to take into account the dynamics of monopoly, such as the impact of monopoly in stifling innovation, we may be underestimating monopoly's negative impact on the economy. Yet we may be overestimating the net negative impact by failing to consider the benefits of monopoly. In short, the jury is still out. Economists have yet to provide a conclusive answer to the question, How significant is the cost of monopoly to an economy?

Summary

Whether monopoly ought to be controlled or to be free from government regulation is a complex issue. The control option follows directly from a comparative static comparison between the monopoly and perfect competition models. Not only does the monopoly set a higher price and produce less than the competitive firm, and so causes an unrecoverable deadweight loss, but it is also less efficient than the competitive firm and leads to a poorer allocation of scarce resources. The static comparison further implies that controlling monopoly is not only desirable but also possible. Tax policy can recoup some of the lost consumer surplus. Even better, antitrust policies that prevent monopolies from forming or that dissolve existing monopolies can preserve or restore all of the benefits of the competitive marketplace.

The issue becomes more complicated when monopoly is analyzed in a dynamic context. Some economists have argued that implementing antitrust policy is itself costly. Moreover, not even the monopolist is immune from competition. Rarely will the product controlled by the monopolist be so unique that it has no substitutes. Moreover, given the right incentives, domestic and foreign producers will penetrate the monopolist's market. These economists conclude that intervention should be resisted as both costly and unnecessary.

Other economists are less patient with the market. They feel that monopolists can employ limit pricing policies to maintain their domination over the market. Morever, it's likely that a monopolist will retard the rate of technological growth and innovation. Public control of monopoly, they claim, is superior to a "hands-off" attitude.

Intervention has been the norm in the case of public utilities, where dissolving the monopoly would dissipate the economies of scale. Control typically takes the form of price regulation, with average-cost pricing the normal mode. While average-cost pricing does not allocate resources most efficiently, it provides sufficient revenue to cover the utility's costs. Marginal-cost pricing, on the other hand, would better allocate resources, but would force the utility to operate in the red and require government subsidies. Public utility commissions occasionally allow block and/or peak-load pricing techniques, improving resource allocation while still covering the utility's costs.

Has the impact of monopoly on the American scene been catastrophic, discomforting, or negligible? This, too, remains an unresolved controversy. Some have calculated the deadweight loss of monopoly to be insignificant, but others have taken issue with the methodology and have concluded otherwise. The dynamics of monopoly muddy the waters even further. At best, most economists would prefer competition to monopoly but are agnostic about monopoly's actual impact.

This contrast of perfect competition and monopoly, however, may be unimportant in a modern economy. Neither perfect competition nor monopoly is a significant player in the real world. Far more characteristic of the industrial West are oligopolies, which are the subject of the next chapter.

Key Terms

Average-cost pricing
Limit pricing
Marginal-cost pricing

Peak-load pricing
Public utility

Review Questions

1. Specify the static advantages of perfect competition over monopoly and demonstrate them diagrammatically.

2. *a.* Why is a licensing charge superior to an excise tax as a method of monopoly control?
   b. Would that remain true if the monopoly had practiced limit pricing?

3. Coleco Industries rode its highly profitable Cabbage Patch dolls to amazing success during the mid-1980s. But it was forced to file for bankruptcy in 1988 when the craze ended.
   a. Analyze the downfall of this monopolist.
   b. What general observations about monopoly might be derived from this case?

4. Evaluate the arguments for and against antitrust policy.

5. The Virginia State Board of Pharmacy, a professional organization that regulates pharmacists, authorized itself to revoke licenses for unprofessional conduct. The board also ruled that advertising the price of a prescription drug constitutes unprofessional conduct! The Supreme Court in 1975 found this rule violated the public's First Amendment rights. Do you agree

with the court on economic grounds as well? Explain.

6. *a.* What determines whether a monopoly is "natural"?
   b. Why do natural monopolies pose a dilemma for the policymaker?
   c. Why do regulators favor average cost pricing for public utilities?
   d. Why do economists prefer marginal-cost pricing?

7. How do block pricing and peak-load pricing schemes simultaneously avoid resource maldistribution and eliminate the need for a public subsidy?

8. A computerized parking meter that can be programmed to charge different prices during different times of the day is being tested at Boston's Logan Airport.
   a. Why would Logan be interested in this meter, which is 40 percent more expensive than the run-of-the-mill type?
   b. How would Logan vary the meter rates during the day?

9. *a.* How did Harberger measure the deadweight loss of monopoly in the United States?
   b. Do you accept his conclusion that monopoly's cost to the U.S. economy is insignificant? Explain.

Food for Thought

1. The U.S. Department of Justice investigated 23 northeastern schools, including all the Ivy League colleges, for possible

antitrust violation. The Justice Department contended that officials of these institutions met annually to adjust student aid awards. As a result, the prospective student found herself with the same tuition cost (net of financial aid) no matter which of these colleges she selected. The universities claimed that this method enabled the schools to serve the students best, while the Justice Department implied that such measures limited competition for the best students. Analyze the arguments and explore their economic consequences.

2. When R. D. Percy and AGB Television Research, national TV rating services, suspended operations due to continued losses, they left the entire market to A. C. Nielsen Co. Do the economics of antitrust suggest that Nielsen should be prosecuted, since it now monopolizes the market? Explain.

3. The Anatomical Chart Company of Skokie, Illinois, advertises itself as "the world's only source of real bone skeletons and skulls." Most of its customers are physicians and medical schools, but at $1,995, you, too, can own a real bone human skeleton. It maintains its monopoly by having a secret supply source.
   a. Analyze how control over information limits competition.
   b. Would you insist that the company be forced to disclose its source? Explain.

4. The ever increasing cost of postage has led heavy mail users to send packages and correspondence through private delivery systems.
   a. What economic arguments could explain why it took until the 1980s for such companies to emerge?
   b. Show how private deliverers can operate profitably and thus break the monopoly of the U.S. Post Office.
   c. How would you expect the post office to react?

5. Antitrust prosecution during the Reagan years tended to focus on mergers between companies that produced similar products. Mergers of companies involved in different stages of production (e.g., a lumber company and a furniture manufacturer) typically escaped scrutiny. Do you agree with that policy?

6. *a.* How could regulators control a monopoly by using a price ceiling?
   b. At what level would you set the price assuming U-shaped average and marginal cost curves?
   c. What would be the advantages and disadvantages of this policy as opposed to dissolving the monopoly?

7. Explain the economic rationale of a block pricing policy for a public utility in which greater use of the product led to *higher* utility rates.

Suggested Readings

For details on antitrust economics, see Roger D. Blair and David L. Kaserman, *Antitrust Economics* (Homewood, Ill.: Richard D. Irwin, 1985). A review article by Morton Kamien and Nancy Schwartz, "Market Structure and Innovation: A Survey," *Journal of Economic Literature* 13 (March 1975), pp. 1–37, is somewhat dated but nevertheless will give you a broad taste of the issues.

For additional studies of monopoly's cost, see David Schwartzman, "The Burden of Monopoly," *Journal of Political Economy* 68 (November/December 1960), pp. 627–30; Dean A. Worcester, Jr., "New Estimates of the Welfare Loss to Monopoly, United States: 1956–1969," *Southern Economic Journal* 40 (October 1973), pp. 234–45; and Yale Brozen, *Concentration, Mergers, and Public Policy* (New York: Macmillan,

1982), Chapter 9. The only study that finds a significant impact—in the order of 6 percent of national income—is David R. Kamerschen, "An Estimation of the 'Welfare Losses' from Monopoly in the American Economy," *Western Eco-*

nomic Journal 4 (Summer, 1966), pp. 221–36. Kamerschen's study is criticized in Victor Goldberg, "Welfare Losses and Monopoly: The Unmaking of an Estimate," *Economic Inquiry* 16 (April 1978), pp. 310–12.

Notes and Answers

1. *Hamilton Shoe, Inc.* v. *United Shoe Machinery Corp.,* 392 U.S. 481 (1968).
2. If you're not sure why this is so, check back to Figure 7.10b (p. 236) and the related discussion.
3. What about lost producer surplus? Because the LRMC is horizontal, and thus the long-run supply curve is constant, there isn't any. However, where the LRS is positively sloped, there'd also be a deadweight loss stemming from the producers' side. (Check back to Figure 8.7b, p. 278.)
4. To be sure, it's impossible to rule out a situation where the monopolist is as efficient as the competitive firm. Certainly that's the picture in Figure 12.1. It's also true when the MR = MC output is identical with the minimum point of the AC curve. In monopoly these situations would be fortuitous, whereas in a competitive marketplace, there's pressure to reach minimum cost.
5. 175,000; \$8.25; \$3.85 × 175,000 = \$673,750; (\$8.25 − \$6.90)(175,000) = \$236, 250.
6. Fixed; "No" for all other answers.
7. If the probability of losing the case is 40 percent and the damage equals \$5 million dollars, then the probability of keeping the \$5 million is 60 percent. The average expected gain or loss would be (.60)(\$5 million) + (.40)(−\$5 million) or \$1 million. That net gain turns into a loss under triple damages: (.60)(\$5 million) + (.40)(−\$15 million) = −\$3 million.
8. Two parting observations are worth making in the Hamilton versus United case. First, note the year in which the suit was initially filed and the year in which the Supreme

Court finally ruled. Patience is surely a virtue in major antitrust cases. Second, the courts rejected a most innovative argument. United Shoe claimed that Hamilton had not really suffered any damages since it had undoubtedly passed on the higher machinery leasing costs to consumers!

9. *Polaroid* v. *Kodak,* 641 F Supp. 828 (D. Mass 1986). Polaroid was awarded almost \$1 billion in damages and penalty.
10. Typically, utilities will remedy supply shortages by activating their older plants. Since the MC of these sources is higher, it's analytically equivalent to the rising MC curve used here.
11. Arnold C. Harberger, "Monopoly and Resource Allocation," *American Economic Review* 44, no. 2 (May 1954), pp. 77–87. Note that Harberger and those who followed in his footsteps defined a monopoly industry as one that earned more than average profits, a definition that corresponds more closely to the overall concept of imperfect competition rather than to the narrower definition of a single-firm industry used in this chapter.
12. A bit of arithmetic tolerance is necessary here. The price cut is 50 percent only by dividing the \$2 increase into the latter number, \$4.
13. Richard Posner, "The Social Costs of Monopoly and Regulation," *Journal of Political Economy* 83 (August 1975), pp. 807–28. Those who read Judge Posner's provocative article should also study Franklin M. Fisher, "The Social Costs of Monopoly and Regulation: Posner Reconsidered," *Journal of Political Economy* 93 (April 1985), pp. 410–16.

13

OLIGOPOLY: A GREAT NAME FOR A CONTEMPORARY BOARD GAME

In the factory we make cosmetics. In the store we sell hope.
Charles Revson, Founder of Revlon

All Quiet on the Price Front in Cola Wars
Wall Street Journal Headline, 1989

Learning Objectives

In this chapter you'll learn about:
- Why oligopolies exist.
- The classical theories of oligopoly pricing policies—the Cournot duopoly model, price leadership, and the kinked demand curve.
- The analysis underlying the ways oligopolists compete: discounts, advertising, and quality.
- Game theory and how it is used to explain oligopolistic behavior.
- Methods actually used by oligopolists to set prices and to reduce uncertainty.

Games Economists and Companies Play

The Prisoners' Dilemma

An **oligopoly** is a market dominated by a *few* sellers.

Although the relationship between the famous prisoners' dilemma and **oligopoly,** the subject of this chapter, will become apparent only later, the

429

reasoning involved in this case is challenging in itself. And it is extremely pertinent to oligopoly theory.

The James Brothers, Jesse and Frank, have been brought into the Ranger station charged with robbing the local bank. In line with the standard operating procedure, Frank is interrogated by a lone Ranger and Jesse by another. Each is offered the same deal. Frank's is represented by the following **payoff matrix:**

A **payoff matrix** records the outcomes for a given combination of actions.

	Jesse's options	
	Confess	**Don't confess**
Confess	5 years in prison	Freedom
Don't confess	10 years in prison	2 years in prison

Frank's options

Frank's choices are to confess or to keep his lips sealed. But whether Frank will be freed or imprisoned depends not only on his own actions but on his brother's as well. If Frank doesn't snitch but Jesse implicates his brother, Frank will serve 10 years for his recalcitrance. On the other hand, if he confesses but Jesse doesn't, then Frank's reward for setting his brother up is freedom. If they both confess, they each serve 5 years, while if they both remain steadfast in their protestations of innocence, they are sent up on a lesser charge. As Frank's attorney, what would you advise Frank to do—squeal or remain steadfast?

You realize, of course, that Jesse is being given the same options. That raises a critical distinction between this case and virtually all the others found in earlier chapters: *mutual interdependence*. The optimal choice of one party is intrinsically linked to that of another. Consider now mutual interdependence in a market context.

Coke versus Pepsi

When was the last time you noticed a price difference between a can of Coke and a can of Pepsi, both purchased from the same convenience store? In probing for a reason for such price uniformity, you might consider two possible causes. First, the market is so competitive that long-run equilibrium position has been reached. Both companies have been forced by market pressures to set the lowest possible price to their retailers, and that low price is passed on to consumers. A second explanation might be that the market is not competitive, but the two companies understand that engaging in continuous price competition helps neither and harms both.

The second explanation appears more plausible. Perfect competition requires that sellers be sufficiently numerous so that no single firm can control price, a condition not met in the U.S. soft-drink market. In 1990, for example, Coke accounted for slightly over 40 percent of total U.S. soft-drink sales, Pepsi 32 percent, Dr. Pepper and 7UP shared 16 percent, and the rest divided up the remaining 12 percent. Surely, PepsiCo and Coca-Cola recognize their interdependence.

Yet that interdependence manifests itself in strange ways. First, price competition among the companies is an aberration, not the rule. Moreover, prices do not seem to reflect either demand or cost changes except with a very long lag. Second, one can hardly deny that Coke and Pepsi compete aggressively for market share. Such economic behavior indicates that neither the monopoly model nor the perfect competition model will be very fruitful for understanding oligopoly.

The challenge of this chapter is to explain how oligopolistic firms react to mutual interdependence. We begin with the classical treatment of oligopolistic pricing and then proceed to explore ways in which oligopolists do compete: discounting, advertising, and quality differentiation. We'll then examine the more popular theoretical framework for analyzing interdependence, **game theory.** The chapter then turns to some typical pricing methods actually used by oligopolists as well as the strategies they employ to reduce uncertainty.

This chapter may well be the most important of the market structure chapters in this book. Perfect competition is an important theoretical model, yet you realize that no industries are perfectly competitive. Monopoly occurs in the United States, but it is overwhelmingly regulated. Oligopoly, however, is almost synonymous with big business and, more than anything else, characterizes U.S. capitalism. Whether the oligopolies are **differentiated** or **undifferentiated**—from the manufacture of breakfast foods and light bulbs, assemblers of automobiles and steel sheeting, suppliers of network television broadcasts and long-distance telephone services—we come into daily contact with the products of oligopoly.

Game theory focuses on strategies chosen by interdependent players and the consequences of implementing the strategies.

The products marketed by a **differentiated oligopoly** have unique qualities in contrast to those sold by an **undifferentiated oligopoly,** which are identical no matter who is the producer.

MicroQuery   Which of the oligopolies listed above are differentiated and which undifferentiated?

1

Why Oligopoly?

The reasons underlying both the formation and the perserverence of oligopoly are identical to those used in Chapter 11 to explain monopoly:

efficiency, artificial entry barriers, and government sanctions. But while the theme is the same, understanding oligopoly requires that the theme be played with some minor variations.

Efficiency

Monopoly is efficient when economies of scale are so pervasive that the market can support only one optimally sized firm. Analogously, when the market is sufficiently large to permit the coexistence of but a few optimally sized firms, the efficient outcome is an oligopolistic market. So, if demand for soft drinks is 36 billion quarts per year but least-cost production occurs when a firm is capable of processing 12 billion quarts, then the market has room for only three optimally sized firms.

Artificial Entry Barriers

In theory, and sometimes in fact, collusion remains a source of barriers to entry, preventing competitors from entering a market that is already oligopolistic. Nevertheless, most economists doubt the practical significance of collusion in the United States. Instead, they point to other barriers, the most important of which are:

- Brand names.
- Information.
- Capital requirements.
- Strategic considerations.

Brand Names.   Think of the confidence you have when you buy a Jaguar, an IBM computer, a Sony Walkman, or any of the many other brand-name products you encounter daily. Brand names signify quality, based on a reputation that has been earned over years of sales. In a broader sense, established firms have developed *customer relationships* that strengthen the ties between producers and their buyers. Any competitor that wishes to enter an established oligopoly market must first overcome consumer allegiance to existing brands. While such barriers can be surmounted with sufficient patience and money, the hurdle itself deters entry.

Information Advantages.   The established firm will have assembled a network of contacts and amassed experience. Suppliers and sales outlets are nutured over the years. Similarly, the established oligopolist will be able to call upon an inventory of experience: Which particular advertising agency is best for print ads and which for TV advertising? Which supplier has been flexible on pricing or reliable on meeting supply deadlines? Perhaps even more important in some industries is the experience of the firm's scientists, facilitating the development of new products or the improvement old ones. In general, the battle between the novice and the pro is normally one-sided, and the unwillingness of the novice to engage the pro retards entry.

Capital Requirements.   The deep pockets needed to overcome brand loyalty and to acquire experience are merely examples of the financial demands placed on firms attempting to penetrate an oligopolistic market. The typical established oligopoly in the United States consists of a few giant enterprises. How much capital would you need to set up production facilities to compete with Eastman Kodak in the film market or with Procter & Gamble in the soap and detergent industry? Potential entrants often lack adequate capital, find banks reluctant to finance ventures with but slight prospects of success, or are forced to agree to terms that place them at a cost disadvantage. In short, it's hard, often impossible, to attain the critical mass of finance needed to compete on even terms with existing oligopolists.

Strategic Considerations.   Brand names, superior information, and lower capital costs are side effects of policies that are primarily instituted for purposes other than inhibiting entry. Quite different is **strategic entry deterrence.** Limit pricing, mentioned in connection with monopoly, is equally applicable to oligopolists, who purposely set lower prices in order to deter entry. They may also enter into long-range contracts with suppliers to control the availability of a critical input, forcing potential competitors to develop alternative and more expensive supply channels. In either case, such strategic moves preclude easy entry by those seeking to challenge the oligopolists.

> **Strategic entry deterrence** policies are specifically designed to keep competitors from penetrating the industry.

Government Sanctions

Just as government actions preserve monopolies, so, too, do they maintain oligopolies. Some examples: Import restrictions on cars protect the Big Three automotive oligopolists. Government-supported control over airport gates complicates entry into passenger air transportation. In cities where cab fares are regulated, the quid pro quo of price fixing is regulator-enforced entry restriction.

In short, the answer to "Why oligopoly?" is that a few sellers are able to achieve market control because, for one reason or another, potential competitors are prevented from challenging their dominant position. The paucity of rivals leads to interdependence. In contrast to the perfectly competitive firm, whose production policies follow from the overall movement of the market rather than from the actions of any individual competitor, the oligopolist cannot ignore its fellow oligopolists when making decisions. Interdependence looms large in the models of oligopolistic pricing that are reviewed in the next section. It is the key to understanding both price uniformity and stability among oligopolists.

Formal Oligopoly Models in a Classic Mode

None of the three models surveyed in this section captures the diversity of oligopolistic behavior. In any given industry, one particular explanation may be useful at one time and a second at a different moment, so the theories that follow should be seen as complementary rather than competitive.

The Cournot Model

Duopoly is an industry characterized by *two* sellers.

The French economist Augustin A. Cournot devised one of the first **duopoly** models in 1838. Don't be put off by the strange simplifying assumptions, for the outcome is intriguing and can be applied more generally.

Cour and Not are the only bottlers of some fizzy mineral water; their marginal costs are zero, and both lack the wits to learn from experience. Specifically, each assumes that the other duopolist will not change its output in response to the output decision of the first. But despite their denial of interdependence, each duopolist's actions turn out to reflect the actions of the other.

Begin with the uppermost demand curve in Figure 13.1a, which represents both the industry demand and Cour's demand. Cour sets his price at 6 francs per bottle and produces 12 million bottles daily, in line with the MR = MC criterion. Not realizes that Cour has left a significant segment of the market to her, and she calculates her demand curve in Figure 13.1b by subtracting 12 million bottles a day from the industry demand curve. That generates the lowest demand curve in Figure 13.1b (D_N^1), the corresponding MR_N^1 curve, and the optimum output of 6 million bottles. Back to Cour, who suddenly notices that the public buys 6 million bottles from Not. Cour recalculates his demand curve by subtracting 6 million along the entire length of $D_{industry}$. (Here's where interdependence is recognized.) Cour's new demand and corresponding marginal revenue curves are marked with a superscript 2; optimum output falls to 9 million bottles daily. But if Cour produces less, there's room for Not to expand; her new demand and MR curves are also indicated by a superscript 2. (How much will Not now produce? _____ million bottles.[2])

You can see the pattern: Cour's output is falling. Not's is rising. Where will it all stop? Interestingly enough, a stable equilibrium is possible, and is indicated by the superscript 3 curves in both Figure 13.1a and Figure 13.1b. Take a careful look at Cour's position when he realizes that Not is selling 8 million bottles daily. The maximum demand available to Cour is 16 million bottles (24 less the 8 sold by Not), which means that

FIGURE 13.1   **Cournot Duopoly Pricing**

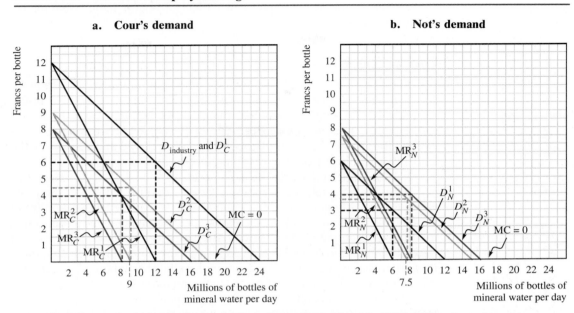

a. Cour's demand   **b. Not's demand**

When Cour enters the industry, he faces the industry demand curve. With MC = 0, optimum output = 12 million bottles per day. Not now enters, and realizes that Cour has already captured half the market, so Not's initial demand curves equals $D_{industry}$ minus 12 million, or D_N^1. That generates MR_N^1 and an optimum output of 6 million units. Back to Cour, who finds that with Not selling 6 million, his demand has fallen to $D_{industry}$ minus 6 million or D_C^2. Cour's optimum output falls to 9 million, which of course enlarges Not's market to D_N^2. This process continues until a stable equilibrium is reached with both Cour (along D_C^3) and Not (along D_N^3) producing 8 million units each.

Cour would sell 8 million. Apply now this very same reasoning to Not. If Cour sells 8 million, then the maximum Not can sell is 16 million and her optimum output will be 8 million. Both will price their product at an identical 4 francs, and neither has any impetus to change output. Consequently each will capture a third of the market, while the final third remains unsatisfied.[3]

MICROQUERY   How does this duopoly result compare to the perfect competitive outcome on the one hand and the monopoly equilibrium on the other?
To perfect competition: _____

To monopoly: _____

4

While price uniformity and market stability are direct consequences of the Cournot model, the assumed naïvité of oligopolistic behavior remains a serious flaw.

Price Leadership

Under **price leadership,** the price set by one oligopolist is adopted by all other oligopolists. An announced, verifiable price is called a **list price.**

In contrast to the Cournot framework and far more consistent with modern economies is the **price leadership** model, which stresses the price-setting role of a single oligopolist, the price leader. However the leader arrives at an announced **list price,** it must be tolerated by the other oligopolists, for should the other oligopolists be dissatisifed and not follow the leader, all will lose from the resulting instability.

A price leader might set the cartel price of Figure 11.7a (p. 386). But in contrast to a cartel, the initiating oligopolistic firm would set the price without explicitly consulting the others. Also, the price leader would not allocate output among fellow oligopolists; each would sell however much it could at the price leader's price. Alternatively, the price leader might park at the Cournot price. Again, as long as the other oligopolists implicity agree, the price remains uniform and stable throughout the industry.

More complex models of price leadership have been developed,[5] but they all share the same essential point: oligopolistic interdependence leads to a uniform and stable price even without explicit collusion.

Price leadership models are characterized by *symmetry*. The followers follow the leader both for price increases and decreases. (Some examples will be found in MicroBits 13.1.) That's not true of the final model—the kinked demand curve.

Competitive Oligopoly: The Kinked Demand Curve

In the kinked demand curve model devised by American economics professor Paul Sweezy in 1939, recognition of interdependence leads to uniform pricing even in the absence of collusion or price leadership. This result follows from an *asymmetric* assumption arrived at independently by each oligopolist: "My fellow oligopolists will follow price decreases but not price increases." The reasoning is straightforward. Because of interdependence, when Huey cuts price, he draws customers away from Dewey and Louie. Self-protection mandates that Dewey and Louie retaliate. But when Huey raises price, customers will be attracted to Dewey and Louie, who have no reason to follow Huey upward.

Pursue the consequences of this behavioral assumption in Figure 13.2, which depicts Huey's present position. Begin with the initial price of $250 for a Huey-made flute; sales are 1,000 monthly. Huey now considers boosting the price to $262.50. But because neither Dewey nor Louie will join Huey in even this modest increase, Huey realizes that his sales will drop drastically. Huey's clients will simply switch to his competitors'

Price Leadership Is Alive and Kicking

1. Automobile Rentals

In recent weeks, Hertz and Avis quietly raised their extra-cost options—and competitors are likely to match. . . . Both companies increased their drop-off charges by as much as 50 percent; dropping a car off more than 1,000 miles from where it was rented now costs $750. They also increased their "collision-damage waiver" to $9.95 a day from $8.95.*

2. Interest Rates

a. On the Rise. "More large banks raised their prime lending rates April 1 to 7¾ percent from 7½ percent, matching moves by Citibank and Chase Manhattan."§

b. On the Fall. "Many large banks cut their prime lending rate to 8½ percent from 8¾ percent. . . . Morgan Guaranty Trust Co. led the way"‖

---

* *The Wall Street Journal,* August 20, 1987, p. 25.

§ April 2, 1987, p. 48.

‖ February 3, 1988, pp. 3, 12.

3. The Challenge to U.S. Steel (Now USX)

The following series of headlines appeared between May 9 and May 13, 1977, in *The Wall Street Journal:*

- "Republic Will Increase Steel Prices; Top 3 Firms Silent as Lykes Follows: Rises Averaging 8.8 Percent, 6.8 Percent Surprise Some"
- "U.S. Steel Undercuts Price Boosts Announced by Republic and Lykes: Concern Plans to Lift Quotes an Average 6 percent June 19"
- "Lykes Price Rise Is Cut to Level Set by U.S. Steel: National Also Will Follow Industry Leader with 6 percent Average Boost on June 19"
- "Republic Steel Rolls Back Boost to Average 6 percent: Inland, Wheeling Also Will Match U.S. Steel Rise; Bethlehem Studies Move"
- "Bethlehem, J&L Join Steel Boosts of Average 6 percent: Moves Make It Certain Price Pattern Established by U.S. Steel Will Prevail"

---

flutes. The demand curve above $250 then will be highly elastic. On the other hand, Huey really can't increase sales very much by cutting price below $250. Since Dewey and Louie join him on the downswing, Huey won't attract any of their customers. At best, all three will pick up some new customers induced by the fall in industry price. The demand curve below $250 therefore will be less elastic and perhaps even inelastic. The result: The kinked demand curve in Figure 13.2 implies that any change in price will be a change for the worse.

That conclusion is borne out even more strongly by examining Huey's optimum profit position. The kinked demand curve gives rise to

FIGURE 13.2   The Kinked Demand Curve

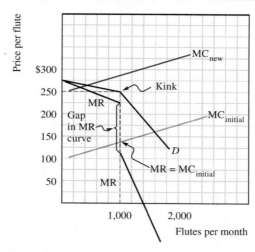

With price equal to $250 per flute, Huey
considers changing the price. If he were to
raise price, his fellow oligopolists would
not follow, and so Huey loses substantial
sales. If Huey were to cut price, Dewey
and Louie would match his price
reductions, and so sales would not increase
by much. Huey's kinked demand curve,
which conforms to this belief in
asymmetrical competitor reaction, leads
Huey to maintain the $250 price, in line
with the equality of MR and $MC_{initial}$.
Indeed, MC can fluctuate anywhere within
the MR gap without leading Huey to
attempt a price change.

an interrupted MR curve, with the gap lying below the $250 price. (You
might want to glance back at Figure 11.6c, p. 384, which is analogous.)
Now with marginal cost given by $MC_{initial}$, you understand that the MR =
MC point occurs at an output of 1,000 and a price of $250. And, of course,
since Dewey and Louie reason identically, Huey's analysis and conclusion is repeated for the others, so that all charge $250.

The kinked demand curve model also suggests an answer to price
stability. Input costs may rise or fall. But as long as marginal costs fluctuate within the range of the MR gap, optimum profit dictates maintaining
price. It's only when marginal cost shifts to MC_{new} that Huey will be
inclined to reprice his product.

Once again, the kinked demand curve model doesn't answer all questions. Indeed, one troubling enigma is how the kink was formed in the first

---

Ditto for the Kinked Demand Curve

1. The Airlines

Two weeks ago, American Airlines and other carriers said that, starting March 16 [1987], they would significantly limit the benefits of new "MaxSaver" fares. But Texas Air Corp., the nation's largest airline, refused to go along, and yesterday American and the others backed off.*

---

* *The Wall Street Journal*, February 27, 1987, p. 4.

2. Aluminum

Bowing to competitive pressure, Aluminum Co. of America and Kaiser Aluminum and Chemical Corp. quietly rolled back a portion of recent price increases on certain automotive products.

The aluminum producers confirmed reports that they are matching the smaller boosts on sheet and bumper stock posted by the Reynolds Metal Co. and Alcan Aluminum Corp.§

---

§ *The Wall Street Journal*, December 16, 1980, p. 4.

---

place. But if the kinked demand curve theory does not provide an all-encompassing analysis of oligopolistic behavior, it nevertheless contributes to a better understanding of pricing policy among oligopolists. (See MicroBits 13.2.)

The Cournot, price leadership, and kinked demand curve theories outlined in this section all explain the absence of price competition in oligopolistic industries. Nevertheless, executives in such markets often complain about the competitive actions of their fellow oligopolists. In truth, restricted forms of price competition are considered acceptable. So, too, is competition in advertising and in product quality, issues that are taken up in the next section.

Competition among the Few: Implicit Prices, Advertising, and Quality

Respectable Price Competition

While oligopolists tend to maintain list prices in order to avoid retaliatory price cutting, or "price wars," they tolerate certain business practices that have the effect of shaving prices implicitly. In the automobile industry, manufacturers rarely reduce sticker prices, but they offer special deals when sales are slow. Low interest rate financing, cash rebates, option packages at reduced prices, and longer warranties all are in fact price reductions, but they're never announced as such. Oligopolists in the processed-food industry compete with cents-off coupons,[6] cash rebates, and merchandise premiums. The airlines shave prices with free mileage plans and vacation package deals that combine air, hotel, and car rentals. These examples are only suggestive; surely you can find others. But they do have some interesting implications, one of which will be explored here.

An Interpretation.   When you consider that many price-cutting options are more expensive to institute than a simple price reduction—coupons, for example, entail design, printing, distributing, and redeeming costs—you must wonder, Why don't manufacturers choose the cheaper expedient of temporarily reducing price?

Figure 13.3 suggests one possible answer. Consumers respond differently to price hikes that restore list-price reductions as opposed to the implicit price increases that accompany the termination of discounts. If

FIGURE 13.3   Discounts versus List Price Reductions

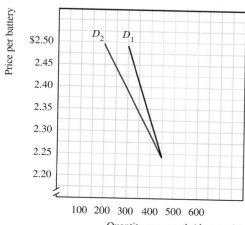

A price reduction from $2.49 to $2.24 per 9-volt Celladur alkaline battery can be achieved either by cutting the list price or by distributing a 25 cents off coupon. In either case, quantity demanded rises along D_1 from 300,000 to 450,000. But an asymmetric reaction occurs if the list price is raised, in which case consumers react by moving up D_2 and reducing quantity demanded from 450,000 to 200,000. If the coupon is not reissued, quantity demanded moves along D_1 and returns to 300,000.

consumers are conditioned to a "normal" price that is synonymous with a list price, then might not the following sequence occur? Hypothesize that consumers have become accustomed to a list price of, say, $2.49 for a 9-volt Celladur alkaline battery. Either reducing that list price by a quarter or sending out a "25 cents off" coupon would move the quantity demanded down on D_1 to 450,000 per month. But despite the identity of reactions on the downside, the two alternative policies may give rise to a difference in consumer perceptions. A reduction in the list price is interpreted as a decline in the normal price, or what the commodity should sell for. Consequently, when price is increased to its former level, consumers feel that they are being exploited. On the other hand, when purchasers receive a discount coupon, they have positive feelings and do not resent paying the nondiscounted price once they've used up the coupon.

This difference in perceptions leads to two different market reactions, indicated by D_1 and D_2. When the coupon is used or expires, consumer quantity demanded reverts to the starting point on D_1. But when the price is first cut and then raised, the movement down on D_1 is followed by a movement up on D_2—a response that reflects consumer distaste with the increase in price.

If such is the reasoning of oligopolists, you can well understand why they maintain fixed list prices and compete with various discount incentives.

Competition in Advertising

Neither price discounts nor advertising is necessary in a perfectly competitive market. But in oligopolistic markets, more so differentiated oligopolies than undifferentiated ones, advertising can divert sales from other oligopolists and so increase the revenues of the successful advertiser. That's why oligopolists account for a large percentage of TV and print media advertising on the national level.

How Much Advertising? The View from the Firm. The economics of advertising is simple in principle if complex in practice. In theory, successful advertising shifts the demand curve outward, enabling the oligopolist to sell more at the same price, to raise prices and sell the same quantity, or to raise both price and quantity sold.[7] The first quote at the beginning of this chapter suggests this underlying objective of Revlon's advertising strategy: to sell hope rather than cosmetics. The increase in demand is presumably quantifiable and can be measured against the increased costs that advertising requires. A profit-maximizing oligopolist should advertise as long as the marginal revenue from advertising exceeds its marginal cost. In fact, this analysis is identical to that discussed in connection with the firm's search costs and revenues (Figure 8.9, p. 286).

Quality versus Price

Oligopolists compete in the quality of the product they sell, offering a better product at a higher price. The quality versus price decision is also simple to sketch out on the conceptual level, but again, converting theoretical into practical conclusions is complicated indeed.

Finding Optimum Quality.   Figure 13.4a compares three alternatives facing a jeans manufacturer in an oligopolistic market. The demand curves represent jeans of three different qualities, with the quality of $3 > 2 > 1$. Since higher-quality jeans cost more to produce, each demand curve is paired with its appropriate marginal cost curve.

Figure 13.4a represents the initial phase of a straightforward method for resolving which quality of jeans the firm should market. Treat each quality as a different product and determine profit-maximizing price and quantity for each. (You'll have to do this on your own by first providing MR curves in this panel.) Then calculate the profit for each quality, using the fact that $TR = PQ$ and a constant $MC = AVC$, so that $TVC = (AVC)Q$. (For these calculations, let $TFC = \$100,000$). Figure 13.4b plots the profits for each quality, so that the oligopolist merely has to find the

FIGURE 13.4   An Oligopolist Selects a Price-Quality Package

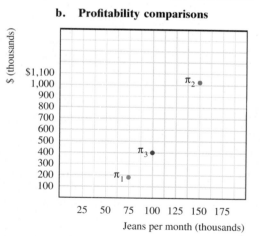

a.   **Three price-quality options**

b.   **Profitability comparisons**

a.   As quality improves, demand shifts rightward, but costs rise, too. The producer can calculate the optimum price and quantity for each option. You can do that by first supplying the appropriate MR curves.

b.   Having determined price and output, the producer can calculate total revenue for each option. Given constant MC curves and a $100,000 total fixed cost, the producer can calculate TC. The three profit points indicated here are the result of these calculations. Clearly, option 2 is optimal.

highest profit point and backtrack to Figure 13.4a to find the corresponding quality and price. In this case, it's quality 2.

Quality Differentiation.   As a matter of fact, the either-or choice of the jeans example in Figure 13.4 precludes marketing a **product line.** Many oligopolists offer consumers a variety of qualities, catering both to those who seek economy in price and to those for whom price ranks lower in priority than quality. The advantage of quality differentiation is identical to that of the third-degree price discrimination model of monopoly (Figure 11.6, p. 384). The producer extracts additional profits by catering to individual tastes. (The potential for abuse is examined in MicroBits 13.3.)

A supplier's **product line** consists of a variety of products that are similar to each other in terms of function but that vary in quality and price.

The early days of the Ford–General Motors competition highlights the contrast in policies. Henry Ford insisted on offering customers one type of car. When asked about the range of colors available for the car, Ford is reputed to have answered: "People can have the Model T in any color—so long as it's black."[8] Right from the start, GM offered a varied product line—the corporation was formed by merging a number of automobile manufacturers—and so attracted a broad range of economic classes to its showrooms. The supremacy of GM in domestic automobile sales can be traced to this product line policy, even though now all automobile manufacturers pursue similar strategies.

In terms of Figure 13.4, the quality differentiator simultaneously faces all three demand curves, produces all three products, and sells them at the appropriate prices. Profits then are the sum of π_1, π_2, and π_3.

Game Theory: Strategic Decision Making

Game theory was designed to analyze strategic choices under conditions of interdependence. Its robustness enables it to deal with collusive and noncollusive behavior, single and repeat decisions, and certain and uncertain situations.

Oligopoly and the Prisoners' Dilemma

Let's return to Frank James's choices at the chapter's opening, but let's rephrase them into an oligopoly situation. Instead of being accused criminals, Frank and Jesse are now corporate managers who must decide their pricing strategies. Frank's payoffs are listed in the following matrix:

		Jesse's options	
		Maintain	**Undercut**
Frank's options	**Maintain**	$10 million	−$5 million
	Undercut	$15 million	$1 million

The Gullible Consumer: The Rule of Thumb that Sucks

While consumers can easily distinguish certain quality aspects of common household products, evaluating quality often requires technical competence that is beyond the ability of the typical consumer. (Recall Chapter 1's dilemma of finding a competent and honest mechanic.) Indeed, even in the case of foods and beverages, blindfolded consumers have frequently been unable to distinguish between brands.

One thing, however, is sure: quality costs. So we expect that higher quality comes at a premium price. That presumption has led to a rule of thumb: If it's more expensive, it's better. While this rule is often true, it can become an instrument of exploitation in the hands of an unscrupulous seller. Why offer better quality at a higher price? Why not, instead, just raise the price and let consumers believe they're acquiring a better quality product? (In terms of Figure 13.4a: Price out D_3 and MC_1.*)

———————

* $P = \$16.25$; $Q = 275,000$; $TR = \$4,468,750$; $TC = \$787,500$; $\pi = \$3,681,250$.

These numbers, as well as the solutions to Figure 13.6a, are based on solving two equations: (1) $Q = a - b\text{MR}$, and (2) $P = c - dQ$.

In this particular case:

$$Q = 300,000 - (30,000/\$30)\text{MR}.$$

That's not an uncommon occurrence and has been practiced by major firms as well as minor ones. Some years ago, General Motors angered Oldsmobile buyers who discovered that GM had substituted Chevrolet engines in the more expensive Oldsmobile. Beech-Nut executives were convicted in 1987 for selling cheap sugar water instead of the expensive apple juice they claimed they were producing. Some years ago, a student told me about his lipstick manufacturer father, who sold a premium brand, high-priced lipstick and a cheaper lipstick that were identical products!

The moral: Consumer beware.

———————

Since $MC = \$2.50$ and in equilibrium $MC = MR$, we can find the optimum Q by substituting $\$2.50$ for MR, yielding

$$Q = 300,000 - (10,000)(2.50) =$$
$$300,000 - 25,000 = 275,000.$$

Substitute 275,000 for Q in the second equation to determine P:

$$P = \$30 - (\$30/600,000)(275,000) = \$30 -$$
$$(\$8,250/600) =$$
$$\$30 - \$13.75 = \$16.25.$$

Try solving for one of the other price/quantity points in Figure 13.6a if you've not already done so.

THE BORN LOSER

Source: Copyright © 1967 *Born Loser*, reprinted by permission of NEA.

Frank can maintain his own price no matter how Jesse reacts, or he can undercut whatever price Jesse sets. If he maintains his price and Jesse implicitly cooperates by mimicking Frank's price, then Frank's payoff matrix indicates a gain of $10 million. On the other hand, if Jesse undercuts Frank, then Frank stands to lose $5 million as his customers abandon Frank's firm. On the other hand, Frank can undercut Jesse, with two possible results. If Jesse will maintain his price no matter what, then Frank stands to attract Jesse's customers and so profit $15 million. If Jesse matches the price cut and a price war starts, then neither gains the other's customers, but the lower price does bring new demanders into the market and so Frank gains $1 million.

What would you advise Frank?

A **dominant strategy** occurs when one player's best strategy is entirely independent of the strategy chosen by the other player.

Actually, Frank's **dominant strategy** is to undercut Jesse's price, for Frank will then always be better-off irrespective of Jesse's price policy. If Jesse always maintained his price, then Frank's undercutting would bring in $15 million in profits instead of only $10 million had he maintained the status quo. Similarly, had Jesse started a price war, then by joining in, would Frank gain $1 million instead of losing the $5 million that passivity would have cost.

MICROQUERY

What is the dominant strategy of Frank, the alleged bank robber—confess or bluff it out? Why? _____

9

Turn now to Jesse. Should he maintain price or undercut? That, of course depends on Jesse's payoff matrix. If Jesse's matrix is symmetrical to Frank's, so that we could simply reverse the names, then clearly Jesse's dominant strategy would also be to undercut. And since each will undercut the other's price, each will profit $1 million.

But suppose Jesse's matrix looked like this:

		Frank's options	
		Maintain	**Undercut**
Jesse's options	**Maintain**	$10 million	$1 million
	Undercut	$15 million	−$2 million

Jesse has no dominant strategy. What's optimal for him depends on Frank's course of action. If Frank were to maintain price, then Jesse should undercut. But if Frank undercut, then Jesse should maintain his price. In this situation, Jesse must put himself in Frank's shoes, identify Frank's strategy, and then act in his own best interest.

Perfect Information.   The solution is simple if we can assume that Jesse is fully informed about Frank's payoff matrix. Then, knowing that Frank's optimal strategy is to undercut, Jesse will maintain. Although Frank gains $15 million and Jesse only $1 million, these strategies are nevertheless optimal for each player. In the language of game theory, the players have achieved a **Nash equilibrium.**[10] (If you don't think so, try alternatives.)

A **Nash equilibrium** requires that each player's strategy be optimal, *given the known strategy of the other*.

Variations on a Theme

The game theory approach becomes more complex when the same players play the game more than once or when they are not fully informed about each other. We'll begin with a simpler application.

Cooperative Games.   Although it appears intuitive that from the firm's viewpoint, cooperation is better than competition, game theory provides both a simple rationale and some additional insight. Return to the prisoners' dilemma. The dominant strategy of each prisoner is to confess. Depending on the action of the other, the worst outcome is five years of imprisonment; the best is freedom. But clearly, if Frank and Jesse could collude, their joint optimal strategy is not to confess. The same is true for our pricing managers in the symmetrical game. Competition yields the undercutting strategy, with $1 million in profits for each. With a cartel agreement, both would maintain price and come away with $10 million each.

Repeated Games.   Yet all is not well. Why shouldn't Frank convince Jesse not to confess, rat on Jesse, and then go free, while Jesse is put away for 10 years? Indeed, if this game is not repeated, then that may well be Frank's optimal strategy.[11]

In contrast to the prisoners' dilemma example, real-life pricing strategies are devised by companies that expect to confront each other repeatedly. This opens up the game horizon to signals, threats, and credibility issues. For example, the antitrust laws make explicit collusion risky and potentially unprofitable. However, companies might cooperate implicitly by signaling their willingness to collude. An oligopolist may publicize its price lists, which certainly informs buyers, but simultaneously lets competitors know its pricing policy. The same is true for media messages about forthcoming price changes.

Signals combined with threats will improve the chances for cooperation. But for a threat to be effective, it must be credible. A "tit-for-tat" strategy, or "Do unto others as they do to you" strategy, is credible because the threat is carried out. Thus, Jane Duopolist maintains a high price as long as Joe Duopolist does. But should Joe decide to cut price, Jane reacts in the next period by cutting her price. If Joe reads the message and raises price in the third period, Jane reacts in the fourth by raising price as well. (Look again at the steel example in MicroBits 13.1. Microbits 13.4 provides an instance of threat/counterthreat.)

Rational Irrationality.   Credibility might pose some difficulty for the oligopolist whose dominant strategy is to maintain price, for the threat to undercut fellow oligopolists will be disregarded as irrational. But if you play this game at a still deeper level, even such threats might prove credible if the threatening party can develop a reputation for taking irrational actions. Consider a policy of strategic entry deterrence that sends the following signal to potential competitors: "Yes, we'll cut our nose to spite our face. And we'll keep on cutting as long as it takes to convince you that you're not welcome." It may well prove effective.

Imperfect Information.   The certain payoffs of the prisoners' dilemma give way to uncertainty in the business setting. Rivals don't know each other's payoff matrices, and so cannot fathom each other's strategies. That forces them to approach the potential outcomes probabilistically. In

---

MICROBITS 13.4

Credible Threats in the Airline Industry

When Northwest Airlines lowered prices on nearly empty night flights from Minneapolis to the West Coast, Continental quickly matched the reductions. But the Continental cuts were only for a day or two. In a recent civil antitrust suit against Northwest, Steven B. Elkins, senior director of marketing systems for Northwest, testified:

> We felt that what they were doing was trying to send us a message that they didn't want us setting reduced night coach fares in those markets. . . . We didn't think it particularly appropriate for Continental to be telling us that . . . , and so we essentially tried to tell them to knock it off and leave us alone.

The message was conveyed by a Northwest fare reduction announcement. Fares from Houston, a Continental hub, to the West Coast were to be cut for a few days. Apparently, such threats and counterthreats are common in the airlines industry. Indeed, Mr. Elkins wished his staff to live by the Golden Rule, by which he meant, "I did not want my pricing analysts initiating actions in another carrier's market like Chicago for fear of what that other carrier might do to retaliate."

Source: *The Wall Street Journal*, October 9, 1990, pp. B1, 10.

such instances, some of the earlier conclusions need to be reconsidered. For example, whether a player should cooperate or compete may depend on the probabilities involved.

Let Frank assume that Jesse is a loose cannon but a man who keeps his word, so Frank just doesn't know whether Jesse will maintain price or not. If the probability of Jesse's choosing each option is 50 percent, then undercutting still remains the dominant strategy, but collusion is even better. After all, Frank's expected profit from undercutting = (.5)($15 million) + (.5)($1 million) = $8 million, while collusion guarantees a profit of $10 million. On the other hand, if the probability of Jesse's pursuing a price war strategy is only 25 percent while it's 75 percent certain that Jesse will stick to his price, then Frank's expected profit from undercutting is (.75)($15 million) + (.25)($1 million) = $11.5 million, so Frank ought to refuse Jesse's offer of collusion.

The Cournot Model Once Again

The Cournot scenario explored previously in this chapter can be reinterpreted as a game in an uncertain setting. Each duopolist in this game assumes the strategy of the other duopolist is to maintain output. However, neither duopolist knows the precise output of the other, and so each must deal with a number of contingencies.[12] Cour can assume that Not will produce anywhere from zero to the entire market demand, and Not can assume the same of Cour. Each must then calculate his or her optimal output given the unknown output of the other. Table 13.2 shows the options facing each.

A **reaction curve** plots out the response of one strategist to the expected actions of another.

Figure 13.5 plots out the **reaction curves** of the duopolists.[13] At the intersection, each party produces 8 million bottles of mineral water. But more important, each expects, and in fact discovers, that the other will do so. Thus, the intersection of the reaction curves identifies a Nash equilibrium.[14]

TABLE 13.2   Cour's and Not's Output Strategies

Cour's Strategy		Not's Strategy	
Not's Expected Output	*Cour's Reaction*	*Cour's Expected Output*	*Not's Reaction*
0	12	12	6
6	9	9	7.5
7.5	8.25	8.25	7.875
8	8	8	8
10	7	7	8.5
12	6	6	9

FIGURE 13.5   Cour's and Not's Reaction Curves

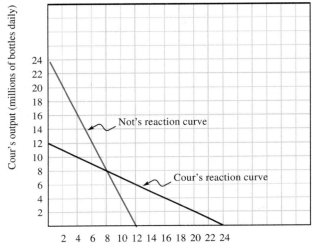

Cour's reactions to all possible output levels that Not could set determine Cour's reaction curve. The same applies to Not. At 8, 8, they achieve a Nash equilibrium. Cour's expected reaction as envisaged by Not is matched by Not's actual behavior and vice versa.

This taste of game theory has sampled some of its major features, but it has not been exhaustive. You might think about one complication. What happens when the market is shared by a number of oligopolists, so that in addition to either competition or collusion, it now becomes possible for some to collude against others? How are decisions made such as who joins the group and who gets left out?

In **markup pricing** (or **full-cost pricing**) oligopolists calculate product price by adding a specific percentage to their average costs. **Target pricing** is a variation of markup pricing, the specific percentage added to costs being the desired rate of profit.

Oligopoly Pricing Practices: From Theory to Reality

While the theories of oligopoly pricing discussed earlier in the chapter yield surprisingly useful results, they still leave gaps in economists' understanding of oligopoly pricing. Do the theories really describe oligopolistic pricing behavior? How, for example, is the price achieved in the case of the kinked demand curve? Some insight into the pricing process can be gleaned from two common methods actual used by oligopolists to determine price: **markup pricing** (or **full-cost pricing**) and **target pricing**.

Markup Pricing

As the name implies, an oligopolist pursuing a markup pricing strategy first calculates average production and overhead costs and then adds to these costs a given percentage to cover profit. Sounds easy, and in a sense, it is. Full-cost pricing is popular because most managers can calculate their average costs.[15] In addition, practitioners of markup pricing believe that this method will always be profitable, since price always exceeds cost.[16] Moreover, in many industries using full-cost pricing, a standard industry markup is traditional. So, if the average cost of production of air conditioners is $200 and the standard markup is 60 percent, then the price of an air conditioner equals $200 + (.60)$200, or $320.

The clear advantage of the markup procedure is its focus on the known—production costs—and its ignoring of the unknown—marginal costs, elasticity of demand, competitors' prices. In other words, full-cost pricing avoids grappling with the many uncertainties that plague any producer operating in imperfectly competitive markets. And using the traditional markup conforms to another one of those implicit oligopolistic pricing practices that deters retaliation.

But this ostrichlike posture may turn out to hide significant disadvantages. If you were in charge of pricing air conditioners and discovered that your competitor had set the price of a nearly identical air conditioner at $275, would you still maintain the $320 price? Or, if you found that your production backlog already stood at three months' time, would you not be tempted to raise price? As a matter of fact, many producers adhere to a **flexible full-cost pricing** strategy, where the full-cost price is adjusted either upward or downward in response to market pressures. In many ways, this procedure verges on marginal cost/marginal revenue pricing. But in doing so, it also upsets oligopolistic pricing standards and may initiate a price war.

In **flexible full-cost pricing** the percentage added on to average cost is adjusted to reflect market conditions.

Markup pricing is paradoxical. When sales fall, prices are raised, and when sales rise, prices are lowered. This perversity stems from the inclusion of fixed costs in the full-cost calculation. As sales fall, total fixed costs must be apportioned among fewer units, raising ATC. But if price is some percentage above ATC, then a decline in demand forces the full-cost pricer to raise prices instead of lowering them to offset the drop in sales.

Target Pricing

A firm's **standard volume** is the anticipated average output over a given period of time.

Target pricers avoid the perversities of markup pricing by setting prices on the basis of average output rather than current output. Producers know that demand for their product will fluctuate over time, be it within a year or over a period of years. They calculate their ATC at **standard volume** and add to that a target return, frequently a desired return on investment.

Figure 13.6 examines both the setting of a target price and the impact of fluctuations on price and output over time. The average total curve for light bulbs is shown, but it is related to capacity utilization rather than to the volume of sales. Costs per unit fall as capacity is used more fully, but they rise quickly as they approach capacity. Let's assume that the firm expects sales to fluctuate over three years but that the standard volume equals 75 percent of capacity. The ATC curve at 75 percent tells management that costs will average 30 cents per bulb. With a target return on investment of 15 cents at the standard volume, the price is set at 45 cents per bulb, for a 50 percent markup over cost. Now if the average demand curve is as depicted in Figure 13.6, the firm will achieve its targeted rate of return.

What happens if demand falls to D_{weak}? Under target pricing, the price remains at 45 cents, capacity usage falls back to 55 percent, and the profit margin drops to 5 cents a unit. True, the target pricer doesn't lower price to compensate for the weakness in demand, but neither will the

FIGURE 13.6   Target Pricing

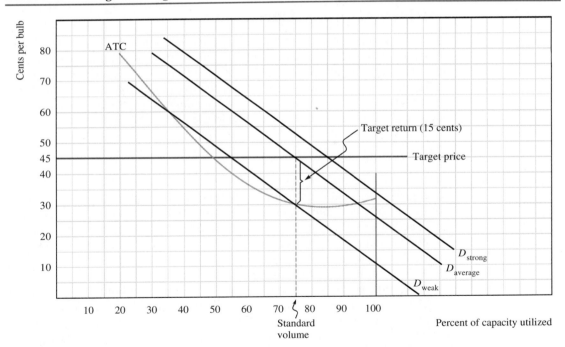

Having selected a standard volume of 75 percent and a target return of 15 cents, the target pricer will set a price of 45 cents. When demand is average, the target return is achieved. But even though the target return will not be gained if demand is weak or if it will be exceeded because demand is strong, the target price will be maintained.

firm's price setters raise it in line with their higher average costs. Instead, they believe that the period of slack demand will end and will be offset by D_{strong}, where capacity utilization will be 85 percent and the profit margin will grow to 16 cents.

While target pricing is another explanation for price constancy in oligopoly, it appears at variance with marginal pricing. Yet appearances may be deceiving, for if all oligopolists pursue the same target pricing strategy, they will achieve a stable kink price and eliminate price competition. Or, in game theory terms, implicit cooperation will achieve a Nash equilibrium. Moreover, common cost changes—an increase in the price of a major input or a rise in industrywide wages—lead to a uniform industry response. The uncertainty that envelops one oligopolist's pricing policy is eliminated, because all have selected a common method.

Pricing uncertainty is only one of the types of uncertainty that affect oligopolists. Other types of uncertainty can be reduced through a planned policy of expansion, an activity that is often associated with oligopoly.

[E]merging from Uncertainty

Firms expand for a variety of reasons and in a number of different ways. One popular method is the merger,[17] which, though not unique to oligopolistic markets, has played and continues to play an important role in the growth of big business. One reason for the popularity of consolidations stems from the fact that *mergers reduce uncertainty*. Because uncertainty comes in different guises, so, too, do the merger responses.

Horizontal and Vertical Mergers

A combining of firms selling the same product is called a **horizontal merger,** while a combining of firms that are linked in the production or distribution chain is called a **vertical merger.**

The most straightforward types of combinations are **horizontal** and **vertical mergers.** In each instance, the benefit to the merged firms is evident. In the case of a horizontal merger, the combined firm captures a larger share of the market, faces fewer rivals, and reduces the uncertainty about profitability that accompanies competition. Profits may also rise if the merger leads to economies of scale.

In contrast, a vertical merger reduces the uncertainty that stems from relying on suppliers or buyers in the production-distribution chain. Henry Ford was the prime mover in vertically integrating his Ford Motor Company in the years after World War I. He had been stymied by wartime restrictions on raw materials as well as postwar skyrocketing prices. So, Ford embarked on a course of action that by the mid-1920s would see the company acquire (by outright purchase or merger) timberlands, a Brazilian rubber plantation, and coal and iron ore mines. The raw materials were shipped to Ford manufacturing plants on a Ford-owned railroad or in Ford-owned vessels, to be processed into intermediate products, and then into the manifold products that were either sold as replacement parts or used in the assembly of automobiles and tractors.[18] Similarly, Radio Shack fabricates electronic replacement components that are used in manufacturing its ready-to-use products. It sells both the finished goods and the components in its Radio Shack retail chain, assuring its sales outlets of an unimpeded flow of products.[19]

A **conglomerate merger** involves the combining of two firms in unrelated industries.

The **conglomerate merger,** currently the most popular form of combination, limits uncertainty by reducing a firm's reliance on a single industry for profit generation. By merging across industries, the component firms diversify much as did the individual investor in Chapter 3. When Sears, Roebuck (America's largest retailing corporation) acquired Dean, Witter (the nation's fourth largest securities broker) and Coldwell Banker (the country's largest real estate broker), all three companies stood to benefit. If retailing turned weak for a time, profits in financial services and real estate could compensate, and if the housing market turned soft, the other components of the conglomerate could keep profitability up.

The growth of firms by horizontal, vertical, or conglomerate expansion poses a series of policy issues that are examined in Chapter 14. But before turning to public policy and oligopoly, it's worthwhile to crystalize the varied lessons of this chapter by examining the Pepsi-Coke competition.

Coke versus Pepsi, II

Let's refresh our memories. Pepsi and Coke jointly control over 70 percent of the U.S. soft-drink market, distributing their beverages mainly through franchised bottlers. The prices they charge, by and large, are identical at any given retail outlet. Despite some exceptions, prices have tended to remain stable (when adjusted for economywide inflation) over long periods of time. That's true despite the fact that U.S. soft-drink consumption rose from 31 gallons per capita in 1977 to approximately 47.5 gallons (or over 500 12-ounce cans) per capita in 1990, a 53 percent increase. In volume terms, 1990 per capita soft-drink consumption was nearly as large as consumption of the next two most popular beverages, coffee and beer, and two and a half times as great as the third, milk.

To better understand the soft-drink oligopoly, it will be useful to answer a few questions:

- Why have prices been so uniform and rigid?
- How do Pepsi and Coke compete?
- What type of entry barriers maintain the oligopoly structure?
- How have Coke and Pepsi reduced uncertainty?

Soft-Drink Pricing

A Coca-Cola bottler in Virginia does not compete against any other seller of Coke, for the bottler's franchise guarantees territorial integrity. The same is true for the Pepsi franchisee.[20] Consequently, the only type of competition each has to fear is from the other and, to a minor extent, local and private-label brands of soft drinks. The local Pepsi and Coke bottlers, being the big leaguers in their markets, recognize their interdependence, which can be manifested in a number of ways:

- Explicit collusion.
- Implicit collusion.
- Repeated games.
- Price wars.

Collusion. The Justice Department successfully prosecuted a number of price-fixing cases against some East Coast regional bottling companies in the mid-1980s. Both Coca-Cola and PepsiCo claim that collusion violates company policies and that these instances are exceptions to the general practice.

Implicit Collusion. "Live and let live" may be the consequence of price leadership. But when two large oligopolists dominate the market, one is hardly likely to cede the leadership position to the other. More likely, the kinked demand curve provides a realistic explanation of why prices are not cut when, say, more expensive sugar is replaced by less expensive corn syrup. Since price reductions will be quickly imitated, there's no profit in initiating such cuts. At the same time, each firm would like nothing more than to capture market share from the other. Thus, neither would follow price increases.

Repeated Games. PepsiCo and Coca-Cola are involved in a repeated game. Each is sufficiently strong and motivated to pursue a tit-for-tat policy, and each is aware that such is the strategy of the other party. Consequently, each realizes the benefit of cooperation.

Price Wars. Nevertheless, such cooperation may break down. One party may feel that the payoff matrix of the other argues against retaliation. Or perhaps the payoff matrix of the price cutter has changed, so that price cutting becomes a dominant strategy. When that happens, one cuts and awaits the countermove. In the case of Pepsi versus Coke, it's not clear who started the cola wars of the mid-1980s. But once the battle for foodstore sales began, Coca-Cola and PepsiCo fought tooth and nail for market share. This Cournot-type competition was ultimately recognized as mutually destructive, and the price war ended in a Nash equilibrium.

Elton John versus Ray Charles

Competition in advertising has replaced competition in pricing between the two major soft-drink companies. The oft-repeated slogans of both brands are supplemented by endorsements from stars of the entertainment and sports worlds.

PepsiCo and Coca-Cola have also used cents-off coupons and quality claims as competitive devices. Each company tries to convince the public that its particular brand is superior in taste.[21] Market expansion is another way in which Pepsi and Coke compete. Both have actively pursued a policy of overseas expansion, penetrating into markets where soft-drink consumption is substantially lower than it is in the United States.[22] They have also battled each other for major fountain service accounts.[23]

Entry Barriers

Brand names and advertising expenditures surely are key elements in solidifying the market in the hands of Coke and Pepsi over existing rivals as well as potential entrants. But their stranglehold is strengthened further by marketing arrangements with retailers, in which the bottlers pay for installing display cases and featuring their brands in local advertising. Coca-Cola and PepsiCo have also successfully used "calendar marketing agreements," whereby each pays a supermarket chain to feature its brand at the lowest price for a week.

A broader product line also inhibits entry. Some 30 years ago, both Coca-Cola and PepsiCo had only one brand each. They have since introduced diet brands, noncaffeinated colas, new flavors, and juice-based carbonated drinks. In the case of low-calorie and noncola drinks, Pepsi and Coke responded to the threat from Royal Crown's RC Cola and 7UP. Diet Coke and Diet Pepsi have risen to the top of the low-calorie list, surely helped to that prominence by their brand names.

The entry deterrent impact of brand names, advertising, and product line expansion appears to have been a side effect of other objectives. The two major brands have not, however, ignored strategic entry deterrence. In 1986, PepsiCo announced plans to acquire 7UP, and Coca-Cola sought to buy up Dr Pepper. That would have bottled up the soda oligopoly even further. The merged firms would have then jointly controlled 81 percent of the market and would have eliminated their closest rivals. Because of government intervention, the mergers were not consummated and market concentration was not intensified. Nevertheless, we might imply from all these moves that neither Coca-Cola nor PepsiCo welcome entry and competition, hardly a surprising conclusion.

Reducing Uncertainty

Although the antitrust authorities prevented PepsiCo and Coca-Cola from merging horizontally, the latter has been actively pursuing vertical mergers. During the 1980s, Coca-Cola began to alter its franchise-dominated structure by buying out two of its largest bottlers and taking equity positions in others, forming a subsidiary corporation, Coca-Cola Enterprises. The stated reason for these vertical mergers was to enhance bottling and distribution efficiency and to give Coca-Cola greater quality control over its product.

The picture on conglomeration is mixed. Until recently, both corporations sought the advantages of diversification by moving into new product areas. In 1960, Coca-Cola acquired Minute Maid, the largest domestic producer of concentrated fruit drinks, as the first of its moves to become a broad-based beverage producer. That was followed in 1964 by the purchase of Texas's Duncan Foods, a coffee, tea, and hot chocolate manufacturer and distributor; Belmont Spring Water in 1969; and Taylor Wines in 1977. Coca-Cola also bought Aqua-Chem, a manufacturer of water-pollution-control equipment, and Cleaver-Brooks, a major producer of steam and hot water generators. In 1982, Coca-Cola acquired Columbia Pictures Enterprises, the movie and TV production company. But it reversed its corporate strategy in 1989, and divested itself of all its acquisitions except for Minute Maid. Coca-Cola now specializes in soft drinks, but it still is diversified, except that it's spreading its risks geographically rather than along product lines.

To PepsiCo, diversification has meant the relative downgrading of its initial beverage orientation. It began by acquiring Frito-Lay, the potato chip company, in 1965. PepsiCo's president explained the synergy: "Potato chips make you thirsty; Pepsi satisfies thirst."[24] In the next two decades, PepsiCo expanded into the fast-food area, acquiring Pizza Hut and Taco Bell; entered the leisure-time activities market (Wilson Sporting Goods); and became a major force in trucking and the leasing and moving of heavy equipment. But like Coca-Cola, PepsiCo also reversed gears, though not as drastically as its archrival. PepsiCo remains a beverage and food conglomerate, although it, too, has not neglected geographical diversification.

In short, the soft-drink oligopoly displays many of the characteristics suggested by microeconomic theory. Pricing for the most part, if not collusive, is consistent with the implicit cooperation suggested by the theory of the kinked demand curve or by the repeated game version of game theory. Game theory easily explains the cola wars as well. And although Coca-Cola and PepsiCo do not often compete explicitly on the price of soft drinks, each relentlessly seeks to capture its rival's market share through coupons, advertising, and quality competition. Market expansion plays a significant role in their corporate strategies as well. Both oligopolists defend themselves against competitors by the strength of their brand names and the extensiveness of their advertising. Attempts by both Coca-Cola and PepsiCo to limit competition by acquiring competitors, however, have been stymied by the antitrust authorities. Finally, both companies have expanded by mergers, with Coca-Cola's strategy now more attuned to vertical mergers and PepsiCo's to conglomeration.

Summary

Oligopoly is born and flourishes for any number of reasons. The market may be too narrow to warrant more than a limited number of optimally sized firms. Such artificial entry barriers as brand names, better information, high capital requirements, and strategic entry deterrence may keep the market closed to newcomers. And government policies may exclude new entrants. But whatever the cause, the paucity of competitors forces the oligopolists to recognize their interdependence. The lack of price competition is one vital consequence.

Economists have devised a number of formal oligopoly models to explain price uniformity and stability. Sampled in the chapter are the Cournot duopoly paradigm, the price leadership model, and the theory of the kinked demand curve. In the Cournot model, a seesaw battle for sales leads to a stable market-sharing arrangement, while in a price leadership situation, firms in the industry imitate the pricing decisions of the leader both upward and downward. Price uniformity also emerges from the kinked demand curve model, but for a different reason. Since each firm believes that the other oligopolists will follow price cuts but not increases, leaving prices alone turns out to be the profit-maximizing strategy for each firm.

The absence of price rivalry does not mean that oligopolists don't compete in other ways. Temporary discounts in a variety of guises are acceptable modes of competition, as is advertising the virtues of the product. Offering a product line with different qualities of the same good or service is a common competitive practice, although such a practice does open the door to abuse. It's not too difficult to pass off a lower-quality product as a higher-quality one, especially when price is used as an index of quality.

Game theory is uniquely suited to examine strategies that can be employed by limited numbers of interdependent producers. Such strategies may be extremely simple or very complex. For example, when an oligopolist plays a nonrepeated game, has perfect information, and can field a dominant strategy, the dominant strategy dominates. On the other hand, when there's no dominant strategy, when information is imperfect, and when the relationship is prolonged, the choice of strategies is less clear-cut. Coming into play then are such considerations as the degree of imperfection in the information and the credibility and significance of retaliation. Despite these complications, game theory has become a powerful tool in explaining oligopolistic behavior.

From theory, the chapter turns to actual oligopoly price setting. Among the more popular methods oligopolists use are markup (or full-cost) pricing and target pricing, which are keyed to each firm's costs. Yet it is misleading to believe that oligopolists can ignore market structure in setting prices. No oligopolist can determine desired profit margins and profit targets and then markup prices without taking into account the possible reactions of fellow oligopolists. Both markup and target pricing, when standardized in the industry, have another advantage. With oligopoly costs likely to be similar, a common pricing practice will assure that prices will be similar as well.

The chapter ends by suggesting that mergers and acquisitions, which are a common feature of U.S. oligopolies, serve not only to expand the oligopolist's domain but also to reduce uncertainty. Horizontal mergers reduce competition, vertical mergers provide greater control either over supplies or outlets, and conglomerate mergers diversify the oligopolist's profit base into other industries.

This chapter has examined the positive theory of oligopoly, and for the most part eschewed its normative implications. But because oligopoly is the most significant market structure in much of the world, its benefits and disadvantages deserve to be considered as well. That's the task of Chapter 14.

Key Terms

Conglomerate merger
Differentiated oligopoly
Dominant strategy
Duopoly
Flexible full-cost pricing
Game theory
Horizontal merger
List price
Markup pricing (or full-cost pricing)
Nash equilibrium

Oligopoly
Payoff matrix
Price leadership
Product line
Reaction curve
Standard volume
Strategic entry deterrence
Target pricing
Undifferentiated oligopoly
Vertical merger

Review Questions

1. Explain what your decision-making process would be if you were faced by a prisoners' dilemma game and
   a. It was a one-shot deal.
   b. You and your partner anticipated a continuing relationship.

2. What barriers to entry are likely to preserve an oligopoly? Explain and give examples of each.

3. List after each of the following entries the model of oligopoly that best explains the industry's behavior. Justify your selection. (Note: All of these cases are based on real events.)

   a. Tire manufacturers raised prices by 10 percent following the sharp rise of petroleum prices after Iraq invaded Kuwait. _____

   b. American Airlines, a traditional price leader, announced special low fares for vacation travelers. It is likely that other U.S. carriers will match the reduction. _____

   c. GM raised prices for some equipment options following a similar move by Ford. However, Chrysler, Toyota, and Honda were not expected to follow.
   _____

d. Bethlehem Steel trimmed a planned price increase, and other steelmakers are expected to do the same. _____

e. Apple Computers increased prices across the board, following a rise in the price of memory chips. Most other computer manufacturers had already increased their prices. _____

f. Although GM reduced the length of warranty coverage on new cars, neither Ford nor Chrysler are cutting theirs. _____

g. Five airlines will meet the price hike announced by TWA and Texas Air. _____

h. Coffee prices surge after the international coffee board agrees to reduce export quotas. _____

4. *a.* Find the Cournot equilibrium in Figure 13.1 if the MC for both producers is 3 francs.

    b. Sketch out the producers' reaction curves and find the Nash equilibrium.

5. *a.* Distinguish between a differentiated and an undifferentiated oligopoly.

b. Give some examples from U.S. industry of each.

c. In which case are advertising expenditures likely to be greatest? Explain.

d. Contrast the role of advertising in perfectly competitive and oligopoly markets.

6. Why might a producer of a product line be tempted to raise price without improving quality? Explain with the aid of a diagram.

7. *a.* Find the Nash equilibrium in the game depicted below. (The first number in the payoff matrix is Clyde's expected profit, the second, Bonnie's.)

    b. When would collusion be worthwhile in a nonrepeating game for Bonnie? for Clyde?

    c. How would your answer change if the game were repeated?

8. *a.* Why is full-cost pricing apt to move prices inversely with demand changes?

    b. How does a target pricing procedure avoid this error?

    c. Is such flexible pricing consistent with oligopoly and its presumed price stability?

		Bonnie's options	
		Maintain	**Undercut**
Clyde's options	**Maintain**	$30; $50	$10; $40
	Undercut	$40; $20	$20; $10

Food for Thought

1. What do the following quotations indicate about oligopoly?

    a. "On average, manufacturers paid $5.1 million to get a new product or line extension on grocery store shelves nationwide" (*The Wall Street Journal*, November 26, 1990, p. B1).

    b. "Major brands of pet foods are almost

equally nutritious [so] there is little brand loyalty.'' (*The New York Times,* December 16, 1990, p. C5).

c. ''Over the past few months, both Procter & Gamble [Pampers and Luvs diapers] and Kimberly-Clark [Huggies] have cut the number of diapers in their packages, leaving prices the same.'' (*The Wall Street Journal,* February 5, 1991, p. B1).

d. ''The Justice Department said it will try to block . . . the proposed sale by Eastern Airlines to United Airlines of its landing and take-off slots and passenger gates at Washington National Airport. . . . United . . . already is the dominant carrier at [nearby] Dulles Airport. . . . The acquisition of the Eastern assets would make United the second-largest carrier at Washington National. . . .'' (*The Wall Street Journal,* February 15, 1991, p. 4).

2. Show that in a Cournot case with three participants, each oligopolist will supply a quarter of the demand, and one quarter of the demanders will be priced out of the market.

3. a. How does advertising affect an oligopolist's elasticity of demand?

   b. Explain how the price policy of a successful advertiser would change if the firm were (i) a price leader, (ii) a follower, (iii) anchored at the kink, and (iv) pursuing a target pricing formula.

4. Three types of discriminating monopolists were discussed in Chapter 11. Would this concept be appropriate in an oligopoly setting? Why or why not?

5. You are a potential entrant in a monopolized market with the payoff matrix depicted below. (The first number is the monopolist's profit, the second, yours.) The monopoly may disregard your potential entry and always maintain a high monopoly price or can anticipate your entry and try to forestall it by setting a lower limit price. In either instance, once the price policy is announced, it's maintained.

   b. Would your decision change if the monopolist announces an ironclad guarantee, which states that he'll pay each customer 50 percent of the sales price should the buyer find a cheaper price quote elsewhere? What happens to the payoff matrix?

6. When GM raised automobile prices during the slack demand period of 1990, one GM dealer commented: ''They may as well raise prices when they're not selling cars.'' Try to make economic sense out of this statement.

7. Why do you think that Coca-Cola reversed its product diversification program after 1989?

		Potential competitor's choice	
		Emulate monopolist's price	Limit price
Monopolist's options	**Monopoly price**	$25; $5	$20; $8
	Limit price	$15; $3	$10; $1

Suggested Readings

About all you'd ever want to know about modern industrial organization in general and specifically about oligopoly theory can be found in the two-volume *Handbook of Industrial Organization* edited by Richard Schamlensee and Robert D. Willig (New York: North-Holland, 1989). The articles range from the accessible to the highly technical, but you really ought to take a look. For a change of pace, read Robert Axelrod's *The Evolution of Cooperation* (New York: Basic, 1984). This entire book is devoted to tit-for-tat strategies and their implications in settings as diverse as business strategy, war, and biology. In between lies the brief piece by Steven C. Salop, "Strategic Entry Deterrence," *American Economic Review* 69, no. 2 (May 1979), pp. 335–38.

Notes and Answers

1. The first of each pair is differentiated. There are obvious distinctions between different breakfast cereals, automobiles, and TV shows, but no perceptible differences between light bulbs, steel sheets, and the long-distance services provided by AT&T, MCI, and U.S. Sprint.

2. 7.

3. The mathematical solution runs as follows: The market demand curve is $P = 12 - 1/2Q$, where Q is the combined output of the duopolists (i.e., $Q = Q_1 + Q_2$). TR for Cour equals PQ_1, which equals $(12 - 1/2Q)Q_1$, which can be expanded to $12Q_1 - 1/2(Q_1 + Q_2)Q_1 = 12Q_1 - 1/2Q_1^2 - 1/2Q_1Q_2$. Cour's MR $(\delta TR_1/\delta Q_1) = 12 - Q_1 - (1/2)Q_2$. Since MC is given as 0, the equilibrium equation is: $0 = 12 - Q_1 - (1/2)Q_2$. Solve now for Q_1: $Q_1 = 12 - (1/2)Q_2$. Similarly, $Q_2 = 12 - (1/2)Q_1$. Substituting the latter expression into the former yields: $Q_1 = 12 - 1/2(12 - 1/2Q_1) = 12 - 6 + 1/4\ Q_1 = 6 + 1/4\ Q_1$. Consolidating the Qs on the left side and factoring out leads to: $Q_1(1 - 1/4) = 6$, which solves to: $Q_1 = 8$. Since Not's solution is symmetrical, $Q_2 = 8$. Total output is 16, which, when inserted into the price equation, yields $P = 3$.

4. Since price would be driven down to MC in the long run and MC equals zero, price would be zero and quantity supplied would be 24 million bottles daily. In other words, mineral water would be a free good, and all who thirsted for mineral water could take as much as they wanted. The monopolist, on the other hand, would set price and quantity at 6 francs and 12 million bottles daily, respectively, as did Cour before he was aware of Not's existence.

5. The appendix to this chapter considers a price leadership case where one firm accounts for a substantial share of industry output and the remaining firms are relatively small.

6. In 1991, over 300 billion coupons were distributed in the United States, and 7.5 billion, with a total value of over $4 billion, were redeemed.

7. What's happened to the oligopolist's elasticity of demand?

8. Cited in Allan Nevins and Frank Ernest Hill, *Ford: Expansion and Challenge, 1915–1933* (New York: Charles Scribner's Sons, 1957), p. 395.

9. Frank should confess, for if Jesse confesses, then Frank would be imprisoned for 5 years instead of the 10 years he would serve had he not confessed. And if Jesse doesn't confess, Frank goes free.

10. John F. Nash, a Princeton University mathematician, first published this equilibrium criterion in 1950.

11. Of course, Jesse can do the same to Frank. That leads to a complicated game along the lines, "He thinks that I think that he thinks that I think . . ." Whether one confesses and sets up the other or they both confess cannot be determined in advance.

12. Phrasing this model in game theory language

avoids the strained assumption that each duopolist remains ignorant of the actions of the other.

13. The equations for the reaction curves, $Q_1 = 12 - 1/2Q_2$ and $Q_2 = 1/2Q_1$, are derived in note 3.

14. You might test yourself by explaining why the intersection of the reaction curves is indeed a Nash equilibrium.

15. Or so they believe. Actually, while calculating accounting costs of production is simple, calculating the true economic costs—including opportunity costs—requires a degree of sophistication that not all business executives possess.

16. You understand that this is also not necessarily correct, since this pricing policy may itself engender losses. Think about a situation where profit maximization dictates a price below ATC but above AVC. What price will a full-cost pricer choose?

17. The term *merger* in this context includes other forms of acquisitions, such as asset purchases of existing companies or the creation of new entities that replace the merged firms.

18. See Nevins and Hill, *Ford,* Chapters 8 and 9. This book constitutes one volume of a masterly trilogy that focuses on Henry Ford and the Ford Motor Company, but encompasses the entire automotive industry and its impact on American civilization from its beginnings through the first half of the 20th century.

19. An innovative motive for vertical mergers is connected with rate regulation. When a firm such as a public utility finds its prices and profits regulated by a utility commission, a vertical merger can circumvent the impact of regulation. Let's say a telephone company merges with a manufacturer of telecommunications equipment. Management then inflates the costs of the equipment, and the telephone company appeals for higher rates on the basis of the increased costs. The monopoly profits that regulation precludes the phone company from earning are downstreamed to the unregulated equipment arm. Other reasons for vertical mergers including tax shifting motives are discussed in Roger D. Blair and David L. Kaserman, *Antitrust Economics* (Homewood, Ill: Irwin, 1985), pp. 283–95.

20. "Pepsi sells more cheaply in the Washington, D.C. suburb of Warrenton, Va. than it did in the city. Because of the territorial exclusivity, the Warrenton Pepsi bottler is prohibited from selling in the city so that the Washington Coca-Cola bottler is protected from competition as well." Cited from a Federal Trade Commission report in J. C. Louis and Harvey Z. Yazijian, *The Cola Wars* (New York: Everest House, 1980), p. 330.

Territorial exclusivity was violated to some extent by the operation of "bootleggers," who shipped Pepsi and/or Coke across territories. Louis and Yazijian, *Cola Wars* (p. 331) cite the case of one California chain that bought all of its Pepsi and most of its Coke from bootleggers, saving 15 to 25 percent per case over the local bottler's price, prima facie evidence of market control by the bottler.

21. In a cola taste test conducted for *The Wall Street Journal,* "70 percent of the 100 . . . tasters were mistaken about [the brand] they were drinking," (June 3, 1987, p. 32).

22. Some years ago, Pepsi won a contract with the Soviet Union and more recently Coca-Cola gained an exclusive with mainland China.

21. Burger King and Wendy's defected to Coca-Cola in 1990, while the Marriot food service account was won over by Pepsi in 1991.

24. Cited in Louis and Yazijian, *Cola Wars,* p. 118.

APPENDIX
GULLIVER AMONG THE LILLIPUTIANS: A FORMAL PRICE LEADERSHIP MODEL

This appendix supplements the price leadership discussion of the chapter by answering two questions: How does a price leader set the industry price? and Why do the followers follow? The particular model discussed here assumes that the industry consists of a single dominant firm, the leader, who enjoys economies of scale and thus produces at a lower cost than the host of smaller firms that comprise the remainder of the industry.

Take a look at the hypothetical photographic film industry's demand and cost curves in Figure 13A.1. The industry leader, Westman-Kojak, competes with three smaller firms, Fiji, Avga, and Pillory. The fact that the marginal cost curve of the leader lies below the combined curves of the followers is consistent with the leader's presumed low-cost production.

As a first step, calculate the price the leader would set if it ignored the presence of others. (You'll have to supply an MR curve.)

Have you discovered that the MR = MC equilibrium occurs at an output of 60 million rolls per month and a price of $6 per roll? Yet $6 could not become a viable oligopoly price for a very simple reason. Since the followers will also charge $6 per package and would market 85 million themselves in line with their P = MC optimum production position—draw a horizontal price line at P = $6 and see where it intersects the MC$_{followers}$ curve—they would flood the market. After all, at $6, consumers demand only 60 million units, while the combined output of Kojak and the other film manufacturers would come to 145 million.

So, the price leader has to take into account the production of the other oligopolists. Let's say Kojak film is priced at $5 per package. The remaining firms will equate P ($5) and their own MCs and so produce 75 million rolls of film. But if that's the case, their output exhausts the entire demand; there's nothing left for Kojak. The following table lists the demand for industry, for the followers, and for Kojak, under different potential prices.

Price	Industry Demand (Millions)	Supplied by Followers (Millions)	Available to Kojak (Millions)
$5	75	75	0
4	90	65	25
3	105	55	50
2	120	45	75
1	135	35	100

FIGURE 13A.1   Price Determination in a Leadership Situation

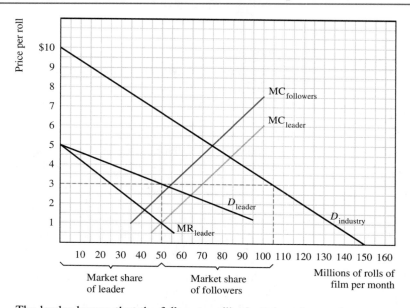

The leader knows that the followers will adopt the price set by the leader. Thus, the leader's demand curve equals the industry demand curve *less* the amount supplied at the set price by the followers. D_{leader} at every point equals $D_{industry}$ minus the quantity produced by the others, which is determined by finding the quantity at which $P = MC_{followers}$. So, if the leader sets $P = \$3$, then $P = MC_{followers}$ at $Q = 55$ million, leaving 50 million to the leader. With D_{leader} so derived, the leader finds its own $MR = MC$, here $= 50$ million and sets the appropriate price, here \$3. Since all firms now sell at \$3, the leader sells 50 million, the followers sell 55 million and consumers buy 105 million as per the industry demand curve.

Now Westman-Kojak can consider the worst possible scenario: no one buys Kojak unless there's nothing else available. But that's precisely the situation described by the last column of the above table, and enables Westman-Kojak to calculate a worst-case demand curve, the line labeled D_{leader} in Figure 13A.1. Its demand curve generates an MR curve, and now Kojak can act as a monopolist. The market that remains is exclusively in its hands. As Figure 13A.1 shows, $MR = MC$ at an output of 50 million units and a corresponding price of \$3.

You can read off the figure or the table the distribution of the film market between Kojak and the followers at $P = \$3$: Kojak accounts for 50 million units, while the remaining firms share 55 million, meeting the total demand of 105 million.

But Kojak is not the only one satisfied with this situation—so are Fiji, Avga, and Pillory. They snuggle under Kojak's \$3 umbrella and maximize profits, knowing well that should they become greedy and try to expand market share by undercutting Kojak, the leader has the ability to match their lower price and drive price down even further. A price war can lead to their demise, given the fact that Kojak's costs of production are lower than those of its rivals. (Is this a Nash equilibrium?)

This model has an appealing quality in that it purports to explain how a price leader actually sets price. Yet if you really think about it, this analysis points out Gulliver's impotence in the face of the Lilliputians. Would you call the leader dominant when it is forced by the followers to operate on a worst-case scenario?

14

CONTROLLING OLIGOPOLY: ASSURING THE GAME'S INTEGRITY

Sometimes the competition is Pepsi.
Sometimes it is water, sometimes it is wine.
Roberto C. Goizueta, Chairman of Coca-Cola (1988)

If you laid all of the world's economists end to end, you'd never reach a conclusion.
Anonymous

Learning Objectives

In this chapter, you'll learn about:
- The meaning and implications of the structure, conduct, performance view of economic power.
- Methods for measuring oligopoly power.
- The scope of oligopoly in the United States.
- The welfare and efficiency implications of static oligopoly models compared with perfect competition and monopoly.
- The defense of oligopoly markets: why conclusions based on static models may be misleading.
- The contributions of the New Empirical Industrial Organization.
- Antitrust laws and their applicability to oligopoly.

Snap, Crackle, and Divestiture[1]

Oligopolists would do best on the whole to coordinate their policies. However, outright collusion is banned not only in the United States but in many other countries as well. A second best solution from the vantage point of the oligopolists is implicit collusion, which recognizes that interdependence forces oligopolists to commonly confront challenges to their prices, market share, and product lines. The oligopoly models examined in Chapter 13 are predicated on this presumption. They suggest that at the minimum buyers should anticipate implicit collusion among oligopolists, a supposition brought home in the following case.

The Federal Trade Commission, which along with the Justice Department is charged with enforcing the U.S. antitrust laws, filed an antitrust suit against Kellogg's, General Mills, General Foods, and Quaker Oats. The four corporations, marketing over 100 cereal brands, account for more than 90 percent of the nation's cereal sales. Kellogg's alone is responsible for 45 percent of the market.

The FTC did not allege that the four fixed their prices through collusion. Instead, it contended that the cereal manufacturers were oligopolists; their collusion was implicit. Thus, the FTC argued that the four joined in a "tacit conspiracy or agreement not to engage in price competition. Each respondent has recognized that, for price increases to be successful, price competition must be avoided, with the result that respondents follow each other's price increases without challenge." Kellogg's was singled out as the price leader. The FTC also asserted that the companies minimized advertising competition by sharing information about their advertising outlays. The four were similarly charged with doing away with cereal package premiums.

According to the FTC, the cereal oligopolists erected barriers to discourage entry. They refused to expand their production of private-brand cereals. They continuously added new brands that were then heavily advertised, requiring potential competitors to undertake costly marketing campaigns. And, by combining brand-name recognition, advertising, and product line diversity, the four majors dominated supermarket shelf space, so even if competitors could gain a foothold, consumers, facing a wall of major brands, would barely notice the newcomers. The consequent weak sales would initiate a vicious cycle as supermarket managers cut back on the scarce shelf space alloted the new entrants, leading to further sales deterioration. The cereal companies naturally enough contested both the facts and the illegal nature of their mutual interdependence.

Clearly, all cereal eaters had a stake in the outcome of this suit. Nowadays, the manufacturers may be exploiting consumers well beyond the tune of the $128 million estimated by the FTC in the early 1970s. But in all fairness to the big four, we need to evaluate the merits of this case objectively. We must move beyond the theories outlined in Chapter 13 and grapple with some of the practical considerations that are relegated to the sidelines by the simplifying assumptions of economic theory. We need to deal with both conceptual and factual issues and the law as well. Such is the task of this chapter.

The "structure-conduct-performance" (SCP) view of oligopoly is central to this chapter. Briefly, SCP asserts that the structure of the industry determines the conduct of its participants, which in turn determines their market performance. With this framework in mind, the chapter begins by examining the pervasiveness of oligopoly in the U.S. economy. That is followed by an analysis of public policy toward oligopoly along the lines already familiar to you from Chapter 12. We'll first examine the welfare implications of the static oligopoly model in terms of deadweight loss as well as efficiency and resource allocation. But we'll also have to consider such dynamic considerations as innovation and technological change in an oligopolistic market, and evaluate the available evidence on both static and dynamic fronts.

Economists have long voiced dissatisfaction with the conceptual foundations of SCP and so with its conclusions, which have formed the basis for public policy toward imperfect competition. The new empirical industrial organization (NEIO), while still in its early stages, offers an alternative way of marshaling the evidence concerning oligopoly's economic impact. Although at this time NEIO studies have tended to support SCP research, it's premature to tell whether or not NEIO will lead to major revisions in government policy. But clearly the stakes are large, for public policy rests on the answers to two questions:

- Is oliogopoly beneficial or detrimental to the economy?
- If oligopoly is detrimental, what, if any, policies should be implemented to temper its adverse consequences?

Oligopoly in the United States

Public policy toward imperfect competition in the United States has historically been predicated on a linked tripartite division: structure, conduct, and performance. Because of the very *structure* of an oligopolistic industry—few, interdependent firms—the firm's decision makers can *conduct* their affairs in a manner incompatible with competitive behavior. But whether their *performance* reflects this inherent power cannot be answered in the abstract. Let's begin with *structure* to assess the extent of oligopoly in the U.S. economy.

Structure

The first issue a factual analysis of market structure faces is one of definition. You've already seen in Chapter 5 that drawing the borderline between two industries is not inconsequential. Other issues of similar magnitude, such as geographical market demarcation, need to be addressed as well.

Measuring Oligopoly.   The most popular method for measuring oligopoly structure is the **four-firm concentration ratio.** Two other measures of industry power used by economists are the **Lerner index (£)** and the **Herfindahl-Hirschman index (HHI).**

The Four-Firm Concentration Ratio.   The simplicity of the four-firm concentration ratio underlies its popularity: sum up the percentage of the market controlled by the top four and you've got your figure. Table 14.1 ranks 19 industries on the basis of their four-firm ratios. Are you surprised by the high concentration ratios of those listed?

The percentage of the market captured by the four largest firms in the industry is called the **four-firm concentration ratio.** The **Lerner index (£)** equals (Price − Marginal Cost)/Price. The **Herfindahl-Hirschman index (HHI)** is the sum of the market share of each firm squared.

The Lerner Index.   The fame of the Lerner index (£), originated by the late Professor Abba P. Lerner, a most prolific and creative economist, stems from its close relationship with the theory of the firm. For a perfectly competitive industry, price should equal marginal cost, so that £ = 0. But as firms extract greater control over pricing, which is synonymous with ever greater degrees of imperfect competition, the greater the discrepancy should be between price and marginal cost and so the larger the index number is.

TABLE 14.1   **Measures of Concentration for Selected U.S. Manufacturing Industries (by Value of Shipments), 1987**

Industry	4-Firm Concentration Ratio	HHI	Industry	4-Firm Concentration Ratio	HHI
Chewing gum	96	—	Aluminum sheets, plate, and foil	74	1,719
Electric lamps, bulbs, and tubes	93	—	Tires and inner tubes	69	1,897
Motor vehicles and car bodies	90	—	Roasted coffee	66	1,589
Small arms ammunition	88	—	Soaps and detergents	65	1,698
Cereal breakfast foods	87	2,207	Prerecorded records and tapes	63	1,505
Greeting card publishing	85	2,830	Burial caskets	59	1,820
Household refrigerators and freezers	85	2,256	Cookies and crackers	58	1,278
Flat glass	82	1,968	Elevators and moving stairs	52	824
Photographic equipment and supplies	77	2,241	Electronic computers	43	693

NOTE: Dash (—) indicates either not available or not reported.
SOURCE: U.S. Bureau of the Census, 1987 Census of Manufactures, *Concentration Ratios in Manufacturing* (Washington, D.C.: Government Printing Office, 1992), Table 4.

MicroQuery   What is the Lerner index for Mr. Metz of fly-feather fame (Figure 11.3, p. 377) and the oligopolists hovering at the kink in Figure 13.2 (p. 438)? _____ and _____ [2]

Intuition suggests that the Lerner index and demand elasticity are related, too. After all, the more competitive the market, the greater the elasticity of the demand curve facing the firm, and vice versa for a less competitive industry. So, £ and elasticity should move inversely. And indeed that is the case:[3]

$$£ = (P - MC)/P = 1/|\varepsilon|.$$

The Herfindahl-Hirschman Index.   The Herfindahl-Hirschman index (HHI)[4] is particularly useful in fine-tuning the concentration ratio. It enables the observer to distinguish between an industry that is top-heavy like the beverage industry and one where the market is more evenly distributed.

The HHI is 10,000 for a monopoly, since the single producer controls 100 percent of the market. At the other extreme, for a perfectly competitive industry with, say, 100 firms, each firm having captured only 1 percent of the market, the HHI = $1^2 + 1^2 + 1^2 + 1^2 + \ldots = 100$. Now calculate the HHI for a four-firm concentration ratio of 80 where the market is shared equally, and contrast it to a four-firm concentration ratio with three firms sharing 30 percent and the fourth controlling 50 percent. (Assume the remaining 20 percent in each case is distributed equally among 20 firms.)

For the equal distribution, HHI = _____ ; for the unequal distribution, HHI = _____ .[5]

A similar contrast would emerge between the HHI and the four-firm concentration ratio in the soft-drink merger situation mentioned in Chapter 13. The latter would have risen from 81 to 87, or a mere 7 percent, had the mergers contemplated by Coca-Cola and Pepsi come to fruition. The HHI suggests a more substantial impact on industry structure. Once again assume that aside from Coca Cola, PepsiCo, 7UP, and Dr Pepper, the remaining 13 firms each account for only 1 percent of the market. The premerger HHI then equals 2,628.32, while the postmerger HHI comes to 3,383.60, an increase of 29 percent.[6]

Return to Table 14.1 and examine the HHI for the industries appearing there. Notice that the four-firm concentration ratio and the HHI correspond only approximately. Substantial discrepancies are evident. The most concentrated industry measured by the HHI, greeting cards, is ranked below breakfast cereals by the four-firm concentration ratio, while burial caskets, which has a concentration ratio only 4 percent points below the recording industry, has a HHI that is 315 points higher. What does that tell you about the two industries? _____ [7]

Using the Concentration Ratio. Of these three measures of market structure, the concentration ratio retains its popularity because of its simplicity, the HHI is taking a more important role in antitrust intervention, and the Lerner index remains the economist's favorite. But to use any of these measures for normative purposes, we need a criterion to distinguish oligopolistic from nonoligopolistic market structures. In the case of the former, economists who specialize in industrial organization have concluded that a four-firm concentration ratio less than 40 is inconsistent with oligopoly.

Defining Industry and Market. In addition to a criterion for implying oligopoly, we also need an operative definition of industry. Should we measure concentration broadly, as Mr. Goizueta opined in the chapter's first opening quotation, and so focus on a "beverage industry" that encompasses not only soft drinks but also alcoholic and noncarbonated beverages? Or should we limit ourselves to a narrower conception that considers only soft drinks? Clearly, the broader the definition, the lower the concentration ratio, while the narrower the industry, the more frequently oligopoly will be encountered.

Finally, we need an appropriate definition of geographic market, since some firms compete nationally, while others serve regional or local markets. Thus, banking has an extremely low concentration ratio because more than 10,000 commercial banks serve the nation. Yet that statistic is very misleading, because most individuals and businesses deal with local banks. Competition in their city is best measured by the local concentration ratio, not the national one.

The **Standard Industrial Classification (SIC) Code** is a numerical categorization of U.S. industries and their products, running from broad economic sectors (one-digit) to ever finer distinctions and culminating in seven-digit product listings.

Oligopoly's Reign. As a practical matter, most empirical studies of oligopoly use the U.S. Census Bureau's **Standard Industrial Classification (SIC) Code,** which divides U.S. industries into ever finer categories. Broad labels such as manufacturing give way to detailed product levels such as "six- to nine-ounce bottled carbonated soft drinks, nondietetics, containing kola extract." Most studies focus on the four-digit, or "industry," level, which is narrower than manufacturing but broader than the product level. (In the soft-drink case, the four-digit level is "bottled and canned soft drinks.") Yet virtually all economists using this data complain about its inadequacy; the data are too broad in some cases and too narrow in others.[8] Moreover, the SIC is compiled on a national basis and therefore misleads when the relevant markets are regional or local.[9] It also only considers domestic production, and thus ignores the competitive impact of imports, which in some industries makes a significant difference. Finally, virtually all empirical studies are limited to manufacturing; it's the only category for which sufficient data are available.

Having absorbed all these qualifications, take a look at Table 14.2, which breaks down U.S. four-digit manufacturing industries by their four-firm concentration ratios. Certainly, the numbers point to a significant degree of oligopoly in U.S. manufacturing. Using 40 as the dividing line, 197 four-digit SIC industries, or 43.3 percent of the total, are oligopolistic if not monopolistic in structure.

Conduct and Performance

Do those industries that are structurally capable of exerting control over their markets in fact do so? That thorny question has been approached by empirical economists using a variety of methods and data sources. The starting point has been simple: let's see whether concentrated industries (i.e., oligopoly structures) earn a higher rate of profits than unconcentrated ones, which would signify "poor" performance. The simplicity of this formulation, however, hides complex empirical problems, starting with defining profits properly and ranging to distinguishing the impact of concentration on profitability from other causal factors.[10]

Yet despite all the problems, a consistent answer follows: concentration and profitability are positively correlated. The greater the degree of concentration, the higher profits are. (One such study is summarized in MicroBits 14.1.)

TABLE 14.2   Distribution of Four-Firm Concentration Ratios, U.S. Manufacturing, 1982

Four-Firm Concentration Ratio	Number of Industries	Percentage of all Industries
0–19	89	19.6
20–39	169	37.1
40–59	123	27.0
60–79	54	11.9
80–100	20	4.4
Totals	455	100.0

SOURCE: Compiled from the U.S. Bureau of the Census, 1982 Census of Manufacturers, *Concentration Ratios in Manufacturing* (Washington, D.C.: Government Printing Office, 1986), Table 6, pp. 7-51–7-176.

Concentration and Profits: An Empirical Study

Consider the results of a representative study by Leonard W. Weiss:*

$$PCM = .174 + .0007CR - .0003GDR$$
$$+ .0010FCSR + 0.16ASR$$
$$+ .0021COE$$

where PCM = the price-cost (or profit) margin (in percent), CR = the four-firm concentration ratio, GDR = a geographic dispersion index, FCSR = the fixed capital to shipments ratio, ASR = the advertisement to shipments ratio, and COE = the ratio of central office to total office employment. This regression equation includes variables other than the concentration ratio to weed out other influences on profit margin or to correct for improperly defined markets. Thus, two firms with different capital intensities (FCSR) or

_____
* "The Concentration-Profits Relationship and Antitrust," in *Industrial Concentration: The New Learning*, eds. Harvey J. Goldschmid et al. (Boston: Little, Brown, 1974), pp. 184–232. The cited equation appears on p. 228.

advertising and central office expenditures (ASR and COE) could well show different profit margins, but they would be unrelated to the degree of industry concentration. Similarly, national concentration may be meaningless for industries that deal primarily at the regional or local level; GDR adjusts for that.

Applying the data to 399 four-digit industries, Weiss found all the coefficients except the last to be statistically significant, and the explanatory contribution (R^2) of the entire equation to be .40, an acceptable value in cross-section studies.

What does the equation tell us about the concentration-profitability relationship? Look at the coefficient of CR, the concentration ratio. The .07 percent indicates that should the concentration ratio rise by 10 points, the profit margin would rise by (.0007)(10), or $^7/_{10}$ of 1 percent. True, the percentage increase is small, but it's in the expected direction: positive.

The conclusion: Oligopoly leads to market performance that is different from that of the perfectly competitive model.

The Malevolent Implications of the Static Oligopoly Model

Much like the monopoly model of Chapter 11, the static theories of oligopoly reviewed in Chapter 13 picture oligopoly unfavorably when contrasted to perfect competition.

The Price Front

Since theory predicted that firms in concentrated industries will conduct themselves in a manner designed to enhance their profitability, and since the empirical results confirm this relationship, it seems plausible to conclude that oligopolists exploit their customers by charging higher prices than would be set in competitive markets. However, except in the case of collusive oligopoly, the oligopolist's control over price is less absolute than the monopolist's. We would expect lower prices than under monopoly.

The Quantity Front

As in the case of monopoly, oligopolists will have to cut back on the quantity sold on the market in order to maintain the higher price. Once again, oligopolists produce less than their perfectly competitive counterparts, but because of their looser control over the market, they supply more than a monopolist would.

Placing oligopoly between the two extremes of monopoly and perfect competition both in terms of quantity produced and the price increase suggests that the deadweight loss of oligopoly will also be intermediate. Figure 14.1 bears that out.

Figure 14.1 contrasts the Cournot duopoly model of Figure 13.1 (p. 435) with a monopoly outcome on the one hand and a competitive

FIGURE 14.1   The Statics of Monopoly, Oligopoly, and Perfect Competition

a.   Monopoly versus perfect competition

b.   Oligopoly versus perfect competition

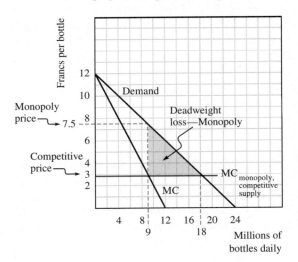
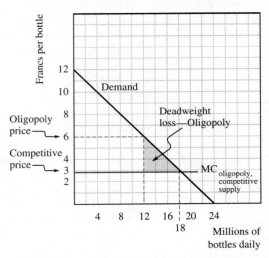

a.   The monopolist, by raising price and reducing output, causes a deadweight loss of 20.25 million francs compared with the competitive equilibrium.

b.   Oligopolists produce more than a monopoly and charge a lower price. Consequently, the deadweight loss shrinks to 9 million francs. If perfect competition were to prevail, however, there would not be a deadweight loss at all.

equilibrium on the other. Figure 14.1a compares monopoly with perfect competition, while Figure 14.1b juxtaposes competitive industry with oligopoly. A marginal cost curve at 3 francs has been added in both diagrams.

Turn first to the left-hand figure. The monopolist faces the industry demand curve, sets output by equating MR to MC, and derives the equilibrium output at 9 million bottles daily priced at 7.5 francs per bottle. Competitive suppliers are portrayed by their MC = supply curve, which is horizontal at 3 francs. In competitive equilibrium, price equals 3 francs and output is 18 million bottles daily.

You can see the deadweight loss to consumers stemming from monopoly in Figure 14.1a. Under competition, consumer surplus equals the area between the competitive price and the demand curve up to the quantity bought, or $\frac{1}{2}(12 - 3)(18) = 81$ million francs. Under monopoly, consumers' surplus is reduced to $\frac{1}{2}(12 - 7.5)(9) = 20.25$ million, which is supplemented by revenues of 40.5 million francs $[= (7.5 - 3)9]$, which the monopolist extracts from demanders. The deadweight loss is thus 20.25 million francs.

Move on to Figure 14.1b. With the market shared equally by Cour and Not, each sells 6 million bottles daily at a price of 6 francs per bottle.[11] With 12 million bottles sold, the deadweight loss shrinks to 9 million francs.

Efficiency

The absence of price competition removes a spur to efficiency both in the short run and in the long run. Like the monopolist, the oligopolist is not forced to operate at the minimum point of its ATC curve. Once again, however, in contrast with monopoly, some pressure is placed on the oligopolist by other oligopolists. Moreover, insofar as entry is easier in oligopoly than in monopoly, the threat of entrants may induce oligopolists to monitor their costs more carefully.

Resource Allocation

The discrepancy between price and marginal revenue and the matching of marginal revenue and marginal cost foster the same sort of resource maldistribution under oligopoly as under monopoly. In both cases, because output will not be driven to the point where MC = P, MSB > MSC. Although increased production would move MSB closer to MSC, output expansion is not in the interest of the oligopolists.

In short, theory and fact fault oligopoly as a less desirable type of market structure than perfect competition. The normative implication follows: control oligopoly or, even better, convert oligopolistic markets into perfectly competitive ones.

In Defense of Oligopoly

The above conclusions seem too simplistic to many economists. They are based on static models that disregard pro-oligopoly rationales. And the "facts" are not that conclusive, either.

Structure, Conduct, and Performance Revisited

The first attack against both theory and evidence builds on the truth known to every student of statistics: correlation does not prove causation. Theory claims that oligopolists are not efficient because they don't need to be. That they are nevertheless profitable is indicative of their market power. And evidence supports at least part of the proposition: industries that are more concentrated are also more profitable.

    The critics of this view challenge the interpretation of the evidence as well as the reasoning of the argument. The correlation of concentration and profitability does not prove that concentration causes profitability. It may well be that high profitability causes concentration. And theory suggests why: economies of scale. If larger firms are more efficient but their long-run cost curves turn up before exhausting demand, there may well be room for a few highly efficient oligopolists. Indeed, only an oligopolistic market structure will yield low-cost production.[12] Proving the inefficiency of oligopoly will require other evidence.

Contestable Markets

The theory of contestable markets (MicroBits 9.4, p. 321) suggests another reason why oligopoly may be consistent with efficiency and proper resource allocation. (You recall that a contestable market is one in which entry and exit are costless, so that the threat of entry by a potential competitor suffices to ensure competitive performance even in an oligopolistic market.) To be sure, in the real world, entry and exit are rarely costless, but even the entry barriers set up by oligopolists are not absolutely insurmountable. True, brand names and scarce capital resources deter entry, yet giant corporations in related industries often have both. Thus, the threat to complacency and the goad to efficiency come not from start-ups, but from oligopolists who cross industry lines. For example, Polaroid announced in 1988 that it would expand beyond its traditional sphere of instant cameras and film to market its own brand of conventional film. It would challenge Kodak, which had captured 80 percent of the $7 billion U.S. market, and Fuji, which had 10 percent. And in the ethnic food market, Campbell Soup invaded the Hispanic market, previously dominated by Goya Foods.

No less important is the potential entry by foreign suppliers. They are familiar with production and marketing methods, they often have the requisite deep pockets, and they frequently come with a polished brand name. If their production facilities are not fully utilized, their entry and exit costs in the domestic market may well be negligible. So, Airbus challenges Boeing; Japanese and Korean personal computers give IBM and Compaq a strong run for the money; the U.S. tire industry meets heavy competition from Michelin (France), Bridgestone (Japan), and Pirelli (Italy); and no one needs to point to the ubiquitous Japanese car.

Contestable market theory, then, suggests that oligopolists will realize the danger to their bottom line that comes from either domestic or foreign potential competitors. That tempers their power, and forces them—in some cases more, in others less—to emulate competitive results.

Long-Run Competition

Even oligopolists face competition in the long run. The various devices that deter entry may operate for a while, but if the incentive is sufficient, oligopolistic markets will be penetrated or circumvented.[13]

Two bits of interesting evidence support this contention. First, take a look at Figure 14.2, which reproduces the results of William G. Shepard's study of the trend of manufacturing competition in the United States

FIGURE 14.2   The Competitive Structure of U.S. Manufacturing, 1958 and 1980

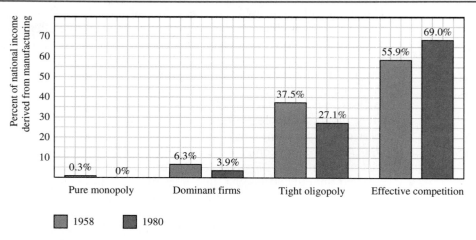

SOURCE: Calculated from William G. Shepard, ''Causes of Increased Competition in the U.S. Economy, 1939–1980,'' *Review of Economics and Statistics* 64 (November 1982), Table 3, p. 619.

between 1958 and 1980.[14] Shepard categorized all industries into four market structure-conduct-performance groups:

1. *Pure monopoly.* Market share of a single firm approaches 100 percent; entry is restricted; prices are controlled.

2. *Dominant firms.* Market share of 50 to 90 percent; no close rivals; high entry barriers; strong price control; excess profits.

3. *Tight oligopoly.* Four-firm concentration ratio above 60 percent; stable market shares; entry difficult; interdependence recognized.

4. *Effective competition.* Four-firm concentration ratio below 40 percent; unstable market shares; flexible pricing; low entry barriers; little collusion; low profitability.

Figure 14.2 shows that between 1958 and 1980, effective competition in U.S. manufacturing rose by 13.1 percentage points while the two oligopoly categories, combined, fell by 12.8 percentage points. Shepard attributes these changes to deregulation, antitrust actions, and foreign competition. Surely your own eyes bear witness to the role of imports in the consumer electronics and photography markets.

A second measure of the dynamics of the market is suggested by Table 14.3, which lists the 10 largest manufacturing, mining, and distribution firms in 1909 and in 1987. That the U.S. economy does not guarantee

TABLE 14.3   **The 10 Largest U.S. Manufacturers by Assets, 1909 and 1987**

*1909 Rank**	*1987 Rank§*
1. United States Steel, now USX (17)	1. General Motors
2. Standard Oil of New Jersey, Exxon (3)	2. Sears, Roebuck (45)
3. American Tobacco, American Brands (52)	3. Exxon, formerly Standard Oil of New Jersey (2)
4. International Merchant Marine	4. IBM
5. International Harvester	5. Ford Motor Co.
6. Anaconda Copper	6. Mobil Oil
7. U.S. Leather	7. General Electric (16)
8. Armour	8. Chevron
9. American Sugar Refining	9. Texaco (91)
10. Pullman Inc.	10. Du Pont (29)

* 1987 rank is in parentheses; lack of number indicates that firm dropped out of the top 100.

§ 1909 rank is in parentheses; lack of number indicates that firm was not listed among the top 100 in 1909.

SOURCE: F. M. Scherer and David Ross, *Industrial Market Structure and Economic Performance* (Boston: Houghton Mifflin, 1990), pp. 68–69.

survival to any firm, no matter how powerful it may appear at any point of time, is evident from a comparison of the two columns. Of the top 10 in 1909, only 1 manufacturer remained in that group in 1987, and the 7 that dropped were not found even among the 100 leaders in 1987. Similarly, 5 of the top 10 in 1987 were not even on the top 100 list in 1909.

Oligopoly and Economic Growth

The static models of the firm ignore the firm's growth over time and thus its contribution to economic advancement. At the core lies a simple question: Will competition or oligopoly encourage more invention, more technological change, and greater economic growth?

Competition may be a poor vehicle for stimulating new methods of production for three reasons:

1. *Lack of internal funds.* With excess profits driven down ever closer to zero in a competitive market, there's just no surplus to devote to research and development.
2. *Difficulty in obtaining external funds.* The absence of significant and long-lasting profits combined with the high risk of failure dampen outsiders' willingness to lend to competitive firms.
3. *Inability to capitalize on innovations.* Because of the competitive firm's small market share, it will be unable to exploit its discoveries sufficiently to recoup its outlays.

Consequently, the competitive firm lacks both the ability and the incentive to initiate new and more efficient methods of production. It is hardly surprising, then, that the major technological innovations of the past half-century were introduced into everyday life by large oligopolistic corporations, from which their very invention often came. Clearly, the ability to amass excess profits enables oligopolies to spend money on research and development and to take the risks associated with potentially fruitless investments. The absence of competitive pressures enables the oligopolist to take the chance that significant and marketable scientific and technological breakthroughs will emerge. And since oligopolists control a significant share of their market, they can capture for themselves the fruits of successful discoveries.

The Competitive Response.   If these arguments were sound, you would expect to find a strong correlation between the degree of industry concentration and innovation. In fact, the evidence is fragile.[15] Read Professor Jesse W. Markham's assessment of a number of such studies:

> As the factual analyses indicate, invention apparently remains largely a matter of individual genius, while innovational effort, however measured, appears to be disproportionately centered in the largest several hundred manu-

facturing corporations, and these large companies qualify (more frequently than not) as oligopolists. . . . [Yet] the evidence confirms that innovational effort is not spread throughout American industry in neat proportion to the concentration indexes for those industries.[16]

In other words, while some degree of concentration is associated with research and development, the fact that an industry is more concentrated does not necessarily mean that it will be more innovative. True, oligopolists have the ability and some incentive to innovate, but they also lack the pressure that characterizes more competitive markets.[17]

The defenders of oligopoly are, then, agnostic. Evidence seeming to demonstrate oligopolistic exploitation can be reinterpreted to be meaningless. Theory that suggests oligopoly is immune from competition doesn't take into account domestic and foreign contestability, nor does it account for the continuous flux in a dynamic economy that weakens the strong and strengthens the newborn. Indeed, oligopoly may demonstrate such positive virtues as fostering new technology and economic advancement and bringing costs down through economies of scale. Oligopoly's defenders contend that the case against oligopoly has been oversold.

The New Empirical Industrial Organization (NEIO)

Economic theory was the foundation upon which empirical studies of industry structure and performance were built. The serious studies, using the fledgling tools of an infant econometrics methodology, began in the 1950s and the blossomed thereafter. They more or less confirmed the theorists' notions that structure and performance were related and that deviations from the competitive marketplace reduced economic welfare.

What's Wrong with the Old Industrial Organization?

In a wide-ranging survey of the new empirical industrial organization, Stanford's Timothy F. Bresnahan focuses on three key differences between the old and the new:[18]

- Accounting data as a source of price-cost margin information.
- The use of cross-industry studies.
- The role of reduced-form empirical equations.

Accounting Data. Accounting records that firms generate for financial and tax purposes have traditionally been the major source of information about industry conduct and performance. These are only obliquely related to such economic concepts as opportunity costs; they arbitrarily allocate fixed costs; and they link depreciation deductions to the tax code rather than to the economic use of assets. Earlier empirical industrial organization studies adjusted wherever possible, but a gap still emerged between the basic data and the kind economists desire.

Cross-Industry Studies.   The SCP model presumes that behavior is universal rather than industry specific. Thus, the SCP methodology implies that there's really no difference between the steel oligopoly and the auto oligopoly. Wherever the structure deviates from the competitive norm, firms are presumed to have and to use their market power, which is reflected then in their performance. Consequently, economists could reach conclusions by generalizing from a broad range of industry studies.

Reduced-Form Equations.   Reexamine Professor Weiss's equation in MicroBits 14.1. Although it seeks to determine the price-cost margin, its explanatory variables are not the ones you'd normally expect, such as demand and costs. It skips over such fundamentals to specify a number of broad-based forces that are thought to determine the profit margin. While using reduced-form estimating equations is certainly legitimate, it is more roundabout than examining the primary determinants of the profit margin.

NEIO economists use the economic theory of oligopoly to model each specific industry. They examine the price-cost structure of each industry directly, attempting to estimate prices and marginal costs within the model. Conduct, which is not measurable in SCP models, can be estimated from the NEIO equations, so that researchers can investigate the relationship between conduct and performance.

The Results

NEIO studies, because they derive industry-specific equations, are less easily generalized. This is compounded by the infant-industry status of NEIO, which means that the number of studies is still small. On the other hand, because NEIO studies estimate prices and marginal costs, the theoretically satisfying Lerner index can be calculated. Table 14.4 lists £ values calculated for a variety of industries.

Bresnahan finds that his review of the NEIO literature permits three qualified conclusions:

1. As is evident from Table 14.4, there's substantial market power in some industries.
2. Anticompetitive conduct does cause high price-cost margins.
3. There's much still to be learned about the relationship between structure and market power.

In short, the NEIO guardedly supports SCP in some of its conclusions. At least on the empirical level, concentration is associated with

TABLE 14.4   **The Lerner Index for Selected U.S. Industries**

Industry	$\pounds$
Food processing	0.504
Coffee roasting	0.55
Rubber	0.049
Textiles	0.072
Electrical machinery	0.198
Tobacco	0.648
Railroads	0.40
Retail gasoline	0.10
Automobiles	0.1/0.34*
Aluminum	0.59

* Varies by type of car; larger in the standard, luxury segment.
SOURCE: Adapted from Timothy F. Bresnahan, "Empirical Studies of Industries with Market Power," *Handbook of Industrial Organization,* vol. 2, p. 1051. Table 17.1. All the studies cited were published between 1981 and 1986.

anticompetitive performance. What that means and implies, however, still remains subject to dispute. The war continues between those who view oligopoly as not that bad and maybe even quite good and those who see oligopoly as straying from the competitive market model and its welfare implications. The resolution of this debate, of course, extends beyond the realm of theory and the interpretation of empirical studies. Policy is at stake, since government control of oligopoly is colored by one's attitude about its consequences. (MicroBits 14.2 surveys briefly the controversy surrounding advertising, which is characteristic of imperfect competition.)

Oligopoly and Antitrust

The jury is still out on the question raised earlier in this chapter: Is oligopoly beneficial or detrimental to the economy? Indeed, no matter how many economists have been laid end to end, the profession still hasn't reached a conclusion. Nevertheless, the thinking of economists has influenced antitrust prosecutions especially in the last decade. Let's begin with a consensus issue: price fixing.

MicroBits 14.2

Advertising: The Public View

Chapter 13 examined advertising expenditures from the viewpoint of the individual firm. Here, we take the broader focus of society as a whole. Of course, no one denies that advertising agencies and major corporate marketing departments employ hordes of advertising executives who directly benefit from advertising expenditures. And undoubtedly the media depend heavily on advertising revenues. Economists, however, wonder whether "we, the people" gain or lose from advertising. Would we on balance be better-off without advertising or with less of it?

The Pros

On the one hand, advertising is an important means of disseminating information about new or altered products, as well as about changes in product price and quality. Certainly, our costs of amassing information are reduced by checking prices in a newspaper or magazine or learning about the virtues of a new product by watching its performance on

TV. Furthermore, advertising may broaden the firm's market, enabling it to take advantage of economies of scale.

The Cons

On the other hand, advertising often provides useless, misleading, or outright incorrect information. Much advertising is sheer waste, because its objective is primarily to neutralize the advertising of a fellow oligopolist. Given a choice, consumers might prefer to see half the money spent on beer advertising used to lower beer prices. Futhermore, do consumers really benefit when advertising aims to differentiate products that are fundamentally identical, such as a generic and a brand-name aspirin? Are we ennobled by deodorant ads that encourage us to ostracize those who don't spray their underarms? Indeed, the very attitude cherished by marketing executives is questioned by many economists and consumer advocates. The latter would strongly dispute the words of one lead-

Price Fixing

Section 1 of the Sherman Antitrust Act (1890) begins as follows:

> Every contract, combination in the fo.m of trust or otherwise, or conspiracy, in restraint of trade or commerce among the several States, or with foreign nations, is hereby declared illegal.

As early as 1897, the Supreme Court ruled that price fixing or market-sharing conspiracies violated Section 1 of the act, a policy that the courts have consistently employed since. (Recall the *Goldfarb* v. *Virginia State Bar* of MicroBits 12.1, p. 410.) Most economists support such rulings, for price fixing impedes competition and provides no discernable benefit except to the pockets of the price fixers.

MicroBits 14.2 continued

ing advertising textbook, which proclaims, "Advertising can add value to a product in the consumer's mind." The rhetorical question of the advertising text—"What do you think most consumers prefer: to buy an unadvertised brand of denim pants or Levi's?"*— would be thought meaningless if the two products wear equally well.

Another issue has been raised: Does advertising contribute to the subversion of competitiveness throughout the economy? Does savvy advertising enable some firms to gain sufficient strength to weaken and ultimately eliminate competition? The competitive impact of advertising has been studied extensively. Unfortunately, the studies are inconclusive. As Comanor and Wilson wrote:

> The weight of available evidence is consistent with the hypothesis that heavy advertising can have substantial anticompetitive consequences. However, because the distribution of advertis-

ing intensities is highly skewed, there is no indication that these effects are pervasive throughout the economy, or even within the manufacturing sector. Rather, they appear to be concentrated in a small number of industries with high advertising-sales ratios and/or high absolute levels of advertising per firm.§

In other words, in some industries advertising has been shown to reduce competition. Yet Comanor and Wilson also cite studies that are consistent with the hypothesis that advertising actually increases competition.

But even if the evidence were overwhelmingly one-sided, the debate would still continue. The role of advertising in a free and open society transcends the economic dimensions; it has philosophical and political overtones as well.

_____

* Courtland L. Bove and William F. Arens, *Contemporary Advertising* (Homewood, Ill.: Irwin, 1986), p. 32.

_____

§ William S. Comanor and Thomas A. Wilson, "The Effect of Advertising on Competition: A Survey," *Journal of Economic Literature* 17 (June 1979), pp. 453–76. The passage cited is from page 470.

Is "Bigness" Bad?

Whether or not domination of a market similarly violates public policy is a more complex issue. Is a monopolistic or oligopolistic structure per se, no matter what conduct or performance results, undesirable? Section 2 of the Sherman Act contains the following text:

> Every person who shall monopolize, or attempt to monopolize, or combine or conspire with any other person or persons, to monopolize any part of the trade or commerce among several States, or with foreign nations, shall be deemed guilty of a misdemeanor.

Does a firm that grows large enough to dominate a market violate Section 2? The courts have vacillated in resolving this question. The

The **rule of reason** views only unreasonable intent and actions as violations of the monopolization prohibition of the Sherman Antitrust Act.

Supreme Court articulated the **rule of reason** in two major antitrust cases in 1911. Only conduct that was unreasonable violated the Sherman Act.[19] That market domination attained through acceptable business behavior was not unlawful was strikingly confirmed in the U.S. Steel case (1920). Despite the fact that U.S. Steel controlled 50 percent of the market, and the "corporation is undoubtedly of impressive size . . . [,] the law does not make mere size an offense. . . . It, we repeat, requires overt acts."[20] To possess the power implied by an imperfectly competitive market structure but not to use it was lawful.

The pendulum swung back in 1945, when the rule of reason was effectively reversed. The structure-conduct-performance model that inextricably linked the three components suggested that the first inevitably led to the rest. Judge Learned Hand of the federal appellate bench ruled that Alcoa had violated Section 2 of the Sherman Act by virtue of its size. It was the sole domestic producer of virgin aluminum ingot.[21] Judge Hand found that congressional intent "did not condone 'good trusts' and condemn 'bad' ones; it forbade all." Given the structure of the aluminum market, even benign conduct by Alcoa that supported its market dominance was illegal behavior.

The structural test has come under increasing attack since the late 1970s. In both court cases and Justice Department actions, behavior once again is the criteria. Price cutting that has the effect of limiting entry is acceptable, for example, provided that costs are not reduced below average costs.[22] This new attitude represents a successful challenge to the static oligopoly models by those confident that market forces effectively restrain anticompetitive behavior even in highly concentrated markets and/or those who believe in the net benefits of large size. It apparently lay beneath the Reagan administration's dropping of an antitrust case against IBM that had begun in the lower courts in 1969 and had been in progress for six years.

Implicit Collusion

Prior to the 1980s, a leaderless oligopoly, or one without evidence of explicit collusion, escaped antitrust prosecution. The absence of a firm with substantial control of the market meant that Section 2 of the Sherman Act was not an issue, while the absence of collusion protected the firms against Section 1 violations. With the rule of reason recapturing the limelight, even an oligopoly with a clear industry leader seems to be safe as well. Does that mean that the anticompetitive performance of oligopoly is protected by law even though interdependence implies collusion? This, of course, was the issue in the FTC's suit against the Big Four cereal manufacturers.

The Cereal Case. You recall the issue: The FTC contended that the oligopoly structure of the market buttressed by the price leadership of Kellogg's was itself unlawful. No less than a monopolist did the presence of the Big Four and their substantial marketing power keep potential entrants out. The few who tried to breach the entry barrier were soon repulsed. Furthermore, the FTC pointed to the deadweight loss suffered by consumers, which would be maintained as long as the market was dominated by the Big Four. The absence of explicit collusion did not alter these economic facts.

This novel application of economic theory could have changed the face of U.S. industry. But in 1982, the FTC chickened out; it dismissed the case. Today, noncollusive oligopoly is beyond the pale of the antitrust laws. Again, this stance presumes either that the market knows best or that oligopoly is on balance superior to perfect competition.

Mergers

Horizontal Mergers. The distinction made Chapter 13 between horizontal, vertical, and conglomerate mergers finds its legal counterpart in the differential treatment of such mergers by the authorities and courts. The ruling law here is the Clayton Antitrust Act (1914), which prohibits actions and combinations that "substantially lessen competition or . . . tend to create a monopoly." Horizontal mergers that either reduce competition or even limit potential competition have been barred under the provisions of the Clayton Act, provided the impact on competition was found to be substantial. The Justice Department issued its own merger guidelines, defining the conditions under which it will initiate antitrust prosecution. The Herfindahl-Hirschman index is ceded a central role in the decision process. The guidelines take into account both the premerger and postmerger HHI. A small increase in the HHI will trigger an antitrust suit if the industry's HHI is already sizable, but only a large increment will lead to Justice Department intervention if the premerger HHI is small. The HHI, however, is not applied mechanically. Evidence on structure is tempered by other considerations, such as entry barriers and efficiency consequences, as theory would recommend.[23]

Vertical and Conglomerate Mergers. Vertical mergers that create barriers to entry, facilitate collusion, or are designed to circumvent rate regulation are also subject to the Justice Department's merger guidelines. Indeed, the doctrine of "foreclosure," or limiting opportunities to competitors through vertical combinations, has a long record of case law behind it. Conglomerate mergers, because they do not reduce competition in any single market, are almost immune from antitrust prosecution nowadays, which accounts for their current popularity.

In general, the prevalent attitude toward antitrust, especially as it concerns oligopoly, is one of benign neglect. This rejection of the activist policy of earlier times reflects a more conservative philosophy about the proper role of government in the economy. But it also can be attributed to economic theory. Neither economic reasoning nor empirical evidence conclusively justifies an active antitrust posture. The fact that static microeconomic theories point to the malevolence of oligopoly insofar as consumer benefits, efficiency, and resource allocation are concerned is tempered by the dynamic aspects of the competitive process. Oligopolists can't ignore potential competitors when entry barriers are low or can be surmounted with relative ease, nor can they feel sheltered over the long run in a vibrant economy. But even if oligopoly limits the benefits to consumers, that may be the price that has to be paid in order to achieve efficient, low-cost production.

Summary

Public policy toward oligopoly can best be understood within the structure-conduct-performance (SCP) framework. If a market structure is less than perfectly competitive, the industry's firms will conduct themselves in light of their power, which leads to performances that depart from those predicted by the model of the perfectly competitive marketplace. The initial step in fleshing out the SCP skeleton is to quantify *structure*. Economists have used the four-firm concentration ratio, the Herfindahl-Hirschman index, and the Lerner index. None are perfect. Today's favorite is the HHI, which is used by the Justice Department as the centerpiece of its merger guidelines. The Lerner index is also enjoying a resurgence, coming to life in the research of the new empirical industrial organization (NEIO) movement. The evidence that springs forth from both the NEIO and the more traditional SCP studies indicates that concentration and performance do move together. The less competitive an industry is, the more profitable it tends to be.

Interpreting the empirical studies is controversial indeed. The traditional view, based on static models of oligopoly, points to high prices, limited quantity, inefficient production, and resource maldistribution as the results of imperfect competition. These conclusions have been challenged by economists who assert that the traditionalists have it backward. Efficiency causes high profits and thus oligopoly. Moreover, oligopolists cannot seal themselves in a protective cocoon. Markets are contestable, and invasion by oligopolists in other industries or by foreign competitors constitutes a real threat. Finally, oligopoly promotes economic growth, since excess oligopoly profits provide funds for research and development and since the control of the market enables the oligopolist to recoup research and development expenses. (The evidence on oligopoly-induced innovation, however, is inconclusive.)

These two views of oligopoly imply altogether different stances with respect to public control of oligopoly. Although both schools support antitrust prosecution of explicit price fixing, they differ as to whether bigness equals badness. The courts, too, have waffled over this issue. Early decisions used the rule of reason to declare unlawful only those firms that had behaved inappropriately. That attitude changed in the post–World War II period, so that a monopoly, or in rare cases an oligopoly, structure itself was taken to imply an antitrust violation even without improper action. More recently, faith in market forces has led both the federal government and the courts to downplay the inherent evil of an oligopolistic structure. That same attitude has shaped current policy with respect to the implicit collu-

sion that occurs in price leadership or kinked demand curve situations. On the merger front, horizontal mergers are more likely to encounter the scrutiny of the antitrust authority than are vertical mergers, while conglomerate mergers tend to be left unchallenged.

On the whole, oligopoly theory and policy remain unsettled issues. This is less true of the final market structure, the subject of Chapter 15.

Key Terms

Four-firm concentration ratio
Herfindahl-Hirschman index (HHI)
Lerner index ($£$)

Rule of reason
Standard Industrial Classification (SIC) Code

Review Questions

1. Explain the advantages and disadvantages of the three measures of industry structure discussed in this chapter.

2. *a.* What are the policy implications of defining both industry and geographic markets either narrowly or broadly?
   b. Cite some actual examples where the breadth of definition would have led to different policy decisions.

3. Compare and contrast the welfare implications of the static theory of oligopoly to monopoly on the one hand and perfect competition on the other.

4. *a.* If firms operating in imperfectly competitive markets earn abnormally high profits, why do some economists reject

   the conclusion that the lack of competition is responsible for their unusual earnings? Explain.
   b. What alternative hypothesis do they offer?

5. Defend oligopoly as superior to perfect competition.

6. *a.* Explain the NEIO criticism of traditional SCP studies.
   b. How do the NEIO results compare to the SCP outcomes?

7. What role has the rule of reason played in antitrust policy?

8. Should economists favor applying the antitrust rules to oligopolistic markets even in the absence of collusion? Explain.

Food for Thought

1. *a.* Calculate the coefficient of correlation between the concentration ratio and the HHI in Table 14.1.

   b. Explain why this coefficient is less than 1.

2. Show and explain why it is possible for £ to be smaller for a monopolist than for an oligopolist.

3. Calculate the deadweight loss along the lines of Figure 14.1, but assume that marginal cost is rising.

4. Use a payoff matrix to demonstrate that although two oligopolists who dominate an industry would benefit from reducing their marketing outlays, neither will do so independently.

5. A new artificial low-calorie sweetener, acesulfame potassium, was approved by the FDA in 1988. To be marketed by a U.S. subsidiary of a German pharmaceutical conglomerate, it will complete directly with saccharin and aspartame. Use this information in fashioning a defense of oligopoly.

6. While Alcoa, the number one aluminum producer in the United States, remains a vertically integrated aluminum company, Reynolds Metals, the number two company, began a program of diversification in 1985. Reynold's consumer products division no longer manufactures only aluminum foil, but waxed paper, plastic wrap, and plastic food bags as well. In addition, Reynolds acquired a substantial interest in two Australian gold mines. Comment on these different strategies both from the business and the legal viewpoints.

7. Obtain a copy of the U.S. Justice Department's merger guidelines and comment on their relationship to the theory of the firm.

Suggested Readings

In addition to the relevant portions of the *Handbook of Industrial Organization* mentioned in the readings section of Chapter 13, you will be amply rewarded by consulting F. M. Scherer and David Ross's classic textbook, *Industrial Market Structure and Economic Performance* (Boston: Houghton Mifflin, 1990). Should you be overawed by Scherer and Ross's abundance of detail, less comprehensive but more modern texts are William F. Shughart II, *The Organization of Industry* (Homewood, Ill.: BPI/Irwin, 1990) and Douglas F. Greer, *Industrial Organization and Public Policy* (New York: Macmillian, 1992). Judge Robert H. Bork's *The Antitrust Paradox: A Policy at War with Itself* (New York: Basic Books, 1979) poses a serious challenge to traditional antitrust theory.

Notes and Answers

1. Based on "Snap, Crackle, and Divestiture," *The New York Times,* April 25, 1976, pp. C1, 9.

2. $(15 - 6)/15 = .60$ and $(250 - 138)/250 = .44$

3. The proof hinges on the relationship between marginal revenue and price, $MR = P(1 + 1/\varepsilon)$, and the equilibrium condition, $MR = MC$. Substitute MC for MR and multiply out the right side to obtain: $MC = P(1 + 1/\varepsilon) = P + P/\varepsilon$. Subtract P from both sides and divide both sides by P: $(MC - P)/P = 1/\varepsilon$.

Since ε is negative, multiply both sides by -1 and rearrange the terms to: $£ = (P - MC)/P = 1/|\varepsilon|$.

4. The index is named after its two independent discoverers, both linked to Columbia University. Professor Albert O. Hirschman, who taught there many years before moving on to Princeton, published his version in 1945, while O. C. Herfindahl devised his formulation for his 1950 Columbia Ph.D. dissertation.

5. For the former, HHI $= 4(20)^2 + 20(1)2 = 1,620$; for the latter, HHI $= 50^2 + 3(10)^2 + 20(1)^2 = 2,820$, a 74 percent increase.

6. Premerger: $40.3^2 + 30.2^2 + 5.4^2 + 5.3^2 + 4.5^2 + 1.3^2 + 13(1^2) = 2,628.32$. Postmerger: $45.7^2 + 35.5^2 + 4.5^2 + 1.3^2 + 13(1^2) = 3,383.68$.

7. The distribution of firms within the casket industry is more uneven than that in the recording industry. You might spend a moment thinking about the public policy implications of this distinction.

8. For an excellent discussion of concentration measures and their problems, see F. M. Scherer and David Ross, *Industrial Market Structure and Economic Performance* (Boston: Houghton Mifflin, 1990), Chapters 3 and 11.

9. Scherer and Ross, *Industrial Market Structure,* p. 78, point out an interesting anomaly: The four-firm concentration ratio in the "bottled and canned soft drinks industry" in 1982 was only 14, because each local bottling firm is counted individually. Since we know that the market is dominated by Coca-Cola and PepsiCo, a better handle on this industry is obtained by examining a five-digit entry, "liquid beverage bases for use by soft drink bottlers," where the four-firm concentration ratio in 1982 was 90.

10. The rate of profit normally is defined as price less *average* cost over price, and so is not a Lerner index, which requires marginal not average cost.

11. Intuition suggests that no more than 18 million will be sold even in a competitive market. Since each duopolist will capture a third of the market, the combined total is 12 million. You can prove this algebraically by returning to the mathematical proof of Cournot equilibrium in Chapter 13 (p. 461), and substituting MC = 3 for the MC = 0 assumption there.

12. An alternative interpretation of the profitability-concentration nexus suggests that innovations, managerial expertise, or even good luck explain both size and profitability. So, although concentration and profitability are correlated, concentration did not cause profitability, nor did profitability cause concentra-

tion. Either explanation torpedoes the conclusion that oligopoly is inefficient. See Scherer and Ross, *Industrial Market Structure,* pp. 430ff. and Chapter 17.

13. Refer back to p. 409 in connection with entry into monopoly markets.

14. William G. Shepard, "Causes of Increased Competition in the U.S. Economy, 1939–1980," *Review of Economics and Statistics* 64 (November 1982), pp. 613–26.

15. Wesley M. Cohen and Richard C. Levin, "Empirical Studies of Innovation and Market Structure," in *Handbook of Industrial Organization,* vol. 2, eds. Richard Schamlensee and Robert D. Willig (New York: North-Holland, 1989), p. 1078.

16. "Market Concentration and Innovation," in *Industrial Concentration: The New Learning,* ed. Harvey J. Goldschmid et al. (Boston: Little Brown, 1974), p. 268.

17. Scherer and Ross, *Industrial Market Structure,* concludes: "[T]heory and evidence suggest a threshhold concept of the most favorite industrial climate for rapid technological change. A bit of monopoly power in the form of structural concentration is conducive to innovation. . . . But very high concentration has a positive effect only in rare cases, and more often it is apt to retard progress by restricting the number of independent sources of initiative and by dampening firms' incentive to gain market position through accelerated R&D" (p. 660).

18. Timothy F. Bresnahan, "Empirical Studies of Industries with Market Power," *Handbook of Industrial Organization,* vol. 2, pp. 1012–57. This section is based on Bresnahan's survey.

19. In both the Standard Oil and the American Tobacco Co. cases (U.S. 221, 1 and 106), the court found that the companies used their power to drive competitors out of business, including undercutting prices in local markets to force their competitors into bankruptcy.

20. 251 U.S. 417.

21. 148 F. 2d 416.

22. One federal court suggested that prices set on a marginal cost basis, even if below ATC, do

not signal monopolization. See *California Computer Products* v. *International Business Machines,* 613 F.2d 727 (9th Cir. 1979). The cases cited in this section and others as well are excerpted in Irwin M. Stelzer, *Selected Antitrust Cases: Landmark Decisions* (Homewood, Ill.: Richard D. Irwin, 1986).

23. See U.S. Department of Justice, *Justice Department Merger Guidelines* (1984) and "Department of Justice and Federal Trade Commission Horizontal Merger Guidelines," *Antitrust & Trade Regulation Report* 62, no. 1559 (April 2, 1992), Special Supplement, pp. S2–13.

15

MONOPOLISTIC COMPETITION IS NEITHER MONOPOLY NOR COMPETITION

If the facts don't fit the theory, change the facts.
Albert Einstein

All professionals are conspiracies against the laity.
George Bernard Shaw

Learning Objectives

In this chapter you'll learn:

- How monopolistic competition differs from monopoly and oligopoly on the one hand and perfect competition on the other.
- How monopolistically competitive prices are determined in both the short run and the long run.
- The roles played by asymmetric information, time and convenience, uncertainty, and location in monopolistic competitive markets.
- The difficulty in deciding whether monopolistic competition is beneficial or detrimental to the economy.

And, as a conclusion to imperfect competition, you'll understand:

- How the models of these chapters relate to actual pricing decisions in regulated natural monopolies, illegal monopolies, oligopolies, and monopolistic competition.

A Puzzling Introduction

A Quiz

Why not begin this chapter by answering two multiple-choice questions?

1. Your car just conked out along U.S. 40, somewhere in the Mojave Desert, hundreds of miles away from home. Fortunately, a passing tow truck hauls your vehicle to the nearest town. Which one of the following diagnoses is the mechanic, after inspecting your car, most likely to propose?

   a. The transmission is shot. ($500 to repair.)

   b. The carburetor is so gummed up that it wouldn't pay to have it repaired. (Used carburetor: $275.)

   c. The battery is dead and is beyond recharging. (New battery: $85.)

   d. The battery cable somehow worked itself loose, and just has to be reattached. (No charge.)

2. Your car has just conked out two blocks away from the shop of the mechanic who has serviced your vehicle for the last five years. You walk over to his garage, and he walks back with you to check over the car. Which of the four options listed is the most likely diagnosis?

Write your answers here: 1. _____ 2. _____

While you're still puzzling over the relevance of these questions, consider a related quandary.

Choosing a Gasoline Station

The locations of 7 neighborhood gasoline stations and the actual price each charged for a gallon of unleaded regular in May 1992 are depicted in Figure 15.1. All of these stations are self-service outlets and, except for Mobil station A, did not distinguish between cash and credit payments. Notice not only the price range—from $1.239 to $1.349—but also that no two adjacent stations had the same price. Notice, too, the discrepancy between the prices charged at Mobil A and Mobil B.

Monopolistic competition is similar to perfect competition in terms of many suppliers and ease of entry and exit, but it is also like monopoly in that firms control price to some degree.

The puzzle lies not in why these gasoline retailers charge different prices but in why consumers let them get away with it. Are drivers acting irrationally by not filling up at the cheapest station, or is there an acceptable explanation for their behavior?

If you believe that gas buyers are acting reasonably because there's a difference in the brands they buy, you'll have discovered the key to this chapter. Markets characterized by **monopolistic competition** offer products that are simultaneously unique and similar. Indeed, the term *monop-*

FIGURE 15.1   Location and Prices of Seven Retail Gasoline Service Stations, May 1992

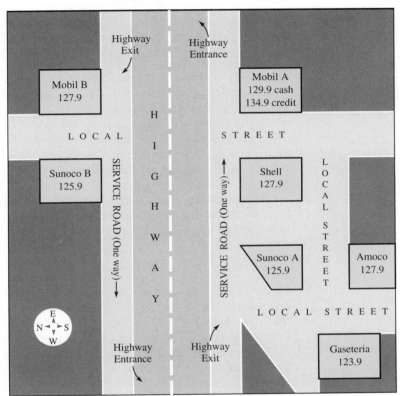

olistic competition itself implies the paradox, for it suggests elements of both monopoly and perfect competition. Like the monopolist, the monopolist competitor has some control over its market and thus over price. But unlike monopoly and oligopoly, with few or no competitors and with entry restricted, monopolistic competition approaches perfect competition with respect to both the extent of competitors and the relative ease of entry and exit.

How these contrasting characteristics determine price in monopolistic competition is the subject of the next section of this chapter. The model is expanded in the third section to bring theory closer to reality. Beyond enhancing our conceptual understanding of monopolistically competitive markets, this broader model casts a different light on public policy toward this market structure, which is taken up in the fourth section. This final chapter on imperfect competition ends by reviewing and exploring further the relevance of imperfect competition models to the world in which we live. Do decision makers in firms act as microeconomic theory suggests they do or should?

The Theory of Monopolistic Competition

Begin with a typical college neighborhood that contains any number of restaurants catering to students, faculty, and staff. Within a few blocks of the campus, you'll find Pepito's Mexicana, Lugosi's Transylvanian Retreat, and André's French Château. Of course, southern dishes are available from Hominy's Grits, Middle Eastern food from the Cedars of Lebanon, Chinese delicacies from Lily Wong, and Italian specialties from Tony's. And don't forget the college dining hall and the ubiquitous McDonald's, Wendy's, and Burger King.

The preparation and sale of meals is the common denominator that links all of these competitors for your patronage. Yet each one is unique to some degree, if only by virtue of its specialized menu.

Equilibrium in the Short Run

Figure 15.2a shows two demand curves, the overall demand for eating out and the specific demand for Lily Wong's place. Common sense dictates that only a part of the entire market will be attracted to Lily Wong's Chinese menu, so Figure 15.2a depicts Lily Wong's demand curve within the entire market demand curve. For example, if every restaurant charged $9 for a dinner, Lily Wong would supply only 3,000 of the 54,000 dinners sold that week.

MICROQUERY   Which demand curve is more elastic at $9? Why? (Hint: $\Delta Q/\Delta P$ on the industry demand curve = 857.14) _____

_____ [1]

Note an important fact. The elasticity of demand for Lily Wong is not infinite, as it would be in the case of perfect competition. That's because a meal at Lily Wong is not identical to a meal at any other restaurant. Lily's unique menu implies that she will not lose her entire clientele if her prices are higher than those of the other eateries in the neighborhood. On the other hand, Lily cannot disregard the other restaurants. The negatively sloped demand curve means that whenever she raises price, she loses customers.

How, then, does Lily set the price of a meal? Figure 15.2b reproduces on an expanded quantity scale Lily's demand curve from Figure 15.2a,

FIGURE 15.2   Short-Run Equilibrium in Monopolistic Competition

a. The industry and the firm	**b. Price determination by Lily Wong**

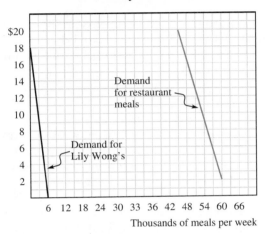

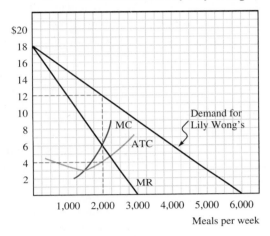

a. The demand for the entire restaurant industry is far greater than that for the individual restaurant.

b. In the short run, Lily Wong can optimize by charging $12 per meal and sell 2,000 meals. Her profits equal $16,000 per week, which you can verify by calculating total revenues and total costs.

sketches in the corresponding marginal revenue curve, adds on Lily's average and marginal cost curves, and finds the output at which MR = MC. In order to sell precisely 2,000 meals weekly, Lily Wong would have to set a price equal to $12 per meal. You can calculate this restaurant's excess profits:

Total revenue: _____

Total costs: _____

Profits: _____ [2]

Equilibrium in the Long Run

Will those excess profits persist? In contrast with the entry barriers that generate long-run excess profits in both monopoly and oligopoly, monopolistic competition presupposes easy entry. So, once other restauranteurs and potential entrants come to realize the Chinese gold mine that Lily Wong has exploited, they, too, enter. The Middle Eastern restaurant that has barely been breaking even closes up for a week, changes its decor, hires an Asian-American chef, and renames itself Cedars of Shanghai. Thomas Ho leases a store, equips it, and hires staff, and within a month the Thomas Ho House serves its first customers.

The presence of new Chinese restaurants doesn't affect the industry demand curve of Figure 15.2a, but it does reduce Lily Wong's share of the market. So, in terms of Figure 15.2b, Lily's demand curve shifts leftward. How far will it shift?

Logic dictates that entry will continue as long as excess profits can be earned and will cease only when excess profits are eliminated. Figure 15.3 depicts the long-run equilibrium for Lily Wong. It satisfies two conditions:

- MR = MC (profit maximization).
- P = ATC (zero excess profit).

You can see that MR = MC at an output of 666.67 meals weekly. Now take a look at the demand and ATC curves above that quantity. At the optimum price of $4, Lily Wong's demand curve is tangent to the restaurant's ATC curve, and so P = ATC. When P = ATC, excess profits are eliminated.

In short, excess profits in monopolistic competition are only ephemeral. The uniqueness of the monopolistic competitor is not absolute, and

**FIGURE 15.3   Long-Run Equilibrium in Monopolistic
Competition**

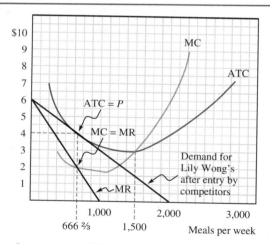

Long-run equilibrium requires that MC = MR and that no excess profits be earned or ATC = P. In this case, that occurs at Q = 666.67, when MR = MC and the demand curve is tangent to the ATC curve. Do you understand why Lily Wong would fare even worse if she tried either to raise or reduce price from its $4 level?

imitators can provide sufficiently close substitutes to draw customers away from the firm earning excess profits.

Gasoline Retailing.   You can now analyze the price structure at the gasoline stations that opened this chapter. The brand name attached to each gasoline convinces the public that each station is selling a differentiated product. We've come to believe gasoline refiner advertising to the extent that many of us have some allegiance to a particular brand. But there's a limit to that loyalty. Do you think drivers would buy as much Shell gasoline if it were to sell for $1.49 per gallon while the prices of its monopolistic competitors remained in the $1.20 range?

Unfortunately, the existence of brand names fails to explain the different prices charged by the Mobil stations in the case. After all, when two stations within a block of each other sell the identical brand of gasoline, why do customers patronize the higher-priced station? The answer to that question requires proceeding a step further with the analysis of monopolistic competition.

Frictions in the Market

The basic monopolistic competitive model assumes frictionless decision making. Specifically, that means each of the following is true:

- Information is costless.
- Time and bother don't matter.
- No uncertainty exists.
- Location is irrelevant.

As we remove each of these assumptions, we'll move closer to actual monopolistic competitive markets.

Information

Demanders, much like firms, search to acquire information about prices and products. But this blanket statement is not true for all buyers, nor even for some buyers all of the time. Some consumers have only limited knowledge about the prices of goods and services available in their neighborhood. They're even less knowledgeable about options in nearby communities. Such demanders will remain oblivious to the lower-priced Mobil station!

Nevertheless, consumer ignorance should not be taken too far, especially given the pervasiveness of advertising. Probably more important than sheer consumer laxity in the price discovery process is our technical incompetence in appraising alternatives. Those who sell to the public take advantage of this cornucopia of ignorance in pricing and marketing their products. Indeed, as mentioned in Chapter 13, higher prices are often taken by consumers to indicate higher quality. If we believe the hype, it's not surprising that customers will pay more for a brand-name gasoline.

Time and Convenience

Of course, we can all become better informed about price and quality. Unfortunately, acquiring knowledge is not a costless activity. At the least, the time spent in search constitutes an opportunity cost to the consumer. Driving to the closest store or shopping mall saves time, and so a modest extra charge for the products or services sold at the closest place is often tolerated.

Saving time is partially a subset of convenience, which encompasses minimizing bother as well. Buyers may be more than willing to pay more for groceries at an outlet that's open day and night, for a pizza from a shop that delivers, or for gas at a service station where attendants also check oil and wipe windshields. The convenience of not having to carry cash may well explain buyers' willingness to pay more for gasoline bought on a credit card at Mobil A than for the same gasoline bought with cash. And the slight savings versus the inconvenience may also explain why Mobil buyers will not travel an extra block to Mobil B, especially if they intend to travel east and enter the highway at Mobil A.

Uncertainty

Check your answers to the two questions that opened this chapter. Are they, in order, *a* and *d*? These are the results obtained from the vast majority of students asked the same questions.

There's a double lesson implicit in this quiz:

- Because we are inadequately informed, we must frequently grapple with uncertainty about product or service quality. We couldn't be bamboozled by a strange mechanic if we really were experts in car repair. Most of us aren't experts, and so we risk paying for a major repair when a simple remedy is at hand.
- Since we try to avoid playing the fool continuously, we've developed damage control measures to help us cope with uncertainty.

One such mechanism is establishing a long-term relationship with a vendor. Honesty becomes the basis for repeat business and a profitable long-lasting relationship. Your mechanic won't charge you for diagnosing and reattaching your loose battery cable, since you've patronized him in the past and are expected to do so in the future.

When you consider that most service stations repair automobiles as well as sell gasoline, it's not surprising that people will buy gas at the station where their cars are repaired. That's their way of cementing the business relationship. They seem to be saying, "I know that you're more expensive than others when it comes to gasoline. I'm willing to pay that extra cost as a sign of good will. But when I come in with a minor problem, I expect that you'll take care of it promptly and at a reasonable price." In short, while price is one element in the relationship between buyers and sellers, buyers may well pay more in order to insure the integrity of the seller.

Location

You don't buy gasoline in Waco, Texas, where it's cheaper than in Philadelphia, Pennsylvania, where you live. Yet you might well shop for a personal computer through the mails as easily as in a local computer store. What's the difference? _____

Obviously, the critical issue is the net savings from shopping elsewhere. The $2 savings on a tank of gasoline doesn't come close to the $1,000 travel costs. On the other hand, you might find the $200 to $500 savings on a mail-order PC well worth the effort required to check out the reliability of the PC and the company shipping it.

In general, consumers consider two types of costs—the cost of the product or service itself at the source and the cost of getting it from the source to the buyer. The price that matters to the buyer is the final, or out-of-pocket, cost, not the price at the source.

Figure 15.4 will be familiar to those who read the appendix to Chapter 10, although the interpretation here differs. Assume that the distance between the grid lines on the horizontal plane represents five city blocks and that cab fare is proportional to the distance traveled, say 20 cents a block. John Law sets up his legal office at point JL, with the vertical bar representing the price he charges for drawing a simple legal document such as a will or an uncontested divorce. For simplicity in exposition here, we provide John with only one competitor, Jane Court, whose office is at JC. As you can see from the diagram, while John charges $100, Jane charges only $75 for the same service. Clearly, those living in Jane's neighborhood will have her prepare documents. But so, too, will those living further away, provided that the cost of a cab does not exceed $25.

Figure 15.4 indicates how the market will be split. Clients living within a radius of 10 blocks will walk to the nearest office. Hence, there's a short horizontal arm on both sides of both John's and Jane's prices, representing the fact that the only cost to those living within walking distance is the lawyer's fee. But those residing further away will take cabs, so the cost to the more distant attorney moves upward along the rising arms. As the diagram indicates, a client residing 85 blocks from Jane's office pays $15 in addition to the $75 legal fee. It stands to reason that Jane will attract more customers, but at some point—in this example,

FIGURE 15.4   Location and the Division of the Market

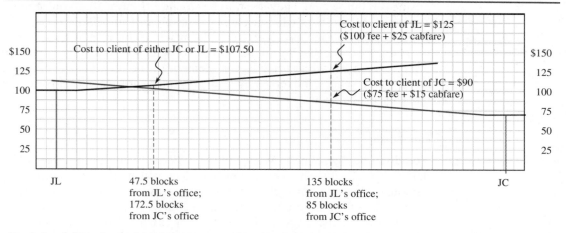

| | JL | 47.5 blocks
from JL's office;
172.5 blocks
from JC's office | 135 blocks
from JL's office;
85 blocks
from JC's office | JC |

Basic legal fees charged by John Law are $100; those charged by Jane Court are $75. But whether a client chooses John or Jane depends not only on the fee but also on the cab fare to their respective offices. All those residing between JL's office and 47.5 blocks to the right will use JL even though his basic fee is $25 more than JC's merely because it costs more than $25 to reach JC's office.

172.5 blocks from Jane and 47.5 blocks from John—the combined costs of fees plus transportation are identical. All those living to the left of the intersection of the arms use John; the remainder turn to Jane.

MICROQUERY   John seeks to expand his client list by matching Jane's price. How will the market be split? _____ Show your results on Figure 15.4.[3]

What does this tell us about our gasoline stations? Since the stations are located at different points along the intersection and since the price differentials are small, the rational consumer, considering transportation costs in addition to fuel prices, may find it less expensive in total to pay a higher pump price for gas at a closer station.

In general, then, location differences may enable monopolistic competitors to charge different prices and yet still dominate the market closest to them.

So, when you discover that two apparently identical products are being sold at different prices by monopolistic competitors, you can attribute it to a number of non–mutually exclusive causes. Buyers may simply be ignorant of the price differentials, they may disregard the higher price simply to save themselves time and/or trouble, they may be willing to pay more in order to build up a long-term relationship with a particular vendor, or they may be willing to pay the higher price if the total costs of the good and service plus transportation are lower. And do not rule out consumer gullibility: they may pay more because they believe they're acquiring a higher-quality good or service. Of course, as MicroBits 15.1 indicates, there's always the oddball.

An Application: The Market Structure of Physicians' Services

The realm of personal service gives ample scope to demonstrate the characteristics of monopolistic competition. Think of physicians, for example, not in their professional role as healers, but as businesspersons selling

---

MICROBITS 15.1

Select Customers

You thought the customer was king? Consider Founde, a discount ladies underwear store in Semba, the rag-trade district of Osaka. The first thing that greets prospective buyers at Mrs. Ayoko Tsuda's shop is a sign proclaiming "Founde chooses the customers."

And chooses them carefully. "Customers these days think that they have the right to do what they want," says the 51-year-old Mrs. Tsuda, "but I do not like the trend. As I am selling at a discount price I am providing a special service, so customers should respect my rules."

Anybody who does not agree is not even allowed through the door. And, by the way, all bags to be left outside, please. Once inside, it is easy to transgress and get thrown out. The merchandise, often manufacturers' seconds, is stacked in cardboard boxes. No rummaging. And any garment taken out for inspection must be neatly folded and replaced. There are signs on the wall to remind customers in case they forget. And signs to

remind them to be well mannered. And signs to tell them to speak good Japanese. Those who do not—or cannot—are out, too. If, by some chance, a customer manages to pass all these tests and is actually allowed to make a purchase, then there are no returns and no refunds.

Despite these amazing rules, shoppers keep coming. Some who have been turned away once try to sneak back later in disguise (or so Mrs. Tsuda says). Some even come from Tokyo, three hours away on the bullet train.

What's the attraction? Partly the low prices; partly Mrs. Tsuda herself, who imposes her take-it-or-leave-it conditions with consummate politeness. She can point to one vindication of her style. Her husband ran a conventional lingerie shop and went bust. She picked up the pieces in 1970, and has thrived ever since.

Source: "Select Customers," *The Economist*, March 19, 1988, p. 69.

therapeutic services to their patients. The general practitioner and the specialist possess skills that in one sense are unique, so the services they offer are differentiated. Yet in most communities, equally talented physicians are readily available. And while barriers to entry do exist, for a licensed physician to enter a local market is far easier than for a newcomer to challenge Firestone Tires or AT&T.[4]

A market characterized by monopolistic competition should reflect a range of prices for the same basic services. Table 15.1 is based on confidential survey information of general practitioner and pediatric fees charged to new patients for a comprehensive examination in three adjacent zip-code areas in a major Connecticut city in 1988.

Notice first that fees differ for both general practitioners and pediatricians between different zip-code regions. The average for pediatricians in area 2 is about half of that in area 1, while the average for general practitioners in region 1 is only three fourths of that in area 2. But notice, too, that even larger differences are encountered within each zip code. In the extreme, the highest fees charged by physicians in area 1 are more than four times the minimum fees.

Why not judge for yourself how well the categories used to explain differences in gasoline prices can be applied to physicians' charges?

Information. The information problem is extremely acute insofar as finding a suitable physician is concerned. Ignorance about the quality of physicians is widespread, and even where information is sought, it often focuses on the physician's bedside manner. The question of technical competence is all too often judged by patients, who truly lack the ability to evaluate a physician's expertise. The tradition against physician advertising, although now undergoing change, has closed one avenue of information. But even those physicians who do advertise are silent about prices. Choosing the right physician is not terribly different from the

TABLE 15.1   The Range of Medical Fees

Zip Code	Number of Patients	Maximum Fee	Minimum Fee	Average Fee
General Practitioners				
1	22	$131	$ 30	$ 83.78
2	9	130	65	110.00
3	11	115	100	101.36
Pediatricians				
1	5	125	30	63.00
2	6	40	30	33.33
3	7	45	35	37.86

dilemma of finding a competent and qualified mechanic mentioned in Chapter 1. Unfortunately, the consequences are far more serious.

Physicians, of course, realize how important recommendations by their patients are. They also understand that, given a good dose of ignorance, patients will not view price as an overriding consideration, even when payment comes directly from the patients themselves. Indeed, it is the rare patient who even asks for a fee schedule. Thus, it's not surprising to find two board-certified physicians affiliated with the same teaching hospital charging different fees for fundamentally identical services.

Time and Convenience.   No one wants to waste hours in physicians' waiting rooms, and so the doctor who is a more efficient scheduler is apt to attract more patients. Convenience in a broader sense may well prove critical to the doctor's economic survival. The physician whose office is difficult to reach, who doesn't return calls, who always seems to be away, and whose office hours conflict with patients' busiest work hours will hardly prove suitable no matter how qualified he or she is.

Uncertainty.   The absence of adequate information leads patients to make decisions in an environment suffused with uncertainty. But, just as in the case of the automotive mechanic, the impact of uncertainty may be minimized by building a strong doctor-patient relationship. The patient normally benefits from finding a highly qualified physician to oversee his well-being and permitting that practitioner to quarterback his medical care. Building a strong doctor-patient relationship reduces the uncertainty that must arise under the alternative: flitting from one physician to another.

But the physician-patient relationship is not a one-way street: the doctor also benefits. A client list provides the physician with a captive market and a smoother income stream.[5] The latter enables the physician to count on a more regular income, while the former provides a greater degree of discretion over fees. That's particularly important in explaining fee differentials. New clients may be influenced by medical charges, but established clients are unlikely to abandon a physician merely because her fees have risen beyond those of comparable doctors.

Location.   Location can account for price differences among physicians in at least two ways. First, it's clear that transportation costs limit the market for medical care to the local area. Only in rare instances will the patient consider the regional or, even less often, the national market.[6] Second, especially within sizable communities, physicians whose offices are conveniently located have an edge over those whose offices are farther away. Knowing this, physicians can insulate their fees to some extent from more distant competitors. It must be conceded, however, that location is not a primary explanation for the fee disparities in Table 15.1.

"On the other hand, what's it worth to you if I don't operate?"

SOURCE: Reprinted from *The Wall Street Journal*; Permission Cartoon Features Syndicate.

Lay persons are expected to conform to the conventional wisdom that physicians are professionals and that money is the last thing on their minds. Surely that's as much an exaggeration as is the money-hungry physician depicted in the cartoon. Physicians are human, have human needs, and are not averse to an affluent lifestyle. Moreover, a medical practice, like any business, entails a host of costs that must be covered if the practice is to survive as an economic entity. Fees are important to physicians, and setting fees is part of their business responsibilities. In sum, while physicians may not ever have heard the term *monopolistic competition,* the medical care market is monopolistically competitive, and doctors act accordingly.

Is Monopolistic Competition Good for Us?

Consumers come into direct contact most frequently with monopolistic competitive markets. So, aside from the theoretical fascination of this market structure, we have a personal interest in understanding whether monopolistic competitive markets improve our overall well-being or detract from it. As in the earlier discussions of monopoly and oligopoly, we will first examine the static model of price determination and then move beyond the narrow formal theory.

The Narrow Static Model: No Redeeming Social Virtues

Return to the long-run equilibrium of Figure 15.3 and note the relationship between the equilibrium ATC and the least-cost ATC. Clearly, from the point of view of Lily Wong, the most profitable output occurs at 666.67

meals, and the lowest cost per meal is $4. But if Lily were able to serve 1,500 meals, she could cut her per meal costs to $3.

Why won't Lily Wong expand output to 1,500? _____ 7

Of course, if this market were perfectly competitive, the industry demand and supply curves would intersect at $3, at which price Lily would indeed sell 1,500 meals.

All of this points to a repeat of the criticisms voiced in connection with the static models of monopoly and oligopoly. The monopolistic competitive industry supplies less output at a higher price and does it less efficiently than would a perfect competitive industry. Consequently, too few resources are devoted to the monopolistic competitive industry.

But there is one significant difference: Monopolistic competition is overpopulated, whereas monopoly and oligopoly have too few firms. You might well ask, "What's wrong with an abundance of firms? After all, doesn't the presence of many similar firms force prices down to a level that more closely approximates perfect competition?"

You can best answer these questions by considering again the relationship between Figures 15.2b and 15.3. Remember how the short-run equilibrium of the former figure spurred on the long-run equilibrium of the latter. What happened? _____

Excess profits visible in Figure 15.2b induced competitors to enter the market, forcing demand downwards. Such entry would continue as long as newcomers could share in the excess profits of the industry. At some juncture in this competitive war, Lily Wong's MR curve would cross the minimum point of the ATC and thus intersect the MC curve as well. Optimum output would occur at 1,500 meals weekly, and per unit costs would be at their efficient minimum. But there's a catch. If you draw that situation onto Figure 15.2b, you'll discover that $P > ATC$ and that Lily Wong will earn excess profits. What happens then? _____

Still more firms enter. But Lily Wong and other restaurants with similar demand and cost curves have just reached the point of lowest-cost production. Additional firms drive the price down but force Lily Wong to operate on the left side of the U-shaped ATC curve. Too many firms! And, because there are too many monopolistic competitors, each firm producing on the left side of the ATC curve operates with unused, and thus wasted, productive capacity.

In fact, the picture is even more appalling, for this portrayal of monopolistic competition makes it look worse than either oligopoly or monopoly. Some of the potentially redeeming virtues that accompany monopoly and oligopoly, such as the possibility of achieving scale economies, are absent in monopolistically competitive markets.

The Revisionist View: Don't Judge Monopolistic Competition Too Harshly

This negative conclusion loses much of its cogency after the rigid assumptions of the simple static theory of monopolistic competition are dropped. Just think of how the conclusion must change merely after the introduction of transportation costs. Efficient delivery of goods and services cannot be judged by production costs alone if the products have to be moved from producer to consumer. Since resource-using transportation now comes into the picture, social benefit is measured by minimizing combined production and transportation costs. The fact that many gas stations or eateries coexist in a neighborhood may simply prove that each is providing efficient service to local consumers.

A similar argument can be made when time and convenience are introduced. The apparent oversupply of physicians, indicated by less-than-full-capacity doctor utilization, reduces the time patients spend between making appointments and seeing their doctor. Who's to say that minimizing the physician's time is more beneficial than saving the patient's time?

Isler   Good Housekeeping

SOURCE: Lawrence Lariar, ed., *Best Cartoons of the Year* (New York: Dodd, Mead 1967).

Perhaps the strongest defense of monopolistic competition is that *variety itself is desirable.* Surely, resources are wasted and production costs inflated in the production of 300 different shades of lipstick rather than a single color. Yes, food is thrown out if restaurants are not filled to capacity at each meal and the menu is too varied. But would you prefer limiting the number of restaurants and reducing the range of their menus? Choice itself is a "good." We all are better able to satisfy our individual preferences by being able to select from different qualities even of the same product. Does economic theory give the policy analyst the right to impose his or her value judgment on the rest of us by declaring there are too many shoe stores or supermarkets in the neighborhood? Is it not the breadth of choice that makes Western economies the envy of the rest of the world?

All of this leads to a much more agnostic conclusion about monopolistic competition. Yes, many firms that produce similar products do coexist in monopolistic competition. But that could be viewed as a benefit, since the very numbers enhance consumer utility.

Policy Issues

Economists' attitudes toward public policy measures in monopolistic competition hinge very much on these alternative interpretations. Is monopolistic competition characterized by an excessive number of firms, or does the variety of similar yet different businesses add spice to the market system?

Banking.   Let's take a specific application. In Chapter 7, the empirical studies of economies of scale in banking turned out to be inconclusive. Some found the long-run ATC in banking to be U-shaped, while other research was more consistent with an L-shape. Many of these cost-curve studies also addressed themselves to a structural question: How did bank costs change as the number of branches increased? It's not hard to think of reasons why operating in a variety of locations might be more expensive than centralizing operations. Each branch office has to be minimally staffed and equipped even if that staff and equipment could be more fully utilized at the home office. Coordination will be more difficult and expensive for a branch network than when all operations are conducted under one roof. Paper and personnel will have to travel between the home office and the branch, and vice versa. Indeed, empirical studies confirm that it is more expensive to operate a branch banking network than it is to run a single-office bank.[8]

Did you know that in most states and in many countries a bank that wishes to open a new branch must obtain permission from the bank regulatory authorities? At least one justification for such regulations is that the banking industry is "overbanked"; too many bank offices in one community lead to each one operating below capacity. The regulators limit the amount of banking offices to assure a more efficient use of society's scarce resources, an inference that's consistent with the simple model of monopolistic competition.

In recent years, that conclusion has been challenged by economists who are uncomfortable with the narrow conceptual framework of the model. Sure, the more banks, the more resources that will be devoted to banking. But that's not synonymous with waste. The public benefits from the convenience of having more accessible banking offices and the variety of services they bring. It's not at all clear that these benefits are outweighed by the presumed redundancy of offices. The challengers insist that the authorities must at the very least demonstrate that the waste exceeds the public benefits before preventing banks from opening new branches.

Conclusion

This chapter on monopolistic competition completes the analysis of imperfect competition, much of which has centered on price and output determination under monopoly, oligopoly, and monopolistic competition. The key rule for output determination, repeated perhaps ad nauseum, is MR = MC, with price then set on the demand curve above the MR = MC output to assure that the actual quantity demanded matches the desired output. You've seen again and again the central role that microeconomic theory attributes to the costs of the producing firm and the demand facing the firm.

The final section of this chapter deals with a simple question: How do firms in different markets actually set their prices? In other words, does economic theory describe only an imaginary world created by economists, or does theory offer insights into the practices of real firms?

Theory Faces Reality: How Imperfect Competitors Price

It's best to begin with a caveat. The practical world of business is far more complex than even the most sophisticated economic models. You certainly don't expect to find pricing executives drawing demand and cost curves, pinpointing the MR/MC intersection, or holding a ruler perpendicular to the quantity axis to discover the price. Firms are often unable to discern their own marginal costs, while demand functions in a world that's undergoing continuous change are shrouded in uncertainty. Moreover, few firms sell only one product, so pricing decisions must deal with a host of related products. Nevertheless, the art of pricing in business enterprises is not random, and by discovering its rules, we can compare theory and reality.

Monopoly Pricing

It's paradoxical that it is virtually impossible to discover how a real-life monopolist would set prices and to compare that to the process predicted by economic theory. This is because economic theory has so convincingly demonstrated the deadweight loss and inefficiency of monopoly that legal, unregulated monopolies exist only in small niches in the economy. We don't really know how, say, an electric utility would behave in an unregulated environment.

Natural Monopolies.   Chapter 12 explored pricing in regulated natural monopolies. You recall that the socially efficient solution of equating price with marginal cost will guarantee bankruptcy for firms with continuously declining long-run average cost curves. Regulatory commissions in the United States normally set $P = $ ATC, with the ATC including some permitted rate of profit. This enables the utility not only to avoid losses but also to attract funds from investors for expansion.

Illegal Monopolies.   The presence of antitrust laws has not eliminated collusion. Indeed, collusion may well be more widespread than we realize, for secrecy is essential to perpetuate this unlawful act. Moreover, the limited resources of the antitrust authorities prevent them from discovering and disclosing more than a handful of violations. Since the only information on cooperation among sellers stems from these antitrust prosecutions, the sample of cases is patently biased. We don't really have any information on the successful practices of those not prosecuted. Nevertheless, two popular methods of collusion can be outlined: outright price fixing and bid rigging.

Outright Price Fixing.   Executives of competing companies meet and set prices. There's no attempt to fix market shares, and the colluders may compete in nonprice ways in order to capture a larger portion of the market. True, no one brings to the table a study of demand and marginal costs for the industry, if only because these meetings are conducted in secrecy and are limited to a few key participants. So, the optimal industry price is never determined. Nevertheless, it is clear that the fixed prices satisfy each of the firms' executives individually. They must cover each participant's costs and provide for a higher return than could be obtained by not colluding.

The antitrust prosecution of some East Coast Pepsi and Coke bottlers is one example of outright price fixing. The government contended that, in 1983, executives of Baltimore's Allegheny Pepsi-Cola Bottling Co. and the Mid-Atlantic Coca-Cola Bottling Co. of Silver Spring, Maryland, agreed to establish prices jointly and abide by them. Allegheny even promised not to reduce prices after Pepsi introduced a cheaper, plastic six-pack package, thus lowering Allegheny's costs.

Bidding Arrangements.   Some larger buyers are able to invite bids from sellers and then contract with the vendor providing the best terms. In such circumstances, competing sellers may rig the bids. Here's a brief excerpt from an article in *The Wall Street Journal* on bid rigging in the electrical contracting industry:[9]

> Federal court records in Pennsylvania show that starting as early as 1967, major contractors set up a complicated rotation system for allocating contracts in that state. The system was based on the size of the bids, whose turn it was to be the "designated hitter" to win a contract, and which of the participants most needed the work. Precise records were kept. . . .
>
> During one secret meeting at a hotel near Pittsburgh airport . . . the president of Sargent Electric Co. of Philadelphia "apologized" to his counterparts "for the mistake" of underbidding a competitor previously designated to receive a contract from U.S. Steel Corp. Sargent even agreed to "lose a turn" obtaining contracts from U.S. Steel Corp. . . .
>
> Prosecuters in North Carolina say executives in that state exchanged information in such an unconcerned, business-as-usual manner that some contractors signed blank bid forms for certain jobs and simply gave them to the designated low bidder to fill out and turn in on their behalf.

In essence, these loose cartel arrangements relieve each seller from price competition. If prices are fixed, clearly there's no price advantage to the buyer from abandoning its present vendor in favor of another. Nevertheless, the buyer still can choose from among sellers on the basis of terms other than price. In the second method, buyers' choice evaporates. True, buyers may be deluded into thinking that choice exists in bid-rigging situations, but the sellers have effectively precluded buyer maneuverability.

Niche Monopolies.   Some markets are monopolistic by default. Like the salamander and fly-feather cases of Chapter 11, such markets are simply not sufficiently attractive to encourage rivals. They're also too insignificant in the total picture to warrant antitrust attention and thus do not provide us with a documented portrayal of price determination. Niche monopolies are an area that merits further investigation.

In sum, information about price determination by a single monopolist is sadly lacking. On the other hand, there's an abundance of information about collusive monopolies in the United States. However, lessons gleaned from price determination under an illegal, but close-knit, monopoly cannot be generalized to cases where such collusion is legal. At best, experience suggests that the set price takes into account producers' costs and includes a profit markup. Demand is considered only in the most general sense, but it surely is not ignored. At the least, it seems clear that industrywide price increases are consistent with movement toward an unknown industry MR = MC equilibrium.

Oligopoly and Monopolistic Competition

Seasoned observers of the U.S. business scene have proposed two mutually exclusive views of price determination in oligopoly and monopolistic competition. They can be summarized as follows:

- Cost determines price.
- Price determines cost.

Cost Determines Price.   How does cost determine price? The markup and target pricing procedures discussed in Chapter 13 begin with cost and add a margin for profits. If such a practice is traditional in the industry, it not only serves to determine price but also implictly deters competition. As long as all the oligopolists have similar costs, which is often true when industrywide wage agreements prevail, the standard markup means that all oligopolists will offer buyers similar prices even without collusion.

Although at first glance it seems that in neither full-cost nor target pricing is there any role for demand, marginal revenue, or marginal cost, such appearances are deceptive. True, in the real world prices seem to be related to average cost, not marginal cost, and demand appears to be ignored. Yet slavish adherence to full-cost pricing is rare. Prices are boosted when demand is strong and cut when maintaining the customary markup keeps customers out of the store. Surely, the familiar end-of-season sales suggest as much. Although costs do not decline as the season moves along, prices are cut to move the merchandise out. Isn't this clear recognition that MR > MC, and that a price cut will increase profits by moving MR closer to MC?

Even the apparent inconsistency between target pricing and marginal pricing is deceiving. The target return itself is not an inflexible constant. Indeed, we would be surprised if in the same industry one firm strove for a 50 percent target return while others aimed at a 15 percent target return. Certainly, the desired target return has to be grounded on an achievable rate, and that must take into account demand as well as costs.

Target pricing is consistent with MR/MC pricing in another sense. Target pricing may well prove to be a profit-maximizing strategy for oligopolists, for if all the oligopolists in a particular industry pursue the same target pricing strategy, they will achieve a stable kink price and eliminate price competition among themselves. Moreover, common cost changes— an increase in the price of a major input or a rise in industrywide wages— lead to a uniform industry response. Since all the oligopolists are more or less affected by the common cost increase, they will all raise price in tandem by adding the target markup to the average cost increase. Thus, oligopolists halt incipient price wars by selecting a common pricing method.

In short, neither markup pricing nor target pricing is purely cost based. In practice, costs are the starting point for the pricing position. But the degree of markup or target return is influenced by market conditions. True, firms do not consciously seek the MR = MC equilibrium. Yet, in most respects, their actions move prices in the direction of that point.

It must be admitted, however, that in one respect practice and theory diverge. Sellers are loath to cut price below full cost. The understanding that profits can at times be best preserved by considering not average total costs but average variable costs is a lesson that many businesspersons find hard to accept.[10]

Price Determines Cost.   A diametrically opposed pricing policy suggests that the starting point for price is demand. Producers examine the competition's price and ask themselves whether they could earn a satisfactory profit by marketing a similar product at about the same price. Cost control then becomes the name of the game.

Here's how *Business Week* has described pricing in the automobile industry:

> Detroit typically works out the cost of a car backward. . . . An auto maker starts by studying the market segment in which a new car will go five or more years down the road. It checks the price of competing models, works out what features it wants, and allows for inflation. The result is a target price for the still-undeveloped car. . . . Then the company figures out whether it can design and build the car cheaply enough to leave a theoretical profit margin of at least 10 percent. Jockeying back and forth between desired price and the cost of production continues up to the moment the car is introduced.[11]

Note that the concept of *cost* in the above description is being used in two different senses; it's important that you not confuse the two. First, decision makers consider the height of the ATC. Given the price, the lower the ATC can be pushed, the greater the profit margin no matter where on the ATC production will actually take place. Second, for a given ATC curve, costs will vary depending on the actual quantity produced. (You might want to sketch out these two interpretations of reducing average costs.)

The fact that the height of the ATC is itself variable is a critical point; it is not consistent with the simplification that underlay the production function of Chapter 7. There, the production function was assumed to be determined technologically, an assumption that surely is valid for some products and services but is inappropriate for many of the diverse goods and services produced in a modern economy.

Think of cars coming out of the showroom. Each is equipped with a brand-new set of tires. But whether the tires are rated to wear for 40,000 miles or only 20,000 miles obviously affects the cost of the car and thus its final price. This observation is equally true for the shock absorbers, the transmission, the windshield wiper mechanism, the carpeting, the seat coverings, and the materials used for the interior finish. Surely, costs can be reduced by using less expensive components.

Such thinking is not limited to the automobile industry. It applies to all sorts of goods and to services as well. Consider, for example, the backward pricing of medical services. Let's say that Dr. Pullem, an oral surgeon, wants to net $300 an hour. The going rate is $100 per extraction, and Dr. Pullem estimates her standard volume at four extractions an hour. The implication: Costs must not average more than $100 per hour. The $100 per hour cost maximum will determine whether the good doctor will hire a dental technician and a secretary or a combination technician-secretary; how much hourly pay will be; and even whether the surgeon will subscribe to current magazines for her waiting room rather than rely on a used-magazine shop.

Arguing that price determines costs again seems to controvert the simple MR = MC analysis of the past few chapters. Yet there's obviously a limit to how far costs can be cut without changing the nature of the product. But a more compelling argument stems from the realization that selecting the appropriate ATC ought not to be viewed as a substitute method but rather as a more sophisticated version of marginal analysis. Price setters must simultaneously determine the appropriate "quality" of the product or service produced—the height of the ATC—as well as the optimum output, the maximum profit position on the ATC. Indeed, would it surprise you to learn that the same automobile manufacturers that determine costs on the basis of price also pioneered the target pricing method based on standard volume? In fact, pricing executives consider both prevailing prices and production costs. Determine how plausible the careful conclusion of the authors of *The Pricing Decision* seems:

> The study results indicated that both costs and market conditions were important ingredients to the determination of specific prices for product lines. The variant of cost-plus pricing frequently used was a percentage markup over costs. Even in those firms where competitors' prices were of prime importance, cost information played a secondary role in assessing whether or not the firm could sell the product line at the established market price. Thus, the literature arguing the costs are of little, if any, importance in the determination of prices must be viewed as suspect with regards to the firms included in our study.[12]

Does price determine cost or do costs determine price? The answer is both! Sellers can neither ignore costs nor disregard demand. Their pricing decision takes both costs and demand into account. It would hardly be

MicroBits 15.2

Pricing of Products Is Still an Art, Often Having Little Link to Costs

At $4.50 a 750 milliliter bottle (about a fifth), Fleischmann's gin was losing ground. More gin drinkers were drinking at home. Fewer were patronizing the bars and cocktail lounges where much of Fleischmann's gin flowed. So Fleischmann's over a period of two years raised its price by $1 a bottle to $5.50.

"The strategy helped incredibly." Ferdie Falk gloats. He's the executive in charge of Nabisco Brands Inc.'s beverage group, which markets Fleishmann's. "Sales were deteriorating; now they're coming up. Sales are considerably above last year." Fleishmann's bottle sales and revenue from gin increased although the gin itself remained the same. Only the price—and the bottle, belatedly—was changed to attract liquor-store patrons. The bottle has a new and apparently more salable oblong shape.

Although merchants of just about everything devote a great deal of time and study to determine what prices to put on their products, pricing often remains an art. In some cases, it does involve a straightforward equation: Material and labor costs plus overhead and other expenses, plus profit, equals price. But in many other cases the equation includes psychological and other factors so subtle that pricing consultants, themselves high-priced, are retained to help assay what the market will bear. . . .

$9.86 versus $9.99

To decide prices, manufacturers usually weigh costs, and prices, on similar products, and then, as an apparel maker puts it, "take a good guess." Herbert Denenberg, a pro-

moter of consumer causes in Philadelphia and former Pennsylvania state insurance commissioner, says that "everybody thinks people go about pricing scientifically. But very often, the process is incredibly arbitrary."

At its 20 factory outlet stores, Cowden Manufacturing, a subsidiary of Interco Inc., St. Louis, prices jeans at just $9.86. Why the 86 cents? "When people see $9.99 they say, 'That's $10,' " says James McAskill, Cowden's general sales manager. "But $9.86 isn't $10. It's just psychological."

Higher prices seem to suggest higher quality. The relation is dubious. The price on a higher quality product may be considerably higher than the product's extra quality. In 1979, University of Iowa professor Peter C. Reisz tried to relate the prices of 679 brands of packaged foods with their quality ratings as determined over 15 years by Consumers Union. His conclusion: "The correlation between quality and price for packaged food products is near zero."

Marketing men, however, sense that consumers are buying more than a mere commodity when they buy some goods. A $100 bottle of perfume may contain $4 to $16 worth of scent. The rest of the price goes for advertising, packaging and profit. Such perfume sells. "Women are buying atmosphere and hope and the feeling they are something special," says Henry Walter Jr., chairman of International Flavors & Fragrances Inc., a major scents manufacturer. "There are very few people who are willing to settle for what will satisfy pure needs."

Low prices also sell. Or so J.C. Penney Co., the big retailer, hopes in the case of its

MicroBits 15.2 continued

bargain $13.50 "plain pockets" jeans and its $18 leisure shirts with fox emblems. Penney does more than concede that the clothes are knockoffs of Levi Strauss & Co.'s $17 jeans and Lacoste's $23 alligator shirts. It insists that they are practically identical. Levi Strauss asserts that the Penney jeans are inferior. Lacoste executives decline to dignify the question by discussing it.

Premium Profit

If different companies sell substantially the same product at different prices, they may also sell their own substantially identical products at different prices. Heublein Inc., for example, believes that consumers want a variety of prices on vodka. Last year, it "repositioned" its Popov brand by raising its price by 8% to an average $4.10 a fifth at retail without changing what went into the fifth. Popov lost 1% of its market share. Heublein moans all the way to the bank; its Popov profits increased by 30% because of the higher price. "We are not going to leave money on the table," says John Powers, a Heublein senior vice president.

Popov remains less expensive than Heublein's premium Smirnoff vodka. Securities analysts and others scoff at Heublein's claim that there is a difference between the vodkas. "U.S.-made vodkas are colorless, odorless, and tasteless," says Marvin Shanker, publisher of Impact, a wine and spirits newsletter. "The cost of producing vodka is pretty consistent irrespective of brand name.". . .

On many goods, retailers first set prices merely by more or less doubling the price they pay wholesale. If the goods don't sell at that price, the retailers mark them down.

Proctor-Silex and other manufacturers are legally prohibited from fixing retail prices, but they do set their wholesale prices with an eye toward their retail customers' pricing policies. A distributor buying directly from the King of Prussia, Pa., manufacturer usually tacks on 12 percent when he resells the product to a retail merchant. The merchant typically adds another 30 percent, although most stores eventually discount all appliances that remain on hand. Otherwise an iron that Proctor-Silex sold at wholesale for $24 will cost about $35 at retail.

Proctor-Silex knows that, and it also knows that a customer who will pay $40 for an iron is a different customer from the one who will pay only $30. The same retail store might not wish to attract both customers for fear of losing its quality reputation with one and its price reputation with the other. That's why Proctor-Silex and its competitors in industry make so many variants of the same product. "Our products are designed and priced with different types of consumers in mind," says a spokesman for General Electric Co.'s major appliance group.

On the other hand, many shoppers appear to pay little attention to price. Last spring, S. C. Johnson & Son, Inc., Racine, Wis., maker of Johnson wax products, asked 800 shopping-mall customers what they pay for air-fresheners. Only 28 percent quoted figures within 15 percent of actual prices, 39 percent quoted figures that were off by more than that and 33 percent had no idea at all what they paid.

"We concluded that when you ask consumers if they are interested in buying a new product at a particular price," says Johnson marketing research director Richard F. Chay, "there's going to be a lot of error."

Source: Jeffrey H. Birnbaum, "Pricing Products Is Still An Art, Often Having Little Link to Costs." Reprinted by permission of *The Wall Street Journal*, © 1981 Dow Jones & Company, Inc. All Rights Reserved Worldwide.

surprising if they cannot precisely discover the point at which MR = MC in a world that is constantly in motion, that cannot provide executives responsible for pricing decisions with all-encompassing and instant information, and that is shrouded in uncertainty. In such an environment, sophisticated pricers realize that precision is impossible, but that their decisions can move prices in the right direction. In considering whether to raise or lower prices, management must evaluate the impact of each decision on the firm's revenues and on its costs. The tyrant that's the market will sooner or later penalize them for the wrong decision.

In short, the economic theory of firm pricing is compatible with real-life experience as long as you recall the caveat expressed in the opening paragraph of this section. To be sure, you won't find business executives practicing pricing along the lines of an intermediate microeconomic theory textbook. But you will find them considering the variables highlighted by microeconomic theory—marginal revenue and marginal cost—whenever pricing decisions have to be made.

MicroBits 15.2 provides a fitting end to this chapter, for it highlights the fact that, ultimately, pricing in a world characterized by imperfect competition is not scientific at all.

Summary

This double-barreled chapter concludes the study of market structures. It first introduced you to monopolistic competition and then exposed you to actual price determination in a variety of markets, the objective being to compare price theory with its real-life analogue. Do executives responsible for pricing decisions act as predicted by theory, or, as the Einstein quotation that opened the chapter mandated, do we have to change the facts to fit the theory?

Monopolistic Competition. Monopolistic competition is characterized by substantial numbers of suppliers of differentiated products. But these goods and services are not so unique that similar ones cannot be produced by other firms. Moreover, barriers to entry and exit in the monopolistic competitive market are relatively low. So, the leverage producers have over price is significantly weaker than the con-trol exercised by the monopolist or even the oligopolist. On the other hand, unlike the firm in perfect competition, the demand curve of the monopolistic competitor is not perfectly elastic. The monopolistic competitor can charge a price that is different from those set by other firms in the market, and so the monopolistic competitor can earn excess profits in the short run. In the long run, however, excess profits attract new firms, forcing demand down until ultimately all excess profits are squeezed out. In long-run equilibrium, MR = MC and P = ATC.

In reality, monopolistic competition operates in a complex environment that preserves price distinctions. Some vendors can maintain higher prices than their competitors because customers are unaware of these price differences or are technically incompetent to compare similar but not identical goods and services. Customers are often willing to pay more if that is the price of reducing the uncertainty that accompanies the purchase of complex and sophisticated goods and services. Establishing a strong and lasting buyer-seller relationship builds mutual trust and confidence, with neither the customer nor the seller interested in sacrificing short-term gains that would permanently damage that relationship. Sellers located closer to customers can charge more for their particular good or service if buyers find that the cost of the seller's product plus the buyer's travel costs are lower. That conclusion is buttressed by considering not only outright travel costs but also the time and convenience of buying in one outlet rather than another. The vendor who offers quicker service and greater convenience can charge more.

Whether monopolistic competition enhances societal well-being or not hinges very much on the implications of the simple versus the expanded model. The simple model leads to a long-run equilibrium that forces consumers to pay a higher price for a lower quantity of output. Production is inefficient because costs are above the ATC minimum, while resources are maldistributed since marginal social benefit exceeds marginal social cost. At the same time, there's a surplus of monopolistically competitive firms in the industry.

The above conclusions are challenged by the refined model. If the consumer saves transportation costs and time, and/or is more conveniently served, and if the consumer treasures certainty to uncertainty, then such benefits must be weighed against the purported disadvantages that accompany monopolistic competition. Indeed, the very fact that monopolistic competition offers variety and opens the path to choice must be included among its benefits. Thus, one cannot conclude a priori that monopolistic competition is worse than perfect competition. In this view, public policy that seeks to restrain monopolistic

competition may well harm the economy rather than improve it.

Price Determination. Price determination in the real world is certainly more complex than any of the models presented in the preceding chapters. Yet it's important to investigate price setting outside of the theoretician's ivory tower. Unfortunately, U.S. monopolies provide little information, for a variety of reasons. Natural monopolies are regulated, so management lacks the freedom to pursue optimal pricing rules. Illegal monopolies can't follow optimization procedures, either, if only because those involved want to minimize the risks of discovery and so are forced to limit the number of people involved. And there's no information available to outsiders on pricing decisions of the unprosecuted niche monopolies such as the salamander king of Chapter 11.

Oligopoly and monopolistic competition are more fertile sources of information about pricing. Two procedures belong to the "cost determines price" category: markup or full-cost pricing and target pricing. The former method sees the decision maker setting the list price by adding a fixed markup to the product's cost, while the latter method involves calculating a markup that represents the firm's desired rate of return. Yet both of these methods lose their cost-based purity in practice since demand and thus implicitly marginal revenue influence the size of the markup. Strong demand leads to higher markups; the opposite occurs when demand turns out to be weak.

An alternative focus is "price determines cost," with the market price of competitors roughly viewed as the maximum achievable. The challenge of the pricing executive is to develop a product that will cost little enough to provide the firm with its desired profit. In essence, costs can be cut by reducing product quality. Yet even here, costs cannot be brought down without limit. Moreover, costs do vary with production volume, so that cost enters by the back door even when price appears to determine costs.

In summary, the broad principles of MR = MC are implicitly understood in real-life pricing decisions. True, no one, least of all the microeconomic theorist, believes that business executives slavishly adhere to the elementary models outlined in the preceding chapters. Yet when management sets prices by considering both demand and costs and is flexible in adjusting price to changes in both demand and costs, it is clearly adhering to the fundamental principles of marginal analysis.

Key Term

Monopolistic competition

Review Questions

1. *a.* Explain why the demand curve facing the monopolistic competitor is more elastic than that facing the monopolist but less elastic than that facing the perfect competitor.
   b. Would these relationships hold true even for a product whose market demand was perfectly elastic or one whose demand was perfectly inelastic? Explain.

2. *a.* Sketch and explain the short-run equilibrium for a monopolistic competitor.
   b. Why does the firm earn excess profits in the short run?

3. *a.* Sketch and explain the long-run equilibrium for a monopolistic competitor.
   b. Why do excess profits evaporate in long-run equilibrium?

4. The demand for a product sold in a monopolistically competitive market increases. Show the short-run and long-run consequences in terms of profits and the number of firms in the industry.

5. *a.* How does the introduction of travel costs and information asymmetries affect the welfare implications of the narrow model of monopolist competition?
   b. As gasoline prices rose sharply in late 1990, many drivers switched from premium unleaded to regular unleaded gas. Of course, if regular gasoline performed adequately, drivers should have been using the less expensive quality even prior to the price hike. What does such consumer behavior suggest about the theory of monopolistic competition?

6. Demonstrate and explain the distribution of customers in Figure 15.4 if cab prices rise by 50 percent.

7. Funeral homes typically price a funeral as a percentage markup on the price of the selected coffin. Does this mean that funeral directors do not take demand and marginal revenue into consideration? Explain.

8. How can price determine cost when most price makers set price on the basis of ATC?

Food for Thought

1. "McDonald's Says Price Cuts Helped Sales in February" read a headline in a national newspaper.
   a. What does this indicate about elasticity of demand for McDonald's products?
   b. Specify the conditions that justify McDonald's pricing policy.

2. The demand for a product sold in a monopolistically competitive market increases. Show the short-run and long-run consequences in terms of profits and the number of firms in the industry if the industry is characterized by increasing costs.

3. Analyze the following excerpts from the *Bulletin of the American Association of Retired Persons* (September 1989) that deal with prescription drug prices:
   a. "Comparative shopping of pharmacies within the same locality produced savings ranging from $8 to $35 on Tagamet, used to treat stomach ulcers" (p. 14).
   b. "Special customer services such as 24-hour service, after-hours emergency service, free delivery, patient profiles and discounts—frequently advertised as 'free'—actually result in an overall 7 percent increase in prices" (p. 14).

4. "Odd pricing" means that retailers list prices ending in numbers other than zero (e.g., $4.98). Since $4.98 is, for all rational purposes, the equivalent of $5.00, why does the retailer provide customers with a 2-cent discount?

5. a. Why is collusion unlikely in a monopolistically competitive setting?

   b. How can you then explain the saga of a coffin retailer who undercut funeral home coffin prices by 30 to 40 percent only to find its supply of coffins cut, a consequence of a funeral-home-induced supplier boycott? (The funeral directors also pressured truckers not to deliver the caskets and imposed handling fees on customer-supplied coffins.)

6. An Irish innkeeper claims that there are too many pubs in Ireland. His own hometown of 120 villagers and some outlying farmers has 3 pubs, while a nearby town of 1,000 inhabitants has 24. Not surprisingly, half of Irish pubs showed no profits in 1987, and few did much better.
   a. Do you agree with the innkeeper's contention? Why?
   b. What could be done to reduce the number of pubs?
   c. On what basis would you recommend your method of reducing the number of pubs?

7. Two alternative retail location strategies are "clustering" and "dispersion." The former occurs when similar businesses (e.g., lamp stores, motels) locate near each other, while the latter refers to a practice common in shopping malls. The mall owner guarantees a particular type of retailer that it will not lease space to a shop carrying a similar product. Why would a monopolistic competitor choose one or the other strategy? (Hint: Think of the relationship between industry and firm demand curves.)

Suggested Readings

Business pricing strategies are discussed in every marketing text. You might consult the relevant chapters of E. Jerome McCarthy and William D. Perrault, Jr., *Basic Marketing* (Homewood, Ill.:

Irwin, 1990) or Paul S. Busch and Michael J. Houston, *Marketing: Strategic Foundations* (Homewood, Ill.: Irwin, 1985). Thomas T. Nagle, *The Strategy and Tactics of Pricing: A Guide to Profitable Decision Making* (Englewood Cliffs, N.J.: Prentice-Hall, 1987) is more of a how-to book. Two economists who have dealt with the theory and practice of pricing are Jules Backman,

Prices: Policies and Practices (New York: The Conference Board, 1961), which, though much out of date, does give an excellent survey of business price setting; and Alan S. Blinder, "Why Are Prices Sticky? Preliminary Results from an Interview Study," *American Economic Review* 81, no. 2 (May 1991), pp. 89–96.

Notes and Answers

1. For the industry, elasticity = $(857.14 \times 9)/54,000 = .14285$, while for Lily Wong, elasticity = $(333.333 \times 9)/3,000 = 1$. So Lily Wong's demand is more elastic. That's not surprising, since the greater the number of substitutes, the more elastic the demand is.
2. $P \times Q = \$24,000$; $ATC \times Q = \$8,000$; $\pi = \$16,000$.
3. The market will now be equally divided, with each lawyer dominating the closest 110 blocks. In your diagram, you should begin JL's T at a height of $75, the right arm perpendicular for 10 blocks (2 boxes), and then rising to the right at a slope (representing the cost of cabs) parallel to the old arm.
4. This statement is not invariably true, for on occasion, community doctors have banded together and prevented outside physicians from penetrating the market. Indeed, Kessel has indicted the medical profession as monopolistic price discriminators. See Reuben A. Kessel, "Price Discrimination in Medicine," *Journal of Law and Economics* 1(1958), p. 20–53.
5. A practice is a marketable asset, which physicians try to sell when they leave the community or retire.
6. Data on average pediatric charges for an office visit with a new patient in 1984 ranged from $44.12 in the Pacific region to $29.25

billed by the average mountain region pediatrician. See Roger A. Reynolds and Daniel J. Duann, eds., *1985 Socioeconomic Characteristics of Medical Practice* (Chicago: American Medical Association, 1985), p. 102. This $14.87 difference would hardly warrant that the San Francisco parent take an ill child to Denver.
7. At that output, MC > MR—in fact, MR is negative—and the price of the $1.50 on the demand curve is below the $3 cost per meal. Instead of earning normal profits at 666.67, Lily will lose ($1.50)(1,500), or $2,250 weekly. Not wise!
8. See George J. Benston et al., "Operating Costs in Commercial Banking," Federal Reserve Bank of Atlanta, *Economic Review* (November 1982), p. 20.
9. Andy Pasztor, "Busting a Trust: Electrical Contractors Reel under Charges that They Rigged Bids," *The Wall Street Journal,* November 29, 1985, pp. 1, 14.
10. That's one conclusion of an interview study of 44 U.S. and Canadian firms. See Lawrence A. Gordon et al., *The Pricing Decision* (New York: National Association of Accountants, 1981), p. 10.
11. *Business Week,* March 1, 1982, p. 110.
12. Gordon et al., *The Pricing Decision,* pp. 9–10.

PART

VI

FACTOR MARKETS

The producing firm demands land, labor, and capital from the factor market, where it faces the suppliers, the owners of the factors. Chapter 16 derives the demand for and supply of labor in perfectly competitive labor markets. Chapter 17 treats markets in which employees are organized into labor unions and employers also exert power over their workers. Not surprisingly, the conclusions that apply to perfectly competitive markets no longer hold in imperfectly competitive factor markets. Chapter 18 focuses on the remaining factors and their incomes: rent, interest, and profit.

16

WAGES IN PERFECTLY COMPETITIVE LABOR MARKETS

I believe that in today's world, $3.35 an hour [the federally mandated minimum wage in 1988] is too close to slave labor for a civilized society to tolerate.

My mother-in-law has worked for five years sewing for a clothing manufacturer at minimum wage—no paid vacation, no other benefits, just lots of complaints about the quality of her work. Her income is below subsistence level, but she feels she has no alternative. I believe that her work is more beneficial to our society than that of any billionaire money manipulator.

Letter to the Editor, *The Wall Street Journal* (October 25, 1988)

Overtime shall be paid at the rate of one and one-half times for all hours worked outside of the regularly scheduled basic workday.

From a contract between the International Brotherhood of Electrical Workers and the Public Service Electric and Gas Company, New Jersey (1980)

Learning Objectives

In this chapter you'll master:

- The relationship between marginal productivity theory and the input market.
- How to derive a competitive firm's labor demand curve.
- Using indifference curve analysis to determine the supply curve of an individual laborer.
- Competitive labor market equilibrium for the industry and for the individual firm's employment decisions.

- Applications concerning various policies used to stimulate employment.
- The challenge posed by the new view of labor markets introduced by modern labor theories.

Should the Minimum Wage Be Increased?

Chapters 8 and 9 suggested to you that competitive product markets are cruel taskmasters. That is no less true in competitive factor markets. Because the inputs into the production process—labor, natural resources, capital, and management skills—are bought and sold in free markets, the reward to each factor supplier, be it in the form of wages and salaries, rents, interest, or profits, hinges on the market-established price for each factor. At times, the input price will richly reward the resource supplier. But the market may also be niggardly, which gives rise to a critical social and economic issue: the minimum wage.

In late 1989, after protracted negotiations between the president and Congress, the minimum wage was boosted from its 1981 level. Figure 16.1 plots the federal minimum wage since its introduction in 1938, when the Fair Labor Standards Act mandated that employees engaged in interstate commerce be paid no less than 25 cents an hour. Despite its apparent inexorable rise to the present $4.25 an hour, the upward movement has been neither smooth nor easily accomplished.

FIGURE 16.1   The U.S. Federal Minimum Wage, 1938–1991

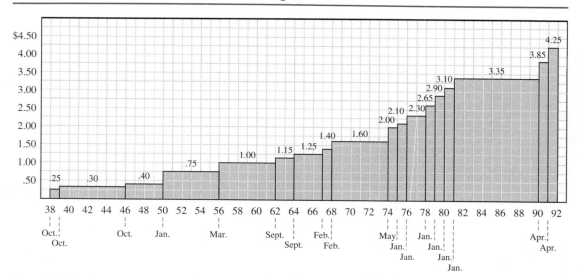

SOURCE: U.S. Department of Labor.

Do you wonder why the wage floor has changed at such a snail-like pace? So, too, do many who believe the present minimum is just too low. Do a simple calculation. Multiply $4.25 by 40 hours by 52 weeks a year, and see how much that comes to. You'll discover that the product is significantly below the 1990 poverty line of $10,419 for a family of three. Or look at this in another way. The historical increase in the minimum wage recorded in Figure 16.1 is in *nominal* terms. Adjusting the minimum wage for increases in the cost of living brings the 1990 minimum down to the 1954 level.

There's a second strain to the moral argument. Western religious tradition believes work to be ennobling, a theme picked up by writers throughout the ages. The words of 19th-century Englishman Thomas Carlyle—"Work alone is noble"—are representative. Even to Karl Marx, who believed religion to be the opiate of the masses, work was the ultimate ethical act. It seems that our conscience leads us to support an increase in the minimum wage.

But students of economics can't vote merely on the basis of an ethical argument. We have a professional responsibility to examine the economic issues involved. We want to ask ourselves, Will increasing the minimum wage lead to the objectives sought? If the answer is no, we could be sympathetic to the idea, but we would oppose the policy on practical grounds.

If, however, the answer is yes, we should then ask, Can the goals aimed for by boosting the minimum wage be achieved in a more efficient manner than by direct intervention in the market? Are there undesirable side effects that could be avoided by proposing alternative options? If the answer to both questions is yes, then we'd oppose the minimum wage increase.

If the answer is no, we'd want to ask another question: What are the costs of the minimum wage boost? We'd want to consider: How much will production costs be driven up, and how will that affect the public? Will an increase in the minimum wage raise unemployment, and if so, how many people and what types of laborers will be unemployed? Which industries will be most affected? Will some states and regions be more burdened than others?

The approach taken in this series of questions is a straightforward one:

- Abstract from the moral dimension in order to consider the economic issues involved.
- Examine the economic questions and their implications in their entirety.
- Calculate whether the overall economic impact is beneficial or detrimental.
- Reintroduce the ethical issues.

It may be that ethics and economics dictate the same decision. But it is equally likely that our economic analysis demonstrates that raising the minimum wage is more damaging than beneficial. Nevertheless, our feelings of propriety may dictate that we advocate a higher minimum wage. There's nothing wrong with that, for we're making this decision with open eyes and full recognition of the consequences.

The economics of the minimum wage constitutes a unifying theme that runs throughout this chapter. By the time you've worked your way through this chapter, you should be able to evaluate the theoretical arguments that are developed, as well as the empirical results introduced, and so reach a preliminary conclusion about the net economic benefits of raising the minimum wage. This chapter and the next deal with the labor market—this one with competitive markets on both the supplier and demander sides and Chapter 17 with either the supplier or the demander straying from the perfect competition ideal. Chapter 18 uses the techniques developed in this chapter to examine the remaining factor markets. You'll shortly discover that there's relatively little new analysis in these two chapters. The old theories are merely applied to factor markets. So if you've navigated this book well up to this point, you'll find your travels from here on not easy but easier. There's but one added complication that stems from the fact that factor demand depends on product prices.

The chapter opens with an analysis of the demand for labor, followed by the derivation of a labor supply curve. It moves on to discover the competitive equilibrium wage and quantity of labor input and to explore the individual firm's reaction to that equilibrium. The fourth section discusses a number of employment-generating policy implications, the impact of taxes on wages and work effort, and the development of markets that are outside the pale of the law. The chapter concludes with a series of labor market theories that are designed to reflect the reality of contemporary labor markets more consciously than the highly stylized model that has been the mainstay of labor market analysis for almost a century. Not surprisingly, this new look has led to some challenging conclusions.

Hiring and Firing: The Employer's Demand for Labor

Who demands labor? In the simple form that constituted the building block of the last few chapters, you followed an entrepreneur who, faced with market-determined input prices, acquired the resources necessary for the production process, combined them optimally (Chapters 6 and 7), and produced some marketable product. The relationship of costs to output in both the short run and long run shared the focus of Chapters 8 and 9 with the nature of perfectly competitive markets, while imperfect competition was the subject of Chapters 11 to 15. In all of these chapters, the firm was the supplier.

We now backtrack to the very same entrepreneur as someone who must marshal the various inputs in order to produce the product. The businessperson is now the demander, seeking labor, physical resources, and capital in order to produce. And no longer is the input price a given. The wage is something that will be determined by the interplay of suppliers and demanders in the competitive market.

Marginal Productivity and the Demand for Labor

Ted manufactures teddy bears, using a relatively simple production process. One group of workers stuffs pieces of polyfoam into synthetic bearskins, another group sews the covers together, still another adds the tongues and eyes, and the last batch of workers places the finished bears in cartons. The multitalented workers are able to perform all of these varied functions with equal skill. Ted assembles the bears in a loft stocked with various cutting and sewing machines, where he also stores his inventories of materials, parts, and boxes, as well as the finished bears prior to shipping. As such, all his costs except labor are fixed. Ted can, on a daily basis, vary the quantity of his workers, who are all paid by the day. The question facing Ted is, How many workers should he call in tomorrow?

The Production Function Again.   You've come across a similar issue in Chapter 6 in connection with the car wash production function. There you saw that the production function could be sliced so that one factor was held constant while the other was varied. Here, too, Ted has fixed commitments to all inputs except labor. So, the first step in determining how much labor he should call in requires that he examine the teddy bear production function. Table 16.1 reproduces the relevant line of the production function.

Notice right at the start that production is impossible without labor. It's equally evident that Ted will not want to employ 10 people, since using the 10th laborer actually causes output to decline! (Remember negative returns?) Precisely how many workers Ted will employ depends on:

- The production function.
- The market price of the bears.
- The cost of labor.

Ted can't know how many bears *can* be produced efficiently without knowing the production function. He can't know how much he stands to earn from bear sales without information about the price of bears. And he won't know about his variable costs of production without knowing the wage rate. Ted must somehow combine all this information in order to arrive at a sensible decision. Let's show him how.

**TABLE 16.1   The Teddy Bear Production Function
(with Factors Other than Labor Fixed)**

Quantity of Labor	Number of Teddy Bears	Marginal Physical Product	Average Physical Product
0	0		_____
1	10	_____	_____
2	24	_____	_____
3	39	_____	_____
4	48	_____	_____
5	55	_____	_____
6	60	_____	_____
7	63	_____	_____
8	64	_____	_____
9	64.5	_____	_____
10	64	_____	_____

Average and Marginal Product Curves

As a first step, complete Table 16.1 by calculating the average and marginal physical product of Ted's labor force. (If you're not sure how, check back to pages 185–186.) Figure 16.2a depicts these calculations in the form of average and marginal physical product of labor curves. Notice that the curves demonstrate increasing, diminishing, and negative returns to labor. (If you can't identify the appropriate regions, glance again at Figure 6.3, page 188.)

The **value of average product (VAP)** equals the average physical product times the price of the product, while the **value of marginal product (VMP)** equals the marginal physical product times marginal revenue.

But these curves are in terms of physical output. Since economic decisions rest on price/cost relationships, the next step is to translate these physical product curves into dollar terms. When the market is perfectly competitive so that the price of bears is fixed, the transformation of product curves to value terms is quite simple. Merely *multiply each physical product by the market price.* Figure 16.2b is identical to its counterpart with but one critical change: the vertical axis is now in dollars, and each point is precisely $20 (the price of each bear) times the corresponding number of Figure 16.2a. The corresponding curves are renamed **value** of **average product (VAP)** and **value of marginal product (VMP)** to reflect the money values.[1]

Ted now has some important pieces of information at hand. He knows that if he hires five workers, the average physical product of each is 11 bears daily or, in dollar terms, $220 per worker. The total physical product of five employees is 55 bears, and the **value of the total product (VTP)** is $1,100. He knows that employing, say, seven workers will bring in still more revenue, $_____, while hiring nine yields $_____.[2]

The Employment Decision: Introducing Wages. The critical importance of the value of marginal product becomes evident when examining the final consideration, the cost of workers. Since wages, too, are determined in a perfectly competitive market and since the quality of labor is uniform, assume a wage of $80 a day. (Please, no comments about this unbearably

The **value of total product (VTP)** is the total revenue derived from selling the production of a given number of inputs.

FIGURE 16.2   Average and Marginal Product Curves for Teddy Bear Production

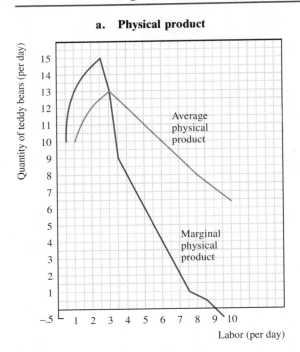

a. Physical product

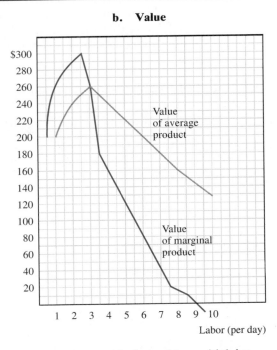

b. Value

a. The APP and MPP curves are derived from the data in Table 16.1, with the production function known and all factors other than labor fixed.

b. The VAP curve is derived by multiplying each point on the APP by the price of bears ($20), while the VMP = MPP × MR. Since bears are sold in a perfectly competitive market, MR = P = $20, so VMP = MPP × $20.

The **marginal outlay (MO)** is the cost of an additional unit of input.

low wage; just bear with it!) This wage is equal to Ted's **marginal outlay (MO),** the marginal cost Ted undertakes in employing an additional person. You now should be able to determine how many laborers will Ted hire by filling in the Hiring Plan column in Table 16.2. (Write in *more* to indicate Ted should add to employment or *less* to signify that employment should be cut back.) At equilibrium, workers should be neither added nor subtracted.

You should reason as follows:

> As long as the revenues earned from hiring an additional worker exceed the worker's cost to Ted, Ted should hire that worker. But do not employ a worker whose additional labor cost exceeds the revenue contributed by the worker. In fact, Ted should hire six workers. (Up to six, the answer is *more*; after six, *less*.)

In general, the equilibrium rule for the employment of a factor of production is MVP = MO, which is the analogue of the MR = MC principle. The reasoning is identical. Employ the input up to the point where an additional unit would cost more than it contributes to the firm's revenue. But the proof of the pudding is in the eating, so why not return to Table 16.2 and calculate for each point the value of total product, which equals total revenue, brought in at each employment position (VAP times

TABLE 16.2   The Employment Decision: VMP and MO

Number of Workers	Value of Marginal Product (VMP)	Marginal Outlay (MO)	Hiring Plan	Value of Total Product (VTP)	Total Labor Cost (TLC)	Residual
0			——	——	——	——
	$200	$80				
1			——	——	——	——
	280	80				
2			——	——	——	——
	300	80				
3			——	——	——	——
	180	80				
4			——	——	——	——
	140	80				
5			——	——	——	——
	100	80				
6			——	——	——	——
	60	80				
7			——	——	——	——
	20	80				
8			——	——	——	——
	10	80				
9			——	——	——	——

FIGURE 16.3   Ted's Hiring Decision

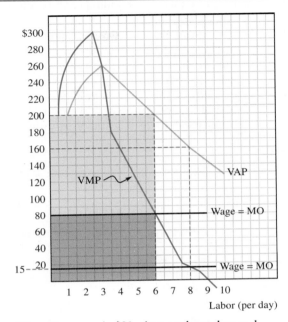

When the wage is $80, then each worker and each *additional* employee costs the firm $80 per day. Unless the marginal contribution to revenue of an additional worker is at least as large as the marginal outlay, hiring that worker would not make good economic sense. What happens to employment should the wage fall to $15?

the number of employees), the total labor (or variable) cost, and then the difference. You'll discover that the largest VTP accrues to Ted when he employs six workers.

Figure 16.3 demonstrates the equilibrium employment. Again, the VAP and VMP curves are identical to those in Figure 16.2b, but an additional line, Wage = MO (Marginal Outlay) is inserted at the wage of $80. VMP = MO at six workers.

Fill in the blanks: At equilibrium,

> The **residual** is the difference between the VTP and the cost of the variable input. It is used to pay the fixed factors of production as well as profits.

The VTP = VAP × Number of workers	$_____
TLC (= total labor costs) = Wage × Quantity of workers	$_____
The difference, or **residual**	$_____ [3]

In Figure 16.3, the lower dark purple box is the TLC, the upper light purple box is the residual, and together they constitute VTP.

Changing Wages.   Let's assume a flood of bear stuffers drives wages down to $15 daily. Figure 16.3 shows a horizontal Wage = MO line at $15 that crosses the VMP curve above eight laborers. Hiring eight workers, each costing $15 daily, forces the employer to fork out $120. But the VAP of each of these employees is $160 (the point on the VAP above eight workers), so that revenues are $1,280, leaving a residual of $1,160 for the other productive factors. Verify these numbers from Figure 16.3.

MICROQUERY   Will the firm employ one or four workers at a wage of $200? _____
                    _____ 4

Draw in, now, a wage at $260 per worker per day and calculate the following:

Number of workers hired	_____
Total labor cost	$_____
Value of total product	$_____
Residual	$_____

You see that when the wage is $260, the total labor cost equals the value of total product ($780), so that there's no residual at all. And the question that springs to the fore is, Should the firm produce at all, since there's nothing left to pay any of the other factors of production?

This situation appeared in a different guise in Figure 8.5 (p. 273), where the price of bicycles had fallen to the point where variable costs were just covered but fixed costs were not. In this bear production case, labor, the variable factor, can be paid from the revenue inflow, but none of the fixed costs can. In other words, with wages at $260 per day, the firm has reached its shutdown point, where it's immaterial whether it remains open or closed.

Ted's Demand for Labor.   The time has come to put these preceding paragraphs together in a coherent manner. Table 16.3 lists the various wage rates and Ted's employment decision. Clearly, the lower the wage rate, the more workers Ted hires. Is this not the underlying information for drawing Ted's demand curve for labor? Indeed, is the demand curve not the VMP curve in Figure 16.3 below the VMP/VAP intersection?

The Market Demand for Labor.   Just as in Chapter 8 the individual firm's MC curve became its bicycle supply curve and the sum of the individual supply curves became the market supply curve for the bicycle industry,

TABLE 16.3   The Demand Schedule for Teddy Bear Production Workers

Daily Wage	Workers Employed	Daily Wage	Workers Employed
$280	0	$80	6
260	3	40	7
160	4	15	8
120	5	0	9

so analogously can we determine the demand curve for bear industry labor. Add Ted's labor demand curve to the labor demand curves of Plush Bears, Qute Bears, Kuddly Bears, and all the other bear manufacturers, and you'll discover a negatively sloping demand curve for bear labor. The lower the wage, the larger the number of workers sought will be. (See Figure 16.6b on p. 543.)

On, then, to the supply curve.

Working or Not: The Employee's Supply of Labor

Labor supply theory begins at the level of the individual and makes the plausible assumption that people work because they have to, not because they want to. The wage merely compensates individuals for relinquishing their leisure to supply labor.[5]

"*Of course you're not having any fun, Clooney
—that's why it's called work.*"

SOURCE: Reprinted by permission of United Media.

Indifference Curve Analysis Again

The individual has a choice—to work more or to work less—with the understanding that the less she works, the less she will earn and the less she will consume.

Figure 16.4a depicts Sharon's indifference curves, plotting two "goods": consumption against leisure. (Ignore the budget lines for the moment.) Of course, leisure has a daily limit: 24 hours. Notice that if you measure leisure from the origin, as you normally would, its converse, labor, can be read leftward from 24 hours to the origin.

Take a look at U_3. Sharon is equally happy whether she earns and consumes $160 a day, requiring her to work 14 hours (with 10 hours of

FIGURE 16.4   Sharon Decides about Work Hours

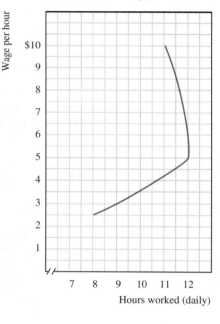

a.   Sharon's indifference map

b.   Sharon's labor supply curve

a. The indifference curve–budget line tangencies trace out Sharon's working hour decisions. When the hourly wage is $2.50 ($60/24), she wishes to work only 8 hours, spending the other 16 hours in leisure. But she reevaluates her decision as the wage rises. How many hours will she work at a $5 wage? A $10 wage? How much time will she spend resting in each case? How much will Sharon earn?

b. As the wage rises from rather low hourly rates, the quantity of labor rises. But beyond $5, wage boosts reduce the quantity of labor supplied. (Can you explain why?)

leisure), or $110 daily, requiring her to work 11 hours (with 13 hours leisure). They are both points on the same indifference curve. Of course, points on U_2 and U_1 are even less satisfactory. Note, too, that the MRS is declining as Sharon spends more hours in leisure-time activities.[6]

In short, the trade-off between spending and leisure is in principle no different from the trade-off between spending on two goods. For any individual, choices can be represented by an indifference curve map.

The Budget Line.   How much Sharon earns and spends versus how much time she devotes to nonwork activities depends not only on her preferences but also on her earning options. That, in turn, depends on the hourly wage and the number of hours she works. Consider an hourly wage of $10. If Sharon works 24 hours, she earns the maximum possible, $240. On the other hand, if she does not work at all, she earns nothing. Sharon's options are spelled out by the budget line that connects $240 and 24 hours, with a slope (equal to the hourly wage) of $10, assuming that she can work as many hours as she wishes.

Labor/Leisure Equilibrium.   Sharon will maximize her satisfaction by striving for the highest indifference curve she can achieve consistent with the budget constraint. In Figure 16.4a that's on U_3; she'll earn $110 daily by working 11 hours.

MicroQuery   How many hours would Sharon work if the wage were only $2.50 an hour? _____

You're correct if you answered eight, for she would now have to deal with the lowest of the budget lines depicted in Figure 16.4a. She'll enjoy 16 hours of leisure; work 8 hours; and, at $2.50 an hour, earn $20 a day.

Sharon's Supply of Labor.   Examine now the three budget lines, each representing a different wage, and Sharon's response to them. With the hourly wage at $2.50, her equilibrium amount of labor supplied is 8 hours; with the hourly wage at $5, she'll work 12 hours; and with the wage reaching $10, she'll work 11 hours.

Figure 16.4b plots Sharon's reactions on a price/quantity axis. As the hourly wage rises from $2.50 to $5, Sharon's quantity of labor supplied increases. But as the wage rises from $5 to $10, the supply curve bends back on itself, and the actual quantity of labor supplied falls. The resulting supply curve of Sharon's labor seems irregular but is fully consistent with her indifference curve map. You'll find nothing in this backward-bending labor supply curve that does not correspond precisely to Sharon's equilibrium positions. MicroBits 16.1 explains the backward bend using income and substitution effects.

MicroBits 16.1

The Mystery of the Backward-Bending Labor Supply Curve Resolved

Two stimuli are released simultaneously with a boost in the hourly wage. On the one hand, every hour of labor is now worth more, and so the opportunity cost of every hour of leisure has risen. That would impel the individual to work more. But there's another hand. Because the higher wage permits the worker to work as many hours as before yet earn more, the worker may well opt to enjoy some of the fruits of the higher pay by cutting back on hours worked. In a sense, the higher in-

come enables the worker to "buy" some more leisure. Indeed, one can well imagine a situation in which a worker's appetite is sated so that any boost in income will be met by a proportionate cutback in hours. The interplay of these two opposing forces leads to the backward-bending labor supply curve.

The two figures here deal with Stanley, who will work more as his wage rises, and Geraldine, who will work less when her wage increases. Let's look at Stan's *substitution*

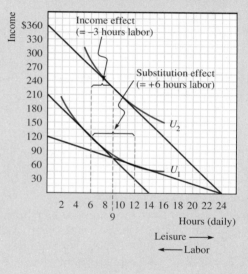

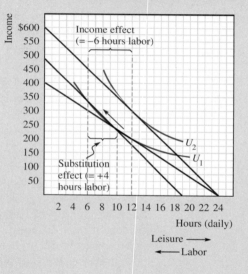

Overtime Pay.   Figure 16.5 uses indifference curve analysis to explain why employers pay higher hourly rates for overtime work. Gwendolyn earns $10 an hour at the cosmetic counter of Lacy's Department Store. Gwen's budget line–indifference curve tangency at U_1 shows her working eight hours per day. But when holiday time comes and the retailer's volume increases, Gwendolyn will be asked to stay longer. Her enlight-

MicroBits 16.1 continued

effect first. As the left figure indicates, keeping satisfaction unchanged but tripling the wage from $5 to $15 induces Stanley to work six hours more. He moves along U_1, substituting work for leisure in line with the higher opportunity cost of each leisure hour (shown by the steeper slope of the new budget constraint). As a result of the substitution effect, Stan shifts from his initial position of 12 hours leisure to only 6 hours.

The increase in the wage rate, however, also engenders an *income effect*. In essence, Stanley can work as much as before but can do better because of the higher wage. The income effect leads him to desire more leisure and so catapults Stan to a higher indifference curve, U_2. The new equilibrium urges him to spend nine hours in nonwork activities rather than six.

For Stan, the substitution effect of working six more hours outweighs the income effect that urges him to work three hours less. The net effect is a 15-hour workday at $15 an hour, for an income of $225. (Would Stanley's supply curve have a positive or a negative slope? _____*)

Turn now to the right figure and Geraldine, who was graduated with a B.A. in economics and found a job at $16.67 an hour. Her preferences led her to work 14 hours a day and earn about $233. When Geraldine's hourly pay goes up to $25, she also moves along U_1, and substitutes four more work hours for her leisure time. However, Geraldine's indifference map indicates a very strong income effect that moves her onto U_2 and 12 leisure hours. For Geraldine, the income effect has overwhelmed her substitution effect, so that the increased wage leads Geraldine to reduce her net work effort by two hours. (How does Geraldine's supply curve look—positively or negatively sloped? _____§)

Most individuals are both Stanleys and Geraldines. If they are represented by a normal indifference map, you'll discover that the substitution effect will dominate at low wages and the income effect will weigh more at high wages. Try it out!

A survey by the U.S. Bureau of Labor Statistics partially bears out these conclusions. The research reports that "most workers are satisfied with the number of hours they currently work, although one out of four—especially young people and low earners—would prefer more hours and more money; very few would trade income for leisure time."‖

‖ Susan E. Shank, "Preferred Hours of Work and Corresponding Earnings," *Monthly Labor Review* 109, no. 11 (November 1986), pp. 40–44.

---

* Positive.

ened employer offers Gwen time and a half, which will commence only after her eight-hour day is completed. In terms of the diagram, a new budget line is introduced at the old equilibrium with a slope of $15 instead of $10. The new equilibrium finds Gwen working an extra two hours at the overtime rate.

FIGURE 16.5   Overtime Pay

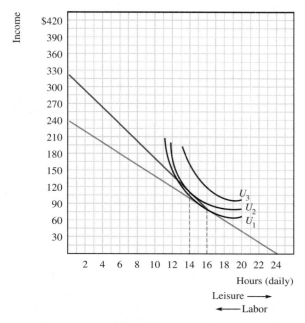

Gwendolyn sells cosmetics at a local
department store, where she works happily for
eight hours daily at $10 per hour. Around
holiday time, the store stays open longer.
Lacy's offers Gwen $15 to work beyond her
normal day, leading to a more steeply sloped
budget line and a new equilibrium. Gwen now
works 10 hours. How much does she earn?

Labor Supply for the Market.   Although indifference maps are unique to
an individual and can't be added up, the resulting supply curves can be.
Figure 16.6b assumes that the market supply for teddy bear labor is positively sloped.

Labor Market Equilibrium

Figure 16.6b juxtaposes the labor supply curve with the market demand
curve for labor. In our presumed perfectly competitive labor market, the
equilibrium wage turns out to be $80 a day for bear industry employees.

    How does the market wage affect Ted? Since Ted will not pay more
than the competitive wage and since he will not be able to obtain workers
at less than $80 per day, the market wage becomes a "given" to Ted.
Figure 16.6a adds the $80 wage onto Ted's VMP and VAP curves, which
leads Ted to employ six workers.

FIGURE 16.6   Equilibrium in the Market and the Firm

a. Ted's firm

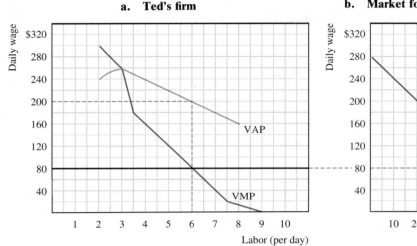

b. Market for bear industry workers

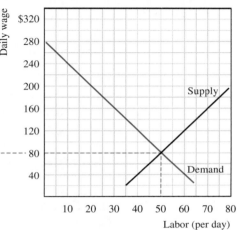

a. At a market wage = $80 per day, Ted hires 6 workers. Calculate his total labor cost, the VTP, and the residual.

b. The individual worker supply curves are aggregated into the market supply curve, and the individual firm demand curves are combined to form the market demand curve. In equilibrium, the daily wage equals $80, and the quantity of labor supplied = the quantity of labor demanded = 50,000 days.

You can calculate the total labor costs, the value of the total product, and the residual. Why not do it here and check it against Figure 16.3?[7]

Actually, this analysis of the competitive market for labor is the starting point for any of the applications and policy implications. But realize at the outset that the legitimacy of the implications hinges on the appropriateness of the assumptions. Clearly, a conclusion that is correct for a competitive market need not hold true for a market that lacks a competitive thrust on either the employers' or the employees' part.

Public Policy Applications

Minimum Wage Laws Revisited

You now have in hand the tools to consider the economics of the minimum wage. The simple analytics of the impact of minimum wage laws can be easily framed in terms of Figure 16.6. Without intervention, the market wage of $80 per day leads to employment in the teddy bear industry of 50,000 employees a day and in Ted's firm of six workers.

Fix now a minimum wage of $120 per day by drawing in a horizontal line in both parts of Figure 16.6 at that wage. If you examine Figure 16.6b, you'll immediately notice a discrepancy between the 40,000 quantity demanded and the 60,000 quantity supplied. The excess supply represents workers seeking but unable to find employment.

The above lesson is obvious to Ted. He's quite willing to hire six workers at $80, for the marginal worker earns his marginal outlay. But it no longer pays Ted to hire six workers if he is forced to pay each another $40 a day. At $120 per day, VMP = MO only at five workers. So, Ted reaches his new equilibrium by reducing employment.

Elasticity Revisited.   How much unemployment will this 50 percent increase in the minimum wage cause? You should surmise that the answer hinges on the elasticity of the demand curve. If the demand curve is very elastic, then even a small percentage increase in wages causes a substantial percentage decline in employment. On the other hand, if the demand for labor is relatively inelastic, then the number of workers released will be far fewer.

Elasticity not only influences employment but also affects total outlays on labor. The elasticity at the $80 equilibrium price equals 2/5, using the geometrical formula of Chapter 5. Recall that when demand is inelastic, an increase in price leads to a rise in total revenue. In this case, a rise in the wage when demand is inelastic leads to an increase in total labor revenues. Check it out by multiplying initial wages by quantity demanded and comparing it to the quotient after the minimum wage is imposed.[8]

Are you curious about the actual elasticity of labor demand? Take a look at MicroBits 16.2, which deals with quantitative measures of the effect of the minimum wage laws in the United States.

Programs to Increase Employment

If minimum wage laws decrease employment, what type of policies could be used to increase employment? Take a brief look at three popular programs: maintaining unchanged the existing minimum wage laws, subsidizing employment, and "workfare."

Stabilizing Minimum Wage Laws.   The economic logic behind stabilizing the minimum wage is simple and carries over directly from the analysis of minimum wage laws. If minimum wage laws increase unemployment, then decreases in the minimum wage increase employment. You can easily see from Figure 16.6 that if the minimum wage is reduced below $120, the excess supply of labor is reduced. Indeed, unemployment will be eliminated if the minimum wage law is abolished and the market equilibrium reasserts itself.

Because it is not politically realistic to turn the clock back, those opposed to minimum wage legislation satisfy themselves with resisting increases. In practice, however, the continuous upward thrust in U.S. consumer prices means the real minimum wage has been steadily eroding, even taking into account the occasional increases in the nominal minimum wage.

Subsidizing Employment.   Under both the Work Incentive Tax Credit Act (1979) and the Targeted Jobs Tax Credit Act (1978), Congress authorized private employers a tax credit of 50 percent of the first $6,000 of wages paid to specific eligible workers. Thus, the $6,000 wage costs the employer only $3,000.[9]

You can work out the analytics of this subsidy by using Figure 16.7b, which depicts a market equilibrium and Figure 16.7a, which depicts a firm equilibrium. To simplify, assume that the government is willing to pay a per unit subsidy of $25 per worker per day, so that the employer, instead of having to pay the market wage of $50 from the firm's pocket, has to shell out only $25. Your task is to show the impact of the subsidy on firm and industry employment. (Hint: Since a per unit subsidy is precisely the reverse of a per unit tax, you can refer back to Figure 8.8, p. 283.)

FIGURE 16.7   Subsidizing Employment

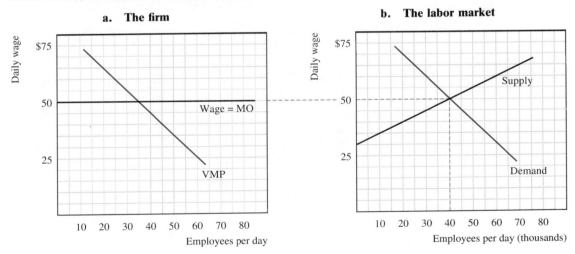

a.   A new equilibrium wage and consequently an altered quantity of labor demanded will follow a change in the cost of labor to the firm.

b.   You'll have to draw a new supply curve to demonstrate the impact of a $25 wage subsidy.

MicroBits 16.2

Empirical Estimates of the Impact of the Minimum Wage on the U.S. Economy

The relationship between increasing the minimum wage and the consequent decline in employment is analytically straightforward. Finding that impact in the real economy is something else. Surprisingly, numerous studies that have searched for the inverse relationship have found it, despite the differences in variables examined, time periods, and methods used. A representative study by James F. Ragan,* is reported here (although some simplifying adjustments have been made).

Ragan's basic equation to explain employment of a specific group, say, white teenage males who were not in school, was as follows:

$$N/P = a_0 + a_1U + a_2\text{MIN} + a_3\text{POP} + a_4\text{PSE} + e$$

---

* James F. Ragan, Jr., "The Effect of a Legal Minimum Wage on the Pay and Employment of Teenage Students and Nonstudents," in *The Economics of Legal Minimum Wages* ed. Simon Rottenberg (Washington: American Enterprise Institute, 1981), pp. 11–41. The most extensive survey of the impact of the minimum wage on the economy can be found in the seven-volume *Report of the Minimum Wage Study Commission* (Washington, D.C.: Government Printing Office, 1981).

where all variables were in logarithmic form and where

N/P = The fraction of a subgroup employed.

U = The unemployment rate of males aged 25 to 54, used to capture the impact of the overall business cycle on the group.

MIN = The minimum wage variable.

POP = Population of the subgroup relative to total population aged 16 and older.

PSE = The percentage of the subgroup enrolled in *p*ublic *s*ervice *e*mployment.

e = The random or error term.

Consider white males aged 18–19 who are not in school, so that N/P is the employment rate of this specific group. The above equation suggests that the percentage of this group actually employed can be explained by four systematic factors (and e a random factor):

• The overall employment rate (U). As the economy strengthens and the unemployment rate for prime-aged males falls, the employment rate for 18- to 19-year-old white males should increase.

• The minimum wage rate (MIN). One should expect that the higher the minimum wage, the lower the percentage of white male teenagers employed.

MicroBits 16.2 continued

- A supply variable (POP) that takes into account the actual numbers of white male 18–19-year-olds relative to the total working population. Presumably, the larger the supply, the lower the employment rate.
- Youth enrollment in government manpower programs (PSE). Clearly, the larger the percentage of the group engaged in this type of employment, the higher their employment rate.

Ragan used data from 1963 to 1972 and arrived at the following equation:

$$N/P = -0.17 - 0.099U - 0.13\text{MIN} \\ - 0.008\text{POP} + 0.55\text{PSE} \ (R^2 = 0.752)$$

Notice that the signs of the independent variables are as predicted. An inverse relationship exists for N/P and both U and POP, while a positive relationship was found between N/P and PSE. For present purposes, however, the critical finding is the inverse connection between the minimum wage variable and the employment rate: The higher MIN is, the lower N/P is. Moreover, since *the value of the coefficient in a logarithmic function is the elasticity,* this equation states that a 10 percent increase in the minimum wage will reduce the employment of 18- to 19-year-old white males who are not in school by 1.3 percent.

Ragan's study is typical of a number of studies that were surveyed by Charles Brown, Curtis Gilroy, and Andrew Kohen in 1982. Their overall conclusion is worth citing:

The most frequently studied group in the empirical literature is teenage. Time-series studies typically find that a 10 percent increase in the minimum wage reduces teenage employment by one to three percent. . . . We believe that the lower half of that range is to be preferred. . . . Cross-section studies of the effect on teenage employment produce a wider range of estimated impacts, . . . from 0 to over 3 percent, but estimates from 0 to .75 percentage points are most plausible.§

One final point: In light of the decline in the real minimum wage over the 1981 to 1990 period mentioned earlier, we should have expected teenage employment to have increased. As a matter of fact, Charles Brown‖ sets out some simple ratios to examine the 1981 to 1986 period, where the erosion of the minimum wage for teenagers was around 20 percent. Professor Brown finds himself surprised by the relatively minor impact that the decline in the real minimum wage had on teenage employment. Whether behavior in the 1980s differed from that in earlier periods or whether other reasons explain the discrepancy, the earlier consensus may be unraveling. We may no longer share a generally accepted *quantitative* estimate of the impact of the minimum wage law on employment.

---

§ Charles Brown, Curtis Gilroy, and Andrew Kohen, "The Effect of the Minimum Wage on Employment and Unemployment," *Journal of Economic Literature,* 20 (June 1982), pp. 487–528.

‖ Charles Brown, "Minimum Wage Laws: Are They Overrated?" *Journal of Economic Perspectives* 2, no. 3 (Summer 1988), pp. 133–46.

Workfare.   Both minimum wage legislation and tax credits influence the demand for labor. In contrast, workfare is designed to affect labor supply. Conventional wisdom insists that individuals living on "welfare" have lost the incentive to work. Indeed, Figure 16.8 suggests how this claim can be justified.

Consider Malcolm, an unskilled laborer whose indifference map is shown in Figure 16.8. At the minimum wage of $4.25 an hour, Malcolm would earn $42.50 before expenses should he be able to work 10 hours daily. But Malcolm could do better by not working if he were entitled to a daily welfare payment of $50.[10] The straight line at $50 reaches U_5 at $50 and no work, a position that dominates Malcolm's given budget line and tangency.

But the diagram suggests a less obvious conclusion. Would Malcolm want to work if the welfare payment were only $35 per day? The diagram demonstrates that Malcolm still reaches a higher indifference curve at $35

FIGURE 16.8   The Disincentive Effect of Welfare Payments

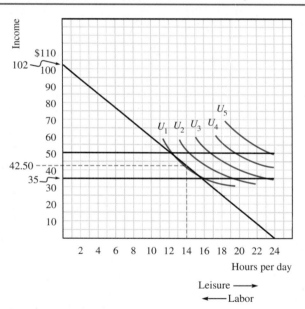

At the $4.25 minimum wage and no welfare option, Malcolm would work 10 hours and earn $42.50, putting him in equilibrium on U_1. With a fixed welfare payment of $50, Malcolm can reach U_5 providing he doesn't work at all. But note, too, that even a welfare payment of $35, which is less than the income he earned by working, will induce Malcolm to cease working, enabling him to reach U_3 instead of U_1.

and no employment than working for 10 hours per day, implying that the system encourages the rational welfare recipient to remain unemployed.

Workfare represents the government's attempt to counter this disincentive effect. Since 1982, a number of states have required able-bodied welfare recipients to work in order to obtain welfare payments. The federal government adopted this idea as part of the Family Support Act (1988). The government provides work options in the public sector for certain welfare recipients deemed physically and mentally able to work; refusal can lead to a termination of public funding.

Taxes and Wages

Indifference curve analysis is a fruitful method for examining the impact of taxes on labor supply. Under the U.S. tax withholding system, income and employment taxes are deducted before an employee ever receives his or her paycheck, so that take-home pay is always less than income earned. If we make the reasonable assumption that workers are motivated by take-home pay rather than gross income, then indifference curve analysis can be used to analyze the impact of an alteration in tax rates on labor effort. Will raising taxes induce people to work more or less?

C.D. Slaughter is employed by The Whole Hog, a processor of pig products. He works a 40-hour week at $10 (after taxes) per hour, and so brings home $400 weekly. Figure 16.9a shows his equilibrium work effort and income. Now, income taxes are raised to bring his net hourly wage to $8. Sketch in the new budget line and indicate Mr. Slaughter's new equilibrium.

If you've drawn in the new line properly, you'll discover that the lower take-home pay has induced Mr. Slaughter to work about 5 hours less. (His substitution effect has outweighed his income effect.)

This outcome is dictated by the structure of the indifference map. Figure 16.9b shows the reverse for his son, Lamont Slaughter, who works about 5 hours more in response to the same tax boost.

It follows that C.D. could be induced to work more if his taxes were cut! Try it in Figure 16.7a by increasing wages to $12 an hour.

Lest you consider this analysis sterile, think back to the 1988 presidential election campaign. Among the economic policies endorsed by President Bush was the **Laffer curve,** which appears in Figure 16.9c. The relationship between tax rates and labor supply is shown to be backward bending. An increase in tax rates above point *M* reduces labor input; a decrease from *N* increases labor input. If the bulk of U.S. workers are better represented by Mr. Slaughter senior than by his son, then tax cuts will prove effective in raising labor input. But they will be counterproductive if U.S. workers are found on the Laffer curve below *M*.

What does the empirical evidence suggest? In a survey of labor supply models, Mark Killingworth found income elasticities for men to range

The **Laffer curve** posits a backward-bending relationship between tax rates and labor supply.

FIGURE 16.9 The Laffer Curve

a. C.D. Slaughter's indifference map	**b. Lamont Slaughter's indifference map**	**c. A hypothetical Laffer curve**
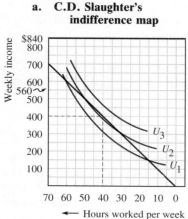	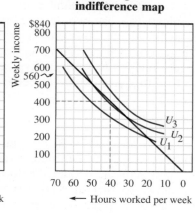	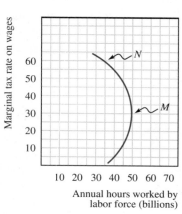

C.D. works 40 hours weekly at $10 per hour. What happens if tax increases reduce his hourly wage to $8? Alternatively, how does C.D. react to a tax cut that increases his hourly wage to $12?

Lamont works 40 hours a week at $10 per hour. What happens if tax increases bring the wage down to $8 per hour? Alternatively, how does Lamont react to a tax cut that brings his hourly wage up to $12?

If the labor supply curve for the entire labor force is backward-bending with respect to tax rates, then the impact of a tax change on hours worked depends both on the direction of the change and the initial position. A cut in taxes from an initial position at N increases labor input, while a cut when starting at M reduces hours worked.

from -0.33 to 0 and for women from -0.75 to -0.10.[11] In other words, an increase in income due to a tax cut would at best *not* decrease men's labor input, but might decrease it by as much as one third of the income change. For women, the decrease in labor input could be even more substantial. But if we also consider the substitution effect—after all, the tax cut increases the take-home pay for each hour worked and should induce the substitution of labor for leisure—the results are less clear-cut. Killingworth's survey revealed a range of labor supply elasticities for men from -0.40 to 0.3 and for women from -0.07 to 0.90.

Taxes, Wages, and the Underground Economy. The Laffer curve suggests that higher taxes may induce workers to reduce the quantity of labor supplied. But a second alternative may be even more plausible, since workers may not want to see their take-home pay being eroded: supply labor and don't pay the tax. Tax withholding laws preclude that option for most employees in their primary employment. But it is possible through self-employment outside of normal working hours. So, a computer programer acts as a software consultant, a teacher provides private lessons on weekends, a painter takes on odd painting jobs during her spare time, a carpenter builds cabinets in the evening, and so forth.

Markets in illegal goods or services, or activities that are intrinsically permitted by law but in which the participants do not comply with the income and/or sales reporting mandates of the authorities all fall under the umbrella of the underground economy.

Welcome to the **underground economy,** where incomes are not reported and taxes are not paid. The worker deals directly with the customer, neither of whom have any particular incentive to enforce government tax policy. And when payments are made in cash, the paper trail that checks would leave is also eliminated.

The economics of tax avoidance is readily analyzed with the aid of Figure 16.10. Recall C.D. Slaughter of Figure 16.9. In the absence of an income tax, he worked 40 hours and earned $400 each week. This combination represents the initial equilibrium in both Figure 16.9a on U_2 and Figure 16.10a on indifference curve U_4. If you've worked out the impact of the tax on C.D. in Figure 16.9, you should have derived the equilibrium

FIGURE 16.10   Tax Avoidance Incentives

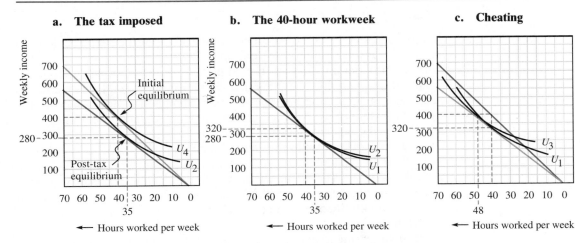

| a. The tax imposed | b. The 40-hour workweek | c. Cheating |

When a tax lowers the effective hourly take-home pay, a new equilibrium on a lower indifference curve replaces the initial equilibrium.

When the employee is required to work a fixed number of hours per week (e.g., 40) then U_2 becomes unattainable. Instead, a disequilibrium position at 40 hours work and $320 is imposed on the employee, forcing him to U_1.

In order to restore income to the previous level, the employee seeks additional work at the same gross wage of $10. The $10 per hour will also be the net wage, since he doesn't pay income tax on these extra earnings. The new equilibrium is attained at $400, requiring 48 work hours—the tangency of the new budget line segment with U_3.

shown in Figure 16.10a on U_2: C.D. works only 35 hours and takes home $280 (35 hours at $8 per hour).

As a matter of fact, few workers can choose the number of weekly hours they wish to work. Most jobs have defined workweeks, and the only option facing the employee is take it or leave it. Given that choice, C.D. puts in his 40-hour week despite the tax boost and his preference for a shorter workweek. Figure 16.10b finds C.D. forced to a lower indifference curve, U_1, which is *not* tangent to the budget line at 40 hours work.

C.D. now considers an alternative. He'll put in the 40-hour workweek, earn $320 after taxes, and try to recoup the lost income by working in the underground economy. There, he'll earn his $10 per hour, and by pulling in eight more hours will take home the same $400 as before. Figure 16.10c shows his new equilibrium. A new budget line with a slope of $10 per hour is drawn in at the 40-hour work disequilibrium, representing his new option. C.D. can reach a new equilibrium point on U_3 at $400, although he now works 48 hours.[12] As you can see, C.D. is better off on the U_3 tangency than at either the 35-hour, $280 equilibrium or the 40-hour, $320 disequilibrium.[13]

Illegal Markets

It's just one step from the economics of illegal reporting to the economics of illegal markets. Labor in the cocaine market, for example, comes in at both the production and distribution ends, but the analysis is identically simple. Legal activities pay less than do illegal ones, and for some illegal activities, far less. You need not be an economist to understand the options, but why not use the analytic tools you've learned in this chapter to sketch out the labor supply consequences?

Figure 16.11 presents the indifference map of Lester, a typical unskilled urban teenager. On the one hand, he can work in a fast-food establishment at, say, $5 per hour. On the other hand, Lester can push drugs at an hourly rate of $50. Draw in the two budget lines, and find Lester's weekly income from both alternatives as well as his labor and leisure hours.

The surprising implication of Figure 16.11 is not that so many people are tempted to engage in illegal drug sales but that so relatively few are. This puzzle is partly resolved by considering the moral dimension of drug dealing. Another clue was suggested in connection with Chapter 1's discussion of the risk involved in criminal activity. In the particular case of drug selling, not only does the pusher face arrest and a prison term, but also the high income derived illegally makes the pusher a prey to extortion or worse. All too often, cutthroat competition in the drug business is precisely that, although a bullet in the head is more typical. For many individuals, the risk-adjusted wage of pushing lies below the legal market wage, so that legal occupations are better paying on balance.

FIGURE 16.11   The Economic Attraction of Illegal Activities

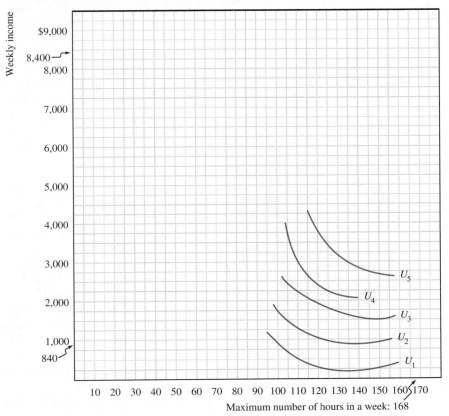

Given the indifference map depicted here and an individual's occupational choice—the legal position paying $5 per hour and the illegal one paying $50 per hour—which one will be chosen? How many hours will be devoted to each alternative? What will be the respective earnings?

Shopping for an Improved-Quality Labor Market Theory

Modern labor market theory has grappled with one obvious feature of the labor market that was ignored for many decades and may have bothered you in this chapter as well. Labor is not a homogeneous input. People differ in abilities, in attitudes, and in behavior. Finally, in competitive circumstances, not only do different firms pay similar workers divergent wages, but also within a single firm apparently similar workers are paid differently. Finally, since workers can be motivated to be more productive either through economic rewards or through psychological techniques, treating humans like machines is too much of an oversimplification. The simple supply and demand analysis that purports to determine equilibrium wages and employment fails to reflect such complexities. The rest of this chapter is concerned with theories that grapple with the labor market as it is, explicitly taking into account the roles of uncertainty, asymmetric information, and wage differences. Specifically, you'll be introduced to three related labor market theories: job search, implicit contracts, and efficiency wages.[14]

Shopping: The Analysis of Job Search

The Employee.   It's not only employers who seek the best workers; workers also search out the best employers.[15] Job search is a two-way street, entailing costs and benefits in an uncertain environment for both sides.

Think ahead and imagine yourselves about to graduate. You're in the process of exploring employment options. On the one hand, you're going to spend time discovering the available jobs, the firms you'd like to work for, mailing résumés, interviewing, and ultimately evaluating your offers. Aside from the actual expenses, search involves an opportunity cost—the income not earned by accepting the last best offer. And the more you search, the more you're apt to pass up earlier and, in retrospect, better offers. It certainly is plausible to assume that the marginal cost of search rises the longer you extend your search.

But there's also a benefit to the extended search. The more you search, the more likely you are to discover new opportunities and better-paying jobs. If we make the reasonable presumption that you try your best opportunities first, then as you expand your search you also reduce the likelihood that you'll find better offers. In other words, the marginal benefit from expanded search declines with the extent of the search.

Return to Figure 8.9a (p. 286) for a diagrammatic analysis. But now relate the diagram not to the firm but to you, the prospective employee. You understand that it pays to search only as long as the marginal benefit of search exceeds its marginal cost. Optimum search occurs when MB = MC. When you've reached that point, stop looking and take the best job that's still available.[16]

The Employer.   The employer's job search also entails actual expenditures and opportunity costs. The personnel department must sift through the applicant batch to identify the most suitable employees, interview the best of them, verify and evaluate the information obtained, and make a decision that remains shrouded with uncertainty until the employees have proven themselves. The opportunity costs associated with search stem from the fact that unfilled positions mean lost output. Presumably, employers also face a rising marginal cost curve, for the more they search, the more potential employees they can screen. But they simultaneously risk losing good candidates to other employers. On the other hand, like the employee, marginal benefits from extended search decline. The more applicants they interview, the lower the probability they'll find still better ones than those already seen. So, the employer, too, runs through an exercise depicted by Figure 8.9a, hiring when the MB of search equals its MC.

Introducing job search suggests that the competitive marketplace cannot guarantee that the workers most suited for specific jobs will in fact be found in those jobs. Because of the various search costs, workers may rationally stop the job hunt before finding just the right position. Employers may find it equally rational to hire workers who meet a certain minimal level of competence rather than continue the search to find the perfect employee.

Another implication: Equally proficient workers at different firms, or even within a single firm, may earn different wage rates even in a perfectly competitive labor market because of divergent job search cost/benefit propensities.

The Value of a College Degree.   Wouldn't both potential employees and employers benefit from reducing the costs of search? Using educational certification as a **screen** or **signal** is a common method of cutting search costs. Most universities will not hire faculty members without a Ph.D. Many white-collar positions require a college degree, and many blue-collar jobs that do not will be filled first by college graduates. Yet one can justifiably claim that a Ph.D. does not make a good college teacher, nor will someone with a B.A. in sociology prove to be a better insurance salesman. Those who believe in the usefulness of signals claim that a degree serves as a proxy for a number of desirable job-related characteristics such as intelligence, ability, and motivation. It's an efficient shortcut for reducing search costs.[17]

Screens or **signals** are proxies for job-related tests used by potential employees and/or potential employers when direct job-performance testing is either impossible, difficult, or expensive.

The Invisible Handshake

Job search, which is costly both to the hiring firm and the new employee, ends once the worker joins the firm. But employment costs continue as both the employer and the employee begin to invest in each other. New employee training can be an expensive undertaking for the employer, especially for those firms that require new employees to undergo formal training. Even when training is more informal as senior workers "break in" the new hands, it's also costly in terms of personnel time and of errors by the new employees.

New hires invest time in trying out their firms, learning more about their duties and what is expected of them in a manner that could not be gleaned as an outsider. True, they're being paid during this discovery period. But the new employees may be disappointed with any number of job-related factors. Their expenses include lost time, a precious, irretrievable commodity. Less prosaically, there's an opportunity cost: they'll always be a step behind their peers who began earlier at another firm.

The challenge of the firm, having searched for, discovered, and trained new employees, is to devise a strategy to retain those employees it wishes to keep. An explicit labor contract, binding the particular employee to a specific employer, would not be enforceable in the courts; it verges on violating the antislavery amendment to the Constitution. Moreover, any formal wage contract that fixes wages or salaries adversely affects incentives. For example, if Fred knows that he can anticipate an annual 5 percent wage increment as long as he performs the minimum amount of work, Fred has little incentive to produce more than that minimum.

An **implicit contract** commits employers and employees to a mutually beneficial long-term employment relationship in the absence of explicit contractual arrangements.

Instead, in many firms, labor and management engage in an **implicit contract,** or in Arthur Okun's picturesque phrase, an "invisible handshake,"[18] an understanding that employer and employee cooperate for their mutual interest. This implies that the employer will pay fairly, will provide proper working conditions, and will assure the worker of some degree of employment stability. The employee in return will contribute an honest day's labor, will perform reliably and steadily, and will be committed to the firm's goals.

Seniority refers to the length of a worker's employment in a given firm.

Implicit contract theory, with its emphasis on the investment by the employer in the employee, helps explain the prevalence of deferred compensation schemes. Basically, such practices as merit raises, **seniority** benefits, and promotion from the ranks accrue to individual workers only after they have spent some time with the firm. The message the employer is sending by paying the worker more the longer he or she is attached to the firm is twofold:

- If you keep your part of the performance bargain, you'll be rewarded by pay increments.
- If you stay on long enough so that I can recoup my investment in you, you'll benefit from longevity increases and promotions.

Implications.   Implicit contracts theory casts a new light on a puzzling phenomenon. Why, when product demand declines, do few firms cut wages across the board, opting to lay off workers instead? Indeed, the firings occur in reverse order of seniority, with those having the greatest seniority facing the least risk of layoffs. Implicit contract theory suggests that this option benefits both the firm and the employees.

Offering job security and maintaining pay schedules clearly benefits the senior employee. But even the more recent recruit benefits if she's not among the first to be dismissed. Moreover, the longer the junior employee stays with the firm, the more stable her job becomes. Indeed, all but the newest employees benefit from a "last in, first out" employment policy rather than a fluctuating wage practice. The employer gains in at least three ways: reduced employee turnover, improved employee morale and productivity, and lower average wages.

• *Reduced employee turnover.* The incentive for the employee to remain translates into lower search and training costs for the employer. A second benefit from retaining existing workers is asymmetric information: you know whom you've got; you don't know whom you might pick up!

• *Improved employee morale and productivity.* Worker morale is enhanced when wages are maintained and seniority is respected in firing. As with reduced turnover, the reason also stems from asymmetric information. It's sensible to assume that management is better informed about the firm's profitability than are workers. That discrepancy can create a credibility gap. Employees may view reports about reduced demand and pressure on profits as ploys to lower wages and increase profits at their expense. The resulting employee resentment can easily turn into worker inefficiencies and higher production costs. On the other hand, preserving wages and laying off new employees is unlikely to be viewed as a management plot. That the firm continues to employ the more costly senior workers despite falling output, sales, and profits is viewed favorably by the workers.

• *Lower average wages.* Long-run labor costs may be lower as a result of a wage preservation policy accompanied by firing new hires rather than saving all jobs and instituting an across-the-board wage cut whenever product demand falls. The reason has to do with employee attitudes toward risk. Imagine the following scenario. Zeneida has just been hired at $300 a week with no guarantee of job stability. When she begins work, however, she is offered an employment insurance policy. For $25 weekly, Zeneida would be guaranteed work at that salary for a year. If Zeneida sufficiently values job security over wages, then she should buy the insurance. On a companywide scale, if other workers are similarly risk-averse, as is thought to be the case, and employers are better able to protect themselves against income fluctuations, then firms could provide this insurance themselves. They would offer their employees a lower wage combined with an implicit contract of job security. In essence, the employer, in exchange for its implicit employment commitment, pays Zeneida only $275 a week instead of $300.

Of course, not every firm will find it profitable to act in this way, nor will every employee be satisfied with a particular employer's implicit contract. The link that bonds employers and employees even when labor market conditions change is not forged of steel. Employers who disappoint employee expectations or who, over time, fail to react to, say, increases in market wages will see their labor force eroding. And the better workers are likely to leave first. The worker, too, must make it worthwhile for the employer to adhere to the implicit contract. There's absolutely nothing to prevent the employer from releasing the worker whose performance is substandard. For both parties, the implicit contract is only an informal commitment, not a sentence of penal servitude.

This invisible handshake stands in clear contrast to the flexibility implied by the classical theory of supply and demand. As you well know, if the demand for, say, math teachers in Minneapolis rises, leading city schools to boost the pay of math teachers, other cities will have to match the increase or watch teachers emigrate. Indeed, in the short run, Minneapolis will attract mathematics teachers from other areas. Even within the city, some men and women who are capable of teaching mathematics but who, for one reason or another, had elected to pursue other activities will respond to the higher wage offer. That reaction, of course, epitomizes the increase in the quantity of labor supplied. And classical theory is symmetrical. If demand falls, wages are cut and employment is reduced.

Implicit contract theory visualizes a different scenario. It does not see workers continually searching for better-paying jobs in their industry and region. Nor do employees leave their jobs immediately upon discovering better employment prospects. Similarly, employers do not fire workers if the labor market loosens up. They normally do not cast aside their existing workers to employ cheaper new hires in their place. This inertia also applies to wages. Even in competitive markets, employers do not reduce the wages of existing workers if market wages fall. It doesn't necessarily pay to violate the implicit contract. In terms of supply-demand analysis, the wage rate may not be forced down to the intersection of the supply and demand curves. Both firms and employees are in equilibrium even though there's a discrepancy between the quantity of labor supplied and demanded.[19]

While both the analysis of job search and implicit contract theory can explain a number of labor market phenomena without resorting to differences in the quality of labor, the final theory to be discussed recognizes that no two workers are really alike.

Wages and Labor Quality[20]

That labor quality is not uniform and that information is scarce and thus expensive form only part of the story. As mentioned earlier, information is also asymmetrically distributed. The worker knows about her own abilities and motivation; the employer has to discover the truth about the quality of the specific candidate, hopefully before committing the firm to hiring and training her. What if the potential employee unwittingly supplies the employer with a signal by which to judge the worker's ability?

An **efficiency wage** is the cost of a unit of labor adjusted for the individual worker's productivity.

Efficiency wage theory suggests that such is reality. And some marvelous consequences follow.

Role-play an employer facing two potential hires, both seemingly equally qualified. Hazel expects $35,000 a year as a middle-level financial executive, while Trudy asks for only $25,000. Which one would you hire?

At first blush, you'd hire Trudy. But consider asking yourself the following question: Why is Trudy willing to work for so little and why does Hazel demand so much? That might set you thinking along these lines: Either Trudy doesn't know what the market wage is—in which case, she's naive—or she isn't worth more than $25,000. On the other hand, Hazel is asking for $35,000 because she's really worth that much. She thinks she's a highly productive individual and challenges the firm that is serious about quality personnel to meet her price. If true, Hazel's cost to the firm on an efficiency wage basis will be lower than Trudy's, so that you'd hire Hazel. (This is quite analogous to the consumer's buying the higher-priced product because it is deemed sufficiently superior to justify the higher price.)

Implications.   Consider just one implication of this view of the labor market. Should an employer pay more than the minimum wage even if the firm can obtain all the labor it wishes at the minimum wage? Efficiency wage theory suggests that the firm attracts better-quality labor by offering more than the minimum wage.

Efficiency wage theory upsets another feature of the labor demand and supply model explored earlier. The prevailing assumption throughout much of the text is the independence of the production function from the wage.[21] But what if the worker's productivity is affected by the wage, so that the higher the wage, the more productive the worker. Actually, it has long been understood that if a higher wage enables the worker to be better nourished, the employee will be physically capable of better work. Indeed, that argument has been used to advocate higher wages in the developing world or among migrant unskilled farm labor in this country. But even in the industrial sector of modernized economies, paying a higher wage may lead to greater productivity under certain conditions. Just to cite one possibility: If the workers believe that the least productive workers will be fired and if they further know that employment in other firms in the industry pays less, then the workers' incentive to shirk is minimized. The relatively higher wage induces a greater labor effort per hour of work and more work over the year due to less absenteeism.

Higher wages may even drive down total labor costs. Consider the employer-employee relationship as an analogue to the agent-principal problem you read about at the outset of Chapter 8. If the worker's (i.e., agent's) self-serving objective is to obtain the most pay for the least effort and management's (i.e., principal's) goal is to get the most worker effort for the least pay, then these different agendas inevitably breed conflict.

The principal must devise strategies for inducing the agent to generate maximum labor effort rather than just to turn up daily and go through the motions. One such strategy is using supervisors to monitor labor input. But monitoring is costly. A higher wage combined with the threat of job loss for poor performance is an alternative that economizes on monitoring costs and conceivably reduces total labor outlays.

Back to the Minimum Wage.   Might not the above implications suggest that increasing the minimum wage can prove beneficial? For all those earning the minimum wage, the increase boosts the opportunity cost of losing the job. The result is more labor input per worker and thus more productivity. If productivity and the wage rise by the same proportion, then the firm's cost per unit of output remains unchanged, and presumably there's no reason for the firm to rid itself of employees.

Take this one step further. MicroBits 16.2 mentioned Professor Brown's surprise that the decline in the real minimum wage since 1981 had a relatively minor impact on teenage employment. Efficiency wage theorists would not be nonplussed. They would posit that the fall in the real minimum wage induced teenagers to slack off. So, the lower hourly cost of labor was offset to some degree by a fall in labor productivity. Firms would simply not be as interested in hiring many more less-productive workers.

Efficiency wage theory challenges economists to rethink some of the basic concepts in labor economics. It certainly has led to a more sophisticated understanding of the labor market. Indeed, all these new developments have deepened our comprehension of labor market operations. The old hasn't been dumped overboard; it's been refined and expanded. In the process, however, economists have forced themselves to reexamine some old truths. As a result, many economic theorists have taken a more agnostic posture. Indeed, a strange picture is evolving. On the one hand, the new developments have shown economists once again how effectively the market functions. (For example, wage discrepancies among individuals may well reflect differential productivities rather than inefficiencies in the market.) On the other hand, the new advances in theory have led other economists to question the efficacy of the market in a world of uncertainty and asymmetric information. (For example, could some type of government intervention lead to the development of a cheaper screening device than a college degree?) We've started on a new path in these last years; it's too early to tell where it will lead.

Summary

The exciting adventures of Ted, manufacturer of teddy bears, opened the chapter. Ted was confronted with a simple question facing all producers: How much labor to hire? He discovered that the solution to the employment puzzle depended on unearthing three types of information:

- The production function, which would tell him how many teddy bears different quantities of workers could manufacture, given commitments to other production inputs.
- The price at which the teddy bears could be sold, which would tell Ted how much revenue different amounts of employees would bring in.
- The cost of each laborer.

The first two of these elements enabled Ted to calculate the value of marginal product (VMP) for different numbers of workers, while the wage provided Ted with his marginal outlay (MO). Since the VMP informed Ted how much each additional worker contributed to the firm's revenues and the MO told Ted how much each additional worker added to the firm's costs, he found the optimal quantity of labor by VMP = MO.

With employment totally dependent on the production function, the market price of bears, and the wage, wage hikes to teddy bear workers (the other elements in the trinity remaining unchanged) would induce Ted to cut back on employment in order to maintain his optimum production. Similarly, if wages were to fall, Ted would find it profitable to hire more workers. Thus was generated Ted's demand curve, which when combined with the demand curves of all teddy bear manufacturers leads to the market demand for teddy bear workers.

Labor supply takes off from a different angle. Work is assumed a "bad," leisure, a "good." But work has as its compensation a wage, and so most individuals are willing to sacrifice some amount of leisure in order to earn some income. Indifference curve analysis permits us to visualize the derivation of a labor supply curve by varying the wage and discovering how much work our subject is willing to undertake. (One unusual feature of labor supply is the possibility of a backward-bending supply curve, so that at some high wage, the worker actually wants to work less.) Of course, the combined supply curves constitute the supply of labor for a particular type of labor.

The market wage and the equilibrium quantity of labor supplied and demanded are determined in a competitive labor market when a downward-sloping demand for labor curve crosses an upward-sloping supply of labor curve. Shifts in either the supply or demand curve will lead to a change in the equilibrium wage and quantity.

A policy issue that has long intrigued economists and public policymakers, and for which this simple model emits a powerful voice of caution, is the impact of a minimum wage law. As Chapter 2 has already shown, intervening in a competitive market by setting a floor below which price cannot drop leads to a decrease in quantity demanded and a discrepancy between quantity demanded and quantity supplied. Imposing a minimum wage in a competitive labor market means creating unemployment. And, in fact, empirical studies of the U.S. teenage labor market bear this conclusion out, although the impact appears rather small. The chapter also examined other employment-oriented policies and demonstrated that imposing taxes creates tax-evasion incentives, including the birth of illegal markets. Indeed, more surprising than the presence of an underground economy in the United States for a variety of goods and services is its limited nature.

In recent years, microeconomic theorists have devoted a great deal of effort to constructing new models of the labor market. Underlying this quest is the belief that the simple supply and demand model inadequately stylizes the labor market's complex nature. The chapter outlined three such models: job search, implicit contracts, and efficiency wage theories. Job search focuses on shopping for employment and comes directly to grips with the uncertainty faced by both the job seeker in finding a job and the firm in discovering the right employee. Since search is a costly activity with increasing marginal costs and decreasing marginal benefits for both the seeker and the employer, at some point both will decide that they've searched long enough, and hiring will take place. (That's true even when using various cost-saving screening devices to weed out undesirable firms or applicants.) However, because individual seekers and firms have different cost/benefit calculations, it's not plausible to expect all firms to offer the same wage nor for each individual hired to receive the same pay. Thus, the unique equilibrium wage of the supply-demand model just doesn't exist in the job-search universe.

A similar conclusion emerges from implicit contract theory but for a different reason. Firms invest in their new employees not only search costs but also training expenses. In return, they anticipate that their employees will stick around for a while. Employers realize, of course, that they must induce their workers to remain with the firm by providing them with such benefits as merit raises, seniority bonuses, and promotion prospects. Perhaps most important to many workers is employment security. On the other hand,

employees, too, must deliver. This understanding constitutes an implicit contract between employers and employees, an invisible handshake that benefits both parties.

Implicit contract theory leaves room for non-market-clearing wages and employment. A rationally acting firm may well pay more than the market-clearing wage to maintain the allegiance of its labor force. Similarly, it may be sensible to maintain wage scales and lay off in inverse seniority order rather than cut wages across the board.

Finally, efficiency wage theory relates wages to productivity. For any number of reasons, a higher wage may reflect or induce higher productivity. So, it's not certain at all that increasing wages reduces a firm's quantity of labor demanded for labor. Increasing wages may even increase labor demand if the wage hike induces so large a productivity increment that labor cost per unit of output actually falls. If that's the case, then economists might want to rethink the impact of an increase in the minimum wage. Perhaps by raising the minimum wage, employment will actually increase.

The jury is still out on these newer theoretical developments. But the latter conclusion will be developed in Chapter 17, which analyzes imperfectly competitive factor markets. In those circumstances, an increase in the minimum wage can truly buttress rather than retard employment.

Key Terms

Efficiency wage
Implicit contract
Laffer curve
Marginal outlay (MO)
Residual
Screen or signal

Seniority
Underground economy
Value of average product (VAP)
Value of marginal product (VMP)
Value of total product (VTP)

Review Questions

1. Describe the impact each of the following will have on the teddy bear firm's demand for labor, and in each instance, sketch out the before and after VAP and VMP curves:
   a. An increase in the quantity of capital.
   b. An innovation that causes each worker to be 50 percent more productive.
   c. A decrease in the market price of bears.
   d. An increase in the wage rate.

2. Explain why you should agree or disagree with the following statement: "Production will only take place in the production function region of diminishing returns."

3. Why will employment equilibrium occur only where VMP = MO?

4. Use indifference curve analysis to derive an individual's supply of labor curve.

5. Summarize and evaluate the arguments presented in this chapter in favor of and against minimum wage legislation.

6. Show on Figure 16.8 and explain the impact of a $20 welfare payment.

7. a. How do the job search and implicit contract theories explain differences in worker pay even when a number of individuals are performing identical tasks?
   b. Are such differences consistent with the classical theory of wage determination? Explain.

8. How does efficiency wage theory explain the apparent paradox that higher wages can be consistent with lower labor costs?

Food for Thought

1. Use VAP and VMP curves to demonstrate why an employer might want to hire Ms. A, who asks for a $50,000 annual salary, rather than the less demanding Mr. B, who asks for $40,000.

2. Refer to Figure 16.4a. How would Sharon's indifference map and supply curve look if she would never work for less than $60 per day?

3. Sketch an indifference map and a supply-of-labor curve for a workaholic.

4. Refer to Figure 16.5. Why doesn't Lacy's just offer Gwen a straight $15 an hour instead of overtime pay? Draw in the proper budget line on Figure 16.5 and find the new equilibrium.

5. Some economists have proposed a teenage minimum wage that is less than the legal minimum.
   a. What effect would that have on teenage employment?
   b. How would such an amendment affect overall employment?

6. Use indifference curve analysis to demonstrate why most individuals work at legal rather than illegal jobs.

7. Graduate schools of economics use the graduate record exam (GRE) to help determine admission even though the correlation between graduate performance and GRE scores is not very strong. Does search theory provide a rationale for this practice? Explain.

Suggested Readings

Among the textbooks you might consult for further details about labor economics are Daniel S. Hamermesh and Albert Rees, *The Economics of Work and Pay* (New York: HarperCollins, 1988).

The November 1986 issue of the *Monthly Labor Review* contains a special section on "The Time We Spend Working," a survey on U.S. worker behavior.

Among the less complex articles on implicit contract theory is the survey by Costas Azariades

and Joseph E. Stiglitz, "Implicit Contracts and Fixed-Price Equilibria," *Quarterly Journal of Economics* 98 (1983 Supplement), pp. 1–22. That entire issue is devoted to implicit contract theory. Profit sharing as a strategy for resolving the labor-management agent-principal conflict is proposed by Martin L. Weitzman in *The Share Economy: Conquering Stagflation* (Cambridge, Mass.: Harvard University Press, 1984).

Notes and Answers

1. Since the market is perfectly competitive, P = MR, so that the physical values on both curves are multiplied by the same number. This will not be true when the product market is not perfectly competitive.
2. $1,260; $1,290.
3. $1,200; $480; $720.
4. The best way to answer this question is to perform the calculations for each point. You'll then discover that the residual will be larger when four are employed. Indeed, whenever the MO curve intersects the VMP curve twice, as in this instance, optimal employment is always at the larger quantity.
5. "Leisure" in the labor economics literature describes all time spent in nonmarket activities. It includes relaxation time but also encompasses various home-based but non-marketed production such as taking care of one's own children or do-it-yourself home repair.
6. When she only spends 10 hours in leisure, she's willing to give up $20 for an additional hour, while when she already enjoys 13 hours of leisure time, Sharon is only willing to give up $10 for an additional hour. Conversely, if you wanted to compensate her for lost leisure time, the amount of compensation would vary depending upon how much leisure time she's already enjoying. At 13 hours, you could get her to work by paying her $10, while at 10 hours, you'd have to pay her $20.

7. This analysis is an exact analogue to the determination of the optimum output and profits by a competitive firm once the market price of the product is determined by the supply and demand for the product.
8. ($80)(50,000) = $400,000, as opposed to ($120)(40,000) = $480,000.

    Some have argued that in this case, all workers are better off. If a representative unemployed worker is indifferent between not working and receiving $50 a day or working and earning $80, then the 40,000 who remain working at the $120 wage could pay, say, $15 a day to the 10,000 who lost their jobs and *all* would gain. The workers who retain their jobs would be earning $105 (after the $15 deduction), which is better than working for $80 a day. On the other hand, the unemployed would be receiving $15 × 40,000 = $600,000 to be distributed among 10,000 or $60 each, which is more than they consider the utility equivalent for not working. A minor practical problem arises, of course: How do you identify those unemployed because of the minimum wage alteration and induce the remaining employed to part with some of their wages to support these unemployed?
9. Actually, the saving is somewhat less, since the $6,000 wage is a normal business expense and is thus subtracted from taxable income when computing the firm's income tax liability. If the firm is in the 25 percent marginal

tax bracket, then a $6,000 expense actually reduces profits by only $4,500. So, the $3,000 savings to the firm is only a $1,500 addition to net income.

10. The assumption here is that should Malcolm work, he would lose a dollar of welfare payment for each dollar earned. So, whether he works 10 hours a day or not, the maximum daily income he could receive is $50. As absurd as this assumption sounds, this 100 percent tax on earnings was a common feature of welfare programs not too many years ago. Only with welfare reform in the 1970s were welfare recipients permitted to retain some percentage of their earnings, a policy that attenuated the disincentive effect.

11. Mark Killingworth, "A Survey of Labor Supply Models," *Research in Labor Economics* 4 (1981), Tables 1–4.

12. This fortunate equilibrium was planned. The equilibrium could be anywhere else, too, as long as it was to the left of 40 hours. But then, C.D. would not be earning precisely $400, which would further complicate the issue.

13. If C.D. were not, he'd obviously not work more than 40 hours. On the other hand, while it's certainly possible that the free-choice, shorter workweek position is preferred to the 48-hour week, that is not a viable option. Why not try to sketch out these alternatives to test your understanding?

14. Human capital theory, which also addresses labor market reality, must be deferred until capital theory is examined in Chapter 18.

15. A best-seller some years ago was Robert Levering, Milton Moskowitz, and Michael Katz, *The 100 Best Companies to Work for in America* (Reading, Mass.: Addison-Wesley, 1984).

16. Shopping for a job is no different from shopping for, say, a new car. You prepare by obtaining information from advertisements and brochures, narrow down your choices to a few models, and then start visiting showrooms to compare prices. The broader your search, the greater the probability of finding the precise vehicle you wish at just the right price. But the more you search, the smaller is the probability that the next dealer will offer you a better deal than you've already come across. Moreover, the more time you spend looking, the more likely it is that some car you were seriously considering will already have been sold to someone else.

17. That position has been challenged in recent years in a few discrimination-related court cases. Employers have been forced to justify their job-search criteria on job-specific qualifications rather than general rules of thumb.

18. Arthur Okun, *Prices and Quantities: A Macroeconomic Analysis* (Washington, D.C.: The Brookings Institution, 1981), p. 89. The phrase is meant to remind you of Adam Smith's more impersonal "invisible hand."

19. In some circumstances, this case is analogous to the buffer stock agency (BSA) case of Chapter 8. Firms might be willing to warehouse their labor force much as the BSA stores commodities, the assumption being that over time demand will rise again and the now-surplus labor will be fully utilized.

20. Much of this section is based on the excellent survey by Joseph E. Stiglitz, "The Causes and Consequences of the Dependence of Quality on Price," *The Journal of Economic Literature* 25, no. 1 (March 1987), pp. 1–48.

21. The exception consisted of the section in Chapter 6 in which the rigid assumptions of the production function were removed. There, too, the role of worker motivation replaced the sheer mechanistic relationship of the theoretical production function.

WAGES IN IMPERFECTLY COMPETITIVE MARKETS

In May, June, July and August, we will begin work at Sunrise and leave off at 6 o'clock P.M. reserving one hour for breakfast and two for dinner. In December, January and February, we will get breakfast before going to work, begin work at 45 minutes after Sunrise, reserving one hour for dinner, and work until Sunset.

Proposed Rules to Regulate the Work of the Journeymen, Shipwrights, Joiners, Caulkers, and Mast Makers of Philadelphia (September 1830)

Did you see what the senate voted for yesterday? A week's work is to consist of thirty-six hours. I doubt very much if the people working now will agree to an increase in time of work like that. We stick to the old American principle of only working when the boss is looking.

Will Rogers

Learning Objectives

In this chapter, you will discover:

- How labor demand must be modified when product markets are imperfectly competitive.
- What happens to the analysis of labor demand when labor is not the only variable input.
- How wages and employment change when the labor market operates under conditions of imperfect competition.
- That game theory can help explain labor-management bargaining and strikes.
- That unions and management often cooperate for their mutual benefit.
- The evidence of unionization's impact on workers and the economy.

A word of advice: Students seem to have a great deal more trouble with the analysis covered in this chapter than in most others. You will simplify your task by thoroughly understanding the few new terms you come across in the analytic section of this chapter. They should become almost second nature to you.

Nummi[1]

Although unions account for not quite a fifth of the U.S. labor force, their public presence and political influence is much greater. This chapter begins by describing two distinct modes of labor-management relationships.

Nummi may well represent the wave of the future in worker-management relations. Nummi, or New United Motor Manufacturing Inc., the joint General Motors–Toyota automobile manufacturing venture headquartered in Fremont, California, has convinced the skeptics that even unionized American workers can produce automobiles as efficiently as the Japanese can. Certainly, the Nummi workers were far more cost-effective than their counterparts in the United States. The Chevy Novas produced in Fremont took only 20 hours to assemble and ranked second in a 1986 survey of automobile quality. And worker satisfaction appeared high. These numbers stand in sharp contrast to the now-closed GM Framingham, Massachusetts, plant, where it took 28 hours to assemble a comparable vehicle, which did not even rank among the top 15 in terms of quality.

Recently, however, sharp criticism has been levied against the Nummi techniques. Critics have charged that the plant's productivity stems not from worker-management cooperation, but from "management by stress." They cite Nummi's absence policy as an example. Any worker who misses 3 days during any 90-day period for any reason receives an "offense." The worker is dismissed after accumulating four offenses. Both management and labor representatives deny such charges. They hail cooperation, not confrontation, as the labor-management style at Nummi.

"Confrontation not cooperation" seems an appropriate heading to the negotiations between the United Food and Commercial Workers (UFCW) union and John Morrell & Co., which is the subject of MicroBits 17.1.

Clearly, management-labor relations between either the UAW and Nummi or the UFCW and Morrell cannot be described by the techniques used in the last chapter, just as the wide spectrum of American industry could not be correctly analyzed with the perfectly competitive model of the firm. Imperfect competition in both the product and factor markets opens up a variety of possibilities:

· Imperfect competition in the product market combined with perfect competition in the factor market.

- Asymmetrical factor market competition, with either the employer overshadowing the workers or the union dominating the firms.
- Symmetrical power relations—a strong union facing a powerful employer.

Each of these cases will be analyzed in this chapter.

Unions benefit their members by obtaining a large slice of the firm's given income pie. But such confrontation is not the only way union members can benefit. Unions can help the pie expand—Nummi being one example—so there's more for everybody. So, this chapter will also deal analytically with how labor can gain from a cooperative approach. Chapter 17 ends by discussing the deadweight losses of imperfect competition in labor markets. It begins by modifying the straightforward model of labor demand described in Chapter 16.

Refining the Demand-for-Labor Curve

The demand for labor presented in Chapter 16 assumed that teddy bears were sold on a competitive product market and that labor was the only variable factor of production. What happens to the demand for labor if either of these assumptions is violated? To anticipate, the basic negative slope of the demand curve is retained, but its elasticity will be altered.

Complication 1: Imperfect Competition in the Product Market

The demand curve for labor derived in Chapter 16 presumed that Ted could sell as many bears as he wished at the $20 competitive market price. That enabled Ted to calculate the value of the marginal product of labor by multiplying the marginal physical product curve by $20. The resulting VMP curve turned out to be Ted's demand for labor curve.

What would happen if Ted sold bears in an imperfectly competitive market? If teddy bears were more charming than his competitors' ursine products, the demand curve for Ted's teddy bears would no longer be horizontal but have a negative slope. The second and third columns of Table 17.1 hypothesize Ted's new demand curve, while the first two columns reproduce the labor input–bear output relationship specified in Table 16.1.

The **marginal revenue product (MRP)** equals the *change* in the VTP divided by corresponding *change* in the quantity of labor input ($\Delta VTP/\Delta Q_L$).

Column 4 lists total revenue from bear sales, calling it *value of total product* (VTP) to emphasize its relationship to labor input. It is simply price times quantity. (You should be able to fill in the blanks in this column as well in the columns to its right.) Notice that VTP takes on the typical parabolic shape of total revenue under imperfectly competitive conditions. As price falls, VTP first rises, reaches a maximum, and then declines. Corresponding to the value of marginal product (VMP) of Table 16.2 (p. 534) is the **marginal revenue product (MRP)** (column 5). Like the

---

MICROBITS 17.1

Local Unions Accept Pay and Benefit Cuts to Try to Rescue Jobs

Estherville, Iowa. When John Morrell & Co. announced plans to close beef-processing operations here in November, "everybody was worried," says Dean Hanson, who had slaughtered cattle and cut up beef at the plant for 25 years.

Mr. Hanson, who is 47 years old, says he figured that his job would be saved because he had enough seniority to transfer to Morrell's pork operations next-door. But closing the beef plant still would mean the loss of 350 jobs at Esterville's biggest employer. "We were concerned about that 350," Mr. Hanson says. Many laid-off beef workers would probably have left the town of 8,000, he says, and property values would have fallen.

John Morrell, a unit of United Brands Co. in New York, didn't close its beef plant last month as scheduled. At the 11th hour, workers voted 400 to 226 . . . to cut base wages in the beef plant by $2 an hour to $8.69, to take benefit cuts, and to freeze wages for a year. They cut maximum vacations from six weeks to four, agreed to work four extra hours per week, and agreed to a reduction in sick pay.

In return, John Morrell, which was said to be losing $2 million a year in its beef operations, even as it made money in pork, agreed to keep the beef plant open, to show its books to the local union and to pay workers 20 percent of the beef plant's profits, should there by any. John Morrell also created a labor-management committee to give workers a voice in plant operations, and the company said it will invest $2 million in the plant during the next three years.

The whole affair began when Lee Bishop. John Morrell's senior vice president for administration, came to town last May and announced that the beef portion of the company's beef and pork plant would close on Nov. 8. Labor costs under the company's national agreement with the UFCW, he said, were too high for the company to compete with the likes of Iowa Beef Processors Inc., which has driven other beef packers out of business with its modern plants and tough labor tactics. . . .

[The local attempted to reach an agreement with the packer, but the effort failed.] So the local appealed for help to Mr. Anderson at UFCW headquarters. John Morrell, Mr. Anderson said, wanted labor rates at Estherville to match those of Iowa Beef's plant in Dakota City, Neb. But John Morrell locals elsewhere would have had to approve that cut, which was unlikely. Mr. Anderson told Estherville about the union's employee dislocation service.

"The international started getting us used to the idea that our beef plant was going to close and that there was nothing they could do about it." says Mr. Lowe of the local negotiating committee. "They said that 350 beef plants had closed in the last 10 years and we were just another notch on the wheel." . . .

MicroBits 17.1 continued

It wasn't until six days before the plant was to close that things really heated up. Local union leaders had hoped the international would extract a bargaining proposal from Morrell. But when that didn't happen, rank-and-file members clamored for the local to take matters into its own hands.

Then John Morrell played its trump card. Although its Estherville pork operations were making money, it announced that it would close that business too (next May) because overhead costs would make the pork processing unprofitable after the beef plant had closed. Mr. Bishop says the company also wanted lower labor costs in pork because it dreads the entry of Iowa Beef into that business late next year.

In Estherville, notice of the pork plant's closing sent a shiver through the workers who had hoped to transfer to pork once the beef plant closed. "The rank and file said, 'We want to know what the company has to offer,'" says Merlyn Wee, one of the 450 pork workers. "We were mandated to go and find out." . . .

Local union leaders weren't too happy with the negotiations either, because the company, for the first time, had told them how big a wage cut it wanted. "When the committee left that meeting" says Mr. Dalen, the chief steward, "we had no intention of meeting with the company again."

"Panic at the Plant"

"But we had our minds changed when we got to work," he says. "Everything started to panic at the plant."

Rank-and-file workers demanded to vote on whatever the company proposed, Mr. Dalen says. So, reluctantly, the local called a vote the day before the plant was to close.

The final approval pleased community leaders but angered other UFCW locals and led Bob Tuttle, Estherville's union president, to resign.

"Morrell used the threat of a plant close-down to extort millions of dollars of wages and benefits from the workers," says Jack Smith, the business agent for the UFCW local in Sioux Falls, S.D., where Morrell has another plant. He doesn't like the precedent.

The Estherville negotiating committee, however, says it got a better deal than those separately obtained after long strikes by UFCW locals at Iowa Beef plants. "This agreement could be the greatest thing to hit packing if it's treated with respect on both sides," says Mr. Lowe of the negotiating committee. Workers say that management attitudes at the beef plant are better, and workers are told more about day-to-day productivity. The company lets the local see its books each week, and they are beginning to show a small profit. . . .

Robert Weber, who succeeded Mr. Tuttle as president of the union local, sees good news and bad news in what happened in Estherville. "It's kind of like being mugged, he says. "Maybe they take your wallet and jewelry, but you're still alive."

Source: Janet Guyon, "Local Unions Accept Pay and Benefit Cuts to Try to Rescue Jobs." Reprinted by permission of *The Wall Street Journal*, © 1981 Dow Jones & Company, Inc. All Rights Reserved Worldwide.

TABLE 17.1   Production of Teddy Bears under Imperfect Competition

(1) Quantity of Labor	(2) Quantity of Teddy Bears	(3) Price of Teddy Bears	(4) Value of Total Product	(5) Marginal Revenue Product	(6) Average Revenue Product
0	0	$30	$ 0		$ 0
				$280	
1	10	28	280		280
				320	
2	24	25	600		300
				—	
3	39	22.05	860		——
				140	
4	48	20.83	1,000		250
				—	
5	55	19.27	1,060		212
				—	
6	60	18	——		——
				10	
7	63	17.30	1,090		155.71
				–__	
8	64	16.72	1,070		133.75
				−50	
9	64.5	15.81	1,020		133.33
				–—	
10	64	15	——		——

VMP, the MRP is the contribution to total revenue obtained by employing an additional laborer.[2]

MICROQUERY   How is MRP different from MR? _____

_____

[3]

The MRP comes under two sources of downward pressure as more labor is hired.

* In common with Table 16.1, diminishing returns to labor sets in after the third worker. Thus, the marginal product of labor declines as each additional worker contributes less to total physical production than did the previous worker.
* In contrast with Table 16.2, where the VMP declines only because of diminishing returns, Table 17.1 reflects a second downward push. More teddy bears can be sold only by reducing price. Marginal revenue, instead of remaining constant, declines as well.

Take a look at the impact of employing an eighth worker and the resulting output growth from 63 to 64 bears. Diminishing returns are represented by the fact that the *seventh* worker's marginal output was three bears, while the *eighth* worker's contribution is only one bear. So, even had price remained at $17.30, the seventh worker would have increased Ted's revenues by $17.30 × 3, or $51.90, while the eighth worker's contribution was only $17.30. But now for the double jeopardy. In order for Ted to sell 64 teddy bears, he has to cut price from $17.30 to $16.72, and to price all 64 bears at $16.72. Ted's 58-cent price cut on each of the 63 bears that he sold previously means that his revenue is reduced by $36.54. The net effect of hiring one more worker thus equals $16.72 − $36.54, or −$19.82, the value you'll have inserted in column 5.

The **average revenue product (ARP)** equals VTP divided by the corresponding quantity of labor.

Finally, the **average revenue product (APR)** tells you the sales contribution of the average worker for any given number of workers. Using the same row in Table 17.1, you can see that the eight workers manufacture 64 teddy bears, which Ted then sells for $16.72 each. This value of total product of $1,070, when allocated to each of the eight workers, produces an average sales income per worker of $133.75. (Conversely, multiplying ARP by the quantity of labor gives you the VTP).

You might find it useful to compare Table 17.1 to Tables 16.1 and 16.2 to see for yourself the impact of the negative demand curve for teddy bears. The impact is made evident as well by contrasting Figure 16.2b with Figure 17.1, which plots the final two columns of Table 17.1 against the quantity of labor. But the entire distinction may be encapsulated by answering the following question: If the cost of labor per day is $80, how many workers will Ted hire? _____

An answer of *four* would indicate that you've correctly applied the technique of Chapter 16 here. Ted would hire workers to the point where the last worker's contribution to revenue—MRP—equaled the firm's marginal outlay on a worker. In terms of Figure 17.1, equilibrium is achieved where the horizontal marginal outlay line at $80 crosses the MRP above four workers. Ted would not be acting intelligently to employ labor whose MRP < MO, since the cost of any employee beyond MRP = MO would exceed the worker's addition to Ted's revenues. Similarly, Ted would not stop short of MRP = MO, since the firm's revenues could be increased more than its costs by hiring additional employees.

Two additional observations are worth making:

- Had Ted been operating in a perfectly competitive bear market, an $80 wage would have induced Ted to employ six workers, not four workers. That result stems from the fact that the MRP curve slopes down more sharply than does the VMP curve.
- The MRP, like the VMP curve, is Ted's demand-for-labor curve. You can prove this by changing the wage and tracing out the MRP = MO intersections.

FIGURE 17.1 **Employment Decisions When the Labor Market Is Perfectly Competitive but the Product Market Is Imperfectly Competitive**

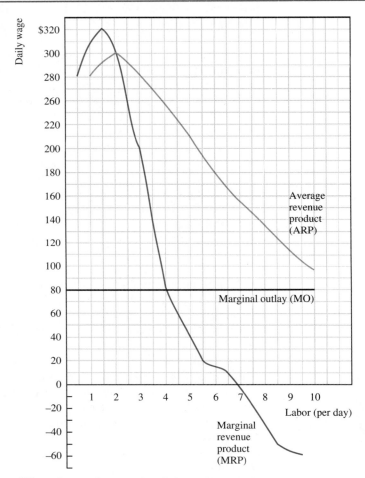

When the product market is imperfectly competitive, so that more can be sold only by cutting price, the MRP replaces the VMP as the demand curve for labor. The competitive labor market ensures that the MO = the wage. Where is employment equilibrium? How much will the daily wage be? How much will the employer pay in labor costs? What will the residual be?

The moral of the story is that the fundamental analysis of Chapter 16 remains sound when the product market is not perfectly competitive but the labor market is. However, the employer must then take into account the impact of extra employment not only on production but on pricing and the firm's earnings as well.

Complication 2: Two Variable Factors of Production

Ted could purchase additional machines to manufacture bears or rent more vans to ship his output. Such flexibility would certainly be more descriptive of the real world than presuming that only labor is variable. Assume, then, Ted can vary capital, too. For simplicity, let's restore perfect competition to the teddy bear market, so that the demand for labor is represented by the VMP.

What happens when wages rise and both labor and capital are variable? For a given dollar outlay on inputs, an increase in wages means that the firm must cut back either on labor, on capital, or on both. (In terms of the isoquant analysis of Chapter 7, an increase in the price of one factor of production forces the producer onto a lower isoquant for the same outlay. Check out Figure 7.3 on p. 214 to refresh your memory.)

Follow carefully this chain of events:

- The reduction in capital usage diminishes the total physical product of labor. Think back to the production function grid of Figure 6.1: *Reducing the amount of capital lowers the output obtained from any given amount of labor.* In other words, the producer is forced to shift down to a lower TPP curve.
- The lower TPP is, the lower, too, the APP and the MPP will be. The reduction in APP $(= \text{TPP}/Q_{\text{labor}})$ follows from the arithmetic. The APP's numerator is lower for any given amount of labor input. The lower TPP also alters its slope and hence reduces the MPP.
- The lower the MPP, the lower the VMP. The VMP is simply the MPP times the price of the output. Since output price hasn't changed but the MPP has fallen, the VMP must fall.

Table 17.2 compares the different marginal physical products when the cost of labor is $80 and $100. At the lower wage, the firm can use more capital for a fixed amount of expenditures, and so would look at labor's marginal productivity as represented by the middle column, while at the higher wage, less capital is used and therefore the smaller MPP (final column) becomes relevant.

Figure 17.2a plots the two marginal physical product of labor curves, while Figure 17.2b plots the corresponding VMP curves. Which VMP curve is the demand for labor?

TABLE 17.2   A Comparison of the Marginal Product of Labor in Teddy Bear Production with Differing Capital Inputs

Quantity of Labor	Marginal Physical Product of Labor, Capital Input Higher	Marginal Physical Product of Labor, Capital Input Lower
1	10	8
2	14	12
3	15	14
4	9	8
5	7	6
6	5	4
7	3	2
8	1	0.5
9	0.5	−0.5
10	−0.5	−2

FIGURE 17.2   The Demand for Labor When Both Labor and Capital Can Be Varied

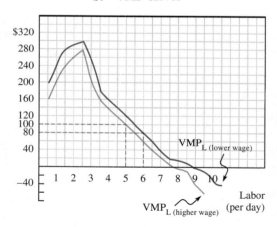

a.   **MPP curves**

b.   **VMP curves**

a.   When more capital is utilized, then the MPP_L will be higher *for any given quantity of labor* than when less capital is used in conjunction with labor.

b.   Since $VMP_L = MPP_L \times$ Price of output in a competitive product market, the differences in the MPPs are mirrored by the differences in the VMPs. (The lower wage permits greater capital usage and so corresponds to the higher MPP.) You'll have to supply the demand-for-labor curve by yourself.

The answer, of course, is neither. When capital inputs vary in response to wages, the VMP curves must also shift. But we can relate points on the VMP curves to a specific amount of capital used. We know that the upper VMP curve is appropriate for the larger amount of capital consistent with the $80 wage, while the lower VMP curve comes into play when the wage equals $100. From the intersection of the wage and the appropriate VMP curve, we can read the number of employees Ted will hire—six when the wage is $80 and five when the wage is $100. Those two points must lie on Ted's demand-for-labor curve, which you should draw onto Figure 17.2b and label "demand for labor." Other points on the new demand-for-labor curve will be derived similarly. Specify a wage, find from the firm's isoquant map the impact of that wage on the firm's desired capital usage, derive the corresponding MPP and VMP curves, and locate the employment consistent with the new VMP curve and wage. Clearly, the demand-for-labor curve when more than labor is variable will be more elastic than its counterpart demand-for-labor curve when only labor is variable.

In summary, when the product market is characterized by imperfect competition or when the firm will modify its use of other inputs when wages change, the demand-for-labor curve will still take on the typical demand curve shape. To be sure, its elasticity will depend on the precise factor and product market circumstances. But in all cases, the lower the wage, the large the quantity of labor demanded.

Power Plays: Employer–Employee Relationships in Imperfectly Competitive Labor Markets

The conclusion of the preceding section holds also when the labor market is characterized by imperfect competition. Let's begin with a monopoly of labor suppliers—a union—facing a group of competitive users of labor. This case will be followed by its converse: a single employer hiring laborers who compete against each other. The final scenario depicts a unified group of workers facing a single employer. In all instances, we'll assume a perfectly competitive product market and focus only on the labor market.

Labor Monopoly

Let's put our teddy bears to sleep and shift to a labor market for craftsmen fabricating precision optical instruments. Act I, which has already been completed, saw competition in the labor market settle on a wage of $12,000 per year consistent with the supply and demand curves pictured in Figure 17.3. As Act II opens, the workers have just formed the Opticians, Periscopers, Telescopemakers, Instrumenters, and Clarifiers Asso-

**FIGURE 17.3   Labor Monopolist Faces Perfectly Competitive
Labor Users**

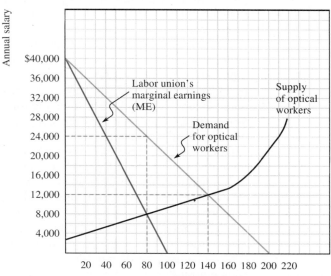

When perfect competition prevails on the labor market, supply and demand forces will induce an equilibrium at an annual wage of $12,000. When the workers join forces and become a labor monopoly, the union members' marginal earnings fall more rapidly than does the demand curve for their services. Their monopoly position leads to a search for the position that equates labor supply with their marginal earnings. The wage consistent with S = ME is $24,000, the point on the demand curve above S = ME. (Note the impact of unionization on employment.)

---

ciation (OPTICA), and have adopted the three musketeers' motto, "All for one and one for all." They are particularly interested in raising their wages so as to maximize the group's income. In concept, this is no different from a product cartel, and analytically, we can deal with a labor monopoly in precisely the same manner as an oil cartel.

Total labor income depends on two conflicting forces. On the one hand, the more workers who are employed—a movement downward along the demand curve—the more workers who will start to receive income. On the other hand, since additional workers will be hired only at lower wages, those previously working at the higher wage must now supply their labor at the new, lower wage, too. Those already working find their income decreasing.[4] Hence, the union's **marginal earnings (ME)** curve, which has been inserted into Figure 17.3, must slope more steeply than the demand curve for the same reason that a product MR curve is steeper than the product demand curve.

Marginal earnings (ME) are the changes in total labor income for a given change in the quantity of labor demanded.

On the labor supply side, the individual union members have distinct work-leisure preferences. Consequently, they differ in the minimum wage levels that would induce them to offer their labor supply to the labor users. The rising labor supply curve in Figure 17.3 is analogous to a marginal cost curve that portrays the costs of bringing more of the scarce product into the market.

You can complete the rest of the story. The union maximizes labor income by equating ME and supply. To find the optimum wage, the union moves up to the demand curve above the ME = Supply intersection. The quantity of labor employed by the firms in the industry will simply be the quantity of labor demanded at the union wage. In Figure 17.3, the optimum annual wage per worker is $24,000, corresponding to 80,000 workers. Total labor income equals the annual wage times quantity, or $1.92 billion.

Notice a further analogy to the cartel. At the union monopoly wage, only 80,000 OPTICA members are employed. Yet the supply curve indicates that 210,000 are willing to work at that wage. The pressure by the unemployed must force down the wage unless the union takes countermeasures. Union members could share the wealth by redistributing their gains to those not working or by dividing the available worktime among the total number of workers. A more common tactic among some unions is to restrict union membership and prevent employers from hiring non-union labor.

The Company Store

The refrain of a song popularized in the 1950s by Tennessee Ernie Ford ran as follows:

> Y'load 16 tons and waddayeh get?
> Another day older and deeper in debt.
> St. Peter don't y'call me, 'cause I can't go.
> I sold my soul to the company sto'.

A two-fold exploitation of coalminers emerges from this stanza. First, hard work at measly wages left the miner with insufficient income to buy even the bare survival minimum. Second, because mining corporations typically built company towns on their vast landholdings near the mines, rented living quarters to the miners and their families, and operated the only community store, they in fact dictated the expense budget of the miners as well. The last line in the refrain alleges that in the absence of alternative retail outlets, prices in the company store were set to keep the miners in perpetual serfdom.

Monopsony occurs when the market is dominated by a single buyer.

When the employer effectively dominates the labor force, being the sole demander in a market where labor is not organized, **monopsony** replaces the monopoly model just analyzed.[5] In monopsony, the demand

TABLE 17.3   Marginal Outlay in Monopsony

Quantity of Labor	Annual Wage	Total Labor Cost ($ Millions)	Marginal Outlay per Worker
100	$10,000	$ 1	
200	15,000	3	$20,000
300	20,000	6	30,000
400	25,000	10	40,000
500	30,000	15	50,000

curve is untouched, but the shape of the marginal outlay curve is significantly altered. Examine Table 17.3.

The first two columns portray a simple supply curve relationship. The higher the wage, the greater the number of individuals who would supply their labor. Since the employer pays the same price for each equal-quality laborer, the firm that hires 300 workers must pay each worker $20,000 a year. The third column lists the annual total labor cost, the product of the annual wage and the quantity of labor supplied and used. When the acquirer of labor services operates on a competitive labor market, the firm's marginal outlay (MO) and wage are equal since the firm will be able to hire additional labor at the going market rate. A monopsonist employer, however, must raise the wage to attract more labor, and must pay all its workers the higher wage. Thus, the monopsonist's marginal outlays rise more sharply than do wages, as you see in the final column.[6]

How does the monopsonist decide on employment and wages? Keep the two-step monopoly analogy in mind as you look at Figure 17.4, and you'll find the going relatively smooth.

1. The rule for optimum employment is equating the demand for labor to the MO. Employ it here to find the number of workers the firm should hire by dropping a perpendicular from the labor demand = MO intersection to the labor quantity axis. The labor force optimum is 300 workers.

2. Now ask yourself, What's the minimum wage necessary to induce 300 laborers to work? That information is provided by the supply curve, which specifies the number of workers available at each wage. The annual wage must be $20,000.[7]

How much does labor cost the firm? Just multiply the wage times the quantity of labor. You realize, of course, that the monopsonist gains from exerting its leverage. If the market were competitive, the wage would have been $27,500 instead of $20,000.[8]

The Minimum Wage Law Revisited.   Here's a quick problem for you: What would be the impact of a minimum wage law that guarantees workers an annual wage of $27,500 if Figure 17.4 represents the actual labor situation? Realize that passage of such a law would eliminate the upward slope of the monopsonist's marginal outlay curve, for if each additional laborer costs the monopsonist $27,500, then the firm's MO = $27,500. Draw onto Figure 17.4 the new MO, and write here the quantity of labor employed, _____, and the impact on employment, _____.[9] Since there is no longer any reason for the monopsonist to pay less than the minimum wage, total labor income rises as well.

In such circumstances, minimum wage laws could be justified on the grounds of efficiency as well as on ethical grounds. Neutralizing monopsony power and the resulting increased output is accompanied by ending labor exploitation.

Whether in fact U.S. industries are characterized by monopsony is, of course, an empirical question. Nowadays, few economists would accept such a general view, although some specific markets might well be monopsonistic. (See MicroBits 17.2.) Much more representative of U.S. manufacturing is the final analytic group, bilateral monopoly.

FIGURE 17.4   Monopsony

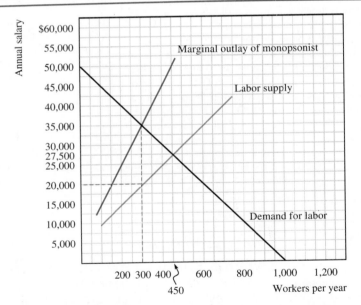

Because the monopsonist must pay higher wages to attract new employees and because these higher wages must also be paid to workers hired earlier, the monopsonist's MO curve rises more rapidly than does the supply curve. Equilibrium employment occurs where MO = the demand for labor, who are then paid only $20,000, the salary needed to induce 300 workers to join the firm.

MicroBits 17.2

If Adam Smith Were Pope

To the Editor:

John J. Fialka's May 19 page-one article about the growing number of aging, impoverished nuns gives a good account of a classic case of labor-market distortion. Mr. Fialka accurately describes the symptoms of what economists call "monopsony." Monopsony refers to a situation where the wages of labor are held below the level that would emerge in a competitive market. In the case of most priests and nuns this occurs because they are not in a position to bargain with the employer of their own choice. In order for Catholic clergy or religious to relocate, they must be granted permission by a bishop or similar administrator.

The perpetual nature of the labor contract effectively limits employment choices, making it difficult for competitive bidding to take place. By contrast, in most Jewish and Protestant denominations employment contracts allow more freedom, allowing most ministers and rabbis to seek competitive bids for their services. As a consequence, average compensation for rabbis and ministers is much greater than for Catholic clergy. In 1979 (the last year available) mean compensation rates were: $13,650—Protestant, $25,000—Jewish and $3,000—Catholic. Moreover, the payment of market salaries for Protestant and Jewish clergy has assured those religions an abundance of clergymen and women, while the Catholic Church suffers an acute shortage.

The American Catholic bishops' pastoral letter on the U.S. economy was highly critical of market institutions. However, the bishops could learn a great deal about the benefits of market economics, their own institution and the failure of alternative systems. Catholic priests and nuns are precious people who sacrifice a lot to take up their noble profession. They could be helped immensely if they simply had the freedom to contract for their labor services, a basic right of market systems. The priest shortage would be gone and the exploitation of nuns would be greatly alleviated.

Source: Reprinted from *The Wall Street Journal* by permission of William Orzechowski. Mr. Orzechowski is chief economist, The Tobacco Institute, Washington, D.C., and adjunct professor of economics at George Mason University, Fairfax, Virginia.

Bilateral Monopoly

Bilateral monopoly occurs when a monopoly seller faces a monopsony buyer.

When labor unions face powerful employers, imperfect competition characterizes both sides of the negotiating table. This case of **bilateral monopoly** leaves the microeconomic theorist with an indeterminate solution. Figure 17.5 shows you why.

The employer's demand curve for labor leads the union to calculate its marginal earnings curve, and in combination with its supply curve, to insist that the employer pay each worker $35,000 annually, which implies employment of 300 workers. But the employer, using the labor supply curve, computes its marginal outlay curve and wishes to hire the 300

FIGURE 17.5   Bilateral Monopoly

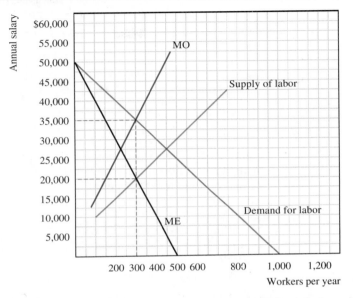

The labor union maximizes its revenues by equating supply and ME, demanding a salary of $35,000. On the other hand, the monopsonist optimizes by setting its demand for labor = MO and offering a salary of $20,000. Since the monopolist and the monopsonist must come to an agreement, the salary will be found within the $20,000–$35,000 range. The precise salary, however is indeterminate theoretically, and will depend on the collective bargaining strategies and goals of the employer and the labor union.

workers at an annual wage of no more than $20,000. This theoretical stalemate will, in the world of real employers and employees, be resolved by negotiations. Since no party can impose its will upon the other, some compromise will have to be reached.

Game Theory and Bilateral Monopoly.   The theory of games offers some interesting insights to collective bargaining strategies. Both management and labor can either settle amicably or tough it out. The latter alternative may force the union to engage in a prolonged strike, which is costly both to workers and to management. Management may opt to close down either temporarily or permanently if it can't obtain a satisfactory settlement, but that's costly to both parties as well.

Consider the following two scenarios. (Each number in the payoff matrix is in millions of dollars. The first number refers to labor, the second to management.)

		Management	
		Tough stance	**Compromise**
	Tough stance	5, 5	15, 2
Labor			
	Compromise	2, 15	10, 10

In the first situation, both parties suffer from lost incomes if they tough it out and a prolonged strike or lockout ensues. If one party is willing to compromise after a brief strike or lockout, a small gain is attained by the weaker negotiator, while the other party gains substantially more. On the other hand, if they both settle, no time is lost and they both gain.

What actually will happen? Both sides have dominant strategies that compel them to play hardball. Each one loses from the attempt to bring the other to its knees.

Now vary the scenario a bit.

		Management	
		Tough stance	**Compromise**
	Tough stance	2, 4	10, 6
Labor			
	Compromise	5, 10	15, 5

Labor's dominant strategy is to compromise, while management's is to take the opposite tack from labor. So, when labor compromises, management remains intransigent. In the consequent Nash equilibrium, management ends up with two thirds of the pot.

What happens, however, if management is unsure of labor's payoff matrix? Labor may then adopt a tough negotiating position until the very last minute, threatening to strike unless its demand are met. Of course, for the union to make its threat credible, workers must be willing to support the union's strike call. If management calls the bluff, then the union settles.[10] However, if the union's bluff is believed, then management gains most by compromising and keeping the firm operational.

To sum up, the world of imperfect competition in the labor market adds a new dimension to the analysis of wage and employment determination. Economic power replaces the passive acceptance of market forces that characterizes fragmented groups of employers and employees. Terms of employment depend on whether a unified labor organization confronts an unorganized group of employers, whether the employer dominates powerless suppliers of labor, or whether the labor market is organized on both sides. The latter situation was described in MicroBits 17.1, which can now be better appreciated, using the tools developed in this section.

Union and Management in an Iowa Slaughterhouse: An Application

John Morrell & Co., as Estherville's largest employer, can with but a bit of exaggeration be considered a monopsonist (refer back to MicroBits 17.1). The UFCW local was a labor monopolist, and so a classic confrontation between a monopsonist and a monopolist is set into motion. There's but one new condition that must be recognized explicitly in this analysis: Morrell's claim that it was losing money in the beef-processing plant.

Figure 17.6 is no more than Figure 17.5 with an added demand curve to sketch out a before-and-after scenario. The 350 workers had been working under an old collective bargaining agreement, which provided them with a wage and benefits package including a base hourly wage of nearly $11. The Demand$_{before}$, Supply, Marginal outlay, and Marginal earnings curves in Figure 17.6 suggest the conditions that led to this earlier agreement. As a monopsonist, Morrell would have preferred to employ 350 workers at an hourly wage of $7.50. The UFCW as a monopolist would have imposed a $14 hourly wage for the 350 employees. The $11 wage was a viable compromise, allowing Morrell to operate its beef-packing plant profitably.

Unfortunately, circumstances, represented in the diagram by a downward shift of the demand curve for labor, changed. The more productive operation of Iowa Beef Processors and the resulting intensification of competition has brought down Morrell's revenues.[11] Morrell presented the UFCW with an ultimatum: Accept a lower wage or we'll close down entirely. Negotiations ensued, but the bargaining range had narrowed considerably. The difference between the supply curve and the demand-for-labor curve at the 350 employment level ranged from $9—the highest the union could obtain—to $7.50—the lowest Morrell could pay to attract the 350 workers. The new agreement brought the wage down to $9 per hour. Morrell gained its objective, and the plant workers were able to make the best of a bad situation.

Before leaving this case study, consider a number of additional points.

- Realize the roles of uncertainty and asymmetric information.
  Each party knows its own position and its final offer, but neither

FIGURE 17.6   *John Morrell & Co. v. The Estherville UFCW*

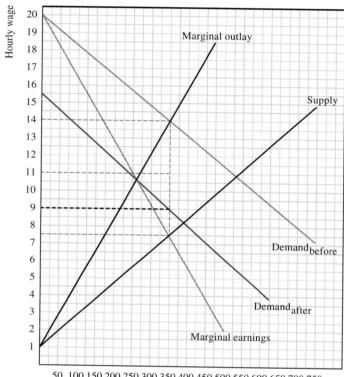

Bilateral monopoly initially led to a range of wage possibilities, from a $14 maximum to a $7.50 minimum. The actual contract calls for a $9 hourly wage. When the beef packer insists that competition has intensified and the labor demand curve has shifted down, the range narrows to between $9 and 7.50. In this instance, the workers have done the best under the circumstances, with 350 remaining employed at $9 per hour.

side is informed about the ultimate stand of its opponent. The shoe in the Morrell case obviously was on the other foot from the second game scenario discussed earlier. The UFCW could only guess whether Morrell's threat to close down the plant was a bargaining ploy or a decision that would have been implemented in the absence of wage concessions.

· Notice the skill that Morrell used to make its threat credible. At first, Morrell limited its position to closing the beef plant. It later escalated the stakes by threatening to shut down its Estherville pork plant as well. That frightened the more senior workers, who had had less to fear from the beef plant's closing. Their intended transfer to the pork plant would be stymied by Morrell's shutting it down. The credibility of Morrell's threat strengthened management's position and helped bring down the wage.

Clearly, the real world is far more complex than the models of imperfect competition in the labor market. Nevertheless, the models suggest the variables economists ought to examine when analyzing actual situations. Theory also hints at the kind of responses that can be expected once perfect competitive assumptions are abandoned.

The Two Faces of Unionism: Theory and Fact

The analysis of the preceding section, as well as the tone of this chapter and Chapter 16, was that of labor-management confrontation. Certainty, a good deal of U.S. labor union history validates this picture. Yet the daily interactions between employees and employers are normally peaceful. A confrontation model of labor-management behavior does little justice to the day-to-day operation of the modern business. Moreover, in much of the contemporary labor scene, businesses have learned to work together with unions for common goals rather than to view each other as antagonists.

Richard B. Freeman and James L. Medoff in their book *What Do Unions Do?*[12] contrast the monopoly face of unions with the "collective voice/institutional response" face. The monopoly aspects of unionism are precisely those that were discussed earlier. Unions, by unifying workers, act as a labor monopolist, thereby raising wages above the competitively set wage. Moreover, unions can use their power to inhibit efficient operations, forcing, for example, the employer to hire redundant workers or setting the pace of an assembly line slower than optimal.

The collective voice/institutional response face or, for short, the *cooperative* mode, refers to an alternative way of looking at economic behavior. For example, unions and management may prevent frictions from escalating into conflicts by setting up channels of communication, allowing labor to speak with a uniform voice and management to respond. Freeman and Medoff point out that

> The voice/response face directs attention to the possibility that, because of incomplete information, lack of coordination in an enterprise, and organizational slack, management can respond to unionism in more creative ways, which may be socially beneficial. . . . [It follows that] unions have some positive effects on productivity—reducing quit rates,[13] inducing management to alter methods of production and adopt more efficient policies, and improving morale and cooperation among workers.[14]

When unionization leads to improved productivity, firm revenues increase, but labor can benefit as well. By enlarging the dimensions of the revenue pie, workers obtain larger absolute returns even when the shares of both labor and management are left unchanged. Return to Figure 17.2b, which can help drive this point home. Presume the lower VMP curve represents the firm prior to unionization. At $80 a day, the employer hires only 5.5 workers, for a daily labor cost of $440. Now if unionization increases productivity, so that the upper VMP curve becomes the new demand for labor, the union faces three options:

· It could assign another half a worker to the firm.
· It could maintain the labor force at 5.5 workers. But because the workers are now more productive, the employer would be willing to pay each $100 instead of $80.
· It could split the benefit, increasing the numbers of workers to, say 5.75, and raise the wage. (What would the new wage be? ____[15])

Nummi Once Again

The Nummi model of labor-management relations contrasts these two faces of union life in the United States today. "Management by stress" suggests the conflict mode, with Nummi management being the dominant force. UAW members realize that if they don't work harder and smarter, the U.S. automotive industry will be unable to protect itself from further inroads by foreign competitors, and their jobs will jeopardized. That unpleasant realization makes workers agree to more productive techniques.

But the cooperative model is evident as well. Teamwork and worker rotation within the team both enhance productivity by giving workers some control over their assignments and by reducing the tedium of assembly-line work. Workers' responsibility for quality control reduces the number of assembly defects. Management's promise of employment security means that workers need not resist new technology, and indeed benefit from productivity-enhancing suggestions.

In short, at Nummi both management by stress and labor-management cooperation exist side by side. And so it is elsewhere. At times, the Dr. Jekyl face predominates, and at other times it's sweet Mr. Hyde.

Unions and Wages: An Empirical Review

Because the models suggest that unions can raise wages either by using their monopoly power to increase the share of labor in total firm income or by stimulating worker productivity to increase everyone's share, two empirical questions can be raised:

1. Have unions in the United States in fact raised wages?
2. If they have, has the wage increase come through socially beneficial productivity boosts or socially inefficient monopoly power?

Unionization and Wages

Analytically, it's difficult to see why anyone should question whether
unions have raised wages. Certainly, the models in this chapter all virtually dictate a yes response. Moreover, simple data comparisons, such as
those in Table 17.4, involving unionized versus nonunionized workers
almost always show the former earning more than the latter. It really only
seems to be a question of how substantial the difference is.

And yet the issue is not that simple. Can you be certain that union
membership alone accounts for the difference in wages between union
members and nonmembers?

Economists have tried to resolve the union/nonunion issue by building sophisticated econometric models that carefully specify the many
elements that can lead to wage differences among workers. One such
difference, of course, will be membership in a labor union. Using such
sources as the *Current Population Survey*, researchers obtain data on
wages and on the corresponding other variables. MicroBits 17.3 summarizes one typical econometric study.

Using econometric methodology has enabled economists to calculate
the **wage gap**. W. Gregg Lewis surveyed over 50 econometric studies that
used the *Current Population Survey* data covering 1970 to 1979.[16] He
discovered that the wage gap ranged from 5 to 24 percent. Lewis himself,
in a labor of obviously immense detail, further adjusted the results of an
even larger number of individual studies, using a variety of data sources
and methodologies, to make them more comparable. That narrowed the

> The **wage gap** is the
> difference between
> union and nonunion
> wages thought to
> result only from
> unionization.

TABLE 17.4   Median Weekly Full-Time Earnings, Wage and Salary Workers, 1990

| | Union | | Percentage Difference* |
Occupation	Member	Nonmember	
Managerial and professional	$610	$608	0.3
Technical, sales, and support	466	365	27
Services	418	241	73
Precision production, craft, repair	586	422	30
Operators, fabricators, laborers	466	300	55
Farming, forestry, fishing	373	251	48

* (Member wage − Nonmember wage)/Nonmember wage.
SOURCE: U.S. Bureau of Labor Statistics, *Employment and Earnings*, January 1991, p. 231.

MicroBits 17.3

Measuring the Impact of Unionization on Wages

Consider the following regression equation:

$$\ln W_i = a_0 + a_1 E_i + a_2 U_i + a_3 F_i + e$$

where

W = Wages (specifically, average hourly earnings).

E = Labor quality (measured by the average educational level of the labor force).

U = Unionization ratio (or the percentage of production workers covered by collective bargaining agreements).

F = Employment discrimination (measured by the percentage of females in the labor force).

The subscript i's stand for each of 19 specific manufacturing industries in the data set, while the e is the random term.

This equation, one of many tested by Ashenfelter and Johnson,[*] suggest that wages in each manufacturing industry depend on the quality of labor, the extent of unionization, and the degree of discrimination. They expected that the higher the educational level of workers and the more pervasive unionization, the higher wages would be. On the other hand, the more discrimination toward women the industry exhibits (or alternatively, the more attractive the industry is for reasons other than wages[§]), the lower wages will be. Using ordinary least squares, the economists found

$$\ln W_i = -1.72 + 0.77E + .382U - .473F$$
$$[R^2 = .939]$$

The signs were as anticipated. Most important, the equation validated the expectation that unionization resulted in higher wages. The authors also tested for other possible determinants of wages including the level of concentration in the industry—presumably, the more concentrated, the higher the wage—and the percentage of workers living in the south—unions are weaker in the south, so wages should be lower—but neither variable proved significant.

---

[*] Orley Ashenfelter and George E. Johnson, "Unionism, Relative Wages, and Labor Quality in U.S. Manufacturing Industries," *International Economic Review* 13, 3 (October 1972), pp. 488–508.

[§] Ashenfelter and Johnson surmised that women are more likely to avoid industries that offer less attractive working conditions. Employers must compensate workers in the form of higher pay in order to induce them to work under poorer conditions. So, the lower the percentage of women in the industry, the higher should wages be.

---

wage gap range to 12 to 20 percent over 1967 to 1979.[17] Lewis concluded that, on average, union wages were 15 percent higher than nonunion wages, everything else being the same, a conclusion that is consistent in principle with the analysis of this chapter but attaches a number to the broad generalizations of economic theory.

Unionization and Costs to the Economy

Having established that unions have raised wages for their members, the follow-up question is, Has the wage boost been beneficial or costly for the economy as a whole? That question is exceptionally difficult to answer in an empirically precise way. But we can employ an approach used in connection with monopoly: measure the deadweight loss of unionization. Albert Rees performed such a calculation for 1957 and discovered the impact to be 0.14 percent of GNP.[18] Using data for 1981, Freeman and Medoff estimated the union monopoly impact at no more than ⁴/₁₀ of 1 percent of GNP.[19]

The actual adverse impact of unionization on the economy may even be less significant for at least two reasons:

1. *Efficiency wage theory.* Efficiency wage theory claims that if employers have to pay more for labor, they will be induced to employ higher quality labor. In efficiency wage terms, the union monopoly wage is no higher than the lower-quality, nonunion wage.

2. *Productivity increasing effects of unionization.* If unionization has been responsible for increased productivity that would not have occurred in its absence, then it's clear that at least some of the increase in wages was compensated for by greater labor productivity. It's misleading to measure the triangle under a fixed labor demand curve and call that a deadweight loss if the marginal product curve was actually shifted up because of unionization.

In short, neither the analysis nor the numbers bear out the fact that unionization has imposed substantial costs on the U.S. economy. Indeed, economists cannot be certain that unionization has had a detrimental impact on the overall economy. Nevertheless, before ending this subject, we ought to consider whether militant unionization is necessarily in the best interests of union members or whether a more modest union stance is apt to prove more beneficial.

Are Unions Their Own Worst Enemy?

At least three arguments can be advanced that suggest a union adversely effects the wages of its members in the long run even though the short-run impact is positive.

By raising the wage rate

- Unions induce employers to substitute cheaper production factors such as capital or nonunionized labor for unionized labor.
- Unions indirectly persuade firms to migrate to areas—including foreign shores—where unions either do not exist or are weaker.
- Unions spur on labor-saving technology, which reduces the demand for production inputs in general and labor in particular.

For any or all of these reasons, the reduction in the demand for unionized labor over time can offset the initial, temporary gain for the unionized sector. Only if the beneficial cooperative response impacts of unionization offset the negative monopoly response will unionization prove to be a long-run positive force both for union members and the economy in general.

Summary

Imperfect competition in labor markets adds a new dimension to the perfectly competitive models of Chapter 16. Product markets are not perfectly competitive. Moreover, when almost a fifth of the labor force is unionized and when unions are critical players in some strategic economic sectors, imperfect competition as reflected in union-management relations cannot be ignored.

The trade-off between wages and employment is implicit in the negatively sloped demand-for-labor curve. While Chapter 16 derived the demand curve from conditions of perfect competition in the product and labor markets, assuming that labor alone was the variable input, this chapter examined how the demand curve changes when neither conditions exist. When the product market is characterized by imperfect competition, the marginal revenue product curve replaces the value of marginal product curve. While the VMP drops because of declining marginal physical product, the MRP is negatively sloped for an additional reason: falling marginal revenue. The net result is a downward sloping MRP curve, which is also the demand-for-labor curve, but it is more steeply sloped than the VMP curve.

The analysis of labor demand becomes more complicated when two inputs are variable. Now, the microeconomist must take into account interactions between the two inputs (say labor and capital) when the price of one changes. If wages rise, the same dollar outlay buys not only less labor but, in line with isoquant analysis, also less capital. The reduction in the amount of capital used in conjunction with labor reduces labor's productivity, which shifts the marginal physical product curve downward. (Think this through carefully; it's heavy stuff. If you're not sure, read the text again.) The upshot is that an increase in the wage does not reduce the demand for labor along a given VMP curve (which would presume capital was fixed), but forces the demand to hop onto a lower VMP curve. The opposite happens, of course, for a wage reduction, leading to a more elastic demand for labor when inputs other than labor can be varied.

Wage determination becomes the focal point when the labor market itself is characterized by imperfect competition. The analogue to the product monopoly occurs when monopoly labor suppliers face unorganized demanders. The union equates its marginal earnings curve (similar to a monopolist's MR curve) to the labor supply curve (analogous to the MC curve). The resulting wage is higher than the competitive wage, hardly a surprising outcome. In the monopsony case, the single employer faces a competitive labor supply. The optimum wage is determined by equating the marginal outlay curve with the firm's labor demand curve. The wage turns out to be lower than the competitive wage. In the bilateral monopoly case—a monopolist facing a monopsonist—the wage is theoretically indeterminate. Although it's easy to find its upper and lower boundaries, the actual wage will depend on the negotiating strengths and abilities of the two parties.

The models explored to this point dealt with the "monopoly face" of labor, which views unions as confrontational. Labor unions either try to prevent exploitation of their members or attempt to gain sufficient economic power to do some of their own exploiting. But modern unions also show a cooperative side, working together with management to increase labor productivity. The monopoly face envisions labor as trying to enlarge its slice of a fixed pie; the cooperative face views unions as working with management to bake a larger pie.

Chapter 17 concludes with an examination of two empirical issues: Have unions raised wages? and if so, Have unions done so through exploiting their monopoly power or by increasing labor productivity? Most studies conclude that unionization causes a wage gap favoring organized workers. It's much less apparent whether that wage gap is the result of the monopoly or the cooperative face. The few investigations of the deadweight loss of union monopoly show a very small loss. But such calculations may well overstate the actual impact, so a definitive conclusion remains elusive at this moment.

The complex analytics of the labor market that were highlighted in Chapter 16 and in this chapter may have been frustrating. You're in good company if you had to read through these chapters, especially this one, more than once. Chapter 18, which deals with rent, interest, and profits, will be less taxing.

Key Terms

Average revenue product
Bilateral monopoly
Marginal earnings

Marginal revenue product
Monopsony
Wage gap

Review Questions

1. *a.* Redo Table 17.1 and Figure 17.1 to indicate an increase in the demand for bears, shifting each point on the demand curve for bears up by $10.
   b. Calculate the new demand curve for bear stuffers.

2. *a.* Why does the MRP differ from the VMP?
   b. How does that affect the demand for bear stuffers?

3. *a.* Explain and show the impact of a decrease in the wage rate on production and the demand for labor if both labor and capital are variable inputs.

   b. Would your answer differ in principle if labor and land were the variable inputs?

4. *a.* Explain why a labor monopoly must calculate its marginal earnings curve.
   b. Show how an increase in labor demand will change the wage and employment position of a labor monopoly facing unorganized employers.

5. *a.* Why is a monopsonist interested in the firm's marginal outlay curve?
   b. Show how a monopsonist uses the MO curve to set a wage when faced by unorganized employees.

6. *a.* Why is the wage/employment equilibrium indeterminate in bilateral monopoly?

   b. Show the deadweight loss of bilateral monopoly.

7. Show how a productivity improvement could increase both wages and the residual.

8. Why might labor unions, in successfully increasing benefits for their members, win the battle but lose the war?

Food for Thought

1. Draw and explain the difference between the demand for labor facing a monopsonist that sells its product in (*a*) a perfectly competitive market and (*b*) a monopoly market.

2. Physician earnings, while still well above the U.S. average, have stopped growing at the pace of earlier decades. Part of the explanation lies in the alleged surplus of physicians. An American Medical Association report in 1986 recommended that states and medical schools review admission standards with a view to reducing the number of specialists and foreign-trained physicians.

   a. What is the relationship between earnings and the supply of physicians?

   b. Translate the AMA proposals into the appropriate model of this chapter to demonstrate the impact of the recommendations.

   c. Do you agree that there's a surplus of physicians, at least in some specialties?

3. *a.* Sketch and explain the market equilibrium for a first-degree discriminating monopsonist.

   b. Compare the deadweight loss of (*a*) to that of a nondiscriminating monopsonist.

4. "GM and Ford Press Suppliers of Parts to Roll Back Prices" read a headline in early 1991. GM and Ford, suffering from a sales slump, demanded that parts prices be cut back immediately by 3 percent.

   a. What does this pressure indicate about the relationship between the manufacturers and their input suppliers?

   b. Use the models of this chapter to explain the economic reasoning that underlay this insistence.

   c. Why didn't GM and Ford insist on these price cuts when vehicle sales were stronger?

5. In discussing a baseball strike, Susan Lee of *The Wall Street Journal* (June 30, 1981, p. 30) wrote, "Baseball is . . . a textbook illustration of bilateral monopoly. And the strike is no more than the owners' monopsony power . . . pitted against the monopoly power of the players. . . ." Sketch out and explain why this bilateral monopoly led to a strike.

6. Some firms have offered unions pay hikes linked to productivity increases.

   a. Explain and evaluate the economic reasoning that ties wages to productivity.

   b. What are the likely limits to such links?

   c. How can productivity improvements be attributed empirically to labor on the one hand and management on the other?

7. Explain how a policy of permitting strikers to collect unemployment insurance would affect labor market equilibrium when the market is characterized by (*a*) monopsony and (*b*) bilateral monopoly.

Suggested Readings

Labor economics textbooks cover both theoretical and institutional details. You might consult F. Ray Marshall, Vernon M. Briggs, Jr., and Allan G. King, *Labor Economics* (Homewood, Ill.: Richard D. Irwin, 1984); or Daniel S. Hamermesh and Albert Rees, *The Economics of Work*

and Pay (New York: HarperCollins, 1988). Richard B. Freeman and James L. Medoff, *What Do Unions Do?* (New York: Basic, 1984) is a highly readable study of U.S. labor organization objectives and their results.

Notes and Answers

1. This case is based on John Holusha, "No Utopia, but to Workers It's a Job," *The New York Times,* January 29, 1989, Sec. 3, p. 1.
2. The semantic distinction between VMP and MRP is meant to emphasize that the MRP is used when the product is sold on an imperfectly competitive market, and so is related to the falling MR curve.
3. MRP examines the extra revenue from the viewpoint of utilizing an additional *worker*. It answers the question, How much will an additional laborer contribute to the firm's revenues? The MR looks at the extra revenue from the vantage point of an additional *unit of output* and responds to the question, How much will the production of one more unit of product add to the firm's revenues?
4. The analogy with a product demand curve and its marginal revenue curve under conditions of imperfect competition should be evident.
5. Monopsony can be found on product markets as well. Can you think of any examples?
6. Remember, MO $= \Delta TLC/\Delta Q_L$. Test yourself by calculating the marginal outlay at, say, 300 workers. The firm must pay $25,000 not only to the 100 new employees (= $2.5 million), but also grant a $5,000 raise to the 300 workers already earning $20,000 (= $1.5 million). So, the extra 100 workers drive the wage bill up by $4 million for a MO of $4,000,000/100, or $40,000 per worker.
7. In the monopoly case, after matching the MR and MC, you move *upward* to the demand curve to find the optimum price. In this monopsony situation, after discovering the

Demand = MO intersection, you move *downward* to discover the optimum wage.
8. Actually the gain from monopsony is better defined by calculating the residual. To simplify the problem, assume labor alone is variable and so the labor demand curve equals the VMP. An alternative to calculating the VTP by multiplying the VAP and the quantity of labor—since the VAP is not supplied—is to sum up the area underneath the VMP curve up to the number of workers employed. If you do that for the two cases, you'll discover that for the monopsony, the VTP = $(1/2)(50,000 - 35,000)(300) + ($35,000)(300)$ = $15 million. Subtracting from that the $6 million wage bill leaves the monopsonist with a residual of $9 million. The VTP for the competitive case equals $17,437,500, and after deducting the higher wage costs of $12,375,000, the competitive firms share a residual of only $5,062,500.
9. 450; increase by 150 workers.
10. The union may not settle if the game is repeated over time. This explains why strikes occur even though the pay lost to the workers during the strike far exceeds the benefits they gain when the strike is finally settled.
11. Remember, a lower product price reduces the entire family of value-of-product curves, including the VMP = demand for labor curve.
12. Richard B. Freeman and James L. Medoff, *What Do Unions Do?* (New York: Basic Books, 1984).
13. This point fits in well with the argument made in the last chapter that quits are costly, since

their replacement requires search and training expenses.

14. Freeman and Medoff pp. 11, 13.
15. Draw a line from the labor axis at 5.75 to the higher VMP curve. It will touch at about $90.
16. W. Gregg Lewis, *Union Relative Wage Effects: A Survey* (Chicago: University of Chicago Press, 1986), p. 176.
17. Freeman and Medoff, *What Do Unions Do?* p. 46, report a range of 21 to 32 percent, using data from the 1970s.
18. Albert Rees, "The Effects of Unions on Resource Allocation," *Journal of Law and Economics* 6 (October 1963), pp. 69–78.
19. Ibid., p. 267. Even if one were only to consider the monopoly impact in the unionized sector of the economy, using Freeman and Medoff's figures still leaves a deadweight loss of no more than 2 percent. Note, however, that none of these calculations take into account the indirect impact of union wages. If employers pay nonunion labor more in order to prevent unionization, then the nonunion wage is higher than the true competitive wage and thus the deadweight loss is underestimated.

18

RENT, INTEREST, AND PROFITS

Rembrandt, Portrait of Titus *(3/15/63)*	$ 2,234,400
Valesquez, Juan de Pareja *(10/27/70)*	5,544,000
Turner, Juliet and Her Nurse *(5/29/80)*	7,040,000
Turner, Seascape Folkestone *(7/5/84)*	10,023,200
Mantegna, Adoration of the Magi *(4/18/85)*	10,449,000
Manet, La Rue Mosnier aux Paveurs *(12/1/86)*	11,088,000
van Gogh, Sunflowers *(3/30/87)*	39,921,750
Pontormo, The Halberdier *(5/31/89)*	35,200,000
van Gogh, Portrait of Dr. Gachet *(5/15/90)*	82,500,000

Date of Most Recent Sale in Parentheses.[1]

*Minneapolis police . . . announced they would no longer assist the
20,000 motorists who lock themselves out of their cars each year.
Within 3 days, local entrepreneurs set up a 24-hour "doorman" service
called Car-Help.*

The Wall Street Journal (April 16, 1987)

Learning Objectives

In this chapter you'll learn about:

- Rent and quasi rent, the returns to an input whose supply is fixed in the long run and short run, respectively.
- The indifference map analysis of lending.
- The demand for investment and the explicit analysis of the role of time in investment decisions.
- Students investing in themselves, acquiring "human capital" during the years they devote to their education.

- The meaning and role played by the profit motive in a market economy.
- The importance of proper factor pricing in achieving appropriate allocation of resources.

Values for the Living and Dead

Out-of-This-World Incomes

This chapter is a cleanup batter, touching base with payments to factors of production other than labor. That should lead you to ask—after glancing at MicroBits 18.1, which lists some very impressive salaries from the entertainment, sports, and business worlds—Aren't these people earning income for their labor? A moment's reflection should convince you that, for the most part, the answer is no. Certainly, Madonna, Michael Milken, and Ozzie Smith do not earn astronomical incomes by supplying their labor in the conventional sense of the term. You'll shortly see that these returns are more akin to rents than to wages.

Pinto versus Pinto: How Much Is a Life Worth?

This chapter also develops a method to estimate the value of human life, an issue that typically arises in the course of a damage suits involving life-taking negligence. Here's an actual case.[2]

It was a dark Texas night when Steve Green drove his Ford Pinto onto Highway 224, dimming his lights as he saw a car approach along the road. Suddenly a horse loomed in front of him, and before he could brake, his Pinto hit the pinto. Momentum propelled the animal into the windshield header, which collapsed under the weight. Mr. Green stopped the car, checked his two children who were in the back seat, and then discovered that the head of his wife, Kelly Sue, had been bashed in by the collapsing roof.

Kelly Sue's death prompted a damage suit against the owner of the horse and the Ford Motor Company. The former was accused of negligence for letting his horse roam freely, while Ford was taken to task for faulty design of the 1980 Pinto. The owner of the horse settled out of court, but Ford elected to go before a jury.

The attorney representing the Green estate contended that the Pinto's roof should have been able to withstand the impact. The jury agreed and awarded Steve and his children damages of $1.5 million.

Damages consisted of three components. First, the estate was entitled to medical and funeral expenses incurred on behalf of Kelly Sue. Second, as the trial judge charged the jury, the estate was entitled to

MicroBits 18.1

Star Gazing

The table below lists some superstar incomes from the sports, entertainment, and business worlds. The data represent pretax incomes from the individuals' primary source of earnings.

Entertainment*	Income (in millions)
Bill Cosby	$58
Kevin Costner	50
Oprah Winfrey	42
Johnny Carson	30
Steven Spielberg	27
Baseball§	
Bobby Bonilla, New York Mets	$6.1
Danny Tartabull, New York Yankees	5.3
Ruben Sierra, Texas Rangers	5.0
Dwight Gooden, New York Mets	4.9
Frank Viola, Boston Red Sox	4.7

Business‖	
Anthony O'Reilly, H. J. Heinz	$75
Martin J. Wygod, Medco Containment	34
Leon C. Hirsch, U.S. Surgical	23
John C. Malone, Tele-Communications	19
Richard K. Eamer, National Medical	17
Miscellaneous	
Michael R. Milken, junk bond salesman (1987)	$550
Mike Tyson, boxer¶	54
Benji, dog	1

* Source: 1991 income from *Forbes*, September 20, 1991, pp. 113–14.

§ Source: 1992 salary, pro-rata share of signing bonus, and other guaranteed payments from *The New York Times*, February 25, 1992.

‖ Source: 1991 salary, bonus, and long-term compensation of chief executive officers, *Business Week*, May 4, 1992, p. 143.

¶ When you consider that Tyson earned over $20 million for his title match against Spinks, whom he knocked out in 91 seconds, this surely must be the largest per minute income ever recorded, with Spinks, the loser, coming in second. Note, however, that boxing champions and major contenders do not earn income with any degree of regularity. Source for Tyson: *Business Week*, May 1, 1989, p. 51.

Any loss to the decedent's estate. Loss to the decedent's estate is the present value of the increase, if any, that would have accumulated in the estate during the remainder of the decedent's life, had the decedent's life not ended. (p. 1116)

Finally, the survivors were entitled to compensation for loss of "companionship, society, and services" resulting from Kelly Sue's death. How would you go about assessing the "loss to the decedent's estate"?

The major new element introduced in the second part of this chapter arises from the need to reconcile disparate payment flows. Kelly Sue would have earned her income over a lifetime, but Ford had to pay upon the conclusion of the trial. If money paid earlier is worth more than funds received later, making Ford pay Kelly Sue's estate the total loss would have overpenalized Ford and overcompensated the estate. Some method for translating later payments into earlier receipts must be used.

In fact, this decision is not terribly different from those management makes in acquiring productive assets. They pay for capital assets much earlier than they profit from their fruits. How firms decide whether and how much to invest is also examined in the second section.

Finally, profits are as much an income to profit earners as are wages to wage earners. And although the quest for profits played a key role in the analysis of supply and in the previous chapters on market structure, the time has come to reflect a bit on the nature of profit and the profit motive in a market economy. Finally, we'll have to pull together some of these disparate threads and weave them into a tapestry.

Rent

The return to an input whose *long-run* price elasticity of supply is zero is called a **rent.**

Not only are apartments rented, but so are cars, ski equipment, excavation machinery, power tools, and even office "temps." When economists use **rent,** however, they refer only to the return to factors of production that are in fixed supply in the long run. Because the supply of vehicles, sporting equipment, capital goods, and even apartments can be increased, the returns to the owners of these assets are not technically rents.

The Supply of a "Fixed" Resource

When the supply is fixed only in the *short run,* the return is a **quasi rent.**

Although it's always important to distinguish between short-run and long-run supply, that distinction is especially crucial when discussing rent. In the short run, the total supply of many resources is fixed. There's only so much petroleum recoverable from existing wells, only so much labor obtainable from the existing population, and only so much operating time available from the existing stock of machinery. Consequently, until the supply is expanded, the returns earned by the owners of these factors are rentlike. Indeed, they are called **quasi rents.**

Virtually all resources are expandable in the long run. Exploration leads to the discovery of new oil fields, government decisions to loosen immigration laws bring in their wake a larger labor force, and capital-goods manufacturers can increase machinery production. (Recall the discussion of supply elasticity in Chapter 5; even such an apparent fixed resource as land can be expanded by landfill methods.) In all these instances, the supply constraints on seemingly limited resources can be overcome given adequate incentives. Consequently, the application of the pure rent concept is bound to be limited.

One additional point needs to be made here: Economists define rent by considering the entire supply of the resource rather than examining it from the viewpoint of the individual firm. The fact that the supply of commercial real estate suitable for fast-food restaurants in Los Angeles in 1992 is limited makes that a rent issue, even though the supply facing McDonald's or Wendy's is not similarly constrained.

Rent.   Despite its limited scope, pure rent continues to play a role in policy debates. Perhaps even more important, the idea of rent facilitates our understanding of phenomena that imbed rental elements, even though they do not give rise to pure rents.

Visualize the situation depicted in Figure 18.1, which is more or less true for most colleges in the United States. The campus of Dreary College contains only five large lecture halls capable of seating 500 students. The number of classes that can be accommodated during a single semester equals the number of halls times the number of available hours divided by the average number of hours per class.

Assume that each class meets three hours weekly, students will not attend classes scheduled earlier than 8:00 A.M. nor are they willing to leave later than 9:00 P.M., and students will just not come in during the weekend. With 12-hour daily availability on a five-day schedule for each hall, no more than 100 classes, or $[5 \times (12 \times 5)]/3$, can be accommodated per semester. Thus, Figure 18.1 sets the perfectly inelastic supply curve of classroom space per week at 100.[3]

To turn to the demand for this space, imagine that each academic department is charged a fixed price per hour of lecture hall use. The chairpersons of the departments with large enrollments face a trade-off. They can use the large classrooms, which, though costly, economize on faculty, or opt for smaller classrooms but spend more to staff the more numerous classes. A budget conscious chairperson will cost out the two alternatives and choose the least costly. Since the more the college charges for space, the less desirable using the lecture halls will be, the quantity of space demanded will vary inversely with the cost of the space—hence the college's demand curve in Figure 18.1, which is the sum of each department's separate demand curve for space.

You have suddenly been appointed director of space usage. Among your tasks is to price the lecture halls. How would you do that? _____

Figure 18.1 indicates that lecture halls would be fully utilized if each class-hour cost $1,500. Any higher price will leave you with wasted space; any lower charge will lead to an excess demand that cannot be met from existing capacity.

FIGURE 18.1

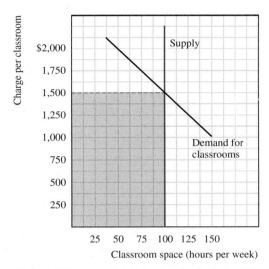

The equilibrium price per classroom is $1,500, the price that equates the fixed supply with the quantity demanded.

This $1,500 charge—if we ignore the short-run nature of the scenario—is the *rent* per class. Total rent, the amount paid for using this resource that is in fixed supply, is simply the rent per class times the number of class-hours, or the shaded area in Figure 18.1.

Carry this analysis just one bit further. Burgeoning enrollments lead to an increase in demand (at every price) by 25 hours. What happens to the rent? Draw in the new demand curve, calculate the new rental per classroom, and derive the total rent: _____ 4

Notice an important result: since the elasticity of supply equals zero, quantity supplied doesn't change. The increase in demand causes a proportionate increase in price and in total rent. Consequently, economists often refer to rent as a *price-* or *demand-determined return.*

Applications

The analysis of rent leads to some interesting implications, two of which are considered here: rent taxes and rentlike incomes.

Taxing Rent.   When the demand for a product that generates a rent increases, the rental income of the supplier also increases. That raises an equity issue. What did the rent earners do to merit the increased incomes? Some economists feel that such unearned returns can justifiably be taxed away. But there's an economic argument supporting a rent tax as well. A tax on rent will not affect the supply of the resource. Think of a tax on urban property. The owner will supply the same quantity of space whether it's taxed or not, since the alternative is not supplying it at all and receiving no income. So, in contrast to the supply-reducing impact of the taxes discussed in Chapters 5 and 9, a rent tax embodies no production disincentive.

Draw a supply and a demand curve, as in Figure 18.1, onto Figure 18.2, where the abscissa is labeled "Apartments" and the ordinate represents the monthly payment per apartment. Assume a $500 payment as the equilibrium. Now the government imposes a tax on the landlord of $100 per month per apartment. The landlord, of course, tries to shift that tax onto the tenants, and so raises the price to $600 per month. Since the $600 is not an equilibrium price, which remains at $500, the landlord is forced to absorb the full burden of the tax. Of course, for the moment, the number of apartments on the market remains unchanged.

The "for the moment" qualifier adds an important caveat to the above conclusion. The given volume of apartments is fixed only in the short run. Over time, landlords can opt not to repair deteriorating build-

FIGURE 18.2   The Impact of a Tax on an Input Whose Supply Is Perfectly Inelastic

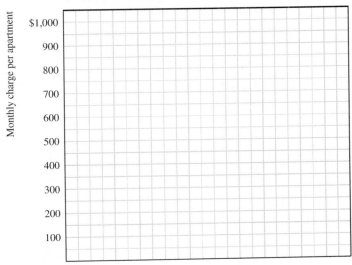

Draw in supply and demand curves to achieve an equilibrium price of $500. (Be sure the slopes of the curves match the assumptions of this problem.) Show that a $100 tax on apartments will be absorbed by the landlord.

ings or not to replace them. The stock of housing can decline if the tax so cuts into landlord income that it no longer pays to replace existing facilities. That's true of taxes on petroleum wells or coal mines as well, even if the tax is assessed on the number of wells or mines rather than on the oil or coal extracted. Taxes do alter the incentive for construction or for exploring for new reservoirs of natural resources. That's because, strictly speaking, the payment a landlord obtains for "renting" space is not a rent but a quasi rent.[5]

There are, as mentioned in Chapter 5, some items whose supply is fixed in the long run as well. Dead artists cannot create additional paintings, nor can expired sculptors increase the supply of their chiseling. In such cases, the supply can be diminished through destruction but never augmented. Consequently, while the price can rise or fall in line with shifts in the demand curve—the first citation at the beginning of this chapter suggests a trend of rising demand for works by the old masters—a tax imposed on collectibles cannot be escaped even in the long run. Those unfortunates who owned ancient coins when the tax was imposed will be unable to pass on the tax by reselling the coins to other numismatists.

Rentlike Incomes.   In some ways, human talent is analogous to works of art. Few of us are endowed with rare gifts that are marketable, be it in the world of entertainment, sports, or business. Hence, pushing up the salaries of major league ballplayers is hardly likely to augment the pool of talent available to the majors.

Now it's clear that if talent was not remunerated at least as well as its next best alternative, the price elasticity of supply would not be zero throughout the supply curve. Nevertheless, once the level of that opportunity cost was surpassed, the supply curve would turn vertical. Ask yourself, Had Springsteen earned $5 million less, would he have performed less?

The supply curve of Melinda Superstar is depicted in Figure 18.3. A normally shaped demand curve also appears in the figure, the presumption being that at too high a price, booking agents would switch to some other personality. The equilibrium salary is set by the market at $9 million per year. Isn't Melinda's income basically a rent? Above $50,000, Melinda's total income is solely demand determined. Yet because the curve is not perfectly inelastic, the entire return can't be considered purely a rent. The portion of Melinda's supply curve that is not perfectly inelastic gives rise to labor income, while the vertical segment constitutes the source of Melinda's rent. Similarly, the equivocal *perhaps* that *Business Week* gave as an answer to its question "Is the Boss Getting Paid Too Much?" suggests that the high compensation of major corporate leaders contains a significant rent component. Indeed, it remains to be proven whether star-level executive compensation causes higher corporate profits.[6] In short,

FIGURE 18.3 Melinda Superstar's Rent

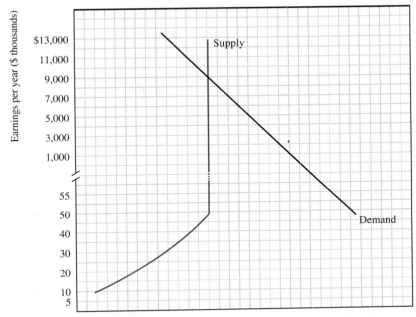

At any income above $50,000, Melinda's earnings are determined only by demand.

the individuals listed in MicroBits 18.1 receive the bulk of their income from rents because of their unreproducible talents.

If taxes on land won't be shifted onto demanders, the same appears true for the rents people receive from their talents or good fortune. Since they would hardly be likely to devote less effort to their present occupation if they were to be taxed, say, 50 percent of all income above $1 million, such a tax would not cause any change in resource allocation. (Whether that would be fair or not is another issue.)

Recap

Rent, then, is a return to a factor of production whose long-run supply is fixed, while quasi rent accrues to inputs whose supply is inelastic only in the short run. When the long-run supply curve is perfectly inelastic, the return to the factor is entirely determined by demand. A stronger demand raises the rent, but does not bring forth additional units of the factor.

Consequently, reducing the return to the factor will not reduce the quantity supplied either, so that a tax on the rent-earning input will not affect the amount provided. But be careful: the validity of this conclusion rests on the time dimension of the perfectly inelastic supply curve. Should the supply curve possess some degree of elasticity in the long run, higher taxes will reduce supply. The exceptions to the exception occur for those assets that cannot be reproduced (e.g., collectibles) or unique talents whose rents are out of sight.

Interest

Interest, like rent, has a colloquial meaning that is somewhat different from its interpretation by economists. For example, for tax purposes, the Internal Revenue Service insists that we report our interest income, so we dutifully list interest paid by banks for our deposits, by corporations and government for our purchases of bonds, and all interest received from personal loans. And if someone asked you, "What interest rate are you paying on your student loans?" you would most probably answer whatever number that's recorded on the loan document.

Yet the conventional usage of interest is inappropriate for economic decision making. Would you lend out $10,000 for a year (repayment guaranteed) at an interest rate of 12 percent when you anticipated the inflation rate over the year would equal 20 percent? Surely not. Upon repayment, you'd receive $11,200, consisting of the $10,000 in principal and the $1,200 interest payment. But you understand that inflation would not only have chewed up your interest, but also have actually eaten into your principal. Just to keep the purchasing power of your principal intact, you'd have to get $12,000 back.

The **nominal interest rate** is calculated by dividing the actual interest paid by the lender by the principal value of the loan. The **real interest rate** adjusts for inflation by subtracting the expected rate of inflation from the nominal interest rate.

A 12 percent **nominal interest rate** when the inflation rate is 20 percent constitutes a negative **real interest rate,** which simply means that you're getting back less than you put in. But even if the rate of inflation were 10 percent and you were receiving a positive 2 percent real interest rate, the nominal interest rate is deceptive. You're not earning the 12 percent you think you are, but only 2 percent. Economists believe that both borrowers and lenders understand that inflation erodes their purchasing power, and consequently base their financial decisions on real, not nominal, interest rates. Hence, the interest rate in this text is synonymous with the *real* interest rate.

Why Do Lenders Earn Interest?

One puzzle that economists have sought to answer is, Why do borrowers offer interest to lenders? Couldn't they obtain risk-free funds without paying interest?

Positive time preference describes the behavior of an individual who prefers present consumption to future spending.

The answer hinges on the crucial behavioral assumption that people exhibit **positive time preference.** They would rather have their funds than part with them even briefly and therefore must be compensated to induce them to divert funds from their own control and their own purposes.

Figure 18.4 uses the indifference curve apparatus to lay out why lenders have to be paid interest. In structure and implications, it's quite similar to the indifference curve analysis of labor supply (Figure 16.4, p. 538). Let's set the scene. Vashti has no income, but has fortunately received a payment of $100,000 from Royal Insurance for termination of employment. Unfortunately, however, Vashti's doctors have just diagnosed a terminal illness and have predicted that she will not live more than two years. Vashti now has to plan her two-year consumption pattern, realizing that the more she consumes in the present year, the less

FIGURE 18.4   Vashti's Indifference Map for Consumption Now versus Tomorrow

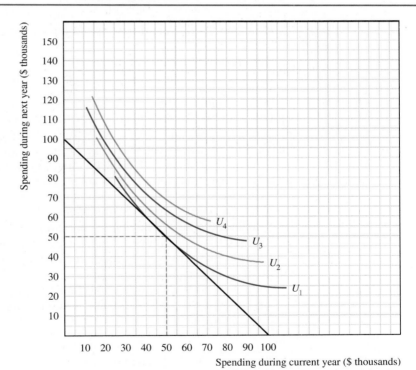

When no interest compensation is offered Vashti, she spends $50,000 in each of the two years; there's no reason for her to lend out any funds. But if she can earn interest, then lending becomes worthwhile. The actual dollar amount of lending will vary with the interest rate, as you will see by drawing in budget lines for $i = 10$, 20, and 30 percent.

remains for future consumption. The lowest budget line in Figure 18.4 represents Vashti's options in the absence of inflation—assumed henceforth—and without any possibility of earning interest—assumed just for the moment. Vashti's budget line connects this year's consumption of $100,000 to an equal value of future consumption.

The indifference map in Figure 18.4 displays Vashti preferences for spending in the two time frames. The marginal rate of substitution shows how many dollars of future spending she's willing to give up in order to increase current consumption by a dollar. Since neither present nor future consumption is a "bad," the indifference curves are convex to the origin, and the MRS is negative. As you can see from the diagram, in the absence of an interest inducement, Vashti's tangency on the lowest budget line leads her to spend $50,000 this year and $50,000 next year.

Enter Abigail, who offers to pay Vashti a 10 percent interest rate for a one-year loan. How does Vashti react? This option opens for Vashti a new budget line that stretches from $100,000 on the *x*-axis to $110,000 on the *y*-axis.[7]

How much will Vashti now spend during the present year?	$_____
How much will she lend to Abigail?	$_____
How much will Vashti have to spend next year?	$_____ [8]

Draw in additional budget lines to represent interest rates of 20 and 30 percent; read off the amounts that Vashti is willing to lend at these different interest rates; and list them in Table 18.1.[9] (Precision may prove elusive, but your answers should be in the neighborhood.)

Figure 18.5a plots Table 18.1 to derive Vashti's supply curve for loanable funds, the amounts she's willing to lend at various interest rates. It looks quite similar to a backward-bending supply-of-labor curve.

Of course, the assumptions that went into this brief tale are extreme. Nevertheless, the idea of paying a premium in order to induce individuals with positive time preference to sacrifice present consumption is not unrealistic. Other things remaining equal, the potential lenders will lend only if sufficiently compensated.

One final comment: You realize that everyone is a potential lender, with his or her own supply-of-loanable-funds curve. Adding them all to-

TABLE 18.1   Vashti's Loanable Funds

Interest Rate	Amount Lent	Interest Rate	Amount Lent
0	$0	20%	$_____
10%	_____	30%	_____

FIGURE 18.5   The Demand and Supply of Loanable Funds

a. Vasthi's supply of loanable funds

b. The market for loanable funds

c. Ted's demand for investment funds

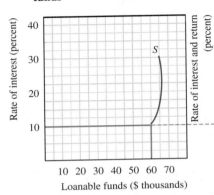
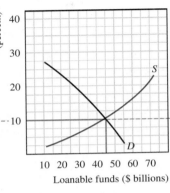
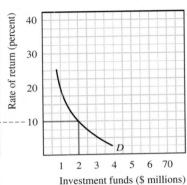

a. Vasti's backward-bending supply-of-funds curve is based on her indifference map (Figure 18.4). When the actual interest rate is 10 percent, she will lend $60,000.

b. The market demand and supply curves for loanable funds determine the interest rate and the quantity of funds borrowed and lent.

c. The demand for investment funds is obviously related to the demand for real capital. Like other factors, the demand for capital is negatively sloped because of the principle of diminishing returns.

gether yields the market supply-of-loanable-funds curve displayed in Figure 18.5b. (See MicroBits 18.2 for the actual shape of the supply curve.)

Why Do Borrowers Pay Interest?

Clearly, if potential lenders won't lend unless they receive an interest payment, potential borrowers will be unable to borrow unless they pay interest. But what's in it for the borrower?

The brief answer is increased profits. If additional funds would enable the firm to obtain resources with which it could improve its return beyond the cost of borrowed funds, or if it could invest in machinery that would lower its costs or raise its productivity above its borrowing costs, profit maximization decrees that funds should be borrowed.

This simple proposition is the nucleus around which the demand for loanable funds revolves. But to understand how the demand for funds is related to the interest rate, we must first introduce explicitly the concept of time as it affects the borrower.

Time, Compounding, and Discounting.   Both to the lender and the borrower, funds now are worth more than funds later. This is quite apparent

---

MICROBITS 18.2

Do Higher Interest Rates Encourage Saving?

Pure theory is ambivalent about the shape of the supply-of-savings curve. Individual savers may exhibit a backward-bending supply curve, and the aggregate saving curve can be drawn to indicate that saving either increases or decreases as interest rates rise. Empirical economists have grappled with this issue for years. Here's a summary of one representative contribution.

Professors Irwin Friend and Joel Hasbrouck approached the saving decision indirectly by examining why people spend rather than save.* One typical equation related consumption to permanent and transitory income,§ wealth, and interest rates. All data were adjusted to eliminate the impact of inflation, while the consumption, income,

and wealth variables were reduced to a per capita basis to abstract from variations in population. Using least-squares regression techniques on quarterly data from 1952 to 1980, Friend and Hasbrouck obtained

$$C_t = 0.225 + 0.712\ YP_t + 0.084\ YT_t \\ + 0.022\ W_{t-1} + 0.145\ R_t$$

where

C = Consumption.
YP = Permanent income.
YT = Transitory income.
W = Household wealth.
R = The expected real rate of interest on tax-free municipal bonds.

---

* Irwin Friend and Joel Hasbrouck, "Saving and After-Tax Rates of Return," *Review of Economics and Statistics* 65, no. 4 (November 1983), pp 537–43.

§ Permanent income is an estimate of earnings over one's lifetime. The earnings during a particular year, however, may be more or less than a year's share of permanent income. The difference between the individual's actual annual income and his permanent income is transitory income.

---

from the lender's point of view. The earlier the lender receives the funds back, the earlier can they be lent out again to earn additional interest. An interest return of 10 percent on a one-year $1,000 loan pays back $1,100 at the end of the year, which can then be lent out again at 10 percent. Ten percent of $1,100 is $110, for a total two-year return of $210. In contrast, a 10 percent annual return on a two-year loan paid at maturity brings in only $200. The secret ingredient in the first alternative is **compound interest.**

Compound interest occurs when the earned interest is added to the principal and in the next period interest is paid on the new principal.

The following is the basic formula for compound interest:

$$P_t = P_0(1 + i)^t$$

where

P_t = Principal at some later time, t.
P_0 = The original principal.
i = The interest rate.

MicroBits 18.2 continued

The subscripts refer to the time periods, which in all cases but the wealth variable are contemporaneous. (All absolute numbers are in thousands of 1972 dollars.) The R^2 value was .711, and all the variables were statistically significant.

What does the equation imply about the relationship between saving and interest rates? The positive sign of R_t indicates that an increase in interest rates will increase consumption. But if consumption rises when interest rates move up, then saving must decline, since by definition saving equals income minus consumption. Nevertheless, other empirical results forced Friend and Hasbrouch to reach an agnostic conclusion:

The evidence . . . indicate[s] that at the present stage of knowledge, we have no sound basis for alleging either a strong positive or negative after-tax rate of return effect on saving.

Other economists have been more positive. Michael J. Boskin, for example, wrote in 1978‖ that

A variety of functional forms, estimation methods, and definitions of the real-after-tax rate of return invariably lead to the conclusion of a *substantial positive interest elasticity* of private saving. [italics added]

Does it really matter whether the savings supply curve is positively or negatively sloped? The answer will be yes if you agree with those economists and public policymakers who believe that the U.S. saving rate is abysmally low and that raising aggregate savings is a national priority. Whether public policy should be directed at raising or lowering interest rates depends critically on the slope of the savings supply curve.

‖ Michael J. Boskin, "Taxation, Saving and the Rate of Interest," *Journal of Political Economy* 86, no. 2, supplement (April 1978), pp. S3–S27.

Using the above numbers:

$$\$1,210 = \$1,000(1 + .10)^2$$

This compounding formula can be manipulated to answer a different question. Let's say someone wanted to sell you a government bond that guaranteed payment of $1,210 two years from today. If the interest rate you could earn on your savings was 10 percent annually, what is the maximum price you'd be willing to pay for the offered bond? The intuitive answer is $1,000, since you could buy a security today with your own $1,000, and in two years receive back $1,210. Your intuitive reasoning is merely the compound interest formula expressed as follows:

$$PV = P_t/(1 + i)^t$$

The **present value (PV)** of an investment is the sum of the flow of returns **discounted,** or adjusted, by the appropriate interest rate.

This procedure, which calculates the **present value (PV)** of an investment, is known as **discounting.** It can be applied to real investments as well as to financial investments and to multiperiod returns as well as to single payments.

Present Value and Capital Investment.   There's a two-stage process for using present value calculations in investment decisions.

1. Compute the present value of the investment.
2. Compare the present value to the purchase price of the investment.

Assume Ted, whose teddy bear manufacturing firm was discussed in Chapter 16, has contracted with a toy retailer for a given volume of sales over the next five years. Ted could decrease his costs and thus increase his returns by purchasing a bear-stuffing machine to replace some labor, but that machine will disintegrate at the end of five years. Ted's calculations indicate the following stream of increased revenues that are certain to accrue from acquiring the machine:

Year 1	Year 2	Year 3	Year 4	Year 5
$200,000	$240,000	$288,000	$345,600	$414,720

What's the maximum price Ted should be willing to pay for the machine, considering once again an interest rate of 10 percent? You might be inclined to advise Ted not to pay more than $1,488,320, the sum of the returns. But this response ignores the role of time. A payment coming at the end of the fifth year is not quite the same as a return at the end of the first year. Delay has an opportunity cost, which must be taken into account in investment calculations.[10]

So, Ted has to calculate the present value, using an expanded version of the discounting formula:

$$PV = \frac{\$200,000}{1.1} + \frac{\$240,000}{(1.1)^2} + \frac{\$288,000}{(1.1)^3} + \frac{\$345,600}{(1.1)^4} + \frac{\$414,720}{(1.1)^5}$$

$$= \$181,818 + \$198,347 + \$216,379 + \$236,049 + \$257,508$$

$$= \$1,090,101.$$

Each return is discounted by the known interest rate and the proper exponent. Thus, the $288,000 that will be available only in the third year is discounted by $(1.1)^3$. The calculated present value of $1.09 million means that this particular income stream is worth *today* $1.09 million, not $1.49 million.

On to Step 2. Ted must compare the current cost of the equipment to its present value. Since the investment rule is "Invest as long as the present value is not less than the current cost of the investment," Ted would gain from purchasing the bear-stuffing machine as long as its price was no more than $1,090,101.

The "Rate of Return" Investment Criterion.   The PV = Cost rule can be reformulated in a slightly different manner. Instead of leaving the cost of investment for the second step, it's entered right from the start. The interest rate, which represents the cost of financing the new investment, however, is deferred to the second step. A new concept—the **rate of return (r)**, which measures the profitability of the investment—now emerges from the first stage. The formula is as follows:

The **rate of return** (*r*) of an investment is the number that discounts the flow of revenue to equal the cost of the investment.

$$C = \frac{R_1}{1 + r} + \frac{R_2}{(1 + r)^2} + \frac{R_3}{(1 + r)^3} + \cdots + \frac{R_t}{(1 + r)^t} + \frac{S}{(1 + r)^t}$$

where

C = The known cost of the equipment.
R = The known annual return.
S = The known salvage value.
r = The unknown rate of return.

If the bear-stuffing machine cost $1 million and the rest of the information remained identical, the solution would be obtained as follows:

$$\$1,000,000 = \frac{\$200,000}{1 + r} + \frac{\$240,000}{(1 + r)^2} + \frac{\$288,000}{(1 + r)^3} + \frac{\$345,600}{(1 + r)^4} + \frac{\$414,720}{(1 + r)^5}$$

MICROQUERY   Why not simply sum up the returns and divide them by the cost to obtain a rate of return of 44.832 percent? ————————————————— [11]

A calculator programmed for financial calculations would show you that r = 20 percent, meaning that a bear-stuffing machine that has precisely this time pattern of cost savings and could be purchased for $1 million would provide a rate of return to the purchaser of 20 percent per year.

Again, onto the second step, which now requires comparing the rate of return with the rate of interest. Would Ted be willing to pay a lender an interest rate of 10 percent yearly? The answer is obvious. He could use the borrowed funds to buy the bear-stuffing machine and earn a return that was double its cost. Profit-maximization considerations dictate the following three-part rule:

- Borrow as long as $r > i$.
- Don't borrow when $r < i$.
- Be indifferent when $r = i$.[12]

The Demand for Investment.   Since the rate of return of Ted's first ma-chine exceeded by a substantial margin the cost of funds, Ted certainly should look into acquiring a second one. But remember a key proposition of marginal productivity theory: increasing any single factor while keep-ing the other factors of production fixed leads to diminishing returns to the variable factor. In this case, Ted's acquisition of the second machine is unlikely to garner for him the same rate of return. The new capital equip-ment yields a lower MPP and a smaller VMP. The Rs in the numerator will come down, and so must the rs. But as long as the rate of return on the second piece of equipment is no less than 10 percent, Ted should invest in that one, too.

There's an interesting conclusion implicit in this scenario. We know that the VMP curve of an input is the firm's demand curve for that factor of production. We also know that the VMP and r move in the same direction: the more capital acquired by the firm, the lower the VMP and the smaller the marginal rate of return. Hence, the demand curve for the firm's borrowing can be directly related to its rate of return. *The more the firm borrows, the lower will be the rate of return it will obtain from its additional use of capital.* Figure 18.5c uses this reasoning to sketch out Ted's demand for investment funds.

Figure 18.5c also contains a horizontal line at 10 percent that indi-cates the interest rate facing the firm. The rule of invest as long as $r > i$ leads the firm to demand $2 million to acquire capital.

A further implication follows from the negatively sloped demand-for-funds curve. Just as the firm already in equilibrium in terms of its labor force will hire more workers if the wage falls, so, too, will the firm borrow additional funds for investment purposes if the interest rate comes down. See for yourself: Had interest rates been 7.5 percent instead of 10 percent, how much would the firm have borrowed? $_____ .[13]

To recapitulate: Figure 18.5a shows an individual's saving decisions as they vary with changes in the rate of interest. Figure 18.5c depicts the firm's capital accumulation decisions, as they relate to the rate of return. The obvious next question is, How are the actual return on capital and the interest rate determined? The simple microeconomic theory of rates of return and interest in a perfectly competitive capital market is displayed in Figure 18.5b. You've already seen that the supply curve represents the market supply of all potential lenders. The demand curve in Figure 18.5b is derived by summing the individual funding demands of all potential borrowers. In this simple model, where borrowers and lenders bid to demand and supply funds under perfectly competitive conditions and which excludes financial intermediaries such as banks, the 10 percent equilibrium interest rate = the rate of return is found at the intersection of the supply and demand curves. Of course, this market rate then becomes the interest rate facing each individual borrower and lender. So, in Figure 18.5a, Vashti lends $60,000, while in Figure 18.5c, Ted borrows $2 mil-lion.

It's simple now to calculate Vashti's earnings and Ted's loan payments. Once the interest rate is determined in the market, Vashti's interest income equals the interest rate times the amount she lends. Similarly, Ted's interest costs equal the rate he pays times the amount the firm borrows. The firm's marginal rate of return on capital will, in equilibrium, equal the interest rate, too, and certainly will move in the same direction.[14]

Investment Uncertainty

It's rare that decision makers can calculate the present value or rate of return accurately, for the Rs in the numerator of the equations depend upon many variables that are beyond the firm's control. An investment's net returns, as well as its time pattern, hinge on the unknowable answers to such questions as: Will demand meet up to expectations? Are future output and input prices correctly estimated? Will government actions change the competitive environment? And the longer an investment's life is, the more uncertain its returns will be.

Dealing with Uncertainty.   Perhaps an extreme but not unrealistic example concerns airline investments in aircraft. In October 1990, United Airlines placed an order for up to 68 Boeing 777 jetliners, a new twin-engined, 360-seater that Boeing had yet to manufacture. Even with rumored 25 percent discount off the $100 million list price per plane, United's investment exceeded $5 billion. Moreover, the useful life of a jetliner runs into decades, although the majors will sell off their planes well before they wear out. United's decision to go with Boeing and the size of its order hinged not only on the purchase price and financing terms, but also on expected demand on United's routes over many years. That in turn depended on travel trends, airfares, competition in the airline industry, and so on. But these variables themselves depended on others; fares, for example, were related to fuel prices.

United handled this complex decision by using "Valerio's Black Box," an extremely sophisticated economic model developed by Lou Valerio, a United economic analyst. The model, which understandably is top secret, presumably captures the various components of the investment decision and their interrelationships in an uncertain world. Ultimately, the model churns out either a present value or a rate of return for various options, leaving management to choose among them.

The Payback Criterion

The **payback criterion** is the number of years that an investment is expected to take to recoup its initial cost.

A more typical method, especially for shorter-lived and less complex investment decisions, is the **payback criterion.** The company estimates the number of years that it will take for an investment to pay back its initial outlays and compares that to a preset payback criterion. Thus, a three-year payback criterion means that the investment must cover its costs in no more than three years.

The typical U.S. corporate payback criterion is three to four years, which really means an annual rate of return of 25 to 33 percent. Such rates are significantly above historical U.S. real interest rates, which implies that had firms invested more they would have increased their revenues. This, however, is not true if uncertainty is taken into account. Since future events can turn apparently sound investment decisions into major catastrophes, companies leave a healthy margin for error. The demand for substantial rates of return means that firms are implicitly saying, "Even if we overestimated our returns by 20 to 30 percentage points, we'd still end up in the black."[15]

How Much Is a Life Worth? The Resolution

The same reasoning used for calculating the present value of an investment can be applied to the value of a life. Although the emotional loss can never be restored, a life cut short also entails a replaceable economic loss to the survivors. The deceased could have earned income over his or her lifetime, although the precise value of those earnings is not easy to quantify. We ought to estimate not only the pay increments the deceased would have earned—taking into account not only merit and seniority increases but also the rate of inflation—but also such things as the deceased's likelihood of surviving until retirement and the possibility of being unable to work full-time either because of layoff or illness. Finally, income earned over time must be adjusted to its present value, since if the plaintiffs win the negligence suit, the payment will be made soon after, while the earnings of the decedent would have accrued over a longer period of time.

How were these elements combined in the Green case described earlier in this chapter? Let's focus on the economic loss to the estate, for which the judge charged the jury:

In determining this amount, you may consider:
a. What the decedent earned in the past;
b. What the decedent might reasonably have been expected to earn in the future; and
c. The decedent's age, ability, life expectancy, health, habits, industry, sobriety, and thrift. (pp. 1116–17)

In addition to the concept of present value that comes into play, notice the treatment of uncertainty in the second item ("might reasonably have been expected to earn") and in the third ("life expectancy"). In fact, the plaintiffs hired economics professor Nelson Crick of Portland State University to come up with a figure for the economic loss.

To minimize potential controversy over uncertainty, the plaintiff's attorney asked Dr. Crick to present a conservative estimate of the economic loss. The witness did so in stages. First, the professor gathered data on life expectancy and work life expectancy. Kelly Sue was nearly 21 at the time of her death and could have been expected to live another 59 years and work 24.5 years. Professor Crick then obtained data on the value of a housewife's services in the home, which in 1984 came to $10,847. Since Mrs. Green would have provided those services to the household, namely, Mr. Green, only over *his* lifetime, Professor Crick multiplied $10,847 by Mr. Green's life expectancy of 47.2 to reach a loss of services equal to $511,978. Third, Professor Crick calculated the loss of future earnings based on the average earnings for a female high school graduate. In 1983 that equaled $9,147 per year, which, when multiplied by Kelly Sue's work life expectancy rounds off to $224,000. The next step involved subtracting Kelly Sue's personal consumption, since, had she survived, some percentage of her services to the household and her earnings would have been used by herself rather than by the other family members. On the basis of a study done at Cornell University, Professor Crick subtracted 27 percent, reaching a total economic loss of slightly less than $575,000.

But remember that this sum would have accrued to the family over decades, and so Professor Crick had to provide a present value figure. He avoided this calculation by a method often used in such cases—offsetting the discount rate against future wage increases. His reasoning: Had Kelly Sue's future earnings grown by 5 percent a year and had the appropriate discount rate also been 5 percent, then plugging an additional 5 percent into the numerator and denominator of the present value formula would not have changed the present value. The professor admitted under examination that in fact the increase in wages would most likely have been larger, and so his assumption provides a smaller sum than had a less conservative method been used. The expert witness also noted that in calculating lost wages, he had assumed Kelly Sue would have earned the average wage, a more conservative estimate that eliminated the possibility that she could have found a better-paying job.[16]

A final note: Life is irreplaceable, and calculating a value seems rather callous. Nevertheless, would you have been happier had the family of Mrs. Green not been awarded anything?

Human Capital

The concept of present value has also been applied to investment decisions that individuals make about their own future, especially in the area of education.

Think about it for a moment. Most of you reading this text will devote four years of your life to college. You may continue on to a graduate or professional school, spending even more time on your studies. Obviously, you and/or your parents undergo substantial expenses. In addition, there's a heavy opportunity cost. While you're in school, you're unlikely to work at a full-time job and thus earn a living income. Why spend so much on yourself?

Human capital, the personal analogue of physical capital, is the investment embodied in an individual.

Although economic rewards are not the only reason, surely potential earnings constitute a major part of the answer. You believe that building up your **human capital** now will pay significantly larger dividends over your lifetime. You expect that the return on your education will more than compensate for your costs during your school years.

Like the firm investing in real capital, the rational student must calculate costs and benefits. How much more are you going to earn over your lifetime as a result of your education? How much is it costing you? But, again analogously to the investor, you realize that the returns will accrue to you only over time, while the costs are immediate. In order to calculate your costs and benefits more accurately, you must discount future earnings by some rate of interest. Otherwise, you'd be overstating the true value of the benefits. (See MicroBits 18.3.)

Implications. Human capital theory has some interesting implications for labor market issues. One reason why education and income are correlated is that the employer is willing to pay more for a better-educated and presumably higher-quality worker. Surely this makes sense in the training of skilled workers or professionals. It's quite clear why some students are willing to spend megabucks to attend private colleges. The better education they presumably receive pays off in their enhanced job prospects upon graduation.[17]

A second implication concerns choice of professions. The time required for medical specialty training ranges from 6 years to become a general practitioner to 10 years to become a neurosurgeon. Why, then should anyone become a neurosurgeon and invest four more stressful years at very high opportunity costs?[18] It's clear that the rewards for intensive and prolonged study must be commensurate with the effort. If not, some physicians may well conclude on the basis of cost/benefit calculations that it's just not worth it to invest that many more years. So, if you ever wondered why neurosurgeons charge more per hour than do general practitioners, it all boils down to the fact that the former embody greater amounts of human capital and expect to be paid for their investment in themselves. The same applies to salary differences among professions. That's why elevator operators earn less than druggists and why secretaries earn less than executives with M.B.A. degrees.

Profits

The concept of profits as the driving force of business enterprise is central to a capitalist economy. Without the lure of profits, entrepreneurs would have little, if any, incentive to start a business or keep it running. In a real sense, then, profits are a return to a factor of production in the same way that wages are a return to labor, rent to fixed-supply inputs, and interest to providers of capital. The factor of production, however, is a less tangible, more nebulous "entrepreneurship" or "management," and profit is, in a sense, the reward to the person or people who put it all together.

Accounting versus Economic Profits

Despite the apparent clarity of the concept, profit is shrouded in confusion. A common error is to ignore the distinction between accounting profits and economic profits. Students of accounting familiar with a profit-and-loss statement know that net profits equal sales revenues minus the costs of sales and overhead. When taxes are subtracted, the result is called, not surprisingly, net profits after taxes. While these calculations meet both accounting and Internal Revenue Service standards, they normally overstate the economic profits of the firm, since they fail to take into account opportunity costs.

Consider the following for instance. Flora owns a flower shop, which employs just one worker in addition to herself. To start the shop, Flora invested $50,000 of her own funds and borrowed another $25,000. Monthly running expenses involve the cost of the flowers, sundry sup-

---

MicroBits 18.3

How Much Is a Baccalaureate Worth?

The "College Edge" figures on the next page indicate quite clearly that a college-educated person will earn more than an individual whose education ceased after high school. For the last four decades, college graduates earned about 40 percent more than high school graduates.

The return on an investment in college must be less than 40 percent for two reasons. First, focusing on earnings ignores the costs of education. Second, education outlays occur early in an individual's career, while the benefits accrue over a lifetime.

The Sam and Gordon figure on p. 621 sketches out a simplified example of two time patterns of earnings and costs. Gordon joins the labor force right after his high school commencement. At 18, he starts earning $20,000 a year. To keep the arithmetic simple, assume away income taxes and further assume that the pay increases Gordon receives until he retires at 62 just compensate for inflation. In short, Gordon's real income remains a constant $20,000 for 44 years, the straight line in the figure. Sam, on the other hand, decides to attend college, which costs him between $4,500 and $19,000, the tuition and fees in a public or private college, respectively. In addition, consider the opportunity cost in terms of forgone wages, assuming that

MicroBits 18.3 continued

The College Edge

Comparing the median income of college-educated men and women and high-school-educated men and women.

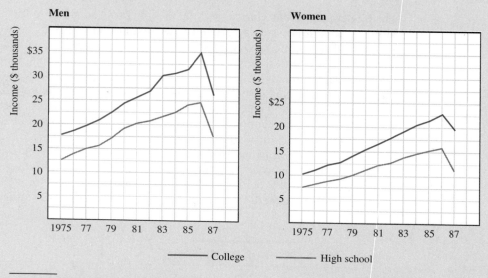

* Includes only workers out of school 10 years or less, based on census data analyzed by Jonathan Bound, University of Michigan.

SOURCE: Reprinted by permission of *The Wall Street Journal,* © 1988 Dow Jones & Company, Inc. All Rights Reserved Worldwide.

Sam could have earned as much as Gordon had Sam begun working right after high school. So, Sam's lost income equals $20,000 for each year of his four-year college stay, and his total costs can be rounded off to $30,000. On the other hand, when Sam completes his education, he'll earn $30,000 a year for the rest of his life. Sam's earning pattern, as depicted in the figure, shows that for the first four years, Sam's earnings are a negative $30,000, while for the rest of Sam's productive life until retirement, his earnings are a positive $30,000 annually. Is the extra $10,000 a year worth the initial costs?

You can answer this question by first calculating Sam's rate of return on college education. On the left side of the equal sign is the four-year cost and on the right side the 40-year difference in earnings.

$$\frac{\$30,000}{1+r} + \frac{\$30,000}{(1+r)^2} + \frac{\$30,000}{(1+r)^3} + \frac{\$30,000}{(1+r)^4} =$$

$$\frac{\$10,000}{(1+r)^5} + \frac{\$10,000}{(1+r)^6} + \cdots + \frac{\$10,000}{(1+r)^{40}}$$

MicroBits 18.3 continued

Sam and Gordon

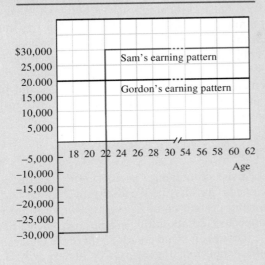

To solve for r, move the left-hand side of the equality to the right-hand side, so that

$$0 = -\frac{\$30,000}{1 + r} - \frac{\$30,000}{(1 + r)^2}$$

$$-\frac{\$30,000}{(1 + r)^3} - \frac{\$30,000}{(1 + r)^4}$$

$$+\frac{\$10,000}{(1 + r)^5} + \ldots + \frac{\$10,000}{(1 + r)^{40}}$$

With the proper software, you'll discover that r, the discounted annual rate of return, yields 4.92 percent, meaning that taking into account the time pattern of both costs and returns, Sam's investment in a college education returns a smidgen less than 5 percent. (A variety of economic studies have shown the actual return to range between 10 and 15 percent.)

Whether that return pays depends, as for any investment, on the interest rate. Imagine that Sam, in order to finance his education

and living expenses, would have had to borrow $30,000 for each of his four college years. Had the real interest rate on the borrowing been 4 percent, the investment in education would have been worthwhile. But had the real interest rate been 8 percent, the interest cost would have exceeded the rate of return, and Sam would have found it more profitable not to attend college.

Of course, the decision to attend college is far less cut-and-dried. Other economic elements—such as the risk of unemployment, which is less for the college graduate than for the high school graduate, and the fact that a job requiring a college degree is likely to be both more interesting and less physically demanding—as well as cultural and social factors come into play in the attend/not attend decision. Moreover, it's quite clear that overall calculations are not helpful for the individual. For each of us, the decision is not a general "work versus education" option, but specific types of work versus specific types of education. Surely a highly skilled blue-collar worker can earn more than a college student who specialized in a major for which there's little demand.

Despite these caveats, studies examining decisions of more versus less education (high school vs. college, Ph.D. vs B.A.) as well as choice of majors indicate that student enrollments do vary directly with the rate of return.* So, even if students are generally unaware of the precise returns to education in general and to the various types of education in particular, they behave as if they understood human capital theory.

---

* Although Richard S. Freeman's *The Over-Educated American* (New York: Academic Press, 1976) is now dated, it nevertheless provides a useful and readable survey of economic decision making by the demanders of education.

plies, and wages, as well as overhead—interest on the loan, rent, and utilities. The first two columns of Table 18.2 list the annual accounting income statement for Flora's Flower Boutique, and indicate a profit of $30,000.

The accounting statement, however, has left out two sources of opportunity cost. First, the fact that Flora herself works in the shop surely entitles her to a salary. At a minimum, she ought to earn at least as much as her worker. Second, Flora's own funds are invested in the business, forfeiting the interest she could have earned had she put those funds in a bank or lent them to someone else. These $26,000 opportunity costs must be subtracted before calculating Flora's economic profits. As the final column in Table 18.2 indicates, Flora's true profits come to $4,000, rather than the $30,000 accounting profits.

Excess versus Normal Profits

Economic profits consist of two components: normal profits and excess profits. You came across excess profits in two different contexts—the temporary excess profits of the perfect competitive market and the permanent excess profits of imperfect competition. When competitive firms are in equilibrium without excess profits and a sudden increase in demand leads to an increase in price, then existing firms will temporarily earn excess profits. These excess profits will self-destruct, for their very existence brings forth new entry and additional supply sufficient to wipe out the abnormal profit level. The same is true when a cost-saving innovation is introduced. Those who first introduce the innovation will earn excess profits, but they, too, will find profits returning to normal levels once other firms imitate the pioneers. This scenario does not emerge under monopoly or oligopoly conditions. Where new entry is constrained, the monopolistic or oligopolistic firm can maintain the excess profit position for substantial time periods.

TABLE 18.2   Accounting and Economic Profit Statements for Flora's Flower Boutique

Category	Accounting Calculation	Economic Calculation
Revenues	$100,000	$100,000
Costs		
Flowers and other materials	35,000	35,000
Employee labor	20,000	20,000
Owner's labor		20,000
Rent & utilities	12,000	12,000
Loan interest	3,000	3,000
Interest on owner's funds		6,000
Net profit	30,000	4,000

Why Profits?

Profits encourage two related aspects of economic activity: (1) innovation (including risk taking) and (2) the efficient organization of production. Perhaps the major economic benefit that accrues from the profit motive lies in innovation. If we consider an entrepreneur as an individual who identifies and exploits opportunities—take a look at the second quotation at the opening of this chapter—we have to wonder what motivates an entrepreneur to go out on a limb, often risking his capital and always risking his time and effort, if not for the rewards of success. To be sure, luck often plays a role, but lucks works better for those who are prepared to seize the opportunity (see MicroBits 18.4).

"Oh, I believe in free enterprise, sir--I'm just not good at it."

Source: Reprinted from *The Wall Street Journal;* Permission Cartoon Features Syndicate.

Innovations come in all forms, some revolutionary (Henry Ford's mass production techniques, Steven Jobs's Apple computer), some less so (Walt Disney's cartoons, Ray Kroc's franchising McDonald's), and some eminently forgettable.[19] Some innovations improve existing products, others introduce new products, and still others alter production techniques. Innovations enrich the product mix available to consumers and producers alike, and, when they are directed at production methods, increase the productive efficiency of the economy.[20] Indeed, the profit motive is enjoying new prestige in the East European former communist bloc nations.

As important as entrepreneurship is, however, it is only the initial source of profits. Entrepreneurs are not necessarily good organizers. Indeed, the insights, drive, and motivation that make for successful innovators often lead them to be impatient and intolerant managers. The ability

---

MICROBITS 18.4

A Gallery of the Greatest

Notice in these two vignettes the distinct types of innovations introduced by Messers. Disney and Kroc. Yet both were risk takers as well as innovators.

Walt Disney (1901–1966)

When Walt Disney left Kansas City for Hollywood in 1923, he carried sketches for his first film project, "Alice in Cartoonland," featuring a live actress cavorting with cartoon figures. Working in a converted garage, and with brother Roy running the business side, Walt produced several Alice features. Mickey Mouse arrived in 1928, and other icons of everlasting childhood followed.

Walt wasn't much of a cartoonist (he hired great animators), but he was a perfectionist and a terrific idea man. His classic feature-length cartoons—"Snow White and the Seven Dwarfs," "Pinocchio" and "Fantasia"—while visually daring and hugely popular, were very costly to produce.

Government contracts for wartime propaganda and training films kept Disney studios solvent in the 1940s. Disney was one of the first film makers to recognize the power of television. His theme park, Disneyland, spawned another industry and cemented the Disney legend.

Raymond A. Kroc (1902–1984)

Is it ever too late to strike it rich? Ray Kroc was a 52-year-old milkshake-machine salesman when he called on one of his best customers, a small chain of Southern California hamburger stands run by the McDonald brothers. Excited by what he saw, he bought the franchise rights. Seven years later, in 1961, Kroc bought the company for what seemed a pricey $14 million, including interest costs. At his death in 1984, his McDonald's Corp. stake was about $500 million.

Kroc, a high-school dropout, had bounced from job to job most of his life. He sold real estate in Florida, peddled paper cups in the Midwest and played professional jazz piano. His blueprint for selling fast food—cleanliness, uniform prices and speed (with fantastic customer service), transformed eating-out habits. With 1988 sales of $16 billion by franchise and company-owned restaurants, McDonald's Corp. qualifies as the world's largest food service.

Source: "A Gallery of the Greatest," *The Wall Street Journal*, June 23, 1989, p. B2. Reprinted by permission of *The Wall Street Journal*, © Dow Jones & Company, Inc. All Rights Reserved Worldwide.

---

to organize the production, marketing, finance, personnel management, and other functions of a modern business; to negotiate and compromise; to motivate others—in short, to manage—is crucial to both the evolving firm and the already established business. It often happens that a good idea dies stillborn because the innovator lacks the ability to market the product successfully. Management is an essential skill, and its return is also called profit.

Recap.   Profit as a return to entrepreneurship and management works along these lines: An entrepreneur notices a gap in the market. She discovers a product that will fill the gap, and either by herself or with the assistance of a skilled manager, produces and markets the product. If the product indeed fills a need and proves successful, the company will grow, profits will be earned, and the entrepreneur and manager will share in those profits.

But the nature of the competitive market guarantees that innovations will be replicated. Profits lure imitators, each one hoping to capitalize on the success of the innovator. Ultimately, a new competitive market will have been created, and profits are reduced to the level that eliminates further inducement to entry. Clearly, then, the profit motive serves a highly useful economic and social function.

Income and Efficiency

Profits are simultaneously the stimulus to innovation and the reward of the successful entrepreneur. Similarly, wages and interest rates serve as signals to business firms, indicating how best to channel their demands for labor and capital. At the same time, wages and interest rates determine the incomes of the suppliers of labor and capital. The failure to understand the dual role of factor prices has often led to confused policy-making.

Interest and Profits in a Socialist Context

Socialist ideology has caused interest to be underpriced and profits and the profit motive to be rejected in socialist economies. The allocational consequences of these decisions were not foreseen by the socialist planners, although they did not surprise Western economists. When the management of government-owned enterprises is charged low or even zero interest rates for capital use, it selects capital-intensive production techniques. But is capital really that cheap? Don't the machine-building industries require raw materials, intermediate products, labor, and machines in order to produce output? Surely, efficient use of investment goods mandates a price that reflects their scarcity and their opportunity costs. The Soviet Union erred by overinvesting in capital goods and underinvesting in labor-intensive techniques.

The same point is equally pertinent to profits. Marxist ideology views the capitalist as the exploiter; eliminate the profit motive and you'll also eliminate worker exploitation. Thus, until recently, in socialist economies the state owned most, if not all, businesses. But if there's no reward to private entrepreneurs for innovation, why should anyone bother to introduce new products or new production techniques? That's no less true for the executives and workers of government-owned businesses. Rarely have they shared in the "profits" of enterprises operating in the black. Instead, the difference between revenues and costs has been removed by taxes that have been channeled to cover the losses of other state firms. Such reallocation of profits eliminates the incentive of managers and workers in the profitable firms. At the same time, it stifles any movement toward greater efficiency in the unprofitable enterprises.[21]

And so, socialist economies have, for the most part, been bypassed by the innovations of the past decades. Only belatedly, for example, is the computer revolution beginning to penetrate East European factories and service outlets. Private ownership of land and capital, free markets, and competition are now emerging in the socialist bloc, as the people in socialist nation after nation have forced economic liberalization upon reluctant bureaucracies and a deteriorating economic system.

Profits in a Capitalist Economy

Many individuals oppose the profit motive even in as capitalist an economy as that of the United States. In part, such opposition reflects the socialist ideal that people should work for the good of all rather than merely for their own benefit. However noble that sentiment is, no national economy has been able to operate in that vein.

Historically, at least in the United States, the late-19th-century opposition to the excesses of the trusts and their exploitation of both the consuming public and their employees left a legacy of distrust against business power. The distaste for profits is buttressed insofar as the economy fails to meet the competitive ideal and continues to support restraints on competition that benefit the few at the expense of the many.

In part, too, there's an ethical revulsion against "profiteering," which usually is defined by the person who uses the phrase to mean "profits in excess of what I believe they ought to be." Thus, the thousands of dollars each AIDS patient spends yearly on AZT appears to be unjustifiable. Similarly, an article in *The Wall Street Journal* headlined "Profiteering on Rubber Gloves Suspected" relates that the AIDS crisis has led to a ballooning increase in the demand for gloves used by nurses and physicians. The reporter notes "complaints of suspected profiteering, price-gouging, and other unethical practices," which some distributors attributed to "smaller, recently arrived suppliers. . . . The big U.S. manufacturers' have behaved well.' "[22] This belief in fair pricing behavior stands in sharp contrast to the role of the price mechanism as an allocating and signaling device. Moreover, in suggesting self-restraint on profits, the argument works at cross-purposes with the profit motive as the quickest way to increase the quantity of goods that are in short supply.

For all of these reasons, profit earners tend to be on the defensive even in capitalist economies. Economists do not claim that the social, political, or ethical system of a nation must be subservient to the economic mechanism. Certainly, economics is a means to nobler ends. But economists are professionally committed to point out the costs of alternative policies. In the case of an antiprofit ethic and policies designed to enforce that attitude, the cost is a loss in economic system efficiency. Reducing profits through fiscal or regulatory policies weakens the desire of entrepreneurs to perform the tasks that lead to a more efficient and faster-growing economy. We may discover that we have no alternative but to restrain the profit motive, but we should not ignore the fact that there is a cost attached. As in most economic decisions, there's no such thing as a free lunch.

Summary

The present chapter is devoted to the returns earned by the factors of production other than labor: rent, interest, and profit. *Rent* is unique because it accrues to resources that are in fixed supply even in the long run. When the short-run supply curve is perfectly inelastic—think of commercial or residential real estate in a given neighborhood, a specific type of labor, or known reservoirs of petroleum or natural gas—then the return is called a *quasi rent*. In either instance, the fixed nature of the supply curve means that prices can change only through shifts in the demand curve.

Taxation of pure rent has two advantages: the tax cannot be shifted, nor will the tax cause a decrease in the quantity supplied. While the pure rent case is rare, taxation of the art of deceased painters or sculptors or on the earnings of talented superstars is also not shiftable, nor will a supply response be likely.

In discussing *interest* earnings, it's critical to distinguish between the nominal interest rate and the real interest rate, which is the nominal rate adjusted for the expected rate of inflation. Lending and borrowing decisions are based on the real rate. Lenders, who are characterized by positive time preference, need to be induced by the payment of interest to forgo control over their savings. A supply of loanable funds can be derived by using indifference curve analysis, varying the interest rate, and tracking the changes in equilibrium points.

Borrowers are willing to pay interest as long as the rate of return on investments financed by borrowing is at least equal to the rate of interest. To make that decision requires calculating the rate of return on investment, taking into explicit account the role of time. After all, the investing firm spends funds on expanding its plant or acquiring machinery in the near future, while the return to investment occurs over a range of time.

An interesting analogy to business investment is investment in human capital. Indeed, the theory of investment is equally applicable to such questions as: Is a collegiate education profitable? Ought a police officer spend time and money studying for promotional examinations? In light of the education or skill requirements, what career should an individual choose?

Profits are the final return discussed in this chapter. Economic profits differ from accounting profits because the former encompass not only expenses but also opportunity costs. The role profits play in an economy hinges on their source. Market control, either through collusion or with the consent of government authorities, leads to long-run excess profits. In addition to redistributing income from the buyers to the sellers, these persistent profits may result in an efficiency loss to the economy.

Profits serve a positive function in a competitive marketplace. Entrepreneurs are willing to take risks and innovate in order to earn profits. Businesspeople involve themselves in the efficient management of their firms because of the profit motive. Indeed, the profit motive is the driving force in a capitalist economy. Unlike the market control case, however, the competitive marketplace assures the entry of imitators, so that the initial profits earned by the innovator are driven down to a minimum level.

Despite the fact that profits play a critical role in assuring the vitality of the market economy, critics of the profit motive have tended to put its proponents on the defensive. To be sure, economic efficiency is not the primary goal of society. Yet, ignoring efficiency is costly. The latter fact is well demonstrated by the decades of economic stagnation of planned socialist economies. The economic revolution in the East, with country after country dismantling its inflexible command economy and replacing it with a market-oriented free-enterprise system, revitalizes the profit motive as it fashions an increasing role for the private business sector.

Key Terms

Compound interest
Discounting
Human capital
Nominal interest rate
Payback criterion
Positive time preference

Present value
Quasi rent
Rate of return (*r*)
Real interest rate
Rent

Review Questions

1. Table 18.2 lists "rent and utilities" as a cost of production at Flora's Flower Boutique, which presumably helps determine the selling price of the shop's flowers. But earlier on, the chapter asserted that rent is determined by price. Reconcile this apparent paradox.

2. Would a subsidy to landlords in inner cities be an efficient method of assisting poor urban tenants with their rent payments? Explain.

3. *a.* Why should the income earned by highly talented individuals be considered a rent rather than a return on the labor they supply?

    b. Would you favor a law that imposed stiffer tax rates on such individuals? Explain.

4. *a.* Use indifference curve analysis to explain why individuals with positive time preference lend only if they're paid interest.

    b. Would that be true for people whose time preference is negative? Explain.

5. *a.* Why is the present value concept important for investment decisions?

    b. How is present value related to discounting?

    c. Would you advise a firm to invest in equipment that costs $425,000 and returns in three years $200,000, $250,000, $75,000, respectively? The firm could borrow at a real interest rate of 5 percent per annum. Use the present value method.

d. How would your answer differ if the nominal rate was 5 percent and prices were falling at an annual rate of 1 percent?

e. Calculate the real rate of return for the investment detailed in question (c) above.

f. Would you recommend that the firm undertake the investment?

6. a. Why does the demand for investment curve demonstrate a negative slope?

b. The government wishes to stimulate investment. Explain the advantages and disadvantages of government intervening to fix a below-market interest rate in a competitive loanable funds market.

7. How does human capital theory explain why

a. Tenured professors earn more than nontenured faculty members?

b. Professors with a Ph.D. earn more than those with only an M.A.?

c. Professors of finance earn more than professors of linguistics?

8. a. Since profits are the residual left to the owners of a firm after costs have been subtracted from revenues, why would it not be wise to tax profits more heavily than wages?

b. Why might it be sound public policy to tax permanent excess profits more heavily than temporary excess profits?

Food for Thought

1. High prices for art encourage forgery. (Some authorities believe that as much as 20 percent of the Andy Warhol prints on the market may be forged.)

a. Draw an equilibrium art market before and after the introduction of forgeries.

b. Does it matter that the forgery market is characterized by asymmetric information (i.e., the seller knows it's a forgery, but the buyer doesn't)?

c. How does the practice of museums, which purchase but rarely sell, affect the value of the artwork still in the market? Sketch out and explain.

2. Gentrification, the renewal of urban areas by the affluent, has led to increasing rents in inner-city apartments and commercial establishments. Those moving in tend to chase out existing tenants, who are frequently among the poor, as well as neighborhood shops. What would be the economic consequences of a real estate tax on the more expensive apartments combined with a subsidy of equal value to be spent on the neighborhood poor?

3. a. Show and explain the impact of an Oscar on the recipient's rent.

b. A professor of economics at Princeton was lured to the Wharton Business School in 1989 by a reputed annual salary offer of $250,000. How could you determine how much of this salary is a rent?

4. Use income and substitution effects to explain the backward-bending supply of loanable funds curve.

5. a. Your old car needs a new carburetor, which costs $500. Alternatively, you could junk the vehicle and buy a new

used car for a net cost of $5,000. What factors would you consider in making this repair versus replacement decision?

b. How does uncertainty influence your decision? Elaborate.

c. Would managers having to choose between adding on components to upgrade their PCs and buying newer models face the same factors? Explain.

6. The following letter was written by an irate flier:

> Pirates are active again in the Caribbean Sea. This time they are airlines. Anyone reserving a seat . . . becomes a victim. The airlines demand all of your ticket money four months in advance . . . or the reservation is null and void. No interest is offered or paid. The airline takes your money and collects interest or invests it in other profitable projects.

a. Does implicit airline borrowing from travelers at a zero interest rate contradict the presumed positive time preference of individuals?

b. If not, what do the airlines offer fliers as payment?

c. The writer believed "the major airlines practiced monopoly on whatever routes they control" as the explanation for not paying interest. Do you agree?

7. Fewer people would be killed or maimed in vehicular accidents if roads were built with fewer curves, were better lit, and had safer median separators. Yet neither the authorities nor the public itself seems to be terribly concerned with reducing the death or accident rate. How can this attitude be reconciled with the presumed pricelessness of human life and suffering?

8. a. Use human capital theory to explain the relationship between wages and seniority.

b. Contrast the human capital explanation to the job search and implicit contract theories of the last chapter.

Suggested Readings

Although Henry George's *Progress and Poverty* (New York: Schalkenbach Foundation, 1958) was first published in 1882, it remains an eminently readable polemic in favor of the rent tax. Interest rate and investment theory, which straddle microeconomics and macroeconomics, has a long history with contributions by many famous economists. They are nicely summarized at the level of an intermediate microeconomics student in J. W. Conard, *An Introduction to the Theory of Interest* (Berkeley: University of California Press, 1966). Meghnad Desai, "Profit and Profit Theory," in *The New Palgrave: A Dictionary of Economics,* vol. 3, ed. John Eatwell, Murray Milgate, and Peter Newman (New York: Stockton Press, 1987), pp. 1014–1021, provides a succinct review of the history and contemporary controversies on profit. The benefits and disadvantages of the price system in socialist and capitalist economies are lucidly analyzed in Arthur M. Okun, *Equality and Efficiency: The Big Tradeoff* (Washington, D.C.: Brookings Institution, 1975).

Notes and Answers

1. Except for the last two entries, prices were reported by Christie's International to *The Wall Street Journal,* May 19, 1987. The Pontormo and van Gogh were reported in *The*

New York Times, June 1, 1989, and May 20, 1990.

2. The original case, *Green v. Denney and Ford Motor Co.,* was tried in Circuit Court, Multnomah County, Oregon (Case no. A8304-02482) in June 1985. Ford's appeal to the Oregon Supreme Court was denied in January 1988.

3. Obviously, over time, other classrooms can be remodeled and new buildings can be constructed, so, strictly speaking, this a quasi-rent scenario.

4. The rightward shift of the demand curve by 25 leads to a new rental price of $1,750 and a total rent of $175,000.

5. The return to the land underlying the buildings is, for all intents and purposes, a rent, since the land area itself is normally neither increased nor decreased. Consequently, a real estate tax on the land itself could not affect supply.

6. *The Economist* (June 17, 1989, p. 79) reported on a study of executive compensation by Professor Graef Crystal of the University of California at Berkely. "He found that a company's size, its recent performance and the riskiness of its business all helped to predict a boss's pay—but only imprecisely. Most of the variation in pay, in fact, seems to have no explanation but boardroom whim."

7. Had Vashti been willing to lend the entire $100,000 to Abigail—and so consume nothing during the present year—she would have been able to spend $110,000 during the second year.

8. About 40,000; 60,000; and 66,000.

9. Be sure you list the amounts Vashti saves, not the amount she spends. Note, too, that the slope of the budget line $= 1 + i$.

10. An intuitive way of seeing this point is asking yourself, Would I rather receive a payment stream of $1,488,320 as Ted expects or receive it in one lump sum at the end of the first year? Remember that the payment is guaranteed and inflation is assumed to be zero, so there's no risk of default or decline in the purchasing power of the payments.

11. Again, this procedure ignores the fact that the returns flow in over time, not all immediately.

12. In most cases, the decision to invest will be the same whether the $PV = C$ or the $r = i$ criterion is used.

13. About $2.4 million.

14. You will often find interest and rate of return on capital used interchangeably. But they really are distinct concepts and ought not be confused. *Interest* refers to the amount paid by a borrower to a lender, while the *return on capital* is, broadly, the profit rate earned on an investment.

15. Corporate profits are nowhere near 25 to 33 percent, suggesting that the actual rate of return to investment is significantly lower.

16. Professor Crick was questioned under cross-examination on both these points. Might not the estate have earned from careful investment a larger interest rate, making for a higher discount rate, and thus a smaller present value? Might Ms. Green have earned no more than the minimum wage, reducing the value of her future earnings? The defense attorney's summation, by the way, did not challenge Dr. Crick's estimates, and the jury accepted them in calculating the award.

17. Signaling theory, mentioned in Chapter 16, suggests an alternative explanation for student willingness to pay the substantially larger tuition of private institutions. While the education of students attending public colleges may not differ significantly from those attending private colleges and certainly the best graduates of public universities are likely to outperform the average graduates of private universities, it is nevertheless true that the prestige of the better-known private universities rubs off on their students. Employers use the source of the degree as a screening device.

18. Although the opportunity cost of a medical student is low, being merely the cost of someone who has completed a college education, the opportunity cost of a physician who decides to specialize further equals that of a completed, but not specialized, M.D.

19. Among the latter, Toto, Ltd., a Japanese bathroom fixtures company, is marketing a "paperless toilet" that sprays warm water from several directions and then blows warm

air and scent. It also keeps the seat warm in winter and automatically washes the bowl, all for less than $3,000. In the wings is Toto's "intelligent toilet," which will record the protein and sugar levels in the urine as well as blood pressure, temperature, weight, and pulse.

20. Implicit in this view of the profit motive is a belief that public welfare is increased by the introduction of a new product as long as purchasers are willing to pay a price sufficiently high to cover the entrepreneur's cost and profit. This puts Britain's "Dial-a-Poem" in the same category as the U.S.'s "Dial-a-Porn," a view hardly acceptable to all. However controversial this type of normative argument is, an intermediate microeconomics text is not the place for an in-depth discussion of the issue.

21. See Janos Kornai, "The Hungarian Reform Process: Visions, Hopes, and Reality," *Journal of Economic Literature* 24 (December 1986), pp. 1687–1737, for an excellent and readable analysis of an economy that is undergoing reform simply because the Hungarian socialist economic system has failed to deliver.

22. Peter Truell, "Profiteering on Rubber Gloves Suspected," *The Wall Street Journal,* June 9, 1988, p. 6.

VII

GENERAL
EQUILIBRIUM AND
EPILOGUE

The two chapters that compose Part VII pull the textbook together in different ways. Chapter 19 focuses on the interdependence of the product and factor markets. It explains how a change in one market repercusses through other markets and, in doing so, leads to some surprising policy implications. Chapter 20 challenges you to "do it yourself." You've spent a semester mastering microeconomic theory and seeing it applied to many diverse situations. It's your turn now to try your hand. Measure success, however, not by nailing the suggested answers but by approaching the questions with the insight you've developed during the past semester. Zero in on the critical issues, seek sensible approaches, and don't be disconcerted if you can't provide precise solutions. The most interesting questions facing economists have yet to be resolved.

GENERAL EQUILIBRIUM AND ECONOMIC WELFARE

Trade could not be managed by those who manage it if it had much difficulty.
Samuel Johnson (1779)

Tariff: A scale of taxes on imports, designed to protect the domestic producer against the greed of his consumer.
Ambrose Bierce (1875)

Learning Objectives

In this chapter, you'll learn:

- How product and factor markets are interrelated.
- How a change in one market sends repercussions through other markets.
- About the conditions for general equilibrium among consumers, producers, and factor suppliers.
- How to interpret the Edgeworth box in both exchange and production scenarios.
- About the role of the contract curve and its relationship to optimal consumption and production decisions.
- About the efficiency and resource allocation implications of the production-possibilities frontier.
- Why perfect competition in both product and factor markets leads to optimal satisfaction and production, and why monopoly doesn't.
- Why economists both favor and question free-trade policies.

- About the paradoxical conclusions that stem from the theory of the second best.
- About the policy implications of general and partial equilibrium analysis.

Staying Dry

This chapter deals with two distinct yet related topics: simultaneous equilibrium in all markets and efficiency in the market economy. The tie that binds these topics is perfect competition. Economists have demonstrated that simultaneous equilibrium exists when all markets are perfectly competitive and that perfectly competitive markets maximize the economy's efficiency.

Up to this point, the text's overall structure simplified the analysis by artificially breaking up the economic system into product markets (Parts II through V) and factor markets (Part VI). When you read that buyers and sellers together determined the price of goods and services, the text did not bother much with pricing the inputs used in production. Then when you discovered how wages and other factor prices were set, the text ignored, for the most part, the market for the goods and services produced by the factors of production. This chapter puts decision making in the product and input markets together, as befits reality. Consider the following case.[1]

While the disposable diaper has captured 85 percent of the U.S. diaper market, the cloth diaper still hangs around. Indeed, environmentally conscious consumers seem to be among the vanguard of a trend to switch back to cloth. Anything that is likely to raise the price of cloth diapers not only has environmental implications but also directly affects the pocketbooks of parents of infants and the profits of diaper-service companies, which buy over 1 million dozen cloth diapers annually.

The overwhelming bulk of diapers sold to the diaper-service companies is imported from China. The only U.S. manufacturer that has woven cotton cloth into diapers is Gerber Products' Curity brand, whose plant is in Pelzer, South Carolina. Thus, when a quota on diaper imports was proposed, the battle lines were quickly drawn. (The accompanying cartoon wonderfully clarifies the issues.) On the one hand stood Gerber, whose monopoly was being undermined by the imports, and its workers who were directly employed in manufacturing the diapers. They were supported by the textile industry, which advocates quotas on cloth and apparel imports that compete with domestic manufacturers. Presumably, too, disposable diaper manufacturers would not object to import constraints, since the fewer cloth diapers brought into the country, the larger the market for disposables would be.

SOURCE: *The New York Times,* August 17, 1986.

Arrayed in opposition were an amorphous grouping of environmental, consumer, and business interests. The former noted that disposable diapers already accounted for 3 to 4 percent of all solid waste going into the landfills, which were nearing capacity and were unlikely to be supplemented over time. Less competition would mean higher prices for the consumers of cloth diapers, repeating the price hikes of 1987 after temporary quotas were imposed. Diaper services were the third interested party, since higher diaper costs would lead to higher service charges, which would cut into demand. Finally, the men and women employed as launderers, packagers, drivers, and administrative staff in the nation's diaper-service companies would lose out if the quota was imposed.

In short, the proposed change in the rules of the game affected not only the product market for cloth diapers but that for disposable diapers as well. The impact would also be felt by the workers and other input suppliers to both markets. This type of complex interrelationship is grist for the mill of the present chapter.

This chapter begins with a descriptive overview of the interface between product and factor markets, which is followed by a more formal specification of the conditions for simultaneous equilibrium in all markets. The chapter then turns to the second issue: efficiency in the competitive marketplace. The next two sections examine efficiency in consumption and production. You'll then discover that consumers achieve the greatest benefit and that the economy's resources are most efficiently allocated when markets are perfectly competitive. All this leads to a simple conclusion: *An economy characterized by perfect competition will not only reach equilibrium in all markets, but will maximize consumer benefit at the minimum resource cost.*

These consequences of the competitive model form the basis for the applications segment, which is largely devoted to international trade issues. The analogue to perfect competition in an international context is free trade, so you'll examine both free-trade and protectionist arguments. The chapter concludes with some final thoughts about general equilibrium and competitive markets, focusing on some of the complexities that the simple static model ignores. It also reflects on the appropriate use of the broader model of interrelated markets in contrast to myopic models that focus on only one market at a time. Clearly, there's room for both approaches in the analysis of microeconomic policy.

Combining Product and Factor Markets

An Overview

General equilibrium exists when *all* markets in the economy are simultaneously in equilibrium. **Partial equilibrium** refers to equilibrium in a particular market without considering repercussions in other markets.

To give you an initial sense of **general equilibrium** analysis, let's begin by integrating product and factor markets using the **partial equilibrium** analysis of the text. A. Tom Smasher, the nuclear physicist who works in a cyclotron as a supplier of skilled labor to the research project and who earns $85,000 in annual salary, is the same Tom who relaxes in his cabin cruiser on weekends. Tom spends some of his income on fuel, maintenance, nautical supplies, and docking facilities in addition to the usual purchases of the typical family. Tom's neighbor, Sally Saver, has absolutely no interest in boating. Her lifestyle led her to buy $1.23 million in corporate bonds over the last 15 years, which earn for her each year $75,168 in aftertax interest income. Sally spends $12,045 on food, clothing, rent, and utilities and thus participates, albeit thriftily, in a variety of product markets.

In truth, Sally and Tom are no different from most of us. We all wear at least two hats. On the one hand, we are (or will be) suppliers of factors of production. On the other hand, we are demanders of a whole range of goods and services. Similarly, business firms participate in the product market as producers, but are demanders in the factor market. The task of business management is to fashion from the various inputs they acquire products that can be profitably sold to demanders. Figure 19.1 schematically portrays these interrelationships.

Focus on the center illustrations of Figure 19.1. At the far left is Tom, and the line emanating upward represents Tom's demand for boat supplies and food. Projecting downward is a single line, representing Tom's labor supply. Next to Tom stands Sally, from whom lines similarly flow upward and downward. The one going upward represents her demand for food and housing, while the one moving downward is her supply of loanable funds.

Moving to the right now, notice two firms: Chris Craft, which outfits and maintains cabin cruisers, and Sloppy Joe's a neighborhood food em-

FIGURE 19.1   The Market Economy

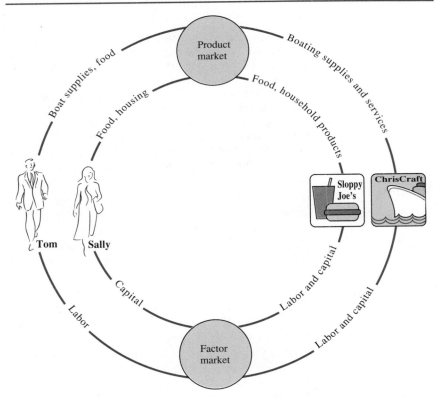

Participants in a market economy are both demanders and suppliers. Individuals supply factors and demand products. Firms supply products and demand factors. The circular nature of the diagram symbolizes the interrelationship of product and factor markets.

porium. Both firms are suppliers of goods and services, represented by the lines going upward. The firms must also be demanders of the production inputs needed to bring their supplies on the market, as indicated by the lines running downward.

Finally, the two circles on the top and bottom of Figure 19.1 represent the product and factor markets, respectively. In the product market, demand for goods and services is brought together with supply. It is here that prices and quantities of products are determined. Analogously, input prices and quantities are determined in the factor market. The circle formed by the figure as a whole is meant to show the interrelationships of the participants in this crude representation of a modern market economy.

You can break into this circle at any point, so let's see what happens if the government, in a wave of financial righteousness, cuts back on grants to cyclotron projects. The impact of this tightness will not be felt immediately, but ultimately Tom will be called in to the director's office and told something like this:

> You know, we lost that $57 million grant we thought we had in our pocket. So, we've been forced to rethink our ongoing projects and revamp our priorities. Unfortunately, the project you've been working on these past years has been downscaled, and we're going to have to cut back on our expenses by phasing it out. Tom, you know how much we all appreciate your valuable contribution. But short of a new infusion of funds, I have to break the unfortunate news that as of the next fiscal year, we no longer will be able to carry you on our budget. It's nothing personal, of course, and we're certainly going to try our best to come up with alternative funding. But I think I owe you this news now, so that you can begin to plan your next steps.

Well, among the first of Tom's next steps will be a reduction of boat expenditures. The demand line from Tom to the product market thins out, a move soon felt by Chris, as Figure 19.2a shows. This drop in demand in the competitive market leads sellers to cut boating supply prices in the product market but nevertheless end up with a smaller quantity demanded and supplied.[2]

But the story can't stop here. If Chris sells less, he's going to order fewer variable inputs—products from his suppliers and labor. Chris will tell Popeye, the most expendable of his stockboys, "This is your last week on the job, Popeye. We just can't use you anymore. But keep in touch; you never know if business will pick up again."

Sketch onto Figure 19.2c the reduction in the demand for unskilled labor. You'll see that the decrease in labor demand brings with it a reduction in wages and a decreased quantity of labor supplied and demanded.

Let's return now to Tom and Sally. Tom understands that the market for physicists in general is likely to be weak for some time and that he'll have to cut back on his standard of living in the long run. But to cushion

FIGURE 19.2   **Market Linkages**

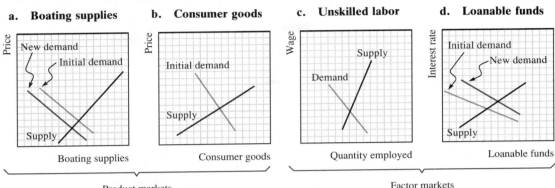

a.   **Boating supplies**   b.   **Consumer goods**   c.   **Unskilled labor**   d.   **Loanable funds**

Product markets   Factor markets

a.   When Tom cuts back on his demand for boat-related expenditures, price and quantity sold decline.

b.   What happens to price and quantity when Sally buys more consumer goods?

c.   How does Popeye's loss of his job affect the labor market?

d.   Tom's decision to borrow leads to a stronger demand, causing interest rates and borrowing to increase.

the impact on his family's lifestyle, Tom decides to borrow some funds from his neighbor. Sally agrees, and the results of the new relationship appear in Figure 19.2d. The demand for loanable funds shifts rightward to represent Tom's additional demand for finance, driving up the interest rate and raising Sally's income as well. Sally's new income enables her both to spend and to save more, whereupon she decides to buy soft drinks rather than continue to drink water from the faucet. And so, when Sally leaves Sloppy Joe's, she's also left a little bit more of her income there as well. Take a look at Figure 19.2b now and draw in the new demand for the products sold in Sloppy Joe's. What happens to price and to quantity demanded and supplied? _____ Of course, everything increases.

Put yourself in Joe's shoes now. He's felt an increase in demand, which will in turn lead him to increase his demand for inventory and other inputs. But because interest rates have gone up and the price of unskilled labor has gone down, Joe will reconsider how he'll handle the new inventory when it comes in. Should Joe buy a new handtruck and make do with his existing labor as he'd been thinking about all along, or should he now tip the scales toward labor rather than capital? Surely, you'd recommend that Joe should substitute the cheaper labor for the more expensive capital. He might just hire Popeye, who wandered in looking for a job as a stockboy.

The story cannot end here, but we will have to leave it for now. You realize that a Pandora's box has been opened. Once you start, the ramifications extend throughout the links that chain together the components of a modern market economy. Anything that affects any demander or supplier in Figure 19.1 will reverberate on others, which in turn will affect still others. We started at an implicit equilibrium. Will we ever again reach a general equilibrium?

Input-Output Analysis: An Application

Are U.S. exports more labor intensive or capital intensive? Since anecdotal evidence suggests that labor is relatively more expensive in the United States than is capital, we ought to be producing and thus exporting capital-intensive products and importing labor-intensive goods and services. Indeed, you could confirm this by eyeballing U.S. exports—from capital-intensive agricultural products to passenger jets and military equipment.

Yet anecdotal evidence can be misleading, so the economist, like the scuba diver, probes beneath the surface. U.S. exports are themselves end products of a vast interrelated production process that consists of millions of components and subcomponents. We must therefore examine the labor and capital intensity of the entire production chain. That requires a general equilibrium approach.

Input-output economics is the Nobel Prize–winning innovation of Wassily Leontief, the Russian-born American economist. This empirical adaptation of general equilibrium theory examines the quantitative interdependence among industries. Table 19.1 reproduces a summary U.S. input-output table for 1977.

Take a look at the row labeled "Manufacturing." In 1977, the manufacturing sector provided agriculture with $26,198 million of inputs; mining with $7,425 million; and so on. It also met the needs of final demanders—consumers, investors, government, and foreign users—to the tune of $578,483 million,[3] so that the total output of the manufacturing sector was over $1.35 trillion.

The columns represent the value of inputs used by that sector. Thus, manufacturing used agricultural inputs worth almost $64 billion, mining inputs in excess of $77 billion, and so forth. The last entry, $1.35 trillion, is the sum of all the inputs used by manufacturing from the other sectors, and is by definition equal to the sum of manufacturing output.

In a pathbreaking application of input-output analysis, Professor Leontief employed his input-output matrix to expose the factor intensity of U.S. exports and imports. He first determined the relative labor and capital proportions that characterized each sector. He then simulated a proportionate increase of $1 million in exports and compared the outcome to an equal rise in the output of U.S. industries that competed with im-

TABLE 19.1   Condensed 1977 U.S. Input-Output Table (Millions of Dollars)

	Inputs							Final Demands	Total Outputs
	Agriculture	Mining	Construction	Manufacturing	Trade and Transportation	Services	Other		
Outputs									
Agriculture	31,930	29	934	63,714	733	4,745	172	27,405	129,663
Mining	275	5,566	2,397	77,704	372	19,794	1,217	−29,295	78,031
Construction	1,383	2,923	303	8,706	7,182	32,058	4,971	206,809	264,334
Manufacturing	26,198	7,425	98,337	517,408	30,714	93,117	3,301	578,483	1,354,983
Trade and transportation	7,463	1,726	28,970	88,262	30,795	27,283	2,274	323,867	510,639
Services	13,056	9,875	20,934	101,615	90,507	188,910	6,226	648,710	1,079,832
Other	355	292	844	10,375	4,050	9,521	492	220,583	246,512
Value added	49,003	50,195	111,615	487,199	344,286	704,404	227,859	1,976,562	
Total inputs	129,663	78,031	264,334	1,354,983	510,639	1,079,832	246,512		

SOURCE: Adapted from Ronald E. Miller and Peter D. Blair, *Input-Output Economics: Foundations and Extensions* (Englewood Cliffs, N.J.: Prentice-Hall, 1985), p. 425.

ports. The increase in final products would cause a chain reaction throughout the matrix. More automobiles would mean greater demand for engines, windows, steering wheels, and so on, which would in turn require more subcomponents as well as transportation, services, and so on. Professor Leontief was thus able to sum up the changes in capital versus labor demands in the various sectors, not only in the end-product category. His startling conclusion: U.S. exports in 1947 relative to import substitutes were labor intensive, not capital intensive![4]

MICROQUERY   Can you see how input-output analysis could be used to determine the economic impact of an arms reduction pact between two countries? Of stricter pollution controls?

General Equilibrium Conditions

General equilibrium exists when the economy is characterized by a consistent set of prices that brings quantity demanded and supplied into equality in all markets. When that occurs, neither consumers, producers, nor factor suppliers have any incentive to change. Let's examine the conditions for such an equilibrium in a stylized microeconomy that consists of two individuals (Jack and Jill), each consuming two products (compact discs and tapes), two firms (CompactDiscMaker, CDM, and TapeFabricator, TF) and two factors of production (skilled and unskilled labor). Let's examine each sector separately.

Consumers.   In a competitive economy, prices of tapes and compact discs will adjust until

1. Jack and Jill together buy all the discs and tapes supplied by CDM and TF.
2. Jack and Jill are each satisfied with their respective purchases of discs and tapes and will not want to buy more of either commodity.

This in turn requires Jack to find his equilibrium by equating his marginal rates of substitution between discs and tapes to their prices and Jill to do likewise. While Jack and Jill need not have identical indifference curves and so will end up with different disc-tape combinations in equilibrium, the following must hold:[5]

$$\text{MRS}^{\text{Jack}}_{\text{disc/tape}} = \text{MRS}^{\text{Jill}}_{\text{disc/tape}} = \text{Price}_{\text{tape}}/\text{Price}_{\text{disc}}$$

Producers.   Consistency requires that (1) the prices paid by Jack and Jill for discs and tapes be those charged by CDM and TF, respectively; (2) the prices are those derived from each firm's maximum profit condition ($\text{MR} = \text{MC}$); (3) the quantity of discs sold by CDM equals the sum of Jack and Jill's individual demands, and so also for TF; and (4) neither CDM nor TF has any incentive to raise its own profits by penetrating the other's market.

You certainly understand that these conditions would hold true if CDM and TF were representative firms in perfectly competitive industries. Then for each firm, $\text{ATC} = \text{MC} = \text{MR} = P$. Price would be forced down to the minimum average cost, and profits would be driven down to a level that deters entry.

Factor Demanders.   Production of both tapes and discs requires skilled and unskilled labor, which are assumed to be hired in perfectly competitive labor markets. Thus, in equilibrium, both CDM and TF face a single wage for each type of labor.

The decisions facing both firms are analogous to those that challenged Jack and Jill: how much of the two factors to acquire, given their respective productivities. And just as Jill's strong preference for discs over tapes would mean she would be willing to pay more for discs, so, too, skilled labor's greater productivity in disc manufacture would mean that CDM would be willing to pay more for skilled than for unskilled labor.

Does that mean that CDM and TF will use the same amount or even the same proportion of the two grades of labor? Not necessarily. Just as Jill's preferences may differ from Jack's, so, too, may the production functions of tape and disc manufacture diverge.

In short, equilibrium for the firms as factor demanders requires the following:

- Each firm would face identical wages (w) for each skill category.
- Each firm would employ skilled (sl) and unskilled (ul) labor so that its $\text{MRTS}_{ul/sl} = w_{sl}/w_{ul}$.[6]
- The combined quantity demanded of both CDM and TF for each labor type would equal the quantity supplied.

You realize that these conditions are met if the labor markets are characterized by perfect competition.

Factor Suppliers.   The workers who supply the two grades of labor will discover that labor market equilibrium occurs when: (1) the quantity supplied of each type of labor equals the totals demanded by the two firms; (2) each individual worker is indifferent to working for either CDM or TF, since they both pay the same wage rate for a given skill; and (3) all workers are satisfied with their levels of skill. That is, the salary differentials do not induce workers to trade off leisure time for skill acquisition.

General Equilibrium.   When the consumer, producer, and factor markets are perfectly competitive, the resulting prices in each market will lead quantity supplied to equal quantity demanded. The prices paid to the factors of production along with factor productivity will determine production costs for each product, which in turn will give rise to the supply curve of each competitive producer. Factoring in consumer demand for each product will determine their equilibrium prices and market-clearing quantities. Presto—general equilibrium! But realize that general equilibrium theory is more than a specification of the conditions under which it will arise. Perhaps most useful is its focus on the interrelated nature of the economy. Change any single element, and the permutations reverberate throughout the economy.

Consumer Equilibrium in an Exchange Economy

The existence of general equilibrium under conditions of perfect competition raises another issue: Is perfect competition efficient? Although you've run across this question in the static models of individual markets, the time has come to ask whether it's true for the economy as a whole. We'll begin with a consumption-only economy.

Beneficial Trade

Our story begins after producers have already manufactured 100 compact discs and 200 tapes. Somehow Jack has acquired 40 discs and 80 tapes, while Jill owns 60 and 120, respectively. The dimensions of the Edgeworth[7] box in Figure 19.3 are determined by the total amount of goods

FIGURE 19.3   Jack and Jill Trade

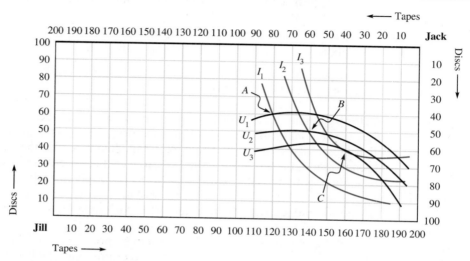

With both Jack and Jill finding themselves initially at *A* on U_1 and I_1, respectively, trading tapes and discs with each other can improve each one's satisfaction. If Jill trades 20 discs to Jack for 40 tapes, both reach the highest indifference curve possible (I_3 and U_3, respectively) from voluntary cooperation. Equilibrium occurs at the tangency of the indifference curves, since further trading will move both to lower indifference curves.

available, so that the rectangle's height equals 100 discs and its length 200 tapes. Jill's initial position at *A* is found by measuring discs upward from the lower left corner and tapes rightward. Jack's endowment at *A* is measured from the upper right corner, with discs moving downward from that origin and tapes leftward. Notice, too, that *A* represents the intersection of two indifference curves, one from Jill's *I* set, which radiates from the lower left origin, and one from Jack's *U* set, which stems from the upper right.

Could Jack and Jill improve their position by trading? Let Jill offer Jack 10 discs in exchange for 20 tapes. If this trade were consumated, Jack and Jill would find themselves at *B*, placing both on a higher indifference curve. In fact, they'll continue to trade until one or the other can no longer benefit from exchange, which occurs when Jack and Jill's indifference curves are tangent to each other at *C*. See for yourself by asking Jill to give up some more discs or Jack one more tape. They'll move to a lower indifference curve! At tangency, Jack and Jill have reached a **Pareto consumption optimum.**

Take a look at Jill's equilibrium for a moment. Jill has been trading off one disc for two tapes, or a relative price (P_{tapes}/P_{discs}) of 1/2. You could, if

A **Pareto consumption optimum** is achieved when it is impossible to increase the welfare of one individual without reducing the welfare of some other individual.

you wish, draw in a budget line with a slope ($\Delta Q_{discs}/\Delta Q_{tapes}$) of 1/2 tangent to Jill's final position. (See Figure 19.4.) That, of course, would be consistent with Jill's $MRS_{disc/tape} = P_{tapes}/P_{discs}$. It's equally true for Jack, since Jack's highest reachable indifference curve, U_3, is also tangent to the budget line. If the price ratios were set in a perfectly competitive market, then the Pareto optimum condition of joint tangency is also consistent with the consumer sector general equilibrium condition specified earlier, namely:

$$MRS_{disc/tape}^{Jack} = MRS_{disc/tape}^{Jill} = Price_{tape}/Price_{disc}$$

Repeated Starts and the Contract Curve

A consumption contract curve is the locus of tangencies of two indifference curve maps.

Jack and Jill's final Pareto optimal position contrasts sharply with their initial endowments. But we can start with any initial distribution of discs and tapes and then determine whether one or both can gain from exchange. Using the same reasoning as before, trade will prove beneficial until two of Jack and Jill's indifference curves are tangent. Figure 19.4 displays a series of such tangencies and the **consumption contract curve,** the line that connects all the Pareto optimum positions.

FIGURE 19.4   The Contract Curve

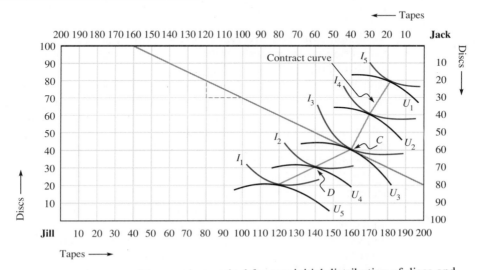

A Pareto optimum position can be reached for any initial distribution of discs and tapes as long as Jack and Jill trade. The contract curve connects these joint tangencies.

Three propositions follow:

1. *Any position off the contract curve is less than Pareto optimal.* That's true since by moving toward the contract curve one party can gain without the other losing. Hence, the combined satisfaction of both parties will increase.

2. *The contract curve is neutral about the distribution of wealth.* Is *D* better than *C*? If you're Jack, *D* is better, while Jill prefers *C*. Moreover, the initial endowments maybe inequitable from some viewpoints. We might have strong personal feelings about how wealth and income ought to be distributed in society. But the contract curve cannot by itself validate or nullify any such belief. It takes the distribution as a given.

3. *There is no unique price ratio implicit in the contract curve.* Price ratios between discs and tapes can be computed at any tangency position, as you can see by calculating relative prices at point *D* and comparing them to *C*.[8]

Producer Equilibrium

The box diagram and the contract curve can be applied to factor markets and production as well as to consumption. Some interesting implications follow.

Optimal Factor Utilization

We'll stick with our two types of labor, which are the only inputs in the production of both tapes and discs. Figure 19.5 begins with an initial supply of both skilled and unskilled labor used by the two manufacturers. That supply is once again given by the dimensions of the box, which shows that 300 units of skilled and 450 units of unskilled labor are employable.[9] Figure 19.5 depicts two sets of isoquants. The isoquants of Tape-Fabricator rise from the southwest corner, with the three depicted showing production of 6,000, 12,000, and 20,000, respectively. The numbers on CompactDiscMaker's isoquants increase as the isoquants move from the northeast to the southwest. The isoquant tangencies are connected by a **production contract curve.**

A **production contract curve** is the locus of tangencies of two isoquant maps.

Visualize a market in which the two producers can trade unskilled for skilled workers and an initial position, *S*. Now draw isoquants for CDM and TF that intersect at *S*. You can see that CDM would relinquish some unskilled workers in exchange for more skilled employees, a proposition acceptable to TF. Both would reach the contract curve at *T*.

Examine the *T* position more closely. Let's assume that skilled labor costs $140 a day and unskilled $40 a day. Further, assume that both firms

FIGURE 19.5   Factor Market Optimum

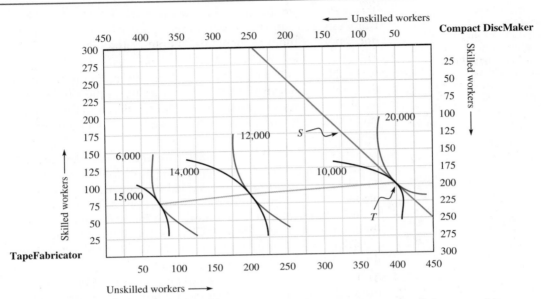

The contract curve, which connects isoquant tangencies, represents Pareto optimum positions for tape and disc production. Any move away from the contract curve reduces the output of one or both producers in an inefficient manner.

can spend $30,000 on labor. Calculate first TF's outlays at T, where the isocost curve is tangent to its 20,000 isoquant. As you can read off the grid, TF uses its $30,000 to employ 100 skilled and 400 unskilled workers. It will manufacturer 20,000 tapes at an average cost of $1.50 per tape.[10] TF spends its available funds to achieve the highest output possible and simultaneously optimizes its use of skilled and unskilled labor.

Is this an equilibrium to CDM as well? You can show it is by filling in the following grid.

	Amount of labor demanded by CDM	Labor cost
Skilled		
Unskilled		

Total labor cost _____

Average average cost _____ [11]

A number of conclusions emerge:

A **Pareto production optimum** occurs when increasing the output of one producer reduces the output of some other producer.

1. T *is a **Pareto production optimum.*** Because CDM's and TF's isoquants are tangent to each other, neither industry can produce more without reducing the output of the other.

2. *Maximum production is achieved for the given distribution of labor.* Neither CDM nor TF would gain by reducing the input of the more expensive skilled workers and using the savings to employ more unskilled laborers. That would undo the isoquant-isocost tangency of each, reducing production without reducing total costs.

3. *The distribution of labor is not identical across industries.* At T, CDM uses four skilled laborers for each unskilled worker while TF uses only one fourth of a skilled worker per unskilled employee. That follows from the construction of the isoquants, which arbitrarily assumed a more skill-intensive production function in the disc industry. Clearly, the optimal usage of inputs depends not only on factor costs but also on factor productivity.

4. *At* T, *the labor market is in equilibrium.* Since each firm pays the same wage to each category of labor, workers are content where they are. Were this not so, workers would move to the firm that pays better, which would change the distribution of workers among our two producers. Also,

5. *At* T, *the average cost of a disc is double that of a tape.* While this relationship is true only at one point of the contract curve, it will become significant later in this chapter, so keep it in mind.

The Production-Possibilities Frontier

The production-possibilities frontier (PPF) plots the maximum achievable production of any combination of products for a given quantity of inputs and production functions.

The production contract curve suggests that when resources are fully and efficiently utilized, an increased production of discs can be achieved only by manufacturing fewer tapes, and vice versa. This production trade-off between discs and tapes is depicted in the **production-possibilities frontier (PPF)** of Figure 19.6. The combinations of disc and tape output that constitute Figure 19.5's contract curve are transposed directly to Figure 19.6, so that *T* in Figure 19.5 corresponds to *C* in Figure 19.6.

Any combination of tapes and discs that lies inside the frontier—and thus is not on the contract curve—indicates inefficiency. At *M*, for example, production of either tapes or discs or both could be increased without decreasing the output of the other. The frontier also distinguishes between the attainable and the unreachable. A point such as *N* that lies outside the PPF represents a production impossibility, since there aren't

FIGURE 19.6   The Production-Possibilities Frontier

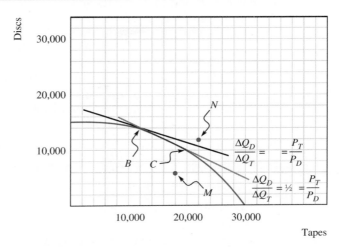

The production-possibilities frontier, which separates
achievable quantities of disc and tape production from the
unattainable, is concave to the origin, indicating an increasing marginal rate of transformation.

sufficient resources in the economy at the moment to attain those production levels.

The Shape of the Production-Possibilities Frontier.   The changing trade-
off between tapes and discs is evident in the bowed-out shape of the PPF.
The slope at *B* is 1/3, indicating that three tapes will be gained for a unit
decrease in disc production. The one tangent to *C* has a slope of 1/2,
indicating that one disc less yields two more tapes. This relationship,
known as an increasing **marginal rate of transformation (MRT),** has an
economic explanation that is rooted in the different production functions
for the manufacturer of discs and tapes.

The **marginal rate of transformation (MRT)** measures the amount of one product that must be sacrificed in order to increase output of a second product by a single unit.

Consider the following scenario. Seno E. Val and her brother, Heerno
E. Val, who jointly own TF and CDM, realize that disc production requires more skilled workers per unit of unskilled employee than does tape
manufacture. They know that switching, say, four skilled employees and
one unskilled co-worker from disc manufacture to tape production means
that they're removing an efficient combination from the disc unit and will
be using it less effectively in tape production. (The partners might be
forced to use some of the skilled workers at jobs that do not utilize their
talents.) Production would rise in the tape industry and fall in the disc
industry. Hence, the MRT must be negative. The more tapes, the fewer
discs.

But an *increasing* MRT claims more. When disc production takes place at *B* and the industry has loads of skilled labor, transferring some resources to tape production would entail a relatively small disc production loss for an increase in tapes. The slope at *B* of 1/3 indicates that one less disc yields three more tapes. But when the E Vals have made further inroads into their disc labor force, as at *C*, further cuts in disc production would be more expensive in terms of lost output. With the slope at *C* at 1/2, transfers of labor from disc to tape manufacture means that the loss of one disc yields them only two additional tapes.[12]

Pulling It Together: General Equilibrium and Pareto Optimality

The production-possibilities frontier offers a menu. It says nothing about where production will take place, because it relates only to supply. But our indifference curve analysis allows us to reintroduce demand.

Figure 19.7 reproduces Figure 19.6 but adds an indifference map that somehow amalgamates the entire community's preferences for tapes and discs and renumbers the axes to allow for additional producers. You can see that *M* is not an equilibrium because production could increase and

FIGURE 19.7   Consumer-Producer Equilibrium

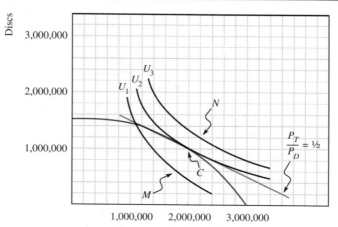

At a price of $3 per disc and $1.50 per tape, consumers and producers reach a Pareto optimum. Consumers demand and producers supply 1 million discs and 2 million tapes, which is consistent with efficient production and the maximum satisfaction of consumers.

enable the community to reach a higher indifference curve. Similarly, N cannot be an equilibrium, since the two industries cannot produce enough product to reach N. Where, then, is equilibrium? _____

You're right if you wrote C. It is both attainable and is the highest indifference curve that can be reached. It is Pareto optimal in resource allocation. The community attains the products it wants in the quantities it desires without any waste of resources.

Perfect Competition and Pareto Optimality

Pareto optimality in consumption, production, and resource allocation will be reached if the economy is characterized by perfect competition. Let's examine each sector to see why this is true.

Producers. Competitive producers are in equilibrium when for each Price = Marginal cost = Average cost. Hence, when the average cost of producing a disc is $3 and that of a tape is $1.50, as you saw in connection with T in Figure 19.5, then the marginal costs must be $3 and $1.50, respectively, as well. But in competitive equilibrium, marginal cost and price are equal, so that the price per disc must be $3 and the price per tape must be $1.50.

In a more general sense, if for CDM

$$P_{disc} = MC_{disc}$$

and for TF

$$P_{tape} = MC_{tape}$$

then dividing the latter by the former leads to the following:

$$MC_{tape}/MC_{disc} = MRT = P_{tape}/P_{disc}$$

In our case, the price ratio is 1/2, indicating that discs are twice as expensive to produce as tapes.

Finally, if all this is true for such representative firms as CDM and TF, it must be equally true for all disc and tape manufacturers. If each of our firms represented 2 percent of their respective industries, then total output would be 1 million discs and 2 million tapes.

Consumers. We've already established that Jack and Jill were in equilibrium when their respective marginal rates of substitution equaled the price ratios. But if the competitive price ratio is 1/2, they're in equilibrium at C in Figure 19.4. Moreover, all 10,000 consumers, clones of Jack and Jill, end up by demanding 1 million discs and 2 million tapes at those prices, which is precisely the total production of the two industries. Thus, C in Figure 19.7 is the competitive equilibrium for consumers as well.

Factor Suppliers. Since C is identical to T on the contract curve of Figure 19.5, both CDM and TF are in equilibrium with respect to the demand for skilled and unskilled labor. Moreover, given competitive markets for skilled and unskilled workers, the ratio of skilled to unskilled wages will be reflected by the slope of the isocost line, which is tangent to each firm's isoquant, so that $\text{MRTS}_{ul/sl} = w_{sl}/w_{ul}$. The total supply of both skilled and unskilled workers is absorbed by TF and CDM and, by extension, the other firms in both industries.

To summarize: When all product and factor markets are perfectly competitive, the economic system reaches a Pareto optimum that can be described in a series of equations:

$$\text{MRS}_{\text{discs/tapes}} = P_{\text{tapes}}/P_{\text{discs}} \tag{1}$$

$$\text{MRT} = \frac{\text{MC}_{\text{tapes}}}{\text{MC}_{\text{discs}}} = \frac{P_{\text{tapes}}}{P_{\text{discs}}} \tag{2}$$

$$\text{MRTS}_{ul/sl} = w_{sl}/w_{ul} \tag{3}$$

Equation (1) is the Pareto efficient condition for consumers. Competitively set prices enable them to reach the tangency position on their highest indifference curves. Equation (2) states that product prices are proportional to product costs, so that producers cannot gain from switching into each others' markets. Moreover, in each product market,

- MC = MR to achieve maximum profit for the competitive producer.
- MC = P, so that MB = MC to attain optimal resource allocation.

Equation (3) declares that inputs are being used optimally; their productivities are proportional to the costs. Shifting resources from one industry to another, or varying the proportions of skilled to unskilled labor, will only reduce output for a given expenditure. Finally, the proportion of the skilled to the unskilled is consistent with the optimum preferences of the workers.

Take this one step further. If perfect competition enables the economy to reach Pareto optimality and if, as we've seen earlier, general equilibrium prevails when prices are such as to clear all markets, then this Pareto optimal position is also consistent with general equilibrium. The economy under perfect competition, Adam Smith's "invisible hand" incarnate, permits us to paraphrase Voltaire's Doctor Pangloss: A competitive equilibrium result is the best of all possible worlds.

Monopoly Misallocations

The efficiency and satisfaction-maximizing solution of the perfectly competitive market system may perhaps be most clearly visualized by briefly considering a contrast: monopoly in the product market. Let's assume that TF is the only manufacturer of tapes and can successfully bar all potential entrants. As a monopolist, TF would restrict output and raise price. Jack and Jill would change their spending patterns, buying fewer tapes and more discs. Similar changes would take place in factor markets, as the excess labor in the tape industry shifted into disc production.

Figure 19.8 reproduces Figure 19.7 to contrast the two cases. When TF now raises the price of each tape to $6 and cuts production to 1.2 million tapes, the price ratio changes from 1/2 to 2, reflected in the budget line passing through *B*. Consumers now optimize with respect to the new budget line and find their tangency at *B*, acquiring 1.2 million tapes and 1.4 million discs. But they're now on U_1, not on the higher U_2.

Note the discrepancy between the price ratio facing consumers and the marginal cost ratios facing the manufacturers. Tapes are cheaper to produce but more expensive to buy. The MRT at *B* equals 1/3, showing that it costs only a third as much to produce a tape as it does to manufacturer a disc. Yet consumers face prices that make a tape twice as expensive as a disc. Clearly, resources are not being put to their best use. Or to put it simply, a movement from *B* back to *C* would not endanger the firms'

FIGURE 19.8   Competition versus Monopoly

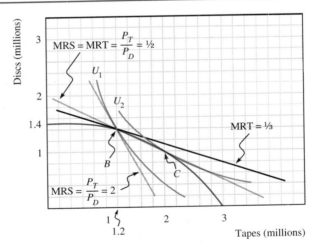

With a higher price for tapes imposed by the monopolist, the new price ratio facing consumers is $P_T/P_D = 2$. Their optimal position is the tangency at *B*, which is also consistent with the cutback in tape production by the monopolist. In contrast with the perfect competitive output at *C*, *B* indicates too many resources devoted to disc production, too few devoted to tape production, and a lower level of consumer satisfaction.

efficiency—since both *B* and *C* lie on the PPF—but would increase consumer satisfaction. Only two components of the triple crown of Pareto optimality—consumption and productive efficiency—are attained when monopoly is present. Optimal resource allocation falls by the wayside.

Applications: International Trade

Whether Jack and Jill are nationals of a single country or residents of two countries is irrelevant to the analysis of Figure 19.3. Both parties benefit from trade as they rid themselves of products they value less in exchange for those they value more. International trade as well as trade between regions of the same country becomes more complicated by introducing not only different demands but also different production capabilities. Some countries or regions are more suited for certain types of production than others are either because of climatic conditions; natural endowments of minerals, labor force qualities, capital abundance, or sophistication; or suitable technology.

The Benefits of Trade

Consider the simple two-country model depicted in Figure 19.9. Urania and Venusa are two bordering nations assumed to be initially self-sufficient in the production of both food and clothing. Their production-possibilities frontiers are based on competitive product and factor markets. To avoid clutter, the indifference maps are not pictured here. But we shall assume that for Urania the tangency of an indifference curve and the frontier occurs at 30 tons of food and 60 million clothing units, while for Venusa the tangency is found at 60 tons of food and 30 million clothing units. As both parts of the figure indicate, this is the pretrade equilibrium in each nation. Notice, too, a price line drawn in at this tangency. Food is half as expensive as clothing in Urania and twice as expensive as clothing in Venusa.

Suddenly, isolation ends. Venusans rush to Urania to buy the cheaper food, just as Uranians stream to Venusa to buy the less expensive clothing. Both food and clothing prices adjust until a new price ratio, represented by the $P_C/P_F = 1$ lines in both diagrams, emerges. Of course, a shift in relative prices affects production in both countries. The new production equilibrium in Urania is shown in Figure 19.9a at 60 tons of food and 40 million units of clothing, while in Figure 19.9b, Venusans produce 60 millions units of clothing and 40 tons of food.

Work out an apparently strange consequence of trade:

Before trade, total production of food = _____

After trade, total production of food = _____

Before trade, total production of clothing = _____

After trade, total production of clothing = _____

By permitting each country to produce more of the product it produces most cheaply, total production expands.

And if total production increases, so, too, must total consumption. Consumers are no longer bound by the production-possibilities frontier of their own country, nor are they subject to their pretrade price ratios. Instead, they face a single price ratio of 1 : 1 no matter where they reside, permitting them to consume at the tangency of their indifference curves with the world price ratio. Figure 19.9a assumes that such a tangency occurs at the coordinates of 70 million units of clothing and 30,000 tons of food. Uranian consumers are clearly in a better position posttrade than pretrade, since they're consuming as much food as before and more clothing. In order to achieve the new consumption equilibrium, Uranians will

FIGURE 19.9   The Benefits of International Trade

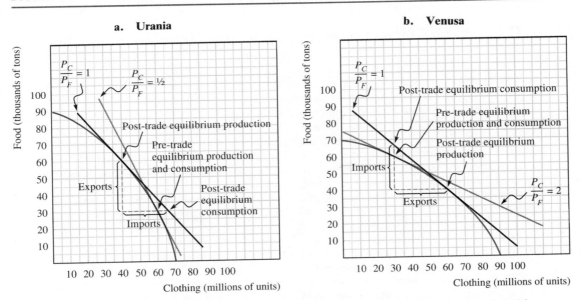

Without trade, Urania produces and consumes 30,000 tons of food and 60 million units of clothing, while Venusa produces and consumes 60,000 tons of food and 30 million units of clothing. With trade, leading to new purchasing and production opportunities and consequently changes in relative prices, Uranians produce 60,000 tons of food, export half, and import 30 million units of clothing. The imports, when added to domestic clothing production of 40 million units, provide Uranians with 70 million units of clothing. Trade has increased their consumption by 10 million clothing units without any decrease in food consumption.

You can trace out the mirror image of this story for Venusa to demonstrate that Venusans will end up with more food and no less clothing.

have to export 30 tons of food and import 30 million units of clothing. (Examine Venusa to see its gain as well as its exports and imports. Not surprisingly, it is the mirror image of Urania.) MicroBits 19.1 discusses the potential gains from trade to the United States if worldwide constraints were to be reduced.

Resisting Free Trade

Trade must be mutually beneficial, for were it not so, voluntary exchanges would not take place. But that does not mean trade benefits everyone. Consider workers in the Uranian clothing industry. Because clothing was relatively expensive, skilled clothing laborers would earn higher wages. Shifting them to food production, which values their skills less, means that their wages will fall. The opposite happens to workers with skills in stronger demand.

MICROBITS 19.1

GATT, The Uruguay Round, and the Gains from Trade

Among the measures used by many nations to pull themselves out of the depression years of the 1930s were home market protection from imports combined with export-promotion programs. Nations soon recognized the consequences of such beggar-thy-neighbor actions, since the exports of one nation were the imports of the others. All together could not export more and import less! In 1947, 23 nations joined in a General Agreement of Tariffs and Trade (GATT), which pledged them to undertake multinational negotiations to improve the flow of international trade and established a small permanent secretariat. GATT has grown to almost 100 nations, which account for over 80 percent of world trade, and has conducted seven rounds of trade-liberalizing multinational negotiations since its inception. But GATT's mission is not yet completed. Indeed, international trade is far from free.

The latest series of negotiations began in

1986 in Uruguay. Aside from further reducing tariffs and other impediments to trade, especially in agriculture and textiles, the Uruguay Round seeks to form international commitments to protect intellectual property such as patents and copyrights, bring services such as telecommunications under GATT, set up international standards for foreign investment regulations that impede trade indirectly, and integrate the developing economies more fully into GATT.

Since vital national interests are involved, the bargaining has been tough and prolonged. The United States has pushed for further liberalization to aid American exporters. But consumers will benefit as well. The Office of the U.S. Trade Representative, which is charged with conducting GATT negotiations, has estimated that cutting tariffs and other impediments to trade by a third would boost U.S. GNP by $1.1 trillion (in 1989 dollars) by the 21st century.

The presence of noncompetitive markets and frictions also contributes to resistance to free trade.

The Absence of Perfect Competition.   Trade damages domestic firms that were earning excess profits. If, for example, the monopoly of Uranian clothiers was destroyed by the invasion of Venusan clothing imports, the excess profits of the former would be eliminated. And if Uranian clothing workers were sharing in these profits, both owners and employees would oppose clothing imports.

Frictions.   In the real world, resources do not shift effortlessly from one industry to another, from one skill category to another, or from one region to another. Clothing manufacturers will not readily junk their machinery and become food producers. Dress cutters will not effortlessly master the skills needed to repair complex farm machinery, nor will clothing designers be easily converted into farmhands. Moreover, neither cutters nor designers will simply pick themselves up from urban manufacturing centers to move to rural farm regions. To be sure, in the long run such transitional frictions will work themselves out. But in the interim, which may take years, the costly transition leads those involved to resist change.

The Diaper Case

We can now return to the battle over import quotas on diapers. Those now using cloth diapers—parents who buy them directly or who rent them from diaper services—as well as all those engaged in the diaper-service industry opposed import restrictions. They stood to lose from the subsequent reduced quantities and higher diaper prices. The domestic cloth diaper producer and its workers, who would benefit from the higher prices they could charge, favored quotas.

General equilibrium contributes to the analysis of this conflict in two ways. First, by linking factor and output markets, we understand better why not only Gerber management and stockholders favored quotas, but also why workers in the diaper industry and the textile industry in general sided with the company. Similarly, those arrayed in opposition were not only the firms but also their employees and suppliers. An import quota on cloth diapers would impose direct gains or losses on all these parties.

Second, competition leads to Pareto optimal conditions in both production and consumption, resulting in economywide efficiency and maximum satisfaction. Thus, noncompetitive practices stemming from domestic monopolies or from protection against imports moves the economy away from Pareto optimality. The distortion of the price structure caused by stifling competition warps decisions in industries that are only peripherally related or not related at all, leading to resource misallocations throughout the economy.

If so, what might a neutral observer suggest? The initial step appears to involve tallying up the gains and losses to those parties most directly affected by the new policy. The analyst might then employ cost/benefit criteria and oppose a quota if the consequent losses to those most involved exceeded the gains to the beneficiaries. This antiquota position would be buttressed by the knowledge that the rest of the economy would suffer additional losses caused by the quota-induced distortions.

The diaper case seems straightforward on these grounds: only 60 people worked in the Gerber diaper manufacturing operation. The worst-case scenario would find these individuals unemployed. But their income loss would be mitigated by unemployment insurance as well as by a special safety net for those unemployed through import competition. At the other end, price increases jeopardized the incomes of the 40,000 workers of the diaper services, not to speak of the cost to consumers who bought the diapers directly. Given this lopsided cost/benefit calculation, it's disturbing that at the end of 1988, China's diaper exports to the United States were limited to 40 percent of its 1988 exports. But there's a happy ending to this case. The quotas weren't effective, and in 1992 Gerber abandoned its role as a vertically integrated diaper manufacturer. Instead of weaving its own cloth, it will buy cotton cloth and sew it into diapers. Diaper purchasers will benefit as Gerber's production costs fall.

Dumping

Dumping occurs when a product sells for less abroad than it costs to be produced at home.

Should imports be permitted to enter the United States when their prices in the United States are below production costs in the exporting country? In truth, this practice, known as **dumping,** is illegal. U.S. law counters dumping by imposing tariffs that increase the prices of imports to the level of their domestic competitors.

While your gut feeling might be sympathetic to a price-equalization policy, your intellect might raise some questions. If the Japanese are willing to sell computer chips or minivans at a loss, why shouldn't American computer manufacturers and potential van buyers be permitted to take advantage of cheap import prices? If trade is beneficial because it reduces some prices and so enables consumers to reach higher indifference curves, as Figure 19.9 indicated, wouldn't still lower prices be even better? Should we cater to the selfish interests of domestic producers and their suppliers who benefit from the protection afforded by antidumping legislation? Wouldn't equalizing prices reduce U.S. consumer utility?

The static case against antidumping policies seems strong, yet we should distinguish between temporary and more lasting dumping strategies. Had Japanese van manufacturers overestimated demand and so overproduced, their selling off their excess inventory in the U.S. market is a temporary phenomenon. Such transient dumping would seem to impose few, if any, adverse domestic long-run consequences and might not warrant retaliation. But that does not hold true when dumping is part of a marketing strategy whose aim is to drive domestic producers out of business. If the dumper then gains control over the market and forces domestic prices up, the long-run costs to domestic consumers might well outweigh the short-run benefits.

A country employs **strategic trade policy** to gain advantage over its trading partners.

A similar consideration conditions the arguments over **strategic trade policy.** Some economists who sympathize with free trade still favor protectionist broadsides to blast open anti-import barriers. For example, U.S. suppliers have accused Japan of fencing in its own industries while taking advantage of easy entry into the U.S. market. U.S. trade negotiators have threatened to retaliate, even though protectionist measures harm the U.S. economy. (MicroBits 19.2 describes another meaning of strategic trade policy.)

The Theory of the Second Best

Strategic trade policy suggests that an apparently worse outcome may be superior to a seemingly better one if the best cannot be attained. Of the three options U.S. policymakers face in the previous case, clearly the best is barrier-free trade between Japan and the United States. Second best, at least from the U.S. consumer's viewpoint, is a U.S. economy open to imports even if the Japanese economy remained closed. Worst are barriers that limit trade between the countries. Yet strategy may dictate pursuing the worst policy. To be sure, if the strategy succeeds, the outcome turns out to be the best. But there's no guarantee the strategy will work. Nor is there any assurance that the future gains will outweigh the losses imposed on U.S. consumers during the period of protectionism.

A similar type of argument applied to static general equilibrium theory was developed by Professors R. G. Lipsey and Kelvin Lancaster in their classic article, "The General Theory of Second Best."[13] They demonstrated that when some of the Pareto conditions are unattainable in some markets, trying to achieve them in others could turn out to be poor public policy. Consider the following two examples.

Monopoly versus Competition.   The scene opens on a raisin bran monopoly, which, by definition, violates the Pareto optimal conditions. Although the best solution is to restore competition, that is impossible for some unknown reason. At the same time, oat cereal manufacturers are subject to government price control. The issue: Should the government set price for oat cereal at the $MC = P$ competitive level?

The obvious answer is yes, since any other price would cause a misallocation of resources. A higher price, for example, would reduce the quantity demanded of oat cereal and result in fewer resources devoted to

---

MICROBITS 19.2

Strategic Trade Policy and the New International Economics*

What happens to the argument for free trade when at least some international markets are imperfectly competitive? Will a hands-off government trade policy remain optimal when some industries are characterized by substantial economies of scale or if expensive technology, accompanied by extensive research and development efforts, has significant positive spillovers into other sectors of the domestic economy? Strategic trade policy explores such cases and concludes that free trade is not necessarily the best policy.

---
* This is the title of a book edited by Paul Krugman (Cambridge, Mass.: MIT Press, 1986). The arguments are summarized in Krugman's *The Age of Diminished Expectations: U.S. Economics Policy in the 1990s* (Cambridge, Mass.: MIT Press, 1990), Chapter 9, "Free Trade and Protectionism."

Consider a Cournot duopoly market for space probes consisting of a French company and an American company. The reaction curves of Figure 13.5 (p. 449) can be applied here, as they are in the accompanying figure. Aeronautica U.S. assumes that Aerospatiale France is interested in maintaining market share, but does not know the production plans of its rival. The same is true for Aerospatiale France. The reaction curves of each define their responses to the possible output of the other, leading to a Nash equilibrium that splits the market equally.

When Aeronautica U.S. suddenly announces its intention to capture a larger share of the international market, the French company ignores the threat. Since the duopolists have reached a Nash equilibrium, the French manufacturer understands that as long as it doesn't change its output, the old output remains optimal for the U.S. firm.

---

oat cereal production. But consider that very argument as it relates to raisin bran. The higher oat cereal price would divert some individuals to the bran market, which would respond by expanding raisin bran output. Since too few resources were devoted to the monopolized raisin bran market, the increase in production would improve resource allocation. Under appropriate cost and demand curves, the improved resource distribution in raisin bran manufacture exceeds the poorer allocation in oat cereal output.

Average versus Marginal-Cost Pricing. The theory of the second best might well justify average cost pricing in natural monopolies rather than the apparently allocation-optimizing marginal-cost pricing. (See pp. 416–17.) The subsidy that must be provided to the natural monopoly under marginal-cost pricing entails collecting revenues elsewhere in the economy. It just isn't clear that taxing some goods and services and thus

MicroBits 19.2 continued

Let the U.S. government now intervene and offer Aeronautica a subsidy for every space probe exported. This change in the rules of the game makes Aeronautica's threat credible, shifting its reaction curve rightward. The new Nash equilibrium leaves it with a larger share of the market at the expense of its rival. Hence, intervention benefits U.S. industry.

Similar arguments are also used to justify government involvement when developing a new technology is so expensive and the world market so limited that only one firm will survive. Once the first firm undertakes serious entry moves, it deters potential competitors, and so will capture for itself and its nation the entire world market. Strategic trade policy again makes the threat credible, and assures the monopolization of the international market by its national.

Strategic trade policy theoreticians have exercised extreme caution concerning the practical impact of their message. They are aware of the problems of identifying the industries to support, the possibilities of retaliation, and the difficulties of measuring potential gains. Moreover, they are wary of becoming the intellectual justification for self-interest groups that will pervert strategic trade policy for their own narrow purposes.

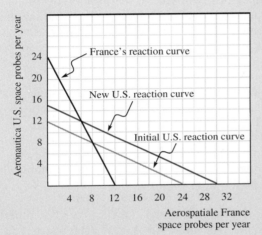

changing prices and the distribution of resources will be a better solution than not subsidizing the natural monopoly and not collecting an equivalent income through taxation.

Final Thoughts

Some Questions

The model elaborated in this chapter was well behaved. Indifference curves and isoquants were all convex to the origin and the production-possibilities frontier was concave. However, at many points in the preceding chapters you came to grips with less manageable assumptions. You faced consumers with corner solutions or firms subject to economies of scale. The general equilibrium model is rich enough to adjust to such conditions. But the policy conclusions that emerge may not necessarily coincide with those derived from the simple model outlined in this chapter. The presumed superiority of perfect competition is the most evident victim, which should not come as a surprise. You saw in numerous contexts that perfect competition can provide inferior solutions. Consider again some examples.

Economies of Scale.   What happens when economies of scale characterize production? In such an industry, competition will be doomed, since the lower costs of the larger firm will enable it to undercut its smaller rivals. But the resulting monopoly will not adhere to the Marginal benefit = Marginal cost outcome of the competitive marketplace, since that would lead to prices below average costs. Perfect competition is no longer Pareto optimal.

Externalities.   A similar conclusion emerges when some industries exhibit external economies or diseconomies. The Pareto optimality conclusion based implicitly on the identity of private and social costs breaks down in the presence of externalities. Unless such externalities can be internalized, advocating a competitive market economy will mean that too few resources are devoted to industries with external economies and too many to industries demonstrating external diseconomies.

Efficient Monopoly.   Those who find substantial virtues in imperfect competition will also quibble with the optimality of perfect competition that emerges from general equilibrium theory. The static model fails to consider that oligopolies stimulate beneficial research and development or reduce the risk of introducing new products. Insofar as these arguments are valid—and that's still being debated—the Pareto optimality implications of perfect competition are undermined.

Frictions, Asymmetric Information, and Uncertainty.   Finally, the static model of competitive equilibrium that optimizes welfare and efficiency assumes away a host of issues that deserve to be considered when employing it as a source of policy recommendations. Change rarely proceeds smoothly. The transition difficulties as one policy regime replaces another benefit some at the expense of others. But even ignoring the distribution of gains and losses, it cannot be assumed that the long-run benefits of change more than compensate for its losses if the transition costs are also included. In addition, information gaps that give rise to asymmetric information and the uncertainty that exists abundantly in the real world mean that the fundamental prerequisites of the perfectly competitive model are practically unattainable.

In short, the perfect competitive model can still serve as an economic policy ideal. But the general equilibrium theory's conclusion of Pareto optimality under perfect competition on welfare and efficiency grounds is undermined. If the stringent set of assumptions that generate the stark contrast between perfect and imperfect competition do not apply, then the conclusions can rightfully be questioned. At this juncture, an agnostic position cannot easily be dismissed.

A Practical Evaluation: General versus Partial Equilibrium Analysis

Positing that, in the long run, general equilibrium can be achieved under certain conditions brings to mind Lord Keynes's famous dictum: In the long run, we're all dead. Nevertheless, general equilibrium warns us against reaching hasty conclusions based on considering a part rather than the whole.

General equilibrium theory insists that we pay attention to the manifold repercussions of even the slightest economic change. Sure, imposing pollution controls on coal users will raise the price of high-sulphur coal and thus decrease its demand. But the imposition will also raise the demand for cleaner-burning fuels, which will change the distribution of incomes—shifting incomes away from coal companies to oil corporations, from domestic producers to foreign producers, from coal-producing states to oil-supplying regions. When you realize that West Virginian coalminers have different consumption patterns than do oil drillers living in the Persian Gulf, that Arab oil sheiks buy Rolls Royces while Oklahomans acquire stretch limos, you begin to mosey along the general equilibrium trail. But you've got to follow it further, for every one of these changes will affect demand for all kind of products. And do not ignore the suppliers to each of the industries. Not only will coal mining decline, but so, too, will demand fall for the manufacturers of equipment used in coal mining—heavy machinery of various sorts, behemoth earth movers, and coal railcars. At the same time, resources used in oil production—offshore drilling rigs, pipelines, helicopters—will experience greater demand.

That is not to assert that every economic problem must be examined from a general equilibrium viewpoint. Surely, as one moves further away from the source, the impact lessens, and for practical purposes can be ignored. (Will imposing antipollution measures on the coal industry significantly affect the demand for photographers?) Indeed, if not for this reason, the theory of the second best would virtually do away with most types of policy intervention. The skill of the microeconomist will be manifest in realizing where to draw the line between impacts that ought to be considered and repercussions that may safely be disregarded.

Summary

Market linkages lie at the center of general equilibrium theory. Although partial equilibrium analysis that separately analyzes consumer, producer, and factor markets facilitates understanding, in reality all markets are interrelated. As a stone thrown into a calm pond sends ripples throughout the water, so will the slightest change in one market spread out through the economic system. If the price of computer modems falls, not only will the quantity of modems demanded rise, but so, too, will the demand for computers and telecommunication services, the income of computer equipment manufacturers and retailers, the wages of modem manufacturing workers and installers, and all the individuals and firms who directly or indirectly experience the initial rise in demand. Others, such as the manufacturers of faxes or mail services and those dependent on them, will experience a decrease in demand. And the ripple expands, touching more and more participants in the economy.

General equilibrium theory develops a methodology for analyzing these ripples. In the two-person, two-firm, two-factor case discussed in this chapter, the equilibrium conditions can be specified once the principle of Pareto optimality is accepted. If every participant in the economy is willing to exchange, produce, or supply resources as long as he or she stands to gain, then it becomes possible to find a mutually compatible series of equilibrium points for all market participants. Using the tape and compact disc markets of the chapter for one more time, the equilibrium conditions are as follows:

$$\text{MRS}_{\text{discs/tapes}} = P_{\text{tapes}}/P_{\text{discs}} \qquad (1)$$

$$\text{MRT} = \frac{\text{MC}_{\text{tapes}}}{\text{MC}_{\text{discs}}} = \frac{P_{\text{tapes}}}{P_{\text{discs}}} \qquad (2)$$

$$\text{MRTS}_{ul/sl} = w_{sl}/w_{ul} \qquad (3)$$

Equation (1) states that consumers achieve indifference curve–budget line tangency, which is their optimum. Equation (2) states that product prices are proportional to product costs, so that producers cannot gain from switching into each others' markets. Equation (3) declares that inputs are being used optimally; their productivities are proportional to their costs. Shifting resources from one industry to another or varying the proportions of skilled to unskilled labor will only reduce output for a given expenditure. Finally, the proportion of the skilled to the unskilled is consistent with the optimum preferences of the workers.

When all markets are characterized by perfect competition, market prices will reflect demand and scarcity, and the result will be a Pareto optimum. Thus, the market prices facing consumers in equation (1) are the lowest possible prices suppliers could achieve and still remain in business. Moreover, as equation (3) indicates, producers allocate scarce resources to those functions that use them most effectively. Equation (2) finally shows that firms have no incentive to switch from their product to those of other industries. Graphically, the community indifference curve will be tangent to the production-possibilities frontier, demonstrating that not only are resources optimally allocated in line with resource costs and consumer demands, but that consumers can't do any better.

Pareto optimality in a competitive environment lends strong support to the notion of free trade and economists' general opposition to trade barriers. Eliminating impediments to trade promotes international competition and enables consumers in the trading countries to take advantage of the production efficiencies of their respective nations. To be sure, economists recognize that not everyone benefits from removing tariffs, quotas, and other barriers. Nevertheless, most economists would insist that those advocating protectionist policies demonstrate convincingly that free trade will cause extensive and permanent damage to the economy. Otherwise, economists would say, pursue a free-trade policy.

The policy implications of the theory of general equilibrium, especially as it supports a procompetitive policy, have been questioned on a number of grounds. The theory of the second best admits the superiority of a procompetitive policy throughout the economy. But if competition is not universal, then a piecemeal procompetitive policy may lead to a poorer allocation of resources than one that promotes some noncompetitive results. For instance, the theory of the second best suggests the paradoxical conclusion that resource allocation will improve in some circumstances if the government imposes a tax on a competitive industry rather than on a monopoly. Moreover, competition is also not always appropriate when markets are characterized by economies of scale, externalities, frictions, asymmetric information, or uncertainty. As in most cases, economic policy is pragmatic.

Economists generally favor competition over monopoly. But most are intelligent enough to avoid dogmatic solutions. Instead, the professional economist will examine each problem or policy recommendation within its own framework, evaluate its likely consequences, and only then reach a conclusion.

Chapter 20 expands on the theme of applying economics to actual problems. It then invites you to practice what this textbook has preached.

Key Terms

Consumption contract curve
Dumping
General equilibrium
Marginal rate of transformation
Pareto consumption optimum

Pareto production optimum
Partial equilibrium
Production contract curve
Production-possibilities frontier
Strategic trade policy

Review Questions

1. *a.* What is the essential difference between general and partial equilibrium analysis?
   b. Analyze the impact of increasing the federal minimum wage according to both general and partial equilibrium analysis. Are your conclusions different?

2. *a.* Why is the tangency of two consumer indifference curves a Pareto optimum?
   b. Could a Pareto optimum position still be reached if the government transferred assets from one trading partner to the other? Explain.

3. Examine the accompanying box diagram. Then,

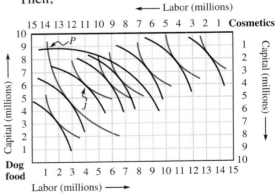

a. Explain why resource allocation is better at *J* than at *P*.

b. Find the relative price of capital to labor that will lead to an equilibrium at *J* under conditions of perfect competition among inputs.

c. Generate a contract curve.

d. Show that a coalition of capital owners will lead to inefficient resource allocation.

4. *a.* Why is the production-possibilities frontier concave to the origin?

b. Why is the economy's optimum position at the tangency of the community's indifference curve with the PPF?

c. Explain how a change in community preferences will upset the previous equilibrium and how a new equilibrium will be restored.

5. *a.* Demonstrate and explain why trade among countries with different factor endowments benefits both countries.

b. If trade is beneficial, why do many countries impede imports?

6. Two trade-related articles appeared on a single day in 1991 on a single page of *The Wall Street Journal*. One was headlined "European Nations Face U.S. Duties on Paper Exports," and related that certain European firms had been dumping paper used for magazines and catalogs. Anti-dumping duties of 25 to 41 percent were going to be imposed. The second article dealt with Japan's opening up ever so slightly its virtually closed rice market.

a. Since lower-cost paper should help hold down magazine prices, why should the U.S. government impose tariffs on cheap paper imports?

b. Who would benefit and who would lose from the tariffs?

c. Since Japanese consumers pay substantially more for domestically grown rice than for imported rice, why is this new policy expected to allow rice imports equal to only 5 percent of the domestic demand?

7. *a.* Explain the theory of the second best.

b. Sunscreen lotions are controlled by an oligopoly that cannot be dismembered by antitrust prosecution. On the other hand, beach umbrellas are produced in the competitive marketplace. The government intends to raise revenue by imposing a tax. Which industry should it tax according to the theory of the second best? Explain.

8. Does the general equilibrium model convincingly demonstrate that competition is the optimal type of industry structure? Prove your thesis.

Food for Thought

1. You and your sibling receive the same allowance from your parents. Could you achieve Pareto optimality if

a. Trade among siblings were prohibited?

b. Trade were permitted? Would the equilibrium you would achieve if trade were permitted be superior to *C* in Figure 19.3?

2. Tape production is characterized by a fixed production function, while compact disc production can employ factors in variable proportions.

a. Draw a box diagram indicating these production functions and indicate the resulting contract curve.

b. Draw the production-possibilities frontier.

3. *a.* Draw the PPF for two industries that are characterized by economies of scale.
   b. Find the Pareto optimum position for production and consumption given the above and a normally shaped community indifference curve.
4. *a.* Find the new equilibrium in Figure 19.7 after production-enhancing technology is introduced only in the disc industry.
   b. How can you explain that in this new equilibrium, more tapes will be produced even though tape production technology was not changed?
5. U.S. businessmen opposed to a trade agreement with Mexico that would further open the domestic trade market to Mexican exports note that (*a*) Mexican labor costs are substantially lower than U.S. labor costs and (*b*) Mexican firms do not have to comply with the stringent and costly environmental protection regulations that are imposed on U.S. producers. What counterarguments might a free-trade economist suggest?

6. The figures below show two straight-line production-possibilities frontiers. Urania is a large country, Venusa a small one.
   a. Can Venusa and Urania gain from trade? (Assume that the new world price ratio is identical to Urania's pre-trade ratio.)
   b. What and how much will each import from the other?
7. How would you measure the benefits and the costs of a 5 percent decrease in the tariff on sugar? Be sure to distinguish between the short- and long-run impacts.
8. Explain strategic trade policy in terms of game theory.

a. **Urania**

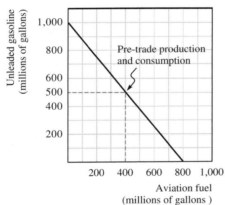

Aviation fuel
(millions of gallons)

b. **Venusa**

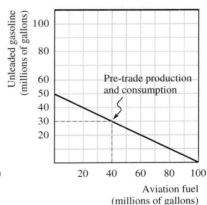

Aviation fuel
(millions of gallons)

Suggested Readings

Francis M. Bator, "The Simple Analytics of Welfare Maximization," *American Economic Review* 47, no. 1 (March 1957), pp. 22–59, while more sophisticated than the title implies, is the granddaddy of all geometric treatments of general equilibrium theory.

General equilibrium theory is a staple of international trade theory, so any international trade text such as Dominick Salvatore, *International Economics* (New York: Macmillan, 1991), will provide both analytic and policy-oriented treatments. The case for free trade is ably presented for the nontechnical reader by Jagdish Bhagwati, *Protectionism* (Cambridge, Mass.: MIT Press, 1988).

Notes and Answers

1. Adapted from "Diaper Import Quotas Under Fire," *The New York Times,* May 31, 1988, pp. D1,2.
2. You might swallow the substantial changes in demand and supply depicted in this scenario more readily by imagining that each participant represents a group of people. Also, note that the underlying assumption in each of these instances is that only the particular curve being singled out shifts; the others are unchanged.
3. The sum of the Final Demand column as well as the Value Added row is GNP.
4. The Leontief paradox has engendered two opposing responses. One accepts Leontief's fundamental conclusion. Indeed, Faye Duchin, in "Technological Change and International Trade," *Economic Systems Research* 2, no. 1 (1990), uses input-output data for 1963 to 1977 to indicate the paradox still flourished. The other rejects Leontief's results, arguing that they stem from technical flaws and unacceptable assumptions. (For example, the matrix assumes only two factors of production, and each factor admits no quality differences.)
5. Check back to Chapter 4 if you're not sure of this condition.
6. Check Chapter 7 if you need to be refreshed.
7. Francis T. Edgeworth was an outstanding 19th-century British economist.
8. The slope at D is $\frac{1}{3}$.
9. Two assumptions should be made explicit. First, producers' funds suffice to absorb the available factor supply, and, second, demand for their products justifies their employing the available supply.
10. $\frac{TC}{Q} = \frac{\$30,000}{20,000} = \$1.50.$
11. CDM uses 200 skilled and 50 unskilled workers, costing \$28,000 and \$2,000, respectively. This total labor cost of \$30,000 for the 10,000 discs produced means that ATC equals \$3. Notice that together CDM and TF use all the available labor.
12. The same analysis would apply if workers were switched from tape to disc production. Try it.
13. R. G. Lipsey and Kelvin Lancaster, "The General Theory of Second Best," *Review of Economic Studies* 24 (December 1956), pp. 11–32. Although the article is highly technical, its central theme and at least some of the details can be handled by students who have reached this point in the text.

20 EPILOGUE: TESTING YOUR SKILLS AS A MICROECONOMIST

The biggest single advantage that economists have is their way of thinking. It comes naturally to them to think in terms of alternatives and to trace the implications of alternative lines of action within the logical framework of an economic system. They are alive to the interaction of economic forces within that system and hence to the full economic impact of policy decisions.

Sir Alec Cairncross (1984)

All's well that ends well.

Shakespeare

Learning Objectives

In this chapter, you'll be exposed to:

- A brief restatement of the lessons of the text, with its focus on analysis, quantification, and relating to the real world.
- A number of actual cases whose understanding requires you to exercise the microeconomic mode of thinking that you've been exposed to during the semester.

The Last Straw

Having gone through a tough semester of intermediate microeconomics, you've almost surely been forced to focus on each chapter as an individual entity. The only opportunity to see part of the forest rather than the trees has been at exam time, where perforce you've had to assimilate material from a number of chapters. Nevertheless, you've probably not been able to afford the luxury of extracting some of the key lessons that all economists share and that distinguish them from other social scientists. Instead of suggesting that you review the entire course again during your leisure time—which you certainly are eager to do—both altruism and efficiency warrant devoting a few pages to save you the time and trouble.

This chapter rests on the assumption that students want to walk away from a course with something valuable and useful for the future. That's certainly true about economics students, if for no other reason than they want their money's worth. This final chapter challenges you to think about a number of economic issues as economists would. As in real life, some issues are trivial and others are important. Hopefully, all will help you see the economics involved clearly.

The Lessons of the Text

Although economists tend to be skeptics, they do agree about many things. They certainly share the basic approach to economic issues, the mastering of which may well be the most important contribution of a microeconomics course. As you have seen repeatedly throughout this text, economists analyze, test, and try to reach practical conclusions. Analysis involves conceiving a theory and then following it through to its logical consequences. These conclusions, however, are most frequently characterized in qualitative terms, such as, "When price rises, quantity demanded will fall." In some instances, statements such as this suffice. Most often, however, the theory will prove far more useful if quantitative estimates are provided, for example, "The price elasticity of demand is −1.3." That's where empirical investigations come into play; they clothe the naked theory in numbers. Finally, while a good number of economic theorists keep their heads in the intellectual clouds, doing theory for theory's sake, most economists use economics to provide answers to real-life issues. In order to do that, they must appreciate that economic investigations, both analytical and empirical, rarely provide the incontrovertible truth.

Analysis

Economic analysis provides its practitioners with a method of thinking about issues. Its three key stages are (1) simplification, (2) specifying alternatives within the framework of objectives, and (3) evaluating alternatives in terms of their targeted goals.

Simplifying.   All theory is a simplification of reality. The theorist focuses on the elements thought to be significant and downplays those believed less important. That is why, as you saw in Chapter 19, economists are satisfied on the whole with the partial equilibrium approach rather than the more encompassing general equilibrium framework.

Specifying Alternatives. Simplification is a trait shared by all theoreticians, be they physical or social scientists. Perhaps the most characteristic feature of economic thinking is the profession's focus on *alternatives*. An economist always conceives of a range of options in analyzing or evaluating issues. The profit-maximizing firm, for example, considers the type of product it should produce, the level of output it should set, and the combination of inputs it should use. Municipal administrators searching for additional revenue evaluate options, too: increase real estate levies, sales taxes, or license fees; borrow the funds from local banks or from the bond market; use political clout to obtain additional funds from the state or federal government; or, reversing direction, eliminate the spending projects that mandated the extra funding in the first place.

Evaluating. Each alternative has a different outcome. While some policymaker—a senior corporate executive, an individual entrepreneur, a civil servant, or a political leader—normally makes the final decision, the economist's task is to lay out and evaluate the merits and demerits of the choices.

In this process, the economist concentrates on the *marginal*. An economist normally disregards the past, about which nothing can be done. Her eyes are to the future. It's *marginal* cost and *marginal* revenue or *marginal* benefit that matter. That a business invested only last year in a machine with an expected service life of five years is irrelevant if a competitor is acquiring a still more modern and cost-effective piece of equipment that will undermine the existing price structure.

Examining the marginal is the beginning. The economist also requires evaluation criteria. In some instances, the objective is framed in terms of dollars and cents: maximum profit, minimum cost. In cases where a pure monetary criterion is inadequate, economists frequently turn to the *cost/benefit* approach, which was used in this text in connection with environmental issues. The economist examines the costs of each option (including the crucial *opportunity costs*), compares them to the benefits, and reaches educated conclusions that are set before the decision-making authority.

Will sound economic advice always prevail? Not necessarily. To follow through with the municipal authority example, an economist may well point out that the least costly way of raising extra revenue, taking all economic considerations into account, is to increase real estate taxes by 5 percent. Nevertheless, the mayor may opt for borrowing the money. In light of the forthcoming election, he fears the political consequences of an immediate tax hike more than the impact of a costly bank loan, which has less of a direct effect on the voters' pockets.

Testing Economic Theory

You understand that qualitative answers rarely help in evaluating alternative courses of action. For centuries, economists were the social scientists who were number-oriented. They have always tried to "prove," or at least buttress, their theories by reference to readily certifiable facts. And their evaluations perforce involved quantitative expression. Contemporary economists have become far more sophisticated in using numbers. Not many decades ago, an economist would have been quite satisfied to discover a negative relationship between sales of various-size firms and their costs of production. He would have felt confident in concluding that the industry in question was characterized by economies of scale. No longer today. Studies of economies of scale use sophisticated multiple regression techniques. Econometricians seek to discover the quantitative link between cost and size while explicitly accounting for the influence of other forces that contribute to cost differences between firms.

Econometrics is in many ways the hallmark of contemporary economics. Some econometricians operate on the cutting edge of this specialty, devising ever better methods of distinguishing between hypotheses, testing theories, and forecasting. Others are users rather than innovators. They apply econometric techniques to a broad spectrum of issues, seeking the crucial quantitative estimates. Thus, oil industry econometricians play around with fuel demand models, while economists working for regional authorities attempt to predict demand for airport facilities by projecting future travel demands. Public-policy-oriented economists examine the impact on environmental pollution of various control schemes, the effect on various industries or regions of tariff-reduction policies, the competitive impact of alternative tax regimes, the financial reserves needed to keep medicare on a fiscally sound basis, and so on.

Few economics majors are likely to make a career out of econometrics, either as theoretical or practical econometricians. That objective is even more remote for those of you not majoring in economics. Turning you into such specialists was not the purpose of providing an econometric example whenever practicable. Instead, the goal was to convince you that when you're thinking about an economic issue and have done the necessary mental analysis, your next step should turn in the direction of quantification.

Realize, however, that neither economic theory nor econometric evidence is likely to prove conclusive on any specific issue. Theory, because it abstracts, can point out directions and likely consequences, but it can never take into account all the practical exigencies of a specific case. Econometric results are based on past data, and no one can honestly say the future will be precisely like the past. Nor will the result of an average apply to a particular case. A bit of skepticism is always healthy.

The Practical

You are certainly aware by now that economic principles can be applied to a variety of actual problems. On the one hand, microeconomic theory permits us to understand, evaluate, and reach conclusions. (Yes, raising the tax on beer is likely to reduce drunken driving. No, imposing controls on entry will not bring prices down.) On the other hand, these very same applications point out the complexity of the real world, which dictates that theory be applied with appropriate caution.

Two elements that complicate reality are related to *information* and *uncertainty*. Much of the standard work in microeconomic theory assumes that every participant in the economy has internalized all the relevant information needed to reach the best decisions. That obviously is not true. Contemporary economic theorists have recognized this weakness and in recent years have devoted a great deal of effort to information issues. The importance of search costs have now been recognized in all areas of microeconomic theory. Signaling theory, which suggests how we devise shortcuts in order to economize on the costs of acquiring information, has become a useful adjunct to the analysis of search. Finally, *asymmetric information* plays a critical role in understanding the real world. Economists realize that when some market participants are better informed than are others, their actions can be expected to reflect that edge.

Uncertainty characterizes our entire life. We rarely know the consequences of our own actions, much less the outcomes of actions by others. Even sure bets don't always turn out as expected.

Finally, in dealing with the practical consequences of economics, remember to distinguish between immediate and subsequent effects. The distinction between the *short run* and the *long run* cropped up throughout the text. Often the short-run outcome is reversed in the long run. For example, higher state corporate taxes may raise government revenues in the short run. But if they drive sufficient enterprises out of business or induce them to move to other states, tax income will actually fall.

It's important to realize that while both the short run and the long run matter in some cases, often the practical course involves focusing on one time horizon to the exclusion of the other. It depends on the problem at hand and the viewpoint adopted. For example, a planner of pension strategies will fashion a diversified portfolio that will increase its value over decades; current stock price fluctuations are really irrelevant. On the other hand, a speculator who moves in and out continuously may have a horizon as short as a quarter of an hour; his short run is truly short. In fact, U.S. corporate managers have been contrasted unfavorably with their Japanese counterparts over this very distinction, the latter praised for their long-run view and the former blamed for their preoccupation with the short run.

If you were asked to summarize the approach of the economist to economic issues, you could succinctly state the following:

* Seek the essential issues.
* Analyze and evaluate the alternative options, remembering the importance of the marginal.
* Estimate the quantitative impact of the various courses of action, not forgetting opportunity costs.
* Be wary of precision. Instead, try to ascertain and calculate the potential impact of the many unknowns that might upset your conclusions.
* Be cognizant of the time frame within which you're operating.

Applying Economic Thinking: Practical Microeconomic Reasoning

The next few pages pose a number of practical issues. Use your semester's exposure to microeconomics to analyze them. (The idea is to understand the issues, not to draw diagrams. Sometimes diagrams will prove helpful, but they're an aid, not the objective.) The cases all appear first; you'll find some suggested answers following. Note, however, that rarely will there be a unique answer, so if your own analysis doesn't coincide with that offered here, don't take that to mean you're necessarily wrong. In this instance, the challenge lies in playing the game, not in winning it. Try, however, to understand why your answer differs from the one given.

You should adopt a dual viewpoint when examining the cases: (1) the perspective of the individual, be it the consumer, the firm, or the factor supplier or demander; and, where appropriate, (2) the impact on society, considering efficiency, welfare, and income distribution.

1. Rewarding Good Grades. *Behavior modification* is a fancy term psychologists coined to describe techniques of reward and punishment. Our parents seemed to know intuitively that the "carrot and stick" method could induce us to behave as they wished.

In January 1988, Cleveland public schools began a behavior modification experiment that encompassed all 32,000 pupils in grades 7 to 12. For each grade of A, a student earned $40; for each B, $20; and for each C, $10. The money was held for the student until graduation, when it could be applied either for college or job-training expenses. Private donations to fund the program designed to reduce the school dropout problem had already reached the $5 million mark by late 1987.

Evaluate the likely success of this scheme.

2. Repairing the Old Car. Your '83 Firebird has passed the 70,000 odometer mark, and it's beginning to feel its age. Indeed, your mechanic diagnosed the sounds you were hearing as a likely $600 transmission repair job.

Should you repair it?

Businesses, of course, face similar problems all the time in terms of equipment repair versus replacement. What decision criteria might they want to employ?

3. Supply-Oriented versus Demand-Inhibiting Policies and the Drug Trade. The crack epidemic manifests itself through all economic and social strata, with costs that extend beyond the harm individuals do to themselves. Violent crime is the addict's means of financing his habit. Banks become victims of cash-laundering schemes, while legitimate businesses are taken over by organized crime. The law enforcement apparatus becomes suspect as corruption becomes endemic. Yet despite all the federal and local resources designed to slow down imports and arrest pushers, barely a dent has been made in the drug trade.

The revenues of the industry are immense, reaching into the billions of dollars annually. In terms of structure, the cocaine industry appears to be oligopolistic on the manufacturing and importing side, with monopolistic competition characterizing the distribution end. With the price elasticity of demand being about -0.06, a reduction in supply by just 1 percent would cause price to rise by 16.67 percent. You understand that such a policy would actually *increase* the profits of the drug suppliers and enable them to devote more resources to circumvent the supply constraints. It would also force addicts to steal more and more often.

Is there an alternative? Could demand-inhibiting policies provide a more effective solution? (You might sketch out a supply and demand diagram and examine the implications of both supply- and demand-limiting policies.)

4. Public Library Revenues. The free public library is a tradition throughout America. The libraries are funded from general public revenues, having virtually no independent sources of income. (Some do charge a user fee for best-sellers, and virtually all impose a fine for overdue books, but such revenues are the proverbial drop in the bucket).

Why not charge borrowers on a per item basis? If you do opt to levy fees, how would you decide a pricing policy?

5. Keeping Cool. Landlords of rental apartments in the United States typically provide tenants with refrigerators and ranges. The gas and/or electricity used is normally paid for by the tenant, which has led to a curious anomaly.

A more electricity-efficient refrigerator requires more insulation, which makes it more expensive to purchase than a less efficient appliance. But the costs of the inefficiency are not borne by the landlord. While tenants would prefer a cheaper-operating if more costly refrigerator, the incentive structure facing landlords induces them to buy the less expensive refrigerator.

Can you devise a method for reconciling the interests of the two parties most immediately concerned so that everyone benefits?

Do you also see that the costs of the existing incentive structure affect not only the landlords and their tenants?

6. Drug-Selling Physicians.   Physicians prescribe medicine; should they sell it to their patients, too? A congressional bill introduced in 1987 that would have barred doctors from selling the prescriptions they recommend was supported by a number of druggist associations. They argued that patients need independent advice on drugs and that drug-selling physicians face conflicts of interest. The Federal Trade Commission opposed the measure as a restriction of competition. What do you think?

7. The Landlord's Rental Dilemma.   You own a shopping mall that is 95 percent occupied. A potential tenant for the vacant space, which has now been unrented for half a year, offers to lease the space for $4 a square foot, a 20 percent discount from the usual $5 per square foot that you've charged all the other tenants.

Should you accept the offer?

You might consider an answer based on the following advertisement by a major hotel:

Introducing the Late-Night Countdown Package: The Later You Check In, the Less You Pay

	Check in from:
8 P.M.	$80
9 P.M.	$70
10 P.M.	$60
11 P.M.	$50

8. Airport Security.   Airport security has become a growing concern as more people fly and as weapons and bombs become increasingly difficult to detect. Although standard security procedures in the U.S. include X-raying all hand baggage and passing individuals through metal detectors, enforcement varies from airport to airport, from airline to airline, and from time to time. Some experts have recommended more stringent security measures, including visual as well as X-ray inspection of both carry-on and shipped luggage and personal inspection of passengers.

What are the economic issues involved?

How it worked

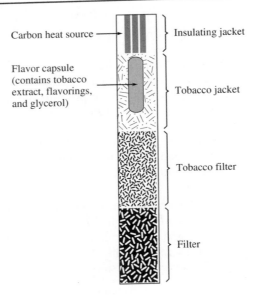

Carbon heat source

Insulating jacket

Flavor capsule
(contains tobacco
extract, flavorings,
and glycerol)

Tobacco jacket

Tobacco filter

Filter

The carbon heats, but does not burn, the
tobacco jacket and the flavor capsule to
produce a ''smoke'' that is cooled by
passing through a tobacco filter and then a
conventional filter.

9. Premier Goes Up in Smoke.   The illustration is a cutaway of Premier,
the smokeless cigarette introduced in 1987 by RJR-Nabisco after seven
years and $300 million of research, development, and test marketing. The
impulse was clear. Both antismoking sentiment and damage suits for lung-
cancer deaths related to smoking were on the rise. In addition to these
general industry problems were RJR's projected falling sales. Smokers of
its leading brands—Camels, Winston, and Salem—were concentrated
among older and blue-collar Americans, a demographic group that was on
a downtrend. Premier was to provide the pleasures of tobacco without the
fatal drawbacks, and so recapture RJR's declining share of the U.S. cigarette market.

   Alas, Premier met strong consumer resistance. As one distributor
commented, ''Premier is a great idea. But it has a lousy taste.'' Part of
that problem stemmed from the fact that Premier had to be lit with a high-
quality butane lighter, as buyers discovered when reading the four-page
instruction booklet that accompanied each pack. Moreover, more than a

quick puff was needed to ignite the cigarette; the smoker had to puff and puff to get Premier started. (Wags quickly called this "the hernia effect.") And while Premier was advertised as a "cleaner smoke . . . substantially reducing many of the controversial compounds of regular cigarettes," RJR never forthrightly claimed that Premier was not cancerous. To add insult to injury, the very antismoking groups who were expected to endorse Premier actually opposed it, arguing that it was an untested drug. The 25 percent price premium over regular cigarettes didn't help either. On February 28, 1989, after just five months of test marketing, Premier was withdrawn.

How can a major U.S. corporation—its 1988 tobacco sales revenues exceeded $7 billion, commanding about a third of the U.S. cigarette market—flop so badly?

10. The Minimum Wage and Unemployment.   George P. Brockway is a liberal businessman who headed W. W. Norton publishers before he retired and became a columnist for *The New Leader*. The following sentence appears in his April 3–17, 1989, article headed "Minimum Wage vs. Maximum Confusion":

> Anyone who bothers to look at the record, however, will find that employment has risen in seven of the eight years when the minimum wage has been raised; and the one year employment fell (1975) was a time of severe recession when the drop was expected for other reasons.

Has Brockway discovered a rising demand curve for labor, or is he dissembling?

11. Insider Trading.   It is against the securities law of the United States for an insider to trade on the basis of "private information." While the precise definitions of *insider* and *private information* are still being tested in the courts, the principle is clear. An individual who has information that could affect the security prices of a particular company as a result of some relationship with the company—a high-level corporate executive, a secretary to such an executive, an attorney who is privy to corporate secrets, a printer who has possession of a corporate announcement in the course of the publication process—may neither directly nor indirectly profit from that information. Nor may such information be passed for profitable speculation by others. The SEC and the Justice Department may act to impose both criminal and civil penalties upon the violators of these statutes, as they successfully did in a series of insider trading cases during the late 1980s.

Equity considerations aside, are such laws apt to increase the efficiency of security markets?

12. Patents and Copyrights.   Albert Einstein was a clerk in the Swiss patent office. But short of finding employment for latter-day Einsteins, are there societal purposes served by giving an individual or a firm exclusive use of a product, process, or creation?

If, for argument's sake, you insist that patents are desirable, how would you determine the number of years for which a patent should be granted?

13. Monetary Policy. As the central bank of the United States, the Federal Reserve fulfills its responsibility for macroeconomic control by varying the quantity of money and interest rates in the economy. But interest movements do entail microeconomic consequences as well. What might they be? Should the Fed be cognizant of and concerned with such microeconomic impacts?

14. Faculty Unions. The faculty members of the college you attend may be members of a labor union. Chances are, however, that they're not, since at the end of the 1980s, less than a third of all faculty members were unionized. This poses the following question: If labor unions coalesce the weak individual power of faculty into a united economic bloc, why have so many faculty members worked against their apparent own best interests?

15. Art for Art's Sake. Chapter 18 opened with a list of prices paid for various works of art. Certainly, the high price for art and other collectibles reflects the demand for such rare works. Nevertheless, not all demand reflects the desire of the final purchaser, be it an individual, a corporation, or a nonprofit institution such as a museum, to enjoy the artwork. To some extent, and perhaps even primarily, art is bought because it will appreciate and can, after some years, be sold at a higher price. In other words, while demand determines the price, the price also determines the demand. Is there a way out of this circularity?

Suggested Answers

1. Rewarding Good Grades. The goal is specified: reducing the number of dropouts. Since conventional educational methods had failed to motivate sufficient students, Cleveland tried incentives based on monetary rewards directly related to performance. The idea is analogous to an employer rewarding workers for higher productivity. It might work!

But two questions need to be raised in connection with this program.

Is the $10 increment for each higher grade a sufficient motivator? Will the D student really expend a great deal of effort to raise his grade to a C for a mere $10? Clearly there is some amount of extra money that will induce sufficient extra effort, but the precise marginal sum remains an empirical unknown. The Cleveland experiment may enable us to discover the most effective dollar motivator.

Could the $5 million spent on inducements be more effectively used in other ways? Would hiring additional guidance counselors or devising more stimulating teaching methods prevent greater numbers of dropouts at the same cost? The answer to this question would depend on the information on types of retention programs currently in use.

By the way, *The New York Times* (January 22, 1989, p. A36) reported that the first two semesters of the experiment saw individual payments ranging from $10 to $400, but did not provide even a hint of the program's success.

2. Repairing the Old Car.   Repair versus replace decisions are shrouded in uncertainty. Even when the repair effectively resolves the problem at hand, you're always left wondering, What will go wrong next? and When will it go wrong?

In all such cases, both age and intensity of use have to be taken into account. Replacing the transmission on a heavily driven vehicle is worthwhile only if you can expect other major parts to last a while. But at 70,000 miles, you begin to worry about the need for a valve job, replacement of the exhaust system, rebuilding of the carburetor, and so on.

Costs, too, have to be taken into account: Repair costs on the one hand and replacement costs on the other. If you can assume significant reliability in a replacement, then you will have to weigh the cost of the replacement, which won't break down, against the probably lower cost of repair but a greater likelihood that something will go wrong.

There's one additional ingredient: opportunity cost. The lower repair cost may only comprise the direct dollar outlay. Keeping a vehicle idle in the repair shop may also constitute an expense. The firm whose delivery van breaks down delays shipments, which causes customer dissatisfaction and ultimately lost sales. The individual owner of a car forever breaking down may be less inconvenienced, the opportunity costs involving the time and transportation expenses spent going to and from the mechanic, but they're surely greater than zero.

3. The Drug Trade.   If you've sketched out supply and demand diagrams, you'll have noticed that reductions in supply reduce the quantity marketed but also raise price. Further, given the inelastic nature of the demand for cocaine and crack, the revenue rectangle expands as price rises. Assuming costs per unit relatively constant, larger revenues also mean higher profits.

But if demand is restricted, then the demand curve shifts downward, leading not only to a reduced quantity marketed but also to lower prices and profits. Demand-inhibiting policies appear to make more sense than do supply-oriented moves.

Of course, such theoretical conclusions are premature. They fail to deal with a key question: What are the costs *versus* the benefits of demand-control measures relative to those that influence supply? And once you consider costs and benefits, the natural follow-up question is, Might an optimal policy response not use both demand- and supply-oriented measures?

Examine Figure 20.1, which assumes a demand curve with a constant elasticity of -0.06. The D_1, S_1 equilibrium position shown replicates 1989 U.S. estimates for a kilogram (2.2 pounds) of cocaine selling on the retail market for \$40,000 and total sales of 2,500 *tons*. Notice the impact of a decrease in the supply curve to S_2: Price rises by \$10,000 per kilogram and quantity sold falls by 50 tons. But continuously working on the supply side means rapidly rising prices for given reductions in supply.[1] If you assume, as is likely, that it's easier to cut back supply when supply is large and harder to restrict supply when supply is smaller, then demand-restricting policies become even more plausible. Look at the equilibrium

FIGURE 20.1   Antidrug Policies: Supply-Constraining versus Demand-Restricting

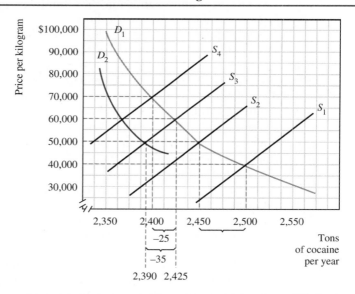

Begin with D_1 ($\varepsilon_p = -0.06$) and S_1, implying an equilibrium price of \$40,000 per kilogram and 2,500 tons sold. Restricting supply to S_2 raises price by \$10,000 and quantity supplied falls by 50 tons. Further supply-oriented measures are even less effective. For a shift from S_3 to S_4, for example, a \$10,000 price rise leads to only a 25-ton reduction in sales. However, an equivalent demand shift from D_1 to D_2 ($= S_3 - S_4$) would reduce sales by 35 tons. (Notice also its impact on price and thus on profits.)

of D_1 and S_3, with a \$60,000 price and sales of 2,425 tons. A reduction in supply to S_4 brings price up by \$10,000 per kilogram, but sales fall by only 25 tons. You can seen that a cutback in demand from D_1 to D_2, which is the equivalent of a reduction in supply from S_3 to S_4 (look along the \$60,000 line) would be even more effective than the supply-oriented policy. Sales would fall by 35 tons. Moreover, note the demand policy's impact on price; it falls by \$10,000 per kilogram. This reasoning underlies the switch in antidrug policy between the Reagan and Bush administrations. The former program focused almost entirely on supply controls and met with only a small measure of success, while the latter attacked both supply and demand.[2]

An analogous problem is faced by the immigration authorities. With wage rates and living standards in the United States among the highest in the world, this country acts as a magnet to attract immigrants. Congressional limits on immigration are implemented by the Immigration and Naturalization Service (INS). Given the long and open land and sea borders, the task of sealing the United States against illegal immigrants is immense, and success has been quite small. (Over 1 million illegal immigrants were apprehended in 1988, but immigration officials believe that at least 2 million crossed the borders without proper documentation that year.) Moreover, the more illegals interdicted by the INS, the more profitable smuggling becomes. Indeed, smuggling of immigrants has evolved from a small-scale, localized operation to an organized, worldwide network, with 1988 charges running as high as \$30,000 per person.

The Immigration Reform and Control Act of 1986 supplemented the enforcement budget of the Border Patrol, a supply-side measure. But it also provided for substantial penalties on employers of illegal immigrants and imposed upon them the burden of assuring themselves that their workers were legal residents of the United States. The objective of this provision of the law was demand-oriented: if illegal immigrants could not find jobs, the incentive to migrate into the United States would be reduced.[3]

It's easier for an economist to justify antidrug policies than it is to rationalize immigration restraints. From an overall economic point of view, drug abuse constitutes a heavy burden to the individual users and to society as a whole. But even on the simplest level, you can see how immigration differs. Immigration, by increasing the supply of labor, reduces domestic costs of production and so benefits the consuming public as a whole, as well as the producer who uses the immigrant labor. The presumption is also that the working immigrant improves his or her level of living, for, were it not so, a reverse flow, emigration, would be evident. The losers are those U.S. laborers who compete with the immigrants. It's not at all clear that the losses of the losers offset the overall gains that result from immigration. Moreover, the United States from its beginning has been a nation of immigrants, and its success can in no small measure be attributed to the many immigrants who have and continue to spur America on to ever greater achievements.

4. Public Library Revenues.   Public libraries do not supply public goods in the meaning of Chapter 10. The borrower of a book obtains direct satisfaction from reading it, so the benefit is primarily personal. Moreover, the borrower can be easily identified and thus can be charged directly. In fact, charging library borrowers for best-sellers shows not only that it can be done, but that it is done. Why not charge everyone on a per book/per day basis? After all, is book lending any different from renting out video films? Indeed, that is precisely what private libraries, which can be found in some cities, do.

Time rather than price is the allocation mechanism used by public libraries. Limits of a week or two may be imposed on books in strong demand; for virtually all books, libraries insist upon some finite borrowing period (say, a month). Instead of allocating books to those willing to pay the price, libraries allocate by first come, first served. Is this method more efficient than allocating on the basis of price?

How would you set borrowing fees? In the absence of significant competition from private lenders, the public library's monopoly would only be limited by the ability of the public to buy rather than borrow. Clearly, you'd have to charge less than the retail price of the books. But you'd also want to price the borrowing privilege high enough to assure that the library covers at least its costs. You might also consider a discriminatory pricing policy, since there are significant differences in the elasticities of different books.

You'd also have to deal with two potential threats to the viability of your library. First, too high a price could induce entry from private book lenders. Second, a resale book market might emerge, much as has occurred with textbooks. Consumers may find it worthwhile to purchase a new book if a significant share of the price could be recouped by selling it as a used book. Both these reasons might induce library policymakers to implement a limit pricing policy as discussed in Chapter 12. From a broader efficiency perspective, however, might we not wish to encourage a competitive book lending industry?

5. Keeping Cool.   Actually, a broad range of issues falls into this category, characterized by the fact that two independent parties are involved in the purchase, one as the decision maker and the other as the buyer. How about an example quite close to home? The professor teaching this microeconomics course selected the text, but you, the student, had to buy it. Price is important to you, but far less so, if at all, to faculty. Similarly, a physician prescribing a drug rarely knows the retail cost of the item, while you, as the patient are far more price conscious. (The price elasticity of demand to the faculty member or the physician will be close to, if not zero.)

One solution to all these cases is to make it worthwhile for the decision maker to take price into account in making the choice. Since it's the purchaser who profits from the broader perspective of the decision maker and who loses from the latter's not considering price, it sounds plausible for the purchaser to share some of the gain with the decision maker.

How about a rebate from each student to the professor equal to half of the difference between the average price of all textbooks in the subject area and the one actually ordered? (If the average micro text price was $60 and the professor selected a text priced at $50, each student would have to pay the professer $5. Note, however, the asymmetry. Professors are hardly likely to pay students for ordering texts priced above the average!)

Some similar scheme might work between landlords and tenants, with the tenants offering to pay some part of the increased costs of a better-insulated refrigerator, recouping their outlays from lower operating costs.

Actually, electricity users in general should be interested in encouraging such results, since it would lower their overall electric bills. The reasoning is as follows. Electric utilities build their plants to handle peak loads. The more inefficient appliances there are in operation, the more capacity will be needed, and the larger the capital investment of utilities. Since regulators normally base the rates they permit utilities to charge on their capital stock, the larger the investment, the higher the price. So, a policy that keeps utility capital down will also hold down electricity rates.

The direct savings from lower operating cost might suffice to induce tenants to negotiate with landlords. Or, as an alternative, regulators might prohibit landlords from installing refrigerators with lower than a specified energy efficiency ratio.[4]

6. Drug-Selling Doctors.   The problem here is virtually the reverse of the last case. Instead of the physician being uninterested in the price of drugs because the patient pays, the drug-selling doctor has a financial incentive to prescribe the medication yielding the most profit.

Can the professional ethics that mandate that the doctor consider the patient's best interest work with sufficient force to overcome the physician's patent self-interest? That's the concern of the druggists. But they, too, are interested parties, since drug-vending physicians will compete with druggists. (Remember the opticians' opposition to open market sale of glasses; see p. 370.)

Under which mechanism would consumers be best served? You might want to examine an analogous case: physician-owned medical laboratories. In an extensive article entitled "Patients for Sale—Warm Bodies: Doctor-Owned Labs Earn Lavish Profits in a Captive Market," two reporters from *The Wall Street Journal* illustrated the conflicts that can occur when physicians own an interest in medical facilities. They cited a 1983 study by Michigan Blue Cross–Blue Shield (see the table below) that seems to support their anecdotal evidence:

	20 Physician-Owned Laboratories	20 Independent Laboratories
Average payment	$44.82	$25.48
Average number of tests per patient	6.23	3.76
Range of payments	$21.33–$123.18	$7.15–$30.33
Range of tests per patient	3.42–20.72	1.67–4.68

As in many cases of economic policy, the answer is not clear-cut; there are pros and cons on both sides. Yet, policymakers will have to reach a conclusion, weighing out as best they can the costs and benefits of the options. In fact, one might want to experiment with different options in different regions and assess the results after some time interval has elapsed.

7. "Premier" Goes Up in Smoke.   One does not expect a major U.S. oligopolist to make a multimillion-dollar error. Indeed, with industry's presumed ability to manipulate consumer taste through advertising, success should be virtually guaranteed. Yet, as the Premier case testifies, consumers are not always willing dupes. The marketing experts failed to anticipate smoker resistance to poor taste and high price, while proving in retrospect too overconfident about smokers' fears of cancer. This is merely another example of the "Edsel effect," named after the highly touted "revolutionary" automobile introduced by the Ford Motor Company in 1957; $250 million went into developing a car with an oval grille, dual headlights, and an automatic transmission controlled by buttons on the steering wheel. By 1959, less than 111,000 Edsels had been sold, and a reluctant Henry Ford II scrapped the memorial to his father, Edsel. (Incidentally, Edsels are now collectibles.) Product failures are not rare. PepsiCo found its Slice, a fruit-juice based carbonated soft drink fizzled out after a few years, while 7UP Gold failed despite strong brand-name identification and a $10 million advertising budget. In fact, the freedom to make mistakes and to pay the ultimate price—failure—is crucial to the efficient operation of a market economy.[5]

What is perhaps most startling is the fact that RJR management was well aware of the defects discovered by consumers during test marketing. It seems, however, that senior executives lulled themselves into a false sense of optimism, believing what they wanted to believe rather than objective evidence that should have counseled caution. How true is

Robert Burns's line: "The best laid schemes o' mice and men/Gang aft a-gley."

This case also emphasizes an important point in analyzing real-life economics. While it's refreshing to learn that business executives are humans rather than mere profit-calculating machines, it also implies that profit maximization is no more than a useful first approach to understanding business decision making.

8. The Landlord's Rental Dilemma.   Begin with the hotel's pricing policy, which shows hotel room rental charge falling as the evening progresses. Why? Examine two conflicting forces:

- An unrented room is a perishable good with a very low variable cost of production (linens, some electricity, a few toiletry items), which, if left vacant, is wasted.
- However, an unrented room is potentially rentable and thus potentially income earning. Renting out a room at $50 means an opportunity cost of $40 should a guest willing to pay $90 materialize.

Hotel management faces a dilemma: Will a renter willing to pay $90 turn up, in which case the opportunity cost is incurred, or will no guest appear, in which case potential revenue is lost? Management hedges its bet by playing probabilities. As the hours pass, the probability of finding a full-paying guest diminishes. So, from 8:00 to 9:00 P.M., the hotel is saying; "We'll take a $10 chance. If a full-paying guest does show up, we'll lose $10, but we won't cut down rates so low as to lose $40." However, by 11:30 P.M., chances of renting to a full-paying guest are rather slim. As long as the $50 rental covers variable costs, it's better to collect some income than leave rooms empty.

That same dilemma faces the shopping-mall landlord. The space that has been idle for half the year has incurred few variable costs but substantial opportunity costs. Renting it out at a discount means that revenue starts coming in even though it's less than others are paying. On the other hand, leaving it empty keeps open the possibility of renting it out at the full price in the future. One crucial question is, How long will the landlord have to wait to find another tenant? You can see that if the wait is too long, the higher future revenues will not compensate for the lower rental collected over a longer period of time. And don't forget to do a present value calculation, since the $4-per-square-foot rental starts now, while the potential $5-per-square-foot rental begins only at some future date.

There's a further uncertainty to be considered. Would the landlord face irate tenants, who upon learning that the new tenant is paying 20 percent less than they are, insist upon a similar discount? An even if the angry tenants could not renegotiate existing contracts, could they press for a reduction in rent upon maturity of their present leases?

The return to the landlord is a quasi rent, since supply of space is fixed in the short run. While income distribution between the lessor and the leasee will depend on whether the lease is settled at $4 or $5 per square foot, the amount of space supplied in this particular location will remain unaffected by the final rental price.

9. Airport Security.   The cost of improved security can be separated into the fixed costs of machinery, the variable costs of security personnel, and the costs to the flying public of the extra time as well as the passed-on costs of intensified scrutiny.

Consider two extremes: no security check and very extensive procedures. The out-of-hand expenses in terms of security-related costs are zero for the first option. On the other hand, laxity in security precautions increases the probability of skyjacking and explosions, costing time; planes; and most of all, human lives. The opposite policy reverses the costs. By strict scrutiny involving searching every piece of baggage, be it stored or carry-on; by frisking each passenger; and by submitting every airport and airline employee with access to the planes to security monitoring, you can virtually guarantee the elimination of airport and airplane terrorism. But the cost would be a multiple of the present system, with substantial delays on the part of passengers, who would have to arrive at the airport many hours before departure to submit to inspection.

Of course, in-between methods could be devised, including a policy of random full-scale checking. For each policy, the costs of the security measures would have to be balanced against the costs of a less intrusive method, and the benefits would have to be evaluated as well.

Should uniform procedures be required, or should the market play a role in deciding on the appropriate degree of security? In the United States, with most airports owned by government entities, airport security must lie with the airport authority, not with the airline companies. But what about security measures affecting passengers? Would you favor a uniform policy for all airlines or would you let airlines compete not only by fares but by safety as well? Would some airlines take strict precautions in order to establish a record, so that they could advertise "Fly safely with Safeway Airlines"? Others might opt to be more lax and advertise "Save time with Streamline; come to the airport just moments before departure, use our express check-in, and be in your seat in a jiffy." The public would be the ultimate arbiter, implicitly trading off safety for speed by choosing whether to fly with Safeway or Streamline.

10. The Minimum Wage and Unemployment.   Brockway may have fallen victim to the identification problem mentioned in Chapter 2's appendix. If the economy is characterized by overall growth, then industry demand curves are continually shifting upward. If demand for labor grows more rapidly than supply, as is normally the case during periods of economic growth, then equilibrium wages should rise. (Sketch it out for yourself to verify this statement.)

When a minimum wage is imposed, then in a static picture, employment will fall below the equilibrium. But in a dynamic situation, as long as the increase in the minimum wage does not overtake the shifting demand curve, both wages and employment can rise. (Draw a minimum wage onto the first set of supply and demand curves in your diagram, and then keep on raising it. You can see under what conditions such increases will be consistent with rising employment. You can also maneuver the minimum wage to force employment down.)

You understand that a line connecting the minimum wage, quantity employed coordinates in the various pairs of supply and demand curves is meaningless. Indeed, had the minimum wage not risen over time, employment would have increased even more! Brockway need not be apologetic about his apparent exception—that in 1975, employment fell as the minimum wage rose. It's not at all surprising to find that the combination of a recession-induced decline in demand and the minimum wage hike drives employment down.

11. Insider Trading.

Modern security markets have multiple objectives:

- Providing firms with sources of funds.
- Providing individuals and firms with an outlet for surplus funds.
- Efficiently matching both investors with funds users and stock buyers with sellers.

Firms that require funds for expansion, for replacement investment, or for any number of reasons will, under a variety of circumstances, turn to securities markets rather than to banks or other lenders. The stock market provides the issuing firm with long-term capital in exchange for which stock buyers obtain a stake in the firm's ownership and thus a share in its profits. This primary securities market is an important component of financing economic expansion and contrasts with the much larger secondary market, which trades in outstanding shares.

In either case, credibility is a key ingredient for market success. How much confidence would you have in the market if, after buying a new issue, you discovered that the corporation's board of directors was selling out the bulk of its holdings? If that could happen, wouldn't investors be wary and less willing to acquire shares in the first place? Wouldn't this reduce the ability of the market to finance new investment? Similarly, those not privy to inside information would be reluctant participants in the secondary market.

In short, insider trading that results from asymmetric information reduces the volume of activity, since the potential losers will cut back on their participation. By preventing insiders from profiting from their information, the equity market becomes not only more equitable but also more attractive to a larger number of players. That makes the stock market more competitive and thus more efficient in carrying out its objectives.[6]

12. Patents and Copyrights.   Incentive is the underlying motive for patents and copyrights. Inventors would be less willing to invest their time and money should they be unable to recoup the fruits of their success. After all, would you play a game in which you would bear the entire costs of your failures and share with others the fruits of your successes? Few doubt the need for such protection. But all realize the flip side of the coin: patent protection provides the inventor with monopoly control and all its consequences.[7]

The positive incentive effect combined with the negative monopoly impact sets the stage for the key issue: How long need this protection be provided? This empirical issue involves calculating the minimum number of years of protection sufficient to recoup costs and provide adequate profits. Extending the patent beyond that time would encourage monopoly profits with no compensating societal benefit. In fact, U.S. federal law grants patents for 17 years, while copyrights on literary works provide 50-year protection. Although these numbers are arbitrary, occasionally evidence of rational thought can be discovered. In the case of "orphan" drugs such as AZT, for example, the Food and Drug Administration permits more extensive patent protection because the expected market is small and thus the producers' risks are abnormally high.

Note that rarely do patents provide an absolute defense against emulation. Patents that engender fantastic profits encourage others to search for alternatives that are effectively similar but sufficiently different to circumvent the legal protection.

13. Monetary Policy.   By playing around with interest rates, the Federal Reserve affects the relative price of capital and labor. When the Fed forces interest rates upward, not only does it reduce the demand for investment in absolute terms as the $r = i$ intersection shifts upward and backward, but it also makes capital more expensive relative to labor. Other things being equal, this shift in the isocost curve leads to a new tangency position that encourages more labor-intensive production methods than previously. The converse, of course, is true when the Fed loosens its monetary policy and brings interest rates downward. Capital use is then encouraged relative to labor.

This microeconomic implication has led some economists to conclude that economic growth, which is encouraged by more intensive use of capital, should be stimulated through loose monetary policies. The inflationary potential of such moves would then be offset by a tight fiscal policy, especially one that taxes individuals and so holds down consumption. Of course, higher tax rates on individuals might also discourage investment in education and thus human capital, which is typically financed from consumer income. It would also mean less income available to save as well as consume. Obviously, the quantitative outcomes of these various policies as well as the time dimension of the impact need to be assessed before reaching a conclusion.

14. Faculty Unions.   Faculty members, of course, may not be rational. They may be less interested in their own well-being than are other members of society. But that's really a poor hypothesis upon which to base an analysis. Surely, we can find a better answer as to the poor success of labor unions with university faculty members.

Two main objectives of labor unions are improved wages and related fringe benefits and enhanced job security. The latter, however, is less critical to faculty members than to most workers, since faculty members in most U.S. colleges and universities can earn permanency through the tenure process. Although tenure does not guarantee absolute protection—a tenured professor can be fired for cause (e.g., regularly failing to meet classes) or financial exigency (e.g., the closing down of an entire department or division)—the whims of the chairperson or dean cannot result in dimissal. Since during the 1980s most faculty members in U.S. institutions of higher learning were tenured, the job security issue affected only the untenured minority. So, if every faculty member voted on the basis of self-interest, the majority would have opposed unionism insofar as job security was concerned.[8]

Wages and fringe benefits are another matter. In order to understand resistance to unionization in the money arena, you should know that faculty salaries in the absence of unionization are based on each faculty member's negotiating with the administration. Now, divide the faculty into two groups—those earning above the average and those earning below. Unionization should benefit those earning below the average, while those earning above the average would lose. So, at least 50 percent would oppose unionization because it could actually lead to losses in their benefits. Moreover, in private universities, accurate information on salaries is not readily available. Most faculty members normally don't know whether they are earning more or less than their colleagues. All of the optimists or naive faculty members who believed themselves to fit in the upper half, even if they were not, would be inclined to vote against unionization.

You might counter, "Wouldn't salaries rise for everybody under unionization, so the average argument is irrelevant?" Even if true, this supposition is not the whole truth. First, unionization doesn't provide only benefits; there are costs attached. Union dues have to be paid. But even more important to faculty members, who tend to be individualists and who treasure their independence, unionization imposes an additional set of rules and regulations that restrain faculty freedom. Salaries would have to rise by enough to more than offset these very real costs. Many professors believe that the marginal monetary benefits would be less than the marginal noneconomic costs. Second, the counterargument fails to take into account expectations. If most faculty members felt that they could do better through personal negotiation than through schoolwide bargaining, the majority would oppose unionization even if average wages rose.

In reality, noneconomic reasons do enter in faculty decisions about unionization. Like many white-collar workers, faculty members often identify with management rather than with labor. And they feel more control over their jobs than does the typical white-collar worker. Economic considerations are not the most compelling force in the life of faculty members. Most understand that they could do far better financially working outside of the university. The satisfaction they achieve from working with students, from performing research, and from living in a university environment is something that most do not wish to change. Unionization would create added tensions, and the gain for many would not be worth the adversarial relationship between faculty and administration that is bound to arise under unionization.

Two other considerations are also germane. First, the voluntary American Association of University Professors (AAUP) provides some of the protection that unionization would give. (AAUP, for example, has established notification requirements, so that a faculty member denied tenure will be informed with sufficient time to search for alternative employment.) However, AAUP has little muscle to apply to university administrators. Second, the low unionization rate also reflects labor law insofar as private universities are concerned. The Supreme Court ruled in *National Labor Relations Board* v. *Yeshiva University* [100 S. Ct. 856 (1980)] that faculty is management and thus is not protected by the federal collective bargaining statutes. That decision makes it virtually impossible to organize faculty unions in the face of administration opposition.

15. Art for Art's Sake.   Any speculative market, be in the art market or the stock market, can be rationally irrational. It's irrational in the sense that expected price determines demand, but the higher price fueled by anticipations then justifies further expected price increases. The generation of speculative bubbles is not a new phenomenon.[9] And bubbles can burst. But until they do, they seem to be self-generating. John Maynard Keynes described such speculative markets as follows:[10]

> Professional investment may be likened to those newspaper competitions in which the competitors have to pick out the six prettiest faces from a hundred photographs, the prize being awarded to the competitor whose choice most nearly corresponds to the average preferences of the competitors as a whole; so that each competitor has to pick, not the faces which he himself finds prettiest, but those which he thinks likeliest to catch the fancy of the other

competitors, all of whom are looking at the problem from the same point of view. It is not a case of choosing those which, to the best of one's judgment, are really the prettiest, nor even those which average opinion genuinely thinks the prettiest. We have reached the third degree where we devote our intelligence to anticipating what average opinion expects the average opinion to be. And there are some, I believe, who practise the fourth, fifth, and higher degrees.

The individual who bucks the tide will, for the most part, lose. Except at the bottom or top turning points, the market trends down or up, so the winning strategy entails "go with the flow." The individual, even recognizing the fundamental irrationality of the expectation, would be rational by also acting irrationally.

By the way, historically counting on appreciation in the art market would not be very profitable strategy. Aside from the few works of art that have appreciated dramatically, the individual investor would have profited more over the past 50 years by holding onto a diversified portfolio of common stocks.

Concluding Words of Wisdom

The microeconomic theory course has a well-deserved reputation for being the toughest course in the economics major and one of the roughest in the entire college curriculum. Some of you will assuredly agree; others will have found it challenging but manageable. Some of you may even agree that the course has confirmed the remark that opened Chapter 1 and probably came from an evidently frustrated student of intermediate microeconomics: "Economics is stating the obvious in terms of the incomprehensible." Yet the majority of you who will not pursue a career in economics, as well as the few who will, should take away an approach to problems that face you both as an individual and as a citizen of your community.

Think through the alternatives, estimate the costs and benefits of the various options, pay due attention to the uncertainties that are an integral part of any problem, and come to a reasonable conclusion. It will certainly help if you can be lucky. And remember a final word of wisdom: It's better to be affluent and healthy than to be poor and sick!

Notes and Answers

1. The air force has been called in to assist the customs service in identifying aircraft suspected of transporting drugs. A Government Accounting Office study found that in 1987, the air force spent $2.6 million and caught six carriers, making but 10 arrests; $260,000 per arrest seems an inordinately large sum.

2. On the supply side, the Bush administration proposed increasing aid combined with financial incentives to the major Latin American sources of drugs. Demand-restricting measures included stronger enforcement measures and penalties against users along with additional spending on the construction of prisons. Demand would also be attacked through increased funding for drug treatment, drug testing measures, and more education.

3. One consequence that policymakers did not expect but that should have been anticipated was the stimulation of a new industry: the provision of forged immigration and residence papers.

4. This proposal imposes the burden on the landlord, which has further consequences. My thanks to Elias C. Grivoyannis for calling my attention to this issue. See his *Refrigerator Standards: An Energy Conservation Issue for Policymakers* (Albany, N.Y.: Public Utility Law Project, 1986) for further details and a different solution.

5. It must be pointed out, however, that on occasion, the U.S. government has intervened to prevent major corporations from failing. Thus, Chrysler Corporation was saved from paying for its errors in 1979, as was the Continental Illinois Trust Company in 1984. These rescues raise an important policy issue:

Are some companies too big to be permitted to fail?

6. Henry Manne, *Insider Trading and the Stock Market* (New York: Free Press, 1966) makes an ingenious and perhaps ingenuous argument for insider trading. He contents that insider trading encourages entrepreneurship, for it provides insider-innovators with an extra fringe benefit.

7. Aside from the obvious controls over price and quantity, a patent also enables the owner to keep the invention off the market if that's the most profitable course of action. An excellent review of the economics of patents can be found in Chapter 17 of F. M. Scherer and David Ross, *Industrial Market Structure and Economic Performance* (Boston: Houghton Mifflin, 1990).

8. Among the nontenured, those who expected to obtain tenure in the near future could also be expected to vote against unionization on job security grounds.

9. See the interesting account of a number of early bubbles in Charles Mackay, *Memoirs of Extraordinary Popular Delusions and the Madness of Crowds* (London: Richard Bentley, 1841). Notice the publication date!

10. John Maynard Keynes, *The General Theory of Employment, Interest, and Money* (London: Macmillan, 1957), p. 156.

Answers to Even-Numbered Problems

Chapter 1 Review Questions

2. Yes, since goods were abundant, no choices had to be made.

4. *a.* The four assumptions of microeconomic theory are (i) people are motivated by self-interest; (ii) people are rational—they think out the consequences of all possible courses of action, and choose the one that best meets their egoistic goals; (iii) microeconomic humans live in a world that is frictionless; and (iv) they never face uncertainty, and so their decisions, based on full knowledge of the consequences, can be implemented with ease.

   b. The precision that the four assumptions imply becomes fuzzy when any of them is dropped. For example, the price of a brand-name cologne is raised; theory predicts that sales should fall. Will they? Consider the following scenarios: (i) my neighbor owns a perfumery, and I feel compelled to buy there even though the price is higher; (ii) if this specific cologne is associated with some pleasant experience, so that emotion rather than reason dictates action, some consumers will not cut back on purchases; (iii) if I am unaware of a lower cologne price available from competitors or if the nearest alternative source of the cologne is inconvenient, then I pay the higher price; and (iv) perhaps the price will rise still higher next time I need cologne—if so, I'll actually increase my purchases now rather than wait for later. In all of these "for instances," the prediction of straightforward demand theory has been rejected.

6. *a.* Rational people examine the benefits and costs of selecting different occupations. Among the benefits are earnings, prestige, and so on. Among the costs are the necessary training; difficulty of the job; and, in the case of an illegal occupation, the chances of being caught and being subject to penalties. The rational individual weighs all of these elements and selects the occupation in which the benefits when compared to the costs are greatest.

   b. If a life of crime was a rational choice initially and the probability of being caught and jailed was correctly calculated from the start, then returning to criminality is still rational.

   c. Economic theory suggests that crime can be deterred by increasing either the probability of being caught, the severity of punishment, or both. This in turn suggests greater expenditures on law enforcement combined with tougher penalties, for example, tougher plea bargains and heavier sentences for first offenders.

Chapter 1 Food for Thought

2. The underlying thesis is that drug pushers are profit motivated and that addicts are not likely to respond to changes in drug prices. Remove the profit incentive, and pushers will leave the business. A successful demand-limiting program will cause prices to fall and cut sufficiently into the pushers' profit margin to diminish the attractiveness of the drug trade. At the same time, low prices will not encourage addicts to expand their habits, nor

will they induce those who are not addicted to experiment with drug use.

4. The moral question is, Should criminals be permitted to benefit from their criminal acts? As long as crime is reprehensible, most people would agree that punishment, not reward, is society's proper response. And since the victim is the person who suffered most directly from the criminal's action, it seems morally just to use such profits to indemnify the victim.

   As to the economic dimension, allowing criminals to profit from books and movies that depict their lifestyle increases the benefits of criminality and so encourages it. Certainly such a policy clashes with deterring crime.

6. Perhaps the answer lies in law-abiding citizens who believe that it's just the proper thing to do. That, of course, is a nonrational decision. But there may also be a rational calculation: it's cheaper than not paying it. For example, if the fee for an hour's parking is 25 cents, the chance of being caught is once in 50 times (2 percent), and the fine is $15, then the saving from not feeding the meter 50 times is $12.50. But you're certain to be caught once and pay $15.

Chapter 2 Review Questions

2.

	Demand	Quantity Demanded	Price	Supply	Quantity Supplied
War tensions rise	Increase	Increase	Increase	Unchanged	Increase
Penalties for spying are reduced	Unchanged	Increase	Decrease	Increase	Increase
A tax is imposed on spies	Unchanged	Decrease	Increase	Decrease	Decrease
Technical advances reduce the need for on-the-spot espionage	Decrease	Decrease	Decrease	Unchanged	Decrease
A maximum salary that is less than current pay is imposed on spies	Unchanged	Increase	Decrease	Unchanged	Decrease

4. *a.* The agency responsible for enforcing the ceiling must sell from its own sources and charge no more than the ceiling price. But unless it has unlimited supplies to meet the market demand, it must ultimately succumb to nonmarket devices, such as imposing criminal penalties for selling or buying at prices above the mandated ceiling.

   b. An illegal market develops because both sellers and buyers stand to gain.

Sellers' profits will be higher at an above-ceiling price, and some buyers are willing to pay the higher price in order to gain access to the goods.

c. On the positive side, those individuals who obtain the price-controlled goods at a below-market price obviously benefit. However, all those who are unable to purchase the good even though they are willing to pay the mandated price, and certainly those who would pay more, lose out. More generally, government controls over market-determined prices short-circuit the price mechanism, which results in a less efficient distribution of resources for the entire economy.

6. In any cobweb situation, buyers base their purchases on current prices, while sellers rely on current prices to plan production that will reach the market in the next period. In the case of an exploding cobweb, where the supply curve is relatively flat and the demand curve steep, sellers react more vigorously to current prices than do buyers. So, starting at point *a*, with quantity supplied low, demanders bid up the price to *b*, which induces sellers to provide *c* in the next period. But that large quantity supplied leads to a drop in price to *d*, inducing a substantial cutback in the next period's quantity supplied, *e*. And so on forever.

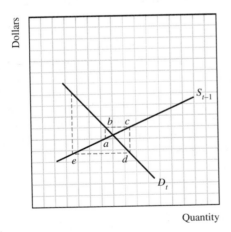

8. Landes and Posner argue that the present system of adoption combined with the lack of a legal market in white children conspires both against the natural mothers who seek to place their children out for adoption and the adoptive parents.

Natural mothers of white children have little financial incentive to proceed through the legal adoption system, while prospective adoptive parents cannot legally pay a fee that would be commensurate with their desire for a white child. The excess demand portrayed in the diagram below enables adoption agencies to use nonprice rationing to allocate the limited quantity of white children available for legal adoption. When the rules of the market are applied to white children—as they are in the illegal market—then a shortage would be reflected initially in a high price. As price reached the market-clearing level, however, the shortage would disappear because the market would allocate the available white children among those prospective parents willing to pay the market price.

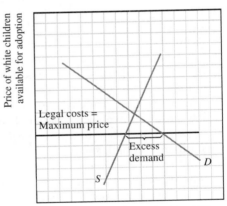

Quantity of white children available for adoption

Chapter 2 Food for Thought

2. *a.* Most tickets to a popular event will have been purchased in advance, and so there's a limited supply to meet the demands of latecomers, as the supply curve in the figure on the next page indicates.

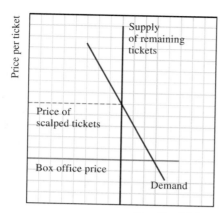

Quantity of tickets

b. Tickets to a specific event are a perishable good; if not sold before the event, they become worthless.

c. Yes, because they are allocating a scarce commodity—the remaining tickets—to those most willing to pay for them.

d. A number of possible reasons may be advanced. First, since stadium managers cannot precisely forecast actual demand, they may opt to err on the side of caution. They may prefer selling out at a lower price rather than price themselves into a near-empty stadium. Second, they may value the goodwill of customers. Charging prices that are thought to be exorbitant hurts their reputation and thus may reduce future sales. The gain in short-run profits may not be worth the loss in profits over a longer time horizon. Third, the organization of ticket sales is bureaucratic and not flexible. The costs of shifting to a more flexible organization—having the box office act as a scalper—may just not be worth the extra revenues collected.

4. *a.* Profit-motivated landlords will abandon buildings when the returns from the building (primarily rent) do not cover their operating costs. Abandoning the property becomes less costly than maintaining ownership. Of course, urban blight is the inevitable consequence of enough landlords acting this way.

b. If public policy dictates that tenants be subsidized, an appropriate subsidy to tenants combined with market-determined rentals would enable landlords to cover their costs and earn a suitable profit.

6. The advantage of a free market in blood, human organs, and surrogate motherhood is linked to the allocational and signaling functions of the market. Those most willing to pay would obtain these resources. Moreover, the high prices that would follow strong demand would induce an increase in organ supplies, thus alleviating the recognized shortage in donor organs. The objections to permitting a market in human body parts or functions stem from moral qualms about dehumanizing very human resources. The sale of a kidney is just not viewed in the same light as the sale of one's labor. Moreover, many object to the likely distributional impact— the wealthy could easily meet their needs, while the poor could do so with difficulty, if at all. Similarly, the poor are likely to be sellers of organs.

Chapter 3 Review Questions

2. The figures across the top of p. 703 suggest plausible answers.

4. *a.* As long as fashion dictates that people who wear earrings do so in matched pairs, consumers' indifference curves for earrings are right-angled, with the angle located at a ratio of one right earring to one left earring. This indif-

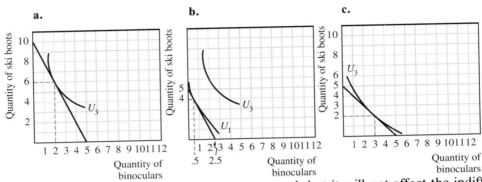

a. **b.** **c.**

ference curve map assures that no matter what the price of right or left earrings is, the consumer will buy them only in a 1 : 1 ratio.

b. Since fashion now permits wearing mismatched earrings, the consumer may at times buy a single earring rather than a pair. Thus, Ilana would not have to replace a lost earring by purchasing a new matched set, but merely by buying a nonmatching replacement. Her indifference curves would no longer be right-angled.

6. Risk aversion is not absolute. It can be compensated by adequate earnings. Since the Treasury securities yield little, Ted would be willing to accept some risk to buy higher-earning, but more risky, securities.

8. The opportunity costs of the time spent in search are the primary costs involved in finding the best professor for a given course. Most students will interview fellow students, especially those who have taken the courses in question. They may also examine published student evaluations of faculty.

Chapter 3 Food for Thought

2. A binding price ceiling that is below the existing market price shifts the budget line of the good whose price is fixed out-

ward, but it will not affect the indifference map, which represents tastes only. The lower price of the price-fixed good will lead to an increase in desired consumption of that good.

4. The rental subsidy—the budget line connecting $1,000 and 15—allows the renter to reach U_3, which is higher than U_2, reached by government providing an income subsidy—the budget line connecting $1,167 and $11\frac{2}{3}$.

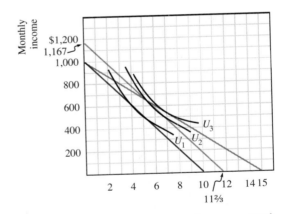

6. Since the gambler likes risk, risk is a "good," and the gambler is even willing to give up some yield (also a good) in order to obtain some risk. As the accompanying figure shows, the gambler's equi-

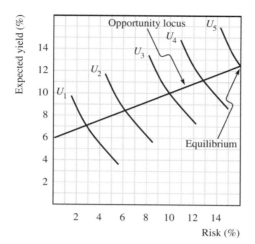

librium will be at the greatest combination of risk and yield achievable, acquiring a portfolio that has only high-yielding, risky securities.

8. The critical point is that search costs will raise the effective price of watches and so will reduce watch purchases. This is in contrast to a situation where search costs are assumed away.

Chapter 4 Review Questions

2. An increase in the price of suits from $100 to $200 shifts the budget line in the left-hand figure below inward and brings purchases down from 12 to 5. The substitution effect accounts for −3, while the income effect of this normal good accounts for −4.

   An increase in the price of pasta from $1 to $2 per pound shifts the budget line in the figure below inward and reduces purchases from 7.5 to 2.5. The substitution effect accounts for −6.5, while the income effect of this *inferior* good accounts for +1.5.

4. The demand curve itself shifted rightward as more people came to realize the advantages of cellular phones. But the supply of cellular phones increased even more as

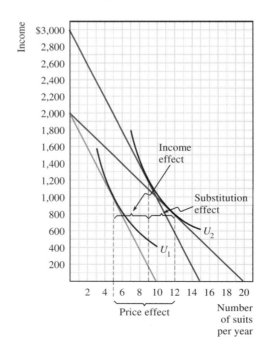

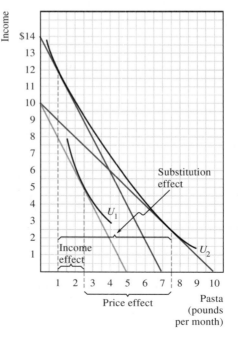

many new companies entered the industry. The resulting increase in sales was accompanied by a fall in price, which had a secondary impact as the lower price on the new demand curve induced consumers to increase their quantity demanded.

6. Price falls as does quantity sold.

Chapter 4 Food for Thought

2. Initial equilibrium with $\dfrac{P_x}{P_y} = 2$ (the grey budget line in the accompany figure) occurs at 8 Borden's and 0 Hershey's. The consumer chooses the cheaper of the two perfect substitutes. When the price of Hershey's falls to three fourths that of Borden's, the consumer buys only Hershey's, but his consumption rises to 12 quarts. The substitution effect, calculated by using the line parallel to the new price line and reaching U_3 at 8 Hershey and 0 Borden, is eight quarts, and the additional movement from U_3 to U_4, four quarts, is the income effect.

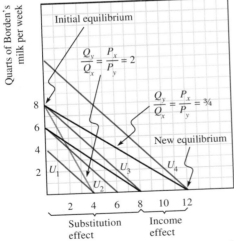

4. Demand theory points us in the direction of gathering information about consumer incomes and tastes. Certainly, we would be more likely to charge a higher price for Skunk among a more affluent clientele than in a poorer community. Moreover, insofar as perfume is a Veblen, or at least a bandwagon, good, efforts would be devoted to instilling a positive image of Skunk in key opinion makers and then advertising these endorsements. Our pricing policy then would reflect the image we wish to convey.

6. While costs differ, costs are but one element in the pricing decision. Demand considerations play an equally important role. Airline managers adapt their pricing policies to take into account the differing demand for cross-country and short flights. They seem to believe that lower fares on cross-country flights will entice substantial numbers of passengers and so increase their revenues. They do not think that similar low fares will encourage traffic on shorter flights and so earn more revenue by keeping the price higher.

Chapter 5 Review Questions

2. *a.* Elasticity at each point on a linear demand curve decreases as the demand curve shifts outward. (See MicroBits 5.1, p. 143.)

   b. Because elasticity at the existing price has decreased, airline management has an opportunity to raise price and thus increase revenues.

4. The statement is true as far as quantity bought and quantity sold are concerned, since a perfectly inelastic demand curve is vertical. However, supply elasticity will determine the price.

6. *a.* Since many car buyers will await the new models, the demand curve for

cars about to become "old" shifts inward and becomes more elastic. When demand has become more elastic, revenues can be increased by reducing price.

b. From the demand-elasticity viewpoint, turkeys ought not to be on sale before Thanksgiving. After all, the higher seasonal demand suggests that sellers ought to raise their prices to increase their sales income. So, one must search for another reason. The concept of a "loss leader" might be the best explanation. Since people who shop for turkeys are usually planning a feast that entails many additional purchases, the sellers seek by their cut-rate turkey prices to capture the rest of their customers' holiday outlays. They hope that these extra sales will more than compensate for the opportunity cost of the discount turkey.

8. a. Nothing. All it says is that the demand curve is negatively sloped.

b. Elasticity is zero; the demand curve is vertical. Thus, cutting book prices will not induce sales. (That's hard to believe!)

Chapter 5 Food for Thought

2. RJR believes the demand for a particular brand of cigarettes is very elastic. By charging a low price for Sterling, it can attract substantial numbers of smokers to this new brand. The high elasticity guarantees that the increased volume more than compensates for the lower price. However, the policy is double edged, for it will also attract smokers who now buy RJR's own higher-priced brands, which may have positive cross-elasticity to Sterling.

4. If in 1984, Inderol was priced at $10 and sold 10 million dosages, then 1984 revenues were $100 million. We're told that price was increased by 20 percent—to $12—and yet revenues did not fall. Quantity sold must have been $100 million divided by $12, or 8.33 million. Elasticity must have equaled 1. But in 1986, price was boosted to $13.92—a 16 percent increase—and sales revenues fell by 60 percent—to $40 million. Quantity sold must have fallen to $40 million divided by $13.92, or 2.87 million. Elasticity must have been greater than one. (Actually, the percentage change in Q $\left(\dfrac{8.33 - 2.87}{8.33} \cong \frac{2}{3}\right)$ divided by the percentage change in P (16 percent) $\cong$ 4.25).

Millions of dosages

6. a. The demand for health care appears to be highly elastic, so that a reduction in health insurance charges would lead to very substantial increases in the use of medical facilities and personnel.

b. Since the demand curve for medical services is negatively sloped, private and public insurers can reduce usage of the medical care system by imposing more of the cost of medical care on the insured. Moreover, the falling demand curve suggests relying less on premiums and emphasizing more cost sharing per visit. When the consumer pays a flat fee for medical insurance that frees him from per visit payments, each visit is in fact costless. He pays the same whether he never visits a physician or visits her daily. Only through some type of usage fee will the consumer be dissuaded from making unnecessary appointments.

8. *a.* Cross-elasticity measures the impact of a change in the price of one item on the quantity demanded of a second. In this case, we're interested in the sign of the cross-elasticity coefficient between beer and whiskey, since a tax on beer will raise beer prices. If the coefficient is negative, so that the increase in beer prices will reduce not only beer consumption but also whiskey consumption, then we can anticipate fewer drunken drivers. But if the coefficient is positive, higher beer prices will lead to increased whiskey consumption. Then the beer tax may prove counterproductive.
   b. Raise taxes on whiskey as well as on beer.

10. Promotions of various sorts such as contests, prizes, coupons; advertising; endorsements by well-known personalities.

Chapter 6 Review Questions

2. *a.* Diminishing returns, because along any row or column, the marginal product diminishes as the variable input increases.

b. Constant returns to scale. Output increases by the same proportion as the proportionate increase in both inputs.

c. At the 200 output level, connect the following three combinations: Hay 4/Fish 1; Hay 2/Fish 2; and Hay 1/Fish 4. Similarly, at the 300 output level, connect Hay 9/Fish 1; Hay 3/Fish 3; and Hay 1/Fish 9.

4. The essential idea, as indicated in the accompanying figure, is that humans and monkeys are substitutes in fruit picking.

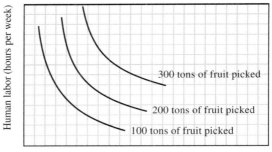

6. *a.* The slope of the isoquant curve. The MRTS indicates how much of one input must be provided to replace a loss of one unit of a second input in order to maintain output unchanged.
   b. When isoquants are convex, the MRTS is falling as we move outward on any input axis. Both the convexity of isoquant and the falling MRTS inform us that as we diminish use of one input by a constant amount, we must compensate for that decrease by adding ever more quantities of the second input in order to keep output constant.

8. One must distinguish between empirical production functions that are based on pure technological relationships (e.g., flowthrough as a function of pipeline size

and horsepower) and those that involve labor and capital as inputs. Labor is not a homogeneous input among people, nor does the same person exhibit identical behavior continuously even in the same setting.

Chapter 6 Food for Thought

2. The trade-off between two inputs has been expanded to include a third, and so the producer has additional options in production.

4. Since a fixed-input production function will exhibit right-angled isoquants, the slope $(\Delta Y/\Delta X)$ is equal either to infinity (the vertical arm), or to zero (the horizontal arm), or at the right angle, the precise trade-off between Y and X.

6. Production theory suggests that industry size depends on the presence or absence of economies of scale. Should economies of scale be insignificant, then the industry will be comprised of small firms. But when economies of scale are significant, then immensity is synonymous with low-cost operations, and the industry will be populated by large firms. A variety of firm sizes can be explained by a horizontal range in the LRATC curve, indicating neither significant economies nor significant diseconomies of scale.

8. *a.* More capital shifts the total product and marginal product curves upward, so that each additional unit of labor employed produces more than before.

   b. Management, which typically introduces the additional capital, argues that it is responsible for the greater productivity. Labor counters by contending that capital without labor is unproductive, and that it is the capital-labor combination that accounts for the greater productivity.

Chapter 7 Review Questions

2. *a.* With machine time now costing only half as much as labor time, the isocost curves swing outward from their origins on the x-axis. For $96, Brad could acquire 24 hours of machine time, as against 12 hours of labor time. The new isocost will enable Brad to reach a higher isoquant and so wash more cars at the same cost as before. At the same time, the relative decrease in the price of machine time induces Brad to use more machine time than before and less labor time for each car washed.

   b. Again, for the same $96 outlay, Brad can now hire a maximum of only 9.6 hours of labor, rotating the isocost curves inward from their origins on the y-axis. This increase in the cost of labor reduces the total volume of cars that can be washed for any given outlay and simultaneously changes the proportions of labor to machine time. Brad will use less of the more expensive labor time.

4. *a.* See the first figure in MicroBits 7.1.
   b. See the second figure in MicroBits 7.1.
   c. See the third figure in MicroBits 7.1.

6. At the plant level: As the physical size of the plant increases, travel distance within the plant imposes costs. At the firm level: Increasing firm size imposes costs of coordination, which includes layers of management and the time it takes to make critical decisions.

8. Since Figure 7.12 shows that each kilowatt hour produced costs less in a larger generating plant than in a smaller one, the correct decision is to build a single giant plant.

10. Indian factories use both capital and labor, so that the isoquant is convex to

the origin and not right-angled. Although labor is assumed to be the cheap factor of production in a labor-abundant society such as India, which suggests that factories should use labor-intensive techniques, the facts dictate otherwise. Labor is not cheap, because it's inadequately skilled and not docile, while capital is subsidized and hence cheap. The outcome is capital-intensive production that emphasizes the cheap capital and refrains from intense use of the more expensive labor.

Chapter 7 Food for Thought

2. The diagram below indicates a trade-off between traffic officers and traffic signals. Both can be used to control traffic, although they are not perfect substitutes. With the isocost curve suggesting that an officer is more expensive than a traffic light, the equilibrium combination consists of six lights and three officers.

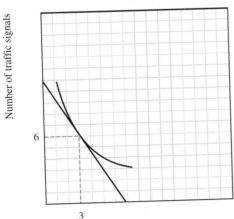

Number of traffic officers

4. *a.* The diagram in the right column shows a convex isoquant and an isocost curve that indicates a far lower cost for faxing than for overnight express delivery. The relatively low

cost of faxing accounts for its intensive use.

b. Because faxes are only imperfect substitutes for overnight delivery services, even at the low fax price there are times when overnight delivery will be preferred (e.g., where original documents are required, packages).

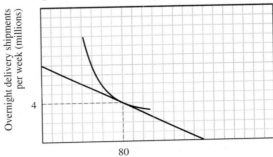

Fax transmissions per week (millions)

6. Although fixed costs are part of total costs, they are not part of the variable costs (by definition). Thus, an increase in fixed costs will raise total and average total costs, but will not change either average variable or marginal costs.

8. Producers have no reason to adopt a labor-saving innovation when labor is cheap and the labor-saving innovation entails expensive capital outlays. On the figure on the next page, if labor and capital were priced identically, the producer would use the labor-saving, capital-intensive innovation to produce 1.5 million units of output at the same cost as the labor-intensive method that yields only 1 million units. However, because labor is so cheap, the labor-intensive method produces 1 million units at the same outlay as the capital-intensive method that produces only 750,000 units.

10. No, because average costs refer to the relationship of costs to output, while the figure shows costs falling over time.

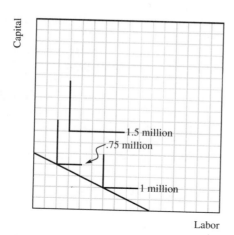

Capital

1.5 million
.75 million

1 million

Labor

Chapter 8 Review Questions

2. The four conditions are: (i) no firm can control price; (ii) all goods or services produced by the competitive firms are identical, so no customer will favor one firm's product over another; (iii) firms can enter and exit the market at will, and (iv) all information needed to function in the market is known to all market participants. Because of these conditions, no buyer or seller can gain any unique advantage over any other buyer or seller.

4.

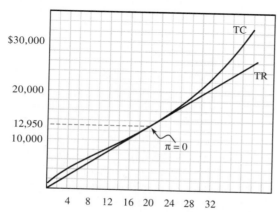

$30,000

20,000

12,950
10,000

TC

TR

$\pi = 0$

4   8   12 16 20 24 28 32

Bicycles per week

6. The statement should properly read, "A firm should continue to operate as long as its revenues cover its *variable* costs." Only then can the firm apply the revenues that exceed its operating costs to its fixed costs and thus reduce total losses. If the firm covers its fixed costs but not its operating costs—assuming operating costs are greater—then it would be less costly to the firm to shut down operations entirely.

8. *a.* Doubling the quota on shirts would shift the supply curve rightward, lower shirt prices, and reduce the deadweight loss to the economy. That would benefit everyone except the domestic shirt manufacturers.

   b. The quota doubling would lead to a market price of $20, which would eliminate this manufacturer's excess profits.

10. Refer back to Figure 8.10. The BSA buys the surplus whenever an excess supply emerges at the stabilized price and sells from the surplus whenever an excess demand emerges at the stabilized price.

Chapter 8 Food for Thought

2. *a.* The issue hinges on whether these plants' overhead costs would have been incurred no matter whether the plants were kept open or shut. If yes, they should have been kept open as long as the sales revenues from those plants would have exceeded the plants' variable costs and contributed something to the fixed costs. If, however, the plants' fixed costs could have been eliminated by shutting the plants, then keeping them open would have made sense only if revenues would

have covered both variable and fixed costs.

b. Yes. "Shutdown costs" seem to mean the total fixed costs that would be incurred if the plant were to shut down, while "operating loss" means that sales revenues are not even covering total variable costs. When an operating loss occurs, it is less costly to shut down altogether than to continue producing.

4. Refer to Figure 8.8, which shows that a steep demand curve coupled with a shallow supply curve puts the burden of the tax on the demander. If the highly inelastic demand of Figure 8.8 belonged to foreign consumers and the elastic supply described domestic suppliers, a per unit tax on suppliers could be shifted onto the foreign demanders.

6. *a.*

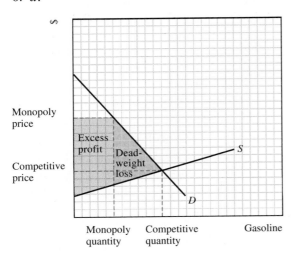

b. No. Although it would redistribute the profits from the monopolist to the government, it would not eliminate the deadweight loss caused by the monopoly pricing policy.

Chapter 9 Review Questions

2. Mr. Martin could not cover his store's operating costs. The competitive market forced him either to improve his efficiency and lower his costs or to close down. He chose the latter.

4. *a.* When the LRATC is consistently falling, the largest firm is optimal.

 b. When the LRATC is horizontal, firms of any size can be equally efficient.

6. As shown in Figure 8.8, p. 283, a tax may be partially borne by suppliers in the short run. They will remain in business as long as the tax does not force price below their average variable costs. But in the long run, firms must cover all of their costs, for otherwise they would not incur fixed costs in the first place. So, if the firms in the competitive industry were in long-run equilibrium, earning zero excess profits before the imposition of the tax, then firms would drop out of the industry until supply contracted sufficiently to force price up to the new long-run equilibrium.

8. *a.* In Figure 2.10a, p. 46, lenders do not lend more than $90 billion yearly, and so demanders obtain only $90 billion. If we assume that the borrowers willing to pay the most obtain loans—even though they pay only 8 percent—then the deadweight loss equals the triangle whose apex is formed by the intersection of the supply and demand curves and whose base is a vertical line above $90 billion that connects the supply and demand curves.

 b. Using the formula for the area of a triangle—$A = \frac{1}{2}$ (Base)(Height)—you derive: Base = 25 cents (per pack); Height = 2 billion cigarettes, or 80 million packs. Hence: (.50)($.25)(80 million) = $10 million.

Chapter 9 Food for Thought

2. *a.* A profit-maximizing producer should always equate MR and MC. Hence, the first phrase is irrelevant.

   b. If firms can easily enter the industry, then merely equating MR and MC does not suffice. The firm must achieve the efficiency consistent with optimal firm size.

4. *a.* The LRATC curve for wood caskets will be U-shaped, with the U occuring at a relatively low level of production. The LRATC for metal caskets will also be U-shaped, but the minimum average cost point will lie to the right of the wood casket cost curve.

   b. Fewer firms would survive. If demand fell very significantly, the competitive nature of the casket industry might well be threatened.

6. As the figure below indicates, A has high fixed costs but low variable costs, while B has low fixed costs but high variable costs. The decision maker would be better off choosing plant B for expected sales that are less than 20 units of output, but selecting A for sales anticipated to be greater than 20 units. Of course, in both cases, revenue from sales would have to exceed costs.

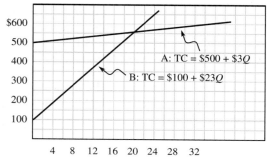

Chapter 10 Review Questions

2. *a.* P   *e.* N
   b. P   *f.* N
   c. N   *g.* N
   d. N

4. *a.* Banning all automobiles would most likely lead to a situation in which costs exceed benefits. Clearly, in the presence of an absolute ban, not only would vehicles used for inessential purposes be prohibited, but so would vehicles used for critical purposes (e.g., cars driven by volunteer emergency medical technicians).

   b. The critical criterion is the cost of pollution reduction. Unequal treatment is appropriate if it is cheaper to reduce pollution by a given amount in that manner.

6. Whether a beach use fee is appropriate or not depends on whether the marginal cost of an additional user is zero or positive. Only in the latter instance is a fee justifiable from an allocational point of view. But even then the charge should not exceed the marginal costs.

Chapter 10 Food for Thought

2. *a.* Each firm faces a choice: stop polluting or buy pollution rights. The decision taken by each firm hinges on the cost of the pollution right versus the cost of prevention. Firms with low marginal pollution abatement costs will demand pollution rights only at a low price, while firms with high abatement costs will be willing to demand such rights at much higher prices.

   b. The demands of individual firms will be added together to determine a "demand for pollution rights" curve, which, when juxtaposed to the fixed supply of pollution rights will determine the price of each right.

c. Once the price is determined, each firm will examine the volume of pollutants it generates and the cost of pollution abatement. If, for example, a firm needs five rights to spew forth 100,000 gallons of polluted water into the drainage system, if each right costs $20,000, and if the marginal cost of cleaning the water before it leaves the plant is $125,000, then the firm keeps costs down by buying five rights for $100,000, saving itself $25,000. On the other hand, a second firm with identical circumstances except purification costs of only $80,000 would not buy any rights and would instead purify its water of pollutants before it is flushed out of the plant.

4. a. The straight-line isoquants in the diagram below denote perfect substitutes. With cans cheaper than bottles, equilibrium lies in the corner with only cans and no bottles.

b. Any action that reverses the relative cost of bottles and cans will lead to a new corner equilibrium on the bottle axis.

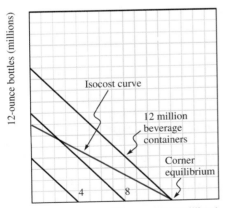

6. Politics as well as economics enters the arena when U.S. polluters impose damage on Canadian residents. Either the United States and Canada must jointly agree to curb pollution at the source, or Canada may be forced to take unilateral action such as imposing tariffs on imports that originate in the offending plants.

8. Since the cost of an additional user of HBO broadcasts is zero, the criterion of marginal benefit equals marginal social cost implies a zero price for this service. Thus, a public policy that stresses allocational efficiency should prevent HBO from scrambling. However, if such a policy were to be imposed, HBO would be unable to prevent free riding and might not generate sufficient revenues to stay in business. Public decision makers will have to choose among alternative policies, each with its own benefits and costs.

Chapter 11 Review Questions

2. At a bit less than $10, the highest possible price in the figure, the monopolist will sell hardly any units. Clearly, this is substantially below the maximum profit position.

4. This is identical to the third-degree discriminating monopolist of Figure 11.6. The critical point is that the demanders can be segregated into groups with different elasticities. The source of the disparate elasticities is immaterial.

6. In Figure 11.6, MC = 50; the price elasticity of demand by business travelers above the intersection of MC and MR is [150/(150 − 250)], or −1.5; and the price elasticity of demand for vacation travelers is [87.50/(87.50 − 125)], or −2.333. Applying the formula to business travelers yields 50/[(1 + 1/−1.5) = 50/(1 − 0.67) = 50/0.33 = 150. For vacation travelers, 50/[1 + (1/−2.333)] = 87.50.

8. Airlines might prefer the relative stability of the price of a major input in their operations. More stable fuel prices permit the airlines to better calculate their costs and thus their own ticket prices.

Chapter 11 Food for Thought

2. Ballpark managers may be concerned with the long-run impact on demand and profits. They may prefer not to be perceived as monopolists who use their power in an extortionate manner.

4. *a.* Students who really don't want to take a chance at missing the performance, and thus have a less elastic demand, pay full price. Those whose demand is

more elastic wait for the price to come down as showtime approaches and hope that they will be able to buy tickets.

b. Unsold tickets are a perishable good, whose life terminates with the performance. The rationale of the owners is that it's better to obtain some revenue than to have the seats unsold.

c. The diagrams below show a monopolist who discriminates in stages. In the first stage, on the left, the monopolist calculates advance-sale prices based on MR = MC. She then sells the leftover tickets as performance time approaches based on a new demand curve and the remaining ticket supply, as in the figure below.

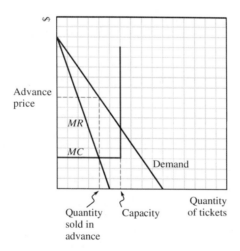
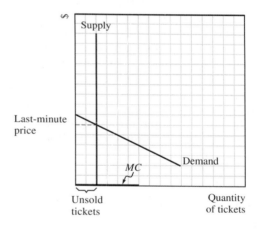

Chapter 12 Review Questions

2. *a.* A licensing fee is a flat tax that affects only fixed costs, while an excise tax is a per unit tax that affects variable costs. Since fixed-cost increases do not change the MR = MC equilibrium while variable-cost increases do, the former do not affect production or prices.

b. The monopolist who practices limit pricing decides for strategic reasons to produce where MC > MR. Although the licensing fee still does not affect MC and so should not bring any change in pricing or production, the imposition of such a fee might induce the monopolist to reconsider the limit pricing policy. Since the fee reduces profits below expected levels, the monopolist might try to restore profits by shifting to a position closer to the MR = MC equilibrium. If that occurs, the difference between a licensing fee and an excise tax disintegrates.

4. The basic antitrust argument is that a monopoly diminishes both allocational efficiency and society's welfare. By restoring competition, prices will come down, production will increase, the deadweight loss will disappear, firms will be forced to be efficient, and resources that were artificially inhibited from moving into the industry will flow toward it. Moreover, a monopolist has the incentive to slow the pace of innovation.

The anti-antitrust argument notes the costs of pursuing an antitrust policy, but it focuses more intensely on the dynamism of the market system. Even a monopoly cannot escape the forces of competition, which will develop substitutes for the monopolized product. Further, while a monopolist may deter domestic competition, it has no control over foreign competition, especially in nondomestic markets. Thus, an antitrust policy really is not needed.

Most economists today feel that antitrust policy is more beneficial than costly and that while ultimately the monopolist may succumb to market forces, there's really little reason to wait for that to happen.

6. *a.* A natural monopoly has a declining LRATC or is characterized by substantial overhead and limited variable costs.

b. Costs can be lower and allocational efficiency higher under monopoly than under perfect competition as the monopolist takes advantage of the economies of scale. But the monopolist may also take advantage of its monopoly powers and so fail to outperform a number of competitive firms.

c. Average-cost pricing permits regulators to force a monopolist to operate at an output that is greater and a price that is lower than the maximum profit position of an unregulated monopolist. At the same time, the regulated price guarantees the monopolist normal profits.

d. Allocational efficiency will be achieved at the point where marginal social benefit equals marginal social cost, which is where $P = MC$.

8. *a.* Most airport parking lots cannot handle the demands on them, which results in roadway congestion during some times of the day and week, while at other times the parking lots have excess capacity. Differentiating the parking rates enables the authority to better allocate the available supply of spaces.

b. The authority would charge more for parking during periods of heavy demand and less during times of weak demand.

Chapter 12 Food for Thought

2. On the surface, Nielsen is a monopolist and should be subject to antitrust prosecution. Yet if Nielsen is not illegally responsible for the disappearance of its competitors, a cogent argument could be made for leaving Nielsen alone. If Nielsen captured the market through its own efforts and now provides efficient service to its customers, then antitrust prosecution would be not only inappropriate but also counterproductive. What message would the business community receive if an efficient producer were penalized for its efficiency?

4. *a.* Until the cost of postage passed some threshold it paid neither for private deliverers to enter the market nor for mailers to use them. Apparently, by the 1980s that threshold had been surpassed.

   b. One could argue that the profit motive forced the private mailers to be more cognizant of the bottom line and so be more sensitive to efficient delivery than the U.S. Postal Service. It might also be true that the private mailers are selective—they limit delivery to localities where a profit can be made. Thus, they are likely to concentrate in high-density urban areas and be less interested in delivering to low-density rural areas. Of course, the more efficient the private deliverers are and the less they charge, the more attractive they become to customers.

   c. We would expect the post office to react on the economic front by improving its efficiency and on the political front by attempting to impose constraints on the private deliverers.

6. *a.* By taking away the discretion of the monopolist to set price, the regulators also remove its incentive to limit production. In the figure on the right, the regulated price becomes the MR curve, since the monopolist cannot charge more and will not charge less than the regulated price.

   b. The regulators would attempt to approximate the competitive market equilibrium, which requires that quantity supplied equal quantity demanded and $P = \text{MC}$.

   c. Could the regulators really determine the competitive market price to impose on the monopolist? Wouldn't the competitive market itself provide more information, and do so more consis-

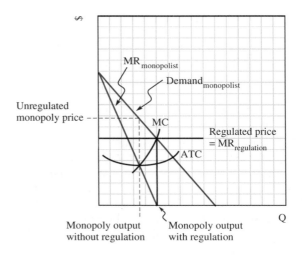

tently, about optimal prices and costs than would the regulators?

Chapter 13 Review Questions

2. Among the artificial barriers erected by oligopolists to deter the entry of competitors are (*a*) brand names, which solidify consumer allegiance to a particular brand such as Sony or Cheerios; (*b*) information, by which the experience gained by existing producers is not easily acquired by new entrants, (*c*) capital, because financial institutions are reluctant to lend to new entrants when success against existing firms is unlikely; and (*d*) strategic considerations, which are specifically designed to deter entry.

4. *a.* The top left diagram on p. 717 sketches in the original equilibrium for Cour, assuming Not is not in the market, with $Q = 9$ million (below MC = $\text{MR}_C^1 = 3$) and $P = F7.5$ on D_C^1. That leads to Not's initial demand curve, D_N^1, and $Q = 4.5$ million and $P = F5.25$. The respective D^2 curves indicate the final equilibrium, with each

Cour's demand

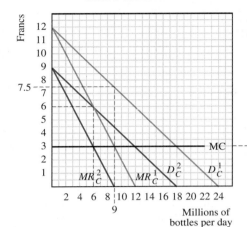

Not's demand

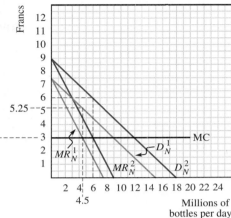

producing 6 million bottles at a unit price of *F*6.

b.

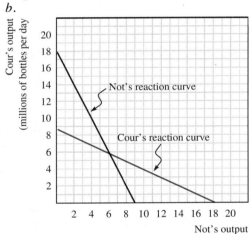

Not's reaction curve

Cour's reaction curve

Not's output
(millions of bottles per day)

6. Since a product line encompasses a number of versions of the same fundamental product, with differences in product quality indicated by price distinctions, the seller might be able to mislead the consumer into buying a higher-priced, lower-quality item. See MicroBits 13.3, p. 444.

8. *a.* Since average fixed costs vary inversely with volume, a decrease in sales leads to a higher AFC, which is passed on under full-cost pricing in the form of higher prices. Sales increases reduce prices as AFC declines.

b. By setting a target price that is independent of actual sales, the firm keeps the price on target even though demand fluctuates.

c. Certainly, if an oligopolist maintains price at the target level, the firm stabilizes its prices. And if all oligopolists adopt the target price convention, then the entire industry will be characterized by stable prices.

Chapter 13 Food for Thought

2. This solution can most easily be worked out mathematically using the technique described in note 3, p. 461. The diagrams on the next page, based on the Cournot example used in this chapter, show that an equilibrium will be reached if each of three oligopolists supplies 6 million bot-

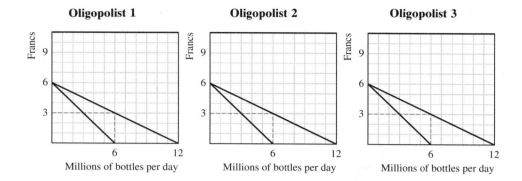

tles daily, or one quarter of the market each, for a total of 18 million bottles. The remaining quarter is left unsatisfied.

4. An oligopolist that produces an undifferentiated product would not practice first-degree discrimination, since sellers can meet their needs from other oligopolists. First-degree discrimination is also unlikely for a differentiated oligopolist, since the degree of differentiation is likely to be small. Second-degree discrimination, or block pricing, is not only possible under oligopoly, but may well be an effective pricing strategy, since consumer allegiance can be solidified using quantity discounts. Third-degree discrimination is also likely, because rival oligopolists often are more competitive in certain locations than in others. Thus, they can charge higher prices in markets where they face less oligopolistic competition and less where they are more strongly challenged by rivals.

6. Although this statement appears to fly in the face of pricing logic—for prices should be cut to induce sales during periods of slack demand—it becomes more plausible in terms of oligopolistic pricing strategy. If GM pursues a target pricing policy that is independent of actual sales volume in any subperiod, then raising the target price during periods of slack sales will encounter less customer resistance than during periods of strong sales. The positive impact of this target price increase on sales and profits is felt later, once demand has increased

Chapter 14 Review Questions

2. *a.* The broader an industry is defined or the larger the market territory, the larger will be the number of firms that comprise the industry or the location. This intensifies competition either in the industry or the area, complicating the proof of allegations of antitrust law violations or forestalling mergers that might restrain trade.

b. Chapter 5's example of the Du Pont antitrust case hinged on the proper definition of the relevant industry, as did the proposed PepsiCo/7UP and the Coca-Cola/Dr Pepper mergers mentioned in Chapter 13. Banking mergers have often depended on the appropriate definition of the geographical market.

4. *a.* Correlation is not causation. Even when two variables are closely related, their relationship does not prove which variable is cause and which effect.

Indeed, both may be the effects of a third cause.

b. These economists argue that economies of scale account for both the high profits and the oligopolistic nature of the market.

6. *a.* The three critiques directed by NEIO economists against SCP studies dealt with (i) inappropriate data, which did not provide the proper information needed to evaluate the argument; (ii) the SCP assumption that behavior is identical across all industries rather than specific to each individual industry; and (iii) the models' use of broad, structural variables rather than the prices and costs that are germane to the economic behavior of individual firms.

b. Many NEIO studies confirm the conclusions of SCP studies that some industries are populated by firms with substantial market power and high profitability.

8. The proper role of antitrust continues to be debated among economists and legal theorists. Those who believe that "big is bad" call for oligopoly to be subject to the antitrust statutes. But for those who believe that competition is alive among existing oligopolists and potential entrants as well as those who view the costs of oligopoly as small relative to its benefits, then antitrust policy ought only to be applied to monopoly or collusive oligopolies.

Chapter 14 Food for Thought

2. Since $\pounds = 1/|\eta|$, elasticity plays a critical role. Although the price elasticity of demand of an oligopolist ought to be greater than that of a monopolist in a given industry, that need not hold true when comparing different industries. When the monopolized industry is characterized by a highly elastic demand curve, the monopolist ends up with a very low Lerner index.

4. In the matrix below, the two competitors can either advertise heavily or lightly. (The payoffs in the boxes list firm A's payoff first and firm B's second.) If firm A elects to advertise lightly and so does firm B, they both walk away with a $15 million profit. However, if A cuts back on advertising, B's optimal strategy is to advertise heavily and garner $30 million. Indeed, heavy spending on advertising is B's dominant strategy. Since the same reasoning applies to A, they'll both advertise heavily and will each take away only $8 million.

	Firm B	
	Advertise heavily	**Advertise lightly**
Advertise heavily	Gain $8 million; Gain $8 million	Gain $30 million; Lose $10 million
Advertise lightly	Lose $10 million; Gain $30 million	Gain $15 million; Gain $15 million

Firm A (rows)

6. The differing business points of view can be expressed in terms of concentration versus diversification. Diversification suggests the firm can offset losses in one activity by gains in a second and so stabilize profits over time. Concentration risks more by putting all the eggs in one basket but may reflect a judgment that the long-term prospects are rosier for aluminum than for a diversified enterprise. It may also reflect management's decision that they are experienced aluminum industry executives who know relatively little about running a diversified conglomerate.

Reynold's diversification may not spare it from antitrust prosecution, since the antitrust laws need not be applied to the entire firm but to each of its disparate components.

Chapter 15 Review Questions

2. *a.* See Figure 15.2b, p. 497.
   b. Since the firm in a monopolistically competitive market has some degree of uniqueness, its price will not be identical to that of firms providing similar products. And, in the short run, the presence of excess profits has not yet attracted additional firms that reduce the demand curve facing the firm.

4. Starting from a long-run equilibrium, represented by the initial demand and MR curves and $P = $ ATC in the diagram at the right, a boost in demand generates the new demand and MR curves. The higher price at the larger quantity exceeds ATC and generates short-term excess profits (purple rectangle). However, as new

firms, attracted by the profits, enter the market, the demand curve in the long run shifts back to the initial position.

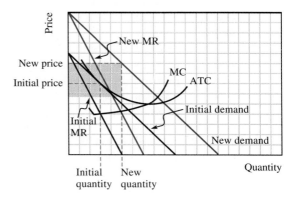

6. When the cab fare rises to 30 cents per block, JL's practice becomes more appealing to those closer to him. As the figure below shows, the new crossover point moves to 58 blocks from JL's office instead of 47.5 blocks.

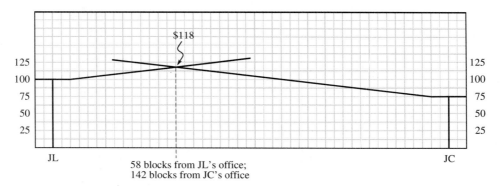

58 blocks from JL's office;
142 blocks from JC's office

8. ATC is not only related to productive efficiency but also to the quality of the final product. A stereo with higher-quality components costs more than one with lower-quality components. Deciding how much a product can sell for profitably will often determine the quality of the final product and hence its costs.

Chapter 15 Food for Thought

2. In the left-hand diagram on p. 721, which combines monopolistic competitive equilibrium with the increasing-cost industry case of the appendix to Chapter 9, the firm is initially in long-run monopolistic competitive equilibrium along the "origi-

nal'' demand, marginal revenue, marginal cost, and average total cost curves. When industry demands increases, so does demand facing the firm, leading initially to higher profits for the existing firms. However, as new firms enter the industry, the industry supply curve moves rightward; price falls; and, as firm demand also declines, profits are eroded. Yet because the industry is characterized by increasing costs, the presence of new firms increases the costs of all firms, as indicated by the new MC and ATC curves. The final equilibrium for the industry is shown on the right at a larger quantity supplied and demanded, and a higher price. This is consistent with an equilibrium for the firm that once again leaves it with no excess profits. The higher price has been offset by increased costs.

Firm

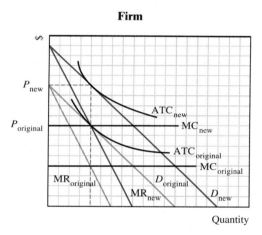

Industry

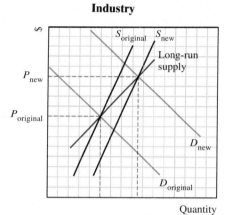

4. Odd pricing is odd from a rational point of view. Nevertheless, marketing experts believe that consumer psychology leads people to group a $4.98 item in a lower $4 category rather than in a higher $5 grouping.

6. *a.* If all Irish pubs were identical and many were not breaking even, then we would expect the number of pubs to decline as the losers left the industry. That would increase the efficiency of the pub industry as a whole, and those cost savings would be passed on to consumers. However, if each pub is unique, then although the losers would exit, their disappearance would also decrease the range of choice available to the public. Consumers will have voted that the uniqueness of the losers is not worth paying the price that would keep them in business. The remaining firms, however, would not necessarily be operated at the minimum point on the industry average cost curve.

b. Various kinds of government policy could then be used to hasten the end of those who would leave the industry anyway. License taxes on pubs or taxes on drinks served in pubs would increase the losses and so force an earlier exit of the losers.

c. Whether it would be desirable for the market to take its course and await the natural demise or to speed up the end depends on whether you believe the industry to be imperfectly or perfectly competitive. Only if the latter were true could a case be made for a policy designed to force exit.

Chapter 16 Review Questions

2. Agree. Production will *not* occur in the region of negative returns, since additional variable inputs lead to smaller output. Production also will not take place in the region of increasing returns, since by moving through this region the producer increases output more than proportionally to the increase in variable input, reducing per unit costs.

4. See Figure 16.4a, p. 538.

6. Accepting a $20 daily welfare payment would not enable Malcolm to reach U_1 and hence would be a worse option than working at the minimum wage.

8. Wage differences can be caused by distinctions in worker efficiency. When a higher-paid employee is significantly more productive than a lower-paid worker, the cost per unit produced will be lower for the former than for the latter.

Chapter 16 Food for Thought

2. The indifference curves would stop at $60, since Sharon is unwilling to trade off any further income for more leisure. (However, more or less leisure at the same $60 would either increase or decrease her satisfaction.) Sharon's labor supply curve no longer will contain the segment below $5 per hour, since a lower wage will not provide her with the $60 daily minimum.

4. The new equilibrium occurs at around $120 earned for eight hours worked, so

Gwen is earning more but not working any additional hours. That defeats Lacy's purpose.

6. Even assuming that people will accept illegal employment provided the reward is appropriate—leading to the concave indifference curves in the diagram below—the returns on illegal occupations, after adjusting for the risk of apprehension and the resulting penalties, are nevertheless low. Hence, the budget line indicates that the return for the same effort earns only $8,000 annually from illegal occupations versus $28,000 for legal work. In equilibrium, this worker will supply 24 times as much labor to legal activities as to illegal ones.

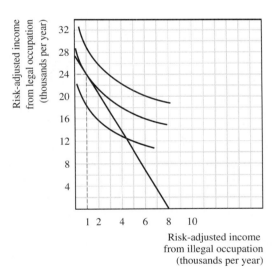

Risk-adjusted income from illegal occupation (thousands per year)

An alternative explanation would incorporate ethical opposition to illegal activities, so that the trade-off would favor legal work. The resulting indifference curves would be very flat, indicating the individual would turn to crime only at a very substantial reward.

Chapter 17 Review Questions

2. *a.* The VMP assumes perfect competition in the product market and is derived by multiplying the MPP by MR, which equals *P*. The MRP is also derived as the product of the MPP and the MR, but is predicated on an imperfectly competitive product market where $P > $ MR.

   b. Because the MR under imperfect competition declines more sharply than its perfectly competitive counterpart, the MRP will also be steeper than the VMP. Since the MRP and the VMP are both demand-for-labor curves, a decrease in the wage rate will lead to greater employment on the VMP than on the MRP.

4. *a.* The labor monopolist is no different from a product monopolist who optimizes profit by calculating the MR = MC position. And, just as the product monopolist finds that demanders can be induced to buy more only by reducing price, so, too, will a labor monopolist have to offer higher wages in order to induce more employment.

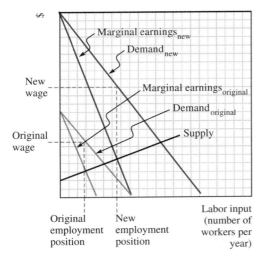

b. In the accompanying figure, demand shifts up from its original position to the new demand curve, leading to a new marginal earnings curve, and both a higher wage and a larger quantity of workers employed.

6. *a.* As Figure 17.5 shows, the optimum monopoly and monopsony positions are such that the best for one party is the worst for the other. Thus, the final equilibrium depends on the economic power and negotiating skills of the two parties, and is indeterminate in the framework of the model.

   b. The deadweight loss equals the triangle formed by the supply and demand curves and the line over 300 workers between \$35,000 and \$20,000.

8. Exercise of union power leads to employer resistance, which in the long run may reduce the demand for labor either by substituting cheaper inputs, introducing labor-saving technology, or relocating beyond the influence of the union.

Chapter 17 Food for Thought

2. *a.* Any increase in the supply of physicians along a downward-sloping demand curve for physicians' services leads to a reduction in physicians' income.

   b. The demand for physicians' services is best described as monopolistically competitive (see Chapter 15), while the productivity and supply of medical personnel hired by physicians can be viewed as typical of most occupations. Hence, the MRP model that opens this chapter well epitomizes the relationship between physicians' operations and their income. With less competition, physicians' fees will be raised, leading to an upward shift of the MRP curve, and hence a higher residual, including a higher return to the physician.

c. Although the AMA's definition of surplus seems to mean reduced physician income, economists evaluate surpluses and deficits in conjunction with market determination of prices and incomes. If the market for medical services were competitive, then any surplus or shortage would prove only temporary, as market forces would bring about a new equilibrium. Hence, a permanent surplus could only result from a policy of artificially raising physician incomes, leading to a discrepancy between quantity demanded and supplied.

4. a. Clearly, the purchasers and suppliers are engaged in a long-term buyer-seller relationship, with contractual arrangements spelling out the obligations of both parties.

b. The presence of contracts limits the scope of competitive markets. Instead, the parties more closely approximate bilateral oligopolists, with parts' costs hinging on bargaining power and strategy. The automobile companies were simply using new tactics to renegotiate the monopoly-monopsony equilibrium along the lines of the slaughterhouse case of the text.

c. One could argue that the reason was inefficiency. Alternatively, the issue is negotiating strategy. While the auto companies might have tried using this type of argument in their negotiations, the suppliers might just have well ignored it.

6. a. When productivity rises, the same amount of input produces more, and so enables the employer to pay workers more without cutting into the firm's profits. At the same time, tying wages to productivity provides an incentive for labor to increase productivity, for it enables the workers to share in the larger revenue pie.

b. The limits are the increased revenues induced by an upward shift of the VTP curve.

c. Labor points to the increase in product and thus revenues brought about by the same amount of labor input. Management cannot prove its contribution so directly, but can point out the cooperating factors without which labor productivity could not have risen.

Chapter 18 Review Questions

2. Although in the short run such payments would only increase the incomes of landlords without affecting the fixed supply of apartments, it might be an effective long-run method of preventing urban blight in instances where rental payments do not cover the operating expenses of the landlords. Moreover, subsidies might increase the stock of low-income housing in the long run. Finally, direct payments to landlords rather than to the tenants would assure that the subsidy reaches the desired party.

4. a. See Figure 18.4, p. 607.

b. Individuals with negative time preference prefer the future to the present. Therefore, they would not have to be compensated for deferring present consumption to a later period.

6. a. The demand for investment curve is related to the principle of diminishing returns. Since the marginal productivity of capital declines as the quantity of capital utilized increases, the discounted rate of return of capital, and hence the quantity demanded, will also decline.

b. The apparent advantage is the stimulation of investment. However, imposing a below-market interest rate also reduces lenders' incentive to supply funds. The excess demand for funds at the below-market rate will lead to an actual decline in investment. This attempt at investment stimulation will be counterproductive unless additional measures, such as government-provided funding, are also introduced.

8. *a.* This question ignores the disincentive effect of taxation. Profit seekers will cut back on their entrepreneurial efforts if their aftertax returns are inadequate.

   b. Taxing permanent excess profits more heavily makes sense when public policy is designed to penalize anticompetitive market structures, which generate such profits.

Chapter 18 Food for Thought

2. Since a tax on apartments that are in perfectly inelastic supply is always borne by the supplier and a subsidy accrues similarly to the supplier, the short-run consequences of the tax-subsidy program are to decrease the net revenues generated by the more expensive apartments and raise them on the cheaper apartments. Depending on the size of the tax and the subsidy, such a policy will either slow down or eliminate gentrification.

4. The supply curve is either negatively or positively sloped depending on the relative strength of the income versus the substitution effect. As interest rates rise, the substitution effect always pushes the lender to lend more, since each additional dollar lent earns a higher return than before. On the other hand, the income effect always pushes the lender to lend less, since the higher interest rate enables the lender to achieve greater future consumption with a smaller reduction in present consumption.

6. *a.* No, for the potential travelers are receiving a payment that is implicit rather than explicit.

   b. Passengers are receiving a claim on a seat to be used in the future. Passengers benefit, since they lock in control over a scarce seat.

   c. While this plea cannot be rejected out of hand provided the term *oligopoly* is substituted for *monopoly*, not paying interest can be explained even if the market were competitive. First, demanders are willing to pay up front, indicating they are gaining utility. Second, the airlines also encounter an opportunity cost upon making a commitment to the passenger: to provide her with a seat on the reserved flight even if the seat could be sold later for a higher fare.

8. *a.* The longer a worker is employed, the greater his experience is and thus the greater his human capital. Furthermore, the longer a worker is employed at a specific firm, the more in tune with the firm's policy she is and the easier she is to supervise, again a human capital contribution. Hence, the more senior an employee, the more that employee is worth to the firm and the greater her wages are.

   b. Job search theory explains wage differentials by different individual calculations of the costs and benefits of searching for jobs combined with similar calculations by employers. Human capital theory attributes wage differentials to differences in the skills, talents, and experience of employees. Implicit contract theory explains long-term relationships between employees and employers on the basis of mutually satisfactory arrangements even when such conditions are not spelled out explicitly in a contract.

The three theories explain seniority payments differently. Human capital theory focuses on the human capital embedded in the older worker. Job search theory suggests that the costs of finding a suitable replacement are greater for the more experienced worker, a condition that the worker realizes. Moreover, the experienced worker understands that his job search costs are likely to be less than those of a new labor force entrant. This cost/benefit calculation by both the employer and employee results in higher wages. Finally, implicit contract theory rewards the worker who has remained with the firm for the long-term commitment. Note, however, that these theories may be viewed as complementary, not competitive.

Chapter 19 Review Questions

2. *a.* When two consumer indifference curves are tangent, an increase in the quantities obtained by one party would necessarily reduce the amounts obtained by the other party. This would violate Pareto optimality, which is defined as the situation whereby no one individual can improve his or her position without making the other party worse off.

   b. Yes, for Pareto optimality is independent of the initial asset distribution of the parties. It merely states that for any given starting combination that is not a tangency position, trade can move one party to a higher indifference curve without moving the other to a lower indifference curve.

4. *a.* Concave production-possibility frontiers presume that both outputs are not perfect substitutes in production. Switching resources from one product to another involves ever-increasing opportunity costs for the product being increased. This will occur even though the same resources enter into the production of both outputs merely because the inputs are used in different proportions.

   b. The PPF frontier represents maximum possible production, whereas the community's indifference curve represents optimum consumption. The tangency indicates the maximum consumption achievable with the community's limited resources.

   c. A new set of community indifference curves will necessarily shift the tangency position. As the demand for one product increases and the other decreases in a competitive market, prices will adjust, leading to supply responses. The new equilibrium will be found once again at the tangency of the PPF and an indifference curve, with relative prices compatible with the new supply/demand situation.

6. *a.* Clearly the users of imported paper would not object. The demand for protection came from domestic paper producers, whose market was threatened by the cheaper imports.

   b. Domestic paper producers would benefit, as would those who supplied inputs to the domestic paper industry. Users of paper that could substitute the cheaper imports for the more expensive domestic paper would be the losers, as would magazine and catalog buyers. Similarly, paper importers and their input suppliers would lose.

   c. Although Japanese consumers undoubtedly would benefit, domestic rice growers would lose out. The political power of the growers seems to overwhelm that of consumers.

8. The narrow assumptions that underlie the simple static model of competition cast doubt on the conclusions reached by general equilibrium theory. The presence of scale economies, externalities, and the possibility that imperfect competition has some virtues in a dynamic setting are circumstances under which perfect competition is not the best possible industry structure.

Chapter 19 Food for Thought

2. *a* and *b*. See the accompanying diagrams immediately below. Essentially, the change in the shape of the isoquant does not change the fundamental nature of the contract curve or the PPF.

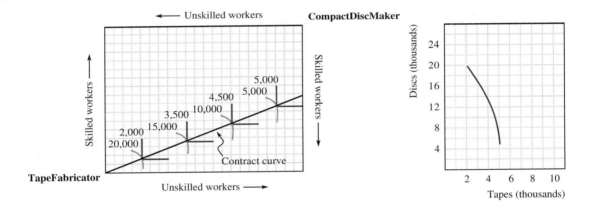

4. *a.* The figure at the right shows the PPF touching the disc axis at an output of 2 million discs instead of 1.5 million, reflecting the increased productivity in disc manufacture. The new PPF becomes tangent to a higher community indifference curve, reflecting greater production and consumption of both discs and tapes.

   b. Although the innovation is unique to disc production, the very fact that discs now can be produced with fewer resources frees inputs for tape production.

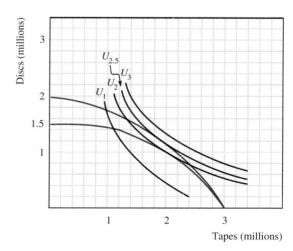

6. *a.* In this "small country case," Venusa gains from trade by riding along Urania's domestic price ratio, which has now become the world price ratio. This new price ratio, depicted in the figure below right, enables Venusa to buy unleaded gasoline more cheaply and sell aviation fuel more dearly. Urania, however, does not gain, as is evident in the figure below.

b. As the diagram indicates, Venusa specializes in aviation fuel production and exports it at the ratio of 1.25 gallons of gasoline for each gallon of aviation fuel. Venusa reaches a new consumption equilibrium along the posttrade price ratio as indicated and exports 50 million gallons of aviation fuel in exchange for 62.5 million gallons of unleaded gasoline.

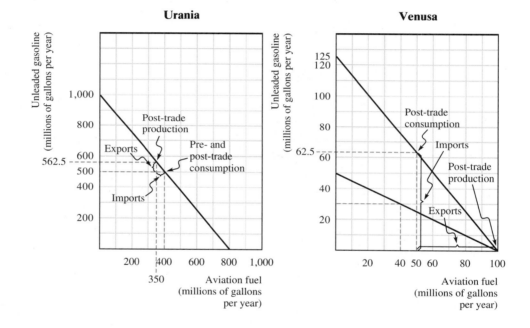

8. The retaliation example discussed in the text (p. 663) can be modeled as in the accompanying grid. Open markets are the best joint strategy, but either Us or Them can do better if an open market policy by one is matched by a restrictive trade policy by the other. If Them move first and impose a tariff, then the best reaction of Us is not to retaliate. However, by Us invoking a strategy of retaliation, Us loses but so does Them. Presumably, Us's willingness to permit its own situation to deteriorate leads Them to reverse its policy, leaving all better off.

		Them	
		Open markets	**Barriers**
Us	**Open markets**	6, 6	3, 7
	Barriers	7, 3	2, 2

GLOSSARY

Agency costs Costs that principals impose on themselves to assure that their agents will act in their best interests. 266

Agent Any person or entity (e.g., management) employed by a principal to implement the objectives of the principal. 264

Allocating mechanism A function of price; price provides available goods and services to those most willing to pay for them. 40

Allocational efficiency The optimal distribution of resources among industries so that the resulting output corresponds to the demands of the decision makers. 314

Asymmetric information When two individuals or groups possess uneven knowledge about an event or a situation. 13

Average-cost pricing When the price of a regulated monopoly is set to equal average total cost. 417

Average fixed costs (AFC) Total fixed costs (TFC) divided by output. 225

Average physical product (APP) Total physical product (TPP) divided by the variable input. 185

Average revenue product (ARP) In an imperfectly competitive product market, the value of the total product (VTP) divided by the corresponding quantity of the variable input. 573

Average total costs (ATC) Total costs (TC) divided by output; or average fixed costs plus average variable costs. 225

Average variable costs (AVC) Total variable costs (TVC) divided by output. 217

Bandwagon (or demonstration) effect When an individual's consumption is conditioned by the consumption of others. 120

Bankruptcy A legal procedure under which a court, having found an individual's or firm's liabilities to exceed its assets, arranges for the orderly distribution of the remaining assets to the bankrupt's creditors. 287

Bilateral monopoly When a monopoly seller faces a monopsony buyer. 582

Block pricing See second-degree discrimination. 383

Budget constraint (or budget line) Diagrammatic representation of an individual's attainable consumption possibilities, given income and the prices of the commodities in question. 78

Buffer stock agency (BSA) An agency charged by an international commodity agreement (ICA) with the mechanics of stabilizing the price of a commodity. 288

Capital-intensive methods Production methods that rely more heavily on capital than on labor. 192

Capital-saving technical change Occurs when a new production method not only increases output for a given amount of input but also uses relatively less capital to do so. 246

Cardinal utility The numerical measurement of satisfaction. 69

Cartel (or collusive monopoly) When competing producers work together as if they were a single firm. 367

Chapter 11 bankruptcy Bankruptcy in which the firm is permitted to continue its operations while delaying payment to its creditors. 287

Comparative statics When economists are concerned with the "before" and the "after" but not with the "in-between." 10

Complements Products that are normally used in conjunction with each other. 152

Compound interest When interest earned is added to the principal and in the next period interest is paid on the new principal. 610

Conglomerate merger The combining of two firms in unrelated industries or markets. 453

Constant returns to scale When equiproportionate increments in inputs result in equiproportionate increases in output. 194

Consumer sovereignty When the production sector of the economy responds to the decisions of the consuming public. 314

Consumer surplus The difference between the amount purchasers would have been willing to pay for a good or service and the actual amount they do pay. 116

Consumption contract curve The locus of tangencies of two indifference curve maps. 649

Contestable markets Markets are contestable as long as firms can enter or leave an industry without being subject to any constraints. 320

Converging cobweb Economic model that moves toward the supply-demand intersection in successive rounds. 53

Cross-elasticity The percentage change in the quantity demanded of a specific good or service in response to a change in the price of some other good or service; $\left(\dfrac{\Delta Q_x}{\Delta P_y}\dfrac{P_y}{Q_x}\right)$. 152

Deadweight loss A loss of production or consumption to some members of the economy without a corresponding gain by others. 279

Decreasing costs When the marginal cost (MC) falls as increasing amounts of variable inputs are combined with a fixed resource. 219

Decreasing returns to scale (diseconomies of scale) When proportional increases in all inputs lead to less than proportional increments in output. 194

Demand curve A pictorial representation of the relationship between price and the quantity desired by buyers per unit of time. 32

Demand function Fundamental economic relationship that relates the behavioral motives that underlie individual or group purchase decisions to the quantities of a specific good or service they wish to buy. 30

Dependent variable The variable to be determined in an econometric equation. 59

Differentiated oligopoly Oligopoly in which the product marketed has some unique qualities. 431

Discounting Determining the present value of an investment by adjusting the flow of returns by the appropriate interest rate. 612

Discriminating monopolist One who is able to charge different prices to different demanders. 381

Diseconomies of scale See **Decreasing returns to scale.**

Dominant strategy In game theory, when one player's best strategy is entirely independent of the strategy chosen by the other player. 445

Dumping When a product sells for less abroad than it costs to produce at home. 662

Duopoly A market characterized by two sellers. 434

Dynamic model An economic model in which the time pattern of reactions is explicitly considered. 15

Econometrics Devising testable economic models and testing them statistically. 16

Economies of scale See **Increasing returns to scale**

Efficiency wage The cost of a unit of labor adjusted for the individual worker's productivity. 559

Elastic When quantity demanded is so responsive that a small percentage price change brings a disproportionate reaction in quantity demanded (i.e., the price elasticity is greater than 1). 139

Elasticity The percentage change of one variable in terms of another. 139

Equilibrium (market balance) Occurs at a price where the quantity supplied equals that quantity demanded. Excess supply = Excess demand = 0. 37

Excess demand When the quantity demanded at a given price exceeds the quantity supplied. 36

Excess profits Those earnings that exceed both the firm's money expenditures and the normal profits that owners receive to cover their opportunity costs. 271

Excess supply When the quantity supplied at a given price exceeds the quantity demanded. 36

Expansion path Connects the isoquant-isocost tangency points for any given set of prices; relates the quantity—and implicitly, the cost—of inputs to output as production changes. 228

Exploding cobweb Economic model that moves away from the supply-demand intersection in successive rounds. 53

Externalities When an economic act spills over to third parties who are not directly involved in the action. 334

First-degree discrimination (or perfect price discrimination) When a monopolist charges demanders the maximum price each is willing to pay. 381

Fixed costs Costs that are independent of the volume of production. 208

Fixed input coefficients In the production function, when two inputs must be used in constant proportions and cannot be substituted for each other in production. 191

Flexible full-cost pricing When the percentage added to average total cost is adjusted to reflect market conditions. 450

Four-firm concentration ratio The percentage of the market captured by the four largest firms in the industry. 470

Free rider An individual who can obtain a service without paying for it. 348

Full-cost pricing See **Markup pricing.**

Futures market An organized mechanism for determining prices prior to the physical availability of the commodity in question. 53

Game theory Focuses on strategies chosen by interdependent players and the consequences of implementing the strategies. 431

General equilibrium When all markets in the economy are simultaneously in equilibrium. 640

Hedger One who uses the futures market to guarantee future prices. 54

Herfindahl-Hirschman index (HHI) A measure of market concentration calculated by summing the market share of each firm squared. 470

Horizontal merger A combining of firms that sell the same product. 452

Human capital The investment embodied in an individual; it is the personal analogue of physical capital. 618

Implicit contract Commits employers and employees to a mutually beneficial long-term employment relationship in the absence of explicit contractual arrangements. 556

Impure public goods Public goods for which either (1) the cost to the marginal user is not zero but there's no easy way to exclude free riders or (2) the user can be charged even though the marginal cost for that user is zero. 350

Income effect The change in the quantity bought that results from a change in the purchasing power of a given amount of income. 106

Income elasticity The percentage change in quantity demanded for a given percentage change in income; $\left(\dfrac{\Delta Q}{\Delta Y}\dfrac{Y}{Q}\right)$. 152

Increasing costs   The rising marginal costs that occur when more and more variable resources are combined with a fixed resource.   217

Increasing returns   When, with one or more inputs fixed, the marginal physical product (MPP) increases with increasing amounts of the variable input employed.   187

Increasing returns to scale (economies of scale)   When equiproportionate increases in all inputs lead to more than proportionate increments in output.   194

Independent variables   The causal or determining forces in an econometric equation.   59

Indifference curve   All points on a single curve represent equal levels of satisfaction.   72

Industry demand curve   *See* Product demand curve.

Inelastic   When the percentage change in price brings a relatively small response in quantity demanded (i.e., the price elasticity of demand is less than 1).   139

Inferior good   A good or service on which individuals spend less as their income rises.   107

International commodity agreement (ICA)   A joint resolution by consuming and producing nations to stabilize the world price of a specific product (typically a raw material).   287

Isocost line   Line on which all points represent combinations of inputs that cost the same.   211

Isoquant   A slice of a production function that indicates equal amounts of output despite differing input combinations.   189

Labor-intensive methods   Production methods that use relatively more labor than capital.   192

Labor-saving technical change   Occurs when a new production method not only increases output for a given amount of input, but also uses relatively less labor to do so.   246

Laffer curve   A backward-bending relationship between tax rates and labor supply.   549

Law of diminishing returns   When one or more inputs are held constant and a variable input is increased, then total physical product (TPP) will increase, but it will do so at a diminishing rate; the marginal physical product (MPP) will fall.   187

Lerner index (£)   A measure of industry concentration calculated by (Price − Marginal cost)/Price.   470

Limit pricing   Setting prices low enough to discourage potential competitors but high enough to earn excess profits.   413

List price   An announced, verifiable price.   436

Long run   A situation in which a firm has not incurred any fixed costs.   207

Long-run equilibrium   When economic conditions are such that no existing firms leave the industry and no new firms enter.   297

Marginal cost pricing   When the price of a regulated monopoly is set to equal marginal cost.   417

Marginal costs   The change in total costs divided by the change in output; ($\Delta TC/\Delta Q = \Delta TVC/\Delta Q$).   208

Marginal earnings (ME)   The change in total labor income for a given change in the quantity of labor demanded.   575

Marginal outlay (MO)   The cost of an additional unit of input.   534

Marginal physical product (MPP)   The change in total physical product divided by the change in variable input; ($\Delta TPP/\Delta Q_i$).   185

Marginal rate of substitution (MRS)   The amount of one good that will be sacrificed in order to obtain one unit of another good without increasing or decreasing the level of satisfaction; the slope of the indifference curve.   72

Marginal rate of technical substitution (MRTS)   The slope of the isoquant; represents the number of units of one input that must be substituted for a second input in order to maintain constant output.   189

Marginal rate of transformation (MRT)   The amount of one product that must be sacrificed in order to increase output of a second product by a single unit; the slope of the production possibilities frontier.   653

Marginal revenue (MR)   Revenue earned by producing an additional unit of output; equals the change in total revenue divided by the change in output ($\Delta TR/\Delta Q$).   270

Marginal revenue product (MRP) In an imperfectly competitive product market, the change in the value of total product (VTP) divided by corresponding change in the quantity of input (ΔVTP/ΔQ_i). 569

Marginal utility The extra satisfaction obtained from consuming an additional unit of a given product or service. 74

Market failure When competition does not provide either the efficiency or the welfare benefits that are anticipated consequences of the competitive process. 334

Markup pricing (or full-cost pricing) When oligopolists calculate product price by adding a specific percentage to their average total costs. 449

Monopolistic competition A market in which there are many suppliers and easy entry and exit (as in perfect competition) but also in which firms control price to some degree (as in monopoly). 494

Monopoly When a single seller (or group acting as a single seller) controls an industry. 366

Monopsony When the market is controlled by a single buyer. 579

Nash equilibrium In game theory, requires that each player's strategy is optimal, given the known strategy of the other player(s). 446

Natural monopoly When the industry is characterized by economies of scale or when monopoly would eliminate costly and unnecessary duplication of resources. 369

Negative externality An externality that adversely affects the bystanders. 334

Negative returns When increasing the variable input leads to output reductions. 187

Neutral technical change Occurs when the same quantity of inputs are used in the same proportions but output is larger. 246

Nominal interest rate The actual amount of interest to be paid to the lender divided by the principal value of the loan. 606

Normal goods Products or services whose consumption increases as income increases and decreases as income decreases. 80

Normal profits The minimum profits needed to induce the owners of a firm to remain in business. 271

Normative economics The type of economics that is concerned with economic policy goals. 16

Oligopoly A market controlled by a few sellers. 429

Opportunity cost The return that could have been obtained had some course of action other than the one actually chosen been pursued. 18

Opportunity locus Diagrammatic representation of the achievable combinations of risk and return. 91

Optimally sized firms Firms that operate at the lowest point on the long-run average cost curve. 297

Ordinal utility The relative degree of satisfaction. 69

Overhead costs Costs not directly associated with production. 209

Pareto consumption optimum Is reached when it is impossible to increase the welfare of one individual without reducing the welfare of some other individual. 648

Pareto production optimum Is reached when increasing the output of one individual reduces the welfare of some other individual. 652

Partial equilibrium Equilibrium in a particular market without considering repercussions in other markets. 640

Payback criterion The number of years that an investment is expected to take to recoup its initial cost. 615

Payoff matrix In game theory, records the outcomes for a given combination of actions. 430

Peak-load pricing When buyers pay more per unit during periods of heavy demand and less when demand tapers off. 419

Planning curves Long-run cost curves; so called to highlight the open choices about all input options. 235

Positive economics The type of economics that deals with describing and analyzing economic issues. 16

Positive externality   An externality that benefits third parties.   334

Positive time preference   The preference of an individual for present consumption over future spending.   607

Present value of an investment   The sum of the flow of returns discounted by the appropriate interest rate.   612

Price consumption curve   On a map of indifference curves, connects equilibrium consumption combinations derived by changing price.   106

Price effect   The total change in quantity demanded resulting from a price change.   106

Price elasticity of demand   The percentage change in quantity demanded divided by the percentage change in price; $\left(\frac{\Delta Q}{\Delta P} \cdot \frac{P}{Q}\right)$.   139

Price elasticity of supply   The percentage change in quantity supplied divided by the percentage change in price; $\left(\frac{\Delta Q}{\Delta P} \cdot \frac{P}{Q}\right)$.   155

Price leadership   When the price set by one oligopolist is typically adopted by all other oligopolists.   436

Price maker   One who exercises discretion over the price to charge customers.   262

Price taker   One who has no control over prices charged.   262

Principal   Any person or entity (e.g., owners) who employs one or more agents to implement objectives.   264

Privatization   Using the private sector to supply goods and services previously produced by the government sector.   353

Producer surplus   The difference between the price necessary to induce suppliers to produce a given level of output and the actual price of that output.   277

Product demand curve (or industry demand curve)   The demand curve for a particular product or for the output of a particular industry.   267

Production contract curve   The locus of tangencies of two isoquant maps.   650

Production function   The function that relates the technologically feasible maximum amount of output for all given combinations of inputs.   180

Production-possibilities frontier (PPF)   Plots the maximum achievable production of any combination of products for a given quantity of inputs and production functions.   652

Product line   A variety of products offered by a supplier that are similar to each other in terms of function but that vary in quality and price.   443

Public good   Any good or service that is desired by the community but would not be adequately provided if it were left to the working of the market.   347

Public utility   An enterprise operating in a market in which demand is too limited to exhaust the firm's economies of scale, thereby subjecting the firm to public regulation.   416

Pure public goods   Public goods for which (1) the cost to the marginal user is zero and (2) the marginal user cannot be excluded from participating in the goods' use.   350

Quantity demanded   The amount of a good or service desired subsequent to a change in the price of that product.   32

Quantity supplied   The amount of a good or service placed on the market subsequent to a change in the price of that product.   34

Quasi rent   The return to an input when its supply is fixed only in the short run.   600

Rate of return (*r*)   The number that discounts the flow of revenue to equal the cost of the investment.   613

Reaction curve   Plots out the response of one strategist to the expected actions of another.   448

Real interest rate   The nominal interest rate minus the expected rate of inflation.   606

Rent   The return to an input whose long-run price elasticity of supply is zero.   600

Residual   The difference between the value of total product (VTP) and the cost of the variable inputs; it is used to pay the fixed factors of production as well as profits.   535

Ridge lines   The lines on an isoquant map that demarcate the region within which production will take place.   192

Risk-averse The quality shown by an individual who prefers safety over risk taking. 89

Rule of reason Views only unreasonable intent and actions as violations of the monopolization prohibition of the Sherman Antitrust Act. 486

Screen (or signal) A proxy for a job-related test used by potential employees and/or potential employers when direct job-performance testing is either impossible, difficult, or expensive. 555

Search costs The expenses, including time and money, involved in obtaining information. 13

Second-degree discrimination (block pricing) When the same customer pays different rates for different quantities of the product purchased. 383

Seniority The length of a worker's employment in a given firm. 556

Shift in demand Occurs when any element of the demand function other than the price of the good itself changes. 33

Shift in supply Occurs when any element of the supply function other than the price of the good itself changes. 34

Short run A situation in which a firm has incurred some fixed costs. 207

Shutdown point The lowest point on the AVC; if the product's price is less than the minimum AVC, the firm will cease production. 274

Signal See *Screen.*

Signaling mechanism A function of price; prices send messages to producers to respond to the demands of the market. 40

Speculator One who hopes to achieve a profit from a favorable discrepancy between the futures price and the spot market price. 54

Spot market A market in which prices for commodities available for current delivery are determined. 53

Standard Industrial Classification (SIC) Code A numerical classification of U.S. industries and their products, running from broad economic sectors (one-digit) to ever finer distinctions, culminating in seven-digit product listings. 472

Standard volume The anticipated average output over a given time period. 450

Strategic entry deterrence Policies that are specifically designed to keep competitors from penetrating the industry. 433

Strategic trade policy Policy employed by a country to gain advantage over its trading partners. 663

Substitutes Products that are used instead of each other. 152

Substitution effect The increase or decrease in the quantity purchased that follows from just a change in relative prices. 106

Supply curve A pictorial representation of the relationship between price and the quantity suppliers wish to sell per unit of time. 34

Supply function Relates the motives behind selling a specific item to the quantities of goods a producer and, by aggregation, all producers wish to sell. 34

Target pricing A variation of markup pricing in which the specific percentage added to costs is the desired rate of profit. 449

Third-degree discrimination When identifiable groups of buyers, each sharing a common characteristic, are charged different prices. 383

Total costs (TC) Total fixed costs (TFC) plus the total variable costs (TVC). 225

Total fixed costs (TFC) The costs associated with the fixed factors of production. 225

Total physical product (TPP) Output measured in physical units (e.g., tons or barrels) rather than in monetary units. 182

Total revenue (TR) Price times quantity. 144

Total variable costs (TVC) The costs associated with the variable factors of production. 216

Transitivity A condition that requires the consumer to be consistent in making choices. 69

Underground economy Markets in illegal goods or services, or activities that are intrinsically permitted by law but in which the participants do not comply with the income and/or sales reporting mandates of the authorities. 551

Undifferentiated oligopoly Oliogopoly in which the product marketed has no or few unique qualities. 431

Unitary elasticity When the percentage change in price is precisely matched by the percentage change in quantity demanded (i.e., when the price elasticity of demand equals 1). 139

Value of average product (VAP) The average physical product (APP) times the price of the product (P). 532

Value of marginal product (VMP) The marginal physical product (MPP) times price (P). 533

Value of total product (VTP) The total revenue derived from selling the production of a given number of inputs. (TPP $\times$ P). 533

Variable costs Costs that vary with output. 208

Variable input coefficients In the production function, when substitution among inputs exists. 191

Veblen effect Explains why the higher the price is of a product, the larger the quantity demanded will be. 120

Vertical merger A combining of firms that are linked in the production or distribution chain. 452

Wage gap The difference between union and nonunion wages thought to result only from unionization 589

X-inefficiency Waste that stems from excessive use of productive resources. 199

INDEX